MyAccountingLab ®

- Web-based tutorial and assessment software where students have more "I Get It" moments.

- Flexible for instructors to easily integrate into their course.

For Instructors

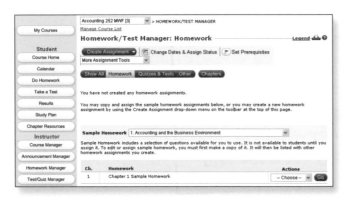

Powerful Homework and Test Manager

- Homework assignments, quizzes, and tests that directly correlate to the textbook.

- Homework guided solutions to help students understand concepts.

- Multiple assignment options including time limits, proctoring, and maximum number of attempts allowed.

Comprehensive Gradebook Tracking

- Automatic grading that tracks students' results on tests, homework, and tutorials.

- Flexible Gradebook with numerous student data views, weighted assignments, choice on which attempts to include when calculating scores, and the ability to omit results of individual assignments.

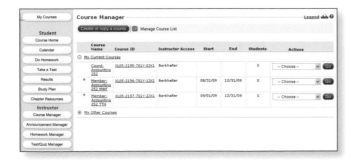

Department-Wide Solutions

- Simplified for departmental implementation with the use of Coordinator Courses—make changes once and they ripple down to all members.

For Students

Interactive Tutorial Exercises

- Homework and practice exercises with additional algorithmic–generated problems for more practice.

- Personalized interactive learning—guided solutions and learning aids for point-of-use help and immediate feedback.

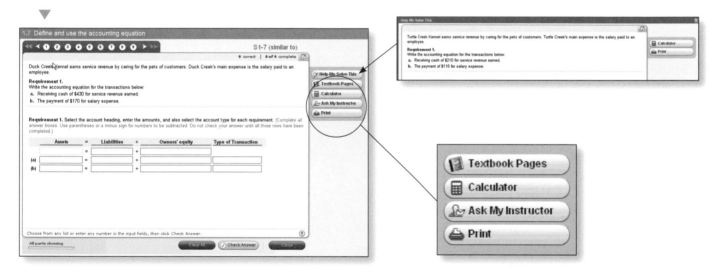

◀ Study Plan for Self-Paced Learning

- Assists students in monitoring their own progress by offering them a customized study plan based on their test results.

- Includes regenerated exercises with new values for unlimited practice and guided multimedia learning aids for extra guidance.

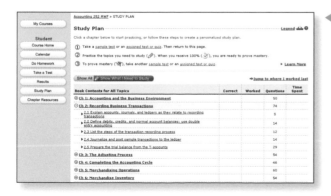

MANAGEMENT ACCOUNTING

Information for Decision-Making and Strategy Execution

SIXTH EDITION

Anthony A. Atkinson
University of Waterloo

Robert S. Kaplan
Harvard University

Ella Mae Matsumura
University of Wisconsin–Madison

S. Mark Young
University of Southern California

International Edition Contributions by

Abhik Kr. Mukherjee
St. Xavier's College, Kolkata

PEARSON

Boston Columbus Indianapolis New York San Francisco Upper Saddle River
Amsterdam Cape Town Dubai London Madrid Milan Munich Paris Montreal Toronto
Delhi Mexico City São Paulo Sydney Hong Kong Seoul Singapore Taipei Tokyo

AVP/Executive Editor: Stephanie Wall
Editorial Director: Sally Yagan
Editor in Chief: Donna Battista
Director of Editorial Services: Ashley Santora
Editorial Project Manager: Christina Rumbaugh
Editorial Assistant: Brian Reilly
Director of Marketing: Patrice Jones
Marketing Assistant: Ian Gold
Senior Managing Editor, Production: Cynthia Zonneveld
Production Editor: Carol O'Rourke
Publisher, International Edition: Angshuman Chakraborty

Acquisitions Editor, International Edition: Arunabha Deb
Publishing Assistant, International Edition: Shokhi Shah
Text Permissions Coordinator: Tracy Metivier
Senior Operations Specialist: Diane Peirano
Art Director: Anthony Gemmellaro
Cover Design: Anthony Gemmellaro
Cover Illustration/Photo: © Image Source/Corbis
Full-Service Project Management: S4Carlisle Publishing Services/Lynn Steines
Cover printer: Courier Kendallville

Pearson Education Limited
Edinburgh Gate
Harlow
Essex CM20 2JE
England

and Associated Companies throughout the world

Visit us on the World Wide Web at:
www.pearsoninternationaleditions.com

© Pearson Education Limited 2012

ISBN 10: 0-273-76998-7
ISBN 13: 978-0-273-76998-9

British Library Cataloguing-in-Publication Data
A catalogue record for this book is available from the British Library

10 9 8 7 6 5 4 3 2
14 13 12

Typeset in 10/12 Palatino by S4Carlisle Publishing Services/Lynn Steines
Printed and bound by Courier Kendallville in the United States of America

This book is dedicated to our
parents and families.

BRIEF CONTENTS

CONTENTS

PREFACE

Intended Audience

The sixth edition of *Management Accounting* targets undergraduate and MBA courses in managerial accounting with a major redesign and several new topics. It integrates state-of-the-art thinking on recent innovations in management accounting including:

- the Balanced Scorecard,
- strategy maps,
- time-driven activity-based costing for product and customer profitability analysis,
- target costing,
- environmental costing, and
- the design of management control systems.

The author team consists of top scholars who have served as advisers to small, medium-sized, and large enterprises in the private, nonprofit, and public sectors. They present a conceptually sound and practically relevant perspective on the role of management accounting information in informing important decisions made by business managers, aligning employees and organizational units with strategic objectives, driving continuous process improvements, and influencing the design of products and services. The sixth edition provides problems and cases drawn from the authors' practical experience including cases from Harvard Business School and the Institute of Management Accountants (IMA) that engage students in strategic and organizational analyses. This action orientation makes the text an excellent fit for management accounting courses taught from a managerial perspective. Although this text is primarily intended for business and accounting students, it will also be useful to practicing managers who would benefit from understanding how to mobilize management accounting to drive value in their organizations.

All Enterprises Need Management Accounting

Management accounting information creates value for all types of organizations: private sector companies attempting to deliver superior and sustainable returns to shareholders, nonprofit and nongovernmental organizations (NGOs) striving to deliver positive social impact to targeted constituents, and public-sector agencies that are empowered to improve the lives of citizens. The common thread across all of these diverse enterprises is how to implement a strategy that delivers long-term value to their stakeholders. Strategy implementation requires decision making that is aligned with strategic goals, continuous improvement of critical processes, motivation and alignment of employees with organizational objectives, and innovation that develops new products and services. This book is the only management accounting book that explains in detail how to use measurement and management systems for sustainable value creation.

New to This Edition

- Chapter 1 introduces the plan–do–check–act cycle as an organizing framework for embedding multiple management accounting processes.
- Chapter 2 is an updated and repositioned chapter on the Balanced Scorecard and strategy maps. It uses an extended example, drawn from an actual company's experience, to illustrate how to develop a Balanced Scorecard and strategy map for a company's new strategy. Placing this chapter at the front of the book helps students to understand the strategic context for the measurement, decision-making, and control topics discussed in subsequent chapters.
- Chapter 3 is an entirely rewritten chapter for introducing students to fundamental cost concepts. Variable, fixed, incremental, relevant, sunk, avoidable, and opportunity costs are explained and illustrated. Students' understanding of the concepts is highlighted through decision-making examples on make versus buy, product abandonment, financial modeling for what-if analyses, and product mix optimization with constrained resources. The chapter ends with several numerical examples that enable students to test their ability to apply fundamental cost concepts in diverse settings. In addition, the chapter contains a new case on product costing and decision analysis in the wine industry.
- Chapter 4, also a major update for the sixth edition, provides the foundation for understanding how cost systems can be designed to assign direct and indirect costs to cost objects, such as products, services, and operating departments. It features an explicit and extensive treatment of capacity measurement and costing that sets the stage for the activity-based costing material that follows in subsequent chapters.
- Chapter 5 covers the measurement and management of product costs through the framework of time-driven activity-based costing. This recent innovation helps product costing to be done in a simple, transparent, accurate, and flexible manner. The chapter features the many ways managers can eliminate losses and improve product profitability once they understand the fundamental economics of their products and services.
- Chapter 6, measuring and managing customer relationships, is an entirely new chapter for the sixth edition. The chapter is new not only to the text but also to most management accounting courses. It features the strategic importance of understanding and transforming customer profitability through decisions on product features, product mix, order pricing, and customer relationships. Entirely new material in this chapter includes the pricing waterfall for measuring customer discounts, promotions, and allowances, and an extended treatment of how to derive customer satisfaction and loyalty metrics for a business unit's Balanced Scorecard.
- Chapter 7 features the role for management accounting information to drive strategy execution through enhanced continuous improvement activities, including lean management, kaizen costing, theory of constraints, cost of quality, six sigma, just-in-time, and benchmarking techniques. As in Chapter 6, new material illustrates how to derive process improvement performance measures for the organization's Balanced Scorecard.
- Chapter 8 introduces students to the total life-cycle costing concept. At the front end, the chapter shows how target costing can inform decisions made during the product design and development stages. Target costing helps companies to develop products that meet customers' functionality requirements at a cost that yields targeted profit margins. New material in the chapter introduces the breakeven time concept for measuring the performance of the product

development process, and the selection of other innovation metrics that companies can incorporate into their Balanced Scorecards. The chapter concludes by examining processes and metrics at the back end of the product life cycle, when consumers dispose of or return their used products.

- The sixth edition drops two topics, capital budgeting and financial ratio analysis, that our research shows are now usually covered in other courses. It retains and updates chapters from the fifth edition on the behavioral and organizational aspects of management accounting, budgeting, and financial and managerial control of decentralized operations.
- Also retained are the valuable HBS cases, first introduced in the fifth edition:
  * Sippican (A) and (B) (integrating time-driven activity-based costing, budgeting, and the Balanced Scorecard),
  * Midwest Office Products (time-driven ABC in a service setting),
  * Chadwick, Inc. (designing a Balanced Scorecard for a pharmaceutical company), and
  * Domestic Auto Parts (building a Balanced Scorecard).
- An additional HBS case is new to the sixth edition:
  * Citibank: Performance Evaluation (the costs and benefits of using multiple performance measures to evaluate performance).

All of these cases are brief for preparation ease and are accompanied by Instructor Case Notes found in the instructor resources.

- The sixth edition also retains the following Institute of Management Accountants cases:
  * How Mercedes-Benz used target costing to develop its new SUV and
  * Precision Systems, Inc.: Improving processes in order entry, with linkages to value-chain ideas (effects on customers, sales representatives, manufacturing, and other internal uses of the order entry information).
- *Readings in Management Accounting*, **Sixth Edition, by S. Mark Young**
  This supplement contains 53 recent and classic business press and academic articles that correlate with the chapter coverage in *Management Accounting*, Sixth Edition. Ideal for additional content reinforcement and for any case-based course, this supplement includes articles from a variety of sources to show the application of management accounting in diverse organizational settings.

Instructor Materials

The following supplements are available to adopting instructors. For detailed descriptions, please visit www.pearsoninternationaleditions.com/kaplan.

- **Instructor's Manual**—teaching tips and additional resources for each chapter.
- **Test Bank**—over 1,200 test questions.
- **Solutions Manual**—solutions for every question, exercise, problem, and HBS case study.
- **PowerPoint slides**—presentations for every chapter.

ACKNOWLEDGMENTS

We would like to acknowledge, with thanks, the individuals who made this text possible.

We appreciate and benefited from the reviews and suggestions of Professors:

Signe Cahn, *Webster University*
Alan Czyzewski, *Indiana State University*
Fara Elikai, *University of North Carolina–Wilmington*
Judith Harris, *Nova Southeastern University*
Kay Poston, *South University*
Barbara Pughsley, *South University*
P. K. Sen, *University of Cincinnati*

For the sixth edition, we also thank the following individuals:

Carol O'Rourke, Production Project Manager
Christina Rumbaugh, Editorial Project Manager
Lynn Steines, Project Manager, S4Carlisle Publishing Services
Stephanie Wall, Acquisitions Vice President

We also gratefully acknowledge Professors Shahid Ansari, Jan Bell, Thomas Klammer, and Carol Lawrence for allowing us to use some of their material on target costing; Professor Priscilla Wisner for permitting us to use her case on the wine industry; Carolyn Streuly for her valuable contributions; and Professor Michael D. Shields and Professor Thomas Lin for their continuing support of the book. The publishers would like to thank Professor Soumya Mukherjee, Maharaja Manindra Chandra College, University of Calcutta, for reviewing the content of the International Edition.

The authors and product team would appreciate hearing from you! Let us know what you think about this book by writing to stephanie.wall@pearson.com. Please include "Feedback about AKMY 6e" in the subject line.

ABOUT THE AUTHORS

Anthony A. Atkinson

A professor in the School of Accountancy at the University of Waterloo, Anthony A. Atkinson received a bachelor of commerce and M.B.A. degrees from Queen's University in Kingston, Ontario, and M.S. and Ph.D. degrees in industrial administration from Carnegie-Mellon University in Pittsburgh. He is a fellow of the Society of Management Accountants of Canada and has written or coauthored two texts, various monographs, and more than 35 articles on performance measurement and costing. In 1989, the Canadian Academic Accounting Association awarded Atkinson the Haim Falk Prize for Distinguished Contribution to Accounting Thought for his monograph that studied transfer pricing practice in six Canadian companies. He has served on the editorial boards of two professional and five academic journals and is a past editor of the *Journal of Management Accounting Research*. Atkinson also served as a member of the Canadian government's Cost Standards Advisory Committee, for which he developed the costing principles it now requires of government contractors.

Robert S. Kaplan

Robert S. Kaplan is Baker Foundation Professor at the Harvard Business School, where he has taught for 27 years. Previously, he served on the faculty and as Dean of the Tepper Business School at Carnegie-Mellon University. Kaplan received a B.S. and M.S. in electrical engineering from M.I.T., and a Ph.D. in operations research from Cornell University.

Kaplan has done extensive writing, teaching, and consulting on linking cost and performance management systems to strategy implementation. He has helped to develop both activity-based costing and the Balanced Scorecard. His 14 books have been translated into 28 languages. Kaplan's most recent books are *The Execution Premium* with David Norton and *Time-Driven Activity-Based Costing* with Steven Anderson. He has also authored or coauthored 21 *Harvard Business Review* articles and more than 100 others in academic and professional journals.

Kaplan was inducted into the Accounting Hall of Fame in 2006 and received the Lifetime Contribution Award from the Management Accounting Section of the American Accounting Association in January 2006. In 2008, his coauthored book, *Relevance Lost: The Rise and Fall of Management Accounting*, received the AAA Seminal Contribution to Accounting Literature Award. His articles and books have also been recognized with several Wildman Medal and AAA Notable Contributions to Accounting Literature Awards.

Kaplan received the Outstanding Accounting Educator Award in 1988 from the American Accounting Association (AAA), the 1994 CIMA Award from the Chartered Institute of Management Accountants (UK) for "Outstanding Contributions to the Accountancy Profession," and the 2001 Distinguished Service Award from the Institute of Management Accountants (IMA) for contributions to the practice and academic community.

Ella Mae Matsumura

Ella Mae Matsumura is an associate professor in the Department of Accounting and Information Systems in the School of Business at the University of Wisconsin–Madison, and is affiliated with the university's Center for Quick Response Manufacturing. She received an A.B. in mathematics from the University of California, Berkeley, and M.Sc. and Ph.D. degrees from the University of British Columbia. Matsumura has won two teaching excellence awards at the University of Wisconsin–Madison and was elected as a lifetime fellow of the university's Teaching Academy, formed to promote effective teaching. She is a member of the university team awarded an IBM Total Quality Management Partnership grant to develop curriculum for total quality management education.

Professor Matsumura was a co-winner of the 2010 Notable Contributions to Management Accounting Literature Award. She has served in numerous leadership positions in the American Accounting Association (AAA). She was coeditor of *Accounting Horizons* and has chaired and served on numerous AAA committees. She has been secretary–treasurer and president of the AAA's Management Accounting Section. Her past and current research articles focus on decision making, performance evaluation, compensation, supply chain relationships, and sustainability. She coauthored a monograph on customer profitability analysis in credit unions.

S. Mark Young

S. Mark Young holds the George Bozanic and Holman G. Hurt Chair in Sports and Entertainment Business and is also professor of accounting and professor of management and organization at the Marshall School of Business, University of Southern California (USC), and professor of communication and journalism at the Annenberg School for Communication at USC. Professor Young received an A.B. from Oberlin College (economics) and a Ph.D. from the University of Pittsburgh.

Professor Young has published research in a variety of journals including *The Accounting Review, Accounting, Organizations and Society*, the *Journal of Accounting Research*, the *Journal of Marketing Research*, and *Contemporary Accounting Research*. Currently, he is on the editorial board of several major journals and was past associate editor for *The Accounting Review*. In 2006, he was a co-winner of the Notable Contribution to the Accounting Literature (with Shannon Anderson) and has won the Notable Contributions to the Management Accounting Literature Award twice—with Frank Selto (1994) and Shannon Anderson (2003). He also received the Jim Bulloch Award for Innovations in Management Accounting Education in 2005. Dr. Young has extensive executive teaching and consulting experience. He has won several outstanding teaching awards including the Golden Apple Teaching Award and is a distinguished fellow of the Center for Excellence in Teaching at USC.

Professor Young also studies the entertainment industry and his book, *The Mirror Effect: How Celebrity Narcissism Is Seducing America* (with Dr. Drew Pinsky) is a *New York Times* bestseller. He also comments regularly in the media and has appeared on *The View, Howard Stern, Fox & Friends*, and CNN's *Situation Room* and has been quoted in the *New York Times, Newsweek, China Daily, Psychology Today, Scientific American Mind*, and the *London Times*.

Chapter 1

How Management Accounting Information Supports Decision Making

After completing this chapter, you will be able to:

1. Understand the major differences between financial and management accounting.

2. Appreciate the historical evolution of management accounting to its present set of practices.

3. Understand how management accounting information is used for strategic and operational decision making.

4. Understand the steps of the plan–do–check–act cycle and how each step defines a unique purpose and role for management accounting information.

5. Be sensitive to the behavioral consequences that result from the introduction of new measurement and management systems.

Research in Motion

In September 2010 Research in Motion (RIM), the producer of the BlackBerry smart phone, announced that PlayBook, its entry into the hot tablet market, would be introduced in the first quarter of 2011. This announcement caused a 3% decline in the value of RIM's shares, which analysts attributed to disappointment that the PlayBook would not be available for the December holiday season as previously expected.

RIM, once a smart phone market leader, was experiencing intense competition. Despite the extraordinary success of its BlackBerry products in the business market segment, new competitors such as Apple's iPhone, which had been developed originally for the consumer market segment, had eroded RIM's market leadership position. Apple's latest hot product, the iPad tablet, had achieved extraordinary success since its launch in March 2010 and RIM was under huge market pressure to respond with its own tablet.

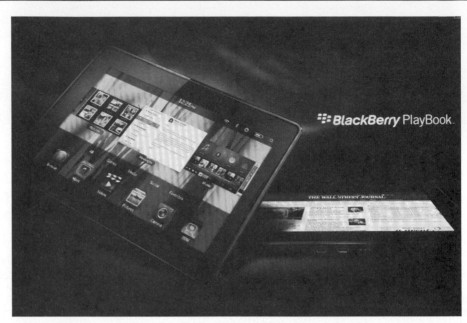

Alamy Images

The situation RIM faced in 2010 vividly illustrates the nature of both corporate strategy (choosing the markets in which it will compete) and business unit strategy (choosing how to compete in a given market segment). The strategic decisions that RIM faced required relevant and timely information, much of which is supplied by management accounting information.

WHAT IS MANAGEMENT ACCOUNTING?

Management accounting is the process of supplying the managers and employees in an organization with relevant information, both financial and nonfinancial, for making decisions, allocating resources, and monitoring, evaluating, and rewarding performance. The reported expense of an operating department, such as the assembly department of an automobile plant or an electronics company, is one example of management accounting information. Other examples are the cost of producing a product, the cost of delivering a service, and the cost of performing an activity or business process, such as creating a customer invoice or serving a customer. Nonfinancial management accounting information includes measures related to customer satisfaction and loyalty, process quality and timeliness, innovation, and employee motivation.

Management Accounting and Financial Accounting

Most students study management accounting after taking an initial course in financial accounting. These two subjects share important similarities since both are based on financial information and other quantitative information about business operations. But they differ in important ways.

Financial accounting has the following attributes:

1. It is retrospective, reporting and summarizing in financial terms the results of past decisions and transactions.
2. It is primarily oriented to external stakeholders, such as investors, creditors, regulators, and tax authorities.
3. It must be consistent with rules formulated by standard setters such as the Financial Accounting Standards Board (FASB) in the United States and the International Accounting Standards Board (IASB) for much of the rest of the world, and local country regulatory authorities, such as the U.S. Securities and Exchange Commission (SEC). These standard setters and regulatory authorities specify the content of the reports, the rules for how the content gets developed, and how the content will be presented.

In contrast, management accounting information has the following attributes:

1. It is both retrospective, providing feedback about past operations, and also prospective, incorporating forecasts and estimates about future events. For both retrospective reporting and prospective planning, management accounting uses both financial and nonfinancial measures.
2. It is oriented to meeting the decision-making needs of employees and managers inside the organization. Ideally, a good management accounting system can become a source of competitive advantage for a company.
3. It has no prescribed form or rules about its content, how the content is to be developed, and how the content is to be presented. All of these get determined by managers' judgments and decisions about what best meets their needs for actionable information and is defined entirely by the needs of managers using the information. No standard setter or regulator specifically influences the design of management accounting information and systems.

Management accounting information must be relevant and helpful to managers, and customized to serve multiple purposes.

A Brief History of Management Accounting

In the early 19th century, management accounting consisted of systems to measure the cost of producing individual products, such as a piece of clothing or a weapon. As enterprises grew in scale and scope, the demands for accurate costing information increased. By the middle of the 19th century, railroad managers had implemented large, complex costing systems that allowed them to compute the costs of carrying different types of freight, such as coal and steel, along multiple routes. This information supported efficiency improvements and pricing decisions. The railroads were the first modern industry to develop and use large quantities of financial statistics to assess and monitor organizational performance. Later in the century, Andrew Carnegie, in his steel company, developed detailed systems to record the cost of materials and labor used in his various mills. Carnegie intensively studied and acted on the information from his systems to continually reduce costs in his mills, and to close mills that he felt were irretrievably inefficient. Carnegie exploited his cost advantage by lowering his prices to levels that competitors could not match if they wanted to stay in business. Thus, Carnegie's excellent costing systems gave him a sustainable competitive advantage in the marketplace and promoted the growth and success of his company.

In the early 20th century, companies, such as DuPont and General Motors, expanded the focus of management accounting beyond cost accounting to management planning and control. These large companies replaced market mechanisms with internal resource allocation to multiple lines of business. Executives needed information, such as return-on-investment by business unit, for coordination and control among these multiple businesses. They used management accounting information to empower and inform the visible hand of management to replace what Adam Smith called the invisible hand of market forces.[1]

These organizations sought to improve efficiency and therefore profitability by internalizing what were previously open market transactions and eliminating the costs of transacting with external agents. The rise of these integrated companies created a demand for measuring the performance of individual organizational units to evaluate their performance through comparisons with stand-alone organizations that performed the same task. For example, an automobile company might want to compare the cost performance of a division that makes transmissions with that of an independent supplier, an application that we discuss in Chapter 3. Managers developed ways to measure the profitability and the performance of their units and continue to use them today, as discussed in Chapter 11 of the book.

After these innovations, the evolution of management accounting practice slowed as senior management interest focused on developing and preparing external financial statements that complied with the new reporting and auditing requirements imposed by regulatory authorities in the 1930s. Only in the 1970s, when American and European companies were under intense pressure from Japanese manufacturers, did interest revive in developing new management accounting tools. These tools included systems that reported on quality, service, and customer and employee performance rather than simple financial summaries of organizational unit performance. Also, major advances were made in measuring the cost of products and services to reflect the increasing importance of indirect and support costs required to design and produce a product, deliver a service, and meet a customer's demands. This text features, and in fact is organized around, many recent innovations in cost, profit, and performance measurement systems.

In summary, the history of management accounting illustrates that innovations in management accounting practice were—and continue to be—driven by the information needs of new strategies as companies became more complex, technologies changed, and new competitors appeared. When controlling and reducing costs were important, innovations in costing systems occurred. When organizations gained advantage from scale and diversification, innovative executives developed new management control systems to monitor and manage their complex enterprises. When competitive advantage shifted to how well a company deployed and managed its intangible assets—customer relationships, process quality, innovation, and, especially, employees, new systems for cost and performance management emerged.

IN PRACTICE

Definition of Management Accounting (2008), Issued by the Institute of Management Accountants

Management accounting is a profession that involves partnering in management decision making, devising planning and performance management systems, and providing expertise in financial reporting and control to assist management in the formulation and implementation of an organization's strategy.

Source: "Definition of Management Accounting," one of a series of Statements on Management Accounting, published by the *Institute of Management Accountants*, 2008, accessed from http://www.imanet.org/PDFs/Secure/Member/SMA/SMA_DefinManAcct_0408_2.pdf, which may be limited to IMA members.

---

[1] Alfred DuPont Chandler, *The Visible Hand: The Managerial Revolution in American Business* (Cambridge, Mass.: Belknap Press, 1977).

The Gap operates retail outlets, such as Banana Republic, Gap, and Old Navy, that target different market segments. Each market segment addresses different customers so the managers in each of the Gap's operating units need different management accounting information to evaluate their performance.

Getty Images, Inc.—Getty News

STRATEGY

This book frames management accounting as a discipline that helps an enterprise to develop and implement its strategy. Of course, this also requires that strategic objectives be linked to reporting on and improving operations.

Strategy is about an organization making choices about what it will do and, equally important, about what it will not do. At the highest level strategic planning involves choosing a strategy that provides the best fit between the organization's environment and its internal resources in order to achieve the organization's objectives. Selecting a strategy forces managers to make choices about what markets the organization should target and how the organization will compete in those markets. The details about how to do strategic planning and the type of information and analysis that strategists use to select a particular strategy are covered in strategy courses. But once a strategy has been selected, the organization needs management accounting information to help implement the strategy, allocate resources for the strategy, communicate the strategy, and link employees and operational processes to achieve the strategy. As the strategy gets executed, management accounting information provides feedback about where it is working and where it is not, and guides actions to improve the performance from the strategy. We can view the iterative strategy execution process through the lens of the **plan–do–check–act cycle**, originally developed for improving the quality of products and processes (see Exhibit 1-1).

Exhibit 1-1
The Plan–Do–Check–Act (PDCA) Cycle

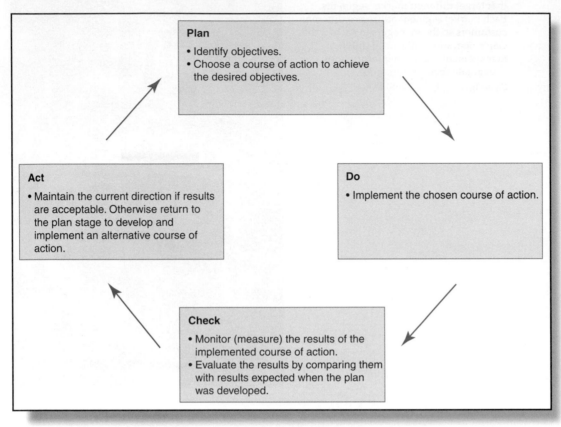

The Plan–Do–Check–Act (PDCA) Cycle

Quality expert W. Edwards Deming helped develop and disseminate the plan–do–check–act (PDCA) cycle, and it is often called the *Deming cycle*. Deming proposed it as a systematic and recursive way to develop, implement, monitor, evaluate, and, when necessary, change a course of action. Although Deming's focus was on improving product and process quality, his idea can be applied to any decision-making activity. We will illustrate how the PDCA cycle can frame the strategic and operational roles for management accounting information.

Plan

The first PDCA step defines the organization's purpose and selects the focus and scope of its strategy. Many organizations start the planning stage by reaffirming or updating their mission statement, which should be a powerful message to people inside and outside the organization about the organization's purpose and the value it intends to create in society. The enterprise's planners then accumulate information about the organization's external environment (political, economic, social, technological, environmental, and legal), its industry situation, and its internal strengths and weaknesses, relative to competitors. Executives use this information to decide on a strategy (a course of action) to achieve the organization's objectives. The planning step uses management accounting information in several ways.

Virtually every company has a mission statement that expresses its fundamental purpose and how it intends to add value to society through its relationships with customers, shareholders, employees, suppliers, and communities. You can find the mission statements for all Fortune 500 companies at the website http://www.missionstatements.com/fortune_500_mission_statements.html.

FedEx has crafted a strong mission statement to express its fundamental purpose to shareholders, employees, customers, and suppliers.
Alamy Images

As one example, FedEx, a Fortune 500 company, provides its mission statement and other aspects of its system of corporate governance at http://ir.fedex.com/governance.cfm.

Chapter 2 introduces the strategy map and Balanced Scorecard, two important management accounting tools for planning, deploying, and communicating the strategy. The strategy map and Balanced Scorecard capture management's beliefs about the drivers or causes of success in achieving an organization's objectives. They also provide a systematic way of identifying the management accounting information needed to communicate, monitor, and evaluate the chosen strategy.

Another essential component for the strategy planning stage is to estimate the cost and profit consequences from a course of action. Managers use cost–volume–profit (CVP) analysis, a widely used financial management tool that is introduced in Chapter 3, for profit planning and financial modeling. The chapter starts with the fundamental cost concepts and cost behavior that are the foundation for CVP analysis. Chapter 3 also discusses relevant cost analysis, which is used to help managers make ongoing business decisions such as whether to make or buy a product component, drop or add a product or department, and add or subtract resource capacity. Chapter 3 provides insight into the critical role management accounting information plays in the support of many of the important planning decisions that arise regularly in organizations.

The financial consequences of a strategy are often translated into a budget, perhaps the most widely used short-term financial planning and control tool. To develop a budget, the organization's financial planners develop a forecast that summarizes the revenue, cost, and profit consequences from the organization's planned activities. Chapter 10 discusses the scope and components of budgeting—an activity you will inevitably confront no matter where your professional career takes you.

Organizations also need to plan for the development of entirely new products and services. Chapter 8 discusses the role of management accounting for designing new products, monitoring the efficiency of the product development process, and assessing the total life-cycle cost consequences from using and disposing of products. End-of-cycle salvage and reclamation costs can be enormous, and information about these future costs for any project are now considered part of any new product development process.

Do

The "do" step of the PDCA cycle involves the implementation of a chosen course of action. In this setting, management accounting information is communicated to front-line and support employees to inform their daily decisions and work activities. Employees use cost, profit, and nonfinancial information to operate and improve processes; market, sell, and deliver products and services to customers; and respond to customer requests. Management accounting information is often used by internal auditing to ensure that the planned strategy and decisions are being faithfully executed. This enforcement role, which is an element of the wider role of corporate governance, has become an important component of the contribution that management accounting information makes in organizations.

Check

The check step in the PDCA cycle includes two components: measuring and monitoring ongoing performance and taking short-term actions based on the measured performance. Management accounting's traditional focus has been on measuring, evaluating, and reporting the costs of ongoing operations. Chapters 4 and 5 develop the nature and elements of systems designed to calculate the cost and profitability of products. Chapter 6 introduces an expanded role for management accounting information by measuring the cost of serving customers and customer profitability. Understanding the profit or loss of a company's multiple products and customers is essential feedback on how well the company's product-line and market strategy is working. Chapter 7 contributes to the check step in the PDCA cycle with its coverage of analyzing and improving operational processes. Chapter 10 describes the traditional financial control tool of variance analysis and Chapter 11 illustrates how management accounting information is used to evaluate overall departmental and business unit performance.

One of this book's innovations is to complement the normal financial focus of management accounting information with extensive treatment of the role of nonfinancial measures of performance. Chapter 2's introduction of the Balanced Scorecard frames the importance and role for nonfinancial information in managers' planning and control decisions. **Nonfinancial information** reports on the critical drivers of long-term financial performance: customers, processes, innovation, employees, systems, and culture. The particular nonfinancial measures most useful for an organization will vary based on its industry and strategy, but generally will include measures of customer loyalty, process quality, and employee capabilities and motivation.

Act

In the final PDCA step, managers take actions to lower costs, change resource allocations, improve the quality, cycle time, and flexibility of processes, modify the product mix, change customer relationships, and redesign and introduce new products. They reward (and occasionally punish) employees based on performance. Rather than a separate chapter or two on the act step of the PDCA cycle, we have embedded such decision making throughout the book. This emphasizes the fact that management accounting should always be informative and actionable for helping the organization implement its plan. As these new actions get implemented, the management team will eventually return to the planning step to assess whether its previous plan is still valid and worth continuing, or whether it has become time to adapt the plan or perhaps introduce a new strategic plan. This launches the enterprise on another trip around its PDCA cycle.

BEHAVIORAL IMPLICATIONS OF MANAGEMENT ACCOUNTING INFORMATION

Thus far we have emphasized the analytic role played by management accounting information for planning, resource allocation, decision making, acting, monitoring, and improving. Although the role of management accounting information is essential for supporting decisions and solving problems, information is never neutral. The mere act of measuring and informing affects the individuals involved. A famous study conducted in the 1920s at the Hawthorne Plant of the Western Electric Company concluded that individuals and groups alter their behavior when they know they are being studied and their performance is being measured. People react when they are being measured. They focus on the variables and behavior being measured and pay less attention to those not being measured. Some people have overstated this effect by declaring, "What gets measured gets done." More accurately, the expression should be "If you don't measure it, you can't manage and improve it," which can be taken as one of the fundamental rationales for studying and implementing management accounting systems.

It is normal, however, as managers introduce or redesign cost and performance measurement systems, for people familiar and comfortable with the previous systems to resist change. These people have acquired expertise in the use (and occasional misuse) of the old system and are concerned about whether their experience and expertise will be transferable to the new system. People also may feel committed to the decisions and actions taken on the basis of information an old system has produced. These actions may no longer seem valid based on the information produced by a newly installed management accounting system. Thus, a new management system can lead to embarrassment and threat, a trigger for reactions against change. The design and introduction of new measurements and systems must be accompanied by an analysis of the behavioral and organizational reactions to the measurements, a topic we discuss extensively in Chapter 9. Even more important, when the measurements are used not only for information, planning, and decision making but also for control, evaluation, and reward, employees and managers place great emphasis on the measurements themselves. Managers and employees may take unexpected and undesirable actions to influence their score on the performance measure. For example, managers seeking to improve current bonuses based on reported profits may skip discretionary expenditures such as preventive maintenance, research and development, and advertising that may improve performance in future periods.

Thus we must be ever vigilant to not only see the analytic, or left-brain, properties of management accounting information but also appreciate the emotional, or right-brain, reactions by individuals to the information used to monitor and evaluate their performance.

SUMMARY

This chapter introduced the role and nature of management accounting within the PDCA planning and control cycle. Management accounting must inform the actions and decisions made by managers and employees. This is why the generation and use of management accounting information must be driven by the organization's strategic choices. Management accounting information also monitors and evaluates the results from implemented decisions. It leads to new actions to improve the implementation of the intended strategy through operational enhancements, decisions about products, processes, and customers, new product introductions, and, perhaps most important, better motivated and empowered managers and employees. But all new measurement and management systems must be introduced with sensitivity to the reactions of employees and managers to the act of measurement.

KEY TERMS

financial accounting, 27
management accounting, 26

nonfinancial information, 32
plan–do–check–act cycle, 29

strategy, 29

ASSIGNMENT MATERIALS

Questions

1-1 What is management accounting? **(LO 1)**

1-2 Give two examples each for financial management accounting information and nonfinancial management accounting information. **(LO 1)**

1-3 Differentiate between management accounting and financial accounting. **(LO 1)**

1-4 What is strategic planning? **(LO 3)**

1-5 Name the management accounting tool that is most relevant to (a) making ongoing decisions regarding making or buying a component, (b) profit planning and financial modeling, and (c) short-term financial planning and control. **(LO 4)**

1-6 Given a selected strategy, how do organizations use management accounting information to implement the strategy? **(LO 3)**

1-7 Briefly explain each of the four steps of the plan–do–check–act cycle. **(LO 4)**

1-8 How can management accounting information produce behavioral and organizational reactions? **(LO 5)**

Exercises

LO 1, 3, 4, 5   **1-9** *The role of management accounting*   Consider the descriptions of management accounting provided in the chapter. Discuss why the associated responsibilities are viewed as "accounting" and how people handling those responsibilities interface with other functional areas in fulfilling the stated responsibilities. What skills and knowledge does one need to fulfill the responsibilities?

LO 3   **1-10** *Management accounting and strategy relationship*   Discuss the relationship between management accounting and strategy.

LO 1, 3   **1-11** *Different information needs*   Consider the operation of a fast-food company with hundreds of retail outlets scattered about the country. Consider the descriptions of management accounting provided in the chapter to identify management accounting information needs for the following:
a. The manager of a local fast-food outlet that prepares food and serves it to customers who walk in or pick it up at a drive-through window
b. The regional manager who supervises the operations of all the retail outlets in a three-state region

c. Senior management located at the company's corporate headquarters. Consider specifically the information needs of the president and the vice presidents of operations and marketing.

Be sure to address the content, frequency, and level of aggregation of information needed by these different managers.

LO 1, 3   **1-12 *Different information needs***   Consider the descriptions of management accounting provided in the chapter to identify management accounting information needs for the following:

a. The managers of (1) a patient unit, where patients stay while being treated for illness or while recuperating from an operation, and (2) the radiology department, where patients obtain X-rays and receive radiological treatment

b. The manager of a nursing service who hires and assigns nurses to all patient units and to specialty services, such as the operating room, emergency room, recovery room, and radiology room

c. The chief executive officer of the hospital.

Be sure to address the content, frequency, and level of aggregation of information needed by these different managers.

LO 3   **1-13 *The elements of quality***   For each of the following products, suggest three measures of quality:

a. Television set
b. University course
c. Meal in an exclusive restaurant
d. Carryout meal from a restaurant
e. Container of milk
f. Visit to the doctor
g. Trip on an airplane
h. Pair of jeans
i. Novel
j. University textbook.

Problems

LO 1, 3   **1-14 *Differences between financial and managerial accounting***   Many German companies have their management accounting department as part of the manufacturing operations group rather than as part of the corporate finance department. These German companies operate two separate accounting departments. One performs financial accounting functions for shareholders and tax authorities, and the other maintains and operates the costing system for manufacturing operations.

Required

What are the advantages and disadvantages of having separate departments for financial accounting and management accounting?

LO 1   **1-15 *Differences between financial and managerial accounting***   The controller of a German machine tool company believed that historical cost depreciation was inadequate for assigning the cost of using expensive machinery to individual parts and products. Each year, he estimated the replacement cost of each machine and included depreciation based on the machine's replacement cost in the machine-hour rate used to assign machine expenses to the parts produced on that machine. Additionally, the controller included an interest charge, based on 50% of the machine's replacement value, into the machine-hour rate. The interest rate was an average of the three- to five-year interest rate on government and high-grade corporate securities.

As a consequence of these two decisions (charging replacement cost rather than historical cost and imputing a capital charge for the use of capital equipment), the product cost figures used internally by company managers were inconsistent with the numbers that were needed for inventory valuation for financial and tax reporting. The accounting staff had to perform a tedious reconciliation process at the end of each year to back out the interest and replacement value costs from the cost of goods sold and inventory values before they could prepare the financial statements.

Required

(a) Why would the controller introduce additional complications into the company's costing system by assigning replacement value depreciation costs and imputed interest costs to the company's parts and products?

(b) Why should management accountants create extra work for the organization by deliberately adopting policies for internal costing that violate the generally accepted accounting principles that must be used for external reporting?

LO 1, 3, 4   **1-16** *Role of financial information for continuous improvement*   Consider an organization that has empowered its employees, asking them to improve the quality, productivity, and responsiveness of their processes that involve repetitive work. This work could arise in a manufacturing setting, such as assembling cars or producing chemicals, or in a service setting, such as processing invoices or responding to customer orders and requests. Clearly the workers would benefit from feedback on the quality (defects, yields) and process times of the work they were doing to suggest where they could make improvements. Identify the role, if any, for sharing financial information with these employees to help them in their efforts to improve quality, productivity, and process times. Be specific about the types of financial information that would be helpful and the specific decisions or actions that could be made better by supplementing physical and operational information with financial information.

Cases

LO 1, 3, 4   **1-17** *Different information needs*   Julie Martinez, manager of the new retail outlet of Super Printing, is pondering the management challenges in her new position. Super Printing is a long-established printing company in a major metropolitan area. The new Super outlet, located at the edge of the parking lot for Western Business School, represents Super's attempt to break into the rapidly growing business for retail digital imaging.

The Super retail store provides a range of copying and digital imaging services for the business school's students, faculty, and administrators, plus other retail customers. Super's primary products are black-and-white copies of documents. Variation exists even in this basic product, however, as consumers can choose from a variety of paper colors, sizes, and quality. Super recently purchased a machine that prints color copies from digital input. Color copies also can be produced in a variety of sizes, paper quality, and paper types, including transparencies for overhead projection and photographic-quality reproductions. Other printing products include business cards, laminated luggage tags, and name badges for conferences, executive programs, and students.

In addition to physical printing, the Super center provides fax services by which individuals can both receive and transmit documents. When incoming faxes are received, a store employee calls the recipient, who stops at the outlet to pick up the document. The center also has several personal computers, both Windows-based and Macintosh, that students rent by the hour for basic computer processing, Internet access, e-mail, and preparing presentations and résumés. Each computer is connected to Super's black-and-white and color printers, enabling students to produce paper copies of their presentations and résumés.

Super has other machines that assemble printed pages into bound documents. Two different binding types are available. The store also sells a limited selection of office supplies, including paper, envelopes, paper clips, glue, binders, tabs, pens, pencils, and marking pens.

Currently, about five employees (including Julie) work at the retail outlet during prime hours (8:00 A.M. to 5:00 P.M.) with two to four people working the evening shift (5:00 P.M. to midnight) when walk-in business is much slower. The number of people working during the evening hours is determined by the anticipated backlog of reproduction work that will be performed during these hours.

Prices for the various products and services have been set based on those of competitors, such as FedEx Kinko's and Staples. Julie receives a daily report on total sales, broken down by cash sales, credit card sales, and credit sales to various programs at the business school; however, she currently does not have a report on expenses such as labor, materials, and equipment for each line of business (black-and-white and color printing, computer services, document preparation, fax services, and sales of office supplies). Thus, Julie is unsure whether each line of business is profitable. Julie is also unsure how efficiently the business is run.

Further, the different business lines require different quantities and types of capital: equipment such as copying and printing machines, computers, and facsimile machines; physical capital such as office space; and the different inventories of paper types, colors, grades and sizes, and office supplies.

If the pilot store that Julie is operating is successful, then the parent company will likely try to open many similar outlets near schools and universities throughout the metropolitan area. For this purpose, the parent company wants to know which business lines are the most profitable, including the cost of capital and space required, so that these lines can be featured at each retail outlet. If some business lines are not profitable, then Super probably will not offer those services at newly opened stores unless they are necessary to build retail traffic.

Required

Identify the management accounting information needs for the following:

(a) An employee desiring to help serve customers more efficiently and effectively
(b) Julie Martinez, the manager of the pilot retail outlet
(c) The president of Super Printing

Be sure to address the content, frequency, and level of aggregation of information needed by these different individuals.

LO 1, 3   **1-18** *Information for employee empowerment*   A U.S. automobile components plant had recently been reorganized so that quality and employee teamwork were to be the guiding principles for all managers and workers. One production worker described the difference:

In the old production environment, we were not paid to think. The foreman told us what to do, and we did it even if we knew he was wrong. Now, the team decides what to do. Our voices are heard. All middle management has been cut out, including foremen and superintendents. Management relies on us, the team members, to make decisions. Salary people help us make these decisions; the production and manufacturing engineers work for us. They are always saying, "We work for you. What do you need?" And they listen to us.

The plant controller commented as follows:

In traditional factories, the financial system viewed people as variable costs. If you had a production problem, you sent people home to reduce your variable costs. Here, we do not send people home. Our production people are viewed as problem solvers, not as variable costs.

Required

(a) What information needs did the production workers have in the old environment?

(b) What information do you recommend be supplied to the production workers in the new environment that emphasizes quality, defect reduction, problem solving, and teamwork?

LO 1, 3, 4   **1-19** *Financial information for continuous improvement*   The manager of a large semiconductor production department expressed his disdain for the cost information he was presently given:

Cost variances are useless to me.[2] I don't want to ever have to look at a cost variance, monthly or weekly. Daily, I look at sales dollars, bookings, and on-time delivery (OTD)—the percent of orders on time. Weekly, I look at a variety of quality reports including the outgoing quality control report on items passing the final test before shipment to the customer, in-process quality, and yields. Yield is a good surrogate for cost and quality. Monthly, I do look at the financial reports. I look closely at my fixed expenses and compare these to the budgets, especially on discretionary items like travel and maintenance. I also watch headcount.

But the financial systems still don't tell me where I am wasting money. I expect that if I make operating improvements, costs should go down, but I don't worry about the linkage too much. The organizational dynamics make it difficult to link cause and effect precisely.

Required

Comment on this production manager's assessment of his limited use for financial and cost summaries of performance. For what purposes, if any, are cost and financial information helpful to operating people? How should the management accountant determine the appropriate blend between financial and nonfinancial information for operating people?

LO 1, 2, 3, 4, 5 **1-20** *Comprehensive performance measurement in public and nonprofit organizations*   Organizations in the public and nonprofit sector, such as government agencies and charitable social service entities, have financial systems that budget expenses and monitor and control actual spending. Explain why these organizations should consider developing a comprehensive set of performance measurements (including nonfinancial measures) to monitor and report on their performance. Provide examples of financial and nonfinancial measures that should be included in such a comprehensive set of measurements.

---

[2] We will study cost variances in later chapters. For the purposes of this case, it is sufficient to recognize that a cost variance represents the difference between the cost actually assigned to a production department and the cost that was expected or budgeted for that department.

Chapter

2

The Balanced Scorecard and Strategy Map

After completing this chapter, you will be able to:

1. Explain why both financial and nonfinancial measures are required to evaluate and manage a company's strategy.

2. Understand how a Balanced Scorecard can represent cause-and-effect hypotheses of a company's strategy across financial, customer, process, and learning and growth perspectives.

3. Explain why a clear strategy is vital for a company.

4. Appreciate the role for a strategy map to translate a strategy into financial, customer, process, and learning and growth objectives.

5. Select measures for the strategic objectives in the four perspectives of a company's Balanced Scorecard and strategy map.

6. Extend the Balanced Scorecard framework to nonprofit and public-sector organizations.

7. Recognize problems that companies may experience when implementing the Balanced Scorecard and suggest ways to overcome them.

Pioneer Petroleum

Pioneer Petroleum was the U.S. marketing and refining division of a large global petroleum company. It operated five refineries and had more than 7,000 branded gasoline stations around the United States, which sold about 25 million gallons of gasoline per day. Historically, Pioneer marketed a full range of products and services. It did, however, match the prices of discount stations operating near a Pioneer station so that it would not lose market share. Pioneer's CEO Brian Roberts had recently learned that Pioneer was the least profitable marketing and refining company in the United States. He decided to turn around the company by implementing a strategy based on a marketing study that had revealed five

Time-sensitive customers prefer self-service gasoline stations.

Alamy Images

distinct consumer segments among the gasoline-buying public (see Exhibit 2-1).

Pioneer's executives saw that price-sensitive consumers constituted only 20% of all U.S. gasoline purchasers. Another segment, Homebodies, had little loyalty to any brand or station. But three segments wanted more than a commodity purchase. After considerable discussion, Pioneer decided on a strategy to offer a superior buying experience to the three top-tier segments: Road Warriors, True Blues, and Generation F3. Also, it would no longer seek to attract price-sensitive consumers by lowering prices to compete with discount gasoline stations.

Exhibit 2-1
Pioneer's Five Gasoline-Buyer Segments

Road Warriors (16%)	Generally higher-income middle-aged men who drive 25,000 to 50,000 miles a year, buy premium gasoline with a credit card, purchase sandwiches and drinks from the convenience store, will sometimes wash their cars at the carwash.
True Blues (16%)	Usually men and women with moderate to high incomes who are loyal to a brand and sometimes to a particular station; frequently buy premium gasoline and pay in cash.
Generation F3 (27%)	(F3—fuel, food, and fast) Upwardly mobile men and women—half under 25 years of age—who are constantly on the go; drive a lot and snack heavily from the convenience store.
Homebodies (21%)	Usually homemakers who shuttle their children around during the day and use whatever gasoline station is based in town or along their route of travel.
Price Shoppers (20%)	Generally aren't loyal to either a brand or a particular station, and rarely buy the premium line; frequently on tight budgets; the focus of attention of marketing efforts of gasoline companies for years.

Roberts faced the challenge of realigning Pioneer to the new customer-focused strategy. The realignment could not be done just at the top. It had to take place at the grass roots. For its strategy to succeed, Pioneer would have to make *everyone* aware of the strategy and accountable for its success. A survey had revealed that employees felt internal reporting requirements, administrative processes, and top-down policies were stifling creativity and innovation. Relationships with customers were adversarial, and people were working narrowly to enhance the reported results of their individual, functional units. Roberts expressed the problem as follows:

> I am accountable for a large organization, spread over a large geographic area. At the end of the day, success comes from individuals at the frontline of operations. You've got an operator at a refinery, sitting in front of a computer screen controlling a process unit at 3 A.M. on Sunday morning when management is not around. My fate is determined by that person's attitude, whether that person is paying attention. Thirty seconds of inattention at the wrong time can shut down that refinery, stopping production. If you're going to drive the business you have to drive it down to that individual who is at the frontline, making the decision.

Pioneer had operated for decades with a centralized structure, organized by functions, such as purchasing, supply chain, manufacturing (refining), distribution, and marketing. Only two people, Roberts and his executive vice president, among Pioneer's 7,000 employees had accountability for a profit and loss statement. Managers of a refinery, pipeline, or distribution facility were responsible for achieving cost targets, while managers of sales districts had to meet revenue targets. To create a more agile organization, Roberts decentralized Pioneer into 17 strategic business units (including regional gasoline sales districts and specialized product units, such as for jet fuels and lubricants) that would be closer to customers. Each business unit would have its own profit and loss accountability. Roberts now faced the problem of how to upgrade the skills of the newly appointed business unit heads who had all grown up within a structured, top-down functional organization:

> We were taking people who had spent their whole professional lives as managers in a big functional organization, and we were asking them to become the leaders of entrepreneurial profit-making businesses, some with up to $1 billion in assets. How were we going to get them out of their historic area of functional expertise to think strategically, as general managers of profit-oriented businesses?

Roberts believed that a major impediment to change was the company's historic focus on achieving short-term financial performance:

> The financial metrics gave us a controller's mentality, reviewing the past, not guiding the future. I wanted metrics that could communicate what we wanted to be so that everyone in the organization could understand and implement our strategy. We needed metrics that could link our planning process to actions, to encourage people to do the things that the organization was now committed to accomplishing.

Roberts struggled with how he could change the performance measurement framework at Pioneer into one that would be better aligned with its new strategy and organizational structure.

Companies use performance measurement systems to perform multiple roles:

- Communicate the company's strategic objectives.
- Motivate employees to help the company achieve its strategic objectives.
- Evaluate the performance of managers, employees, and operating units.
- Help managers allocate resources to the most productive and profitable opportunities.
- Provide feedback on whether the company is making progress in improving processes and meeting the expectations of customers and shareholders.

The challenge is to find the right mix of financial and nonfinancial measures to perform these multiple tasks. Throughout the 19th and 20th centuries, companies like Pioneer Petroleum used only financial metrics to measure their performance. Financial control systems, which we will describe later in the book (Chapter 11), relied on metrics such as operating income and return on investment (ROI) to motivate and evaluate performance. These financial metrics were adequate when the primary assets that generated a company's income and value were physical assets, such as property, plant, equipment, and inventory, and financial assets, including cash, marketable securities, and investments. By the end of the 20th century, however, firms could no longer create value only through their physical and financial assets. They needed to create value through their intangible assets—customer loyalty and relationships, efficient and high-quality operating processes, new products and services, employee skills and motivation, databases and information systems, and, most intangible of all, organizational culture.

With these changes in the factors driving competitive success, financial measures become insufficient for measuring and managing company performance. Consider a company that spends money in the current period to enhance its intangible assets through the following actions:

- Upgrading the skills and motivation of employees.
- Expanding the data captured and shared about processes, customers, and suppliers.
- Accelerating new products through the research and development pipeline.
- Improving the quality and speed of production, distribution, and service processes.
- Enhancing trusted relationships with profitable customers and low-cost suppliers.

All of these actions help to create value for the company. But the financial system treats the spending on such actions as *expenses* of the current period. Thus the company's reported profitability and financial performance decrease during a period when it has actually increased the value of its intangible assets. Or consider the converse situation in which a company cuts back drastically on its spending to train employees, enhance information systems, improve operating processes, develop new products, and build customer loyalty. As such spending declines, reported income and ROI increases, at just the time when the company has likely become less valuable because of the depreciation of its competitive capabilities. Clearly, the financial reports fail to reflect the changes in value that occur when a company either enhances or destroys the value of its intangible assets.

A fundamental principle underlying management accounting is that measurement must support the company's strategy and operations. Some claim "if you don't measure it, you can't manage and improve it." If companies are to get better at managing and improving the value created from their intangible assets, they need a measurement system designed for these types of assets. Several frameworks have been proposed for

Exhibit 2-2
Performance
Measurement
Frameworks

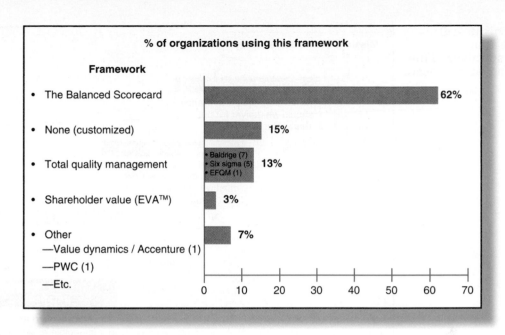

% of organizations using this framework

Framework

- The Balanced Scorecard — 62%
- None (customized) — 15%
- Total quality management — • Baldrige (7) • Six sigma (5) • EFQM (1) — 13%
- Shareholder value (EVA™) — 3%
- Other — 7%
  —Value dynamics / Accenture (1)
  —PWC (1)
  —Etc.

0 10 20 30 40 50 60 70

Source: R. Lawson, D. Desroches, and T. Hatch, *Scorecard Best Practices: Design, Implementation, and Evaluation* (New York: Wiley, 2008).

expanded performance measurement,[1] including those introduced by national and international quality management programs such as the Malcolm Baldrige National Quality Program for performance excellence[2] and the EFQM Excellence model.[3] Among all of the various proposals for improving companies' performance measurement systems, the management accounting system based on the Balanced Scorecard (BSC) has become the most widely adopted around the world (see data presented in Exhibit 2-2). The Balanced Scorecard provides a framework that continues to measure financial outcomes but supplements these with nonfinancial measures derived from the company's strategy. And, the BSC is not restricted to private-sector companies; many nonprofits and public sector entities have also adopted this framework to manage their creation of social value (as we will describe later in this chapter).

THE BALANCED SCORECARD

The Balanced Scorecard (see Exhibit 2-3) measures organizational performance across four different but linked perspectives that are derived from the organization's mission, vision, and strategy. The four perspectives address the following fundamental questions:

- *Financial*—How is success measured by our shareholders?
- *Customer*—How do we create value for our customers?

---

[1] References on organizational performance measurement include Richard L. Lynch and Kelvin F. Cross, *Measure Up! How to Measure Corporate Performance* (Cambridge, Mass.: Blackwell Business, 1995); Robert S. Kaplan and David P. Norton, *The Balanced Scorecard: Translating Strategy into Action* (Cambridge, Mass.: Harvard Business School Press, 1996); and Andy Neely, *Business Performance Measurement: Theory and Practice* (Cambridge, UK: Cambridge University Press, 2002).
[2] NIST: Malcolm Baldrige Excellence Program home page, retrieved November 20, 2010 from http://www.nist.gov/baldrige/
[3] The EFQM Excellence Model home page, retrieved November 20, 2010 from http://www.efqm.org

Exhibit 2-3
The Four
Perspectives of the
Balanced Scorecard

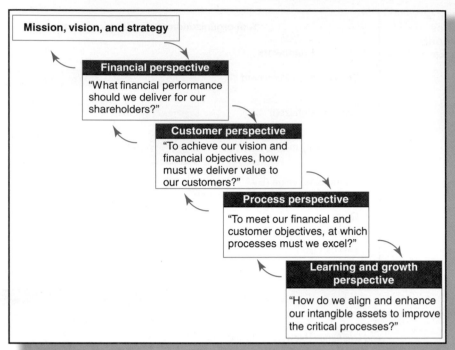

- *Process*—At which processes must we excel to meet our customer and shareholder expectations?
- *Learning and growth*—What employee capabilities, information systems, and organizational capabilities do we need to continually improve our processes and customer relationships?[4]

With the Balanced Scorecard measurement system, companies continue to track financial results but they also monitor, with nonfinancial measures, whether they are building or destroying their capabilities—with customers, processes, employees, and systems—for future growth and profitability. Financial measures tend to be lagging indicators of the strategy; they report the financial impact of decisions made in the current and prior periods. The nonfinancial measures in the three other BSC perspectives are leading indicators. Improvements in these indicators should lead to better financial performance in the future, while decreases in the nonfinancial indicators (such as customer satisfaction and loyalty, process quality, and employee motivation) generally predict decreased future financial performance.

As a simple example of the cause-and-effect linkages across Balanced Scorecard measures, consider the partial scorecard produced by a small manufacturing company. This company's strategy is to win business by producing low-cost, high-quality products, and delivering them on time to its customers (see Exhibit 2-4). The company's financial objective, shown in the financial perspective, is to increase its return on equity (ROE; net income divided by book value). The company expects to generate increased revenues for improving its ROE financial measure by retaining and expanding sales to existing customers. Therefore, it has a customer loyalty objective in its customer perspective, which it measures by (1) percentage of repeat

---

[4] Most organizations implementing the BSC have found four to be the right number for describing their strategy. Some organizations have added a fifth perspective to highlight particularly important aspects of their strategy, such as suppliers, employees, community involvement, or, for nonprofit organizations, social impact. Using fewer than four typically sacrifices metrics that are critical for the strategy.

Exhibit 2-4
A Simple Balanced Scorecard of Linked Objectives and Measures

Strategy map of objectives	Objectives	Measures
Financial — Increase shareholder value	• Increase shareholder value	• Return on equity
Customer — Retain customers, Deliver products on time, Offer competitive prices	• Retain customers • Deliver products on time • Offer competitive prices	• Percentage of repeat customers • Growth in customers' sales • % deliveries made on time • Prices compared to competitors
Process — Reduce process cycle time, Improve process quality	• Reduce process cycle times • Improve process quality	• % improvement in cycle times • Product defect rates • Process yield improvement
Learning and growth — Develop employees' process improvement skills	• Develop employees' process improvement skills	• % employees trained and certified in process improvement capabilities

customers and (2) the growth in year-to-year sales with existing customers. The company's strategy is based on its belief that customers value on-time delivery of orders and low prices. Thus, improved on-time delivery performance and competitive prices are expected to lead to increased customer loyalty, which in turn will lead to higher financial performance. So the predictive metrics of customer loyalty and on-time delivery appear in the scorecard's customer perspective.

The financial and customer measures represent the "what" of strategy, that is, what the company wants to accomplish with its two most important external constituents: shareholders and customers. The process perspective describes "how" the strategy will be executed; it identifies the processes that are most important to meet the expectations of shareholders and customers. For example, short cycle times and high-quality production processes are necessary to achieve exceptional on-time delivery and low prices. Therefore, measures of quality, such as defect rates and yields, and of process cycle time—the time required to convert raw materials into finished products—are used as important process metrics. These are leading indicators for customer loyalty. Measures for the fourth perspective, learning and growth, arise from asking another "how" question: How will employees obtain the skills and knowledge to be able to improve the quality and cycle times of the company's production processes? The company recognizes that its production workers must be well trained in process improvement techniques. Therefore, the learning and growth perspective uses a measure of employees' capabilities to predict improvements in process quality and cycle times.

This simple example shows how an entire chain of cause-and-effect relationships among performance measures in the four Balanced Scorecard perspectives tells the story of the business unit's strategy. The scorecard's objectives and measures identify and make explicit the hypotheses about the cause-and-effect relationships between outcome measures (e.g., ROE and customer loyalty) in the financial and customer perspectives and the performance drivers (i.e., lead indicators) of those outcomes—such as zero defect processes, short cycle-time processes, and skilled, motivated employees—that are measured in the process and learning and growth perspectives.

Exhibit 2-5
Discount Airlines'
Balanced Scorecard

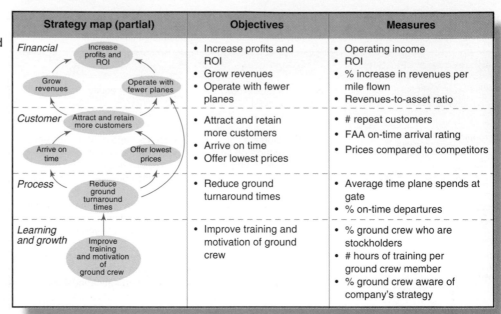

Strategy map (partial)	Objectives	Measures
Financial — Increase profits and ROI, Grow revenues, Operate with fewer planes	• Increase profits and ROI • Grow revenues • Operate with fewer planes	• Operating income • ROI • % increase in revenues per mile flown • Revenues-to-asset ratio
Customer — Attract and retain more customers, Arrive on time, Offer lowest prices	• Attract and retain more customers • Arrive on time • Offer lowest prices	• # repeat customers • FAA on-time arrival rating • Prices compared to competitors
Process — Reduce ground turnaround times	• Reduce ground turnaround times	• Average time plane spends at gate • % on-time departures
Learning and growth — Improve training and motivation of ground crew	• Improve training and motivation of ground crew	• % ground crew who are stockholders • # hours of training per ground crew member • % ground crew aware of company's strategy

Exhibit 2-5 provides another example of performance measures linked across the Balanced Scorecard's four perspectives. Discount Airlines competes by offering low prices and on-time arrivals to its passengers. The diagram on the left side of Exhibit 2-5 shows the cause-and-effect relationships across the four perspectives that describe a key element of Discount's strategy: how it can make money even at low prices by being efficient and low cost in its operations. The high-level financial objective is to increase financial performance, which it measures by operating income and return on investment. Discount has identified two additional financial objectives—revenue growth and asset utilization (fewer planes)—that it believes will drive its high-level financial metrics. If Discount can get two extra flights per day from each airplane and flight crew, its most expensive resources, it can earn higher revenues without having to spend more on these resources.

The company hopes to attract more passengers (and, therefore, revenues) by offering the lowest prices and the most reliable departure and arrival times in the industry. It reflects these objectives in the customer perspective and measures them by prices compared to competitors and by on-time departures and arrivals, again measured relative to industry competitors. A key process that contributes both to the on-time departure customer metric and the asset utilization financial metric is the ground-turnaround process. Discount uses two measures for this critical process: the average time its planes spend on the ground between flights and the percentage of flights that depart the gate on time. By reducing the time its planes spend on the ground, Discount enables its planes to depart on time (meeting a key customer expectation) and get better utilization of its most expensive resources—airplanes and flight crews—enabling Discount to earn profits even at prices that are the lowest in the industry (a key financial objective). In the learning and growth perspective, Discount has an objective to train and motivate ground crews for fast ground turnarounds, much like the training of the pit crew for a race car in the Indianapolis 500 that can change four tires in less than 15 seconds.

The various measures in Discount's Balanced Scorecard include its desired outcomes (the lagging indicators) in the financial and customer perspectives—high return on investment, increased revenues, lower cost per passenger mile flown, and increased market share and customer satisfaction—as well as the drivers (lead indicators) of these outcomes in the process and learning and growth perspectives—fast turnaround times and enhanced employee capabilities and motivation.

This introduction to the Balanced Scorecard shows how a management accounting scorecard of financial and nonfinancial measures can represent the cause-and-effect hypotheses of a company's strategy.

STRATEGY

If companies are to develop a scorecard based on their strategies, they must be clear about what is meant by a strategy. A strategy accomplishes two principal functions. First, it creates a competitive advantage by positioning the company in its external environment where its internal resources and capabilities deliver something to its customers that is better than or different from its competitors. Second, having a clear strategy provides clear guidance for where internal resources should be allocated and enables all organizational units and employees to make decisions and implement policies that are consistent with achieving and sustaining the company's competitive advantage in the marketplace.

Even though companies can select from among many strategies (we will describe three very different strategies later in the chapter), any good strategy should have two essential components[5]:

1. A clear statement of the company's *advantage* in the competitive marketplace, what it does or intends to do differently, better, or uniquely compared to competitors, and
2. The *scope* for the strategy, where the company intends to compete most aggressively, either for targeted customer segments, technologies employed, geographic locations served, or product line breadth.

Consider the advantage and scope for a discount airline, such as Southwest Airlines in the United States:

> *Advantage:*   Offer the speed of airline travel at the price, frequency, and reliability of cars, buses, and trains . . .
> *Scope:*   . . . to price-sensitive travelers who value convenient flights.

This brief statement tells you exactly how Southwest competed against the more established airlines, the customers it targeted to serve, and the benefits it strived to deliver to them.

As another example, consider the advantage and scope statement for the brokerage firm Edward Jones[6]:

> *Advantage:*   Provide trusted and convenient face-to-face financial advice . . .
> *Scope:*   . . . through a national network of one-financial-adviser offices to conservative individual investors who delegate their financial decisions.

---

[5] The strategy statement was introduced in M. Rukstad and D. Collis, "Can You Say What Your Strategy Is?" *Harvard Business Review* (April 2008).
[6] Example taken from Rukstad and Collis, "What Is Your Strategy?"

Infosys was founded in India in 1981 by seven engineers as an IT "body shop"—a firm that deployed skilled IT labor to work, on a contract basis, for clients. Throughout the 1980s and 1990s, the programmer-for-hire business flourished along with the increased global demand for IT systems and maintenance. Infosys soon developed the capabilities it needed to become an outsourcer, executing IT projects for clients from its facilities in India. Its success in executing such complex projects led some clients to hire Infosys to manage software projects end to end, from project architecture to detailed programming. Within a decade, Infosys had shifted its operating model from supplying labor for one segment of a job to designing, managing, and delivering complete software projects.

In the early 2000s, Infosys expanded its portfolio of services beyond traditional IT outsourcing, to partnering with large global clients to transform their businesses through advanced IT products, services, and solutions. In 2005, the firm had only five contracts worth more than $50 million. By early 2008, it had 18 clients generating $50 million or more in revenue and six clients that were generating more than $100 million. These deals usually involved multiple services performed over several years.

As part of the company's transformation from an IT body shop and outsourcer to a trusted transformational partner with large global corporations, the Infosys executive team developed a Balanced Scorecard to provide a comprehensive framework by which it could formulate, communicate, and monitor its strategy. Infosys's CEO explained the role that the BSC played in the company's recent growth:

> The BSC allows us to promote constant change through stretch goals. Since 2002, we have successfully steered the transformation of our company through various stages of its evolution using the Balanced Scorecard. We continue to take on new strategic challenges that require us to manage change. These challenges require us to better execute our strategies comprehensively across the Balanced Scorecard perspectives.

Source: F. Asis-Martinez, R. S. Kaplan, and K. Miller, "Infosys' Relationship Scorecard: Measuring Transformational Partnerships," HBS No. 1-108-006 (Boston: Harvard Business School Publishing, 2008).

Edward Jones' *advantage* is to become the preferred financial adviser to the conservative investor who is willing to follow the advice of a personal, professional counselor. It does not want to be the brokerage firm for the day trader or the do-it-yourself online investor. Its *scope* is the range of locations, typically in a customer's neighborhood, where it can supply an office with a single, self-supporting skilled financial adviser who builds relationships with his or her clients.

BALANCED SCORECARD OBJECTIVES, MEASURES, AND TARGETS

A company should start its process of building a Balanced Scorecard by developing word statements of strategic **objectives** that describe what it is attempting to accomplish with its strategy. Once the company selects and defines its objectives for the four BSC perspectives, it can select measures for each objective. The measures represent a quantitative indicator of how performance on a strategic objective will be assessed. For example, the first two columns in Exhibits 2-4 and 2-5 contain the objectives in each perspective, which are typically written as action phrases—a verb followed by an object—and also may include the means and the desired results. Following are typical Balanced Scorecard objectives:

- Increase revenues through expanded sales to existing customers (*financial*).
- Offer complete solutions to our targeted customers (*customer*).

- Achieve excellence in order fulfillment through continuous improvements (*process*).
- Align employee incentives and rewards with the strategy (*learning and growth*).

However well companies write their strategic objectives, employees will still interpret and translate the words differently when they try to apply the objectives to their day-to-day jobs. Also, unless the objectives can be translated into measures, employees will not know what the status of the objective is today, and whether the company is getting closer or further away from achieving the objective. As stated earlier in the chapter, you can't manage what you don't measure.

Measures describe in more precise terms how success in achieving an objective will be determined. They reduce the ambiguity that is inherent in word statements. Take, for example, an objective to deliver a product or service to a customer on time. The definition of "on time" can differ between supplier and customer. A manufacturer may consider an item on time if it ships the item within a week of the delivery commitment date. A company like Toyota, however, which uses just-in-time production processes with essentially no materials or components inventory, considers an order to be on time only if it arrives within 1 hour of the scheduled delivery time. Toyota is not interested in whether the vendor shipped the item on time; it wants the item to arrive at its factory site on time. Only by specifying exactly how an objective, such as on-time delivery, is measured can a company eliminate ambiguity between suppliers and customers about the definition of "on time." The selected measure also provides a clear focus to employees on how their improvement efforts will be evaluated. Thus, measurement is a powerful tool for communicating clearly what the company means in its word statements of strategic objectives, mission, and vision.

Once the objectives have been translated into measures, managers select targets for each measure. A target establishes the level of performance or rate of improvement required for a measure. Targets should be set to represent excellent performance, much like the par scores on a golf course. The targets, if achieved, should position the company as one of the best performers in its industry. Even more important would be to choose targets that create distinctive value for customers and shareholders. Discount Airlines initially chose "30 minutes at the gate" and "90% on-time departures" as targets for its "fast ground turnaround" process measures. If achieved, such performance would be the best in the industry.

By comparing current performance to the target performance, employees and managers can determine whether the company is achieving its desired level of performance. Thus, performance measures serve multiple purposes: communication, clarification, motivation, feedback, and evaluation. Because performance measures play such important roles, they should be chosen carefully. The Balanced Scorecard framework enables managers to select objectives and measures, derived from their strategy, that are linked together in a chain of cause-and-effect relationships.

CREATING A STRATEGY MAP

Companies use a picture, called a strategy map, to illustrate the causal relationships among the strategic objectives across the four Balanced Scorecard perspectives. Developing a strategy map follows a logical progress. First, identify the long-run financial objectives, the ultimate destination for the strategy. Then, in the customer perspective, select the targeted customers that will generate the revenues for the new strategy and the objectives for the value proposition offered to attract, retain, and grow the business with these customers. In the process perspective, select objectives that create and deliver the customer **value proposition** and also improve productivity and efficiency to improve financial performance measures. Finally, identify the employee skills, information needs, and company culture and alignment that will drive improvement in the critical processes.

A general template for constructing strategy maps is shown in Exhibit 2-6. We will work sequentially through the four Balanced Scorecard perspectives starting with financial at the top and concluding with the learning and growth objectives at the foundation. After describing how to choose objectives for the four perspectives, we provide a specific example of how Pioneer Petroleum, the company featured in the chapter-opening vignette, built its strategy map and Balanced Scorecard.

Financial Perspective

The Balanced Scorecard's financial perspective contains objectives and measures that represent the ultimate success measures for profit-seeking companies. Financial performance measures, such as operating income and return on investment, indicate whether the company's strategy and its implementation are increasing shareholder value. The company's financial performance improves through two basic approaches: *productivity improvements* and *revenue growth* (see Exhibit 2-7).

Exhibit 2-6
Strategy Map Describing How an Enterprise Creates Value for Shareholders and Customers

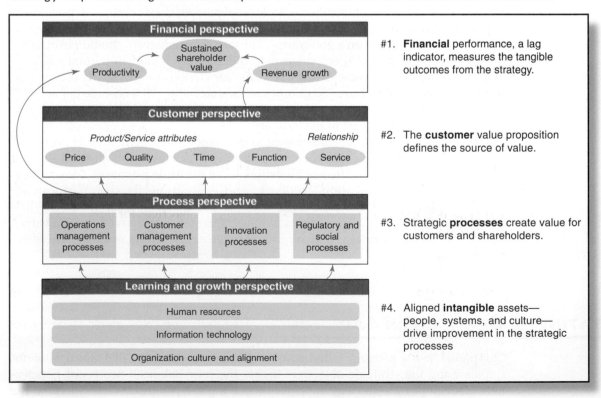

Exhibit 2-7
Financial Perspective Objectives

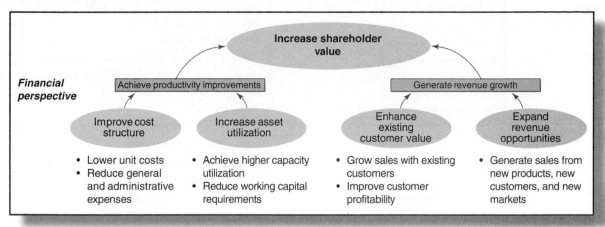

Productivity improvements have two components. First, companies reduce costs by lowering direct and indirect expenses. Such cost reductions enable a company to produce the same quantity of outputs while spending less on people, materials, energy, and supplies. Second, by utilizing their financial and physical assets more efficiently, companies reduce the working and fixed capital needed to support a given level of business. For example, companies can reduce the inventory levels required to support a given level of sales by implementing just-in-time production processes. They can support a higher level of sales with the same investment in plant and equipment by reducing unexpected shutdowns and unscheduled downtime on equipment.

Revenue growth also has two components. First, companies can generate more revenue and income from existing customers, such as by selling them additional products and services beyond the first product or service they purchase. For example, banks can attempt to get their checking account customers to also use the bank for credit cards, mortgages, and car loans. Second, companies generate additional revenues by introducing new products, selling to new customers, and expanding operations into new markets. For example, Amazon.com now sells CDs and electronic equipment, not just books, Staples sells to small businesses as well as retail customers, and Wal-Mart has expanded from its domestic U.S. base into international markets and added new formats at which customers can shop.

Exhibit 2-8 presents frequently used measures for the various financial objectives. Companies usually choose one measure for each objective, and may decide, based on their strategy, not to place all five possible financial objectives for their strategy map or scorecard.

Customer Perspective

The customer perspective should describe how a company intends to attract, retain, and deepen relationships with targeted customers by differentiating itself from competitors. The customer perspective reflects the heart of the strategy. It should contain specific objectives and measures for the strategy's "scope"—how is the company performing with its targeted customers. It also should represent the strategy's "advantage"— the unique combination of product features, services, and relationships it has selected to satisfy its customers' needs better than competitors can. Success in the customer perspective

Exhibit 2-8
Financial
Objectives
and Measures

Objectives	Measures
Increase shareholder value	• Return on capital employed (ROCE) • Economic value added • Market-to-book ratio
Improve cost structure	• Cost per unit, benchmarked against competitors • General, selling, and administrative expenses per unit of output or as % of sales
Increase asset utilization	• Sales/asset ratio • Inventory turnover ratio • % capacity utilization
Enhance existing customer value	• % growth in existing customers' business • % revenue growth
Expand revenue opportunities	• Revenue % from new products • Revenue % from new customers

should lead to improvement in the financial perspective objectives for growth in revenues and profits.

The customer perspective of the Balanced Scorecard typically includes one or two objectives for success with targeted customers. Examples of such objectives include the following:

• Achieve customer satisfaction and loyalty.
• Acquire new customers.
• Increase market share.
• Enhance customer profitability.

Exhibit 2-9 gives examples of typical measures that companies use to measure performance for these four common objectives.

Virtually all organizations, however, try to improve customer measures such as customer satisfaction and customer retention so these measures by themselves do not describe a strategy. They become associated with a strategy only when managers apply them to the customer segments in which they choose to compete (i.e., the *scope* of their strategy statement). A strategy typically identifies specific customer segments that the

Exhibit 2-9
Customer
Outcome
Objectives
and Measures

Objectives	Measures
Achieve customer satisfaction and loyalty	• Customer satisfaction in targeted segments • % repeat customers • % growth in revenue from existing customers • Willingness to recommend
Acquire new customers	• # of new customers acquired • Cost per new customer acquired • % of sales to new customers
Improve market share	• Market share in targeted customer segments
Enhance customer profitability	• Number or percent of unprofitable customers

Discount stores, such as Wal-Mart, offer their customers everyday low prices, though often with limited variety and little consumer assistance.
Alamy Images

company has identified as its target audience for growth and profitability. For example, Wal-Mart appeals to price-sensitive customers who value the retailer's low prices.

Neiman Marcus, on the other hand, targets customers with high disposable incomes who are willing to pay more for high-end merchandise. Price-sensitive customers with low disposable income are not likely to be satisfied with the shopping experience at a Neiman Marcus store, whereas fashion-conscious consumers with high disposable incomes may be disappointed with the selection of clothing offered at Wal-Mart as well as the lack of amenities and salesperson attention they receive at this discounted retail outlet. Therefore, Wal-Mart should measure customer satisfaction, loyalty, and market share only with its price-sensitive customers, while Neiman Marcus would apply these same measures only to segments that feature customers with high disposable incomes. Similarly, Southwest Airlines would want to measure customer satisfaction and loyalty with price-sensitive passengers, whereas Lufthansa would be measuring its performance with business and first-class passengers.

Beyond identifying the segments for measuring these generic customer outcomes, a company must also identify the objectives and measures for the value proposition offered to its customers. The value proposition is the unique mix of product performance, price, quality, availability, ease of purchase, service, relationship, and image that a company offers its targeted group of customers. The value proposition represents the "advantage" of a company's strategy; it should communicate what it intends to deliver to its customers better or differently from competitors.

For example, companies as diverse as Southwest Airlines, Wal-Mart, McDonald's, and Toyota have been extremely successful by offering their customers the "best buy" or *lowest total cost* buying experience in their category. For many years, Dell Computers was the leading seller of personal computers by providing an easy and inexpensive purchasing experience to its customers. The measurable objectives for a low-total-cost value proposition should emphasize attractive prices (relative to competitors), excellent and consistent quality for the product attributes offered, good selection, short lead times, and ease of purchase.

Another value proposition, followed by companies such as Apple, Mercedes, Armani, and Intel, emphasizes *product leadership*. These companies command prices far above the average in their industry because of the superior performance of their products. For example, Italian apparel design companies, such as Armani, offer products to high-end customers who are willing to pay significant price premiums for superior fashion, fit, and fabric. The objectives for companies offering a product leadership value proposition emphasize the particular features and functionalities of the products that leading-edge customers value and are willing to pay more to receive. The objectives could be measured by speed, accuracy, size, power consumption, design, or other performance characteristics that exceed the performance of competing products and that are valued by important customer segments.

A third type of value proposition stresses the provision of *complete customer solutions*. A good example of companies successfully delivering this value proposition is IBM, which offers its customers a one-stop buying experience for a full line of products and services. IBM offers solutions that are tailored to a customer's specific needs for consulting, hardware, software, installation, field service, training, and education. As another example, salespersons at the Nordstrom department store attempt to learn their customers' tastes, sizes, and budgets so that they can suggest entire wardrobes, fully accessorized. This selling strategy generates high customer loyalty and higher average revenue per sales transaction. Many banks strive to profile and understand their customers and offer them integrated financial services including deposit and savings accounts, consumer loans for automobiles and home purchases, insurance, and investment and retirement products, all tied to a lifetime financial plan. Customers at such banks have the convenience of conducting all of their financial transactions, assisted by a knowledgeable account manager, in a single institution and with a common online interface to access all accounts and conduct transactions. Companies that choose to offer a customer solutions value proposition stress objectives relating to the completeness of the solution (selling multiple, bundled products and services), exceptional service both before and after the sale, and the quality of the relationship between the company and its customers.

Exhibit 2-10 displays the value proposition objectives for these three different customer value propositions. Examples of measures that can be used for each value

Exhibit 2-10
Customer Objectives for Three Value Propositions

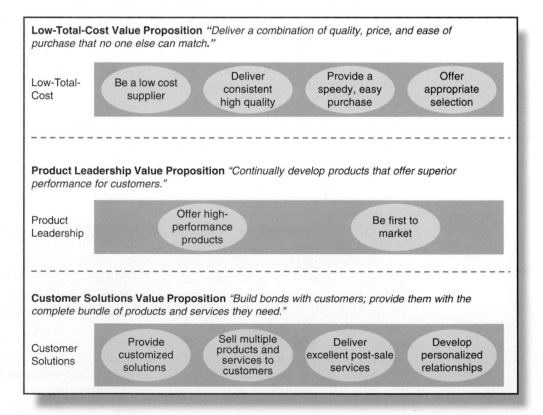

Low-Total-Cost Value Proposition *"Deliver a combination of quality, price, and ease of purchase that no one else can match."*

Low-Total-Cost

| Be a low cost supplier | Deliver consistent high quality | Provide a speedy, easy purchase | Offer appropriate selection |

Product Leadership Value Proposition *"Continually develop products that offer superior performance for customers."*

Product Leadership

| Offer high-performance products | Be first to market |

Customer Solutions Value Proposition *"Build bonds with customers; provide them with the complete bundle of products and services they need."*

Customer Solutions

| Provide customized solutions | Sell multiple products and services to customers | Deliver excellent post-sale services | Develop personalized relationships |

Exhibit 2-11
Customer Value
Proposition
Objectives and
Measures

LOW TOTAL COST	MEASURES
Be a low cost supplier	• Price, relative to competitors • Customer's cost of ownership
Deliver consistent high quality	• # returns; $ value of returns • # and % customer complaints • # incidents of warranty and field service repairs
Provide a speedy, easy purchase	• % on-time delivery • Customer lead time (from order to delivery) • % perfect orders (right product, right quantity, delivered on time)

PRODUCT LEADERSHIP	MEASURES
Offer high-performance products	• Customer innovation rating • Competitive product performance (speed, size, accuracy, energy consumption, . . .) • Gross margins, new products
Be first to market with new products	• Number of products that are 1st to market

CUSTOMER SOLUTIONS	MEASURES
Provide customized solutions	• # customers with profiled preferences
Sell multiple products and services to customers	• # products and services per customer • # clients above $xx million annual in sales
Deliver excellent post-sales services	• Revenues from maintenance, repair, and logistical services
Develop personalized relationships	• # sole-sourced contracts • Client retention

proposition's strategic objectives can be found in Exhibit 2-11. By developing objectives and measures that are specific to its value proposition, a company translates its strategy into tangible measures that all employees can understand and work toward improving.

Process Perspective

The financial and customer objectives and measures reflect the outcomes—satisfied shareholders and loyal customers—from a successful strategy. Once the company has a clear picture of *what* it intends to deliver to its shareholders and customers, it can determine the *how* of its strategy, which are the key processes that accomplish the following:

- Create and deliver the value proposition for customers.
- Achieve the productivity improvements for the financial objectives.

The process perspective identifies the critical operations management, customer management, innovation, and regulatory and social processes in which the organization must excel to achieve its customer, revenue growth, and profitability objectives.

Operations management processes are the basic, day-to-day processes that produce products and services and deliver them to customers. Some typical objectives for operating processes include the following:

- Achieve superior supplier capability.
- Improve the cost, quality, and cycle times of operating (production) processes.
- Improve asset utilization.
- Deliver goods and services responsively to customers.

Starting at the top of the above list, superior supplier capabilities enable the company to receive competitively priced, defect-free products and services that are delivered on time. Lowering the cost of production is important to both manufacturing and service companies. Excellence in production processes also requires improving quality and process times. Improved asset utilization enables the company to produce more output from its existing supply of resources (equipment and people). Finally, the company's strategy might require high-performance processes for distributing finished products and services to customers.

Customer management processes expand and deepen relationships with targeted customers. We can identify three objectives for a company's customer management processes:

- Acquire new customers.
- Satisfy and retain existing customers.
- Generate growth with customers.

Customer acquisition relates to generating leads, communicating with potential customers, choosing entry-level products, pricing the products, and closing the sale.

Customer satisfaction and retention requires excellent service and response to customer requests. Companies operate customer service and call center units to respond to requests about orders, deliveries, and problems. Customers may defect from organizations that are not responsive to requests for information and problem solving. Therefore, timely and knowledgeable service units are critical for maintaining customer loyalty and reducing the likelihood of customer defections.

To *generate growth with customers*, the company must manage its relationships effectively, cross-sell multiple products and services, and become known to the customer as a trusted adviser and supplier. For example, a company can differentiate its basic product or service by providing additional features and services after the sale. A commodity chemical company was able to differentiate its basic product by providing a service that picked up used chemicals from customers and reprocessed the chemicals in an efficient process conforming to environmental and safety regulations for disposal or reuse. This service relieved many small customers from performing expensive environmental processes themselves.

Customer growth can also occur by selling the customer products and services beyond the entry-level product that initially brought the customer to the company. For example, banks now try to market insurance, credit cards, money management services, and personal loans of various types—especially automobile, educational, and home equity—to customers who currently have a basic checking account. Manufacturers of expensive equipment such as medical imaging devices, elevators, and computers sell maintenance, field service, and repairs that minimize the downtime of the equipment. As a customer buys more of a complete set of services from a supplier, the cost of switching to alternative suppliers becomes higher, so growing the business in this manner also contributes to customer retention and higher lifetime customer profitability.

Innovation processes develop new products, processes, and services, often enabling the company to penetrate new markets and customer segments. Successful innovation drives customer acquisition, loyalty, and growth, in turn leading to enhanced operating margins. Without innovation, a company's value proposition can eventually be imitated, leading to competition solely on price for its undifferentiated products and services.

We can identify two important innovation subprocesses:

- Develop innovative products and services.
- Achieve excellence in research and development processes.

Product designers and managers generate new ideas by extending the capabilities of existing products and services, applying new discoveries and technologies, and learning from the suggestions of customers.

The research and development process, the core of product development, brings the new ideas and concepts to market. Although many people believe that the innovation process is inherently creative and unstructured, successful product innovation companies actually use a highly disciplined process to move new ideas to the market, carefully evaluating the product development at specified milestones, and moving the product to the next stage only if they continue to believe that the end product will have the desired functionality, will be attractive to the targeted market, and can be produced with consistent quality and at a cost that enables satisfactory profit margins to be earned. The product development process has to meet its own targets for completion time and development cost.

Regulatory and social processes make up the final process group. Companies must continually earn the right to operate in the communities and countries in which they produce and sell. National and local regulations—affecting the environment, employee health and safety, and hiring and employment practices—impose minimum standards on companies' practices, and companies must comply with these to avoid shutdowns or expensive litigation. Many companies, however, seek to go beyond mere compliance and seek to perform better than the regulatory constraints so that they develop a reputation as an employer of choice in every community in which they operate.

Companies can manage and report their regulatory and social performance along several critical dimensions:

- Environment.
- Health and safety.
- Employment practices.
- Community investment.

Investing in the environment and in communities need not be for altruistic reasons alone. First, an excellent reputation for performance along regulatory and social dimensions assists companies in attracting and retaining high-quality employees, thereby making human resource processes more effective and efficient. Second, reducing environmental incidents and improving employee safety and health improves productivity and lowers operating costs. Third, companies with outstanding reputations generally enhance their image with customers and with socially conscious investors. These linkages to enhance human resource, operations, customer, and financial processes illustrate how effective management of regulatory and community performance can drive long-term shareholder value creation.

Exhibit 2-12 summarizes the objectives for the four process groups, along with possible measures that can be used with each objective.

Exhibit 2-12
Process
Objectives
and Measures

PROCESS OBJECTIVES	MEASURES
OPERATIONS MANAGEMENT	
Improve the cost, quality, and cycle times of operating (production) processes	• Supplier scorecard ratings: quality, delivery, cost • Cost per unit of output • Product and process defect rates • Product cycle times
Improve asset utilization	• Lead times, from order to delivery • Capacity utilization (%) • Equipment reliability, percent availability
CUSTOMER MANAGEMENT	
Acquire new customers	• % leads converted • Cost per new customer acquired
Satisfy and retain existing customers	• Time to resolve customer concern or complaint • # referenceable customers (willing to recommend)
Generate growth with customers	• # products and services per customer • Revenue or margin from post-sale services
INNOVATION	
Develop innovative products and services	• # fundamental new ideas entering product development
Achieve excellence in research and development processes	• # patent applications filed or patents earned • Total product development time: from idea to market • Product development cost vs. budget
REGULATORY AND SOCIAL	
Improve environmental, health, and safety performance	• # of environmental and safety incidents • Days absent from work
Enhance reputation as "good neighbor"	• Employee diversity index • # employees from disadvantaged communities

In developing their Balanced Scorecard, managers identify which of the process objectives and measures are the most important for their strategies. Companies following a product leadership strategy would stress excellence in their innovation processes. Companies following a low-total-cost strategy must excel at operations management processes. Companies following a customer solutions strategy will emphasize their customer management processes.

Typically, the financial benefits from improving processes occur within different time frames. Cost savings from improvements in *operational processes* deliver quick benefits (within 6 to 12 months) to productivity objectives in the financial perspective. Revenue growth from enhancing *customer relationships* accrues in the intermediate term (12 to 24 months). *Innovation processes* generally take longer to produce customer and revenue and margin improvements (24 to 48 months). The benefits from *regulatory and social processes* also typically take longer to capture as companies avoid litigation and shutdowns and enhance their image as employers and suppliers of choice in all communities in which they operate. Achieving overall process excellence generally requires that companies have objectives and measures for improving processes in all four process groups so that the benefits from each process group phase in over time.

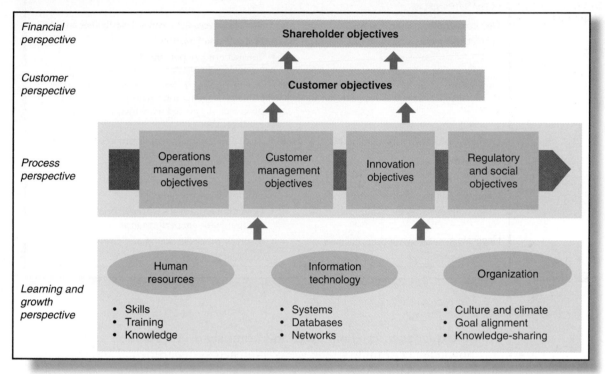

Learning and Growth Perspective

The fourth perspective of the Balanced Scorecard, learning and growth, identifies the objectives for the people, information technology, and organizational alignment that will drive improvement in the various process objectives (see Exhibit 2-13).

It is in the learning and growth scorecard perspective that executives target improvements in their intangible assets—human resources, information technology, and organizational culture and alignment. The following describes typical objectives for the three learning and growth components:

Human Resources

- *Strategic competency availability*—The company's employees have the appropriate mix of skills, talent, and know-how to perform activities required by the strategy.

Information Technology

- *Strategic information availability*—The company's information systems and knowledge applications contribute to effective strategy execution by facilitating process improvements and better linkages with suppliers and customers.

Organization Culture and Alignment

- *Culture and climate*—Employees have an awareness and understanding of the shared vision, strategy, and cultural values needed to execute the strategy.
- *Goal alignment*—Employee goals and incentives are aligned with the strategy at all organization levels.

Exhibit 2-14
Learning and
Growth Objectives
and Measures

OBJECTIVES	MEASURES
HUMAN RESOURCES	
Develop strategic competencies	• % of employees with required capabilities and skills
Attract and retain top talent	• Employee satisfaction
	• Turnover of key personnel
INFORMATION TECHNOLOGY	
Provide applications that support the strategy	• Strategic information coverage: % of critical processes supported with adequate system applications
Develop customer data and information systems	• Availability of customer information (e.g., CRM systems, customer databases)
ORGANIZATION CULTURE AND ALIGNMENT	
Create a customer-centric culture	• Employee culture survey
Align employees' goals to success	• Percent of employees with personal goals linked to organizational performance
Share knowledge about best practices and customers	• # of new practices shared and adopted

- *Knowledge sharing*—Employees and teams share best practices and other knowledge relevant to strategy execution across departmental and organizational boundaries.

Specific examples of learning and growth measures can be found in Exhibit 2-14.

With this overview of identifying objectives and measures in the four Balanced Scorecard perspectives, we can now examine how Brian Roberts and his leadership team developed a strategy map and scorecard for Pioneer Petroleum's new customer-focused strategy.

STRATEGY MAP AND BALANCED SCORECARD AT PIONEER PETROLEUM

Brian Roberts formed a leadership team that included himself, the heads of several large business units and functional departments (such as human resources, finance, and information technology), and a project manager from the finance function to create the division's strategy map and Balanced Scorecard. The team met several times over a three-month period to define the strategic objectives for the strategy map and the accompanying scorecard of measures.

Financial Perspective

The leadership team started by setting an ambitious financial target for the new strategy to achieve: double return on capital employed (ROCE) to 12% within three years from its current depressed level of 6%.[7] The company would achieve its ROCE target by using

---

[7] Return on capital employed = Net income after taxes/[Interest bearing liabilities + Shareholders' equity]. Usually the after-tax interest expense [defined as Interest expense × (1 – Tax rate)] is added back in the numerator of the ROCE ratio so as not to have the mix of financing sources affect this profitability metric.

Exhibit 2-15
Pioneer Petroleum's Financial Objectives and Measures

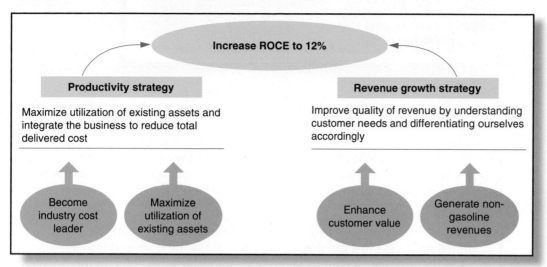

the two financial levers: *productivity* and *growth*. Improving productivity involved two components: cost reduction and asset intensity. Cost reduction would be measured by operating cash expenses versus the industry (using cents per gallon to normalize for volume), with the goal being to have the lowest operating cost per unit of output in the industry.[8] Asset productivity would enable Pioneer to handle the anticipated higher volumes from its growth strategy without expanding its asset base. For this objective, it selected the sales-to-assets ratio to indicate the benefits from generating more revenue (i.e., throughput) from existing assets, plus any benefits from inventory reductions.

Pioneer's revenue growth lever also had two components. The first, volume growth, was to grow sales from its basic gasoline products (and home heating oil and jet fuel) faster than the industry average. In addition to pure volume growth, Pioneer wanted a higher proportion of its sales in the premium product grades. So it set two measures for this growth component: volume growth rate relative to the industry growth rate, and percentage of volume in premium grades.

The second growth component represented the opportunity to sell products other than gasoline to retail customers. An important component of Pioneer's growth theme was a customer-driven strategy built around sales of convenience store products. New revenue could also come from sales of automobile services and products such as car washes, lubricants, oil changes, minor repairs, and common replacement parts. Pioneer set a financial growth objective to develop new sources of revenue, and it measured this objective by nongasoline revenues and margins. Thus, the financial perspective (see Exhibit 2-15) incorporated objectives and measures for both productivity and revenue growth.

Customer Perspective

For the customer perspective, Pioneer started by establishing an objective to continually delight the consumers in its three targeted segments (see Exhibit 2-16). The leadership team decided to measure success for this objective by its market share among the

---

[8] Note that operating expenses exclude the cost of purchased raw materials, such as crude oil. Thus while Pioneer could be the industry leader for its operating expenses, a competitor that had access to lower cost crude oil could have a lower total cost per gallon produced.

Exhibit 2-16
Pioneer
Petroleum's
Customer
Objectives and
Measures

Continually delight the targeted consumer segments by fulfilling their value propositions

Strengthen dealer and distributor relationships to create win-win partnerships

Road Warriors, True Blues, and Generation F3 consumer segments. Measuring total market share would represent an undifferentiated strategy, perhaps no strategy at all.

Pioneer could have selected customer satisfaction as the driver of its segment market share objective. But the leadership team wanted a measure that was more specific to its new strategy. Pioneer's market research had identified the attributes that constituted a great buying experience for customers in the three targeted segments. These included:

- Friendly employees.
- A convenience store, stocked with fresh, high-quality merchandise.
- Immediate access to a gasoline pump (to avoid waiting for service).
- A speedy purchase, including self-payment mechanisms at the pump (to avoid waiting to pay).
- Covered area for gasoline pumps (to protect customers from rain and snow).
- 100% availability of product, especially premium grades (to avoid stockouts).
- Clean restrooms.
- Attractive exterior station appearance.
- Safe, well-lit station.
- Ample parking spaces near convenience store.
- Availability of minor car services.

Pioneer summarized these attributes as offering customers "a fast, friendly serve." But how could all of the attributes of the fast, friendly serve buying experience be measured? Pioneer decided that the consumer's buying experience was so central to its strategy that it invested in a new measurement system: the mystery shopper. Pioneer hired an independent third party to send a representative (the mystery shopper) to every Pioneer station, every month, to purchase fuel and a snack, and evaluate the experience based on specified attributes of a "perfect buying experience." The mystery shopper rating represented the value proposition that Pioneer would offer its targeted customers. If Pioneer's theory of the business was valid, increases in the mystery shopper score would translate into increases in market share in the three targeted segments. Note that Pioneer did not expect that its market share in the nontargeted segments—price shoppers and homebodies—would increase since consumers in these segments did not necessarily value the improved buying experience enough to pay the higher prices Pioneer would charge at the gasoline pump. Over time, Pioneer could use the new data to test the validity of the hypothesis underlying its new strategy. With more than 7,000 retail gasoline outlets, Pioneer could statistically validate whether outlets with high mystery shopper scores generated higher revenues and margins, because of increased purchases by Road Warriors, True Blues, and Generation F3's, than outlets with consistently low mystery shopper scores. In this way, Pioneer would get valuable feedback about both how well the strategy was being implemented in gasoline stations as well as feedback about the linkage from improved buying experiences to increased customer loyalty, revenues, and margins.

The customer perspective, however, was not complete. Pioneer did not sell directly to its end-use consumers. Like companies in many industries, Pioneer worked through intermediaries, such as wholesalers, distributors, and retailers to reach the end-use consumer of its products. Pioneer's immediate customers were independent owners of gasoline stations and distributors of its other petroleum-based products (such as distillates, lubricants, home heating oil, and jet fuel). Franchised retailers purchased gasoline and lubricant products from Pioneer, and sold to consumers in Pioneer-branded stations. If end-use consumers were to receive a great buying experience, then the independent dealers/distributors had to be aligned to Pioneer's new strategy and capable of delivering that experience. Dealers were clearly a critical part of the new strategy.

Pioneer adopted an objective to increase its dealers' profitability so that it could attract and retain the best dealers. The new strategy emphasized creating a positive-sum game, increasing the size of the reward that could be shared between Pioneer and its dealers so that the relationship would be a win–win one.

The higher reward came from several sources. First, the premium prices that Pioneer hoped to sustain at its stations would generate higher revenues. Second, by increasing the market share in the three targeted segments, a higher quantity of gasoline would be sold, and a higher percentage of the purchases would be for premium grades (especially by True Blues and Road Warriors). Third, the dealer would also have a revenue stream from the sale of nongasoline products and services—convenience store and auxiliary car services—a portion of which would also flow back to Pioneer.

Pioneer set an objective to create the win–win relationship with dealers and measured this objective by dealer/distributor satisfaction ratings and profitability.

Process Perspective

With a clear picture about the outcomes desired in the financial and customer perspectives, Pioneer now turned to the objectives and measures for the process perspective. The leadership team wanted strategic objectives in all four process themes:

- Operations management to improve the efficiency, quality, and responsiveness in all of Pioneer's purchasing, refining, and distribution processes.
- Customer management to generate dealer profits from nongasoline revenues.
- Innovation to develop new products and services that could be offered at Pioneer stations.
- Environmental, health and safety performance, and being a better neighbor and employer at all Pioneer locations.

Pioneer included multiple objectives and measures for its basic refining and distribution processes. These stressed low cost, consistent quality, and reduced asset downtime. Most of these objectives would drive improvements in the financial perspective's productivity measures though some related to on-time and on-spec delivery of products to its dealers/distributors.

Objectives for customer management processes supported both the new win–win relationship with dealers and Pioneer's financial objectives. If dealers could generate increased revenues and profits from products other than gasoline, then dealers would place less reliance on profits from gasoline sales to meet their profit targets. This would leave more of a profit share for Pioneer, while still allowing its dealers to be the most profitable in the industry. Pioneer also recognized that another important process objective to drive dealer profitability was having trained dealers be better managers of the gasoline station, service bays, and the convenience store.

An innovation process objective signaled the desire to enhance the buying experience of consumers and profit potential of dealers by developing new offerings at the gasoline station.

Exhibit 2-17
Pioneer Petroleum's Process Objectives and Measures

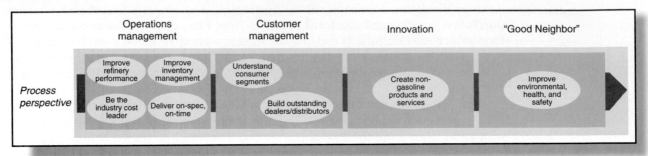

Pioneer also selected objectives and measures related to environmental, health and safety (EHS) performance. Some of the benefits from improved EHS performance contributed to the cost reduction and productivity themes. Roberts believed that safety incidents were an important leading indicator, believing that if employees were careless, leading to personal harm, they were not likely paying much attention to the physical assets of the company either. The EHS measures, however, also contributed to Pioneer being a good citizen in all of the communities in which it produced and sold its products, and for enabling the well-being of its employees.

In summary, Pioneer's eight process objectives (see Exhibit 2-17) supported both its differentiated strategy with consumers and dealers, its financial objectives for cost reduction and productivity, and its social responsibilities.

Learning and Growth Perspective

The final set of objectives provided the foundation for Pioneer's strategy: enhancing the skills and motivation of employees, expanding the role for information technology, and aligning employees to the strategy. The project team identified three strategic objectives for the learning and growth perspective:

Develop Core Competencies and Skills

- Encourage and facilitate our people to gain a broader understanding of the marketing and refining business from end to end.
- Build the level of skills and competencies necessary to execute our vision.
- Develop the leadership skills required to articulate the vision, promote integrated business thinking, and develop our people.

Provide Access to Strategic Information

- Develop the strategic information required to execute our strategies.

Engage and Empower Employees

- Enable the achievement of our vision by promoting an understanding of our organizational strategy and by creating a climate in which our employees are motivated and empowered to strive toward that vision.

Pioneer identified the specific skills and information each employee should have to enhance internal process performance and deliver the value proposition to customers. It measured the percentage of employees who currently had the requisite skills and knowledge as well as the percentage who had access to all of the data and information they needed to excel at process improvement and meeting customers' expectations. It had to defer actual measurement of these two objectives, however, until it could develop the data to support the two new metrics. For the third objective, Pioneer implemented an employee survey designed to measure the awareness people had about the new strategy and their motivation to help the company achieve its targets.

With the learning and growth perspective completed, Pioneer's leadership team now had developed a complete representation of its new strategy. The strategy map, shown in Exhibit 2-18, translated the division's vision and strategy into a visual representation of the cause-and-effect linkages of strategic objectives across the four perspectives. The team also had created a comprehensive Balanced Scorecard (see Exhibit 2-19) that measured performance for each strategic objective. Roberts and other members of Pioneer's leadership team could now communicate the strategy clearly to all business unit leaders and employees throughout the organization.

Exhibit 2-18
Pioneer Petroleum's Complete Strategy Map

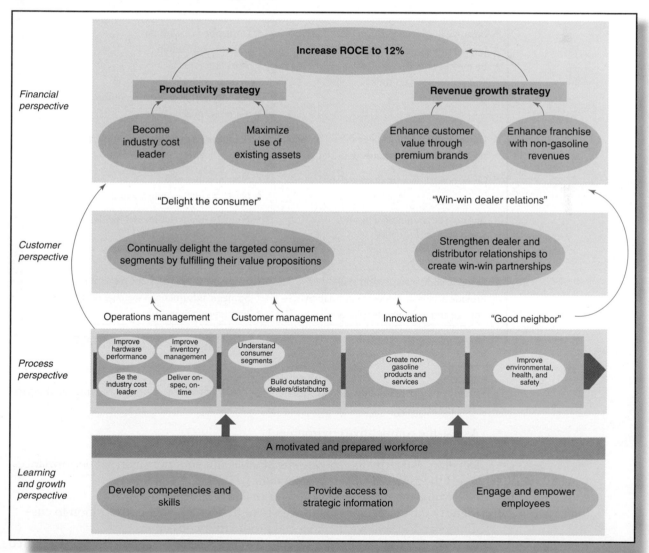

Exhibit 2-19
Pioneer
Petroleum's
Balanced Scorecard

STRATEGIC OBJECTIVES	STRATEGIC MEASURES
FINANCIAL	
• Increase return on capital employed	• Return on capital employed
• Become industry cost leader	• Net margin rank (vs. competition)
• Maximize use of existing assets	• Full cost per gallon delivered (vs. competition)
• Enhance customer value	• Sales to asset ratio
• Generate non-gasoline revenues	• Volume growth rate vs. industry
	• Ratio of premium product sales to total
	• Non-gasoline revenues and margins
CUSTOMER	
• Continually delight the targeted consumers	• Share of segment: Road Warriors, True Blue, Generation F3
• Create win-win relationships with dealers and distributors	• Mystery shopper rating
	• Dealer gross profit growth
	• Dealer satisfaction survey
PROCESS	
• Improve hardware performance	• Unplanned downtime
• Improve inventory management	• Capacity utilization
• Be the industry cost leader	• Stock-out rate
• Deliver on-spec, on-time	• Inventory levels
	• Activity costs versus competition
	• % perfect orders
• Understand consumer segments	• Feedback from consumer focus groups
• Build outstanding dealers/distributors	• Dealer quality score
• Create non-gasoline products and services	• New product ROI
	• New product acceptance rate
• Improve environmental, health, and safety performance	• Number of environmental incidents
	• Days absent from work
LEARNING AND GROWTH	
• Develop competencies and skills	• Strategic competency coverage ratio
• Provide access to strategic information	• Strategic information coverage ratio
• Engage and empower employees	• Employee culture survey

Pioneer had followed a systematic process to develop a strategy map and scorecard for its strategy:

- Assess the competitive environment.
- Learn about customer preferences and segments.
- Develop a strategy to generate sustainable and superior financial performance.
- Select the targeted customer segments.
- Determine the value proposition for the targeted customers.
- Identify the critical internal processes to deliver the value proposition to customers and to achieve the financial productivity objectives.
- Identify the skills, competencies, motivation, databases, and technology required to excel at improving the critical internal processes and customer value delivery.

APPLYING THE BALANCED SCORECARD TO NONPROFIT AND GOVERNMENT ORGANIZATIONS

Strategy maps and Balanced Scorecards are not limited to for-profit companies, such as Pioneer Petroleum. Nonprofit and government organizations (NPGOs) also need to have strategies and measurement systems to communicate and help implement their strategies. Prior to the development of the Balanced Scorecard, the performance reports of NPGOs focused only on financial measures, such as funds appropriated, donations, expenditures, and operating expense ratios. NPGOs, however, cannot be measured primarily by their financial performance. Certainly, they must monitor their spending and operate within financial constraints, but their success must be measured by their effectiveness in providing benefits to constituents, not by their ability to raise money, be efficient, or balance their budgets. The use of nonfinancial measures enables NPGOs to assess their performance with targeted constituents.

In our experience, however, many NPGOs encountered difficulties in developing their initial Balanced Scorecard. First, they did not have a clear strategy. They may have had "strategy" documents that ran upwards of 50 pages, but these consisted only of a lengthy list of planned programs and initiatives that never specified the outcomes the programs and initiatives were intended to achieve. To apply the Balanced Scorecard, an NPGO's thinking has to shift from what it plans *to do* to what it must *accomplish*, a shift from activities to outcomes. Otherwise, any new scorecard will be just a list of key performance indicators of operational performance, not a system to communicate and implement its strategy.

Since financial success is not their primary objective, NPGOs cannot use the standard architecture of the Balanced Scorecard strategy map where financial objectives are the ultimate, high-level outcomes to be achieved. NPGOs generally place an objective related to their *social impact* and *mission*—such as reducing poverty, school dropout rates, or the incidence or consequences from particular diseases or eliminating discrimination—at the top of their scorecard and strategy map. A nonprofit or public sector agency's mission represents the accountability between it and society as well as the rationale for its existence and ongoing support. The measured improvement in an NPGO's social impact objective may take years to become noticeable, which is why the measures in the other perspectives provide the short- to intermediate-term targets and feedback necessary for year-to-year control and accountability.

NPGOs also modify the private-sector scorecard framework by expanding the definition of who is the customer. Donors or taxpayers provide the resources—they pay for the service—while another group, the citizens and beneficiaries, receive the service. Who is the customer, the one paying for the service or the one receiving the service? Many NPGOs treat both as their customers. They place both a constituent perspective and a resource (taxpayer/donor) perspective at the top of their Balanced Scorecards (see Exhibit 2-20). With these changes, NPGOs—as wide ranging in focus as a local opera company, an after-school mentoring program for at-risk urban youth, the Canadian Blood Services, the Federal Bureau of Investigation, and the country of Botswana—have developed Balanced Scorecards that described their strategy and used them to communicate mission and strategy more clearly to resource providers, employees, and constituents.

Exhibit 2-20
The Balanced Scorecard Model for Public Sector and Nonprofit Organizations

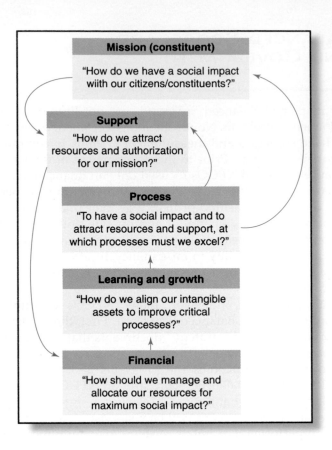

Mission (constituent)
"How do we have a social impact with our citizens/constituents?"

Support
"How do we attract resources and authorization for our mission?"

Process
"To have a social impact and to attract resources and support, at which processes must we excel?"

Learning and growth
"How do we align our intangible assets to improve critical processes?"

Financial
"How should we manage and allocate our resources for maximum social impact?"

IN PRACTICE

A Balanced Scorecard for a Nonprofit Organization

Wendy Kopp founded Teach for America (TFA) in 1989, based on her undergraduate honors thesis at Princeton. Her vision was to ensure that one day all children in this nation would have the opportunity to attain an excellent education. TFA recruited a national teacher corps drawn from talented, highly motivated graduating seniors who committed to teach for two years in urban and rural public schools. TFA's strategy was based on an explicit model of social change in which corps members played two roles. First, they would improve the educational experience and life experiences of existing students through their two-year teaching positions. Second, they would influence fundamental educational reform throughout their lives through their career and voluntary activities.

As TFA scaled to become a nationwide enterprise, it created a Balanced Scorecard to reflect its strategy, as shown in Exhibit 2-21.[9] The social impact perspective contained two high-level objectives: improving the educational performance of today's students and enhancing the educational opportunities for tomorrow's students. For the second objective, TFA created a new metric by reviewing annually the career paths of alumni to determine how they were affecting social change; for example, running for public office, working in public policy, entering school or district leadership, being a truly outstanding classroom teacher, or publishing articles and books about improving education in low-income communities.

[9] Teach for America chose to modify the standard nonprofit template by labeling and sequencing its five perspectives as social impact, constituent, operating processes, financial, and organizational capacity.

Exhibit 2-21
Balanced Scorecard for Teach for America

PERSPECTIVE	OBJECTIVES	MEASURES
Social Impact	• Improve prospects of low-income youth	• Percent of corps members who increase student achievement
		• Principals' rating of corps member performance
	• Impact tomorrow's low-income youth	• Number of alumni engaged in or influencing education
Constituent	• Create engaged corps members	• Percent highly satisfied with TFA experience
	• Produce motivated alumni	• Alumni engagement index
Operating Processes	• Grow size, quality, and diversity of corps member applicants	• Number of highly qualified applicants
		• % African American and Latino corps members
	• Enhance corps member effectiveness	• Corps member satisfaction with training
	• Build a thriving alumni network	• % of alumni attending events
Financial	• Grow and diversify revenue base	• Total revenue
		• # of high net worth contributors
	• Practice good financial management	• Cost per corps member
Organizational Capacity	• Build a diverse team	• % of staff diversity
	• Ensure effective management	• % of key goals met
	• Enhance information technology capabilities	• Staff satisfaction with technology
	• Engage our national board members	• $ raised through board members

The TFA constituent perspective focused on satisfying existing corps members with excellent training and teaching experiences, and the involvement of former TFA corps members in alumni activities. The TFA operating processes stressed recruitment and selection of diverse, high-quality applicants from leading colleges, providing corps members with excellent training before starting their two-year teaching experience, and conducting events that attracted alumni participation. The financial perspective had objectives to improve the funding base and to lower its unit costs (measured by total operating expenses divided by number of corps members). The organizational capacity perspective contained objectives to enhance the talent and diversity of employees and to improve TFA's information technology, plus a new objective of building increased commitments from the national board of directors.

This example illustrates how nonprofit organizations can develop objectives and measures for their strategies. This helps managers of nonprofits to communicate to donors, volunteers, and employees how the nonprofit intends to create social value in the lives of its targeted constituents. The scorecard also gives feedback to managers about whether the enterprise is achieving the outcomes it wants to deliver and the performance of the drivers—operating processes, finances, technology, employees, board members, and volunteers—of the desired social impact.

MANAGING WITH THE BALANCED SCORECARD

Developing a strategy map and Balanced Scorecard is just the start of the journey to performance improvement. Executives must communicate the strategy to all employees since, as Brian Roberts remarked, they are the ones who must implement the strategy. People cannot help implement a strategy that they are not aware of or do not understand.

Once all employees understand the strategy of their operating units, divisions, and corporation, managers ask them to develop personal objectives in light of the broader priorities. Most organizations link *incentive compensation* to the Balanced Scorecard, typically after managing with the scorecard for a year.

The issues of communication, setting objectives, and aligning compensation systems for employees will be discussed in Chapter 9.

Companies must also focus their continuous improvement activities on those processes that have the largest impact on successful strategy execution. Thus, the process improvement approaches described in Chapter 7 will have the largest impact when they are applied to achieve the strategic objectives defined in the Balanced Scorecard's process perspective.

To implement their strategies, companies must have excellent knowledge of their costs. That is why the BSC financial perspective contains objectives and measures to improve productivity and lower costs. The operations management theme in the process perspective emphasizes reducing the costs of products and processes. The next three chapters contain the foundational material for understanding how to develop accurate costing systems that help managers make better decisions about managing and reducing the costs of their processes and products. Chapter 6 extends the cost focus out to customers so that companies can manage their cost of serving customers, resulting in more profitable customer relationships. Chapter 6 will also introduce material on how to develop the nonfinancial measures of customer performance for a company's BSC customer perspective. Measuring and managing innovation processes are often overlooked in a company's performance measurement system. Yet these processes are what enable a company to introduce new product variations and new product platforms. Chapter 8 describes management accounting tools that help employees improve their innovation processes.

Of course, managers must always remember that the success of their strategies will ultimately be evaluated based on how well they deliver superior financial performance. So traditional financial control approaches, including budgeting and resource allocation, discussed in Chapters 10 and 11, remain highly relevant even for 21st-century enterprises.

BARRIERS TO EFFECTIVE USE OF THE BALANCED SCORECARD

Not all companies succeed with developing and applying Balanced Scorecards. Several factors can lead to problems when building a performance measurement and management system around the Balanced Scorecard. Some companies use too few measures—only one or two measures per perspective—in their scorecards. A scorecard with too few measures does not depict enough of the company's strategy and does not represent a balance between desired outcomes and the performance drivers of those outcomes. Conversely, some companies include too many measures, incorporating more than 100 measures, so that managers' attention is so diffused that they pay insufficient attention to those few measures that can make the greatest impact.

Other organizations, unlike Pioneer Petroleum, do not start their performance measurement process by clearly describing their strategy and building their strategy map. Instead they look at measures they currently use, classify them into the four scorecard perspectives, and declare that they now have a Balanced Scorecard. Such key performance indicator (KPI) scorecards will typically use common measures, such as customer satisfaction, process quality, cost, and employee satisfaction and morale, that are certainly worth striving to improve but do not reflect a company's unique strategy. KPI scorecards also arise from capturing the data from a company's quality management approach in a scorecard framework. Again, quality improvement is certainly desirable, but a quality program's focus is to make existing processes better, faster, and cheaper. The metrics drive and evaluate continuous improvement but do not link to a company's differentiating strategy. Thus, such scorecards produce incremental improvements but do not align the enterprise around successful execution of its strategy.

A poor scorecard design, however, is not the biggest threat to successful Balanced Scorecard implementation. When too few or too many measures are present or they are not the right measures, these design defects can be recognized and fixed. The biggest threat is a poor organizational process for developing and implementing the scorecard. Building and embedding a new measurement and management system into an organization is complex and susceptible to at least four pitfalls.

1. **Senior management is not committed.** By far, the largest source of failures occurs when the Balanced Scorecard project is led by or gets delegated to a middle-management project team. Often the impetus for a new performance measurement system arises from the quality group or the finance function. Individuals in these groups see the limitations from attempting to manage with only financial measures and want the organization to adopt a more robust performance measurement system tied closer to strategy or operational improvements, not just financial results. They manage to get approval from senior management to explore extensions of the existing measurement system to include some nonfinancial metrics. But senior management treats this as a local, incremental project and does not understand the need for their entire measurement and management system to change. Ultimately, the lack of understanding and commitment among the senior management team for the new performance measurement undermines the success of any such project led by middle managers. If senior managers are not actively engaged in the project, new measurements will focus on local operational improvements and not be a comprehensive system that senior executives can use to manage the successful implementation of their strategy.

2. **Scorecard responsibilities do not filter down.** In some companies, senior executives feel that only they need to know and understand the strategy. They fail to share the strategy and scorecard with middle managers and with lower level employees on the front lines and in back offices. A successful Balanced Scorecard implementation, while requiring commitment from the senior management team, must involve more than just senior managers. The executive team must communicate the Balanced Scorecard to everyone in the organization so that all employees learn about the strategy and how they can contribute to its successful implementation.

3. **The solution is overdesigned, or the scorecard is treated as a one-time event.** Some failures have occurred when the project team allowed "the best to be the enemy of the good." These teams wanted to have the perfect scorecard. They did not want to launch the scorecard until they were sure they had exactly the right measures as well as valid data for every measure on the scorecard. The teams believed they would have only one opportunity to launch the scorecard, and they wanted it to be the best it could possibly be. So they spent months refining the measures, improving data collection processes, and establishing baselines for the scorecard measures. Eighteen months after the start of the Balanced Scorecard project, management had yet to use it in any meetings or to support their decision processes. When interviewed, several executives at these companies responded, "I think we tried the Balanced Scorecard last year, but it didn't last." The problem was not that it didn't last. It had never begun!

All Balanced Scorecards start with some new measures for which no data currently exist. Sometimes, up to one-third of the measures are not available in the first few months, especially for measures relating to employee skills, information technology availability, and customer loyalty. Managers should initiate new data collection processes for the missing measures and still use the scorecard for their review and resource allocation processes, even without specific data on the new measures.

As the data become available, managers will have an even better basis for their discussions and decisions. However, the management system should be dynamic, and the objectives, the measures, and the data collection processes can be modified over time on the basis of organizational learning.

4. **The Balanced Scorecard is treated as a systems or consulting project.** Some of the most expensive Balanced Scorecard failures have occurred when companies implemented a Balanced Scorecard as a systems project rather than as a management project. Automating and facilitating access to the thousands (or millions) of data observations collected in a company does not lead to a Balanced Scorecard, nor would such a process identify the critical measurements of an organization's strategy not currently being measured at all (recall the missing measurement problem in the preceding pitfall). Also, giving managers more convenient access to an organization's database is much different than having a structured strategy map, with cause-and-effect linkages, for the relatively few (20 to 30) measures that are the best indicators of the organization's strategic performance.

None of these pitfalls is insuperable. In fact, companies, nonprofits, and government agencies around the world have implemented this new strategy execution system and enjoyed considerable success.[10] The leaders of these successful implementers used the scorecard to communicate strategic objectives and measures to all employees and subsequently aligned employees' personal goals and incentives with improvements in scorecard measures. Managers discussed scorecard results at monthly meetings so they could continually learn and improve how to implement their strategy better. The successful organizations used the Balanced Scorecard as their central management system for focusing the organization on the strategy and aligning employees, business units, and resource allocation on achieving dramatic performance improvements for shareholders and customers.

EPILOGUE TO PIONEER PETROLEUM

Shortly after Brian Roberts and his leadership team finished with the Pioneer's strategy map and scorecard (Exhibits 2-18 and 2-19), they asked the newly-appointed heads of all 17 strategic business units to create scorecards for their own units. They did not insist that all 17 scorecards be the same; they preferred that the management teams at each unit be guided by the objectives and measures on the division's scorecard but wanted each business unit to decide what was most important for them, given their local situation. They could eliminate objectives and measures that were not relevant to them and add new ones that better reflected their local competitive situation. Roberts also started an active process to communicate the strategy's strategic objectives and measures to all of Pioneer's employees, and within a year had introduced a variable pay plan that allowed every employee to earn up to a 30% bonus based on performance of the division's and the employee's business unit scorecard. He recalled:

> People got that scorecard out and did the calculations to see how much money they were going to get. We could not have got the same focus on the scorecard if we didn't have the link to pay.

---

[10] A good source to learn about companies, nonprofits, and governmental agencies that had good success implementing their strategies using the Balanced Scorecard is *Palladium Balanced Scorecard Hall of Fame for Executing Strategy,* retrieved April 8, 2010, from http://www.thepalladiumgroup.com/about/hof/Pages/overview.aspx

Roberts met with his 17 business unit heads at least once per quarter to discuss the unit's performance, as revealed by its scorecard. As he described the meetings:

> I went into these reviews thinking they would be long and arduous. I was pleasantly surprised how simple they were. Managers came in prepared. They were paying attention to their scorecards and using them in a very productive way—to drive their organization hard to achieve the targets.
>
> The process enabled me to see how the business unit managers think, plan, and execute. I could see the gaps, and by understanding the manager's culture and mentality, I developed customized programs that made them better managers.

Within two years, Pioneer went from being the least profitable to the most profitable company in its industry. Brian Roberts retired as CEO after five years of industry-leading profitability summarizing what had been achieved:

> We produce a commodity product, with mature processes, using the same assets as our competitors, through standard distribution (ships, pipelines, trucks), ending in public service stations (no secrets; everyone sees what you are doing), and a strategy that can be quickly imitated. Our only secret was that the Balanced Scorecard helped us out-execute our competitors in an open, transparent game.

SUMMARY

Information-age companies succeed by investing in and managing their intangible assets. As organizations invest in acquiring the new capabilities provided by these assets, their success cannot be motivated or measured by the traditional financial accounting model. This financial model, developed for trading companies and industrial-age corporations, does not measure whether the company is building capabilities that will provide future value.

The Balanced Scorecard, a more comprehensive performance management system, incorporates measures derived from a company's strategy. While retaining financial measures of past performance, the Balanced Scorecard introduces the drivers of future financial performance. The drivers—found in the customer, process, and learning and growth perspectives—are selected from an explicit and rigorous translation of the organization's strategy into tangible objectives and measures. The benefits from the scorecard are realized as the organization integrates its new measurement system into management processes that communicate the strategy to employees, align employees' individual objectives and incentives with successful strategy implementation, and integrate the strategy with ongoing management processes: planning, budgeting, reporting, and management meetings. A new performance measurement and management system has its greatest impact when the executive team leads these transformational processes.

KEY TERMS

Balanced Scorecard (BSC), 43	learning and growth perspective, 45	regulatory and social processes, 57
customer management processes, 56	measures, 49	strategy, 47
customer perspective, 44	objectives, 48	strategy map, 49
financial perspective, 44	operations management processes, 56	targets, 49
innovation processes, 57	process perspective, 45	value proposition, 50

Assignment Materials

Questions

2-1 Explain the role of a company's performance measurement system. (LO 2)

2-2 What is a Balanced Scorecard? (LO 2)

2-3 What are the four measurement perspectives in the Balanced Scorecard? (LO 2)

2-4 Explain why the growing importance of intangible assets complements growing interest in the Balanced Scorecard. (LO 1, 2)

2-5 What are the different ways in which a company can manage and improve its intangible assets? (LO 2)

2-6 What two principal functions should a strategy fulfill? (LO 1)

2-7 What is a strategy map? (LO 3, 4)

2-8 Define and explain the role of measures, objectives, and targets, in the Balanced Scorecard strategy map. (LO 2, 3, 4, 5)

2-9 What are the two basic approaches to improving a company's financial performance? (LO 4, 5)

2-10 Describe two broad approaches that companies can use to generate additional revenues. (LO 4, 5)

2-11 Describe two broad approaches that companies can use to improve productivity. (LO 4, 5)

2-12 Why does attempting to improve customer measures such as customer satisfaction, customer retention, customer profitability, and market share not necessarily constitute a strategy? (LO 3, 4, 5)

2-13 What is a value proposition? (LO 3)

2-14 What are the different types of value propositions that a company may offer to its customers? (LO 3, 4)

2-15 Briefly state the broad objectives that must be taken into consideration by an organization that chooses to offer a customer solutions value proposition. (LO 3, 4)

2-16 Explain how a Balanced Scorecard approach is helpful in identifying critical processes and evaluating the processes. (LO 4, 5)

2-17 All of a Balanced Scorecard's measures for processes should be fully controllable by people who perform the work in the processes. Do you agree with this statement? Explain. (LO 4, 5)

2-18 What four categories of processes are useful in developing the process perspective measures for a Balanced Scorecard? (LO 4, 5)

2-19 What are operations management processes within the Balanced Scorecard's process perspective, and what are some typical objectives for operations management processes? (LO 4, 5)

2-20 What are the three important objectives for a company's customer management processes within the Balanced Scorecard's process perspective? (LO 4, 5)

2-21 What are the objectives of a company's innovation process? (LO 3, 4)

2-22 How can a company develop innovative products and services? (LO 3, 4)

2-23 What are some critical dimensions along which to measure regulatory and social processes in the operating processes part of the Balanced Scorecard's process perspective? (LO 4, 5)

2-24 How might a company link its strategy or customer value proposition to a focus on particular categories of processes in the Balanced Scorecard? (LO 4, 5)

2-25 How do the time frames for financial benefits for improvements in the different categories of processes typically vary? (LO 4, 5)

2-26 Discuss the typical objectives of the three components of the learning and growth perspective in the Balanced Scorecard. (LO 3, 4)

2-27 What are several desirable characteristics for a Balanced Scorecard measure? (LO 4, 5)

2-28 What is the nature of the objective(s) that nonprofit and government organizations are likely to put at the top of their Balanced Scorecard and strategy maps? (LO 6)

2-29 What are four common pitfalls in developing a Balanced Scorecard? (LO 7)

Exercises

LO 2, 4, 5   **2-30**   *Balanced Scorecard measures, low-total-cost value proposition*   Identify an organization with the low-total-cost value proposition and suggest at least two possible measures within each of the four Balanced Scorecard perspectives.

LO 2, 4, 5   **2-31**   *Balanced Scorecard measures, product leadership value proposition*   Identify an organization with the product leadership value proposition and suggest at least two possible measures within each of the four Balanced Scorecard perspectives.

LO 2, 4, 5   **2-32**   *Balanced Scorecard measures, customer solutions value proposition*   Identify an organization with the customer solutions value proposition and suggest at least two possible measures within each of the four Balanced Scorecard perspectives.

LO 2, 4, 5   **2-33**   *Balanced Scorecard objectives, cause-and-effect linkages for different value propositions*

Required

(a) Use the objectives below to develop appropriate cause-and-effect linkages across the Balanced Scorecard's four perspectives for the low-total-cost value proposition.
   (1) Increase profit.
   (2) Decrease process defects.
   (3) Increase customer satisfaction.
   (4) Improve employees' process improvement skills.
   (5) Decrease cost of serving customers.
   (6) Increase revenues.

(b) Use the objectives below to develop appropriate cause-and-effect linkages across the Balanced Scorecard's four perspectives for the product leadership value proposition.
   (1) Increase number of products that are first on the market.
   (2) Decrease product development time from idea to market.
   (3) Increase profit.
   (4) Reduce turnover of key design personnel.
   (5) Increase number of new customers.
   (6) Increase revenues.

(c) Use the objectives below to develop appropriate cause-and-effect linkages across the Balanced Scorecard's four perspectives for the customer solutions value proposition.
   (1) Increase revenues.
   (2) Increase customer satisfaction with employees' assistance.
   (3) Increase number of products cross-sold to customers.
   (4) Increase employees' customer relationship skill levels.

LO 5   **2-34**   *Balanced Scorecard measures, environmental and safety dimensions*   Discuss the accuracy of the following statement: "The Balanced Scorecard approach is incomplete because it does not include measures on environmental performance and measures of employee health and safety."

LO 5   **2-35**   *Number of measures*   Respond to the following statement: "It is impossible for an organization to focus on the 20 to 30 different measures that result if each of the four Balanced Scorecard perspectives contains between four to eight measures."

LO 2, 4, 5   **2-36**   *Balanced Scorecard and key performance indicators*   Respond to the following statement: "Our organization has key performance indicators that measure financial and nonfinancial performance, including customer satisfaction, product and service quality, cost, revenues, and employee satisfaction. We therefore have a Balanced Scorecard approach."

2-37 *Balanced Scorecard and key performance indicators* One financial service organization formerly measured its performance using only a single financial measure, profits. It decided to adopt a more "balanced" measurement approach by introducing a 4P Scorecard:

(1) Profits
(2) Portfolio (size of loan volume)
(3) Process (% processes meeting quality certification standards)
(4) People (meeting diversity goals in hiring).

Evaluate the strengths and weaknesses of the "4P Scorecard."

LO 6 **2-38 *Balanced Scorecards for nonprofit and governmental organizations*** Explain how a Balanced Scorecard for a nonprofit or governmental organization typically differs from for-profit Balanced Scorecards.

LO 2, 4, 5 **2-39 *Performance measurement or management system*** Discuss whether the Balanced Scorecard strategy map approach is a performance measurement system, a management system, or both.

Problems

LO 4, 5 **2-40 *Designing a Balanced Scorecard, differentiation strategy*** Why did Pioneer Petroleum, a company following a differentiation strategy, have so many process objectives and measures relating to cost reduction and productivity?

LO 2, 4, 5 **2-41 *Designing a Balanced Scorecard, new strategies, customer measures*** Refer to the *In Practice* description of Infosys on page 48.

Required

(a) Why would a company with Infosys's history find the Balanced Scorecard important for managing its growth and monitoring its performance?
(b) What customer measures would you recommend that Infosys use in its Balanced Scorecard?
(c) What employee measures would you recommend that Infosys use in its Balanced Scorecard?

LO 2, 4, 5 **2-42 *Designing a Balanced Scorecard, new strategies, customer measures*** Refer to the *In Practice* description of Teach for America on pages 68–69. How can Teach for America use its strategy map and scorecard to advance its mission and strategy?

LO 2, 4, 5 **2-43 *Designing a Balanced Scorecard*** Consider the manager of a store in a fast-food restaurant chain. Construct a Balanced Scorecard to evaluate that manager's performance.

LO 2, 4, 5, 6 **2-44 *Developing a Balanced Scorecard within a university*** Develop a Balanced Scorecard that the dean or director of your school could use to evaluate the school's operations. Be specific and indicate the purpose of each Balanced Scorecard measure.

LO 2, 4, 5, 6 **2-45 *Balanced Scorecard for governmental or nonprofit organization*** Organizations in the public and nonprofit sector, such as government agencies and charitable social service entities, have financial systems that budget expenses and monitor and control actual spending. Choose a government agency or nonprofit organization and describe the various perspectives the agency or organization should include in its Balanced Scorecard. What objectives and measures should be included in each perspective, and how might they be linked?

LO 7 **2-46 *Pitfalls in Balanced Scorecard implementation*** A company attempted to build a Balanced Scorecard by fitting the company's objectives and financial and nonfinancial performance measures into the four Balanced Scorecard perspectives. Explain why this approach may not lead to a well-developed Balanced Scorecard.

LO 7   **2-47 Pitfalls in Balanced Scorecard implementation**   A company's chief executive officer (CEO) wanted his company to develop a Balanced Scorecard. After giving considerable thought to who should lead the development, he selected the head of the information technology group because the Balanced Scorecard would obviously involve collecting information leading to the needed measurements. Comment on potential problems with the CEO's approach.

Cases

LO 4, 5   **2-48 Compensation tied to Balanced Scorecard, degree of difficulty of target achievement**[11]   In the mid-1990s, Mobil Corporation's Marketing and Refining (M&R) division underwent a major reorganization and developed new strategic directions. In conjunction with these changes, M&R developed a Balanced Scorecard around four perspectives: financial, customer, internal business processes, and learning and growth. Subsequently, M&R linked compensation to its Balanced Scorecard metrics. To illustrate, all salaried employees in M&R's Natural Business Units received the following percentages of their competitive market salary:

	POOR PERFORMANCE WITHIN INDUSTRY	AVERAGE PERFORMANCE WITHIN INDUSTRY	PERFORMANCE BEST IN INDUSTRY
Base pay	90%	90%	90%
Award based on corporate performance on financial metrics	1–2%	3–6%	10%
Award based on performance on Balanced Scorecard metrics for the M&R division and business unit	0%	5–8%	20%
Total pay as percentage of market salary	91–92%	98–104%	120%

The Balanced Scorecards included numerous metrics. M&R's financial metrics included return on capital employed and profitability, and customer metrics included share of targeted segments of consumers and profitability of dealers. Internal business process metrics included safety and quality indices. Finally, learning and growth metrics included an index of employees' perceptions of the work climate at M&R.

Business units developed their own Balanced Scorecards. In addition to choosing targets for scorecard metrics, the business units chose percentage weights that determined how much the achieved scorecard measures would contribute to the bonus pool displayed in the table. These percentage weights were required to sum to 100%. Furthermore, in connection with the award for performance on the business unit Balanced Scorecard metrics, the business units assigned a performance factor, that is, a "degree of difficulty" of target achievement for each target. The performance factors are similar in concept to those in diving or gymnastic competitions where performance scores depend on the difficulty of the attempted dive or gymnastic routine. The performance factors underwent review by peers, upper management, and the employees whose evaluation and compensation depended on the performance factors. The performance factors ranged from 1.25 (for best-in-industry performance) to 0.7 for poor performance. A target corresponding to average industry performance rated a 1.0 performance factor.

Required

(a) What are some general advantages of and areas of concerns surrounding the linking of compensation to a Balanced Scorecard?

---

[11] Source: Robert S. Kaplan based on analysis of "Mobil US M&R (A): Linking the Balanced Scorecard," Harvard Business School Case # 197025.

(b) Evaluate M&R's approach to linking compensation to multiple measures (Balanced Scorecard measures), including its system of assigning degrees of difficulty to achieving targets. In your response, consider the process that is involved in developing the compensation scheme.

LO 2, 4, 5   **2-49** *Implementing the Balanced Scorecard*   Either by visiting a website or from a description in a published article, find a description of the implementation of a Balanced Scorecard.

Required

(a) Document in detail the elements (objectives, measures, and targets) of the Balanced Scorecard.
(b) Identify the purpose of each Balanced Scorecard element.
(c) Describe, if the facts are available, or infer, if the facts are not available, how the Balanced Scorecard elements relate to the organization's strategy.
(d) Evaluate the Balanced Scorecard by indicating whether you agree that the choice of Balanced Scorecard performance measures is complete and consistent with the organization's plan and stakeholder set.

LO 2, 4, 5   **2-50** *Balanced Scorecard measures*   Refer to the University of Leeds' strategy map at http://www.leeds.ac.uk/downloads/Strategy_map_aw.pdf

Required

(a) What is the strategy for the university?
(b) What will make it distinctive or unique?
(c) What are its advantages and scope?
(d) What measures would you use for each of the strategic objectives?

LO 2, 4, 5, 6   **2-51** *Designing a Balanced Scorecard for a city*   The City of Charlotte, North Carolina, states its vision and mission as follows:[12]

City Vision

The City of Charlotte will be a model of excellence that puts citizens first. Skilled, diverse, and motivated employees will be known for providing quality and value in all areas of service. We will be a platform for vital economic activity that gives Charlotte a competitive edge in the marketplace. We will partner with citizens and businesses to make this a community of choice for living, working, and leisure activities.

City Mission

The mission of the City of Charlotte is to ensure the delivery of quality public services and to promote the safety, health, and quality of life of its citizens.

The city's senior administrative staff has selected the following five strategic focus areas in which the city should try to excel:[13]

- **Community Safety** (evolved from an initial focus on crime and now includes livability, stability, and economic viability of a neighborhood).
- **Transportation** (including maximizing public transit, building and maintaining roads, adopting and implementing land-use policies to support growth and transit goals, and ensuring adequate pedestrian and bicycle connections).

---

[12] http://www.charmeck.org/Departments/Human+Resources+City/City+Mission+and+Vision.htm
[13] See page 35 of the fiscal year 2010 report at http://charmeck.org/city/charlotte/Budget/Documents/FY2010%20Strategic%20Operating%20plan.pdf

- **Housing and Neighborhood Development** (includes adequate code enforcement, developing strategies for affordable housing, and neighborhood and business district involvement in problem identification and solution development).
- **Environment** (includes protecting air and water quality, land preservation, and energy and resource conservation).
- **Economic Development** (includes sustaining prosperity, keeping jobs and the tax base in Charlotte, and building a skilled and competitive workforce).

Required

Develop a Balanced Scorecard for the City of Charlotte. Explain in detail your choice of what appears at the top of your proposed strategy map. Bear in mind that the city's Balanced Scorecard need not include every important service.

LO 4, 5   **2-52 *Designing a Balanced Scorecard*** Wells Fargo's web page (https://www .wellsfargo.com/pdf/invest_relations/VisionandValues04.pdf) states that the company's vision is "to satisfy all our customers' financial needs and help them succeed financially." The brochure also describes the following 10 strategic initiatives:

1. Investments, brokerage, trust, and insurance.
2. Going for "gr-eight"! (Increase the average number of products per customer to eight).
3. Commercial bank of choice.
4. Doing it right for the customer.
5. Banking with a mortgage.
6. Wells Fargo cards in every Wells Fargo wallet.
7. When, where, and how.
8. Information-based marketing.
9. Be our customers' payment processor.
10. People as a competitive advantage.

Required

Based on the annual reports and any other information you are able to find about Wells Fargo or its competitors, develop a Balanced Scorecard for Wells Fargo that will help it achieve its vision and monitor its performance on the strategic initiatives.

LO 4, 5   **2-53 *Designing a Balanced Scorecard for a pharmaceutical company*** Chadwick, Inc.: The Balanced Scorecard (Abridged)[14]

> *The "Balanced Scorecard"[15] article seemed to address the concerns of several division managers who felt that the company was over-emphasizing short-term financial results. But the process of getting agreement on what measures should be used proved a lot more difficult than I anticipated.*
>
> Bill Baron, Comptroller of Chadwick, Inc.

Company Background

Chadwick, Inc., was a diversified producer of personal consumer products and pharmaceuticals. The Norwalk Division of Chadwick developed, manufactured, and sold ethical drugs for human and animal use. It was one of five or six sizable companies competing in these markets and, while it did not dominate the industry, the company was considered well managed and was respected for the high quality of its products. Norwalk did not compete by supplying a full range of products. It

---

[14] Copyright © 1996 President and Fellows of Harvard College. Harvard Business School Case 2-196-124. This case was prepared by Professor Robert S. Kaplan as the basis for class discussion rather than to illustrate either effective or ineffective handling of an administrative situation. Reprinted by permission of Harvard Business School.

[15] Robert S. Kaplan and David P. Norton, "The Balanced Scorecard: Measures that Drive Performance," *Harvard Business Review*, January–February 1992, 71–79.

specialized in several niches and attempted to leverage its product line by continually searching for new applications for existing compounds.

Norwalk sold its products through several key distributors who supplied local markets, such as retail stores, hospitals and health service organizations, and veterinary practices. Norwalk depended on its excellent relations with the distributors who served to promote Norwalk's products to end users and also received feedback from the end users about new products desired by their customers.

Chadwick knew that its long-term success depended on how much money distributors could make by promoting and selling Norwalk's products. If the profit from selling Norwalk products was high, then these products were promoted heavily by the distributors and Norwalk received extensive communication back about future customer needs. Norwalk had historically provided many highly profitable products to the marketplace, but recent inroads by generic manufacturers had been eroding distributors' sales and profit margins. Norwalk had been successful in the past because of its track record of generating a steady stream of attractive, popular products. During the second half of the 1980s, however, the approval process for new products had lengthened and fewer big winners had emerged from Norwalk's R&D laboratories.

Research and Development

The development of ethical drugs was a lengthy, costly, and unpredictable process. Development cycles now averaged about 12 years. The process started by screening a large number of compounds for potential benefits and use. For every drug that finally emerged as approved for use, up to 30,000 compounds had to be tested at the beginning of a new product development cycle. The development and testing processes had many stages. The development cycle started with the discovery of compounds that possessed the desirable properties and ended many years later with extensive and tedious testing and documentation to demonstrate that the new drug could meet government regulations for promised benefits, reliability in production, and absence of deleterious side effects.

Approved and patented drugs could generate enormous revenues for Norwalk and its distributors. Norwalk's profitability during the 1980s was sustained by one key drug that had been discovered in the late 1960s. No blockbuster drug had emerged during the 1980s, however, and the existing pipeline of compounds going through development, evaluation, and test was not as healthy as Norwalk management desired. Management was placing pressure on scientists in the R&D lab to increase the yield of promising new products and to reduce the time and costs of the product development cycle. Scientists were currently exploring new bioengineering techniques to create compounds that had the specific active properties desired rather than depending on an almost random search through thousands of possible compounds. The new techniques started with a detailed specification of the chemical properties that a new drug should have and then attempted to synthesize candidate compounds that could be tested for these properties. The bioengineering procedures were costly, requiring extensive investment in new equipment and computer-based analyses.

A less expensive approach to increase the financial yield from R&D investments was to identify new applications for existing compounds that had already been approved for use. While some validation still had to be submitted for government approval to demonstrate the effectiveness of the drug in the new applications, the cost of extending an existing product to a new application was much, much less expensive than developing and creating an entirely new compound. Several valuable suggestions for possible new applications from existing products had come from Norwalk salesmen in the field. The salesmen were now being trained not only to sell existing products for approved applications, but also to listen to end users who frequently had novel and interesting ideas about how Norwalk's products could be used for new applications.

Manufacturing

Norwalk's manufacturing processes were considered among the best in the industry. Management took pride in the ability of the manufacturing operation to quickly and efficiently ramp up to produce drugs once they had cleared governmental regulatory processes. Norwalk's manufacturing capabilities also had to produce the small batches of new products that were required during testing and evaluation stages.

Performance Measurement

Chadwick allowed its several divisions to operate in a decentralized fashion. Division managers had almost complete discretion in managing all the critical processes: R&D, production, marketing and sales, and administrative functions such as finance, human resources, and legal. Chadwick set challenging financial targets for divisions to meet. The targets were usually expressed as return on capital employed (ROCE). As a diversified company, Chadwick wanted to be able to deploy the returns from the most profitable divisions to those divisions that held out the highest promise for profitable growth. Monthly financial summaries were submitted by each division to corporate headquarters. The Chadwick executive committee, consisting of the chief executive officer, the chief operating officer, two executive vice presidents, and the chief financial officer met monthly with each division manager to review ROCE performance and backup financial information for the preceding month.

The Balanced Scorecard Project

Bill Baron, comptroller of Chadwick, had been searching for improved methods for evaluating the performance of the various divisions. Division managers complained about the continual pressure to meet short-term financial objectives in businesses that required extensive investments in risky projects to yield long-term returns. The idea of a Balanced Scorecard appealed to him as a constructive way to balance short-run financial objectives with the long-term performance of the company.

Baron brought the article and concept to Dan Daniels, the president and chief operating officer of Chadwick. Daniels shared Baron's enthusiasm for the concept, feeling that a Balanced Scorecard would allow Chadwick divisional managers more flexibility in how they measured and presented their results of operations to corporate management. He also liked the idea of holding managers accountable for improving the long-term performance of their division.

After several days of reflection, Daniels issued a memorandum to all Chadwick division managers. The memo had a simple and direct message: Read the Balanced Scorecard article, develop a scorecard for your division, and be prepared to come to corporate headquarters in 90 days to present and defend the divisional scorecard to Chadwick's executive committee.

John Greenfield, the division manager at Norwalk, received Daniel's memorandum with some concern and apprehension. In principle, Greenfield liked the idea of developing a scorecard that would be more responsive to his operations, but he was distrustful of how much freedom he had to develop and use such a scorecard. Greenfield recalled:

This seemed like just another way for corporate to claim that they have decentralized decision making and authority while still retaining ultimate control at headquarters.

Greenfield knew that he would have to develop a plan of action to meet corporate's request but lacking a clear sense of how committed Chadwick was to the concept, he was not prepared to take much time from his or his subordinates' existing responsibilities for the project.

The next day, at the weekly meeting of the Divisional Operating Committee, Greenfield distributed the Daniels memo and appointed a three-man committee, headed by the divisional controller, Wil Wagner, to facilitate the process for creating the Norwalk Balanced Scorecard.

Wagner approached Greenfield later that day:

I read the Balanced Scorecard article. Based on my understanding of the concept, we must start with a clearly defined business vision. I'm not sure I have a clear understanding of the vision and business strategy for Norwalk. How can I start to build the scorecard without this understanding?

Greenfield admitted: "That's a valid point. Let me see what I can do to get you started."

1. Manage Norwalk portfolio of investments
   - Minimize cost to executing our existing business base
   - Maximize return/yield on all development spending
   - Invest in discovery of new compounds
2. Satisfy customer needs
3. Drive responsibility to the lowest level
   - Minimize centralized staff overhead
4. People development
   - Industry training
   - Unique mix of technical and commercial skills

Greenfield picked up a pad of paper and started to write. Several minutes later he had produced a short business strategy statement for Norwalk (see Exhibit 2-22). Wagner and his group took Greenfield's strategy statement and started to formulate scorecard measures for the division.

Required

(a) How does the Balanced Scorecard approach differ from traditional approaches to performance measurement? What, if anything, distinguishes the Balanced Scorecard approach from a "measure everything, and you might get what you want" philosophy?

(b) Develop the Balanced Scorecard for the Norwalk Pharmaceutical Division of Chadwick, Inc. What parts of the business strategy that John Greenfield sketched out should be included? Are there any parts that should be excluded or cannot be made operational? What scorecard measures would you use to implement your scorecard in the Norwalk Pharmaceutical Division? What new measures need to be developed, and how would you go about developing them?

(c) How would a Balanced Scorecard for Chadwick, Inc., differ from ones developed in its divisions, such as the Norwalk Pharmaceutical Division? Do you anticipate that there might be major conflicts between divisional scorecards and those of the corporation? If so, should those conflicts be resolved, and, if so, how should they be resolved?

LO 4, 5   **2-54** *Designing a Balanced Scorecard strategy map for an auto parts manufacturing company*   Domestic Auto Parts (DAP),[16] a $1 billion subsidiary of a U.S. auto parts manufacturing company, manufactured and marketed original and after-market parts for automobile producers in the United States. It distributed products directly to original equipment automakers as well as to large retail chains. DAP was currently number four in market share in the United States out of nine direct competitors. Its 9% return on capital was respectable but less than that of its leading competitors.

DAP's current product line was solid, but it had not introduced new products to the market during the past three years. This had caused its projected revenues to decline and its industry position to slip. As recently as two years ago, DAP was number two in the industry, but competitors Western Auto and Just in Time Automotive had passed it, pushing DAP to number four. Western Auto had introduced higher value products to the market with the use of technology both to manufacture products and in the parts themselves. Western's customers paid a premium price for the improved performance of the company's products.

---

[16] Copyright © 2005 President and Fellows of Harvard College. Harvard Business School Case 2-105-078. This case was prepared by Professor Robert S. Kaplan as the basis for class discussion rather than to illustrate either effective or ineffective handling of an administrative situation. Reprinted by permission of Harvard Business School.

DAP, on the other hand, had protected margins during its revenue decline by aggressively attacking costs. It succeeded in maintaining its gross and operating margin levels but at the cost of limiting plant investment and technology upgrades in manufacturing plants. It was beginning to experience maintenance problems, such as an increase in unscheduled downtime. Also, because it lacked the flexible manufacturing capabilities of competitors, it had to produce to stock rather than to order, causing inventory costs to rise to noncompetitive levels. Company management now recognized that the recent cost cutting had maintained margins in the short term but may have severely affected DAP's ability to compete in the longer term.

To help turn the company around, the parent company had recently hired a new CEO, Ellen Bright. Her job was clearly set out for her—either turn the subsidiary around in two years or close the business. The minimum requirements for continued operations were to achieve 12% return on capital employed (ROCE) and a growth rate faster than the industry's so that it could regain its number one or two position among competitors.

With this directive in hand, Bright held a meeting with her executive team to explain the situation and get their input. She started the meeting by stating:

The only way we can achieve our goal is for each of you and your departments to cooperate to improve our return on capital. Product quality has set us apart in the past. We must regain our high-quality position and grow our revenues and our contribution to the parent company.

My review of the economics and the competitive situation at DAP suggests that we must do three things: we need to grow; we must be customer intimate; and, we must be operationally excellent. And we must do all three things at once to be successful.

Joe [the new chief financial officer brought in by Bright], you and I have been working on the economics required to achieve our financial goals. Why don't you share our initial findings with the group?

Joe Nathan described the financial goals for the turnaround:

Basically, I designed a simple economic model to pinpoint the critical economic drivers needed to reach our goal of a 12% ROCE. We must increase our top line revenue by 50% through innovation and customer relationships, we need to better utilize our capital assets (both current and new)—currently we are operating at 65% on old assets—and we must get to 90% utilization on an upgraded asset base. Finally, we must minimize our total cost structure—today we are operating above the average cost in our competitor group. We need to get to the lowest-cost quartile to compete. These are the key drivers needed to get to the financial results expected by the parent company. We must balance them—one against the other—to achieve our overall goal of 12% ROCE. The question is how are we going to do this? What must we do—what objectives must we set and achieve?

Ellen Bright interjected, "We are going to build a strategy to achieve each of these thrusts. I need your commitment and active contribution." She asked Michael Milton, vice president of manufacturing, for his perspective. Milton said:

I'll admit that we certainly need to get more creative and bring to market new and improved products. But we need to do a lot of our processes better. Supplier management and manufacturing as well as product delivery have to be better coordinated so we can effectively and efficiently get new products to the customer. We need to be on time and on spec just to get the opportunity to sell new products. Key in my mind is managing the supplier pipeline, the raw materials—there is a lot of money to be saved there.

We also need to balance our intense focus on cost cutting with the need to make investments in process improvements and new and upgraded equipment. Unscheduled downtime and the inability to make product switchovers on the manufacturing floor are killing us. Upgraded capital will both reduce our costs and help deliver consistently on time and on spec. We talk a lot about preventive maintenance, but we need to get real about it. This could save us big time in terms of costs and effectiveness. If we don't do these operational things we will have trouble convincing customers to pay a premium price for our products.

David Dillon, head of distribution, described the problems he faced:

At the moment, I don't have the infrastructure tools to create a first-class network of wholesalers and distributors. We need to streamline our distribution process and position ourselves as a strong business partner to attract and retain profitable customers. There are a lot of people out there with great experience and good ideas about how to achieve this, but the department is large and geographically dispersed, and there is no formal way of sharing best practices and best thinking. These steps will help us achieve our grow-revenue goal by getting products to market at a reasonable price in a reasonable time.

Mary Stewart, vice president of marketing and sales, added:

Improving our distribution will be a major factor in our new customer intimacy thrust by providing the opportunity for win–win relationships with our distributor customers and enhancing our reputation for efficiency and organization.
    In addition, we must position ourselves in the market—with the right customers—to be viable. We have recently studied our customer base and found an important segment of the current customer base that is profitable in both the direct and wholesale segments. In fact, 69% of our customers produce 90% of our profit. We went on to determine what these key customers want and will pay for. Both key segments, direct and wholesale, want essentially the same things. They expect us to deliver products on time and on spec. This, however, is expected from everyone in the industry. It's a hurdle that must be passed just to be considered a viable vendor. The differentiator is for a supplier to understand their needs and translate that by continuous communication and productive dialogue. They want a long-term, mutually beneficial relationship with their suppliers. They want superior, technology-sophisticated products from a supplier with a superior reputation and image in the industry. Such a supplier makes their buying decisions less risky.

Rita Richardson, vice president of research and development, responded to the challenge to produce state-of-the-art technologically sophisticated products:

Well, we have some talented people in our R&D group who can produce the kind of products our customers need. But all the products in the world will not be bought without a good marketing communications effort. We need to be able to tell people what we have and how it can benefit them. We need a marketing effort that positions us as an innovator with new and enhanced products to offer. I think it might help to have some of our marketing staff spend time in the R&D department to get a feel for what's going on. Sure some reskilling may be needed to achieve our innovation goals but I think we have a solid base of R&D professionals.

Bright interjected at this point, "I think you have hit on something there, Rita. I think we all need to be more business focused and less functionally focused. The company seems to be suffering because employees know only what goes on inside their own area. This team needs to lead this cross-functional view by example—in what we say and what we do."
    She closed the meeting by challenging the group even further:

None of our objectives can be accomplished without a major commitment from all of us to build a world-class workforce. To operate as an innovator we must change the way we think in this organization. Our employees must value change not resist it. We must reskill large parts—not some—of the organization. This will require training. Training involves both time and money. To support the new workforce we will also need to provide tools to work smarter and harder. We can do this and align the organization through the use of just-in-time technology. This commitment to people and organization is necessary to do the things we need to do to deliver customer benefits and ultimately financial returns.

Required

From the meeting of senior DAP executives, develop a strategy map of objectives, as well as potential Balanced Scorecard measures, for DAP. You can be guided by the following questions:

Financial

1. Who are the shareholders, and what do they want?
2. What are the shareholders' expectations in the following areas?
   (a) Revenue growth.
   (b) Asset utilization.
   (c) Cost improvement.

Customer

1. Who are the customers?
2. What do the customers want? How does DAP create value for them?

Process

1. What processes are most important for creating value for DAP's shareholders and customers?
2. What are the objectives and measures for each process identified here?

Learning and Growth

1. What specific skills and capabilities do DAP's people need in order to excel at the critical processes that you identified in the process perspective?
2. What other objectives can you identify to improve the human resources, information technology, and organization culture and alignment of DAP if it is to succeed with its strategy?

3

Using Costs in Decision Making

After completing this chapter, you will be able to:

1. Understand and be able to explain the important cost-related concepts in management accounting.

2. Understand how cost information supports important management activities such as product pricing, product planning, budgeting, and performance evaluation.

3. Be able to model, interpret, and evaluate the effect of volume changes on costs and profits in simple organizations.

4. Understand the important role of, and be able to use, the relevant cost concept in make-or-buy, product and department abandonment, costing orders, and product mix decisions and be able to apply the relevant cost concept in simple situations.

Nolan Industries

Nolan Industries manufactures control units that are used in high-speed production systems such as pulp and paper manufacturing. The company has two major products: the XR244 and the XR276. Punit Shah, the sales manager at Nolan Industries, is preparing a production plan for the upcoming year and is evaluating a new product opportunity.

Punit is studying the following summary information provided by the finance group at Nolan Industries.

	XR244	XR276
Selling price	$785.00	$955.00
Total costs	470.00	595.00
Profit	$315.00	$360.00
Maximum sales (units)	10,000	15,000
Machine hours (per unit)	2.50	3.00

In recent years the sales mix has been 40% XR244 and 60% XR276 and Punit is wondering, given that XR276 is more profitable, whether a better production mix would include more sales of the XR276. Nolan

Industries has 48,000 machine hours available for the production of these two products. A conversation with the plant accountant suggests to Punit that about 65% of product costs vary with the level of production and that Nolan Industries' total fixed costs amount to $7,500,000.

As he was considering these opportunities, Punit received an e-mail from a customer offering to buy 2,000 units of a specialty product that would sell for $1,200 per unit, have a cost of $820 per unit, and would require 3.5 hours per unit of production time to produce.

Excluding the new product opportunity, Punit is wondering:

1. How many units of each product would he have to sell to break even given the 40/60 mix?
2. What is the maximum number of units he can sell given the machine hours constraint that he faces and given the 40/60 sales mix, and what is the profit at that sales level?
3. Is there a better product mix than the 40/60 split?
4. Finally, considering the new product opportunity, should Punit accept the offer and, if so, what would be the resulting production levels and profit?

HOW MANAGEMENT ACCOUNTING SUPPORTS INTERNAL DECISION MAKING

Chapter 2 identified the role of management accounting in supporting strategy development and in evaluating the results of operations. The balance of this book will develop the various roles of management accounting in supporting the development, implementation, monitoring, and revision of strategy.

In this chapter we discuss cost information and the important role it plays in strategy development and in monitoring the results of implementing the strategy. The use of cost information is pervasive throughout decision-making situations.

Pricing

Organizations use cost information in the pricing decision in two ways. In markets where the organization faces a market-determined price, the organization will use product cost information to decide whether its cost structure will allow it to compete profitably. In markets where the organization can set its price, organizations will often set a price that is an increment of its product's cost—an approach called *cost plus pricing*.

Product Planning

In product planning, organizations use a tool called *target costing* to focus efforts in product and process design on developing a product that has a good profit potential in view of market requirements.

Budgeting

Perhaps the most widespread use of cost information is in budgeting, which is a management accounting tool that projects or forecasts costs for various levels of production and sales activity. Budgets are important in planning, which sets the organization's direction for the budget period. Budgets provide the basis for earnings forecasts that senior executives issue to the stock market.

Performance Evaluation

In performance evaluation, managers compare the actual results from the budget period with expectations that were reflected in the budget to assess how well the organization did in light of its expectations.

Contracting

In cost reimbursement contracts organizations are reimbursed their cost plus an increment for the goods or service they provide under the contract. Governments are frequent and large-scale users of cost reimbursement contracts. Because of the potential for cost manipulation, governments will often prescribe the costing standards that organizations must use when computing reimbursement costs.

VARIABLE AND FIXED COSTS

Variable Costs

A **variable cost** is one that increases proportionally with changes in the activity level of some variable. For example, the activity of making a chair in a furniture factory consumes the wood that goes into the chairs. The acquisition and consumption of the wood creates a cost for wood that increases proportionately with the number of chairs made.

Because there are many possible types of variables, for convenience, a common term used for a variable that causes a cost is **cost driver**.[1] Therefore, the variable cost formula is

$$\text{Variable cost} = \text{Variable cost per unit of the cost driver} \times \text{Cost driver units}$$

Note that the convention is to use variable cost to refer to the total variable cost and variable cost per unit as the variable cost per unit of the cost driver.

The Rose Furniture Company manufactures a single product—a rocking chair. Based on past results, the cost of the wood used to make each rocking chair is estimated as $25. Noting that the cost driver here is rocking chairs, the variable cost equation for wood would be

$$\text{Variable cost of wood} = \$25 \times \text{Number of rocking chairs made}$$

The variable cost of wood graph would look like that shown in Exhibit 3-1. Note that the variable cost line is a straight line that starts at the origin and has a constant slope that equals the variable cost of wood per unit of the cost driver, which is the number of rocking chairs made.

---

[1] As we will see in Chapter 4, the term *cost driver* is also commonly used to describe the method by which indirect costs are assigned to cost objects, such as products, departments, or customers.

Exhibit 3-1
Variable Cost
of Wood at
Rose Furniture
Company

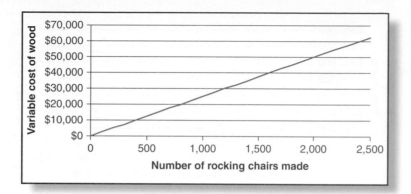

Exhibit 3-1
Variable Cost
of Wood at
Rose Furniture
Company

Two other manufacturing costs at the Rose Furniture Company vary with (i.e., are driven by) the number of rocking chairs made:

- The wages paid to the workers who shape and assemble the various pieces that make up the rocking chairs.
- The cost of supplies such as nails, glue, and stain that are consumed in proportion to the number of rocking chairs made.

Past results indicate that the cost of labor needed for each rocking chair is $30 and the cost of the supplies is $5. Therefore,

> Variable cost for each rocking chair = Variable cost of wood + Variable cost
> of labor + Variable cost of supplies
> = $25 + $30 + $5 = $60

The variable cost equation for rocking chairs will be

> Variable cost of rocking chairs = $60 × Number of rocking chairs made

Finally the Rose Furniture Company incurs variable selling and shipping costs of $20 for each rocking chair sold. This brings the total variable cost of making and selling a rocking chair to $80 (the variable manufacturing cost of $60 plus the variable selling and shipping cost of $20). The equation for all variable costs associated with making, selling, and shipping rocking chairs then becomes

> Variable cost of rocking chairs = $80 × Number of rocking chairs made

Exhibit 3-2 provides the variable cost graph for all variable costs in the Rose Furniture Company.

Exhibit 3-2
Total Variable Costs
at Rose Furniture
Company

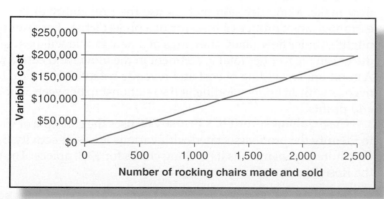

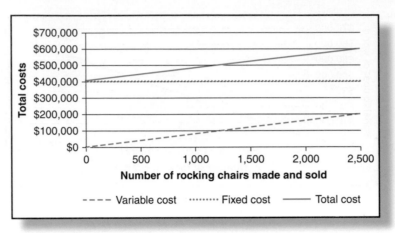

Fixed Costs

A fixed cost is a cost that does not vary in the short run with a specified activity. The defining characteristic of a fixed cost is that it depends on the amount of a resource that is acquired rather than the amount that is used. For this reason fixed costs are often called capacity-related costs.

Examples of fixed manufacturing costs at the Rose Furniture Company are depreciation on factory equipment and wages paid to production supervisors. These costs do not depend on how much of the available machine time or supervisory time is used—they depend only on the amount of capacity that was acquired.

The Rose Furniture Company also has fixed selling and administrative costs. An example of a fixed selling cost is the salary paid to a sales manager. (Note that commissions paid to sales staff are variable costs.) Examples of fixed administrative costs include the salaries paid to head office staff and depreciation on the head office building.

Fixed costs per year amount to $400,000 at the Rose Furniture Company. The total cost equation at the Rose Furniture Company is

Total cost = Variable cost + Fixed cost
$$= (\$80 \times \text{Number of rocking chairs made and sold}) + \$400,000$$

Exhibit 3-3 shows the graph of total costs at the Rose Furniture Company.

COST–VOLUME–PROFIT ANALYSIS

Planners and decision makers like to know the risk associated with the decisions that they make. Many decision makers use the probability of at least breaking even or earning a target profit as a measure of a project's risk. For example, a movie producer might wonder how many showings of a new movie will be required so that the producer can recover her total investment in the movie and earn a required target profit. A good understanding of cost and revenue behavior is critical in providing decision makers with an understanding of the relationship between a project's revenues, costs, and profits.

Cost–volume–profit (CVP) analysis uses the concepts of variable and fixed costs to identify the profit associated with various levels of activity. Suppose that the Rose Furniture Company sells its rocking chairs for $300 apiece. The revenue equation for the Rose Furniture Company will be

Revenue = $300 × Number of rocking chairs sold

Exhibit 3-4
Revenues, Costs,
and Profits at Rose
Furniture Company

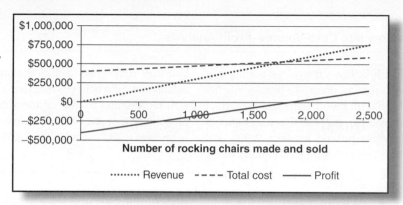

For the sake of convenience, in what follows we will assume that all rocking chairs made in any period are sold. We will simply refer to the cost driver as number of rocking chairs. Therefore, the profit equation for the Rose Furniture Company is as follows:

Profit = Revenue − Total costs = Revenue − Variable costs − Fixed costs
Profit = \$300 × Number of rocking chairs
      − \$80 × Number of rocking chairs
      − \$400,000

Exhibit 3-4, called the CVP chart, shows the revenue, total cost, and profit associated with various levels of rocking chairs made and sold.

Developing and Using the CVP Equation

Recall that earlier we had the following profit equation for the Rose Furniture Company:

Profit = \$300 × Number of rocking chairs
      − \$80 × Number of rocking chairs
      − \$400,000

The difference between total revenue and total variable cost is called the **contribution margin**. The **contribution margin per unit** is the contribution that each unit makes to covering fixed costs and providing a profit. The contribution margin per unit for the Rose Furniture Company is \$220 (\$300 − \$80). Finally, we often have use for the **contribution margin ratio**, which is the ratio of contribution margin per unit to selling price per unit. In the case of Rose Furniture Company, the contribution margin ratio is 73.33% (\$300 − \$80)/\$300. The contribution margin ratio is the fraction of each sales dollar that is available to cover fixed expenses and produce a profit.

We can rewrite this profit equation as

Profit = (\$300 − \$80) × Number of rocking chairs − Fixed cost

We can write the general CVP equation for a single product company as

Profit = Unit sales × (Price per unit − Variable cost per unit) − Fixed cost

or

Profit = Contribution margin per unit × Units produced and sold
      − Fixed costs

For the Rose Furniture Company,

Profit = \$220 × Number of rocking chairs sold − \$400,000

Introducing Uncertainty into Cost–Volume–Profit Analysis

Decision makers like Julie Rose, the owner manager of the Rose Furniture Company, often like to associate the break-even sales level with their beliefs about product sales potential. For example, suppose that Julie believes that sales are uncertain but lie between 1,500 and 3,000 units with all values on this interval equally likely.

You may remember from a statistics course that this means that Julie believes that demand for her chairs is well represented by the uniform distribution and the probability that she will sell at least 1,819 chairs given her beliefs is 78.73% = (3,000 − 1,819)/(3,000 − 1,500).

Planners are often interested in determining the unit sales required to produce a target profit. To see this, we can rearrange the general profit equation to get the following:

$$\text{units needed to be sold} = \frac{\text{target profit} + \text{fixed cost}}{\text{contribution margin per unit}}$$

For the Rose Furniture Company, we have

$$\text{rocking chairs needed to be sold} = \frac{\text{target profit} + \$400,000}{220}$$

The most common use of this equation occurs when the planner calculates the breakeven volume. For example, suppose that Julie is worried about the risk associated with her business and wonders how many rocking chairs must be made to break even (i.e., to achieve a profit of 0 by having the contribution margin just equal the fixed costs). We compute the breakeven level of unit sales for Julie as follows:

$$\text{rocking chairs needed to be sold} = \frac{\text{target profit} + \$400,000}{\$220}$$
$$= \frac{\$0 + \$400,000}{\$220} = 1,819$$

Note that by convention we always round up when finding the required unit sales with this type of analysis.

Because of the huge cost of developing new products in some industries, particularly aircraft and pharmaceutical industries, executives and market analysts pay close attention to the required breakeven sales on new projects and will often use the estimate of the required breakeven sales as a measure of a project's risk.

Variations on the Theme

Suppose that Julie has set the target profit as 20% of revenues. How many rocking chairs will have to be sold to earn this target profit? We have

$$\text{Target profit} = \text{Contribution margin per unit} \times \text{Required unit sales} - \text{Fixed cost}$$

$$20\% \times \text{Revenues} = \text{Contribution margin per unit} \times \text{Required unit sales} - \text{Fixed cost}$$

$$20\% \times \text{Price per unit} \times \text{Required unit sales} = \text{Contribution margin per unit} \times \text{Required unit sales} - \text{Fixed cost}$$

$$(\text{Contribution margin per unit} - 20\% \times \text{Price per unit}) \times \text{Required unit sales} = \text{Fixed costs}$$

$$\text{required unit sales} = \frac{\text{fixed costs}}{\text{contribution margin per unit} - 20\% \times \text{price per unit}}$$

Breakeven on a Development Project

Because of the huge costs of developing new aircraft, airplane manufacturers, and analysts who follow these companies, focus considerable attention on the unit sales required to break even on a new aircraft as a measure of organization risk created by the introduction of a new type of aircraft. In 2010, EADS (the parent of Airbus) CFO Hans Peter Ring said that breakeven on the huge Airbus A380-800, which was introduced in 2007, could be achieved by 2015. The reason it takes so long to break even is because of how many airplanes must be built and sold to recover the development costs and annual fixed production, selling, and distribution costs.

For the Rose Furniture Company, this will be

$$\text{required units sales} = \frac{\$400,000}{\$220 - 20\% \times \$300} = \frac{\$400,000}{\$220 - \$60} = 2,500$$

Until now, we have assumed that Rose Furniture Company pays no taxes. We can easily add to the equation to reflect the impact of income taxes. Suppose the Rose Furniture Company pays a marginal tax rate of 30%. How does this affect the CVP and target profit equations? Suppose Julie wants to know how many rocking chairs must be made and sold to generate a net (after-tax) profit of $100,000 when facing a tax rate of 30%? Here is the equation:

Target profit = [(Contribution margin per unit × Required unit sales) − Fixed cost] × (1 − Tax rate)

Rearranging we find

$$\text{required unit sales} = \frac{\dfrac{\text{target profit}}{1 - \text{tax rate}} + \text{fixed costs}}{\text{contribution margin per unit}}$$

For the Rose Furniture Company the required unit sales would be

$$\text{required unit sales} = \frac{\dfrac{\$100,000}{1 - 0.3} + \$400,000}{\$220} = \frac{\$142,857.15 + \$400,000}{\$220} = 2,468$$

Financial Modeling and What-If Analysis

The CVP analysis that we studied above is an example of financial modeling. The organization's financial circumstances are modeled by an equation that can be manipulated when answering the questions used in a what-if analysis. Decision makers can use their understanding about cost behavior to answer important strategic decisions.

Cost–Volume–Profit Analysis

Consider the business of developing applications for the iPhone. This is an interesting business because the variable cost is essentially zero. Suppose that it costs you $20,000 to hire the programmer and the graphic designer to develop the application. If the application sells for $0.99 and Apple takes 30%, the contribution margin is $0.693 ($0.99 × 70%) per application sold. This means that you will need to sell 28,861 applications to recover your initial investment.

To illustrate, suppose John Jones, the sales manager at the Rose Furniture Company, believes that a $25,000 advertising campaign will increase rocking chair sales by 5% over the current level of 3,000 units. Is this advertising campaign financially attractive?

The incremental cost related to this initiative is $25,000. The incremental benefit will equal the rocking chair's contribution margin per unit of $220 multiplied by the sales increase of 150 (3,000 × 5%) rocking chairs. Therefore, the expected incremental effect on profits at the Rose Furniture Company of undertaking the advertising campaign will be:

$$\text{Incremental profit} = \text{Incremental contribution margin} - \text{Incremental cost}$$
$$= 150 \times \$220 - \$25,000 = \$8,000$$

This sounds like an attractive proposition for John because the expected return is 32% ($8,000/$25,000) on the initial investment. Once again, however, all investments have associated risks and John would need to consider the likelihood of attaining the expected sales increase of 150 chairs.

The Multiproduct Firm

Suppose now that the Rose Furniture Company has expanded and, in addition to making rocking chairs, it is making a kitchen chair. The kitchen chair has variable costs totaling $60 per chair and it sells for $200 per chair, yielding a contribution margin of $140 per kitchen chair. Fixed costs in the Rose Furniture Company have increased by $200,000 to $624,000 with the addition of the chair operations since the kitchen chairs required the acquisition of some new machinery and equipment and production supervisors.

Once again, Julie is wondering about the sales required to break even. With these two products the CVP equation is

$$\text{Profit} = \text{Rocking chair contribution margin} \times \text{Rocking chair sales}$$
$$+ \text{Kitchen chair contribution margin} \times \text{Kitchen chair sales} - \$624,000$$

$$\text{Profit} = (\$220 \times \text{Rocking chair sales}) + (\$140 \times \text{Kitchen chair sales})$$
$$- \$624,000$$

We have one equation in two unknowns, which means that there are infinitely many combinations of rocking chair sales and kitchen chair sales that will allow the company to break even.

Faced with how to deal with the problem of multiple breakeven pairs, developers of CVP analysis used a practical tool to extend their analysis to a multiproduct firm. To illustrate, we continue the example of the Rose Furniture Company supposing that Julie has decided on a target mix of 20% rocking chairs and 80% kitchen chairs.

IN PRACTICE
Estimating the Effect of Unit Sales on Share Price

Some organizations and analysts take volume profit analysis one step further. Instead of stopping with the estimate of sales levels changes on profit, these organizations take the next step of predicting the effect of the resulting profit increase on share price. For example, in April 2010 Apple introduced the iPad. In late June 2010, Apple announced that iPad sales had averaged about 1 million units for the first three months. Some market analysts estimated that every 100,000 units sold of the iPad added 1 cent to Apple's share price.

Exhibit 3-5
Product Contribution Margins at Rose Furniture Company

ROCKING CHAIRS		KITCHEN CHAIRS		BUNDLE	
Price	$300	Price	$200		
Variable cost	80	Variable cost	60		
Contribution margin	$220	Contribution margin	$140		
Number in bundle	20	Number in bundle	80		
Total contribution margin	$4,400	Total contribution margin	$11,200	Total contribution margin	$15,600

This product mix requires setting the number of kitchen chairs produced to be four times the number of rocking chairs produced. We can now substitute kitchen chairs out of the Rose Furniture Company's profit equation as follows:

Profit = ($220 × Rocking chair sales) + [$140 × (4 × Rocking chair sales)]
− $624,000

Rearranging we get

$$\text{rocking chair sales} = \frac{\text{profit} + \text{fixed cost}}{\$220 + (\$140 \times 4)} = \frac{\text{profit} + \$624,000}{\$780}$$

The **breakeven point** is found when the profit is 0, meaning rocking chair sales at breakeven will be 800 ($624,000/$780). Because kitchen chair sales are four times rocking chair sales, the breakeven kitchen chair sales with this ratio of chairs will be 3,200 (4 × 800).

Although several approaches have been used to handle the multiproduct CVP analysis, the following approach, called the *bundle approach*, is the most direct and intuitive.

With a constant product mix, the Rose Furniture Company will sell rocking chairs and kitchen chairs in bundles of 20 rocking chairs and 80 kitchen chairs with each bundle generating a contribution margin of $15,600 as shown in Exhibit 3-5.

With fixed costs of $624,000, the Rose Furniture Company will have to sell 40 ($624,000/$15,600) bundles to break even. Remember that the products are not actually sold in bundles—that is just a computational convenience. This results in the following unit sales for each product.

Rocking chairs made and sold 40 × 20 = 800
Kitchen chairs made and sold 40 × 80 = 3,200

Exhibit 3-6 contains a small income statement showing that these, indeed, are the breakeven quantities for the two products with this product mix.

Exhibit 3-6
Multi-Product Breakeven Results at Rose Furniture Company

ROCKING CHAIRS		KITCHEN CHAIRS		TOTAL	
Units	800	Units	3,200	Units	4,000
Revenue	$240,000	Revenue	$640,000	Revenue	$880,000
Variable costs	64,000	Variable costs	192,000	Variable costs	256,000
Contribution margin	$176,000	Contribution margin	$448,000	Contribution margin	$624,000
				Fixed cost	624,000
				Profit	$0

The Assumptions Underlying CVP Analysis

Many students will complain that there are too many unrealistic assumptions underlying CVP analysis to be practical in most organizations. These assumptions are as follows:

1. The price per unit and the variable cost per unit (and therefore the contribution margin per unit) remain the same over all levels of production.
2. All costs can be classified as either fixed or variable or can be decomposed into a fixed and variable component.
3. Fixed costs remain the same over all contemplated levels of production.
4. Sales equal production.

Note that all these assumptions can be relaxed if the CVP analysis is undertaken in a computer spreadsheet. Indeed, financial modeling that relies on cost and revenue estimates is one of the most valuable and widely used management accounting tools.

OTHER USEFUL COST DEFINITIONS

As you may expect, there are other cost definitions that are important for decision making. We begin our discussion of these other cost definitions by expanding on fixed and variable costs, and then turn to further cost concepts that are useful in decision making.

Mixed Costs

A mixed cost is a cost that has a fixed component and a variable component. For example, your mobile telephone bill may have a fixed component that you pay each month, independent of how many calls you make, and a variable component that depends on the quantity of calls you make.

Suppose that the bill for heating costs in Julie's factory equals $500 per month plus $16 per million British thermal units (BTUs) used. Exhibit 3-7 shows the picture of Julie's factory heating costs for various levels of BTUs used.

Organizations face many types of mixed costs. Examples include the cost of electricity, the cost of labor (where workers are paid a salary plus overtime), and the cost of shipping (where there is a fixed component per shipment and a variable amount that depends on the weight of the shipment).

Exhibit 3-7
Total Heating Cost at Julie's Factory

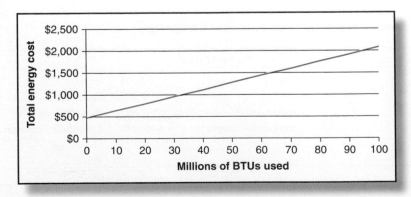

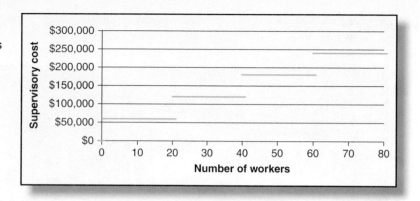

Exhibit 3-8
Step Variable
Supervisory Costs

Step Variable Costs

We often observe step variable costs. A **step variable cost** increases in steps as quantity increases. For example, suppose that a company has a policy of hiring one factory supervisor for every 20 factory workers. If each factory supervisor is paid $60,000, the total cost of supervisory salaries increases in a series of steps with the number of workers as shown in Exhibit 3-8.

Although this type of cost behavior can be modeled directly in any spreadsheet, it is often approximated as if it were a variable cost. Exhibit 3-9 shows what the actual cost looks like and also shows that the linear approximation will sometimes over- and underrepresent costs but, on average, will be correct.

Incremental Costs

An **incremental cost** is the cost of the next unit of production and is similar to the economist's notion of marginal cost. In a manufacturing setting, incremental cost is generally defined as the variable cost of a unit of production. However, the concept is not quite that simple for two reasons.

First, the variable cost per unit may change as production volume changes. For example, in the presence of a learning effect, the variable cost of labor will decrease as cumulative production increases. Also, if a firm operates using overtime, the variable cost of units produced during the overtime period could increase by 50% (time-and-a-half).

Second, if the cost is a step variable, treating the cost as a variable cost will lead to estimation errors as shown in Exhibit 3-9. In that example the incremental supervisory cost is $60,000 as the number of production workers moves from 0 to 1 and is

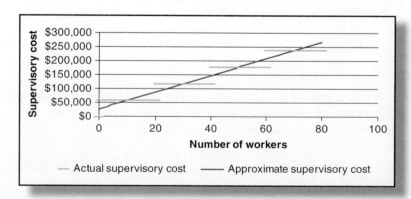

Exhibit 3-9
Linear
Approximation
of a Step Variable
Cost

Just about all of the costs associated with building and operating this dam are fixed costs; the incremental cost of generating an extra unit of electricity is virtually zero.

Shutterstock

zero for all increases in production workers until the number of production workers changes from 10 to 11.

Consider the incremental cost of carrying passengers on a train. Suppose that each railroad car can accommodate 50 passengers. For a particular trip, the incremental cost of adding an additional car is $2,400 and the incremental fuel cost for adding a passenger is $0.05.

Suppose that the railroad company expects 1,825 passengers on the train. The company will provide a train with 37 (1,825/50) cars for a total cost of $88,800 (37 × $2,400) to handle this expected demand. Once this decision is made, this cost becomes fixed. The variable cost will equal the number of passengers that show up multiplied by the variable cost per passenger of $0.05.

Sunk Costs

A **sunk cost** is a cost that results from a previous commitment and cannot be recovered. For example, depreciation on a building reflects the historical cost of the building, which is a sunk cost. Another example of a sunk cost is a lease payment required by a long-term lease.

IN PRACTICE

Sunk Costs

The sunk cost effect is a maladaptive economic behavior that is manifested in a greater tendency to continue an endeavor once an investment in money, effort, or time has been made. [The authors] present evidence that young children, when placed in an economic situation akin to a sunk cost one, exhibit more normatively correct behavior than do adults.

Source: Hal Arks and Peter Ayton, "The Sunk Cost and Concorde Effects: Are Humans Less Rational Than Lower Animals?" *Psychological Bulletin,* Vol. 125, No. 5 (1999): 591–600.

Overcoming the Sunk Cost Effect

Goldman Sachs works to overcome the sunk cost effect by marking all of its holdings to fair value every day. It doesn't want a trader holding on to a position just to defer the recognition of a loss. It forces the daily recognition of a gain or loss, and then leaves it up to the trader to decide whether to continue to hold that position.

For airplane production or building a new weapon system, a company incurs a huge cost before the first one can be built. By adding the development cost to a projected number of planes produced and sold, the company may be attempting to recover what has become a sunk cost. Another example could be a pharmaceutical company that incurs expenses of, say, $1 billion to produce the first pill and then $0.01 for each incremental pill. As it contemplates how much to price, how should it consider the recovery of the $1 billion? Of course, this decision must be much much earlier, before the $1 billion or the airplane's product development cost has been spent.

The notion is that sunk costs should not be considered in subsequent decisions because they cannot be changed. However, because sunk costs so often affect managerial decisions, in practice, the term **sunk cost phenomenon** has evolved. Some people refer to the sunk cost phenomenon as the *Concorde effect* or the *Concorde fallacy*. This is because even though it was apparent that the Concorde, a supersonic passenger jet that was a joint project of England and France, would be unprofitable, the two countries kept investing money because they had already invested huge sums of money. Psychologists attribute this behavior in part to the feeling that people should not waste money.

Consider the plight of Pat Toste who is managing the construction of a new warehouse. Construction is well under way and the construction costs to date amount to $2,500,000. A structural engineer has just discovered a major design flaw. The flaw in the current design can be corrected and the project completed for an additional $4,000,000 or the current construction can be demolished and a new warehouse built for a total of $3,000,000. Pat plans to take the option of correcting the design flaw even though that will cost the company $1,000,000 more than starting over. Pat may not want to look bad in the eyes of the company (assuming that the start-over option is known only to him) or Pat may feel that he does not want to "waste" the sunk costs of $2,500,000.

Studies of practice often attribute the sunk cost phenomenon to a continuing belief in the potential for success despite overwhelming evidence to the contrary. Another popular explanation is that decision makers will often cover up a cost resulting from a bad decision—therefore, the sunk cost becomes a factor in the decision not to address the problem caused by the decision.

IN PRACTICE
Human Behavior and Sunk Costs

Dan Lovallo and Daniel Kahneman argue that successful executives "routinely" engage in "delusional" behavior causing them to overestimate their ability to see a project through to a successful conclusion even in the face of mounting evidence that the project is failing. This behavioral characteristic may be one explanation for the sunk cost effect.

Source: Dan Lovallo and Daniel Kahneman, "Delusions of Success—How Optimism Undermines Executives' Decisions." *Harvard Business Review*, Vol. 81, No. 7 (July 2003): 56–67.

Relevant Cost

A relevant cost is a cost that will change as a result of some decision. Suppose you are thinking about going to a concert this evening. You purchased the $100 ticket several weeks ago. If you go to the concert, you will likely spend $50 on transportation and parking and $70 on snacks and refreshments. You are thinking you really cannot afford the $120 that you will spend this evening but you don't want to "waste" the $100 you already spent. The total cost if you go to the concert is $220 ($100 + $50 + $70). However, the $100 ticket price is sunk and not relevant in the decision you are making today about whether or not to go tonight. The relevant cost is $120 (which is also called the incremental cost).

Richard Thaler, an economist who studies decision-making behavior, provides an interesting example on the other side of this concert story. Suppose in this case there are only immaterial costs of attending the concert and you have lost the ticket; would you buy another ticket to go to the concert? You have already signaled that you get more than $100 of pleasure from the concert, so you should be willing to repurchase the ticket (the loss of the ticket is a sunk cost), but many people would choose not to go to the concert.

Opportunity Cost

Organizations rarely have unlimited amounts of any resource to use when pursuing their activities. For this reason decision makers use various tools, some of which we discuss later in this text, to identify the best uses of limited resources. The notion of opportunity cost arises in this context. Opportunity cost is the maximum value forgone when a course of action is chosen.

To illustrate the idea of opportunity cost, consider the decision facing Lois Leung, a production supervisor at Rubinoff Manufacturing. Lois is wondering how to use the time remaining on a machine that is the bottleneck in the production process. The machine currently has the capacity to handle one more order and Lois must decide between two orders: Order X133 will provide a contribution margin of $12,000, whereas order M244 will provide a contribution margin of $15,000.

If Lois uses the machine time to accept order X133 she will forego the opportunity to accept order M244 and forego a contribution margin of $15,000, which is the opportunity cost of accepting order X133. If Lois uses the machine time to accept order M244 she will forego the opportunity to accept order X133 and forego a contribution margin of $12,000, which is the opportunity cost of accepting order M244.

Choosing the project that provides the highest contribution margin (in this case order M244) will always lead to the same choice as choosing the project that provides the lowest opportunity cost (in this case order M244).

Note that if Lois has the machine capacity to accept both orders, the opportunity cost of each is $0. The opportunity cost of capacity is always zero when there is enough capacity to handle all available demand.

Suppose now that there is a third order, N766, that would provide a contribution margin of $9,000. Since this is not the next best alternative when considering order X133 or M244, it would not change the opportunity cost of accepting either of those orders.

Opportunity cost also provides important insights at the individual product level. Tim Manufacturing produces plastic novelties that are primarily used by customers for promotional purposes. After developing a schedule to produce the orders on hand, Margaret Pierce, the production supervisor, finds that she has 500 hours of molding machine production time still available. Margaret is wondering how to use that time.

	DESK ORGANIZER	PENCIL/PEN HOLDER
Incremental contribution to profit	$2.05	$0.56
Minutes of molding machine time required per unit	2	0.5

After speaking with Mark Thompson, the sales manager, Margaret has identified production opportunities for two products: a desk organizer or a pencil/pen holder. Exhibit 3-10 provides the information that has been identified for the two products.

Mark is enthusiastic about the desk organizer because it provides a higher contribution to the organization than the pencil/pen holder. However, Margaret is more cautious and given her production experience realizes that many more pencil/pen holders could be produced in the 500 molding machine hours available than desk organizers. Margaret quickly determines that with the 500 hours she could produce 15,000 desk organizers [(500 × 60 minutes)/2], providing a total contribution of $30,750 (15,000 × $2.05), or 60,000 [(500 × 60 minutes)/0.5] pencil/pen holders, providing a total contribution of $33,600 (60,000 × $0.56). The opportunity cost of using the machine time to produce the desk organizer is $33,600 and the opportunity cost of using the machine time to produce the pencil/pen holder is $30,750.

The key to evaluating these alternatives is to focus on the contribution that each product makes to the organization in view of its consumption of the molding machine hours. We will return to this idea later in the chapter after we have developed some more management accounting tools and language.

The need to consider opportunity costs is pervasive in decision making. However, opportunity costs are often overlooked. Most students, when considering attending college, will consider the out-of-pocket costs such as tuition and books. Some may even consider the opportunity cost of wages that would otherwise be earned while attending college. However, few students consider the opportunity cost of the four years of working experience forgone while attending college. (As a counterpoint, some college students might point out that the opportunity cost of not attending college is the college experience forgone.) The popularity of part-time college and online university programs may reflect students' desires to avoid some or all of the opportunity costs of getting an education.

Avoidable Cost

A cost that can be avoided by undertaking some course of action is called an avoidable cost. The most obvious avoidable costs are variable costs. If production ceases all variable costs associated with that production process are avoided. Less obvious and more problematic in practice are fixed costs that can be avoided as a result of a course of action.

For example, John Darke, a product manager at Russell Company, is thinking about eliminating a product. All of the variable costs associated with dropping the product will not be incurred (that is, they are avoidable) as well as the salary of the product's sales manager, which is a fixed cost. However, many product costs, such as machine depreciation, are the result of sunk costs that often remain in whole or in part after the product is discontinued. John wonders what costs are avoidable such as depreciation on the machines used to produce the product and depreciation on the factory and warehouse space the product occupies. Estimating these latter avoidable

When companies moved to producing products only when they are demanded rather than stocking inventory, a significant amount of factory floor space was idled. A question facing organizations moving to this production approach was how to measure the cost avoided by moving to just in time manufacturing.
Alamy Images

costs is quite difficult in practice because some machines and factory space may be used by other products or sold.

With these ideas in mind, we now turn to consider how these various cost concepts (sunk, relevant, opportunity, and avoidable) occur in common management decisions. We will look at four types of decisions where these concepts provide useful insights:

1. Make versus buy decisions and outsourcing.
2. Decision to drop a product.
3. Costing order decisions—the floor price.
4. Short-term product mix decisions (with constraints).

MAKE-OR-BUY—THE OUTSOURCING DECISION

As organizations rationalize their operations and focus on exploiting their core competencies, they contract out activities that they believe outsiders can do better or less expensively. Examples include contracting out information technology, housekeeping, laundry, and payroll processing. These outsiders generally focus on a limited set of activities, thereby developing the expertise to perform these activities at consistently high quality and low cost. Deciding whether to contract out for a product or service is known as the **make-or-buy decision**.

Many qualitative considerations go into a make-or-buy decision. These include the reliability of the supplier in meeting quality and delivery requirements and the strategic importance of the activity being outsourced. (For example, any activity that is outsourced could also be purchased from the same vendor by a competitor. So this activity cannot be a source of competitive advantage.) Here we will focus only on the financial considerations of outsourcing.

Contracting Out

A 2007 Ontario Waste Management Association study estimated that the city of Toronto could save at least $10 million a year by contracting out residential waste and recycling collection. The report also noted that private sector waste companies in the area provided the same service for about 20 percent less than the public sector, and that the average private-sector waste collection worker was more than twice as productive as the average city of Toronto worker.

Source: Adam Summers, *San Diego Can Benefit from Private Trash Collection*, retrieved November 22, 2010, from http://reason.org/news/show/1003131.html

Consider an organization that is currently making the part or product being considered for outsourcing. What costs should it consider? The following table summarizes the typical relevant costs in the make-or-buy decision. The financial focus in the make-or-buy decision is whether the costs avoided internally are greater than the external costs that will be incurred when purchasing from a supplier.

INTERNAL COSTS AVOIDED	EXTERNAL COSTS INCURRED
• All variable costs • Any avoidable fixed costs such as the cost of supervisory personnel who would be laid off or machinery that would be sold	• The cost of purchasing the part • Any transportation costs • Any other costs involved in dealing with the outside supplier, ordering the product, and receiving and inspecting it

The following examples illustrate the idea, but first we define some commonly used manufacturing cost categories that are useful in our examples.

Manufacturing Costs

In a typical manufacturing cost system, manufacturing costs are classified into three groups: direct materials, direct labor, and manufacturing overhead. **Direct materials costs** include materials that can be traced easily to a unit of output and are of significant economic consequence to the final product. Similarly, **direct labor costs** are those labor costs that can be traced easily to the creation of a unit of output. Direct laborers are those who physically construct a unit of output. **Manufacturing overhead costs** are all costs incurred by a manufacturing facility that are not direct materials costs or direct labor costs. In particular, materials (such as thread or glue) that are not of significant economic consequence to the final product are treated as indirect materials and their cost is included in manufacturing overhead costs.

Chaps Company

Chaps Company currently makes a component used in one of its major products. The factory accountant has reported the following per unit costs associated with making this component:

Direct materials	$12.54
Direct labor	5.77
Manufacturing overhead	10.00
Total	$28.31

Based on a study of past data, the factory accountant believes that 30% of the manufacturing overhead associated with this product is variable. Moreover, of the fixed costs allocated to this product, about 10% are avoidable if production of this part is discontinued.

Rosa Company has offered to supply this part under a long-term contract for $21.80 per unit. Shipping costs to the Chaps Company factory would be about $0.12 per unit. Rosa Company would require a machine tool to make the part. Chaps Company owns the tool, which cost $25,000 to make. The tool would require rework costing $5,000, which Rosa Company expects Chaps Company to pay for. At the end of the part's life, the tool will have no value. Future demand for this part is expected to be 250,000 units.

Is the Offer from Rosa Company Financially Attractive?

Exhibit 3-11 shows that the total savings per part would be $0.07 per unit or $17,500 (250,000 × $0.07) over the remaining life of the part. The only cost that is not relevant is the $25,000 historical cost of the tool, which is a sunk cost. Note that parts of the fixed costs associated with this product are relevant because they are avoidable. These relevant fixed costs relate to supervisory personnel who would not be needed or a machine that can be sold if the part is discontinued.

This analysis only considers the financial aspects of this decision. Chaps Company would also consider whether Rosa Company could supply a high-quality part and meet production schedules.

Anjlee's Catering Services

Anjlee Desai is the owner-manager of Anjlee's Catering Services. Anjlee's services include planning, preparing, delivering, and serving meals at catered events. Anjlee's unique skill and competitive advantage is her ability to design innovative and tasty meals that can be adapted to meet most cultural requirements.

Demand has increased so much that Anjlee has had to turn down business and this has caused her to think about contracting out some of the activities that, in the past, she has done herself. In particular, Anjlee is considering contracting out the food preparation services. This would allow Anjlee to spend more time with customers taking orders and planning and serving meals. In addition, contracting out the food preparation services will allow Anjlee to expand into providing meals that meet religious requirements by contracting with certified kosher and halal suppliers.

Exhibit 3-11
Contracting Out Production at Chaps Company

Cost Item	Amount	Relevant?	Why
Direct materials	$12.54	Yes	Avoided if purchased externally
Direct labor	5.77	Yes	Avoided if purchased externally
Variable manufacturing overhead (30% × $10.00)	3.00	Yes	Avoided if purchased externally
Fixed manufacturing overhead (70% × 10% × $10)	0.70	Yes	Avoided if purchased externally
Supply price	(21.80)	Yes	Incurred if purchased externally
Shipping	(0.12)	Yes	Incurred if purchased externally
Tool rework cost per unit ($5,000/250,000)	(0.02)	Yes	Incurred if purchased externally
Total savings (additional cost)	$0.07		

Currently the cost of sourcing and purchasing food is about $180,000 per year. The total cost of running her kitchen is $15,000 per month. Anjlee rents her store location and all the equipment in the store for $9,000 per month. If she contracts out the food preparation costs, Anjlee would operate instead from a small office in a building owned by her uncle, which he currently rents for $2,500 per month. The office is currently under a municipal rent control; however, when the lease for the current tenant expires in two months the rent control limit will be increased by 12%. Anjlee pays a driver $60,000 per year to drive the van used to pick up food from supplies and deliver the meals to customers. Depreciation on the van amounts to $3,500 per year and the annual operating costs for fuel and maintenance are $7,500 per year. The van has a residual value of $1,000. Anjlee long ago promised to give the van to her current driver when it is no longer needed.

Based on her current volume of operations, Anjlee's prospective external suppliers have quoted her a cost of $500,000 per year for preparing and delivering the meals to her customers' sites. Based on preliminary discussions with potential customers Anjlee believes that by freeing up her time to concentrate more on sales she can increase her sales by $150,000 per year. Anjlee has estimated that with the prospective suppliers the contribution margin ratio of any new business would be about 20%. Fixed costs would increase by a negligible amount as sales increase.

Should Anjlee Contract with the External Suppliers?

The financial analysis shown in Exhibit 3-12 indicates that, based on Anjlee's estimates, income would increase by $31,900 per year by contracting with the external suppliers. Note that neither the depreciation on the van nor its salvage value is relevant. Depreciation is based on historical cost, which is a sunk cost, and she will not realize the residual value of the van since she has previously promised to give the van to the driver when she no longer needs it. So the residual value of the van is not relevant to this decision. Note, also, that the cost of the van was a sunk cost for this decision; it would not change as a result of whatever action Anjlee takes. An important relevant item is the contribution margin of new business that Anjlee expects to earn from freeing up her food sourcing and food preparation time. Other important considerations in this decision for Anjlee would be her faith that her suppliers would provide quality and timely work.

Exhibit 3-12
Contracting Out Food Preparation Services at Anjlee's Catering Services

ITEM	ANNUAL AMOUNT	RELEVANT?	WHY
Source and purchase food	$180,000	Yes	Avoided if purchased externally
Kitchen costs ($15,000 × 12)	180,000	Yes	Avoided if purchased externally
Rent for current store ($9,000 × 12)	108,000	Yes	Avoided if purchased externally
Driver's salary	60,000	Yes	Avoided if purchased externally
Delivery van operating costs	7,500	Yes	Incurred if purchased externally
External supply price	(500,000)	Yes	Incurred if purchased externally
Rent for new office ($2,500 × 1.12 × 12)	(33,600)	Yes	Incurred if purchased externally
Contribution provided by new business ($150,000 × 20%)	30,000	Yes	Earned if purchased externally
Total savings (additional cost)	$31,900		

THE DECISION TO DROP A PRODUCT

Organizations abandon a product when it is unprofitable either because revenues no longer exceed costs or because another organization offers to buy the rights to the product at a favorable price. For example, in a bid to improve profitability in 2009 General Motors announced that it would drop several of its brands including Pontiac and Hummer. In 2010 General Motors was in talks with a number of prospective buyers to sell its Saturn brand.

Because the focus is on product profitability, the relevant cost analysis involves comparing the costs saved by abandoning the product with the revenues forgone. The analysis of what costs are avoided when a product is dropped can be very difficult. For example, computing General Motors' cost savings from dropping the Pontiac brand is very complex because it involves closing some plants, paying workers severance pay, and incurring environmental cleanup and many other costs.

Messi Company

Messi Company manufactures industrial lathes. The most recent income statement appears in Exhibit 3-13.

The fixed costs allocated to each product include both the fixed costs that are directly attributable to the product and those that could be avoided if the product were discontinued and also corporate fixed costs that would continue if the product were discontinued. The amount of avoidable fixed costs included in the fixed costs for Models X355, X655, and X966 are 55%, 40%, and 20%, respectively.

Messi Company is considering dropping Model X966, which shows chronic losses.

Would Dropping Model X966 Improve the Company's Overall Profitability?

Using the information relating to the avoidable fixed costs, we can produce the income statement shown in Exhibit 3-14. We can now see that, in fact, Model X966 provides the highest contribution of all the products and dropping this product would decrease Messi Company's profitability by $31,548.

In this case sales, variable costs, and avoidable fixed costs are all relevant when evaluating the profitability of each product. The allocated fixed costs that are not avoidable do not change as a result of dropping the product and, therefore, are not relevant to the decision.

Difficulties arise in practice when costs that are attributable to a product (i.e., they reflect the costs of resources that are used exclusively by that product) are only avoidable in the intermediate or long run. Suppose that General Motors

Exhibit 3-13
Product Line
Profitability
Analysis at Messi
Company

	MODEL X355	MODEL X655	MODEL X966	TOTAL
Sales	$23,445	$49,288	$54,677	$127,410
Variable costs	4,722	10,001	14,987	29,710
Fixed costs	14,233	29,722	40,711	84,666
Operating income	$4,490	$9,565	($1,021)	$13,034

All values are in thousands.

Exhibit 3-14
Product
Contribution to
Corporate Fixed
Costs at Messi
Company

	MODEL X355	MODEL X655	MODEL X966	TOTAL
Sales	$23,445	$49,288	$54,677	$127,410
Variable costs	4,722	10,001	14,987	29,710
Avoidable fixed costs	7,828	11,889	8,142	27,859
Product contribution	$10,895	$27,398	$31,548	69,841
Fixed costs				56,807
Operating income				$13,034

All values are in thousands.

IN PRACTICE

Be Wary When Labeling Departments Losers

In many convention hotels, the exercise room, pool amenities, and sometimes food operations operate at losses to support the core product—the sale of room services. Grocery stores often use staples such as milk and bread as loss leaders to attract customers to the store. For this reason milk and bread are often located at the back of stores.

operated a plant that only produced Pontiac automobiles. Since the plant is used exclusively by the Pontiac brand, all of its costs are attributable to that brand. However, not all of the plant's costs are avoidable in the short run if the Pontiac brand is abandoned. In the short run, the buildings must be maintained and taxes and insurance must be paid. In the intermediate or longer run, the plant may be sold or reconditioned to produce another vehicle, thus saving some costs relative to building a new plant. At that point the value to General Motors of the abandoned plant would be a relevant amount to consider in the decision to abandon the Pontiac brand. Also, when closing a plant, some new costs have to be paid (e.g., environmental cleanup costs) that are deferred indefinitely as long as the plant continues to operate.

Organizations often sell an integrated product line where sales of one product affect the sales of others. In this setting additional considerations arise when deciding whether to drop a product.

Buddy's Bar and Grill

Buddy's Bar and Grill is organized into three operating units: a restaurant, a bar, and a games room. Exhibit 3-15 summarizes the results for the most recent year. Buddy is concerned about the continuing losses being reported by the games room and is considering closing it and reallocating the floor space occupied by the games room to the restaurant and bar.

A study of operations yielded the following results:

1. The fixed costs have two components:
   a. The first component is an allocation of the organization's general business costs of $340,000. These costs are allocated in proportion to the floor space occupied by each unit. The floor space occupied by the restaurant, bar, and games room is 1,000, 400, and 600 square meters, respectively.

Exhibit 3-15
Buddy's Bar
and Grill: Area
Profitability
Analysis

	RESTAURANT	BAR	GAMES ROOM	TOTAL
Sales	$1,200,000	$800,000	$100,000	$2,100,000
Variable costs	700,000	375,000	50,000	1,125,000
Fixed cost	320,000	118,000	202,000	640,000
Profit	$180,000	$307,000	($152,000)	$335,000

b. The second component of fixed costs for each unit is the attributable fixed cost relating to rented equipment that can be avoided in full if the unit is closed.

2. If the games room is closed, 400 square meters of the freed up space will be allocated to the restaurant and 200 square meters will be allocated to the bar. Attributable fixed costs in the restaurant and in the bar will not increase if the area is expanded.

3. If the games room is closed and the restaurant is expanded, sales in the restaurant will increase by 10% primarily because the decrease in noise coming from the games room will attract more customers. Variable costs will increase in the same proportion.

4. A study of the bar customers suggests that the patrons of the games room account for about 50% of the bar sales and that half of these sales will be lost if the games room is closed. Variable costs will decrease in the same proportion.

Should the Games Room Be Closed?

We can approach this question in two steps. First, eliminate the allocated costs from the contribution of each of the business units. For example, the allocated cost to the restaurant will be $170,000 {$340,000 × [1,000/(1,000 + 400 + 600)]}. This means that $150,000 ($320,000 − $170,000) is the amount of attributable and avoidable costs associated with the restaurant. We can use the same approach to identify the effect of removing the allocated costs from the bar and games room. The result is shown in Exhibit 3-16.

With the games room closed, restaurant sales will increase to $1,320,000 [$1,200,000 × (1 + 10%)] and variable costs will increase to $770,000 [$700,000 × (1 + 10%)]. In addition, sales in the bar will decrease to $600,000 [$800,000 × (1 − 25%)] and variable costs will decrease to $281,250 [$375,000 × (1 − 25%)]. Exhibit 3-17 summarizes the result.

The result of closing the games room has decreased corporate profit by $6,250 ($335,000 − $328,750). Although this difference is not significant, the analysis does

Exhibit 3-16
Buddy's Bar and
Grill: Effect of
Eliminating the
Allocation of
Corporate Level
Costs

	RESTAURANT	BAR	GAMES ROOM	TOTAL
Sales	$1,200,000	$800,000	$100,000	$2,100,000
Variable costs	700,000	375,000	50,000	1,125,000
Attributable fixed	150,000	50,000	100,000	300,000
Profit	$350,000	$375,000	($50,000)	$675,000
Corporate fixed				340,000
Profit				$335,000

	RESTAURANT	BAR	TOTAL
Sales	$1,320,000	$600,000	$1,920,000
Variable costs	770,000	281,250	1,051,250
Attributable fixed	150,000	50,000	200,000
Profit	$400,000	$268,750	$668,750
Corporate fixed			340,000
Profit			$328,750

illustrate a situation in which the sales by one organizational unit can affect sales in another organizational unit and that these relationships need to be evaluated when consideration is given to dropping an apparently unprofitable product or line of business.

COSTING ORDERS

The order costing problem deals with estimating the cost of unique orders. For example, the manager of an organization that manufactures clothes washers may be asked to quote a price on a one-time order for 10,000 washing machines. Computing the *floor price*, or the minimum price that a company would normally consider for the order, exploits the relevant cost idea by considering the costs that will change as a result of taking the order.

Pepper Industries

Pepper Industries manufactures a wide line of pottery coffee cups that it sells to specialty gift stores. The sales manager has received a request to price a special order from a large consultancy offering to purchase 50,000 mugs that it plans to use for promotional purposes.

The sales manager asked the factory accountant to develop an estimate of the cost to fill this order. The production manager advises that there is plenty of idle capacity to fill this order. The factory accountant replied by submitting Exhibit 3-18.

The following additional information was provided. All variable costs are incremental costs relating to this order. The charge for fixed manufacturing overhead is the standard fixed overhead amount that Pepper Industries allocates to all cups it produces. The fixed manufacturing overhead relates to factory equipment that is used to make the

ITEM	COST
Direct materials – 50,000 @ $0.66 each	$33,000
Direct labor – 50,000 @ $0.23 each	11,500
Variable manufacturing overhead – 50,000 @ $0.15 ea	7,500
Fixed manufacturing overhead – 50,000 @ $0.10 each	5,000
Design costs	1,800
Shipping costs	3,600
Other administrative costs	1,500
Total order cost	$63,900

ITEM	COST	INCREMENTAL
Direct materials — 50,000 @ $0.66 each	$33,000	$33,000
Direct labor — 50,000 @ $0.23 each	11,500	11,500
Variable manufacturing overhead — 50,000 @ $0.15 each	7,500	7,500
Fixed manufacturing overhead — 50,000 @ $0.10 each	5,000	0
Design costs	1,800	900
Shipping costs	3,600	3,600
Other administrative costs	1,500	0
Total order cost	$63,900	$56,500
Cost per cup		$1.13

various products. It will not change in the short run. Design costs are the estimated costs of designing the product for this customer. They reflect a cost of $900 to which is added the standard 100% markup to cover fixed overhead in the design department. The shipping costs are the estimated costs of shipping the completed product to the customer. The other administrative costs represent the cost that is added to each order to reflect fixed administrative costs at Pepper Industries that will not change in the short run.

What Minimum Price per Cup Should Pepper Industries Consider Quoting on This Order?

As shown in Exhibit 3-19, the relevant (incremental) costs to fill this order total $56,500 or $1.13 per cup. This is the minimum, or floor, price that Pepper Industries should consider when quoting on this order. The actual price charged will reflect strategic factors such as the amount of competition (the more unique the organization, the higher the price it likely can charge), the amount of idle capacity, how eager the organization is for new business, the possibility of the price quoted for this business affecting relationships with current customers, and the possibility of future orders. (The opportunity to develop a long-term relationship with the customer will affect the price charged for this order; however, in the long run the organization will need to cover the estimated full costs of filling orders like this.)

Costing Orders and Opportunity Cost Considerations

When there is insufficient capacity to fill an order, costing the order must consider the opportunity cost of accepting the order.

Maggie Company

Maggie Company manufactures a line of backpacks specifically designed for school children ages 8 to 12 years. The backpacks feature licensed graphics of characters popular with this age group. The products sell very well and despite expansion for several years, the company continues to operate at capacity. Exhibit 3-20 summarizes the per unit information relating to this product.

Exhibit 3-20
Profit per Backpack
at Maggie Company

Price	$45.99
Variable costs	24.78
Fixed manufacturing cost	4.33
Profit per unit	$16.88

Exhibit 3-21
Floor Price for a
Special Order at
Maggie Company

Total variable costs ($24.78 + $10.00 + $5.00)	$39.78
Opportunity cost	3.03
Floor price	$42.81

Recently Maggie Company received an order from a large mail-order company asking for a quote to supply it with 10,000 backpacks made to the mail-order company's specifications. The product needed by the company, tentatively called "The Sack," incorporates the design of Maggie Company's current product but includes several additional features. The total incremental costs per unit of The Sack's additional features, relative to Maggie's current product, are $10 for materials and $5 for labor. Because of the additional demand on capacity to add the features needed by The Sack, Maggie Company will have to give up producing and selling one unit of its current product for every seven of the special order product that it produces. Current fixed costs, however, will not change.

What Is the Minimum Price (Floor Price) per Unit That Maggie Company Should Consider Charging for The Sack?

The contribution margin per unit for Maggie Company's current product is $21.21 ($45.99 − $24.78). Therefore, for every seven units of The Sack that Maggie Company makes, it will give up a contribution of $21.21 on the lost unit of its existing product. Expressed on a per unit basis, producing The Sack has an opportunity cost of $3.03 ($21.21 ÷ 7) per unit.

The total relevant cost, or floor price, of The Sack will be $42.81 as shown in Exhibit 3-21.

RELEVANT COST AND SHORT-TERM PRODUCT MIX DECISIONS

Organizations like machine shops and consultancies often face competing demands for their limited production resources. Choices have to be made among the various opportunities that present themselves. Making these choices involves the application of the relevant cost concept.

Fred's Wood Products

Fred manufactures a number of wood products including a cutting board that is sold by several large department stores. The sales manager believes that the product should be upgraded and sold exclusively in high-end stores that focus on kitchenware. Per unit characteristics of the existing product and new product are shown in Exhibit 3-22. The significantly higher profit per unit of the proposed product is what has caused the sales manager to promote the change.

Exhibit 3-22
Evaluating a
Product Redesign
at Fred's Wood
Products

	EXISTING PRODUCT		PROPOSED PRODUCT	
Price		$20.00		$35.00
Direct materials	$3.00		$5.00	
Labor	6.00		12.00	
Selling	1.00		1.75	
Manufacturing overhead	4.50	14.50	7.50	26.25
Per unit profit		$5.50		$8.75

Additional information provided by Fred's accountant indicates that all workers are paid a flat wage irrespective of the number of hours that they work. Labor costs are charged to products at the rate of $24 per hour. Selling costs are 5% of the product price and overhead is charged to products at 150% of direct materials costs. Variable manufacturing overhead costs are about 10% of direct materials costs. Because of commitments to make other products, the maximum number of labor hours that can be used to produce cutting boards is 10,000.

Should Fred Abandon Production of the Existing Product in Favor of the Proposed Product?

Relevant cost analysis suggests that only costs that will change as a result of changing from the existing product to the proposed product should be considered in this decision. Labor costs are not relevant since they are fixed and will not change as a result of this decision. Similarly only variable overhead, which is 10% of the direct materials costs, should be considered in the decision. Finally, selling costs, which are variable and equal 5% of the selling price, are relevant and must be considered. With this information in mind, we can compute the incremental contributions of the existing product and the proposed product, which are $15.70 and $27.75, respectively, as shown in Exhibit 3-23. The proposed product still looks like the preferred alternative.

However, recall that the amount of labor hours available is 10,000 and that the accountant indicated that labor costs are allocated to the products at the rate of $24 per labor hour used by each product. The data in the exhibit provided by the accountant indicate that the existing product uses 0.25 (6.00/24.00) labor hours per unit and the proposed product uses 0.50 labor hours per unit (12.00/24.00).

Put another way this means that the existing product provides a contribution of $62.80 ($15.70/0.25) per labor hour and the proposed product provides a contribution of $55.50 ($27.75/0.50) per labor hour. This means that if the 10,000 labor hours are allocated to the production of the existing product the total contribution to fixed costs will be $628,000 (10,000 × $62.80). Alternatively if the 10,000 labor hours are allocated to the production of the proposed product, the total contribution will be $555,000 (10,000 × $55.50). Clearly, based on the relevant cost analysis the existing product provides the most profitable alternative. Exhibit 3-24 shows the calculation of each product's contribution margin per labor hour.

In this case labor is the constraining factor of production. The approach is to allocate production capacity to the product with the highest contribution margin per unit of the constraining factor of production, which in this situation is the existing product.

Note that in this case Fred will produce 40,000 (10,000/0.25) of the existing boards. Suppose the company can only sell 30,000 boards. In that case Fred would allocate the first 7,500 (30,000 × 0.25) labor hours to the existing product and the remaining 2,500 (10,000 − 7,500) labor hours to the proposed board. This will mean that Fred will produce 30,000 of the existing boards and 5,000 (2,500/0.50) of the proposed boards.

Exhibit 3-23
Contribution Margin Analysis of a Proposed Product Redesign at Fred's Wood Products

	EXISTING PRODUCT		PROPOSED PRODUCT	
Price		$20.00		$35.00
Direct materials	$3.00		$5.00	
Selling	1.00		1.75	
Variable overhead	0.30	4.30	0.50	7.25
Contribution margin		$15.70		$27.75

	EXISTING PRODUCT		PROPOSED PRODUCT	
Price		$20.00		$35.00
Direct materials	$3.00		$5.00	
Selling	1.00		1.75	
Variable overhead	0.30	4.30	0.50	7.25
Contribution		$15.70		$27.75
Labor hours		0.25		0.5
Contribution per LH		$62.80		$55.50

Multiple Resource Constraints

When a company faces multiple resource constraints, the approach described in the previous section for allocating resource capacity will no longer work. We begin our discussion of the alternative approach by illustrating how to solve a simple two-constraint problem and then we turn to consideration of a more general approach.

Harris Chemical

Harris Chemical produces two products, X544 and X588, that are used in the metal coating industry. The two products are made in batches of 1,000 gallons. The company blends two input chemicals Argo and Nevex in a blender to produce the two products. Exhibit 3-25 summarizes the amount of each of the input chemicals required by each of the two products and the amount of blender time required by each product batch as well as the costs of the input chemicals and the cost of operating the blender per hour.

Further analysis reveals that fixed costs comprise two-thirds of the reported blender cost per hour. Each period a maximum of 47,800 gallons of Nevex is available for purchase and a maximum of 900 hours of blender use. There is no limit on the amount of Argo available for purchase each period.

As before, we begin by computing the contribution provided by each product, as summarized in Exhibit 3-26. Note that only the variable hourly cost of $400 ($1,200 × 1/3) for operating the blender is included in computing the contribution of each batch.

We are now at an impasse if we try to apply the approach we considered when there was only one constraining factor of production. We now have two constraining factors of production and must consider them simultaneously. At this point we need to turn to a tool called *linear programming*.

Exhibit 3-25
Product
Information at
Harris Chemical

	PRODUCT	
	X544	X588
Gallons of Argo per batch	700	400
Gallons of Nevex per batch	500	300
Revenue per batch	$33,000	$24,000
Cost per gallon of Argo	12	
Cost per gallon of Nevex	18	
Hours of blender time	6	10
Blender cost per hour	$1,200	

IN PRACTICE
Choosing the Least Cost Materials Mix

You might be interested to know that one of the first decision-making applications of computers in business was to solve the problem of minimizing the cost of dairy feed. Given the various nutritional constraints and the costs of the various ingredients that could be used in the feed, a linear program identified the least cost mix of ingredients that met the nutritional requirements.

Exhibit 3-26
Product Contributions at Harris Chemical

	PRODUCT			
	X544		X588	
Revenue per batch		$33,000		$24,000
Nevex				
Gallons used per batch	500		300	
Cost per gallon	18	9,000	18	5,400
Argo				
Gallons used per batch	700		400	
Cost per gallon	12	8,400	12	4,800
Blender				
Time (hours)	6		10	
Cost per hour	400	2,400	400	4,000
Contribution per batch		$13,200		$9,800

Building the Linear Program

A linear program has three components that we discuss in terms of the Harris Chemicals case:

1. *Objective function*—The objective function is to maximize the contribution margin by producing the best mix of products X544 and X588. Total fixed costs will remain unchanged regardless of the production plan and therefore are not relevant and they are ignored.
2. *Decision variables*—The decision variables are the batches of products X544 and X588 that will be produced.
3. *Constraints*—The two constraints are hours in the blender (900 hours are available) and gallons of Nevex (47,800 gallons are available).

With this information we can construct the linear program. For discussion convenience we will let A be the number of batches of product X544 produced and B be the number of batches of product X588 produced. We then have

$$\text{Maximize } \$13,200A + \$9,800B$$

(This is the objective function, which is the total contribution margin of the production plan.) It is subject to the following constraints:

1. $6A + 10B \leq 900$—This is the blender hours constraint—the left-hand side is the number of blender hours consumed producing X544 and X588, and the right-hand side is the number of blender hours available. The constraint specifies that the amount of blender hours used by the production plan cannot exceed the amount available.

2. *500A + 300B ≤ 47,800*—This is the Nevex constraint—the left-hand side is the gallons of Nevex consumed producing X544 and X588, and the right-hand side is the gallons of Nevex available. The constraint specifies that the amount of Nevex used by the production plan cannot exceed the amount available.
3. *A, B ≥ 0*—This is the non-negativity constraint, which says that production cannot be negative.

In practice, linear programs are solved using computers and specialized software packages. There is a tool in Microsoft Excel and Open Office Calc called *Solver* that can be used to solve linear programs. However, here we will focus on manual solutions to simple linear programs so that you can develop the intuition relating to how linear programs find optimal solutions. The approach we will use is graphical.

The Graphical Approach to Solving Linear Programs

Step 1: Draw the Constraints on a Graph

Exhibit 3-27 graphs the blender constraint. The number of batches of product X588 produced is shown on the vertical (Y) axis and the number of batches of product X544 produced is shown on the horizontal (X) axis. Since each batch of X544 uses 6 blender hours, we can produce 150 (900/6) batches of X544 if we use all 900 blender hours to produce X544. Since each batch of product X588 uses 10 blender hours, we can produce 90 (900/10) batches of X588 if we use all 900 blender hours to produce X588. The line joining these two points on the graph represents the boundary of the area denoting the feasible set of (X544, X588) production pairs. Any combination of batches of production of X544 and X588 that lie on this line or below is feasible since it does not require more blender hours than the 900 hours available.

We can use the same approach to find the end points of the constraint for Nevex availability. The end points are 95.6 (47,800/500) batches of X544 and 159.33 (47,800/300) batches of X588. Exhibit 3-28 graphs both constraints. We have now completed the process of adding constraints.

Remember that for an (X544, X588) production pair to be feasible, it has to lie on or below both lines. In other words for a production pair to be possible, it must be jointly feasible to all the constraints. The area that is jointly feasible to all constraints is called the *feasible production set* or simply the *feasible set*. Exhibit 3-29 shows the feasible set for this problem. The feasible set includes any point on or below the constraint lines shown in the diagram.

Exhibit 3-27
Graphing the Blender Constraint at Harris Chemical

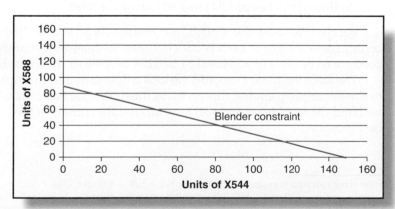

Exhibit 3-28
Adding the Nevex
Constraint at Harris
Chemical

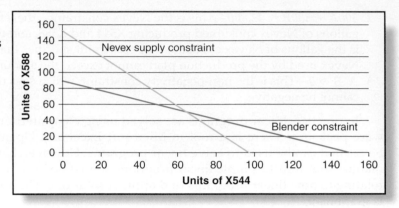

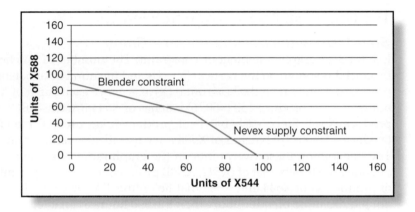

Step 2: Finding the Optimal Solution on the Graph

The trick in linear programming is that the best solution will always be found on the boundary of the feasible set. Moreover, there is no production pair on the boundary of the feasible set that will provide a better solution than a production pair at one of the corners of the feasible set. This means that we only need to look at the corners of the feasible set to find a best solution.

In this case we have four corners:

1. Produce 0 batches of X544 and 0 batches of X588.
2. Produce 95.6 batches of X544 and 0 batches of X588.
3. Produce 65 batches of X544 and 51 batches of X588.[2]
4. Produce 0 batches of X544 and 90 batches of X588.

Because we know the contribution margins of X544 and X588 we can compute the contribution margin of each production pair to determine that the best solution is to produce 65 batches of X544 and 51 batches of X588 as shown in Exhibit 3-30.

The decision maker can add various constraints and multiple decision variables to the linear program but this problem illustrates the basic idea. The linear program will find the feasible set and will hunt around the corners of the feasible set to find the best solution.

---

[2] We have two equations in two unknowns: $6A + 10B = 900$ and $500A + 300B = 47,800$. Multiply the first equation by 30 and subtract the resulting equation from the second equation to get $320A = 20,800$. Therefore, $A = 65$. Substitute $A = 65$ in either of the original constraint equations to find $B = 51$.

Exhibit 3-30
Evaluating the
Production
Alternatives at
Harris Chemical

	X544	X588	Total CM
Contribution margin per batch	$13,200	$9,800	
Batches			
Corner 1	0	0	$0
Corner 2	95.6	0	$1,261,920
Corner 3	65	51	$1,357,800
Corner 4	0	90	$882,000

EPILOGUE TO NOLAN INDUSTRIES

With the tools from this chapter in mind, we can return to the issues Punit was considering at the beginning of the chapter.

Recalling our discussion of both CVP analysis and relevant costs, we know that Punit should begin by computing the contribution margins of the two products. Recognizing that variable costs are 65% of total costs, Punit can compute the contribution margin of the two existing products as shown in Exhibit 3-31.

With this information and recalling that the sales mix is 60% XR276 and 40% XR244, Punit can undertake the breakeven analysis he was wondering about by employing the profit equation we developed in this chapter. If we assume that sales are in batches of 100, then

$$\text{Profit} = (40 \times \text{Contribution margin XR244}) + (60 \times \text{Contribution margin XR276}) \times \text{Batches of 100 sold} - \$7,500,000$$

Noting that profit = 0 at breakeven and rearranging, we have

Batches of 100 sold = 7,500,000/[(40 × 479.50) + (60 × 568.25)] = 140.779
Units of XR244 sold = 5,631.16 (140.779 × 40)
Units of XR276 sold = 8,446.74 (140.779 × 60)

Therefore, with a 40/60 split, Nolan Industries will have to sell 5,632 units of XR244 and 8,447 units of XR276.

You may have realized that a shorter, and perhaps more intuitive, approach to solving this problem is to compute a hypothetical product with a contribution margin that is a weighted average of the two existing products. In this case the hypothetical product would have a contribution margin of $532.75 [(40% × 479.50) + (60% × 568.25)]. Therefore, the number of units of this hypothetical product that would have to be sold to break even would be 14,077.9 (7,500,000/532.75). Therefore, unit sales of XR244 would be 5,631.16 (40% × 14,077.9), and unit sales of XR276 would be 8,446.74 (60% × 14,077.9), which, of course, is the answer we already have.

Exhibit 3-31
Product
Contribution
Margins at Nolan
Industries

	XR244	XR276
Selling price	$785.00	$955.00
Variable cost	305.50	386.75
Contribution margin	$479.50	$568.25

Exhibit 3-32
Breakeven Results
at Nolan Industries

	XR244	XR276	TOTAL
Sales units	5,632	8,447	14,079
Selling price	$785.00	$955.00	
Variable cost	305.50	386.75	
Contribution margin per unit sold	$479.50	$568.25	
Total contribution margin			$7,500,552
Fixed cost			7,500,000
Profit			$552

Exhibit 3-32 provides a profit summary. Recall that by convention all breakeven calculations are rounded up—therefore the profit reported will be slightly greater than the target of 0.

This answers Punit's question about breakeven sales assuming the 40/60 split. Punit now wants to know the maximum sales levels while maintaining the 40/60 split. In this case sales are constrained by the 48,000 machine hours available. If we tackle this problem using the batch approach, we first note that every batch of 100 products will use 280 [(40 × 2.50) + (60 × 3)] hours. Therefore, the maximum number of batches that can be produced will be 171.43 (48,000/280). This means that the maximum number of XR244s that can be produced will be 6,857.14 (171.43 × 40) and the maximum number of XR276s that can be produced will be 10,285.71 (171.43 × 60). As shown in Exhibit 3-33, various combinations of rounding suggest that the best production plan to maintain an approximate 40/60 mix is to produce 6,856 units of XR244 and 10,286 units of XR276 with a resulting profit of $1,632,472.

Note that tackling this problem using the hypothetical product would follow this path. The hypothetical product would require 2.8 hours per [(0.4 × 2.5) + (0.6 × 3)] hours per unit meaning that a maximum of 17,142.86 (48,000/2.8) units of the hypothetical product could be produced. At this point you should be able to complete the analysis to show that this results in the same solution as the batch approach.

Now Punit wants to know whether the 40/60 mix is really the best. From the discussion in the chapter you should recall that what we need to do, since there is only one production constraint in this problem, is to compute each product's contribution per machine hour. Exhibit 3-34 shows these calculations.

	XR244	XR276	TOTAL
Sales units	6,856	10,286	17,142
Selling price	$785.00	$955.00	
Variable cost	305.50	386.75	
Contribution margin per unit sold	$479.50	$568.25	
Total contribution margin			$9,132,472
Fixed cost			7,500,000
Profit			$1,632,472
Machine hours per unit	2.50	3.00	
Total machine hours used	17,140	30,858	47,998

Exhibit 3-34
Product Contribution Margins per Unit of the Constraining Factor of Production at Nolan Industries

	XR244	XR276
Sales units	6,857	10,285
Selling price	$785.00	$955.00
Variable cost	305.50	386.75
Contribution margin per unit sold	$479.50	$568.25
Machine hours per unit	2.50	3.00
Contribution margin per machine hour	$191.80	$189.42

Exhibit 3-35
Best Product Mix of XR244 and XR276 at Nolan Industries

	XR244	XR276	TOTAL
% of Total sales	56.61%	43.39%	
Sales units	10,000	7,666	17,666
Selling price	$785.00	$955.00	
Variable cost	305.50	386.75	
Contribution margin per unit sold	$479.50	$568.25	
Total contribution margin	$4,795,000	$4,356,205	$9,151,205
Fixed cost			7,500,000
Profit			$1,651,205
Machine hours per unit	2.50	3.00	
Total machine hours	25,000	22,998	47,998

Exhibit 3-36
New Product Contribution Margin Analysis at Nolan Industries

	XR244	XR276	NEW
Selling price	$785.00	$955.00	$1,200.00
Variable cost	305.50	386.75	533.00
Contribution margin per unit	$479.50	$568.25	$667.00
Machine hours per unit	2.50	3.00	3.50
Contribution margin per machine hour	$191.80	$189.42	$190.57

Since XR244 has the highest contribution per machine hour, we now know that we should make as many XR244s as we can. We have the capacity to produce 19,200 (48,000/2.5) units of XR244, but we can only sell 10,000 units. Therefore, we should allocate 25,000 (10,000 × 2.5) hours of machine time to produce 10,000 units of XR244. That will leave us with 23,000 (48,000 − 25,000) hours of machine time to produce 7,666 (23,000/3) units of XR276. This results in a 56.6/43.4 split and produces a profit of $1,651,205 as shown in Exhibit 3-35.

Finally Punit wants to know whether the new product offering is a good deal. Once again we need to compute each product's contribution margin per machine hour. Exhibit 3-36 shows this calculation.

Punit's questions can easily be answered using Excel tools. If interested, in Excel set up a spreadsheet that identifies the total contribution associated with a production plan. Then you can use Excel's *Goal Seek* tool to answer a question like finding the breakeven point and Excel's *Solver* tool to find the best production plan. Exhibit 3-37 presents the optimal production plan found by Solver.

Exhibit 3-37
Best Product Mix with the New Product at Nolan Industries

	XR244	XR276	NEW	TOTAL
Units sold	10,000	5,333	2,000	17,333
Selling price	$785.00	$955.00	$1,200.00	
Variable cost	305.50	386.75	533.00	
Contribution margin per unit	$479.50	$568.25	$667.00	
Total contribution margin	4,795,000	3,030,477	1,334,000	$9,159,477
Fixed cost				7,500,000
Profit				$1,659,477
Machine hours per unit	2.50	3.00	3.50	
Machine hours used	25,000	15,999	7,000	47,999

If we follow the rule of allocating machine time in order of contribution per machine hour, we will produce XR244 first, then the new product, and finally XR276. Given that the maximum number of units of the new product we can sell is 2,000, you should be able to show that the production plan shown in Exhibit 3-37 is the best one.

SUMMARY

This chapter provided a review of many of the cost concepts in management accounting and provides an important foundation for the remaining chapters in this book.

The chapter stressed that the primary role of management accounting is to support decision making inside the organization. Therefore, unlike financial accounting, which is driven by reporting requirements specified by accounting bodies and governments, management accounting is driven by the information needs of decision makers inside the organization.

The chapter provided an introduction to CVP analysis, which forms the basis for the spreadsheet-based financial modeling that is used by virtually all organizations. Indeed, many analysts attribute the explosive growth in sales of personal computers in the late 1970s and early 1980s to the development of spreadsheet software, such as VisiCalc and Lotus 1-2-3, which could be used for financial modeling. The basic CVP analysis reviewed in this chapter classifies costs as variable, fixed, and mixed. More complex cost behavior is easily modeled using spreadsheets.

The chapter also introduced the decision-making principle that the only relevant costs in a decision are those costs that change as a result of the decision. The relevant cost concept was explored in the context of the make-or-buy decision, the decision to drop a product or department, the order decision, and the short-term product mix decision.

The discussion in the chapter pointed out that practice frequently witnesses violations of the relevant cost principle—one of the most common violations being the sunk cost phenomenon. The consequence is that decision makers need to avoid introducing irrelevant data into their decision making.

KEY TERMS

avoidable cost, 101
breakeven point, 95
capacity-related cost, 90
contribution margin, 91
contribution margin per unit, 91
contribution margin ratio, 91
cost driver, 88
cost–volume–profit (CVP)
  analysis, 90

direct labor cost, 103
direct materials cost, 103
fixed cost, 90
floor price, 109
incremental cost, 97
make-or-buy decision, 102
manufacturing overhead cost, 103
mixed cost, 96

opportunity cost, 100
relevant cost, 100
step variable cost, 97
sunk cost, 98
sunk cost phenomenon, 99
variable cost, 88
what-if analysis, 93

ASSIGNMENT MATERIALS

Questions

3-1 What are some different managerial uses of cost information? (LO 2)

3-2 Explain the difference between variable costs and fixed costs. (LO 1, 2, 3)

3-3 What does the term *contribution margin per unit* mean? How is the contribution margin used in cost analysis to support managerial decisions? (LO 1, 2, 3)

3-4 Explain the difference between the *contribution margin ratio* and *contribution margin per unit*. (LO 1, 2, 3)

3-5 What does the term *breakeven point* mean? (LO 1, 2, 3)

3-6 What is a mixed cost? Give an example of a mixed cost. (LO 1, 3)

3-7 What does the term *differential cost* mean? (LO 1, 2, 3)

3-8 How do step variable costs differ from marginal costs? (LO 1, 2, 3)

3-9 Why should decision makers focus only on the relevant costs for decision making? (LO 1, 2, 3, 4)

3-10 What are *sunk costs*? Explain whether they are relevant costs. (LO 1, 2, 3, 4)

3-11 What behavioral factors may influence some managers to consider sunk costs as being relevant in their decisions? (LO 1, 2, 3, 4)

3-12 What is meant by the term *relevant cost?* (LO 1, 2, 3, 4)

3-13 When is the opportunity cost of a capacity equal to zero? (LO 1, 2, 3, 4)

3-14 What is meant by the term *floor price?* (LO 1, 2, 3, 4)

3-15 Provide an example of a fixed cost that would be relevant to a make-or-buy decision, and an example of a fixed cost that would not be relevant to such a decision. (LO 3, 4)

3-16 What qualitative considerations are relevant in dropping a product decision? (LO 4)

3-17 What is an opportunity cost that is relevant in a make-or-buy decision? (LO 1, 4)

3-18 In analyzing whether to drop a product or department, what are two difficulties that arise related to the impact on costs or revenues? (LO 3, 4)

3-19 "Prices must cover both variable and fixed costs of production." Do you agree with this statement? Explain. (LO 3, 4)

3-20 "When production capacity is constrained, determine what products to make by ranking them in order of their contribution per unit." Do you agree with this statement? Explain. (LO 3, 4)

3-21 "When production capacity is limited and it is possible to obtain additional customer orders, a firm must consider its opportunity costs to evaluate the profitability of these new orders." Do you agree with this statement? If so, what are the opportunity costs in this context? (LO 3, 4)

3-22 What are the three components of a linear program? (LO 4)

Exercises

LO 3   **3-23** *Classification of variable and fixed costs* Classify each of the following as a variable or fixed cost with respect to a unit of production:
  a. Salaries of production supervisors.
  b. Steel used in automobile production.
  c. Wood used in furniture production.
  d. Salaries for factory custodial staff.

e. Depreciation of factory equipment.

f. Lubricants for machines.

g. Electricity used to operate a specific machine.

h. Wages of production workers.

i. Rent for a factory building.

j. Glue used in furniture production.

k. Maintenance for production equipment, performed every month.

l. Paper used in newspaper production.

LO 3   **3-24** *Classification of variable and fixed costs*   Classify each of the following as a variable or fixed cost with respect to a unit of product that is sold:

a. Commissions paid to sales personnel.

b. Advertising expenses.

c. Salaries of staff processing orders.

d. Salary of the chief executive officer.

e. Depreciation of a shipping truck.

f. Protective packaging for each unit of product.

g. Insurance for corporate headquarters.

h. Gasoline used to deliver products.

LO 3   **3-25** *Cost classification*   Percy's is a small hamburger shop catering mainly to students at a nearby university. It sells hamburgers and vegetarian burgers and is open for business from 11:00 A.M. until 11:00 P.M., Monday through Friday. The owner, Percy Luk, employs two cooks, one server, and a part-time janitor. Because there is no space for dining inside the shop, all orders are takeout orders. Moreover, almost all orders are for one burger. Percy prepared the following partial list of costs incurred last month:

Burger ingredients

Cooks' wages

Server's wages

Janitor's wages

Depreciation on cooking equipment

Paper supplies (wrapping, napkins, and bags)

Rent

Advertisement in local newspaper

Required

Classify these costs as variable or fixed with respect to the number of burgers served.

LO 3   **3-26** *Breakeven analysis*   Klear Camera Company is considering introducing a new video camera. Its selling price is projected to be $1,200 per unit. Variable manufacturing costs are estimated to be $360 per unit. Variable selling costs are 20% of sales dollars. The company expects the annual fixed manufacturing costs for the new camera to be $4,200,000.

Required

(a) Compute Klear's contribution margin per unit and contribution margin ratio.

(b) Determine the number of units Klear must sell to break even.

(c) Klear is considering a design modification that would reduce the variable cost of the camera by $200 per unit. Explain whether this change will cause Klear's breakeven point to increase or decrease when compared to the initial plans.

LO 3   **3-27** *Breakeven analysis and target profit for a hospital*   Morton Medical Institute operates a 1,000-bed hospital and offers a number of specialized medical services. Morton's hospital facility and equipment are leased on a long-term basis. The hospital charges $3,500 per patient-day. On the basis of past cost data, Morton has estimated its variable costs as $800 per patient-day. Fixed costs are $4,000,000 per month. The hospital's administrator has estimated that the hospital will average 4,000 patient-days per month.

Required

(a) How much will the hospital need to charge per patient-day to break even at this level of activity?

(b) Refer to the original data in the problem. How many patient-days must Morton average each month to earn a target profit of $200,000 per month?

> LO 3   **3-28** *Breakeven analysis and target profit, taxes*   Patterson Parkas Company's sales revenue is $50 per unit, variable costs are $30 per unit, and fixed costs are $180,000.

Required

(a) Compute Patterson's contribution margin per unit and contribution margin ratio.

(b) Determine the number of units Patterson must sell to break even.

(c) Determine the sales revenue required to earn (pretax) income equal to 20% of revenue.

(d) How many units must Patterson sell to generate an after-tax profit of $120,000 if the tax rate is 40%?

(e) Patterson is considering increasing its advertising expenses by $40,000. How much of an increase in sales units is necessary from expanded advertising to justify this expenditure (generate an incremental contribution margin of $40,000)?

> LO 3   **3-29** *Breakeven analysis, target profit*   Last year, Revlyn Co. recorded sales revenues of $2,500,000, variable costs of $1,000,000, and fixed costs of $180,000.

Required

(a) At what sales dollar level will Revlyn earn a before-tax target profit of $600,000?

(b) At what sales dollar level will Revlyn break even?

> LO 3   **3-30** *Multiple-product target profit*   A&Z Company sells products both domestically and internationally. Fixed costs totaled $5,000,000 last year. In an effort to increase its total sales volume, A&Z plans to spend an additional $1,280,000 in advertising next year. Expected average prices and variable costs appear below.

	DOMESTIC	INTERNATIONAL
Price per unit	$50	$40
Variable costs per unit	$30	$16

Because of the increased advertising, A&Z expects to sell 300,000 units domestically and 200,000 units internationally next year.

Required

Using the expected sales mix, determine the number of units that A&Z must sell in each market in order to earn income of $200,000 next year.

3-31 *Multiple-product breakeven analysis* Florida Favorites Company produces toy alligators and toy dolphins. Fixed costs are $1,290,000 per year. Sales revenue and variable costs per unit are as follow:

	ALLIGATORS	DOLPHINS
Sales price	$20	$25
Variable costs	8	10

Required

(a) Suppose the company currently sells 140,000 alligators per year and 60,000 dolphins per year. Assuming the sales mix stays constant, how many alligators and dolphins must the company sell to break even per year?

(b) Suppose the company currently sells 60,000 alligators per year and 140,000 dolphins per year. Assuming the sales mix stays constant, how many alligators and dolphins must the company sell to break even per year?

(c) Explain why the total number of toys needed to break even in part a is the same as or different from the number in part b.

LO 2, 3   **3-32** *Pricing and impact on demand* Andrea Kimball has recently acquired a franchise of a well-known fast-food restaurant chain. She is considering a special promotion for a week during which hamburger prices would be reduced $0.40 from the regular price of $1.09 to $0.69. Local advertising expenses for this special promotion will amount to $4,500. Andrea expects the promotion to increase sales of hamburgers by 20% and French fries by 12%, but she expects the sales of chicken sandwiches to decline by 8% (because some customers, who otherwise may have ordered a chicken sandwich, will order a hamburger instead because of its attractive low price). The following data have been compiled for sales prices, variable costs, and weekly sales volumes:

PRODUCT	SALES PRICE	VARIABLE COSTS	SALES VOLUME
Hamburgers	$1.09	$0.51	20,000
Chicken sandwiches	1.29	0.63	10,000
French fries	0.89	0.37	20,000

Required

Evaluate the expected impact of the special promotion on sales and profits. Should Andrea go ahead with this special promotion? What other considerations are relevant in this decision?

LO 1, 2, 3, 4   **3-33** *Variable and fixed costs, profitability of order, opportunity cost* Healthy Hearth specializes in lunches for health-conscious people. The company produces a small selection of lunch offerings each day. The menu selections may vary from day to day, but Healthy Hearth charges the same price per menu selection because it adjusts the portion sizes according to the cost of producing the selection. Healthy Hearth currently sells 5,000 meals per month. Variable costs are $3 per meal, and fixed costs total $5,000 per month. A government agency has recently proposed that Healthy Hearth provide 1,000 meals next month for senior citizens at $3.50 per meal. Volunteers will deliver the meals to the senior citizens at no charge.

Required

(a) Suppose Healthy Hearth has sufficient idle capacity to accommodate the government order for next month. What will be the impact on Healthy Hearth's operating income if it accepts this order?

(b) Suppose that Healthy Hearth would have to give up regular sales of 500 meals, at a price of $4.50 each, to accommodate the government order for next month. What will be the impact on Healthy Hearth's operating income if it accepts the government order?

LO 1, 4   **3-34 *Relevant and sunk costs*** Don Baxter's 6-year-old Impala requires repairs estimated at $6,000 to make it roadworthy again. His friend Aaron Bloom suggested that he buy a 6-year-old Ford Escort instead for $6,000 cash. Aaron estimated the following costs for the two cars:

COSTS	IMPALA	ESCORT
Acquisition cost	$24,000	$6,000
Repairs	6,000	0
Annual operating costs: gas, maintenance, insurance	2,900	4,000

Required

(a) What costs are relevant and what costs are not relevant for this decision? Why?
(b) What should Don do? Explain.
(c) What quantitative and qualitative factors are relevant to his decision? Why?

LO 1, 2, 4   **3-35 *Relevant and sunk costs*** Gilmark Company has 10,000 obsolete components carried in inventory at a cost of $30 each. They can be sold as they are for $5 each. They can be reworked, however, at a total cost of $75,000 and sold for $12 each.

Required

Determine whether it is worthwhile to rework these components.

LO 1, 2, 4   **3-36 *Relevant and sunk costs*** McKinnon Company's plant manager is considering buying a new grinding machine to replace an old grinding machine or overhauling the old one to ensure compliance with the plant's high-quality standards. The following data are available:

OLD GRINDING MACHINE	
Original cost	$60,000
Accumulated depreciation	48,000
Annual operating costs	20,000
Current salvage value	6,000
Salvage value at the end of 5 years	0

NEW GRINDING MACHINE	
Cost	$60,000
Annual operating costs	8,000
Salvage value at the end of 5 years	1,000

OVERHAUL OF OLD GRINDING MACHINE	
Cost of overhaul	$35,000
Annual operating costs after overhaul	13,000
Salvage value at the end of 5 years	500

Required

(a) List all relevant costs and when they are incurred.
(b) What costs should the decision maker consider as sunk costs?
(c) What should the plant manager do? Why?

3-37 *Relevant costs and revenues: replacement decision* Joyce Printers, Inc., is considering replacing its current printing machines with newer, faster, and more efficient printing technology. The following data have been compiled:

CATEGORY	EXISTING MACHINES	NEW MACHINES
Original cost	$80,000	$120,000
Annual operating costs	$50,000	$30,000
Remaining useful life	5 years	5 years
Salvage value after 5 years	$5,000	$10,000

The existing machines can be disposed of now for $40,000. Keeping them will cost $20,000 for repair and upgrading.

Required

Should Joyce Printers keep the existing printing machines? Explain.

LO 1, 2, 4 **3-38 *Make-or-buy and relevant costs*** The assembly division of Davenport, Inc., is bidding on an order of 50,000 smart phones. The division is eager to get this order because it has a substantial amount of unused plant capacity. The variable cost for each smart phone is $140 in addition to the cost of the display and touchscreen component. The divisional purchasing manager has received two bids for the component. One is from Davenport's electronics division. This bid is for $35 per unit, although its variable cost is only $30 per unit. The other is from an outside vendor for $34 per unit. Davenport's electronics division has sufficient unused capacity for this order.

Required

(a) Determine the relevant costs for this order for the assembly division under both internal and outsourcing arrangements.
(b) Determine the relevant costs for this order for Davenport as a company under each of the sourcing arrangements.

LO 1, 2, 4 **3-39 *Make-or-buy*** Kane Company is considering outsourcing a key component. A reliable supplier has quoted a price of $75.50 per unit. The following costs of the component when manufactured in-house are expressed on a per unit basis:

Direct materials	$25.50
Direct labor	15.00
Variable overhead	28.50
Fixed overhead	10.00
Total costs	$79.00

Required

(a) What assumptions need to be made about the behavior of overhead costs for Kane in order to analyze the outsourcing decision?
(b) Should Kane Company outsource the component?
(c) What other factors are relevant for this decision?

LO 1, 2, 4 **3-40 *Make-or-buy, opportunity cost*** Premier Company manufactures gear model G37, which is used in several of its farm equipment products. Annual production volume of G37 is 10,000 units. Unit costs for G37 are as follows:

Direct materials costs	$60
Direct labor costs	30
Variable overhead costs	40
Fixed overhead costs	20
Total costs	$150

Alternatively, Premier can also purchase gear model G37 from an outside supplier for $135 per unit. If G37 is outsourced, Premier can use the facility where G37 is currently manufactured for production of another gear— model G49. This would save Premier $120,000 in facility rental and other costs presently incurred.

Required

Should Premier make or buy G37? By how much will Premier be better off by choosing your decision rather than the alternative?

LO 1, 2, 4   **3-41** ***Make-or-buy, relevant costs, and opportunity cost*** Fab Motors has manufactured compressor parts at its plant in Pitcairn, Indiana, for the past 25 years. An outside supplier, Superior Compressor Company, has offered to supply compressor model C38 at a price of $200 per unit. Current unit manufacturing costs for C38 are as follows:

Direct materials	$80
Direct labor	60
Variable overhead	56
Fixed overhead	17
Total costs	$213

Required

(a) Should Superior Compressor's offer be accepted if the Pitcairn plant is presently operating below capacity?
(b) What is the maximum acceptable purchase price if the plant facilities are fully utilized at present and if any additional available capacity can be deployed for the production of other compressors?

LO 2, 4   **3-42** ***Dropping a segment*** Roger's Relaxation Center analyzes the profitability of three operating units: its restaurant, bar, and gym. Revenues, variable costs, and attributable fixed costs (which can be avoided if the unit is eliminated) for each unit are as follows:

	RESTAURANT	BAR	GYM
Revenue	$520,000	$325,000	$180,000
Variable costs	240,000	60,000	50,000
Attributable fixed costs	70,000	25,000	55,000

Roger, the owner, is considering converting the gym area into an expanded restaurant area.

Required

(a) Ignoring remodeling costs, by how much will the restaurant segment margin have to increase for the center's income to be at least as high as it is now?
(b) What other considerations will Roger want to consider before making the decision to eliminate the gym unit to expand the restaurant area?

LO 2 **3-43** *Special order pricing* McGee Corporation's Olympia plant produces a module used in automobile manufacturing. The company's practical capacity is 4,000 modules per week. The selling price is $900 per module. Production this quarter is 3,000 modules per week, and all of the modules produced are sold each week. Demand is expected to remain steady. Total costs of production this week at the level of 3,000 modules were $300,000 of fixed costs plus $2,400,000 of variable costs.

Suppose that a new customer's supplier has an emergency need for 1,500 modules to be delivered next week and that the plant cannot schedule overtime production. Consequently, McGee would have to give up some of its current sales to fill the new order. Total selling and administrative costs would not change if McGee accepts the order.

Required

What is the minimum (floor) price that McGee should charge for the new order?

LO 2 **3-44** *Special order pricing* Shorewood Shoes Company makes and sells a variety of leather shoes for children. For its current mix of different models and sizes, the average selling price and costs per pair of shoes are as follows:

ITEM	AMOUNT
Price	$20
Costs:	
Direct materials	$6
Direct labor	4
Variable manufacturing overhead	2
Variable selling costs	1
Fixed overhead	3
Total costs	$16

Shoes are manufactured in batch sizes of 100 pairs. Each batch requires 5 machine hours to manufacture. The plant has a total capacity of 4,000 machine hours per month, but current monthly production consumes only about 80% of the capacity.

A discount store has approached Shorewood to buy 10,000 pairs of shoes next month. It has requested that the shoes bear its own private label. Embossing the private label will cost Shorewood an additional $0.50 per pair. However, no variable selling costs will be incurred for fulfilling this special order.

Required

Determine the minimum (floor) price that Shorewood Shoes should charge for this order. What other considerations are relevant in this decision?

LO 2, 4 **3-45** *Export order* Berry Company produces and sells 20,000 cases of fruit preserves each year. The following information reflects a breakdown of its costs:

COST ITEM	COSTS PER CASE	TOTAL COSTS
Variable production costs	$24	$480,000
Fixed production costs	12	240,000
Variable selling costs	6	150,000
Fixed selling and administrative costs	8	90,000
Total costs	$50	$960,000

Berry marks up its prices 40% over full costs. It has surplus capacity to produce 20,000 more cases. A French supermarket company has offered to purchase 15,000 cases of the product at a special price of $34 per case. Berry will incur additional shipping and selling costs of $5 per case to complete this order.

Required

What will be the effect on Berry's operating income if it accepts this order?

LO 2, 4   **3-46** *Profitability of order and extra shift decisions*   The manufacturing capacity of Ritter Rotator Company's plant facility is 60,000 rotators per quarter. Operating results for the first quarter of this year are as follows.

Sales (36,000 units at $10)	$360,000
Variable manufacturing and selling costs	198,000
Contribution margin	162,000
Fixed costs	99,000
Operating income	$ 63,000

A foreign distributor has offered to buy 30,000 units at $9 per unit during the second quarter of this year. Domestic demand is expected to remain the same as in the first quarter.

Required

(a) Determine the impact on operating income if Ritter accepts this order. Assume that if the company accepts the order, it foregoes sales to regular domestic customers. What other considerations are relevant in this decision?

(b) Assume that Ritter decides to run an extra shift so that it can accept the foreign order without forgoing sales to its regular domestic customers. The proposed extra shift would increase capacity by 25% and increase fixed costs by $25,000. Determine the impact on operating income if Ritter operates the extra shift and accepts the export order. What other considerations are relevant in this decision?

LO 2, 4   **3-47** *Shelf mix decision*   Superstore is a large discount supermarket. Profits have declined, so the manager has collected data on revenues and costs for different food categories. The following data pertain to some of the frozen foods that Superstore sells. To facilitate comparisons, the manager has listed average price and cost information for each category in equivalent square-foot packages:

	ICE CREAM	JUICES	FROZEN DINNERS	FROZEN VEGETABLES
Selling price per unit (square-foot package)	$12.00	$13.00	$24.00	$9.00
Variable costs per unit (square-foot package)	$8.00	$10.00	$20.50	$7.00
Minimum square footage required	24	24	24	24
Maximum square footage allowed	100	100	100	100

The manager wants a maximum of 250 square feet devoted to the four categories in this table.

Required

(a) Given the manager's constraints, and assuming that the store can sell whatever is displayed on the shelves, what shelf mix (i.e., what number of square feet for each category in the table) will maximize Superstore's contribution margin from these four categories?

(b) What other factors might the manager consider in deciding on the amount of shelf space per category?

LO 2, 4   **3-48** *Product mix decision*   Boyd Wood Company makes a regular and a deluxe grade of wood floors. Regular grade is sold at $16 per square yard, and the deluxe grade is sold at $25 per square yard. The variable cost of making the regular grade is $10 per square yard. It costs an extra $5 per square yard to make the deluxe grade. It takes 15 labor hours to make 100 square yards of the regular grade, and 20 labor hours to make 100 square yards of the deluxe grade. There are 4,600 hours of labor time available for production each week. The maximum weekly sales for the regular and the deluxe model are 30,000 and 8,000 square yards, respectively. Fixed production costs total $600,000 per year. All selling costs are fixed.

Required

What is the optimal production level in number of square yards for each product?

Problems

LO 3   **3-49** *Cost classification and target profit*   Walt's Woodwork Company makes and sells wooden shelves. Walt's carpenters make the shelves in the company's rented building. Walt has a separate office at another location that also includes a showroom where customers can view sample shelves and ask questions of salespeople. The company sells all the shelves it produces each year and keeps no inventories. The following information pertains to Walt's Woodwork Company for the past year:

a. Units produced and sold	50,000
b. Sales price per unit	$70
c. Carpenter labor to make shelves	600,000
d. Wood to make the shelves	450,000
e. Sales staff salaries	80,000
f. Office and showroom rental expenses	150,000
g. Depreciation on carpentry equipment	50,000
h. Advertising	200,000
i. Sales commissions based on number of units sold	180,000
j. Miscellaneous fixed manufacturing overhead	150,000
k. Rent for the building where the shelves are made	300,000
l. Miscellaneous variable manufacturing overhead	350,000
m. Depreciation for office equipment	10,000

Required

Make appropriate assumptions about cost behavior and assume that direct labor costs vary directly with the number of units produced. How many units must the company sell in order to earn a pre-tax profit of $500,000?

LO 2, 3   **3-50** *Introducing a new product, profitability*   Santos Company is considering introducing a new compact disc player model at a price of $105 per unit. Santos's controller has compiled the following incremental cost information based on an estimate of 120,000 units of sales annually for the new product:

Direct materials cost	$3,600,000
Direct labor cost	$2,400,000
Variable manufacturing overhead	$1,200,000
Sales commission	10% of sales
Fixed cost	$2,000,000

The sales manager expects the introduction of the new model to result in a reduction in sales of the existing model from 300,000 to 240,000 units. The contribution margin for the existing model is $20 per unit.

Required

(a) Determine the total impact on Santos's profit from the introduction of the new model.
(b) Should Santos introduce the new model? Explain.

LO 3   **3-51**   *Cost behavior and cost classifications*   Shannon O'Reilly is trying to decide whether to continue to take public transportation to work or to purchase a car. Before making her decision, she would like to compare the cost of using public transportation and the cost of driving a car.

Required

(a) What activity measure should Shannon use as she estimates the cost of driving?
(b) What should Shannon view as incremental (variable or out-of-pocket) costs of driving from home to work?
(c) What are some fixed costs of driving a car?
(d) Suppose that if Shannon purchased a car, she would use it to take a 2-week scenic vacation by car. What activity measures might Shannon use to estimate her vacation and lodging expenses?

LO 1, 3   **3-52**   *Cost behavior and decisions*   Second City Airlines operates 35 scheduled round-trip flights each week between New York and Chicago. It charges a fixed one-way fare of $200 per passenger. Second City Airlines can carry 150 passengers per one-way flight. Fuel and other flight-related costs are $5,000 per one-way flight. On-flight meal and refreshment costs average $5 per passenger. Flight crew, ground crew, advertising, and other administrative expenditures for the New York–to–Chicago route amount to $400,000 each week.

Required

(a) How many passengers must each of the 70 one-way flights have on average to break even each week?
(b) If the load factor is 60% on all flights (that is, the flights are 60% full), how many flights must Second City Airlines operate on this route to earn a total profit of $500,000 before taxes per week?
(c) Are fuel costs variable or fixed?
(d) What is the variable cost to Second City Airlines for one additional passenger on a flight if the passenger takes a seat that would otherwise go empty?

LO 2, 3   **3-53**   *Breakeven point and competitive contribution margin analysis*   Johnson Company and Smith Company are competing firms that offer limousine service from the Charlesburg airport. While Johnson pays most of its employees on a per-ride basis, Smith prefers to pay its employees fixed salaries. Information about the selling prices per ride and cost structures of the two firms is given below.

Cost Category	Johnson Company	Smith Company
Selling price per ride	$30	$30
Variable cost per ride	24	15
Contribution margin per ride	6	15
Fixed costs per year	$300,000	$1,500,000

Required

(a) Calculate the breakeven point in the number of rides for both firms.
(b) Draw two graphs plotting profit as a function of the number of rides for the two firms.
(c) Explain which firm's cost structure is more profitable.
(d) Explain which firm's cost structure is riskier.

LO 3   **3-54** *Multiple breakeven points*   Last month, Capetini Capacitor Company sold capacitors to its distributors for $250 per capacitor. The sales level of 3,000 capacitors per month was less than the single-shift capacity of 4,400 capacitors at its plant located in San Diego. Variable production costs were $100 per capacitor, and fixed production costs were $200,000 per month. In addition, variable selling and distribution costs are $20 per capacitor, and fixed selling and distribution costs are $62,500 per month. At the suggestion of the marketing department, this month Capetini reduced the sales price to $200 and increased the monthly advertising budget by $17,500. Sales are expected to increase to 6,800 capacitors per month. If the demand exceeds the single-shift capacity of 4,400 capacitors, the plant needs to be operated in two shifts. Two-shift operation will increase monthly fixed production costs to $310,000.

Required

(a) Determine the contribution margin per capacitor last month.
(b) Determine the sales level in number of capacitors at which the profit-to-sales ratio would be 10% for last month.
(c) Determine the two breakeven points for this month.
(d) Determine the sales level in number of capacitors at which the profit-to-sales ratio this month is the same as the actual profit-to-sales ratio last month. Is there more than one possible sales level at which this equality would occur?

LO 2, 3   **3-55** *Effect on costs of volume changes*   Capilano Containers Company specializes in making high-quality customized containers to order. Its agreement with the labor union ensures employment for all its employees and a fixed payroll of $80,000 per month, including fringe benefits. This payroll makes available 4,000 labor hours each month to work on orders the firm receives. The monthly wages must be paid even if the workers remain idle because of a lack of work. If additional labor hours are required to complete jobs, overtime costs $30 per labor hour.

Each job requires 4 labor hours for machine setup and 0.05 labor hour per container. Variable costs are $1.60 per container for materials and $8.00 per labor hour for manufacturing overhead expenses. In addition, the firm must pay $20,000 per month for selling, general, and administrative expenses, and $36,000 per month lease payments for machinery and physical facilities.

In April, the firm won 90 orders, of which 60 were for 800 containers each and 30 for 1,600 containers each.

Required

Determine the total costs for April.

LO 1, 2, 3, 4 **3-56** *Profitability of orders and opportunity cost* Dawson Company produces and sells 80,000 boxes of specialty foods each year. Each box contains the same assortment of food. The company has computed the following annual costs:

COST ITEM	TOTAL COSTS
Variable production costs	$400,000
Fixed production costs	480,000
Variable selling costs	320,000
Fixed selling and administrative costs	200,000
Total costs	$1,400,000

Dawson normally charges $25 per box. A new distributor has offered to purchase 8,000 boxes at a special price of $22 per box. Dawson will incur additional packaging costs of $1 per box to complete this order.

Required

(a) Suppose Dawson has surplus capacity to produce 8,000 more boxes. What will be the effect on Dawson's income if it accepts this order?

(b) Suppose that instead of having surplus capacity to produce 8,000 more boxes, Dawson has surplus capacity to produce only 3,000 more boxes. What will be the effect on Dawson's income if it accepts the new order for 8,000 boxes?

LO 1, 2, 3, 4 **3-57** *Costing orders, profitability, and opportunity cost* Wedmark Corporation's Cupertino, California, plant manufactures chips used in personal computers. Its practical capacity is 2,000 chips per week, and fixed costs are $75,000 per week. The selling price is $500 per chip. Production this quarter is 1,600 chips per week. At this level of production, variable costs are $720,000 per week.

Required

(a) What will the plant's profit per week be if it operates at practical capacity?

(b) Suppose that a new customer offers $480 per chip for an order of 200 chips per week for delivery beginning this quarter. If this order is accepted, production will increase from 1,600 chips at present to 1,800 chips per week. What is the estimated change in the company's profit if it accepts the order?

(c) Suppose that the new customer in part b offered $480 per chip for an order of 600 chips per week and that Wedmark cannot schedule overtime production. Consequently, it would have to give up some of its current sales to fill the new order for 600 chips per week. What is the estimated change in Wedmark's profit if it accepts this order for 600 chips per week?

LO 1, 4 **3-58** *Relevant costs, equipment replacement decision* Anderson Department Stores is considering the replacement of the existing elevator system at its downtown store. A new system has been proposed that runs faster than the existing system, experiences few breakdowns, and as a result promises considerable savings in operating costs. Information on the existing system and the proposed new system follows:

CATEGORY	EXISTING SYSTEM	NEW SYSTEM
Original cost	$450,000	$575,000
Remaining life	5 years	5 years
Annual cash operating costs	$80,000	$8,000
Salvage value at present	$100,000	—
Salvage value in 6 years	$10,000	$100,000

Required

(a) What costs are not relevant for this decision?

(b) Should Anderson Department Stores replace the existing elevator system?

LO 1, 3, 4   **3-59** *Incremental revenues and costs, special order*   Genis Battery Company is considering accepting a special order for 80,000 batteries that it received from a discount retail store. The order specified a price of $12 per unit, which reflects a discount of $3 per unit relative to the company's regular price of $15 per unit. Genis's accounting department has prepared the following analysis to show the cost savings resulting from additional sales:

Costs	Cost per Unit without the Additional Sales (100,000 Units)	Cost per Unit with the Additional Sales (150,000 Units)
Variable	$7.50	$7.50
Fixed	$4.50	$4.00

No additional fixed costs will be incurred for this order because the company has surplus capacity. Because the average cost per unit will be reduced from $4.50 to $4.00, Genis's president believes that a reduction in the price to $12 is justified for this order.

Required

(a) Should the order for the 80,000 units at a price of $12 be accepted? What will be the impact on Genis's operating income?

(b) Is the accounting department's analysis the best way to evaluate this decision? If not, what alternative method can you suggest?

(c) What other considerations are important in this case? Why?

LO 1, 4   **3-60** *Relevant costs, sunk costs, product replacement decisions*   Syd Young, the production manager at Fuchow Company, purchased a cutting machine for the company last year. Six months after the purchase of the cutting machine, Syd learned about a new cutting machine that is more reliable than the machine that he purchased. The following information is available for the two machines:

Category	Old Machine	New Machine
Acquisition cost	$300,000	$360,000
Remaining life	4 years	4 years
Salvage value now	$100,000	—
Salvage value at the end of 4 years	$4,000	$6,000

Annual operating costs for the old machine are $140,000. The new machine will decrease annual operating costs by $60,000. These amounts do not include any charges for depreciation. Fuchow Company uses the straight-line depreciation method. These estimates of operating costs exclude rework costs. The new machine will also result in a reduction in the defect rate from the current 5% to 2.5%. All defective units are reworked at a cost of $1 per unit. The company, on average, produces 100,000 units annually.

Required

(a) Should Syd Young replace the old machine with the new machine? Explain, listing all relevant costs.

(b) What costs should be considered as sunk costs for this decision?

(c) What other factors may affect Young's decision?

LO 1, 4   **3-61** *Make-or-buy*   Beau's Bistro has a reputation for providing good value for its menu prices. The desserts, developed by the pastry chef, are one of the distinctive features of the menu. The pastry chef has just given notice that he will relocate to another city in a month and has volunteered to share some of the dessert recipes with the next pastry chef. Beau has been concerned about the Bistro's declining profits but is reluctant to raise prices because of the competition he faces. He decided this was an opportune time to consider outsourcing dessert production. Beau solicited bids for dessert production and delivery and is evaluating two bids as well as the alternative of hiring a new pastry chef who would make the desserts in-house. The first bid is from a gourmet dessert provider who would fill the Bistro's current dessert demand for $5,500 per month and would periodically introduce new gourmet desserts. The second bid is from a dessert provider who would provide high-quality, traditional desserts to fill Bistro's current demand (in terms of servings) for $5,000 per month. Beau has identified the following costs per month if the desserts are made in-house:

Ingredients	$500
Pastry chef labor	3,500
Assistants' labor	1,500
Variable overhead	200
Total	$5,700

Required

(a) What qualitative factors are relevant for this decision?

(b) Would you advise Beau to outsource dessert production? Provide reasons for your decision.

LO 1, 4   **3-62** *Outsourcing and ethics*   Hollenberry, Inc., is a successful mail-order catalog business with customers worldwide. The company's headquarters is in a small town some distance from any major metropolitan area. Sales have grown steadily over the years, and the call center facilities are currently inadequate for the sales volume. Management is deciding whether to outsource the call center operations to a company specializing in such operations. If the call center is outsourced, most of the current employees would lose their jobs because they do not wish to relocate to the new call center location, close to a major metropolitan area. Many of the employees have been with Hollenberry for more than 20 years. Regardless of where the call center is located, customers will call a toll-free phone number. If the call center is outsourced, however, more multilingual operators would be available. Hollenberry has identified the following costs of operating the call center in-house:

Labor	$650,000
Building rent	60,000
Phone charges	35,000
Other overhead costs	42,000

If the call center is outsourced, the related office equipment would be sold to the new call center operations for $20,000. The equipment was originally purchased at a cost of $100,000. The building will no longer be rented, and call center employees will have the opportunity to transfer to the outside call center, in which case their salaries will be paid by the outside call center. The other overhead costs are associated with maintaining the building and office equipment for the current call center.

If Hollenberry outsources the call center and the same number and pattern of calls occur next year, Hollenberry will pay the new call center firm $700,000 for the year.

Required

(a) What costs are relevant to the decision to outsource the call center?
(b) What qualitative factors are important in this decision?
(c) What should Hollenberry do? Provide reasons for your recommendation.

LO 1, 4 **3-63 *Dropping a product*** Merchant Company manufactures and sells three models of electronic printers. Ken Gail, president of the company, is considering dropping model JT484 from its product line because the company has experienced losses for this product during the past three quarters. The following product-level operating data have been compiled for the most recent quarter:

CATEGORY	TOTAL	JT284	JT384	JT484
Sales	$1,000,000	$500,000	$200,000	$300,000
Variable costs	600,000	300,000	100,000	200,000
Contribution margin	$400,000	$200,000	$100,000	$100,000
Fixed costs:				
Rent	$50,000	$25,000	$10,000	$15,000
Depreciation	60,000	30,000	12,000	18,000
Utilities	40,000	20,000	5,000	15,000
Supervision	50,000	15,000	5,000	30,000
Maintenance	30,000	15,000	6,000	9,000
Administrative	100,000	30,000	20,000	50,000
Total fixed costs	$330,000	$135,000	$58,000	$137,000
Operating income (loss)	$70,000	$65,000	$42,000	($37,000)

In addition, the following information is also available:

- Factory rent and depreciation will not be affected by a decision to drop model JT484.
- Quarterly utility bills will be reduced from $40,000 to $31,000 if JT484 isdropped.
- Supervision costs for JT484 can be eliminated if dropped.
- The maintenance department will be able to reduce quarterly costs by $7,000 if JT484 is dropped.
- Elimination of JT484 will make it possible to eliminate two administrative staff positions with combined salaries of $30,000 per quarter.

Required

(a) Should Merchant Company eliminate JT484?
(b) Merchant's sales manager believes that it is important to continue to produce JT484 to maintain a full product line. He expects the elimination of JT484 will reduce sales of the remaining two products by 5% each. Will this information change your answer to part a? Explain.

LO 2, 4   **3-64 *Drop unprofitable product or department*** Perform an Internet or electronic library search on "close underperforming departments," "unprofitable products," or a similar phrase to locate an example of a company that has closed unprofitable stores or dropped unprofitable products or services. Describe the cost, revenue, and other issues that the company considered in making the decision.

LO 2, 4   **3-65 *Product mix and overtime decisions*** Excel Corporation manufactures three products at its plant. The plant capacity is limited to 120,000 machine hours per year on a single-shift basis. Direct material and direct labor costs are variable. The following data are available for planning purposes:

PRODUCT	TOTAL UNIT DEMAND FOR NEXT YEAR	SALES PRICE PER UNIT	DIRECT MATERIALS COST PER UNIT	DIRECT LABOR COST PER UNIT	VARIABLE OVERHEAD COST PER UNIT	MACHINE HOURS PER UNIT
XL1	200,000	$10.00	$4.00	$2.00	$2.00	0.20
XL2	200,000	14.00	4.50	3.00	3.00	0.35
XL3	200,000	12.00	5.00	2.50	2.50	0.25

Required

(a) Given the capacity constraint, determine the production levels for the three products that will maximize profits.

(b) If the company authorizes overtime in order to produce more units of XL3, the direct labor cost per unit will be higher by 50% because of the overtime premium. Materials cost and variable overhead cost per unit will be the same for overtime production as regular production. Is it worthwhile operating overtime?

LO 1, 2 3, 4   **3-66 *Profitability of order, opportunity cost, and capacity*** Hudson Hydronics, Inc., is a corporation based in Troy, New York, that sells high-quality hydronic control devices. It manufactures two products, HCD1 and HCD2, for which the following information is available:

COSTS PER UNIT	HCD1	HCD2
Direct materials	$60	$75
Direct labor	80	100
Variable overhead	100	125
Fixed overhead	80	100
Total costs per unit	$320	$400
Price	$400	$500
Units sold	2,000 units	1,200 units

The average wage rate including fringe benefits is $20 per hour. The plant has a capacity of 15,000 direct labor hours, but current production uses only 14,000 direct labor hours of capacity. Hudson can, if desired, hire additional direct labor up to its capacity of 15,000 direct labor hours.

Required

(a) A new customer has offered to buy 200 units of HCD2 if Hudson lowers its price to $400 per unit. How many direct labor hours will be required to produce 200 units of HCD2? How much will Hudson Hydronic's profit increase or decrease if it accepts this proposal? (Assume all other prices will remain as before.)

(b) Suppose the customer has offered instead to buy 300 units of HCD2 at $400 per unit. How much will the profits increase or decrease if Hudson accepts this proposal? Assume that the company cannot increase its production capacity beyond 15,000 direct labor hours.

(c) Answer the question in part b assuming that the plant can work overtime. Direct labor costs for the overtime production increase to $30 per hour. Variable overhead costs for overtime production are 50% more than for normal production.

LO 2, 3, 4   **3-67** *Capacity and product mix decisions, linear programming*   Xu Company makes two types of wood doors: standard and deluxe. The doors are manufactured in a plant consisting of three departments: cutting, assembly, and finishing. Both labor and machine time are spent on the two products as they are worked on in each department.

In planning the production schedule for the next month, management is confronted with a labor shortage and the knowledge that some machines must be shut down for major maintenance and repair. The following information pertains to the estimated levels of capacity of direct labor hours and machine hours available next month in the three departments:

	DEPARTMENTS		
CAPACITY AVAILABLE	CUTTING	ASSEMBLY	FINISHING
Machine hours	40,000	40,000	15,000
Labor hours	8,000	17,500	8,000

Direct labor and machine hours required per unit of each product are as follows:

	DEPARTMENTS		
PRODUCT HOURS	CUTTING	ASSEMBLY	FINISHING
Standard:			
Direct labor hours	0.5	1	0.5
Machine hours	2	2	1
Deluxe:			
Direct labor hours	1	1.5	0.5
Machine hours	3	3	1.5

The estimated demand for the next month is 13,000 units of standard doors and 5,000 units of deluxe doors. Unit cost and price information are as follows:

ITEM	STANDARD DOORS	DELUXE DOORS
Unit selling price	$150	$200
Unit costs:		
Direct materials	$60	$80
Direct labor	40	60
Variable overhead	10	15
Fixed overhead	10	5

The average wage rate is $20 per hour and variable overhead cost is 25% times direct labor cost. Direct labor and machine availability in individual departments cannot be switched from one department to another.

Required

(a) Determine whether the direct labor hour and machine hour capacities are adequate to meet the next month's demand.

(b) How many units of each product should the company produce to maximize its profits?

(c) Suppose that as a result of process improvements, the deluxe model only requires 1.2 machine hours in finishing and 0.8 labor hour in cutting. How many units of each product should the company produce to maximize its profits?

(d) Suggest other alternatives the company might consider to satisfy the estimated demand for both products.

LO 2, 4   **3-68** *Client mix decision*   Spencer Grant, a financial planner, contacts and meets with local individuals to assist with financial planning and investments in Spencer's employer's investment services company. Spencer receives no fee for financial planning advice, but in addition to his salary, he receives commissions on client investments in the investment services company. Commission rates vary across different investment products. Spencer's employer pays office and phone costs and also reimburses Spencer for business-related travel. Satisfied clients have recommended Spencer to their friends, and Spencer now finds himself with more clients than he can handle in the 40 hours per week he would like to work. To analyze where to most profitably spend his time, Spencer has classified his current set of customers into the three groups listed here. The hours devoted per customer include direct contact time, travel time, and research and follow-up time for the clients. Spencer will introduce clients he is unable to serve to one of his colleagues.

	CUSTOMER GROUP		
	A	B	C
Average investment in company products per month	$900	$600	$200
Hours devoted per customer per month	3	1.5	0.5
Average commission percentage	6%	5%	4%
Current number of customers	20	60	120

Clients in group A are generally interested in hearing about new investment products that Spencer's company is offering and will usually invest sizable amounts in new products after meeting with Spencer or conversing with him on the phone. Clients in group B will also invest but generally in smaller amounts than clients in group A. Clients in group C appreciate meeting with Spencer because of the excellent advice he provides in planning for retirement and other future expenses but have little discretionary income to invest. Group C clients also generally invest in products with a lower commission rate for Spencer. However, Spencer maintains contact with these clients because he anticipates they will become more profitable as their careers develop.

Required

(a) Based on the data given, what client mix will maximize Spencer's monthly commissions, assuming he works 160 hours per month?

(b) What other factors should Spencer consider as he makes his decisions about his client mix?

Cases

LO 2, 3   **3-69** *Estimating total labor costs*   Dr. Barbara Benson is the head of the pathology laboratory at Barrington Medical Center in Mobile, Alabama. Dr. Benson estimates the amount of work for her laboratory staff by classifying the pathology tests into three categories: simple routine, simple nonroutine, and complex. She expects a simple routine test to require 2 hours, a simple nonroutine test to require 2.5 hours, and a complex test to require

4 hours of staff time. She estimates the demand for each type of test for June through August to be the following:

Month	Simple Routine	Simple Nonroutine	Complex
June	800	250	450
July	600	200	400
August	750	225	450

Laboratory staff salaries, including fringe benefits, average $3,600 per month. Each worker works 150 hours per month. If the hospital workload exceeds the available staff time, Dr. Benson has the tests performed at a neighboring private pathology laboratory that charges $80 for a simple routine test, $100 for a simple nonroutine test, and $160 for a complex test.

Dr. Benson is thinking of employing 20 to 27 workers. Because of the difficulty in hiring reliable workers, Barrington's chief administrator has instructed her to employ laboratory staff for no shorter a period than one quarter.

Required

(a) Determine how many workers Dr. Benson should employ over the quarter to minimize the costs of performing the tests. What is the minimum cost?
(b) Suppose the easy availability of experienced laboratory staff allows Barrington Medical Center to change staffing loads each month. Determine the number of workers Dr. Benson should hire each month in these circumstances to minimize the costs of performing tests. What is the minimum cost?

LO 1, 2, 4 **3-70** *Value proposition, CVP analysis, fixed costs, and opportunity costs* Nordstrom, Inc. (http://www.nordstrom.com) and Saks Fifth Avenue (http://www.saksfifthavenue.com) are upscale retailers. Using the following sources, answer the questions below.

- Each company's history reported on its web page (from "About Us" at the company's home page, link to the company's history).
- Statements of each company's vision or mission.
- "Nordstrom Accelerates Plans to Straighten Out Business," *Wall Street Journal* (October 19, 2001).
- "Nordstrom Regains Its Luster," *Wall Street Journal* (August 19, 2004).
- "Struggling Saks Tries Alterations in Management," *Wall Street Journal* (January 10, 2006).

Required

(a) What is each company's value proposition as defined in Chapter 2 of this textbook?
(b) What measures did Nordstrom take to reduce costs? How might these reductions affect Nordstrom's ability to fulfill its value proposition?
(c) What fixed costs did Nordstrom incur in hopes of long-term benefits? Have these benefits been realized?
(d) How did Nordstrom's efforts affect the cost–volume–profit elements of sales prices, variable costs, fixed costs, and volume of sales?
(e) How did each company attempt to expand its customer base and how successful were the efforts? Were any opportunity costs associated with Nordstrom's "Reinvent Yourself" campaign or Saks Fifth Avenue's "Wild about Cashmere" campaign?

LO 1, 2, 3, 4 **3-71** *Product mix decision* Aramis Aromatics Company produces and sells its product AA100 to well-known cosmetics companies for $940 per ton. The marketing manager is considering the possibility of refining AA100 further into finer perfumes before selling them to the cosmetics companies. Product AA101 is expected to command a price of $1,500 per ton and AA102 a price of $1,700 per ton. The maximum expected demand is 400 tons for AA101 and 100 tons for AA102.

The annual plant capacity of 2,400 hours is fully utilized at present to manufacture 600 tons of AA100. The marketing manager proposed that Aramis sell 300 tons of AA100, 100 tons of AA101, and 75 tons of AA102 in the next year. It requires 4 hours of capacity to make 1 ton of AA100, 2 hours to refine 1 ton of AA100 further into AA101, and 4 hours to refine 1 ton of AA100 into AA102 instead. The plant accountant has prepared the following information for the three products:

| | COSTS PER TON | | |
COST ITEM	AA100	AA101	AA102
Direct materials:			
Chemicals and fragrance	$560	$400	$470
AA100	0	800	800
Direct labor	60	30	60
Manufacturing overhead:			
Variable	60	30	60
Fixed	120	60	120
Total manufacturing costs	$800	$1,320	$1,510
Selling costs:			
Variable	20	30	30
Fixed	10	10	10
Total cost	$830	$1,360	$1,550
Proposed sales level	300 tons	100 tons	75 tons
Maximum demand	600 tons	400 tons	100 tons

Required

(a) Determine the contribution margin for each product.
(b) Determine the production levels for the three products under the present constraint on plant capacity that will maximize total contribution.
(c) Suppose a customer, Cosmos Cosmetics Company, is very interested in the new product AA101. It has offered to sign a long-term contract for 400 tons of AA101. It is also willing to pay a higher price if the entire plant capacity is dedicated to the production of AA101. What is the price for AA101 at which Aramis is indifferent between its current production of AA100 and dedicating its entire capacity to the production of AA101 for Cosmos?
(d) Suppose, instead, that the price of AA101 is $1,500 per ton and that the capacity can be increased temporarily by 600 hours if the plant is operated overtime. Overtime premium payments to workers and supervisors will increase direct labor and variable manufacturing overhead costs by 50% for all products. All other costs will remain unchanged. Is it worthwhile operating the plant overtime? If the plant is operated overtime for 600 hours, what are the optimal production levels for the three products?

LO 1, 2, 4   **3-72** *Variable and fixed costs in the wine industry, decision making*   A Votre Santé: Product Costing and Decision Analysis in the Wine Industry[3]

Background

A Votre Santé (AVS) is a small, independent winery owned by Kay Aproveche. Kay has a relationship with a grower who grows two types of wine grapes, a Chardonnay and a generic white grape. AVS buys the grapes at the point at which they have ripened on the vine. AVS is responsible for harvesting the grapes and all further processing of the grapes into wine. In 2010,

---

[3] © 2010 Priscilla S. Wisner. Adapted and used by permission of Priscilla S. Wisner.

AVS earned an operating margin of almost $100,000 on sales of $848,000, for an 11.6% margin (see Exhibit 3-38).

The process of winemaking is fairly simple, yet requires much attention to process details. After the grapes are harvested, they are brought to the winery for washing and crushing. The crushing process separates the juice from the pulp, skin, and stems. The juice is used to make the wine; the pulp, skin, and stems are recycled back onto the fields whenever possible or otherwise disposed of. The amount of wine generated from the grapes is dependent each year on a number of climatic and growing factors such as temperature, length of growing season, rootstock, and fertilizers used.

Once the juice is extracted, it moves into the fermenting process. The Chardonnay wine grape is fermented using oak barrels; the oak in the barrels gives flavor to the Chardonnay wine. The barrels are expensive ($500 each), but are sold after four years for $200 apiece to another smaller winery. The juice fermenting in each barrel results in the production of 40 cases of wine. The generic white grape juices are fermented in a holding tank; a full tank would result in the production of 1,500 cases of wine. The fermenting process takes place in a temperature-controlled environment; however, each fermenting method results in some wine loss through evaporation. Kay Aproveche estimates that the Chardonnay will lose approximately 10% of its volume through the fermentation process, while the generic white will lose approximately 5% of its volume. Harvest takes place in the late summer and early fall months; typically, the time elapsed from harvest to final sale is about 11 months.

Exhibit 3-38

Sales	Price	# Bottles		
Chardonnay-Estate	$22	24,000	$528,000	
Chardonnay (non-Estate)	$16	9,000	$144,000	
Blanc de Blanc	$11	16,000	$176,000	
Total revenues		49,000	$848,000	
Product costs				
Grapes			$124,000	
Bottle, labels, corks			122,500	
Harvest labor			14,500	
Crush labor			2,400	
Indirect materials			6,329	
Depreciation			8,100	
Lab expenses			8,000	
Production office			12,000	
Utilities			5,500	
Waste treatment			2,000	
Wine master			15,000	
Supervisor			55,000	
Barrels			4,725	
Total product costs			$380,054	44.8%
Gross margin			$467,946	55.2%
Administrative & sales costs				
Administrative rent & office			$20,000	
Liquor taxes			147,000	
Sales commissions			98,000	
Sales manager			30,000	
Administrative salary			75,000	
Total fixed costs			$370,000	
Operating margin			$97,946	11.6%

Product Information

AVS bottles three wines: a Chardonnay-Estate, a regular Chardonnay, and a Blanc de Blanc. Data related to the three wines is as follows:

- Chardonnay-Estate contains only Chardonnay grapes that are grown for AVS; the expected sales price is $22/bottle. The market demand for Chardonnay-Estate wine is estimated to be 24,000 bottles for 2010.
- Regular Chardonnay is blended by combining the Chardonnay wine left over after bottling the Chardonnay-Estate with the fermented generic wine; the blend mixture is two parts Chardonnay grapes (after fermentation) and one part generic grapes (after fermentation). The different grapes are fermented separately and blended at the end. The expected sales price is $16/bottle.
- Blanc de Blanc wine is made from all remaining generic white grapes; the expected sales price is $11/bottle.

All three wines are bottled at AVS using one bottling line. In a typical year, AVS bottles enough Chardonnay-Estate to meet the predicted market demand, then bottles the regular Chardonnay after blending all remaining Chardonnay wine with the necessary amount of generic grapes. The Blanc de Blanc is the last wine to be bottled, using all remaining generic white grapes. Kay again expects the wines from this harvest year to sell out.

Additional Operational and Cost Data

Chardonnay Grapes

- 2009 harvest: 100,000 pounds
- Purchase price of $85,500
- Expected loss in volume through fermentation and bottling: 10%

Generic White Grapes

- 2009 harvest: 60,000 pounds
- Purchase price of $38,500
- Expected loss in volume through fermentation and bottling: 5%

Winemaking

- Chardonnay grapes are fermented in oak barrels; each barrel results in the production of 40 cases of wine.
- Barrels cost $500 apiece, and can be used for four years and sold for $200 each at the end of four years; assume that you have to purchase all new barrels for the 2009 harvest. The barrels are depreciated over 4 years.
- Generic white grapes are fermented in the holding tank; the tank can hold up to the equivalent of 1,500 cases of wine.

Bottling

- Requires 36 pounds of grapes (post-fermenting) for one case (12 bottles) of wine.
- In the bottling process, the wine is put into bottles, with both corks and labels added during this process. The materials costs associated with the bottles, corks, and labels are estimated to be $2.50/bottle.

Direct Labor

- Harvest labor is paid an average of $7.25/hour. It is estimated that 80 pounds of grapes can be harvested each hour.
- Crush labor is paid an average of $8.00/hour. It is estimated that it will take 300 hours to crush the grape harvest.

Overhead Expenses

- Administrative rent and office expenses: estimated to be $20,000/year.
- Depreciation is charged based on the following equipment schedule:

EQUIPMENT	COST	ESTIMATED LIFE
Tractors	$15,000	10 years
Crushers	$6,000	10 years
Holding tank	$40,000	20 years
Bottle lines	$10,000	10 years
Other production equipment	$15,000	5 years

- *Indirect materials:* Part of the winemaking process involves introducing yeasts and other additives into the wine to help the fermentation process and to help balance the flavors in the wine. Indirect production materials average $1.55 per case of wine.
- *Lab expenses:* Lab expenses of $8,000 are incurred for lab supplies and equipment. The lab is used by the production supervisor and the winemaster to test the grapes and wine at various stages of production.
- *Liquor taxes:* AVS is required to pay a liquor excise tax of $3/bottle on every bottle of wine sold.
- *Production office:* AVS pays a part-time person to help administer the production function. This person orders supplies, reviews and approves production invoices, and performs other administrative functions. The production office budget is estimated to be a flat rate of $12,000.
- *Sales and related:* Kay's sister, Maria, is paid $30,000/year on a contract basis to sell AVS wines. She works through distributors, who are paid $2/bottle for each bottle sold.
- *Supervision:* Kay's brother, Luis, supervises the production of wine from the harvest through the bottling processes. His salary and benefits total $55,000 annually.
- *Utilities:* Utility costs are incurred primarily to maintain a constant temperature in the fermenting process. These are expected to be $5,500.
- *Waste treatment:* After crushing, the pulp, skins, and stems that are left over must be disposed of. One-half of the waste can be recycled back onto the fields as a compost material; the other one-half must be disposed of at a landfill dumping cost of $2,000.
- A winemaster is employed to help formulate and test the wines. This is done on a contract basis; AVS pays the winemaster $5,000 for each type of wine that is formulated.
- Kay's role is to manage the AVS business. Her annual salary and benefits total $75,000.

Required

(a) Create a single company-wide contribution margin income statement (as in the "Total" column in Exhibit 3-6) for AVS that includes each expense category. Also calculate the average revenue and net income for one bottle of wine. (*Note:* Do not break out the variable or fixed costs by type of wine.)

(b) Another grower has available 20,000 pounds of Chardonnay grapes from the 2009 harvest. AVS has the opportunity to buy the juice from these grapes (they have already been harvested and crushed). If AVS could blend these grapes with the generic white grapes (using the 2:1 blend formula) to produce a new Chardonnay wine to be priced at $14/bottle, and require a 15% return on sales for this wine, what is the maximum amount that AVS would pay for a pound of Chardonnay grapes?

(c) Other than the cost of the grapes seen in part b, what factors would you consider to support your purchase of the grapes, and what factors would cause you to reject buying the grapes?

Chapter 4

Accumulating and Assigning Costs to Products

After completing this chapter, you will be able to:

1. Describe the cost flows that take place in manufacturing, service, and retail organizations.
2. Understand the concepts of direct and indirect costs and appropriately classify a cost using these concepts.
3. Develop indirect cost rates for applying overhead costs to products.
4. Evaluate a cost system to determine whether it is likely to distort product costs.
5. Recognize how product and process characteristics define the appropriate structure of a costing system.
6. Design and interpret basic job order and process costing systems.
7. Understand the methods of allocating service department costs to production departments.

Strict's Custom Framing

Strict's Custom Framing provides high-end portrait framing. A large bank, which requires framed portraits of its senior-level managers, has approached Dana Strict, Strict's owner and president, for a quote to supply approximately 400 framed photographs over the next five years.

As part of the process of preparing a quote for the bank, Dana has asked Enid Pierce, the Strict's Customer Framing Controller, to prepare a cost estimate. Enid's preliminary research provided the following information. A professional portrait photographer will supply a photograph, approved by the client, for $700 per manager. The bank will contract with the photographer and pay this cost directly to the photographer.

The bank has specified a standard size and framing materials for all the portraits. The cost of framing materials including the wood frame

Alamy Images

stock, glass, mat, glue, backing, hardware used to hang the finished product, and the plaque engraved with each manager's name will be $350 per portrait. Enid is certain about the costs of these materials since they would be supplied under a fixed price contract by Strict's current suppliers. Strict's staff has packaged and shipped, via courier, a prototype portrait, and the shipping materials and shipping costs, including insurance, will cost $100 per portrait.

What Enid is not sure about are the other costs required to frame the portraits.

The framing process begins by cutting the wooden frame pieces from the stock provided by the supplier. Workers then assemble the wood frame using a jig, glue, and nails. Once the frame is ready, workers add the portrait, glass, mat, and backing. Finally, workers apply the hardware that is used to hang the portrait.

Enid is also uncertain about whether the other costs of manufacturing the frames, such as machine and labor costs, should be included in her estimate of the cost of each portrait.

IN PRACTICE

On the Importance of Understanding Costs in the Restaurant Business

". . . you have got to get the pricing just right. You cannot afford to overcharge or undercharge. That means knowing exactly how much every dish costs to produce and charging 2.5 times the cost." Attributed to David Adjey, celebrity chef and restaurant consultant, by Leon Goldstein, restaurateur.

COST MANAGEMENT SYSTEMS

In this and the next two chapters, we discuss how cost management systems measure the costs of products, services, and customers. Historically, two cost management systems, job order costing and process costing, have been used to cost products and services. Many companies continue to use these two systems. Since the mid-1980s, however, companies have been adopting activity-based costing for products, customers, and services. Cost management systems differ in the way that they assign indirect costs to cost objects. In this chapter, we focus on the two traditional methods: job order and process costing systems.

COST FLOWS IN ORGANIZATIONS

To compute product costs, management accounting systems should reflect the actual cost flows in organizations. Manufacturing, retail, and service organizations have very different patterns of cost flows resulting in different management accounting priorities.

Manufacturing Organizations

Exhibit 4-1 summarizes the manufacturing sequence in a simple organization. Recall from Chapter 3 that manufacturing costs are usually classified into three groups: direct materials, direct labor, and manufacturing overhead. Materials are withdrawn from raw materials inventory as production begins. The cost of the raw materials entered into production is moved from the raw materials account to the work-in-process inventory account. The manufacturing operation consumes labor and overhead items (such as machine time and factory supplies), the cost of which are assigned to production by adding them to the work-in-process inventory account. Overhead costs are assigned (or allocated or apportioned) as determined by the cost system. When manufacturing is completed, work is transferred to **finished goods inventory**, and costs are moved from the work-in-process inventory account to the finished goods inventory account. Finally, when goods are sold their costs are moved from the finished goods inventory account to cost of goods sold.

Although the production and costing process in most organizations is usually much more complex, Exhibit 4-1 provides the basic idea behind all manufacturing

Exhibit 4-1
Cost Flows in a
Manufacturing
Organization

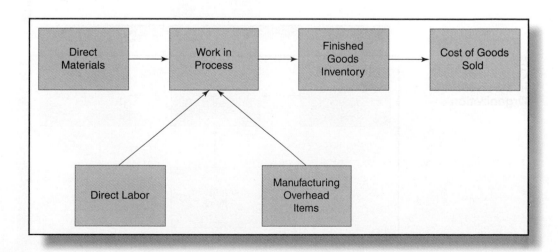

costing systems: to determine the costs that products accumulate as they consume organization resources during manufacturing. We will come back to Exhibit 4-1 later in this chapter as we discuss manufacturing cost accounting in more detail.

Retail Organizations

Exhibit 4-2 summarizes the flow of activities in a retail organization. As goods are purchased, their cost is entered into an account that accumulates the cost of merchandise inventory in the store. Stores incur various overhead costs such as labor, depreciation on the store, lighting, and heating. The primary focus in retail operations is the profitability of product lines or departments. Therefore, costing attention focuses, as in manufacturing operations, on how to allocate various overhead costs to determine, for example, the cost of purchasing and selling products, or department costs. However, unlike manufacturing operations where manufacturing overhead costs often account for about half of total costs to produce goods, merchandise costs in retail organizations can exceed 80% of total costs to purchase and sell goods. Therefore, the potential for distorting the cost of purchasing and selling products through inappropriate allocations of overhead costs is lower in retail organizations than in manufacturing organizations.

Service Organizations

Exhibit 4-3 summarizes the flow of activities in a service organization that undertakes major projects, such as in a consultancy. Unlike retail operations where the major cost item is merchandise, in service organizations the major cost item is usually employee pay. In such service organizations the focus is on determining the cost of a project. Since salaries and wages often comprise 80% or more of total project-related costs,

Exhibit 4-2
Cost Flows in a Retail Organization

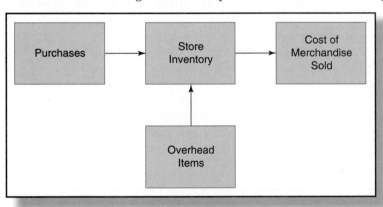

Exhibit 4-3
Cost Flows in a Service Organization

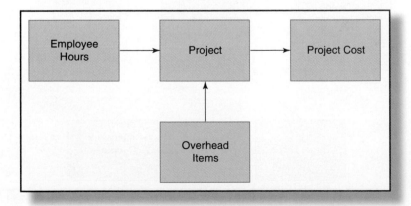

and they can be easily assigned to different projects or services, the potential for cost system distortions in such a service organization is less than in a manufacturing organization. Chapter 6 discusses costing complexities in service contexts where the cost of transacting with an additional customer is small. Examples of such contexts include banking, air travel, and telecommunications.

Because issues surrounding handling production overhead costs are more complex in manufacturing operations, in the following discussions we focus on costing issues in manufacturing organizations. The concepts, tools, and principles of costing in manufacturing organizations also apply in retail and service organizations.

SOME IMPORTANT COST TERMS

Before we develop the key issues in costing we need to develop a few important costing terms that we will use extensively in the discussion that follows.

Cost Object

A **cost object** is anything for which a cost is computed. Examples of cost objects are activities, products, product lines, departments, or even entire organizations.

Consumable Resources

The defining characteristic of a **consumable resource**, also called a **flexible resource**, is that its cost depends on the amount of resource that is used. Examples of consumable resources are wood in a furniture factory and iron ore in a steel mill. The cost of a consumable resource is often called a variable cost because the total cost depends on how much of the resource is consumed.

Capacity-Related Resources

The defining characteristic of a **capacity-related resource** is that its cost depends on the amount of resource capacity that is acquired and not on how much of the capacity is used. As the size of a proposed factory or warehouse increases, the associated capacity-related cost will increase. Examples of capacity-related costs are depreciation on production equipment (the capacity-related resource) and salaries paid to employees (the capacity-related resource) in a consultancy. The cost of a capacity-related resource is often called a fixed cost because the cost of the resource is independent of how much of the resource is used in the short run.

Direct and Indirect Costs

The usual way to proceed in cost classification is to decide whether a cost is direct. If the cost fails the test of being direct it is classified as indirect. A **direct cost** is a cost that is uniquely and unequivocally attributable to a single cost object.

IN PRACTICE
Cost Objects

Most people have experienced cost accumulation for a cost object. If you have had a car serviced, visited a dentist, or ordered from a menu in a restaurant, the services provided to you have been accumulated in some manner to identify the cost of your job.

This printing press provides its owner with the capacity to print newspapers for itself or its clients. The press capacity is defined by the number of hours it is scheduled to operate.
Alamy Images

If a single cost object consumes a consumable resource, the cost of the consumable resource is a direct cost for that cost object. The cost of wood used to make a table in a furniture factory is a direct cost that would be assigned to the table.

It is rare but possible for the cost of a consumable resource to be properly classified as indirect. For example, suppose that a number of different products are shipped to a customer in one truck. The fuel used by the truck is a consumable resource. However, the fuel is jointly used by all of the products being carried in the truck. Therefore, if the cost object is an individual product on board the truck, the cost of the fuel is an indirect cost to that product since all of the products on board the truck jointly consume the fuel.

Any cost that fails the test of being a direct cost is an **indirect cost**. This may sound simple, but disputes in costing about whether a cost (more correctly the resource that created the cost) should be treated as direct or indirect outnumber all other costing disputes.

Most capacity-related costs are indirect. It is unusual for a capacity-related cost to be a direct cost but it is not rare. For example, the cost of production equipment or a factory supervisor that was acquired for and used exclusively by one product is a direct cost for the product. A good test of whether the cost of a capacity resource is indirect is whether the organization would have no use for the resource if the cost object was abandoned.

IN PRACTICE
Indirect Costs

From the time of the Industrial Revolution until the early 20th century, manufacturing operations were mainly labor paced and direct costs comprised the majority of product costs. Since then indirect costs in the form of automation have gradually replaced labor costs and, for many products, are now the major component of total product costs. This increased use of indirect costs in manufacturing has increased the need for costing systems to deal adequately with indirect costs.

In summary, remember that we call the cost of consumable resources variable costs and *almost* all variable costs are direct costs. We call the cost of capacity resources fixed costs and *almost* all fixed costs are indirect costs.

Cost Classification and Context

The classification of a resource (and therefore its cost) as direct or indirect is context specific. Suppose you attend a multiple-campus university. You are a student in the Faculty of Business on one campus. One of your courses is a management accounting course that is offered by the Accounting Department in the Faculty of Business. The course instructor teaches six courses. Let's focus on the salary paid to your management accounting instructor.

If the cost object is the entire university, the university campus, the Faculty of Business, or the Department of Accounting, your instructor's salary is a direct cost. If the cost object is the course you are taking, your instructor's salary is an indirect cost. Why? Because your course is sharing a capacity-related resource (your instructor) with other courses. You might think that an obvious and intuitive approach would be to allocate one-sixth of your instructor's salary to the course you are taking. However, bickering inevitably arises in practice over cost allocations, even ones that seem sensible and intuitive. Exhibit 4-4 provides a summary of common variable and fixed costs and their classifications.

Going Forward

Costing systems first classify costs as direct or indirect. Direct costs are assigned to the appropriate cost object. Indirect costs are allocated to cost objects in a reasonable way, which means that the allocation ideally should reflect the cause-and-effect relationship between the long-run use of a capacity resource by a cost object and the associated cost of that long-run use.

Exhibit 4-4
Attributes of Direct and Indirect Costs

Resource Characteristic	Resource Name	Cost Name	Usual Classification
Consumed by the production process. The total cost of the resource is proportional to the amount of the resource consumed. Examples include: newsprint used to print a paper, plastic used to make laundry hampers, and grain used to make breakfast cereal.	Consumable resource	Variable cost	Direct cost
Provides capacity that is used by the production process. The total cost of the resource is proportional to the amount of the resource that is acquired not how much is used. Examples include: the salary paid to a lawyer, depreciation on factory equipment, and taxes paid on factory property.	Capacity-related resources	Fixed cost	Indirect cost

For the balance of this chapter we will assume that costs that are direct can be reasonably identified and assigned to the appropriate cost object. This assumption allows us to focus on the process of allocating indirect costs to cost objects.

HANDLING INDIRECT COSTS IN A MANUFACTURING ENVIRONMENT

Exhibit 4-5 reviews what we have done so far. The first step is to classify the cost as direct or indirect. If the cost is direct it is assigned directly to the appropriate cost object. If the cost is indirect, it is assigned to an indirect cost pool (there can be one or many). An appropriate portion of the indirect cost is then allocated from the cost pool (or pools) to the cost object (or objects).

We now consider some of the details surrounding the design and use of indirect cost pools.

The simplest structure in a manufacturing system is to have a single indirect cost pool for the entire manufacturing operation. This is the setting depicted in Exhibit 4-1. Examples of indirect costs in a factory setting, which are usually called fixed manufacturing overhead, include heating, lighting, depreciation on factory equipment, factory taxes, and supervisory salaries. In the simple costing system shown in Exhibit 4-1, these indirect costs are accumulated in a single indirect cost pool.

Some organizations create another category called variable overhead, which includes costs for such items as machine electricity usage, minor materials grouped as indirect materials (thread, glue, etc.), and machine supplies. Variable overhead costs are actually direct costs that are too costly and too immaterial (in relation to total product cost) to trace to individual cost objects. An example is the cost of the glue used to make each piece of furniture. These variable costs are accumulated in a variable cost account. Variable overhead costs may be assigned as direct costs. Alternatively, for simplicity, variable overhead costs may be grouped together with fixed

Exhibit 4-5
Costing System Structure

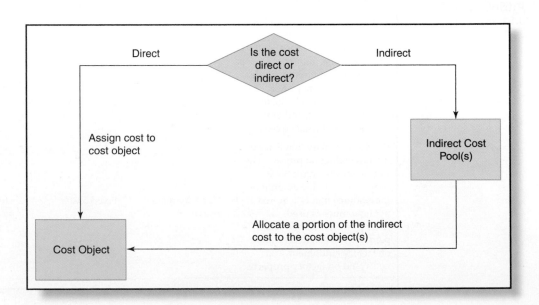

Exhibit 4-6
Cost Flows in a
Manufacturing
Organization

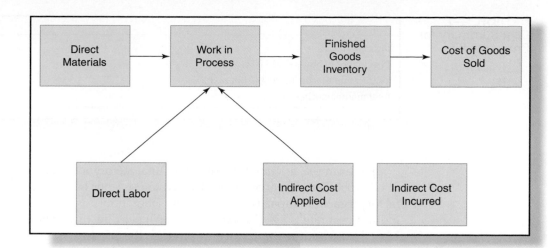

overhead in developing methods for allocating overhead to cost objects. In this chapter, we maintain the "indirect cost" terminology for overhead to emphasize the challenges in allocating fixed manufacturing overhead to cost objects.

Organizations use a separate account (such as "Indirect Cost Applied" in Exhibit 4-6) to record applied indirect costs (that is, indirect costs allocated as production occurs during the year). The resulting situation is shown in Exhibit 4-6, which shows one indirect cost account that accumulates the actual indirect costs that have been incurred, and a second indirect cost account that accumulates the indirect costs that have been applied to production. Later we will discuss the reconciliation between the two accounts, but for now we will focus on how the indirect cost applied account operates.

Because the total indirect costs for the year are not known until after the year end, when all the costs have been accumulated, organizations allocate indirect costs to production during the year using a predetermined indirect cost rate. The first step in developing this rate is to determine the basis, often called the cost driver, which will be used to allocate the indirect cost to production. Cost analysts try to choose a cost driver that best explains the long-run behavior of the indirect cost. In a labor-intensive environment the cost driver of indirect costs in the factory might be labor hours as factory workers use factory space, utilities, and other overhead resources to make products. In a machine-intensive environment the cost driver of indirect costs in the factory might be machine hours because machines consume electricity, lubricants, and other supplies to make products.

Once the cost driver is chosen, cost analysts divide expected indirect factory costs by the number of cost driver units to compute what is called the predetermined indirect cost rate. Other common names for this rate include predetermined overhead rate and cost driver rate. We use these terms interchangeably in this chapter.

The choice of the number of cost driver units to use to determine the predetermined indirect cost rate is a source of debate. We will sidestep that debate for a moment and assume that the cost driver unit chosen in calculating the predetermined indirect cost rate is the factory's practical capacity. We can now compute the predetermined indirect cost rate as follows:

$$\text{predetermined indirect cost rate} = \frac{\text{estimated total factory indirect cost}}{\text{practical capacity in cost driver units}}$$

Exhibit 4-7
Cost Summary for
Product X456

	Unit Cost
Direct materials	$27.89
Direct labor (2 hours @ $25.00 per hour)	50.00
Indirect manufacturing cost (2 hours @ $56.00)	112.00
Total manufacturing cost	$189.89

For example, assume that estimated total factory indirect cost at Tim Company is $14,000,000. The cost analyst has decided to use labor hours as the cost driver, and the factory practical capacity expressed in labor hours is 250,000. The predetermined indirect cost rate is $56 (14,000,000/250,000) per direct labor hour. Therefore for every labor hour used in the factory to produce the product, $56 of indirect cost will be applied to the product. This example uses what is called a predetermined plantwide indirect cost rate since a single indirect cost rate is used for the entire factory. Exhibit 4-7 provides a cost summary for Product X456.

Multiple Indirect Cost Pools

Most organizations use multiple indirect cost pools in order to improve costing. Improvement in costing is defined as the ability of the costing system to more accurately reflect the cause-and-effect relationship between the cost object and the cost of the resources used by the cost object.

Many products require a humidity-controlled atmosphere that is free of any airborne particles. These clean rooms are very expensive to build and maintain and their costs should only be allocated to those products that require their use.

Alamy Images

Indirect cost pool design is considered to be one of the most important choices in costing system design and requires a considerable amount of skill and understanding of the manufacturing process in the organization. The two most widely used alternatives for designing multiple indirect cost pools are to base them on organizational units, such as departments, or activities (sometimes processes), such as setup and manufacturing.

We will continue the example at Tim Company to illustrate multiple cost pools designed around organizational units. Production involves two major activities, which are organized into departments: manufacturing and assembly. Workers in the Manufacturing Department enter large pieces of sheet metal into a computer-controlled machine that cuts the sheets of metal into the pieces needed to make the two products.

Workers in the Assembly Department assemble the pieces of metal and undertake finishing operations such as grinding and coating. Machines do most of the work (called a machine-paced operation) in the Manufacturing Department, and workers do most of the work in the Assembly Department (called a labor-paced operation). Mumtaz Khan, the production supervisor at Tim Company, believes that the current system has the potential to distort product costs because the company's two most important products place very different demands on the manufacturing system, as shown in Exhibit 4-8.

The major difference between the two products is that Product X458 is assembled using fewer but much larger pieces than Product X456. Therefore, relative to X456 it takes longer to cut the pieces for X458 in the Machining Department, but less time to assemble them in the Assembly Department.

It is important to remember that costing system distortions relate to the handling of indirect costs. Direct costs are not subject to distortions caused by inappropriate costing system design relating to the handling of indirect costs. Therefore, in the following discussion we will focus only on the treatment of the products' indirect costs.

Suppose that the plant accountant advises that $9,000,000 of the plant's indirect costs are appropriately assigned to the Machining Department and $5,000,000 of the plant's indirect costs are appropriately assigned to the Assembly Department.

The practical capacity of the Machining Department expressed in machine hours (the assumed cost driver in that department) is 30,000 and the practical capacity of the Assembly Department expressed in labor hours (the assumed cost driver in that department) is 200,000. Therefore we can compute the predetermined indirect cost rate for the two departments as follows:

$$\text{predetermined indirect cost rate Machining Department} = \frac{9,000,000}{30,000} = \$300$$

$$\text{predetermined indirect cost rate Assembly Department} = \frac{5,000,000}{200,000} = \$25$$

Exhibit 4-8
Production Requirement for Products X456 and X458

	PRODUCT X456		PRODUCT X458	
	MACHINING DEPARTMENT	ASSEMBLY DEPARTMENT	MACHINING DEPARTMENT	ASSEMBLY DEPARTMENT
Direct labor hours	0.25	1.75	0.30	0.75
Machine hours	0.15	0.05	0.25	0.06

Exhibit 4-9
Indirect Cost
Allocations for
Products X456
and X458

INDIRECT COST ALLOCATION PRODUCT X456	
From machining (0.15 × $300)	$45.00
From assembly (1.75 × $25)	43.75
	$88.75

INDIRECT COST ALLOCATION PRODUCT X458	
From machining (0.25 × $300)	$75.00
From assembly (0.75 × $25)	18.75
	$93.75

Exhibit 4-9 summarizes the indirect cost allocations resulting from the two-department system.

Note that the indirect cost allocation to Product X458 under the plantwide rate system is $58.80 [(0.30 + 0.75) × $56]. Recalling the earlier calculation of the factory indirect cost allocation to Product X456 in the plantwide rate system, we have the comparative results shown in Exhibit 4-10.

The two-rate system tracks the two products' use of the capacity resources (machine time and labor time) more closely and, therefore, provides a more accurate and meaningful allocation of the costs of the capacity resources the two products use. Note that for Product X458 the allocated indirect cost increases (relative to the plantwide rate approach) because of its heavier consumption of machine time (the more costly resource). For Product X456 the allocated indirect cost drops because it consumed relatively less of the more costly resource.

Cost Pool Homogeneity

Costing distortions can arise when indirect cost pools include costs that have different cost drivers. The following example illustrates this idea.

Cambridge Chemicals

Cambridge Chemicals manufactures two products used for disinfecting sensitive surfaces such as operating theaters in hospitals. The major difference in the two products is that one has an active ingredient that causes the product to have a shelf life of only about 60 days. The other product has virtually unlimited shelf life.

Indirect factory overhead at Cambridge Chemicals amounts to $35,000,000 per accounting period. The factory accountant believes that the practical capacity of the plant is best represented by production volume, which is 2,000,000 liters of product.

Exhibit 4-10
Indirect Cost
Allocations Using
Plantwide versus
Multiple Indirect
Rates for Products
X456 and X458

	PRODUCT X456		PRODUCT X458	
	CALCULATION	AMOUNT	CALCULATION	AMOUNT
Plantwide system	(.25 + 1.75) × 56	$112.00	(.30 + 75) × 56	$58.80
Multiple indirect rate system	(.15 × 300) + (1.75 × 25)	$88.75	(.25 × 300) + (.75 × 25)	$93.75

	PRODUCT	
	X234	X334
Direct materials	$35.00	$44.50
Direct labor	12.00	14.25
Variable overhead	4.25	6.75
Fixed overhead	17.50	17.50
Total cost	$68.75	$83.00
Price	$137.50	$166.00

This results in a predetermined factory overhead rate of $17.50 ($35,000,000/2,000,000) per liter of product. Exhibit 4-11 summarizes the resulting cost per liter estimate for each product, which was doubled to determine the selling price of each product.

Based on complaints that Product X234 seemed overpriced relative to its competitors and X334 underpriced, a cost study was undertaken. This study revealed that approximately $8,000,000 of the indirect overhead costs relate to providing the capacity for setting up production runs. Setup costs are high because the packaging machines have to be carefully cleaned and disinfected to ensure product integrity. Product X234 is usually produced in batches averaging 10,000 liters, whereas X334 is usually produced in batches averaging 1,000 liters.

With this information in mind, the factory accountant organized the fixed manufacturing overhead into two pools. The first pool of $27,000,000 in costs was allocated based on production volume and the second pool of $8,000,000 was deemed to supply setup capacity amounting to 1,000 batches per period. The predetermined rates for volume-driven and setup-driven overhead were then computed as $13.50 ($27,000,000/2,000,000) and $8,000 ($8,000,000/1,000), respectively. This resulted in the product cost estimates reported in Exhibit 4-12.

This example illustrates the costing distortions that can arise when an indirect cost pool includes costs with different cost drivers and where different products use the capacities underlying the indirect costs differentially. In this case Product X334, a heavy user of setup activities, was being undercosted in the volume-based system because significant costs were being driven by setups and not production volume.

Exhibit 4-12
Cambridge
Chemicals: Costs
Based on Volume-
Driven and Setup-
Driven Overhead
Rates

	PRODUCT	
	X234	X334
Direct materials	$35.00	$44.50
Direct labor	12.00	14.25
Variable overhead	4.25	6.75
Indirect overhead		
Volume driven overhead (1 liter @ $13.50)	13.50	13.50
Setup driven overhead ($8,000/10,000)	0.80	
Setup driven overhead ($8,000/1,000)		8.00
Total cost	$65.55	$87.00
Price (total cost × 2)	$131.10	$174.00

Exhibit 4-13
Job Order Costing at Raul Company

Cost Type	Step 1	Step 2	Step 3
Direct costs			
	Materials	Materials	Materials
	5 units of lumber @ $2.50 per unit	None	1.5 units of finish @ $3.50 per unit
	Labor	Labor	Labor
	0.5 labor hour @ $22.50 per hour	0.25 labor hour @ $28.00 per hour	0.75 labor hour @ $18.00 per hour
Indirect costs			
	Cost driver	Cost driver	Cost driver
	Labor hours – 0.5	Machine hours – 0.15	Labor hours
	Cost driver rate	Cost driver rate	Cost driver rate
	$11.00 per labor hour	$55.00 per machine hour	$14.00 per labor hour
Cost calculation			
Materials	$12.50	$0.00	$5.25
Labor	11.25	7.00	13.50
Indirect cost	5.50	8.25	10.50
Total cost	$29.25	$15.25	$29.25
Total product cost	$73.75		

Raul Company

Here is an example that summarizes our work to date.

Raul Company manufactures wooden doors. The manufacturing is done in three steps. In the first step workers glue pieces of wood together to form the door and then trim the door to the required size. In the second step the door is placed on a platform and a computer-controlled router creates the door engraving the customer requires. In the third step the door is treated with the finish specified by the customer and then packed for shipment to the customer. The work in steps 1 and 3 is labor paced and the work in step 2 is machine paced. Each step has its own cost driver and its own cost driver rate.

Exhibit 4-13 summarizes the resource use and the costs for each of the three steps and the total product cost, which is $73.75 ($29.25 + 15.25 + 29.25).

OVERHEAD ALLOCATION: FURTHER ISSUES

Using Planned Capacity Cost

Earlier we mentioned that cost analysts use the planned, not the actual, level of capacity-related costs in computing the cost driver rate. A number of practical reasons are given for this:

1. The annual actual capacity-related costs are not known until the end of the accounting period (which is usually a year), and cost analysts want to compute costs for cost objects such as customers, products, and jobs before the year end.

The U.S. Defense Department said that it pulled certification for a Lockheed Martin Corp system used to analyze costs for aeronautics programs including the F-35 because of a lack of progress in addressing deficiencies. The Pentagon determined that withdrawal of compliance for Lockheed's "earned value management system" at its Fort Worth, Texas, facility was needed to make sure that the company takes corrective steps in a timely fashion, Defense Department spokesman Cheryl Irwin said in a statement.

Earned value management systems, or EVMS, are used by companies to plan, control, and analyze the cost performance of programs and identify potential overruns. The move comes as the Pentagon looks to end years of massive cost overruns on weapons programs.

Source: Adapted from Reuters, *Update 1—Lockheed Cost-Tracking System Loses Certification,* retrieved October 6, 2010, from http://www.reuters.com/article/idUSN0523484020101005

Reuters Limited

2. Using planned rather than actual capacity-related costs sets a benchmark against which to compare actual capacity-related costs at the end of the accounting period.

Reconciling Actual and Applied Capacity Costs

Recall from the discussion above that to manage a system of allocating indirect costs using a cost driver that is based on planned costs, cost analysts use two cost pools for each capacity-related cost. One pool accumulates the actual capacity-related cost incurred during the period. The second pool accumulates the capacity-related cost that has been applied to production. At the end of the year the balances in the two accounts must be reconciled.

Suppose that Watts Company uses a single indirect cost pool and has estimated capacity-related costs to be $10,000,000 for the year. Watts Company uses the practical capacity of the capacity resource, which is 50,000 machine hours, to compute the cost driver rate of $200 ($10,000,000/50,000) per machine hour.

During the year actual capacity-related costs were $9,500,000, which is the balance in the indirect cost pool that accumulates the actual costs. Production required 45,000 machine hours. The balance in the indirect cost applied cost pool will be $9,000,000 (45,000 × $200). The two accounts must be reconciled, which raises the question of what the cost analyst should do with the $500,000 difference. Note that the actual cost is $500,000 greater than the cost that has been applied to production. The cost analyst has to charge this unallocated actual cost of $500,000 to something.

Option 1: Charge the difference between actual and applied indirect costs to cost of goods sold.

The simplest option is simply to charge the $500,000 to the cost of goods sold in the current period. That is, cost of goods sold is increased by $500,000.

Option 2: Prorate the difference between actual and applied indirect costs to work in process, finished goods, and cost of goods sold.

The second approach is to prorate the $500,000 difference proportionately to the ending balances of work in process, finished goods inventory, and cost of goods sold. For example, if the proportion of applied indirect cost in the ending balances of these accounts this period is 25% in ending work in process, 30% in finished goods inventory, and 45% in cost of goods sold, the $500,000 of costs would be used to increase the balance of **work-in-process inventory**, finished goods inventory, and cost of goods sold by $125,000 (25% × $500,000), $150,000 (30% × $500,000), and $225,000 (45% × $500,000), respectively.

Option 3: Decompose the difference between actual and applied indirect costs into two parts: (1) the difference between actual and budgeted indirect costs and (2) the difference between budgeted and applied indirect costs.

This option is the most complex. However, it focuses on developing information that helps identify the reasons for the difference between actual and applied costs and is, therefore, relevant for internal decision-making purposes.

1. The difference between actual and budgeted indirect costs is −$500,000 ($9,500,000 − $10,000,000) which reflects a favorable indirect cost spending variance. (Recall that in the short run this cost is fixed.) The lower actual cost creates a favorable effect on income, relative to the budgeted cost. The difference would be charged directly to cost of goods sold. Note that this charge would *reduce* the balance of cost of goods sold by $500,000.
2. The difference between budgeted and applied indirect costs is $1,000,000 ($10,000,000 − $9,000,000). This difference results from idle capacity. Recall that the machine hours practical capacity was 50,000, whereas the actual machine hours used totaled 45,000. This means that idle capacity was 5,000 (50,000 − 45,000) machine hours with an associated cost of $1,000,000 (5,000 × $200). This idle capacity cost would be charged directly to cost of goods sold.

The net effect of these two steps would be to increase the balance of cost of goods sold by $500,000 ($1,000,000 − $500,000). Although the net effect is the same as in Option 1, in Option 3 management receives more detailed information on reasons for the difference.

Cost Driver Level

The discussion to date has assumed that the appropriate cost driver level is practical capacity. Practical capacity is one of four commonly proposed activity levels used to compute the cost driver rate. The other three are (1) the actual level of operations, (2) the planned level of operations, and (3) the average level of operations.

Using Actual Costs and Actual Cost Driver Activity

Using the actual level of the cost driver to compute the cost driver rate results in what is called *actual costing* since the rate will be computed after completion of the period and will be computed by dividing the actual capacity-related costs by the actual level of the cost driver. This approach is advocated by those who believe that all cost allocations should reflect "actual" costs and is, therefore, motivated by the belief that any approach to allocating indirect costs that uses anything other than actual costs and actual cost driver rates will result in distortion of the costs reported in the income statement and the inventory valuations on the balance sheet. It is reasonable to say that most management accountants reject this approach on the grounds that, first, all costs are estimates and, second, using actual costs disguises the managerial insights provided by the other approaches.

Using Planned Cost and the Planned Level of the Cost Driver

Those who advocate computing the cost driver by dividing planned indirect cost by the planned level of the cost driver argue that this approach provides a practical attempt to allocate planned indirect costs and, therefore, provides a practical and appropriate basis for accurate product costing. Proponents of this approach are most concerned with providing what they call "accurate" costs in the income statement and inventory valuations on the balance sheet.

The first objection to this approach is the same as the objection to the actual costing approach mentioned above, namely, that all cost allocations are arbitrary and it is inappropriate to talk about an actual or accurate cost.

The second, and perhaps more important, objection is that the approach makes no economic sense. Whether costs are used for financial reporting or decision making, most observers argue that they should reflect some economic sense. The problem with this approach is that given capacity-related costs that are fixed, when the planned level of production goes down the cost driver rate will increase, causing the product cost to increase. When the planned level of production goes up, the cost driver rate will go down, causing the product cost to decrease. Given that capacity-related costs are driven by the amount of capacity that was acquired rather than what is used, the notion of a varying cost driver rate does not align with the reality that the capacity-related cost is not changing.

The third objection to this approach is the consequence when management uses cost-plus pricing. Note that as expected demand goes down, the cost driver rate will increase, causing the cost-plus price to increase. Increasing prices in the face of falling demand is never a good strategy and can cause what is called a death spiral. Increasing prices cause demand to fall, which leads to further price increases as the cost driver rate increases the cost-plus price. Consider also the situation in which a government is contracting with a supplier on a cost-plus basis. No rational government contracting agency would ever agree to increased costs and, therefore, prices driven by the contractor facing a falling demand for capacity.

Using Planned Cost and the Average Level of Activity

On the surface computing a cost driver rate using planned indirect cost and the average level of activity over the capacity's life appears to deal with the problems of the two methods just described. The average use of capacity is, after all, the likely activity rate used to justify the acquisition of the capacity, so this approach would seem to reflect the economic basis for the level and cost of the capacity.

The major problem with this approach is that it buries the cost of idle capacity in product cost and provides no clear incentive for management to increase its use of idle capacity. Moreover if this approach results in computing a product cost that should be compared to the long-run market price needed to support this product, the cost will be illusionary since no customer will pay one supplier more for its product simply because the customer is recovering more of the cost of idle capacity through its price than a competitor that has lower idle capacity costs.

Exhibit 4-14
Texas Metal Works: Theoretical and Practical Capacity

		Hours	% of Theoretical Capacity
Theoretical capacity (weekly)	16 hours per day × 5 days per week	80.00	100.00%
Practical capacity deductions			
Allowance for maintenance	0.45 hours per day × 5 days per week	2.25	2.81%
Setup time loss	1.25 hours per day × 5 days per week	6.25	7.81%
Unscheduled repairs and down time	3.75 hours per week	3.75	4.69%
Lost time due to materials shortage	1.8 hours per week	1.80	2.25%
Total time lost each week		14.05	17.56%
Practical capacity		65.95	82.44%

In conclusion, using practical capacity to estimate product cost provides an approach that is not only practical but provides clear decision-making insights and incentives related to dealing with the cost of idle capacity.

Estimating Practical Capacity

Estimating practical capacity begins with an estimate of theoretical capacity. Suppose a machine is nominally available for 100 hours each week. A common rule of thumb is to set practical capacity equal to 80% of theoretical capacity. In other words, allow about 20% of theoretical capacity or, in this case, 20 hours for activities such as maintenance, setup, and repair.

In the case of labor hired for the year, theoretical capacity is 2,080 hours (52 weeks, 40 hours per week). However, workers on average have 3 weeks off and, with breaks, work about 35 hours per week. Therefore, practical capacity is 1,715 hours (49 weeks, 35 hours per week). In this case practical capacity is about 82% (1,715/2,080) of theoretical capacity.

Texas Metal Works

Texas Metal Works (TMW) uses hydroforming to produce a wide variety of metal parts for its customers. The key resource—and key bottleneck—at TMW is the hydroforming machine, which is scheduled for operation 16 hours per day, five days per week. A study of machine use during the past two years suggests that, on average, this machine requires 0.45 hour of maintenance each day, is idle about 1.25 hours each day while it is being set up, requires about 3.75 hours of repairs per week, and is idled 1.8 hours per week due to materials shortages. Exhibit 4-14 shows that the theoretical capacity of this machine is 80 hours each week and that practical capacity is 65.95 hours each week. Put another way, practical capacity is 82.44% of theoretical capacity.

JOB ORDER AND PROCESS SYSTEMS

Job Order Costing

Job order costing is an approach to costing that estimates costs for specific customer orders because the orders vary from customer to customer. At an extreme, each product or service may be unique. Examples of situations in which job order costing might

The staff in this dental office will maintain a sheet that summarizes all of the work done on this patient in order to develop a bill for the actual services provided.

Alamy Images

be used include a consulting engagement for a client, building a nuclear reactor for a power utility, providing a meal from a restaurant menu, or treating a patient in a hospital. In each of these cases the organization providing the product or service will typically assign all direct material and direct labor costs to the job. Then the organization will allocate overhead costs to the job using one of the approaches for handling indirect costs that we discussed earlier.

The purpose of the job order costing system is to accumulate the cost of the job because, due to job differences, costs will vary across jobs. Each job will have a cost that is computed by summing the direct and indirect costs of each department or activity that was used to complete the job.

Process Costing

Process costing is an approach to costing that is used when all products are identical. The total cost of all products is determined by adding up all of the direct and indirect costs used to produce the products and then dividing by the number of products produced to get a cost per unit. Examples of products for which process costing is appropriate are soda drinks, breakfast cereal, plastic water bottles, and routine services such as providing influenza inoculations at a medical clinic.

In this setting cost analysts focus on the components of total product cost. Let's look at an example that illustrates a simple process costing environment.

The National Mint

The National Mint manufactures currency and collector coins. The steps to manufacture pure silver collector coins are as follows:

1. *Melting and casting*—Silver is melted and then cast into bars.
2. *Roughing and finishing*—The silver bars are run through a roughing mill and then a finishing mill to produce strips of silver in the width of the coins that will be made.
3. *Blanking*—The silver strips are run through a blanking machine that punches out blank disks that will be used to make the coins.
4. *Rimming*—The blank disks are put through a rimming machine that puts rims on the blank disks.
5. *Annealing*—Several times during the manufacturing process the blank disks are heated, a process called annealing, to make them less brittle.
6. *Cleaning*—The disks are put through a cleaning tub where they are mixed with water and abrasives to smooth and polish them.
7. *Coin press*—The disks are put into a coin press where they are simultaneously punched on the top and bottom to create the coin. This stamping is done twice.

Each of these seven steps is a process that is required to make the silver collector coins. Cost analysts will accumulate the costs of each process in order to compute the cost of each process required to make the coin. Exhibit 4-15 illustrates what this process costing system might look like to make 100,000 one-ounce pure silver collector coins.

Mint managers will use this process costing information to identify opportunities to reduce process costs. For example, management may feel that the cost of fuel used in annealing is too high and either look for alternative suppliers of the fuel or possibly invest in a new more energy-efficient furnace.

In summary, the focus in process costing is to identify the cost that each process or activity used to make a product contributes to the product's total cost. This cost information is used to highlight opportunities to reduce the overall product cost

Exhibit 4-15
The National Mint: Process Costing for Silver Collector Coins

Cost Item	Melting and Casting	Roughing and Finishing	Blanking	Rimming	Annealing	Cleaning	Coin Press
Cost transferred in from previous process	0	$2,363,000	$2,425,000	$2,467,000	$2,494,000	$2,625,000	$2,679,000
Cost added by this process							
Materials	$2,300,000	$6,000	$1,000	$3,000	$75,000	$23,000	$4,000
Direct labor	18,000	24,000	16,000	9,000	19,000	18,000	25,000
Overhead	45,000	32,000	25,000	15,000	37,000	13,000	45,000
Total cost for this process	$2,363,000	$62,000	$42,000	$27,000	$131,000	$54,000	$74,000
Cost per coin in this process	$23.63	$0.62	$0.42	$0.27	$1.31	$0.54	$0.74
Total cost per coin to date	$23.63	$24.25	$24.67	$24.94	$26.25	$26.79	$27.53
Total cost transferred to next process	$2,363,000	$2,425,000	$2,467,000	$2,494,000	$2,625,000	$2,679,000	$2,753,000

either by reengineering the process or possibly looking to an outsider to undertake one or more of the processes.

Some Process Costing Wrinkles

As you might expect process costing systems are usually more complicated than that shown in Exhibit 4-15. To illustrate one of the more important practical considerations in process costing, consider the following example.

Donald's Ducks

Donald's Ducks has just gone into business to manufacture hand-carved wooden ducks. The manufacturing process begins with a solid block of pine. Each craftsman then uses chisels, small sanders, and polishers to create the final product, which is given a light coat of clear stain.

During the most recent period, 3,500 blocks of wood were entered into production. At the end of the period 2,500 units had been completed and shipped off to customers. Exhibit 4-16 summarizes the costs incurred during the most recent period. Direct materials costs relate almost entirely to the cost of the pine blocks. Direct labor refers to the wages paid to factory employees who carve the ducks. Variable factory overhead refers to the consumables such as chisels, sanding disks, and stains the carvers use. The fixed factory overhead relates to the cost of supervisory and other factory workers and other factory-related costs such as heating, electricity, and depreciation on factory equipment.

If all production had been completed, the process costing would be trivial since the cost of each duck would be computed as $64.00 ($224,000/3,500). The issue that arises in process costing, particularly for financial reporting purposes, is how to account for partially completed work in process. To do this, we use the concept of an equivalent unit of production, which expresses the work equivalent, in finished units of the work, that has been invested in work in process. For example, the equivalent units of 100 units that are 40% complete are 40 (100 × 40%).

Process costing systems use two different cost terms: direct materials costs and conversion costs. Conversion costs include all manufacturing costs that are not direct materials costs; that is, conversion costs consist of labor and factory overhead.

In the case of Donald's Ducks, direct materials costs are $42,000 and conversion costs are $182,000 (80,000 + 8,000 + 94,000). To undertake process costing for this simple example, we begin by identifying the physical flow as shown in Exhibit 4-17.

Next we compute equivalent units. For any units that are completed, the number of equivalent units will equal the number of physical units. So our focus is on the ending work in process. Notice that since all materials are introduced at the start of production, all units in work in process will be 100% complete with regard to materials. Therefore, the equivalent units with respect to materials will equal the physical units and will be 1,000. Now suppose that, on average, the ending work in process is

Exhibit 4-16
Donald's Ducks: Production Costs

Cost Item	Amount
Direct materials	$42,000
Direct labor	80,000
Variable factory overhead	8,000
Fixed factory overhead	$94,000
Total cost this period	$224,000

Exhibit 4-17
Donald's Ducks:
Physical Flows

PHYSICAL FLOW	PHYSICAL UNITS
Opening work in process	0
Started this period	3,500
Units to account for	3,500
Completed and transferred out	2,500
Ending work in process	1,000
Units accounted for	3,500

10% complete with regard to the total work that has to be done to turn the original block of wood into the finished product. Therefore, the work done on the 1,000 blocks of wood in ending inventory is equivalent to 100 (1,000 × 10%) units of conversion work on completed units. Exhibit 4-18 summarizes our work so far.

Next we introduce the costs we need to account for. Exhibit 4-19 summarizes the costs noted in Exhibit 4-16.

The next step is to compute the cost per equivalent unit of work. To do this, we divide the total materials cost by the equivalent units of materials and the total conversion costs by the equivalent units of conversion. Exhibit 4-20 shows this calculation.

Exhibit 4-20 provides important management information since it pinpoints the cost per unit produced for each of the major production activities. The calculation shows that the materials costs per duck is $12 and the total manufacturing cost to convert the raw block of wood into the finished product is $70.

The final step is to use the equivalent cost calculation to allocate the total manufacturing costs to ending work in process and the finished goods. Exhibit 4-21 summarizes how costs would be distributed to ending work in process and finished goods. Note that, as required, all manufacturing costs have been accounted for.

Final Comments on Process Costing

In practice, process costing is more complicated when production involves multiple departments and defective (spoiled) production. However, the principles and the

Exhibit 4-18
Donald's Ducks:
Equivalent Units

			EQUIVALENT UNITS	
PHYSICAL FLOW		PHYSICAL UNITS	MATERIALS	CONVERSION COSTS
Percentage completion				
Ending inventory			100%	10%
Opening work in process		0		
Started this period		3,500		
Units to account for		3,500		
Completed and transferred out		2,500	2,500	2,500
Ending work in process		1,000	1,000	100
Units accounted for		3,500		
Total work done this period			3,500	2,600

Exhibit 4-19
Donald's Ducks:
Equivalent Units
and Production
Costs

PHYSICAL FLOW	PHYSICAL UNITS	EQUIVALENT UNITS	
		MATERIALS	CONVERSION COSTS
Percentage completion			
Ending inventory		100%	10%
Opening work in process	0		
Started this period	3,500		
Units to account for	3,500		
Completed and transferred out	2,500	2,500	2,500
Ending work in process	1,000	1,000	100
Units accounted for	3,500		
Work done this period		3,500	2,600
	TOTAL PRODUCTION COSTS	MATERIALS	CONVERSION COSTS
Costs in opening inventory	$0	$0	$0
Costs incurred this period	224,000	42,000	182,000
Costs incurred to date	$224,000	$42,000	$182,000

Exhibit 4-20
Donald's Ducks:
Costs per
Equivalent Unit

PHYSICAL FLOW	PHYSICAL UNITS	EQUIVALENT UNITS	
		MATERIALS	CONVERSION COSTS
Percentage Completion			
Ending Inventory		100%	10%
Opening work in process	0		
Started this period	3,500		
Units to account for	3,500		
Completed and transferred out	2,500	2,500	2,500
Ending work in process	1,000	1,000	100
Units accounted for	3,500		
Work done this period		3,500	2,600
	TOTAL PRODUCTION COSTS	MATERIALS	CONVERSION COSTS
Costs in opening inventory	$0	0	0
Costs incurred this period	224,000	42,000	182,000
Costs incurred to date	$224,000	$42,000	$182,000
Divide by equivalent units of work this period		3,500	2,600
Cost per equivalent unit	$82.00	$12.00	$70.00
Total costs to account for	$224,000		

objectives remain the same: compute the cost per equivalent unit for each of the components of manufacturing in order to identify where process improvements (i.e., cost reductions) might be possible. Dealing with these more complex issues is left to a more advanced course in management accounting.

Exhibit 4-21
Donald's Ducks:
Costs Distributed
to Ending Work
in Process
and Finished

PHYSICAL FLOW	PHYSICAL UNITS	EQUIVALENT UNITS MATERIALS	EQUIVALENT UNITS CONVERSION COSTS
Percentage completion Ending inventory		100%	10%
Opening work in process	0		
Started this period	3,500		
Units accounted for	3,500		
Completed and transferred out	2,500	2,500	2,500
Ending work in process	1,000	1,000	100
Units accounted for	3,500		
Work done this period		3,500	2,600

	TOTAL PRODUCTION COSTS	MATERIALS	CONVERSION COSTS
Costs in opening inventory	$0	0	0
Costs incurred this period	224,000	42,000	182,000
Costs incurred to date	$224,000	$42,000	$182,000
Divide by equivalent units of work this period		3,500	2,600
Cost per equivalent unit	$82.00	$12.00	$70.00
Total costs to account for	$224,000		
Cost Allocation Work in process ending inventory			
Materials	12,000	= 1,000 equivalent units × $12 per unit	
Conversion costs	7,000	= 100 equivalent units × $70 per unit	
Total work in process	$19,000		
Completed and transferred out			
Materials	30,000	= 2,500 equivalent units × $12 per unit	
Conversion costs	175,000	= 2,500 equivalent units × $70 per unit	
Total cost transferred out	$205,000		
Total costs accounted for	$224,000		

EPILOGUE TO STRICT'S CUSTOM FRAMING

Here is what Enid did to estimate the other costs involved in framing the portraits: First she identified the three departments used to complete the framing. The first department, Manufacturing Division, cut the frame pieces from the stock provided by the supplier and assembled the frames. Enid estimated that the total of all overhead costs in the Manufacturing Division, including labor, machinery, and other supplies was about $675,000. Since work in this department was labor intensive and labor driven, Enid decided that costs in this department were driven by labor hours. Enid estimated that the labor capacity in the Manufacturing Division was 15,000 hours so she estimated the conversion cost per labor hour as $45 per hour ($675,000/15,000). From observing workers prepare the prototype frame, Enid believed that a reasonable estimate of the time required to produce a frame in this department was 0.20 hour.

Exhibit 4-22
Strict's Custom
Framing: Cost
Summary

DIRECT COST		
Materials	$350.00	
Shipping	100.00	$450.00
CONVERSION COST		
Manufacturing Division (0.20 hours @ $45.00)	$9.00	
Finishing Division (0.30 hours @ $25.00)	7.50	
Packaging Division (((0.25 + (0.3 × 2) + 0.50)/60) hours @ $30)	0.68	17.18
TOTAL MANUFACTURING COST		$467.18

The second department in the framing operation is the Finishing Division. In this division workers complete the framing by adding the portrait, mat, glass, backing, and hardware. Enid estimated that the total of all overhead costs in the Finishing Division, including labor, machinery, heat, and other supplies, is about $625,000. Since work in this division is labor intensive and labor driven, Enid decided that costs in this department are driven by labor hours. Enid estimated that the labor capacity in the Finishing Division is 25,000 hours so she estimated the conversion cost per labor hour as $25 per hour ($625,000/25,000). From observing workers prepare the prototype frame, Enid believed that a reasonable estimate of the time required to finish the frames in this department is 0.30 hour.

The third department in the framing operation is the Packaging Division. In this division the frame is placed on the bed of a small machine that wraps the finished portrait first in bubble wrap, cardboard, and then paper before applying a sealing tape. Enid estimated the total overhead costs in this division, which consists of labor and machine overhead, to be $150,000. Since work in the Packaging Division is machine driven, Enid decided that costs in this department are driven by machine hours. Enid estimated the capacity in the Packaging Division to be 5,000 machine hours and the estimated conversion cost per machine hour to be $30 per hour ($150,000/5,000). The time to package a finished product is about 0.25 minute (while the employee placed the product on the packaging machine bed), 0.30 minute per square foot of portrait wrapped, and 0.50 minute to remove the wrapped portrait from the packaging machine and place it in the shipping bin. The size of these portraits is approximately 2 square feet.

With this information Enid developed the cost summary shown in Exhibit 4-22.

SUMMARY

This chapter reviewed the basic elements of costing systems. Costing systems focus on computing the cost of a cost object. Common cost objects are products, customers, product lines, departments, or even entire organizational divisions. A cost that is uniquely and unambiguously attributable to a cost object is called a direct cost. Most, but not all, direct costs are the costs of consumables such as raw materials that

are used to produce a product. The identifying characteristic of a direct cost is that it depends on how much of a resource is used.

Indirect costs are related to the costs of capacity resources such as machinery and factory supervision. The identifying characteristic of an indirect cost is that it depends on how much of the resource was acquired and not how much is used.

Cost analysts assign direct costs and allocate indirect costs to cost objects. Indirect costs are usually allocated using a predetermined indirect cost rate (also called a predetermined overhead rate or cost driver rate), which is computed by dividing the expected cost of the capacity resource by its practical capacity. The costs of indirect resources are accumulated in cost pools that are often organized around departments or activities.

Most organizations have so-called service departments that do not directly produce goods or services for customers, but instead provide services to the departments or activities that produce goods or services. Service department costs have traditionally been allocated to the production departments, where they are accumulated with the production departments' own costs and allocated to the cost objects. The appendix to this chapter explains allocation of service department costs to production departments.

Appendix 4-1

Allocating Service Department Costs

For convenience, in this appendix we will call departments that directly produce goods or services production departments. Factory production departments include machining, assembly, and finishing. Most organizations also have so-called service departments that do not directly produce goods or services for customers, but instead provide services to the departments or activities that produce goods or services. For example, factory service departments include machine maintenance and production scheduling. In a hospital, hospital maintenance and the personnel department are examples of service departments.

Service department costs have traditionally been allocated to the production departments, where they are accumulated with the production departments' own costs and allocated to the cost objects. This appendix explains three methods of allocating service department costs to production departments.

The process of allocating service department costs is best illustrated by an example. Accounting for the costs of service departments begins with accumulating each service department's costs. Recall in what follows that the objective is then to allocate all service department costs to the production departments.

Wellington Regional Hospital

Wellington Regional Hospital (WRH), which is a rural hospital, has four departments: Medical, Surgical, Maintenance, and Administration. (WRH has contracted out housekeeping and cafeteria services.) The Medical and Surgical Departments are production departments, and the Maintenance and Administration Departments are service departments.

For the upcoming accounting period the expected costs in the Maintenance and Administration Departments are $10,000,000 and $25,000,000 respectively.

Ramona Nasser, the WRH controller, has decided that the cost driver for the Maintenance and Administration Departments should be weighted square meters of floor space occupied and number of employees, respectively. Ramona is proposing a weighted cost driver because although the Surgical Department occupies only one-sixth of the floor space occupied by the Medical Department, the maintenance services provided to the Surgical Department are four times more intense than for the Medical Department.

Since the Medical and Surgical Departments must develop their predetermined overhead rates for the upcoming period, Ramona plans to allocate the planned service department costs using the planned service levels.

Exhibit 4-23 presents the planned results for the upcoming period showing the planned service units provided and the planned costs for each of the service departments.

Ramona also advises that the practical capacity of the Maintenance Department is 60,000 square meters of floor space, and the practical capacity of the Administration Department is 750 employees. Therefore, the planned idle capacity of the two departments is 10% [(60,000 − 54,000)/60,000] and 20% [(700 − 560)/700], respectively. Therefore, Ramona will charge $1,000,000 (10%) of the costs of the Maintenance Department and $5,000,000 (20%) of the costs of the Administration Department to the Cost of Idle Capacity account leaving balances shown in Exhibit 4-24 to be allocated.

Exhibit 4-23
Wellington Regional Hospital Planned Service Units and Costs

	MAINTENANCE	ADMINISTRATION	MEDICAL	SURGICAL	TOTAL	TOTAL COST
Maintenance	1,500	2,500	30,000	20,000	54,000	$10,000,000
Administration	110	50	250	150	560	$25,000,000
						$35,000,000

Exhibit 4-24
Wellington Regional Hospital: Adjustment for Idle Capacity

	MAINTENANCE	ADMINISTRATION	MEDICAL	SURGICAL	TOTAL	TOTAL COST
Maintenance	1,500	2,500	30,000	20,000	54,000	$9,000,000
Administration	110	50	250	150	560	$20,000,000
						$29,000,000

Approaches to Allocating Service Department Costs

Direct Method

The **direct method** of allocating service department costs ignores the services provided to the service departments. Dropping the services provided to maintenance and administration results in the following distribution of services, costs, and cost per unit of service.

Because the Maintenance Department provides a total of 50,000 units of service to the Medical and Surgical Departments and the total cost to be allocated is $9,000,000, the cost per unit of service provided is $180 (9,000,000/50,000). Therefore, the Maintenance Department costs to be allocated to the Medical and Surgical Departments are $5,400,000 (30,000 × $180) and $3,600,000 (20,000 × $180), respectively.

Using the same approach the cost per unit of service provided by the Administration Department is $50,000 (20,000,000/400) and the Maintenance Department costs allocated to the Medical Departments are $15,000,000 (300 × $50,000) and $5,000,000 (100 × $50,000), respectively. Exhibit 4-25 summarizes the results. Therefore, the total of all service department costs allocated to the Medical and Surgical Departments are $20,400,000 and $8,600,000 as shown in this exhibit.

Although the direct method is simple, the complaint is that by ignoring the services provided among service departments the direct method introduces the potential for cost distortion.

Sequential Method

The **sequential method** (also called the *step* or *step-down method*) of allocating service department costs partially deals with the complaint that the direct method ignores services provided among service departments by using the following approach.

In the sequential method one of the service departments is chosen to allocate its costs first. That service department ignores services that it provides to itself and allocates its costs to the remaining departments in proportion to the services provided to each department.

Once a service department's costs have been allocated, it is dropped from consideration and the process moves (steps) to the next department. This process continues until all the service departments have allocated their costs. Exhibit 4-26 illustrates the result of using the sequential method with the Maintenance Department allocating its costs first.

Start by computing the service rate ($171.43) for the Maintenance Department by dividing the total cost to be allocated ($9,000,000) by the total service units provided to the remaining departments (52,500). This rate is then used to allocate the Maintenance Department's costs to the remaining departments. For example, the Medical Department is allocated $5,142,857.14 (30,000 × $171.43). (If you are following along these calculations note that the numbers in the exhibit are computed using computer-level accuracy rather than the rounded rate shown in the Exhibit 4-26.)

Exhibit 4-25
Direct Method

		SUPPORT UNITS PROVIDED TO				
	MAINTENANCE	ADMINISTRATION	MEDICAL	SURGICAL	TOTAL	RATE
Direct costs	$9,000,000.00	$20,000,000.00			$29,000,000.00	
Maintenance						
Cost to allocate	$9,000,000.00					
Support units provided			30,000	20,000	50,000	$180.00
Allocation	($9,000,000.00)		$5,400,000.00	$3,600,000.00		
Closing balance	$0.00					
Administration						
Cost to allocate		$20,000,000.00				
Support units provided			300	100	400	$50,000.00
Allocation		($20,000,000.00)	$15,000,000.00	$5,000,000.00		
Closing balance		$0.00	$20,400,000.00	$8,600,000.00	$29,000,000.00	

(left margin label: Support Units Provided From)

As you can see, the Maintenance Department allocates $428,571.43 of its costs to the Administration Department. This cost is added to the Administration Department's direct costs of $20,000,000 resulting in a total of $20,428,571.43 of Administration Department costs to be allocated. Note that the Maintenance Department is now dropped from the process. Following the same steps used by the Maintenance Department, you should be able to compute the Administration Department's cost allocations in the above exhibit. At this point the service department cost allocation process is complete.

Exhibit 4-26
Sequential Method: Maintenance Department Allocated First

		SUPPORT UNITS PROVIDED TO				
	MAINTENANCE	ADMINISTRATION	MEDICAL	SURGICAL	TOTAL	RATE
	$9,000,000.00	$20,000,000.00			$29,000,000.00	
Maintenance						
Cost to allocate	$9,000,000.00					
Units provided		2,500	30,000	20,000	52,500	$171.43
Allocation	($9,000,000.00)	$428,571.43	$5,142,857.14	$3,428,571.43		
New total	$0.00					
Administration						
Cost to allocate		$20,428,571.43				
Units provided			250	150	400	$51,071.43
Allocation		($20,428,571.43)	$12,767,857.14	$7,660,714.29		
Closing balance		$0.00	$17,910,714.29	$11,089,285.71	$29,000,000.00	

(left margin label: Support Units Provided From)

Cost analysts have two complaints about the sequential method. The first complaint is that, although it considers some of the support services provided among service departments, it does not consider all of them. The second complaint is that the order in which the service departments' costs are allocated makes a difference. Exhibit 4-27 illustrates the sequential method with the Administration Department allocating its costs first. You can use Exhibit 4-27, first, to test your understanding of the sequential method and, second, to see, by comparing these results with the results in Exhibit 4-26 of allocating the Maintenance Department first, that order does make a difference.

The Reciprocal Method

The reciprocal method answers the complaints leveled against the direct and sequential methods by considering all support services.

The reciprocal method has two steps. The first step computes the reciprocal cost of each service department. The second step uses each service department's reciprocal cost to allocate its costs.

In step 1 the cost analyst begins by developing a reciprocal cost equation for each service department. The reciprocal cost for each department is the sum of its direct cost and its share (based on share of total use) of the reciprocal costs of all the service departments (including itself). Here, using the abbreviation RC for reciprocal cost, are the reciprocal cost equations for each of the service departments:

$$RC_{Maintenance} = \$9,000,000$$
$$+ (1,500/54,000)\ RC_{Maintenance}$$
$$+ (110/560)\ RC_{Administration}$$
$$RC_{Administration} = \$20,000,000$$
$$+ (2,500/54,000)\ RC_{Maintenance}$$
$$+ (50/560)\ RC_{Administration}$$

With two equations in two unknowns (the reciprocal costs), the analyst can use algebra, or a computer, to solve the equations to find

$$RC_{Maintenance} = \$13,836,226.42$$
$$RC_{Administration} = \$22,664,150.94$$

This completes step 1.

In step 2 these reciprocal costs are used to allocate the service department costs to the production departments. These costs are allocated in proportion to each production department's use of the service department. Here are the resulting service department allocation equations:

Total service department cost allocation
to the Medical Department
$$= (30,000/54,000)\ RC_{Maintenance}$$
$$+ (250/560)\ RC_{Administration}$$
$$= \$17,804,716.98$$

Exhibit 4-27
Sequential Method with the Administration Department Costs Allocated First

| | | SUPPORT UNITS PROVIDED TO | | | | |
		ADMINISTRATION	MAINTENANCE	MEDICAL	SURGICAL	TOTAL	RATE
		$20,000,000.00	$9,000,000.00			$29,000,000.00	
	Administration						
	Cost to allocate	$20,000,000.00					
	Units provided		50	250	150	450	$44,444.44
	Allocation	($20,000,000.00)	$2,222,222.22	$11,111,111.11	$6,666,666.67		
	New total	$0.00					
	Maintenance						
	Cost to allocate		$11,222,222.22				
	Units provided			30,000	20,000	50,000	$224.44
	Allocation		($11,222,222.22)	$6,733,333.33	$4,488,888.89		
	Closing balance		$0.00	$17,844,444.44	$11,155,555.56	$29,000,000.00	

Exhibit 4-28
Summary of Cost Allocations: Four Methods

			ALLOCATION TO	
		MEDICAL DEPARTMENT	SURGICAL DEPARTMENT	TOTAL
	Direct method	$20,400,000.00	$8,600,000.00	$29,000,000.00
	Sequential method 1	$17,910,714.29	$11,089,285.71	$29,000,000.00
	Sequential method 2	$17,844,444.44	$11,155,555.56	$29,000,000.00
	Reciprocal method	$17,804,716.98	$11,195,283.02	$29,000,000.00

(Left margin label: Support Department Cost Allocation Method)

Total service department cost allocation
to the Surgical Department

$$= (20{,}000/54{,}000)\ RC_{Maintenance}$$
$$+ (150/560)\ RC_{Administration}$$
$$= \$11{,}195{,}283.02$$

In practice, the reciprocal method can be implemented using Microsoft's Excel or Open Office's Calc since these spreadsheets are easily programmed to solve systems of equations.

Summary

Exhibit 4-28 provides a summary of the cost allocations provided by the four alternatives.

As you can see either of the sequential methods provides a service department cost allocation that is quite close to the reciprocal method cost allocation. Regrettably, there is no reliable way to predict when any of the alternative methods will provide a good approximation of the cost allocation provided by the reciprocal method. However, as mentioned earlier, the reciprocal method is easily implemented using a computer spreadsheet; therefore, computational convenience is not an issue in choosing a service department cost allocation method. (In fact, programming a computer spreadsheet to undertake the sequential method allocations is the most complicated of the three methods.)

KEY TERMS

applied indirect costs, 153
capacity-related resource, 149
consumable resource, 149
conversion costs, 165
cost driver rate, 153
cost object, 149
cost pool, 152
death spiral, 161
direct cost, 149
direct method (for service
  department allocations), 185

equivalent unit of production, 165
finished goods inventory, 147
fixed manufacturing overhead, 152
flexible resource, 149
indirect cost, 150
indirect materials, 152
job order costing, 162
practical capacity, 153

predetermined overhead rate, 153
process costing, 163
reciprocal method (for service
  department allocations), 186
sequential method (for service
  department allocations), 185
variable overhead, 152
work-in-process inventory, 160

ASSIGNMENT MATERIALS

Questions

4-1   What are the two traditional cost management systems that have been used for product and service costing? What is the current practice in this regard? (LO 1)

4-2   How do the cost flows in a retail organization or service organization differ from those in a manufacturing organization? (LO 1)

4-3   What is a cost object? Give four examples of cost objects. (LO 2)

4-4   Compare the defining characteristic and cost behavior of a consumable (flexible) resource to those of a capacity-related resource. (LO 2)

4-5   Define direct cost and indirect cost and provide an example of each. (LO 2)

4-6   List the attributes of a direct cost. (LO 2)

4-7 What is a single cost driver rate? (LO 3)

4-8 What are predetermined indirect cost rates commonly called in practice? (LO 3)

4-9 Why are costs estimated for individual jobs? (LO 5, 6)

4-10 How are indirect cost rates determined? (LO 3)

4-11 How is overhead cost estimated for individual jobs? (LO 3)

4-12 What are indirect cost pools? (LO 3)

4-13 Why do firms use multiple indirect cost pools? (LO 3, 4, 5)

4-14 What problem arises when cost driver rates are based on planned or actual short-term usage? (LO 4)

4-15 Why are predetermined cost driver rates used when recording job costs? (LO 3)

4-16 "Use of a single cost driver rate when an indirect cost pool includes costs that have different cost drivers (causes of costs) leads to distortions in job costs." Do you agree with this statement? Explain. (LO 4)

4-17 What are the three options for dealing with the difference between actual and applied capacity (overhead) costs? (LO 3, 6)

4-18 How might computing the cost driver rate by using the planned level of the cost driver lead to a death spiral? (LO 3, 4, 6)

4-19 How is practical capacity computed for machines and labor? (LO 3, 6)

4-20 What is job order costing? Describe two situations in which job order costing might be used. (LO 6)

4-21 What is the basic procedure for determining product costs in continuous processing plants? (LO 6)

4-22 What are the similarities and differences between job order costing and multistage process costing systems? (LO 5, 6)

4-23 (Appendix) What is the difference between production departments and service departments? (LO 7)

Exercises

LO 3, 4, 6   **4-24** *Indirect cost rates and the death spiral*   Famous Flange Company manufactures a variety of special flanges for numerous customers. Annual capacity-related (manufacturing overhead) costs are $4,000,000 and the practical capacity level of machine hours is 120,000. The company uses planned machine hours as the cost driver in determining the plantwide cost driver rate. Until last year, the company used approximately 100,000 machine hours per year. Last year, competition increased and demand for the company's flanges fell. In the face of continuing competition, the company estimates that it will use 80,000 machine hours in the coming year. The company sets its prices at 150% of production cost per unit.

Required

(a) What is likely to happen if demand decreases further and Famous Flange continues to recompute its cost driver rate using the same approach?

(b) Advise the company on choosing a cost driver quantity for computing cost driver rates and explain why you advocate your choice of quantity.

LO 3, 4   **4-25** *Theoretical and practical capacity and machine hours*   Kappa Manufacturing Company has 120 machines in its factory. The machines run for three shifts each day. Each machine can be used for production for an average of 6 hours per shift. Assuming that during every shift 1.5 hours are allowed for machine maintenance and break time for machine operators, and that the factory operates for an average of six days per week, what is Kappa's theoretical and practical capacity number of machine hours per week?

LO 3, 6   **4-26** *Practical capacity and labor hours*   Calla Company runs two shifts each day. Workers on average have six weeks off per year and, after training and breaks, average 38 hours per week. What is Calla's practical capacity number of labor hours per year?

LO 6 **4-27** *Job cost* Ernie's Electronics, Inc., delivered 1,000 custom-designed computer monitors to its customer, Video Shack. The following cost information was compiled in connection with this order:

Direct Materials Used

Part A327: 1 unit costing $60 per monitor
Part B149: 1 unit costing $120 per monitor

Direct Labor Used

Assembly: 6 hours per monitor at the rate of $10 per hour
Inspection: 1 hour per monitor at the rate of $12 per hour

In addition, the company applies manufacturing overhead costs to jobs at the rate of $5 per direct labor hour. The selling price for each monitor is $350.

Required

(a) Determine the total cost for this job.
(b) Determine the gross margin per monitor.

LO 6 **4-28** *Job cost* The following costs pertain to job 007 at Graff Auto Shop:

	QUANTITY	PRICE
Direct materials:		
Engine oil	15 ounces	$4 per ounce
Lubricant	3 ounces	5 per ounce
Direct labor	6 hours	20 per hour
Overhead costs (based on direct labor hours)		25 per hour

Determine the total cost for job 007.

LO 3, 6 **4-29** *Job order costing and consulting* Mackenzie Consulting computes the cost of each consulting engagement by adding a portion of firmwide overhead costs to the labor cost of the consultants on the engagement. The overhead costs are assigned to each consulting engagement using a cost driver rate based on consultant labor costs. Mackenzie Consulting's overhead costs are $7.5 million per year, and total consultant labor cost is estimated at $0.25 million per month.

Required

(a) What is Mackenzie Consulting's cost driver rate?
(b) If the consultant labor cost on an engagement is $100,000, what cost will Mackenzie Consulting compute as the total cost of the consulting engagement?

LO 3, 6 **4-30** *Job order costing and cost driver rates* The Brinker Company uses a job order costing system at its local plant. The plant has a machining department and a finishing department. The company uses machine hours to allocate machining department overhead costs to jobs and uses direct labor cost to allocate finishing department overhead costs to jobs. Cost and practical capacity estimates for the current year are as follows:

	Machining Department	Finishing Department
Manufacturing overhead costs	$350,000	$280,000
Machine hours	14,000	1,400
Direct labor hours	3,500	15,400
Direct labor cost	$105,000	$350,000

Required

(a) Determine the cost driver rate for each department.
(b) Cost records for job 101 show the following:

	Machining Department	Finishing Department
Direct materials cost	$8,000	$1,400
Direct labor cost	$250	$800
Direct labor hours	7	35
Machine hours	50	6

Determine the total cost charged to job 101.

LO 3, 4, 6   **4-31** *Single rate versus departmental rates*   Eastern Wood Products has two production departments: cutting and assembly. The company has been using a plantwide cost driver rate computed by dividing plantwide overhead costs by total plantwide direct labor hours. The estimates for overhead costs and practical capacity quantities of cost drivers for the current year follow:

	Cutting	Assembly	Total
Manufacturing overhead	$40,000	$60,000	$100,000
Direct labor hours	2,000	6,000	8,000
Machine hours	4,000	3,000	7,000

Required

(a) Compute the plantwide cost driver rate.
(b) Determine departmental cost driver rates based on direct labor hours for assembly and machine hours for cutting.
(c) Provide reasons why Eastern Wood might use the method in part a or the one in part b.

LO 3, 4, 6   **4-32** *Fluctuating cost driver rates and effect on markup pricing*   Morrison Company carefully records its costs because it bases prices on the cost of the goods it manufactures. Morrison also carefully records its machine usage and other operational information. Manufacturing costs are computed monthly, and prices for the next month are determined by adding a 20% markup to each product's manufacturing costs. The cost driver rate is based on machine hours as follows:

Month	Actual Machine Hours	Month	Actual Machine Hours
January	1,350	July	1,400
February	1,400	August	1,400
March	1,500	September	1,500
April	1,450	October	1,600
May	1,450	November	1,600
June	1,400	December	1,600

Profits have been acceptable until the past year, when Morrison began to face increased competition. The marketing manager reported that Morrison's sales force finds the company's pricing puzzling. When demand is high, the company's prices are low, and when demand is low, the company's prices are high. Practical capacity is 1,500 machine hours per month. Practical capacity is exceeded in some months by operating the machines overtime beyond regular shift hours. Monthly machine-related overhead costs, all fixed, are $70,000 per month.

Required

(a) Compute the monthly overhead cost driver rates that Morrison used last year.
(b) Suggest a better approach to developing cost driver rates for Morrison and explain why your method is better.

LO 5, 6   **4-33** *Process costs*   Fancy Foods Company produces and sells canned vegetable juice. The ingredients are first combined in the blending department and then packed in gallon cans in the canning department. The following information pertains to the blending department for January:

ITEM	PRICE PER GALLON	GALLONS
Ingredient A	$0.40	10,000
Ingredient B	0.60	20,000
Vegetable juice		27,000
Materials loss		3,000

Conversion costs for the blending department are $0.55 per gallon for January. Determine the cost per gallon of blended vegetable juice before canning.

LO 5, 6   **4-34** *Process costs*   Pitman Chemical Company manufactures and sells Goody, a product that sells for $10 per pound. The manufacturing process also yields 1 pound of a waste product, called Baddy, in the production of every 10 pounds of Goody. Disposal of the waste product costs $1 per pound. During March, the company manufactured 200,000 pounds of Goody. Total manufacturing costs were as follows:

Direct materials	$232,000
Direct labor	120,000
Manufacturing overhead costs	60,000
Total costs	$412,000

Determine the cost per pound of Goody.

LO 5, 6   **4-35** *Process costing equivalent units*   The information below pertains to July production at Porter Company's paint factory, which produces paints for household interiors:

	GALLONS	MATERIALS	CONVERSION
Work in process, July 1	3,000	30% complete	20% complete
Started in July	7,000		
To account for	10,000		
Completed and transferred out	6,000	100% complete	100% complete
Work in process, July 31	4,000	25% complete	10% complete
Accounted for	10,000		

Using the weighted-average method, determine the number of equivalent units of production for materials and conversion during July.

LO 7 (Appendix) 4-36 *Service department cost allocation, direct method* San Rafael Company has two production departments, assembly and finishing, and two service departments, machine setup and inspection. Machine setup costs are allocated on the basis of number of setups, whereas inspection costs are allocated on the basis of number of direct labor hours. Selected information on the four departments follows:

ITEM	DIRECT COSTS	NUMBER OF SETUPS	DIRECT LABOR HOURS
Machine setup	$40,000	0	0
Inspection	15,000	0	0
Assembly	25,000	300	200
Finishing	20,000	100	500

Required

(a) Using the direct method, determine the amount of machine setup costs allocated to the two production departments.
(b) Using the direct method, determine the amount of inspection costs allocated to the two production departments.

LO 7 (Appendix) 4-37 *Sequential allocation* Carleton Company has two service departments and two production departments. Information on annual manufacturing overhead costs and cost drivers follows:

ITEM	SERVICE DEPARTMENTS		PRODUCTION DEPARTMENTS	
	S1	S2	P1	P2
Overhead costs	$65,000	$55,000	$160,000	$240,000
Direct labor hours	2,000	1,500	2,000	3,000
Number of square feet	800	1,200	2,400	2,600

The company allocates service department costs using the sequential method. First, S1 costs are allocated on the basis of direct labor hours. Next, S2 costs are allocated on the basis of square footage. The square footage for S1 is assumed to be zero for this purpose. Determine the total overhead costs allocated to each of the two production departments.

LO 7 (Appendix) 4-38 *Direct, sequential, and reciprocal allocation* Ming Company has two service departments (S1 and S2) and two production departments (P1 and P2). Last year, directly identified overhead costs were $300,000 for S1 and $300,000 for S2. Information on the consumption of their services follows:

SUPPLYING DEPARTMENTS	USER DEPARTMENTS			
	S1	S2	P1	P2
S1	0%	40%	30%	30%
S2	25%	0%	25%	50%

Required

(a) Determine the service department costs allocated to the two production departments using the direct method.
(b) Determine the service department costs allocated to the two production departments using the sequential method beginning with the allocation of S1 department costs.

(c) Determine the service department costs allocated to the two production departments using the reciprocal method.

Problems

LO 3, 6 **4-39** *Reconciling actual and applied capacity costs*   Hoyt Company uses a plantwide cost driver rate with machine hours as the cost driver. At the beginning of last year, Hoyt Company estimated its capacity-related (overhead) costs as $15,000,000 for a practical capacity of 100,000 machine hours per year. During the year, actual overhead costs were $14,200,000 and production required 90,000 machine hours.

Required

(a) Determine Hoyt Company's plantwide cost driver rate and calculate the overhead cost applied to production last year.
(b) Suppose the company charges the difference between actual and applied overhead costs to cost of goods sold at the end of the year. Calculate the difference and state whether the result will be an increase or decrease in the previously recorded cost of goods sold.
(c) Suppose now that the company prorates the difference between actual and applied overhead costs to work in process, finished goods, and cost of goods sold. If the proportions of applied indirect cost in the ending balances of these accounts this period are 20% in ending work in process, 45% in finished goods inventory, and 35% in cost of goods sold, by how much will the three accounts be increased or decreased from their previously recorded amounts?
(d) Now suppose that the company wishes to decompose the difference between actual and applied overhead costs to gain further insight into the difference. Compute the difference between actual and estimated overhead cost and the difference between estimated overhead cost and applied overhead cost.
(e) What insight does management gain from the approach in part d as compared to the approaches in parts b and c?

LO 3, 5, 6 **4-40** *Job costing for services*   The Hilton Company sells and services lawn mowers, snow blowers, and other equipment. The service department uses a job order cost system to determine the costs associated with each job for services such as oil changes, tune-ups, and repairs. The department assigns conversion costs through a cost driver rate on the basis of direct labor hours. The cost driver rate additionally includes a markup of 30% on the job's conversion costs in order to provide a reasonable profit for Hilton. The customer's invoice itemizes prices for parts and labor, where the stated labor rate is the department's cost driver rate, which includes direct labor costs, assigned overhead costs, and the 30% markup on conversion costs. Hilton Company's service department estimated the following information for the current year:

Salaries of mechanics	$225,000
Fringe benefits	65,000
General and administrative	16,000
Depreciation	54,000
Billable direct labor hours	6,000

Required

(a) Determine Hilton Company's service department's cost driver rate for assigning conversion costs on the basis of billable direct labor hours.

(b) Job 123 required $52.50 of materials and 0.8 direct labor hour. Determine the price charged for job 123.

LO 1, 6   **4-41** *Job costing and departmental cost driver rates*   The Leblanc Company employs a job order costing system to account for its costs. The company has three production departments. Separate departmental cost driver rates are employed because the demand for overhead resources for the three departments is very different. All jobs generally pass through all three production departments. Data regarding the hourly direct labor rates, cost driver rates, and three jobs for which work was done during June appear below. Jobs 101 and 102 were completed during June, while job 103 was not completed as of June 30. The costs charged to jobs not completed at the end of a month are shown as work in process inventory at the end of that month and at the beginning of the next month:

Production Departments	Direct Labor Rates	Cost Driver Rates
Department 1	$12	150% of direct material cost
Department 2	18	$8 per machine hour
Department 3	15	200% of direct labor cost

	Job 101	Job 102	Job 103
Beginning work in process	$25,500	$32,400	$0
Direct materials:			
Department 1	$40,000	$26,000	$58,000
Department 2	3,000	5,000	14,000
Department 3	0	0	0
Direct labor hours:			
Department 1	500	400	300
Department 2	200	250	350
Department 3	1,500	1,800	2,500
Machine hours:			
Department 1	0	0	0
Department 2	1,200	1,500	2,700
Department 3	150	300	200

Required

(a) Determine the total cost of completed job 101.

(b) Determine the total cost of completed job 102.

(c) Determine the ending balance of work-in-process inventory for job 103 as of June 30.

LO 1, 3, 4   **4-42** *Allocating scheduling service costs*   Airport Coach Service Company operates scheduled coach service from Boston's Logan Airport to downtown Boston and to Cambridge. A common scheduling service center at the airport is responsible for ticketing and customer service for both routes. The service center is regularly staffed to service traffic of 2,400 passengers per week: two-thirds for downtown Boston passengers and the balance for Cambridge passengers. The cost to operate this service center is $7,200 per week normally, but it is higher during weeks when additional help is required to service higher traffic levels. The service center costs and number of passengers serviced during the weeks of August follow:

WEEK	COST	BOSTON PASSENGERS	CAMBRIDGE PASSENGERS
1	$7,200	1,600	800
2	7,200	1,500	900
3	7,600	1,650	800
4	7,800	1,700	850
5	7,200	1,700	700

Required

(a) How much of the service center costs will be allocated to the Boston service and to the Cambridge service if the costs are allocated in proportion to the number of actual passengers?

(b) Suggest an improved approach to allocating the costs and explain why your method is an improvement. Using your approach, how much of the service center costs will be charged to the Boston service and to the Cambridge service?

LO 3, 4, 6 **4-43 *Job cost, markup, and single rate versus departmental rates***   Modern Metalworks Company has two departments, milling and assembly. The company uses a job costing system with a plantwide cost driver rate that is computed by dividing plantwide overhead costs by total plantwide practical capacity direct labor hours. The following cost and practical capacity estimates are for October:

	MILLING	ASSEMBLY
Overhead costs	$120,000	$160,000
Direct labor hours	8,000	12,000
Machine hours	12,000	6,000

The following information pertains to job 714, which was started and completed during October:

	MILLING	ASSEMBLY
Direct labor hours	10	40
Machine hours	18	8
Direct materials costs	$800	$50
Direct labor costs	$100	$600

Required

(a) Determine the cost of job 714.

(b) Suppose that instead of using the plantwide cost driver rate, the company uses machine hours as the cost driver for applying overhead costs in the milling department, and uses direct labor hours as the cost driver in the assembly department. Compute these departmental cost driver rates and determine the cost of job 714 using these rates.

(c) Using the costs you computed in parts a and b, determine the bid price that Modern Metalworks will quote under each cost system if it uses a 25% markup on total manufacturing cost.

(d) Provide reasons why Modern Metalworks might prefer the method in part a or the one in part b.

LO 3, 4, 6 **4-44 *Single rate versus departmental rates***   Bravo Steel Company supplies structural steel products to the construction industry. Its plant has three production departments: cutting, grinding, and drilling. The estimated overhead cost and practical capacity direct labor hours and machine hours for each department for the current year follow:

	CUTTING	GRINDING	DRILLING
Overhead cost	$700,000	$2,400,000	$2,750,000
Estimated direct labor hours	75,000	100,000	125,000
Estimated machine hours	1,000,000	450,000	375,000

Job ST101 consumed the following direct labor and machine hours:

	CUTTING	GRINDING	DRILLING
Direct labor hours	2,400	3,000	5,000
Machine hours	24,000	2,500	4,000

Required

(a) Suppose that a plantwide cost driver rate is computed by dividing plantwide overhead costs by plantwide practical capacity direct labor hours. Determine the overhead cost applied to job ST101.

(b) Determine the departmental cost driver rates and overhead costs applied to job ST101 if machine hours are used as the cost driver in the cutting department and direct labor hours are used as the cost driver for the grinding and drilling departments.

(c) Explain why Bravo Steel might prefer a plantwide rate or departmental cost driver rates.

LO 3, 4, 6   **4-45 *Job costing*** The Gonzalez Company uses a job order costing system at its plant in Green Bay, Wisconsin. The plant has a machining department and a finishing department. The company uses two cost driver rates for allocating manufacturing overhead costs to job orders: one on the basis of machine hours for allocating machining department overhead costs and the other on the basis of direct labor cost for allocating the finishing department overhead costs. Estimates for the current year follow:

	MACHINING DEPARTMENT	FINISHING DEPARTMENT
Manufacturing overhead cost	$750,000	$450,000
Machine hours	25,000	2,000
Direct labor hours	5,000	30,000
Direct labor cost	$250,000	$600,000

Required

(a) Determine the two departmental cost driver rates.

(b) Last month, cost records for job 011 show the following:

	MACHINING DEPARTMENT	FINISHING DEPARTMENT
Direct materials cost	$15,000	$5,000
Direct labor cost	$1,000	$1,600
Direct labor hours	20	80
Machine hours	100	10

Determine the total costs charged to job 011.

(c) Explain why Gonzalez Company uses two different cost driver rates in its job costing system.

LO 5, 6   **4-46 *Process costing*** Connor Chemical Company's plant processes batches of organic chemical products through three stages after starting with raw materials: (1) mixing and blending, (2) reaction chamber, and (3) pulverizing and packing. Connor Chemical's estimates for the total conversion costs for each of the three processing stages are shown in the table below. These costs include production labor assigned to each stage, support labor for performing tasks such as handling the output of the previous stage and setting up for the new stage, and laboratory testing. Additional materials for packing are needed in the pulverizing and packing stage:

	MIXING AND BLENDING	REACTION CHAMBERS	PULVERIZING AND PACKING
Production labor	$253,000	$1,148,000	$370,000
Engineering support	$31,000	$60,500	$22,300
Materials handling	$18,200	$19,200	$29,700
Equipment maintenance	$15,000	$35,200	$9,100
Laboratory expenses	$20,600	$25,400	$5,200
Depreciation	$45,000	$182,500	$51,500
Power	$36,500	$86,000	$22,000
General and administrative	$18,200	$18,200	$18,200
Total conversion costs	$437,500	$1,575,000	$528,000
Total number of process hours	8,750	35,000	8,800

Required

(a) Determine the estimated conversion cost driver rate per process hour for each stage.

(b) Consider two of Connor Chemical's representative products, C206 and C208. Both products are derivatives of ethyl oleate and at the start of the process require the same basic raw materials. Using the information below, determine the total cost of a batch of C206 and a batch of C208:

	C206	C208
Materials:		
Raw materials, beginning of process	$1,525	$1,525
Packing materials	$215	$300
Conversion hours:		
Mixing and blending	10 hours	10 hours
Reaction chamber	20 hours	20 hours
Pulverizing and packing	4 hours	8 hours

LO 5, 6   **4-47** *Process costing equivalent units and product cost*   The information below pertains to October production at Zippy Company's bottling plant, which produces and bottles sports drinks. Each unit consists of a case of 12 bottles:

	UNITS	MATERIALS	CONVERSION
Work in process, October 1	2,000	70% complete	60% complete
Started in October	10,000		
To account for	12,000		
Completed and transferred out	8,000	100% complete	100% complete
Work in process, October 30	4,000	40% complete	25% complete
Accounted for	12,000		
Costs, beginning of October		$1,050	$3,240
Added during October		8,200	22,620
To be accounted for		$9,250	$25,860

Required

(a) Using the weighted-average method, determine the number of equivalent units of production for materials and conversion during October.

(b) Determine the cost per equivalent unit for materials and conversion for October and the total cost per equivalent unit. (Round to two digits after the decimal point.)

(c) Determine whether the cost per equivalent unit for materials and conversion increased or decreased from the previous month.

LO 3, 6, 7 **(Appendix)**   **4-48** *Job bid and direct and sequential allocations*   Sanders Manufacturing Company produces electronic components on a job order basis. Most business is gained through bidding on jobs. Most firms competing with Sanders bid full cost plus a 30% markup. Recently, with the expectation of gaining more sales, Sanders dropped its markup from 40% to 30%. The company operates two service departments and two production departments. Manufacturing overhead costs and quantities of activities for each department are shown here:

ITEM	SERVICE DEPARTMENTS		PRODUCTION DEPARTMENTS	
	PERSONNEL	MAINTENANCE	MACHINING	ASSEMBLY
Overhead costs	$100,000	$200,000	$400,000	$300,000
Number of employees	5	5	5	40
Maintenance hours	1,500	200	7,500	1,000
Machine hours	0	0	10,000	1,000
Direct labor hours	0	0	1,000	10,000

Costs of the personnel department are allocated on the basis of employees and those of the maintenance department on the basis of maintenance hours. Departmental rates are used to assign overhead costs to products. The machining department uses machine hours, and the assembly department uses direct labor hours for this purpose.

The firm is preparing to bid on job 781, which requires three machine hours per unit produced in the machining department and five direct labor hours per unit produced in the assembly department. The expected direct materials and direct labor costs per unit are $450.

Required

(a) Allocate the service department costs to the production departments using the direct method.

(b) Determine the bid price per unit produced for job 781 using the direct method.

(c) Assume that the costs of the service department incurring the greatest cost are allocated first, and allocate the service department costs to the production departments using the sequential method. When allocating personnel costs, assume the maintenance department has 0 employees.

(d) Determine the bid price per unit produced for job 781 using the sequential method in part c.

LO 7 **(Appendix)**   **4-49** *Direct, sequential, and reciprocal allocation*   Boston Box Company has two service departments, maintenance and grounds, and two production departments, fabricating and assembly. Management has decided to allocate maintenance costs on the basis of machine hours used by the departments and grounds costs on the basis of square feet occupied by the departments. The following data appear in the company's records for last year:

ITEM	MAINTENANCE	GROUNDS	FABRICATING	ASSEMBLY
Machine hours	0	1,500	12,000	6,000
Square feet	3,000	0	15,000	20,000
Costs	$18,000	$14,000	$45,000	$25,000

Required

(a) Allocate service department costs to the production departments using the direct method.
(b) Allocate service department costs to the production departments using the sequential method, assuming that the costs of the service department incurring the greatest cost are allocated first.
(c) Allocate service department costs to the production departments using the reciprocal method.

LO 3, 6, 7 **(Appendix)**   **4-50** *Job bid price and direct, sequential, and reciprocal allocations*   Sherman Company manufactures and sells small pumps made to customer specifications. It has two service departments and two production departments. Data on current year operations follow:

	SERVICE DEPARTMENTS		PRODUCTION DEPARTMENTS	
ITEM	MAINTENANCE	POWER	CASTING	ASSEMBLY
Costs	$750,000	$450,000	$150,000	$110,000
Machine hours	0	80,000	80,000	40,000
Kilowatt-hours	40,000	0	200,000	160,000
Direct labor hours	0	0	100,000	60,000

Management allocates maintenance department costs using machine hours, and power department costs using kilowatt-hours. Separate cost driver rates are determined on the basis of machine hours for the casting department and on the basis of direct labor hours for the assembly department. It takes 1 machine hour to manufacture a pump in the casting department and 0.5 labor hour to assemble a pump in the assembly department. Direct labor and material costs amount to $32 per pump.

A prospective customer has requested a bid on a two-year contract to purchase 1,000 pumps every month. Sherman Company has a policy of adding a 25% markup to the full manufacturing cost to determine the bid.

Required

(a) What is the bid price when the direct method is used?
(b) What is the bid price when the sequential method that begins by allocating maintenance department costs is used?
(c) What is the bid price when the reciprocal method is used?

Cases

LO 3, 4   **4-51** *Practical capacity, cost driver rates, and the death spiral*   Youngsborough Products, a supplier to the automotive industry, had seen its operating margins shrink below 20% as its customers put continued pressure on pricing. Youngsborough produced four products in its plant and decided to eliminate products that no longer contributed positive gross margins. The total plant overhead cost is $122,000 per year. Details on the four products are provided here:

	PRODUCTS			
	A	B	C	D
Production volume (units)	10,000	8,000	6,000	4,000
Selling price	$15.00	$18.00	$20.00	$22.00
Materials per unit	$4.00	$5.00	$6.00	$7.00
Direct labor hours per unit	0.24	0.18	0.12	0.08
Total direct labor hours	2,400	1,440	720	320

Youngsborough calculates a plantwide overhead rate by dividing total direct labor hours into total overhead costs. Assume that plant overhead is a fixed cost during the year, but that direct labor is a variable cost. The direct labor rate is $30 per hour.

Required

(a) Calculate the plantwide cost driver rate and use this rate to assign overhead costs to products. Calculate the gross margin for each product and calculate the total gross margin.
(b) If any product is unprofitable in part a, drop this product from the mix. Recalculate the cost driver rate based on the new total direct labor hours remaining in the plant and use this rate to assign overhead costs to the remaining three products. Calculate the gross margin for each product and calculate the total gross margin.
(c) Drop any product that is unprofitable with the revised cost assignment. Repeat the process, eliminating any unprofitable products at each stage.
(d) What is happening at Youngsborough and why? How could this situation be avoided?

LO 2, 3, 4, 6   **4-52** *Alternative job costing systems*   Over the past 15 years, Anthony's Auto Shop has developed a reputation for reliable repairs and has grown from a one-person operation to a nine-person operation, including one manager and eight skilled auto mechanics. In recent years, however, competition from mass merchandisers has eroded business volume and profits, leading the owner, Anthony Axle, to ask his manager to take a closer look at the cost structure of the auto shop.

The manager determined that direct materials (parts and components) are identified with individual jobs and charged directly to the customer. Direct labor (mechanics) is also identified with individual jobs and charged at a prespecified rate to the customers. The salary and benefits for a senior mechanic are $65,000 per year, and they are $45,000 per year for a junior mechanic. Each mechanic can work up to 1,750 hours in a year on customer jobs, but if there are not enough jobs to keep each of them busy, the cost of their compensation still will have to be incurred. The manager's salary and benefits amount to $75,000 per year. In addition, the following fixed costs are also incurred each year:

Rent	$40,000
Insurance	7,000
Utilities	7,000
Supplies	10,000
Machine maintenance	9,000
Machine depreciation	23,800
Total costs	$96,800

Because material costs are recovered directly from the customers, the profitability of the operation depends on the volume of business and the hourly rate charged for labor. At present, Anthony's Auto Shop charges $51.06 per hour for all jobs. Anthony said he would not consider firing any of the four senior mechanics because he believes it is difficult to get workers with their skills and loyalty to the firm, but he is willing to consider releasing one or two of the junior mechanics.

The present job costing system uses a single conversion rate for all jobs. The cost driver rate is currently determined by dividing estimated total labor and overhead costs by expected hours charged to customers. The eight mechanics are expected to be busy on customer jobs for 95% of the total available time. The price of $51.06 per hour is determined by adding a markup of x% to the cost driver rate, that is $51.06 = [1 + x/100] \times$ cost driver rate. Note that all personnel costs are included in conversion costs at present.

The manager is considering switching to the use of two rates, one for class A repairs and another for class B repairs. Electronic ignition system repairs or internal carburetor repairs are examples of class A repairs. Class A repairs require careful measurements and adjustments with equipment such as an oscilloscope or infrared gas analyzer. Class B repairs are simple repairs, such as shock absorber replacements or exhaust part replacements. Class A repairs can be done only by senior mechanics; class B repairs are done mainly by junior mechanics. Half of the hours charged to customers are expected to be for class A repairs, and the other half for class B repairs. Because class A repairs are expected to account for all of the senior mechanics' time and most of the machine usage, 60% of the total costs (including personnel costs) are attributable to class A repairs and the remaining 40% to class B repairs.

Required

(a) Determine the markup of x% currently used.
(b) Determine the two new rates, one for class A repairs and another for class B repairs, using the same markup of x% that you determined in part a.
(c) The following are expected labor hours anticipated for two customer jobs:

Job No.	Class A Repairs	Class B Repairs
101	4.5 hours	1.5 hours
102	None	2.0 hours

Determine the price (in addition to materials) to be charged for each of the two jobs under the present accounting system and under the proposed accounting system.
(d) What change in service mix is likely to result from the proposed price change?
(e) Provide reasons why Anthony might retain the current costing system or change to the proposed costing system.

Chapter 5

Activity-Based Cost Systems

After completing this chapter, you will be able to:

1. Understand how volume-based cost systems distort product costs.

2. Describe why companies producing a more varied and complex mix of products have higher costs than companies producing only a narrow range of products.

3. Design an activity-based cost system that directly traces resource costs to products.

4. Use the information from an activity-based cost system to improve operations and make better decisions about products.

5. Understand the importance of measuring the practical capacity of resources and the cost of unused capacity.

6. Appreciate the role for activity-based cost systems for service companies.

7. Discuss the barriers for implementing activity-based cost systems and how these might be overcome.

Madison Dairy

Christine Lee, the controller of Madison Dairy, was concerned about the company's decline in profitability. In recent years, Madison had diversified into new lines of business yet profits had not kept pace with sales volume increases. Many costs, which Lee thought would be fixed, were turning out not to be; in fact, categories such as factory overhead, warehousing, distribution, and administrative expenses had been increasing faster than sales. She was puzzled with the continual increase in the company's indirect and support expenses.

During the 1990s, Madison Dairy had experienced a major consolidation in its customer base, as small independent retailers became absorbed or put out of business by giants such as Wal-Mart, SuperValu, Target, and Sysco. The buying power from these large distributors and retailers put suppliers' margins under heavy pressure.

Madison had also introduced more specialized packaging, distribution, warehousing, and just-in-time replenishment services in response to demands from its wholesale and retail customers. Madison operated a complex transportation system that offered its customers multiple delivery options. Trucks delivered full loads to supermarkets and their distribution centers, and made direct deliveries of less-than-truckload quantities to convenience outlets and other small retail stores. It also used double-stacked containers to ship frozen loads of ice cream to distribution centers across the United States. And it still made home deliveries of small quantities of milk, cream, and yogurt to insulated boxes outside consumers' homes and apartments.

Madison's plants, responding to customer and consumer demand for high product variety, operated complex production processes. They produced high-volume, standard products in large production runs as well as small runs of special recipes of ice cream, yogurt, and milk.

Madison's standard cost system had excellent data about materials costs and plant operating expenses at the department level. The system allocated factory overhead as a percentage of direct manufacturing costs. The standard costs, however, did not reflect the effects of run size since the system did not incorporate information about the setups or tear downs as machines shifted between flavors, products, and packaging. The unit costs were the same whether the production run lasted for 10 minutes or 10 hours.

Changeovers were costly since some product was lost at the start of each production run until the process stabilized, and also lost at the end

As at Ericson Ice Cream, setups are done between jobs at the manufacturing company pictured here, and are sometimes time-consuming and therefore, costly. Many production and operations-management techniques can reduce setup times. Data about the cost of such labor form part of an activity-based costing system.

Will & Deni McInture/Photo Researchers, Inc.

of each run when the machine had to be stopped and cleaned to prepare for the next product. In addition to the material losses at the beginning and end of each production run, the company incurred a high opportunity cost during changeovers, as expensive machines were not producing salable product. On the filling line, changeovers occurred when personnel had to set up for customers' special labels and containers.

Lee realized that the cost system, which had been developed when the company had a much simpler product line and many fewer delivery and packaging options, no longer reflected the cost of producing its diverse product line, storing and picking the products in the warehouse, and delivering them, through multiple mechanisms, to its highly diverse customer base ranging from a family using one quart of milk per week up through giant customers such as Wal-Mart and Target. She wondered how to obtain accurate cost and profit information for the far more complex environment that Madison now faced. She believed the company could make much better decisions about its product mix, pricing, and operating processes if it had a more accurate understanding of the company's cost structure.

TRADITIONAL MANUFACTURING COSTING SYSTEMS

Chapters 3 and 4 described fundamental concepts in costing. In Chapter 3, you learned about incremental, avoidable, sunk, and opportunity costs and how to use these concepts to make better decisions. Chapter 4 discussed cost system design, how to accumulate expenses in various cost buckets, both production and support, and how to assign service department costs to production departments to calculate cost rates for products and services that are processed through the cost centers.

In this chapter, we discuss systems that assign production costs to products. Product costing systems are important because product volume and mix explain a large percentage of the costs that companies incur. If companies want to influence their costs, they must understand the relationship between the volume and mix of the products they produce and the expenses they incur. Product costs provide the bridge between operating expenses and production output. If poorly designed product costing systems report inaccurate product costs, companies can make poor decisions on resource supply, product mix, pricing, order acceptance, and customer relationships.

Product costing systems start by assigning direct labor and direct materials costs to products. This aspect is straightforward and has been done reasonably well for about a century. For both materials and labor, cost accountants or industrial engineers perform the following computations:

1. Calculate the cost per unit (pound, kilogram, or square meter) of each material used by a product and the cost per hour of each type of direct labor that processes the product.
2. For each unit of product made, determine the quantity (number of pounds, kilograms, or square meters) of each type of material used and the quantity (number of hours) required for each type of labor.

3. For each labor and material type, multiply the cost per unit (or hour) by the quantities used per product, as shown by the following equations:

Materials cost/unit = Quantity of materials/unit of output × Cost per materials unit

Labor cost/unit = Quantity of labor hours/unit of output × Cost per labor hour

4. Add up all of the individual materials and labor costs to obtain the total labor and materials cost of each product unit.

As long as accurate records are maintained about labor time and material usage standards, and about the standard or actual prices of each material and labor type, the company will have good knowledge about the costs of its direct labor and materials inputs for each product it produces.

The main focus of our attention in this chapter is on the assignment of indirect expenses to products. Indirect expenses include the costs of operating machines, scheduling, quality control, purchasing, maintenance, supervision, and general factory support (including building depreciation, insurance, utilities, and housekeeping). Indirect expenses are also called shared or common costs since they support the production of all products and they are not easily traced to individual products in the simple way that direct materials and direct labor costs are.

Historically, manufacturing companies assigned indirect costs, which they often called "overhead," to production departments in simple proportion to the direct labor hours worked in each department, or sometimes through more accurate allocation schemes as discussed in Chapter 4. The manufacturing cost system then divided the indirect costs assigned to each production department by a simple measure of the volume of activity in the department, such as total direct labor hours or total machine hours worked, to calculate an overhead allocation rate for the department. The system used this department-specific overhead cost rate to allocate indirect expenses to the products that were processed through each department.

As an example of a simple product cost accounting system, consider one ice cream manufacturing plant at Madison Dairy. The plant originally produced just two products, vanilla and chocolate ice cream, and enjoyed profit margins in excess of 15% of sales. Several years ago, the plant manager had seen opportunities to expand the business by extending the product line into new flavors that earned premium selling prices. Madison had introduced strawberry ice cream, which required the same basic production technology but could be sold at prices that were 10% higher than vanilla and chocolate. Last year, the company introduced mocha-almond ice cream, which it sold at an even higher price premium. With the increase in product variety came an increase in the plant's overhead costs. These costs were allocated to products based on their direct labor content. Currently, the rate was 240% of direct labor dollars.

Christine Lee, Madison's controller, was disappointed with the recent financial performance of the plant. Exhibit 5-1 shows the product line income statement for a recent and representative month for the plant's operations. The new strawberry and mocha flavors were profitable but the high-volume vanilla and chocolate flavors had just broken even and the overall profit margin was now less than 2% of sales. After subtracting plant general and administrative expenses (not shown), the plant had operated at a loss. Lee wondered whether the company should de-emphasize the commodity vanilla and chocolate products and keep introducing new specialty flavors, which at least had positive operating profits.

Madison's manufacturing manager commented on how the introduction of the new flavors had changed his production environment:

Five years ago, life was a lot simpler. We produced just vanilla and chocolate ice cream in long production runs, and everything ran smoothly,

	Vanilla	Chocolate	Strawberry	Mocha-Almond	Total
Production and sales volume (gallons)	10,000	8,000	1,200	800	20,000
Unit selling price	$3.00	$3.00	$3.30	$3.50	
Sales	$30,000	$24,000	$3,960	$2,800	$60,760
Direct materials	6,000	4,800	720	520	12,040
Direct labor	7,000	5,600	840	560	14,000
Overhead at 240%	16,800	13,440	2,016	1,344	33,600
Total factory expenses	29,800	3,840	3,576	2,424	59,640
Gross profit	$200	$160	$384	$376	$1,120
Gross profit (% of sales)	0.7%	0.7%	9.7%	13.4%	1.8%

without much intervention. Difficulties started when we introduced the strawberry flavor. We had to make more changeovers to stop production of vanilla or chocolate, empty the vats, clean out all remnants of the previous flavor, and then start the production of the strawberry flavor. Making chocolate was simple—we didn't even have to clean out the residual from the previous run if we just dumped in enough chocolate syrup to cover it up. For strawberry, however, even small traces of other flavors create quality problems. And because mocha-almond contains nuts, to which many people have severe allergic reactions, we have to do a complete sterilization of the vat after every mocha production run.

We are also spending a lot more time on purchasing and scheduling activities and just keeping track of where we stand on existing, backlogged, and future orders. I am concerned about rumors that even more new flavors may be introduced in the near future. I don't think we have any more capability to handle additional confusion and complexity in our operations.

Ice cream production at the Madison ice cream plant involved preparing and mixing the ingredients for each flavor in large vats. In a subsequent stage, the ice cream mix was packaged into containers using semiautomatic machines. A final packing and shipping stage was performed manually.

Each product had a bill of materials that identified the quantity and cost of direct materials and labor required for the product. From this information, it was easy to calculate the direct materials costs and direct labor costs for each flavor. Madison's monthly indirect expenses (about $34,000 per month) at the plant were comprised of the following:

Expense Category	Expense
Indirect labor	$12,068
Fringe benefits	6,517
Machinery	15,400
Total	$33,985

Madison's cost system assigned the plant's indirect expenses to products on the basis of each product's direct labor cost. The cost system's current overhead rate was 240% of direct labor cost. Most people in the plant recalled that not too many years ago, before the new specialty flavors (strawberry and mocha-almond) had been introduced, the overhead rate was less than 140% of direct labor cost.[1]

LIMITATIONS OF MADISON'S EXISTING STANDARD COST SYSTEM

Madison's standard cost system is adequate for the financial reporting role of inventory valuation. It is simple, easy to use and understand, and applied consistently from year to year. When Madison's accountants designed the system years ago, production operations were mostly manual, and total indirect costs were less than direct labor costs. Madison's two high-volume products had similar production volumes and batch sizes. Given the high cost of measuring and recording information, the accountants judged correctly that a complex costing system would be more expensive to operate than the company could recoup in benefits from a more detailed assignment of costs.

Madison's production environment, however, had changed. Because of automation, direct labor costs had decreased and indirect expenses increased. As the plant added custom, low-volume flavors, it needed more people to perform scheduling, setup, and quality control and to maintain product specifications. The cost system that was adequate when indirect expenses were low and product variety was limited could now be giving distorted signals about the relative profitability of Madison's different products.

The distortions arise because of the way Madison's existing cost system allocated production costs to products. Many manufacturing companies, like Madison, use only drivers that vary directly with the volume of products produced—such as direct labor dollars, direct labor hours, or machine hours—for allocating production expenses to products. In an environment of high product variety, however, the exclusive use of volume drivers to allocate overhead costs leads to product cost distortion, as illustrated in the following example.

VANILLA FACTORY AND MULTIFLAVOR FACTORY

The Vanilla Factory produces 1 million gallons of ice cream, all the same flavor (vanilla, of course) and all packed in half-gallon containers. The Multiflavor Factory also produces 1 million gallons of ice cream but of many different flavors, recipes, brand names, and package sizes (half-pint, pint, quart, half-gallon, gallon, and two-gallon containers). Multiflavor Factory treats each combination of flavor, recipe, brand name, and package size as a different product (called a stockkeeping unit [SKU]). In a typical year, the Multiflavor Factory produces about 2,500 different SKUs, ranging from specialty flavors and packages, with annual production volumes as low as 50 to 100 gallons per year, up to high-volume standard flavors such as vanilla or chocolate in standard half-gallon packages whose annual production volumes are each about 200,000 gallons per year.

---

[1] The small difference between the budgeted overhead expenses of $33,985 in the table on the previous page, and the overhead assigned to products ($33,600) occurred because Madison used an approximate overhead rate of 240% when assigning costs to products rather than the actual ratio of 242.75%.

Even though both factories make the same basic product, the Multiflavor Factory requires many more resources to support its highly varied mix. It has a much larger production support staff than the Vanilla Factory because it requires more people to schedule machine and production runs; perform changeovers and setups between production runs in the blending and the packaging line; inspect items at the beginning of each production run; move materials; ship and expedite orders; develop new flavor recipes; improve existing products; negotiate with vendors; schedule materials receipts; order, receive, and inspect incoming materials and parts; and update and maintain the much larger computer-based information system. It also operates with considerably higher levels of idle time, setup time, overtime, inventory, rework, and scrap. Because both factories have the same physical output, both have roughly the same cost of materials (ignoring Multiflavor's slightly higher acquisition costs for smaller orders of specialty ingredients and flavors and other materials). For actual production, because all gallons of ice cream are about the same complexity, both the Vanilla Factory and the Multiflavor Factory require the same number of direct labor hours and machine hours for actual production (not counting the higher idle time and setup times in Multiflavor). The Multiflavor Factory also has about the same property taxes, security costs, and heating bills as the Vanilla Factory, but it has much higher indirect and support costs because of its more varied product mix and complex production tasks.

Consider now the operation of a traditional cost system, like the one used at Madison Dairy, in these two plants. The Vanilla Factory has little need for a cost system to calculate the cost of a half-gallon of vanilla ice cream. The financial manager, in any single period, simply divides total expenses by total production volume to get the cost per half-gallon package produced. For a year, divide the factory expenses by the million-gallon capacity to get the cost per gallon (or divide by 2 million to get the cost per half-gallon container produced). For the Multiflavor Factory, the traditional cost system first allocates indirect and support expenses to production cost pools, as described in Chapter 4. Once the traceable and allocated support expenses have been accumulated within each production cost pool, the system allocates the pool's costs to products on the basis of the volume cost driver for that cost center: direct labor, machine hours, units produced, or materials quantity processed. On a per-unit basis, high-volume standard half-gallon containers of vanilla and chocolate ice cream require about the same quantity of each cost driver (labor and machine time, number of units, materials quantity) as the very low volume SKUs, consisting of specialty flavors and recipes packaged in a specialty size. Therefore, Multiflavor's overhead costs would be applied to products on the basis of their production volumes. Chocolate and vanilla half-gallon containers, each representing about 20% of the plant's output, would have about 20% of the plant's overhead applied to them. A low-volume product, representing only 0.01% of the plant's output (100 gallons per year), would have about 0.01% of the plant's overhead allocated to it. The traditional costing system reports, on a per gallon basis, essentially identical product costs for all products, standard and specialty, regardless of the relative production volumes of their flavor, recipe, and packaging SKU combination.

Clearly, however, considerably more of the Multiflavor Factory's indirect resources are required (on a per gallon basis) for the low-volume, specialty, newly designed products than for the mature, high-volume, standard vanilla and chocolate products. Traditional cost systems, even those with multiple production cost centers, systematically and grossly underestimate the cost of resources required for specialty, low-volume products and overestimate the resource cost of producing high-volume, standard products, such as the half-gallon vanilla and chocolate ice cream SKUs.

Christine Lee of Madison Dairy wondered why she could not assign indirect expense costs to products in the same way that standard cost systems assign materials and labor costs to products. That is, why couldn't she obtain the cost of using each unit of overhead or indirect resource, and the quantity of each indirect resource used by each product the plant produced?

After doing some research, she learned that such an approach had recently been introduced, under the name **time-driven activity-based costing (TDABC, or time-driven ABC)**.[2] The new cost system required estimating two parameters, just like for labor and materials:

1. The first parameter is the cost rate for each type of indirect resource. First, identify all costs incurred to supply that resource (such as a machine, an indirect production employee, the computer system, factory space, a warehouse, or a truck). Second, identify the capacity supplied by that resource. The capacity would be the hours of work provided by the machine or production employee, or the space provided by the warehouse or truck. For most resources (people, equipment, and machines), capacity is measured by the time supplied. The resource's cost rate is calculated by dividing its cost by the capacity it supplies, usually expressed as a cost per hour or cost per minute. For warehouses, production space, and trucks, the cost rate would be measured by cost per square foot (or square meter) of usable space. For computer memory, the resource cost rate would be the cost per megabyte or gigabyte.

2. The second parameter is an estimate of how much of each resource's capacity (such as time or space) is used by the activities performed to produce the various products and services (and customers, as we will discuss in the next chapter).

With estimates of these two parameters for each resource and product, the cost assignment can be done simply and similarly to that performed for direct materials and labor costs:

Cost of using resource i by product j = Capacity cost rate of resource i
$\times$ Quantity of capacity of resource i used by product j

For example, take an indirect production employee who specializes in changing over machines from one product to the other. The employee's total compensation is $4,800 per month. The employee has about 120 hours available to perform changeovers each month. This figure is obtained from showing up for work about 20 days per month, being paid for 7½ hours per day, less 90 minutes per day used for breaks, training, quality meetings, and routine machine maintenance. This leaves 6 hours per day available for setting up machines for the next production run. The setup employee's **capacity cost rate** is $40 per hour ($4,800 per month/120 hours per month). Consider now a product that is produced three times during the month, with the setup time for each production run taking 1.5 hours. The product uses 4.5 hours of this indirect production employee's time and would be assigned $180 of cost ($40/hour $\times$ 4.5 hours) this month for use of this indirect employee's time.[3]

Lee decided to implement this approach at Madison Dairy's ice cream factory.

---

[2] The new approach was described in R. S. Kaplan and S. R. Anderson, *Time-Driven Activity-Based Costing* (Boston: Harvard Business Press, 2007).

[3] Whereas direct materials and direct labor cost can be calculated for each unit produced of the product, indirect expenses will get assigned to the total production of the product in a given time period.

Calculating Resource Capacity Cost Rates

Fringe Benefits

Lee started with fringe benefits and immediately realized that these were really part of the cost of the direct and indirect labor resources. The fringe benefits of $6,517 represented 25% of the $26,068 in wages paid for direct and indirect labor. She decided to apply the fringe benefit costs as a simple 25% markup to all direct and indirect labor costs.

Indirect Labor

Lee next turned to the indirect labor expense. Madison had seven production employees who did both the actual work of producing the ice cream as well as all of the production support work. The standard cost accounting system treated the employees as "direct labor" when they ran the production process and "indirect" when they did everything else, such as changing a machine line from one production run to the next, scheduling production runs, ordering and receiving raw materials, and maintaining records on the various products. The plant's cost accounting system estimated the direct labor times required each month for the actual volume and mix of products produced and treated all the remaining time as "indirect."

Madison paid production employees a fixed salary per month of $3,724. Lee added the fringe benefits of 25% (equal to $931) to obtain the total monthly compensation of $4,655 per production employee. For an average month, she estimated that an employee came to work on about 19 days.[4] Employees were paid for 8 hours of work per day, but not all that time was available for productive work. Breaks, training, and meetings consumed about 1 hour per day of employees' time, leaving 7 hours per day available for work. Thus, each employee was available for 133 hours of work each month, leading to the following calculation:

$$\text{Cost rate per employee} = \$4{,}655 \text{ per month}/133 \text{ hours per month}$$
$$= \$35 \text{ per hour}$$

Machinery ($15,400)

The ice cream factory had two identical production lines. It leased all of the machinery on the lines from an outside supplier, and had total current monthly lease payments of $15,400. The production machines were available every working day of the month, or about 22 days per month. The company operated with one daily eight-hour shift. Normal preventive maintenance and minor repairs were performed for one hour each day, leaving seven hours available for productive work on each production line. Thus the total available capacity per machine line was 22 days × 7 hours per day or 154 hours per month.[5] With two machine lines, the plant had machine time available for 308 hours each month.[6] Thus,

---

[4] The estimate of number of days per month came from the following calculation. Employees worked about 228 days per year [365 days in a year less 104 weekend days (52 × 2) when employees did not work, 28 days for holidays and vacation and 5 days for sick days and personal leave]. Dividing 228 days per year by 12 months in a year yields the 19 days per month estimate.

[5] Subtracting 1.0 hour for maintenance from each 8-hour shift per day = 7 hours available per day per production line. Multiply 22 days per month times 7 hours per day times 2 production lines = 308 machine hours available per month.

[6] Calculation of practical capacity can be somewhat more complex than the Madison Dairy ice cream plant situation illustrates. For example, the capacity of Madison's machines could be increased if the company worked a second or third shift. A general rule is to estimate machine capacity based on the number of shifts per week that the company typically works. If the company decides to add shifts, it would increase the production line's quantity of productive hours. Another complication is the existence of peak load or seasonal capacity. More discussion on how to deal with advanced issues in estimating practical capacity can be found in R. S. Kaplan and R. Cooper, *Cost & Effect* (Boston: Harvard Business Press, 1997): 126–132.

$$\text{Cost rate for machines} = \$15,400 \text{ per month}/308 \text{ hours per month}$$
$$= \$50 \text{ per machine hour}$$

Calculating Resource Time Usage per Product

Lee now needed to determine the quantity of time that each product used of each production resource (indirect labor and machines).

Indirect Labor Time

The demand for indirect labor time came from three sources. First, indirect labor scheduled production runs, did the purchasing for a production run, prepared the materials and brought materials to the production line just before a production run. They also inspected the initial output from the production run to ensure that it met the product specifications. Lee assigned an industrial engineer to observe this process over a period of several weeks; he reported back that the time required to order materials, schedule, and prepare for a production run was about four hours, and this time was independent of which flavor was being produced or the size of the production run.

Employees also performed the changeovers from one product to another. Industrial engineers had already established time standards for these changeovers so this information was readily available:

PRODUCT	CHANGEOVER TIME
Vanilla	2.0 hours
Chocolate	1.0 hour
Strawberry	2.5 hours
Mocha-almond	4.0 hours

The time for changing over to chocolate was short since the previous flavor did not have to be completely washed out. Vanilla and strawberry demanded more careful preparation, and mocha-almond required the longest changeover time because of the demanding quality standards for the flavor's special taste and because of the need to flush out all traces of the allergen (nuts) after a production run. Three employees worked as a team to perform each changeover so the setup time for a new batch of vanilla ice cream required six hours of indirect labor time (three employees working for two hours on the setup).

Employees also performed product-sustaining activities each month for each flavor. These activities included maintaining and updating the product's bill of materials and production process on the computer system, monitoring and maintaining a minimum supply of raw materials and finished goods inventory for each product, improving the production process, and performing recipe changes based on customer feedback. This activity took about nine hours per month for each product.

Lee summarized the demand for indirect labor by each product with the following time equation:

$$\text{Indirect labor time/product} = (4 \text{ hours} + \text{product changeover time})$$
$$\times \text{ Number of production runs} + 9$$

For example, if the Vanilla flavor had 10 production runs in a month, its total usage of indirect labor time would be:

$$\text{Vanilla indirect labor time} = (4 + 6) \times 10 + 9 = 109 \text{ hours}$$

The total demands for indirect labor are summarized in Exhibit 5-2.

Exhibit 5-2
Indirect Labor
Hours by Product

	VANILLA	CHOCOLATE	STRAWBERRY	MOCHA-ALMOND
Indirect labor hours—Schedule production runs	4.0	4.0	4.0	4.0
Setup time per run (hours)	2.0	1.0	2.5	4.0
Number employees per setup	3.0	3.0	3.0	3.0
Indirect labor hours per setup	6.0	3.0	7.5	12.0
Indirect labor hours per run: schedule and setup	10.0	7.0	11.5	16.0
Indirect labor—sustain products	9.0	9.0	9.0	9.0

Machinery Time

It was easy to develop the estimates of machine time by product. Machines were either producing products or being set up to produce the next batch of products. The time equation to estimate machine usage was:

$$\text{Machine time per product} = \text{Product run time} + \text{Product changeover time}$$
$$= \text{Product volume (gallons)} \times \text{Run time/gallon}$$
$$+ \text{Product changeover time} \times \text{Number of runs}$$

For example, if Vanilla had 10 production runs producing 8,000 gallons in a month, with processing time of 26 machine hours per 1,000 gallons, its hours of machine usage were:

$$\text{Vanilla machine time} = 8 \times 26 + 2 \times 10 = 228 \text{ hours}$$

Calculating Product Cost and Profitability

Lee had now developed all of the information—capacity cost rates for each resource and capacity demands on resources by each product—that she needed to calculate accurate product costs. She summarized the production data for the four products from the recent month as shown in Exhibit 5-3.

Lee next entered the production data into the two time equations for indirect production labor time and machine time to obtain the resource demand for the four products, as shown in Exhibit 5-4.

Exhibit 5-3
Madison Dairy Ice
Cream Plant
Production Data
(March 2010)

PRODUCTION STATISTICS (MARCH 2010)	VANILLA	CHOCOLATE	STRAWBERRY	MOCHA-ALMOND	TOTAL
Production and sales volume	10,000	8,000	1,200	800	20,000
Direct labor hours per gallon	0.025	0.025	0.025	0.025	
Total direct labor hours	250	200	30	20	500
Machine hours per 1,000 gallons	11	11	11	11	
Total machine run time	110	88	13	9	220
Number of production runs	12	12	8	6	38
Setup time per run (hours)	2.00	1.00	2.50	4.00	
Total setup time (hours)	24	12	20	24	80
Total machine hours	134	100	33	3	300

Exhibit 5-4
Resource Demands
by Product
(March 2010)

Hours of Resource Usage	Vanilla	Chocolate	Strawberry	Mocha-Almond	Total	Cost per Hour
Direct labor	250	200	30	20	500	$35
Indirect labor	129	93	101	105	428	$35
Machines	134	100	33.2	32.8	300	$50

For example, the indirect labor time for vanilla had the following components:

Purchasing and schedule time per run	4 hours
Machine setup time per run	6 hours (2 hours of setup × 3 setup employees)
Indirect labor time per run	10 hours
Number of production runs	12
Production runs indirect labor	120
Product-sustaining time per product	9
Total indirect labor time for vanilla	129 hours

Lee calculated the costs for each product by multiplying the resource usage times in Exhibit 5-4 by each resource's capacity cost rate, shown in the last column in Exhibit 5-4. She summarized the results in the product profit and loss statements shown in Exhibit 5-5.

Lee was initially surprised by the results reported in Exhibit 5-5. She saw that the products previously thought to be the most profitable, strawberry and mocha-almond, were actually the least profitable and in fact had enormous losses as a percentage of sales. Conversely, vanilla and chocolate, previously thought to be breakeven, were actually profitable with profit margins greater than 10% of sales. On further reflection, Lee could see the reasons for the reversals in profit rankings. Vanilla and chocolate were produced in long production runs, so their use of indirect labor and machine setup time were small compared to actual production volumes. Mocha-almond, a specialty product, had small production runs; she noted that its use of indirect labor and machine setup time exceeded the quantity of direct labor and machine run time for the product (see data in Exhibit 5-2). Despite mocha-almond having a unit price that was more than 15% higher than vanilla or chocolate, its price failed, by a large amount, to pay for the cost of its use of indirect labor and machine setup time. In general, the new costing approach clearly revealed that the revenues

Exhibit 5-5
Madison Dairy's
Ice Cream Revised
Product
Profitability
(March 2010)

Product Profit or Loss	Vanilla	Chocolate	Strawberry	Mocha-Almond	Total
Sales	$30,000	$24,000	$3,960	$2,800	$60,760
Direct materials	6,000	4,800	720	520	12,040
Direct labor (including fringes)	8,750	7,000	1,050	700	17,500
Indirect labor usage	4,515	3,255	3,535	3,675	14,980
Machine usage	6,700	5,000	1,660	1,640	15,000
Gross profit (loss)	$4,035	$3,945	($3,005)	($3,735)	$1,240
Gross profit (loss) (% of sales)	13%	16%	(76)%	(133)%	2%

from sales of the specialty strawberry and mocha-almond flavors failed to cover all of the expenses associated with their production.

Madison's previous standard costing system, which allocated overhead costs proportional to direct labor costs, assigned too much overhead cost to vanilla and chocolate, the high-volume simple products, and too few costs to strawberry and mocha-almond, the lower volume and more complex products. In general, not just in the simple example of the Madison Dairy ice cream plant, a company's production of complex, low-volume products requires many more resources per unit to perform setups, handle production runs, and design and support.

We can actually predict when standard costing systems will lead to high errors in estimating product costs. Cost systems that allocate overhead (indirect and support expenses) to products based on the direct labor hours (or any production volume measure) of each product produced will lead to the overcosting of high-volume products and undercosting of low-volume products when the following two situations exist:

1. Indirect and support expenses are high, especially when they exceed the cost of the allocation base itself (such as direct labor cost); and
2. Product diversity is high: the plant produces both high-volume and low-volume products, standard and custom products, and complex and simple products.

With high indirect costs and high product diversity, standard cost systems will always lead to highly distorted product costs, as the Madison Dairy ice cream plant example illustrates.

Possible Actions as a Result of the More Accurate Costing

The more accurate resource consumption and cost information in Exhibits 5-3 and 5-4 provides Madison Dairy's ice cream plant managers with numerous insights about how to increase the plant's profitability. They could attempt to raise prices for the unprofitable specialty flavors to cover their higher per unit production and sustaining costs. Currently, the costs for handling production runs and setting up machines for these two flavors are higher than their direct materials and labor costs. If customers truly value these specialty flavors, they might be willing to pay even higher prices for them. Alternatively, Madison's sales manager could consider imposing a minimum order size for Madison's retail customers so that the specialty products would be produced in larger production runs, thereby reducing the quantity of indirect resources they required. Of course, now that vanilla and chocolate are seen to be profitable, more effort might be devoted to increasing their sales volumes, an action that would not have been encouraged by the profit report in Exhibit 5-1, which showed these to be barely breakeven products for the company. Thus, this more accurate product profitability data signals that Madison Dairy's managers should be considering immediate actions in terms of pricing, product mix, and minimum order size.

Other actions could be directed at improving processes, particularly the processes for indirect and support activities. In the previous standard cost system, the costs of activities to purchase materials, schedule production runs, perform setups, and maintain products was buried in the large overhead pool and, hence, were not visible for improvement opportunities. The main focus had been to reduce direct labor and materials costs since these were the main levers affecting the standard costs. Now Christine Lee could encourage Madison's manufacturing people to redirect their attention to learning how to reduce setup times so that small batches of the specialty flavors would be less expensive (require fewer resources) to produce. They could also search for ways to reduce the times required to do purchasing and scheduling for production orders and to perform the ongoing maintenance of products each month. These would all reduce the demands for indirect labor.

The combined impact of process improvements, repricing, and product volume and mix changes will enable Madison's managers to significantly improve profitability without compromising its ability to offer customers both high-volume standard and low-volume specialty flavor products. The new and more accurate costing system provides Madison's managers with many insights that can be exploited to transform currently unprofitable operations into profitable growth.

IN PRACTICE
Using Activity-Based Costing to Increase Bank Profitability

ATB Financial, a commercial bank based in Alberta, Canada, was offering 200 products and processing more than 12 million transactions per month for its 2 million customer accounts in 160 branches. The Personal Services business offered credit card products, mortgage services, Internet banking, travel protection, loans, and retirement products. The Business Services group offered investment products, tax filing services, merchant processing services, brokerage services, foreign correspondence, and debt financing. A newly formed Investor Services group offered mutual funds, fixed-date deposits, and educational and retirement savings plans.

ATB supported these products with regional and centralized resources, such as call centers and information technology centers. But its existing cost system could not assign the costs of these regional and corporate resources to transactions, products, and customers. The chief operating officer believed that the bank's emphasis on revenue growth in a booming economy had blurred its focus on the bottom line: "When the top line is growing fast, it is easy to hide a ton of sins—we run the risk of overbuilding and giving away profitability."

An ATB project team developed and installed a time-driven ABC system that could accurately calculate branch and product profitability each month. The new system stimulated numerous cost and revenue improvement actions, including the following:

- The time equations in the TDABC model revealed how call-center process times varied by type of call. For example, calls to reset passwords were expensive and frequent. The team developed new procedures to address the root cause for these

calls, and the volume and cost for this type of call soon plummeted.

- Responding to customers' requests to trace items they didn't recognize was a surprisingly high cost process. These costs were often more than the charge for this service and often more than the amount in dispute. The bank established a procedure to either increase the service fee or authorize an adjustment in lieu of handling a trace request on small items.

- The TDABC model enabled the team to discover that differences in capacity utilization explained much of the variation in branch efficiency. The model identified where excess capacity existed by process within each branch. Management could then downsize its branch service and delivery platform to expected demands.

- The project team noticed a marked difference across branches in the cost of human-handled transactions compared with electronic transactions. One human-handled transaction in a branch often led to another as customers who had already waited in line to make a bill payment were likely to make a deposit or withdrawal at the same time. The most efficient branches used "greeters" to direct customers to banking machines or Internet terminals for routine transactions.

Within a year of the ABC project launch, the bank had identified nearly $2 million in annualized profit improvement through revenue enhancement and cost reductions. A senior executive observed, "ABC is now part of our evolution to build a rigorous commercial capability to drive and manage profitability, helping us make the right decisions to drive performance."

Source: "ATB Financial: Guiding Profitable Growth," Chapter 11 in R. S. Kaplan and S. R. Anderson, *Time-Driven Activity-Based Costing: A Simpler and More Powerful Path to Higher Profits* (Boston: Harvard Business Press, 2007): 197–208.

Measuring the Cost of Unused Resource Capacity

Christine Lee noticed that the total profits shown in Exhibit 5-5 ($1,240) were higher than the $1,120 calculated in Exhibit 5-1 by the traditional standard cost system. The time-driven ABC results in Exhibit 5-5 used resource capacity rates calculated from the capacity of the resources (labor and machinery) provided each month. But Madison had operated slightly under capacity during the month of March 2010 as shown in Exhibit 5-6.

With time-driven ABC, the cost of unused capacity is not assigned to products—but it should not be ignored. The unused capacity remains someone's or some department's responsibility. Usually one can assign unused capacity after analyzing the decision that authorized the level of capacity supplied. For example, if the capacity was acquired to meet anticipated demands from a particular customer or a particular market segment, the costs of unused capacity due to lower-than-expected demands can be assigned to the person or organizational unit responsible for that customer or segment. Such an assignment is done on a lump-sum basis to the organizational unit; it should not be driven down to the products actually produced during the period in the unit.

Managers can often assign the cost of unused capacity to a product line, a department, or an executive. For example, if the unused capacity relates to a particular product line—as when certain production resources are dedicated to individual product lines—the cost of unused capacity is assigned to that product line where the demand failed to materialize. Suppose a division manager knew in advance that resource supply would exceed resource demand but wanted to retain the amount of current unused resources for future growth and expansion. Then that unused capacity could be a division-sustaining cost, assigned to the division making the decision to retain the unused capacity. In making such assignment of unused capacity costs, we trace the costs at the level in the organization where decisions are made that affect the supply of capacity resources and the demand for those resources. The lump-sum assignment of unused capacity costs provides feedback to managers on their supply and demand decisions.

Fixed Costs and Variable Costs in Activity-Based Cost Systems

We have seen how an activity-based cost system assigns indirect and support costs to products. Some people believe that such a full cost assignment treats indirect and support costs as "variable," in the sense that they will increase or decrease with short-term changes in the quantity produced of a product or in the number of setups or production runs. This is an erroneous inference as Madison Dairy's ice cream plant clearly shows. All of the production workers are paid whether they are doing production runs and setups or not. And the machine lease payments occur each month whether the machines are producing ice cream or not. If the company does one less setup or one fewer production run, its overall costs will not change, which is why

Exhibit 5-6
Resource Capacity Utilization at Madison Ice Cream Plant (March 2010)

Resource	# Units	Hours Supplied/Unit per Month	Total Hours Supplied	Hours Used (March 2010)	Unused Capacity (Hrs)	Cost per Hour	Unused Capacity ($)
Production labor	7	133	931	928	3	$35	$105
Machines	2	154	308	300	8	$50	$400

many refer to indirect and support costs as "fixed costs." We prefer, however, to refer to such costs as committed, not fixed.

Most expenses assigned by an ABC system are committed because managers have made a decision to supply these resources in advance of knowing exactly what the production volumes and mix will be. Thus the costs of these resources will not vary with actual production volume and mix during the month. But managers can adjust their resource costs by supplying a different quantity of resources for future months. The costs remain fixed only if managers fail to react to changes in demand and capacity utilization. Thus whether a cost is fixed or variable is not an attribute of the cost itself. It is determined by the alertness and willingness of managers to adjust the supply of resources, either up or down, in response to changes in the demands for the work performed by the resource. Committed costs can change (or vary) through the following process:

1. Demands for the capacity resources change, either because of changes in the quantity of activities performed (e.g., changes in number of production runs or products supported) or because of changes in the efficiency of performing activities. For example, if setup times get reduced, fewer resources—employees and machines time—are required to perform the same quantity of setups.
2. Managers make decisions to change the supply of committed resources, either up or down, to meet the new level of demand for the activities performed by these resources.

If the quantity of demands for a resource exceeds its capacity, the result is bottlenecks, pressure to work faster, delays, or poor-quality work. Such capacity shortages occur often on machines, but the ABC approach makes clear that shortages can also occur for human resources who perform support activities, such as designing, scheduling, ordering, purchasing, maintaining, and handling products and customers. Companies facing such shortages increase their committed costs by spending more to increase the supply of resources to perform work, which is why many indirect costs increase over time.

Demands for indirect and support resources also can decline, either intentionally through managerial actions, such as imposing minimum order sizes and reducing setup times, or because of competitive or economy-wide forces that lead to declines in sales. Should the demands for resources decrease, few immediate spending reductions will be noticed. People have been hired, space has been rented, and equipment, computers, telephones, and furniture have been acquired. The expenses for these resources continue even though there is less work for the resources to perform. The reduced demand for organizational resources does lower the cost of resources *used* by products, services, and customers, but this decrease is offset by an equivalent increase in the cost of unused capacity.

After unused capacity has been created, committed costs will vary downward if and only if managers actively reduce the supply of unused resources. What enables a resource cost to be adjusted downward is not inherent in the nature of the resource; it is a function of management decisions—first to reduce the demands for the resource and second to lower the spending on it.

Organizations often create unused capacity through actions, such as process improvement, repricing to modify the product mix, and imposing minimum order sizes on customers. They keep existing resources in place, however, even though the demands for the activities performed by the resources have diminished substantially. They also fail to find new activities that could be done by the resources already in place but not being used. In this case, the organization receives no benefits from its decisions that reduced the demands on its resources. The failure to capture benefits from the actions, however, is not because costs are fixed. Rather, the failure occurs because managers are unwilling or unable to take advantage of the unused capacity they have created, such as by spending less on capacity resources or increasing the volume of work processed by the capacity resources. The costs of these resources are fixed only if managers do not exploit the opportunities from the unused capacity they helped to create.

Thus, making decisions, such as to reduce product variety, solely on the basis of resource usage (the ABC system), may not increase profits if managers are not prepared to reduce spending to align resource supply with the future lower levels of demand. For example, if an action causes the number of production runs to decrease by 10%, no economic benefit will be achieved unless some of the resources previously supplied to perform production runs are eliminated or redeployed to higher revenue uses. Consequently, before making decisions on the basis of an ABC model, managers should determine the resource supply implications of their decisions. We can illustrate this with decisions made by the managers of Madison Dairy's ice cream plant.

Using the ABC Model to Forecast Resource Capacity

Christine Lee formed a small interdepartmental task force, which included representatives of sales, marketing, production, industrial engineering, and human resources, to make recommendations about how to improve profitability at Madison Dairy's ice cream plant. Production people and industrial engineers felt that significant improvements could be made in the setup process and also in the time required to prepare for production runs and maintain product information. They believed that new work procedures would enable the plant to reduce the setup work crew from three to two employees. Similarly, rigorous application of quality management tools would reduce the setup times for both strawberry and mocha-almond by 20%. The production and industrial engineers also committed to process improvements that would reduce the time to prepare for a production run from 4 hours to 2.5 hours, and the time required to maintain a product from 9 hours to 8 hours per month. They summarized all of their process improvement commitments in the following table:

	VANILLA	CHOCOLATE	STRAWBERRY	MOCHA-ALMOND
Setup time per run (hours)	2.0	1.0	2.0	3.2
Indirect labor setup time (hours per run)	4.0	2.0	4.0	6.4
Handle production run (hours per run)	2.5	2.5	2.5	2.5
Sustaining products (hours per month)	8.0	8.0	8.0	8.0

The production people pointed out that in addition to making substantial improvements in performing setups and preparing for a production run, the plant would run more efficiently if it could produce at least 350 gallons in each production run. The sales and marketing members on the task force agreed that they could require customers to either order a minimum of at least 350 gallons of a flavor or else be willing to wait until a batch of small orders could be accumulated to allow a production run of at least 350 gallons.

Sales people suggested that there was considerable price elasticity for the commodity vanilla and chocolate products. They thought that a small $0.10 per gallon price decrease would lead to a 15% to 20% sales volume increase. They also felt that demand would not fall too precipitously for the specialty flavors if a small price increase were imposed. Given the pricing flexibility, they committed to delivering sales that would not require a large number of small production runs. After considerable discussion, the task force agreed on the sales and production plan shown below:

	VANILLA	CHOCOLATE	STRAWBERRY	MOCHA-ALMOND	TOTAL
Selling price	$2.90	$2.90	$3.40	$4.00	$2.96
Sales volume (gallons)	12,000	9,200	1,100	700	23,000
Revenues	$34,800	$26,680	$3,740	$2,800	$68,020
# production runs	15	12	3	2	32

The new sales forecast reflected a 15% increase in gallons sold, and a 12% increase in revenues, from $60,760 (in March 2010) to $68,020. The price reductions and volume increases for the high-volume products would reduce the average selling price per gallon to $2.96 (from the March 2010 average selling price of $3.04 per gallon).

Everyone was excited about the projected sales volume increases and the potential cost savings from the process improvements. But Lee was unsure whether the 15% higher production volume could be handled by the existing two machine lines in the factory. She also wondered how the process improvements would translate into actual cost reductions, especially if the plant ended up needing additional personnel and equipment to handle the higher production volumes. Fortunately, she now had a time-driven ABC model for the plant that she could use to forecast the resource capacity that would be needed with the new sales and production plan.

Lee estimated the quantity of direct labor time required for the new production plan:

	VANILLA	CHOCOLATE	STRAWBERRY	MOCHA-ALMOND	TOTAL
Production and sales volume (gallons)	12,000	9,200	1,100	700	23,000
Direct labor hours per gallon	0.025	0.025	0.025	0.025	
Total direct labor hours	**300.0**	**230.0**	**27.5**	**17.5**	**575.0**

Next she estimated the demand for indirect production labor time.

	VANILLA	CHOCOLATE	STRAWBERRY	MOCHA-ALMOND	TOTAL
# production runs	15	12	3	2	
Handle production run (hours/run)	2.5	2.5	2.5	2.5	
Indirect labor—handle runs	37.5	30.0	7.5	5.0	80.0
Setup time per run (hours)	2.0	1.0	2.0	3.2	
Indirect labor hours per run	4.0	2.0	4.0	6.4	
Indirect labor—total setup hours	60.0	24.0	12.0	12.8	108.8
Indirect labor—maintain products	8.0	8.0	8.0	8.0	32.0
Total indirect labor hours	**105.5**	**62.0**	**27.5**	**25.8**	**220.8**

The total demand for production labor to fulfill the new production plan was 795.8 hours. Lee noted that six employees have a capacity of 798 hours available for work (133 hours per employee × 6 employees). She was surprised and pleased to learn that the new production plan, with a 15% increase in gallons produced, actually required one fewer production worker. The combination of fewer and larger production runs, plus the efficiencies gained from shifting to two-person setup crews and other process improvements, enabled the higher production volumes to be achieved with fewer resources.

Lee had one final calculation to perform: Would the company need another production line, or would it need to operate the existing machines on overtime or add a second shift to obtain additional machine capacity for the higher production volumes? She performed the following calculations to estimate the machine times required for the new production plan:

	Vanilla	Chocolate	Strawberry	Mocha-Almond	Total
Production volume	12,000	9,200	1,100	700	23,000
Machine hours per 1000 gallon	11	11	11	11	
Total machine run time (hours)	132	101.2	12.1	7.7	253
Number of production runs	15	12	3	2	
Setup time per run (hours)	2.0	1.0	2.0	3.2	
Machine setup time (hours)	30.0	12.0	6.0	6.4	54.4
Total machine hours	162.0	113.2	18.1	14.1	307.4

With two production lines, each with a capacity of 154 hours per month, Lee could see that the existing production capacity would be adequate to handle the 15% increase in production volume. The savings from fewer production runs and the 20% reduction in setup times for the strawberry and mocha-almond flavors produced enough new machine capacity to produce the higher production volumes without adding another machine line or requiring overtime or a second shift. This was a vivid example of how process improvements can allow a company to produce more without requiring any increase in total production costs (other than direct materials) and, in fact, allow for a decrease in costs through having one fewer production employee.

Lee quickly generated a pro forma (forecasted) monthly product profit and loss statement by multiplying the planned resource consumption of each product by the cost rate for each resource (right-hand column in Exhibit 5-3) as shown in Exhibit 5-7. All products would be profitable, and the overall profit margin now exceeded 16% of sales, a major improvement from the less than 2% margin earned in March 2010.

Exhibit 5-7
Madison Dairy's Ice Cream Pro Forma Product Profitability

	Vanilla	Chocolate	Strawberry	Mocha-Almond	Total
Selling price	$2.90	$2.90	$3.40	$4.00	$2.96
Sales volume	12,000	9,200	1,100	700	23,000
Revenues	$34,800	$26,680	$3,740	$2,800	$68,020
Direct materials	7,200	5,520	660	455	13,835
Direct labor (including fringes)	10,500	8,050	963	613	20,125
Indirect labor	3,693	2,170	963	903	7,728
Machinery	8,100	5,660	905	705	15,370
Gross profit	$5,308	$5,280	$250	$125	$10,962
Gross profit (% of sales)	15.3%	19.8%	6.7%	4.5%	16.1%

All products would be profitable, and vanilla and chocolate would be achieving the company's targeted rate of 15% of sales.

Lee also noted that a monthly overall income statement for Madison's ice cream plant, shown below, would differ slightly from the last column in Exhibit 5-7:

Sales	$68,020
Direct Materials	13,835
Production Labor: 6 @ $4,655	27,930
Machines: 2 @ 7,700	15,400
Operating Profit	$10,855

The $107 difference is due to the small quantities of unused capacity for the labor and machine resources, as summarized below:

	Hours Supplied	Hours Used	Unused Capacity	Cost Rate	Cost of Unused Capacity
Production labor hours	798.0	795.8	2.2	$35	$77
Machine hours	308.0	307.4	0.6	$50	$30
Total					$107

The cost of this unused capacity is not the cost of the products actually produced during the period. It is a period cost caused by having slightly more capacity than was actually required for the volume and mix of products produced during the period. In this case, the plant is operating at more than 99% of capacity. In other circumstances, the cost of unused capacity could be quite high. If the company were not careful about segregating the cost of unused capacity from product costs, it could get confused by having products report a loss that was caused by an arbitrary allocation of excess capacity costs, not because of inefficient production or lack of adequate margins over production costs. A manager might attempt to raise prices to cover the apparently higher costs at just the wrong time, when the company already has unused capacity, indicating some demand softness in the economy or a weak competitive position. Such a price increase would likely lead to even lower sales volumes in future periods, and higher quantities of unused capacity, in effect the death spiral described in Chapter 4.

Updating the ABC Model

An important issue for any costing model is how to update it, as needed, to keep current with changes in the company's operations. Time-driven ABC models can be modified easily to reflect such changes. For example, Madison's managers may learn that production labor performs activities, such as packaging and shipping products or receiving orders directly from customers, that were not identified for the original model. These additions can easily be incorporated by estimating the time required each time an employee performs the new activity, such as the time required to package a carton of ice cream, or the time required to receive and process a customer

IN PRACTICE
W.S. Industries Uses ABC Information for Continuous Improvement

W.S. Industries, headquartered in Chennai, India, supplies equipment such as insulators, lightning arrestors, transformers, capacitors, and circuit breakers to companies that transmit and distribute electrical power. As competition intensified in the 1990s, the company could no longer pass on cost increases in the form of higher prices. It had to hold its prices constant or even reduce them. W.S. Industries wanted to protect its strong market position in India, where it was among the top three in market share, while expanding aggressively into international markets in Asia, Europe, Africa, and the United States. Among its primary goals for success was to achieve a "quantum improvement in productivity." It turned to ABC as the primary tool to achieve this business objective.

It formed an ABC project team consisting of middle managers from operations, research and development, quality, information systems, and only one finance representative. W.S. wanted operating people to have ownership of the new system, not to feel that it was developed and mandated by finance. The team mapped all process and activities into a database, classifying each as either value added or non–value added (a non–value-added activity, such as moving parts back and forth into inventory, was one that could be eliminated with no deterioration of product attributes).

Employee teams used the new ABC information to suggest continuous improvement projects (CIPs) that would either eliminate nonvalue adding activities or reduce the cost of performing value-adding activities. For example, one team received approval to break down a wall that was causing excessive quantities of internal movement. The team saw from the ABC analysis that the benefits from reduced material movement costs exceeded the cost of the renovation.

The highly unionized workforce was initially concerned about job loss due to successful improvement projects. The company guaranteed that the benefits from the CIPs would be captured by higher sales growth, not job losses. To reinforce the culture of employee empowerment and informed continuous improvement, the company instituted the following reward program:

- A CIP would be eligible for a reward only if it were successfully implemented by a team and the savings were realized without any adverse side effects.
- Expenses to implement the project would be deducted when calculating the actual savings achieved.
- Employees would receive a fixed proportion of the savings either one time or annually if savings continued to occur.
- All rewards would be disbursed equally to all team members in an open forum of all employees.

In the first three years, the company completed 56 CIPs yielding savings of Rs. 13.62 million (about U.S. $300,000). More significantly, factory capacity had increased from 9,000 metric tons of product to 11,700 metric tons per year. Material movements dropped by 15,200 metric ton-meters per day; reductions in waste, scrap, and inventory yielded savings of Rs. 10 million per year; and the available time on bottleneck machines increased from less than 85% to more than 95%. On-time delivery to customers had also improved dramatically.

Source: V. G. Narayanan, "Activity-Based Management at W.S. Industries (A)," HBS No. 101-062 (Boston: Harvard Business School Publishing, 2001).

order. The capacity cost rate for the production employees has already been determined so the system can quickly calculate the cost of the new activity by multiplying the time estimates by the capacity cost rate.

Managers can also easily update the capacity cost rates. Several factors cause a cost rate to change. First, changes in the prices of resources supplied affect the hourly cost rate. If production employees receive an 8% compensation increase, their hourly cost rate increases from $35.00 per supplied hour to $37.80 per hour. If new machines are substituted or added to a process, the cost rate is modified to reflect the change in operating expense associated with introducing the new equipment.

Capacity cost rates also change when the denominator, practical capacity, changes. If working conditions change, such as by increasing the number of holidays, vacation days, or sick and personal leave days or by changing the number of hours worked per day or the time taken for training, meeting, and breaks, then the person maintaining the cost system would recalculate the number of hours available for productive work each month. This is not a difficult calculation to perform.

We have already seen from the Madison Dairy ice cream plant example how employees' quality and continuous improvement efforts enable the same activity to be done in less time or with fewer resources. When permanent, sustainable improvements in a process have been made, the manager of the cost system reduces the unit time estimates—and, hence, the resource requirements—to reflect the process improvements.

Following this procedure, a time-driven ABC model update is triggered by events that require the estimates in the model to be modified. Whenever analysts learn about a significant shift in the costs of resources supplied or about changes in the resources required for the activity, they update the cost rate estimates. Whenever they learn of a significant and permanent shift in the efficiency with which an activity is performed, they update the unit time estimate.

Time Equations

We have already seen how the time estimate to perform an activity, such as changing a machine over for a new production run, can vary based on the product that has just been produced (e.g., mocha-almond to eliminate all traces of allergens) or is about to be produced. Thus processing times can vary based on the specific characteristics of a particular order and task. Time-driven ABC accommodates the complexity of real-world operations with time equations, a feature that enables the model to reflect how particular order and activity characteristics cause processing times to vary.

Consider, as an example, processing a customer's order. Some customer orders arrive over the telephone, others may be faxed in, while many arrive electronically on an automated web page. Each of these may involve different amounts of time for the company personnel to process. For the ice cream plant, suppose that part of the nine, soon to be eight, hours required for each production run includes the time required to receive and process a specific customer order. The ABC project team might estimate the following time equation for the time required to process a customer's order to reflect how the order arrived at the plant:

Indirect labor time to receive a customer order = 1 hour + 2 hours (if telephone order)
+ 1 hour (if fax order)
+ 0.2 hours (if electronic order)

The time equation allows the details of particular orders to be captured simply and incorporated within the model.

As another example, consider the activity of getting orders ready for shipment. If the item is already a standard one in a standard package, the operation may take only 0.5 minute to prepare it for shipment. If the item requires a special package, then an additional 6.5 minutes is required. And if the item is to be shipped by air, an additional 0.2 minute is required to place it in a special bag. The time equation for the packaging process can be represented as follows:

Packaging time = 0.5 + 6.5 (if special handling required)
+ 0.2 (if shipping by air)

The data for the time equations—order types, method of shipment, and all other production characteristics—are typically already in the company's enterprise resource planning system where the order has been entered. Order-specific data enable the particular time demands for any given order to be quickly calculated with a simple algorithm that tests for the existence of each characteristic affecting resource processing time. In this way, the time-driven ABC model can accurately and simply reflect the variety and complexity in orders, products, and customers.

SERVICE COMPANIES

Although ABC had its origins in manufacturing companies, today many service organizations are obtaining great benefits from this approach. In practice, the actual construction of an ABC model is nearly identical for both types of companies. This should not be surprising since even in manufacturing companies the ABC system focuses on the service component, not on the direct materials and direct labor costs of manufacturing operations. ABC addresses the support resources that serve the manufacturing process—purchasing, scheduling, inspecting, designing, supporting products and processes, and handling customers and their orders.

Service companies in general are ideal candidates for ABC, even more than manufacturing companies. First, virtually all of the costs for a service company are indirect and appear to be fixed. Manufacturing companies can trace important components of costs, such as direct material and direct labor costs, to individual products. Service companies have few or no direct materials, and many of their personnel provide indirect, not direct, support to products and customers. Consequently, service companies do not have direct, traceable costs to serve as convenient allocation bases.

The large component of apparently fixed costs in service companies arises because, unlike manufacturing companies, service companies have virtually no material costs—the prime source of short-term variable costs. Service companies must supply virtually all of their resources in advance to provide the capacity to perform work for customers during each period. Fluctuations during the period of demand by individual products and customers for the activities performed by these resources do not influence short-term spending to supply the resources.

Consequently, the *variable cost* (defined as the increase in spending resulting from an incremental transaction or customer) for many service industries is close to zero. For example, a transaction at a bank's automatic teller machine requires an additional consumption of a small piece of paper to print the receipt—but no additional outlay. For a bank to add an additional customer may require a monthly statement to be mailed, involving the cost of the paper, an envelope, and a stamp—but little more. Carrying an extra passenger on an airplane requires an extra can of soda pop, perhaps, a small snack (for most coach-class U.S. flights these days!), and a minor increase in fuel consumption—but nothing else. For a telecommunications company, handling one more phone call from a customer or one more data transfer involves no incremental spending. Therefore, service companies making decisions about products and customers on the basis of short-term variable costs might provide a full range of all products and services to customers at prices that could range down to near zero. In such cases, of course, the companies would receive virtually no recovery of the costs of all of the committed resources they supplied to enable the service to be delivered to the customer.

An activity-based cost system for a service company would be developed in the same way as that for a manufacturing company. We will illustrate with a simple example but not go through an extended example, as we did for Madison's ice cream plant. (*Note:* There will be an exercise in the problems at the end of the chapter for you to practice on.) Consider a retail brokerage company that performs stock and mutual fund trades, account management, and financial planning for its customers.

The broker at a financial services company spends about five minutes to execute this customer's telephone request to purchase a stock.
AFP/Getty Images

Its resources include various types of employees: brokers, account managers, and financial planners, information technology and telecommunications equipment and support staff, and office space and furniture. Let's focus on one resource, one of the company's 225 brokers. Remember that we need to calculate two parameters:

1. The broker's capacity cost rate.
2. How much of the broker's capacity is used by each of the various activities she performs for products and customers.

Capacity Cost Rate

The numerator in the capacity cost rate includes the broker's total compensation and the costs of all other resources deployed to support her. The broker's annual compensation is $65,000, including fringe benefits. The broker works in an 80-square-foot office and the cost of supplying space in that location has been estimated at $125 per square foot per year. Finally, the broker has a leased personal computer, rights to several financial planning and analysis software packages, real-time access to stock pricing and stock research, and support from the company's internal information technology group. The total cost of computer hardware, software, and internal consulting support is about $6,120 per year. This yields the following fully loaded cost for the broker:

Annual compensation	$65,000
Occupancy (80 sq ft @ $125/sq ft)	10,000
Computer technology and support	6,120
Total annual cost	$81,120
Monthly cost	$ 6,760

The denominator of the capacity cost rate equals the time the broker has available for work with customers. She shows up for work on 240 days per year, or 20 days per month. The workday is 7½ hours per day, with 1 hour used for breaks, training, research, and internal staff meetings. Thus the broker has about 130 hours per month (20 days per month × 6.5 hours per day) available for productive work. The broker's capacity cost rate can now be calculated:

Broker capacity cost rate = ($6,760 per month)/(130 hours/month)
= $52 per hour (or, approximately, $0.87 per minute)

Calculating the Time Equation for the Consumption of Broker's Capacity

The broker performs three different activities: performing a stock trade at a customer's request, opening an account for a new customer, and meeting with customers, either over the phone or in person to talk about financial plans and account management. Studies have indicated the typical times required each time one of these activities is performed:

Performing a stock trade transaction	5 minutes
Opening a new account	60 minutes
Meeting with a customer	20 minutes

During a recent month, the broker performed 912 stock trades, opened 4 new stock trading accounts, and had 6 meetings with customers. The total time of the broker associated with the stock trading product line would be calculated as:

$$\text{Broker's time used for stock trading} = (912 \times 5 + 4 \times 60 + 6 \times 20)$$
$$= 4,920 \text{ minutes}$$
$$= 82 \text{ hours}$$
$$\text{Cost of broker for stock trading product line} = 82 \times 52 = \$4,264$$

Stock trading used 82 of the broker's 130 available hours of time during the month. Some of the broker's remaining time might have been used for other product lines, such as mutual fund sales and redemptions, and some might represent unused capacity during the month. This will be determined when the more complete model of resource consumption and costing across all product lines is built.

The preceding calculation for the single broker would be replicated for all of the company's 225 brokers, and a similar set of calculations performed for each of the company's other resources involved in supporting stock trading. The costs of all resources would then be accumulated and matched with the revenues, typically brokerage commissions, earned by trading stocks for customers, to determine the profit or loss from this product line.

Once a complete costing and profitability report has been built, the managers of a service company can contemplate the same set of actions as their counterparts in manufacturing companies: pricing, product mix, process improvements, minimum level of customer transaction volumes, etc. Companies in financial services (banks, insurance companies, and money managers), transportation (airlines, trucking, and railroads), telecommunications, wholesale and retail, health care, and even many government agencies are now using such ABC analysis to understand and improve the economics of their operations.

IMPLEMENTATION ISSUES

Although ABC has provided managers in many companies with valuable information about the cost of their activities, processes, products, services, and customers, not all ABC systems have been sustained or have contributed to higher profitability for the company. Companies have experienced difficulties and frustrations in building and using ABC and profitability models. We can identify several common pitfalls that have occurred and suggest ways to avoid them.

Lack of Clear Business Purpose

Often, the ABC project is initiated out of the finance or accounting department and is touted as "a more accurate cost system." The project team gets resources for the project, builds an initial ABC model, and then becomes disappointed and disillusioned when no one else looks at or acts on the new ABC cost and profitability information.

To avoid this syndrome, all ABC projects should be launched with a specific business purpose in mind. The purpose could be to redesign or improve processes, to influence product design decisions, to rationalize the product mix, or to provide better baselines for pricing decisions. By defining the business purpose at the start, the team will identify the line manager or department whose behavior and decisions are expected to change as a consequence of the information. The decision maker could be the manufacturing or operations manager (for process improvement), the engineering manager (for product design decisions), the sales organization (for managing customer relationships), or the marketing department (for decisions about pricing and product mix).

It is also important not to oversell what the ABC system is capable of doing. Some project teams, carried away by their enthusiasm, promise that ABC will solve all of the company's costing and financial problems. ABC is a strategic costing system that highlights the costs of processes, and the cost and profitability of products, and customers. It is not a good system for providing short-term feedback on process and departmental efficiencies and improvements.

Lack of Senior Management Commitment

A pitfall related to the first problem arises when the finance department undertakes the project without gaining senior management support and buy-in. When this happens, the rest of the organization views the project as done by and for finance people; as a result, no one outside the finance department pays attention to it. Because the finance department is not empowered to make decisions about processes, product designs, product mix, pricing, and customer relationships, no useful actions are taken that lead to increased profitability.

The most successful ABC projects occur when a clear business purpose exists for building the ABC model and when this purpose is led (or at least understood and fully supported) by senior line managers in the organization. A steering committee of senior managers from various functional groups and business units provides guidance and oversight, meeting monthly to review project progress, make suggestions on how to enhance the model, and prepare for the decisions that will be made once the model has been completed.

Even when the ABC project is initiated from the finance group, a multifunctional project team should be formed. The team should include, in addition to a cost analyst or other finance group representative, members from operations, marketing/sales, engineering, and systems. In this way, the expertise from diverse groups can be incorporated into the model design, and each team member can build support for the project within his or her department and group.

Delegating the Project to Consultants

Some projects have failed when they were outsourced to an external consulting company. Consultants may have considerable experience with ABC but not the needed familiarity with a company's operations and business problems. Nor can they build management consensus and support within the organization either to make decisions with the ABC information or to maintain and update the model. Even worse, some companies think they can get an ABC system by buying an ABC software package. The software provides a template to enter, process, and report information, but it cannot provide the thinking required to build a cost-effective ABC model.

ABC consultants and ABC software can play valuable roles for many companies, but they are not substitutes for overcoming the first two pitfalls. Successful ABC projects require top management leadership and sponsorship and a dedicated, multi-functional internal project team. These functions cannot be bypassed just because external consultants and prepackaged software have also been purchased.

Poor ABC Model Design

Sometimes, even with strong management support and sponsorship, the project team gets lost in the details and develops an ABC model that is both too complicated to build and maintain and too complex for managers to understand and act on. In other cases, the model uses arbitrary allocations—frequently percentages, not capacity utilization estimates—to map costs from resources to products and customers. The arbitrary allocations create distortions in the model and destroy its credibility among line managers. Often, the model requires other organizational functions to provide new data and information on a regular basis, increasing their workload without providing corresponding benefits. Under the burden of poor design, the ABC system soon collapses under its own weight and neglect.

As noted, ABC model design should be like any design or engineering project. The project team can start out with a simple high-level prototype, Version 1.0. After various people within the company have a chance to review the output from the model and study the assumptions made in its building, the project team can do more detailed analysis and model extension where Version 1.0 was too simplistic. Over time, the model's design will improve and gain credibility throughout the company. As one vice president of sales insisted, while serving on an advisory committee to the ABC project team:

> We absolutely need credible, valid numbers if we are to have frank discussions with our least profitable customers. Good cost numbers will also help us grow and enhance relationships with our most profitable customers.

The ABC project team should keep end users clearly in mind, get good advice from its senior management steering committee, and make good cost-effective design decisions along the way. These decisions can help avoid the problem of having an overcomplex or nontransparent costing system.

Individual and Organizational Resistance to Change

Not all managers welcome technically superior solutions. Individuals often resist new ideas and change, and organizations have great inertia. The resistance to a new ABC model may not be overt. Managers can politely sit through an ABC presentation about product and customer profitability but continue to behave just as they have in the past; or they will ask the project team to reestimate the model, using a more recent period or at another company site. Sometimes, however, the resistance is more overt. Managers may argue that the company has been successful in the past with its existing cost system; why does it need a new approach? Or, if it has been a finance-led project, they may accuse the finance people of wanting to run the company or not understanding the complexity of the business.

People Feel Threatened

Individual and organizational resistance arises because people feel threatened by the suggestion that their work could be improved. We might not think that a cost model could generate such resistance, but in fact, a more accurate costing model could reveal the following:

- Unprofitable products.
- Inefficient activities and processes.
- Substantial unused capacity.

Managers responsible for these problems could be embarrassed and threatened by the revelation of apparent bad management during their watch. Rather than accept the validity of the ABC model and attempt to rectify the problems (which likely occurred because of inadequacies in the previous cost system, not their own negligence or ineptitude), they may deny the validity of the new approach and question the motives of the people attempting to lead the change. Such defensive behavior will inhibit any effective action.

Chapter 9 includes a discussion of the behavioral issues that arise when implementing new cost control, performance measurement, and management control systems. Resistance is not unique to ABC. It can arise from the introduction of any new measurement or management system or, indeed, any management change initiative. However, as a costing innovation, ABC systems are prime candidates for triggering individuals' and organizations' negative responses to change initiatives. Dealing with such responses requires skills for recognizing and overcoming defensive behavior, skills that managers may not have been taught in their academic studies or in their early job assignments.

EPILOGUE TO MADISON DAIRY

Madison Dairy extended the time-driven ABC system from its single ice cream plant to its entire operations. It was able to track the costs of changeovers in producing and packaging all of its products and the costs of picking, loading, and delivering products to its diverse customer base. The model captured differences in how it entered orders from customers (customer phone call, salesperson call, fax, truck-driver entry, electronic data interchange, or Internet), how it packaged orders (full stacks of six cases, individual cases, or partial break-pack cases for small orders), how it delivered orders (commercial carriers or its own fleet including route miles), and time spent by the driver at each customer location. The model also captured the extra packaging costs for special promotions and customer-specific labels and promotions.

Madison used its time-driven ABC model proactively to become the leading dairy supplier to a national customer. Madison demonstrated that it could identify the specific manufacturing, distribution, and order handling costs associated with serving this customer on the basis of actual order characteristics: DSD (direct store delivery) or shipments to distribution centers, gallon versus pint deliveries, and volume and mix of products. The ABC model facilitated an open, trusting relationship between supplier and customer that differentiated Madison from its competitors.

Madison also became aware that one of its convenience store customers had been overordering and returning product when the date code had expired. To save the high cost of these rebates and returns, Madison offered these retailers a 2% discount if the retailer would manage its own inventory without the return option. In this way, Madison eliminated 95% of out-of-code returns, generating a net saving of $120,000 per year.

Source: The Madison Dairy case was based on an actual company case study; see "Kemps LLC: Introducing Time-Driven ABC," HBS No. 106-001 (Boston: Harvard Business School Publishing, 2006).

SUMMARY

This chapter introduced activity-based cost systems, including why ABC systems produce more accurate costs than standard cost systems, which allocate production overhead proportional to quantities produced. ABC systems drive the cost of indirect and support resources—manufacturing resources in factories and marketing, selling, distribution, and administrative resources—more directly to products by modeling how each product and production run makes demands on the organization's various resources.

An ABC model consists of two fundamental parameters: the costs of supplying each resource's capacity and the demands that each product and production order make on each resource's capacity. The model's developers make appropriate trade-offs in the design of the model, balancing the cost of more accurate measurement for more complex models with the benefits from the greater accuracy.

Managers use the information on activity costs to improve profitability. They can identify high-cost and inefficient processes that are prime candidates for operational improvement projects. Managers also learn about the profitable and unprofitable products and use that information to make better decisions on pricing, product mix, product design, and process improvements that transform unprofitable products into profitable ones.

Despite the apparent attraction of increased accuracy and managerial relevance as a result of using an ABC system, individual and organizational resistance can arise to block their effective use. Finance managers must be sensitive to the conditions that cause such resistance to arise and devise good countermeasures to overcome them.

Appendix 5-1

Historical Origins of Activity-Based Costing

The costing approach described in this chapter is a contemporary version of the original activity-based costing (ABC) method introduced in the 1980s.[7] The original version used a two-stage estimation approach. In the first stage, the project team interviewed and surveyed employees to identify all of the principal activities they performed and asked the employees to estimate the percentages of their time spent on each principal activity. The team used these percentages to assign the cost of the employees to the activities they performed (hence, the origin of the name "activity-based costing"). In a second stage, the project team assigned the activity costs to products based on estimates of the quantity of each activity used in the production of each product.

We illustrate the original ABC approach by applying it to the Madison Dairy ice cream plant example. First, a project team asks the indirect labor employees what activities they perform. They reply with the following three activities: schedule production runs, set up for production runs, and maintain products. They next ask about the percentages of time spent on these three activities, and receive the following estimates:

Schedule production runs	30%
Set up for production runs	60%
Maintain products	10%

The cost of indirect labor plus fringes during March 2010 was about $15,000.[8] So the team estimates the cost of the three activities as follows:

Schedule production runs	$4,500
Set up for production runs	9,000
Maintain products	1,500

This calculation, driving resource costs to activities through estimated percentages of times for each activity, completes the first stage of the cost system. In the second stage, the project team drives the activity costs down to products, using activity cost drivers for each activity. A cost driver represents the output of each activity, such as the following for the three activities performed by indirect labor:

ACTIVITY	COST DRIVER	COST DRIVER QUANTITY
Schedule production runs	Number of production runs	38
Set up for production runs	Number of set up hours	240
Maintain products	Number of products	4

The team calculates activity cost driver rates by dividing each activity cost by its cost driver quantity. The activity cost driver rate represents the costs of the resources used each time the activity is performed.

ACTIVITY	ACTIVITY COST DRIVER RATE
Schedule production runs	$118.42 per production run
Set up for production runs	$37.50 per setup hour
Maintain products	$375 per product maintained

In a final step, the project team multiplies the quantity of cost drivers for each product with its activity cost driver rate to obtain the assignment of indirect costs to individual products. The calculations are summarized on the next page[9]:

This cost assignment of indirect labor cost to products is quite close to that obtained by the time-driven ABC approach used in the chapter (see data in Exhibit 5-4)

---

[7] R. Cooper and R. S. Kaplan, "Measure Costs Right: Make the Right Decisions," *Harvard Business Review* (September–October 1988), 96–103.

[8] Indirect labor wages were about $12,000, plus 25% for fringe benefits; the $15,000 estimate could also be obtained from Exhibit 5-5, which shows the cost of indirect labor used as just under $15,000, and this excludes a small amount of unused labor capacity costs.

[9] Recall that three indirect labor people are used during setups; also all costs are rounded to the nearest dollar.

Indirect Labor Usage	Vanilla	Chocolate	Strawberry	Mocha-Almond	Total	Activity Cost Driver Rate
Number of production runs	12	12	8	6	38	$118.42
Number of setup hours	72	36	60	72	240	$37.50
Number of products	1	1	1	1	4	$375.00
Cost of production runs	$1,421	$1,421	$947	$711	$4,500	
Cost of setups	2,700	1,350	2,250	2,700	9,000	
Cost to sustain products	375	375	375	375	1,500	
Product cost: indirect labor	$4,496	$3,146	$3,572	$3,786	$15,000	

because the employees' estimates of the time they spent on the three activities (30%, 60%, 10%) were remarkably close to the actual percentages of time (which can be calculated as 36%, 56%, 8%) and because the indirect labor employees were operating at nearly full capacity. This example indicates that under the proper conditions, original and time-driven ABC can lead to the same assignment of indirect costs to products. But the original ABC formulation was highly sensitive to employees' subjective estimates of the percentage of time they spent on their various activities and did not handle well the estimate of unused capacity; most employees estimated activity percentages that added up to 100%.

Limitations of Original Activity-Based Costing

Original ABC, while essentially equivalent to time-driven ABC models when time percentages, including unused capacity, are estimated correctly, encountered numerous problems as companies attempted to implement on an enterprise level, the approximate method, based on employees' subjective estimates of time allocations. First, the process to interview and survey employees to obtain their time allocations was time consuming and costly. At one large money center bank's brokerage operation, the ABC model required 70,000 employees at more than 100 facilities to submit monthly surveys of their time. The company had to provide 14 full-time people just to manage ABC data collection, processing, and reporting. A $20 billion distributor required several months and about a dozen employees to update its internal ABC model. Employees also found it intrusive and annoying to continually estimate how much time they spent on various activities. The high time and cost to estimate an ABC model and to maintain it—by conducting interviews and surveys again—became a major barrier to widespread ABC adoption. Also, because of the high cost of continually updating the ABC model, many ABC systems were infrequently updated, leading to out-of-date activity cost driver rates and inaccurate estimates of process, product, and customer costs.

Managers also doubted the accuracy of a system based on individuals' subjective estimates of how they spend their time. Apart from the measurement error introduced by employees' best attempts to recall their time allocations, the people supplying the data—anticipating how it might be used—could bias or distort their responses. At many companies, managers spent more time arguing about the accuracy of the model's estimated costs and profitability than addressing how to improve the inefficient processes, unprofitable products and customers, and considerable excess capacity that the model had revealed.

With original ABC, managers found it difficult to add new activities or add more detail to an existing activity. For example, consider the complexity in an activity, "ship order to customer." Rather than assume a constant cost per order shipped, a company might have wanted to recognize the cost differences when an order was shipped in a full truck or in a less-than-truckload (LTL) shipment, using overnight express or a commercial carrier. In addition, the shipping order could have been entered either manually or electronically, or required either a standard or an expedited transaction. To allow for the significant variation in resources required by each different shipping arrangement, new activities had to be added to the ABC model, and personnel reinterviewed to get their time allocations for reassigning aggregate shipping expenses to all the different shipping activity types.

Such expansion caused many original ABC systems to exceed the capacity of their generic spreadsheet tools, such as Microsoft Excel®, or even commercial ABC software packages. The systems often took days to process one month of data, assuming the solution converged at all. For example, the automated ABC model for a $12 million manufacturer took three days to calculate costs for its 40 departments, 150 activities, 10,000 orders, and 45,000 line items.

Finally, when employees estimated how much time they spent on a list of activities handed to them, invariably they reported percentages adding up to 100%. Few individuals reported that a significant percentage of their time is idle or unused. Therefore, cost driver rates were calculated assuming that resources were working at full capacity. But, of course, operations at practical capacity were more the exception than the rule. When unused capacity was assigned to products, and managers took the normal actions to improve profitability—decrease the production of loss or expensive products, increase production run sizes, and improve process efficiencies—they increased unused capacity even more. But unless the cost of the newly created unused capacity was excluded from future cost assignment to products, the apparent gains from these apparently desirable actions got reallocated back to the remaining products, raising their costs and lowering their reported profitability.

In summary, the process of calculating activity expenses through interviews, observation, and surveys required a time-consuming, error-prone, and costly process to collect the data, an expensive information system to run the model, and a difficult process to update the model in light of changing circumstances. It was also theoretically incorrect in that it included the cost of unused capacity when calculating cost driver rates. All of these difficulties were overcome with the introduction of the time-driven ABC model, which offered the following advantages:

1. It is easy and fast to build an accurate model even for large enterprises.
2. It exploits the detailed transactions data that are available from ERP systems.
3. It drives costs to transactions and orders with time equations that use specific characteristics of particular orders, processes, suppliers, and customers.
4. It provides visibility to capacity utilization and the cost of unused capacity.
5. It enables managers to forecast future resource demands, allowing them to budget for resource capacity on the basis of predicted order quantities and complexity.
6. It is easy to update the model as resource costs and process efficiencies change.

KEY TERMS

capacity cost rate, 196
cost of unused capacity, 203
practical capacity, 210

time-driven activity-based costing (TDABC), 196

time equations, 210

ASSIGNMENT MATERIALS

Questions

5-1 Why are traditional volume-based cost allocation systems likely to systematically distort product costs? **(LO 1, 2)**

5-2 Under what two conditions are volume-based traditional product costing systems most likely to distort product costs? How do activity-based costing systems provide more accurate costs when these two conditions hold? **(LO 1, 2)**

5-3 "When a company produces both high-volume products and low-volume products, traditional product costing systems are likely to overcost high-volume products." Do you agree with this statement? Explain. **(LO 1, 2, 3)**

5-4 What do the terms *activity cost driver* and *activity cost driver rates* mean? **(LO 3)**

5-5 How is a time-driven ABC system updated as resource costs increase or changes in operations occur? **(LO 3)**

5-6 What two sets of parameters must be estimated in time-driven ABC? **(LO 3)**

5-7 How can the information from an activity-based costing system guide improvements in operations and decisions about products and customers? **(LO 4)**

5-8 Why is practical capacity recommended in calculating capacity cost rates? **(LO 5)**

5-9 Why might an organization not experience financial improvement even after using activity-based costing to identify and take action on promising opportunities for process improvements and cost reductions? **(LO 5)**

5-10 What is a TDABC system? **(LO 3)**

5-11 What are some special considerations in the design of cost accounting systems for service organizations? **(LO 6)**

5-12 Why might individuals resist implementation of activity-based costing? **(LO 7)**

5-13 What advantages does time-driven ABC have over original activity-based costing? **(Appendix)**

Exercises

LO 1, 2, 4 **5-14** *Product costing systems and product profitability* Potter Corporation has gained considerable market share in recent years for its specialty, low-volume, complex line of products, but the gain has been offset by a loss in market share for its high-volume, simple line of products. This has resulted in a net decline in its overall profitability. Advise management about specific changes that may be required in its cost accounting system and explain why the existing system may be inadequate.

LO 3 **5-15** *Revising a time-driven activity-based cost system, adding products* Refer to the Madison Dairy ice cream plant example described in this chapter.

Required

(a) Suppose that production-related computer resource expenses of $18,000 per month have been inadvertently overlooked for inclusion in the cost system. Explain how the time-driven ABC model should be updated to reflect this cost.

(b) Suppose that energy costs of $4,000 per month to run the machinery have also been inadvertently overlooked for inclusion in the cost system. How should the activity-based cost model be updated to include this cost, and what will be the effect on the machine hour rate?

(c) If the company wishes to introduce a new flavor, what information is needed in order to determine the cost of producing this new flavor?

LO 3 **5-16** *Revising a time-driven ABC system, cost increases, and process changes* Refer to the time-driven ABC analysis of the Madison Dairy ice cream plant example in the chapter.

Required

(a) Suppose indirect labor costs have increased by 10% from the original setting but all other information remains the same. Determine the total time-driven activity-based costs assigned to each of the four products (flavors) after incorporating the 10% increase in indirect labor costs and prepare an income statement similar to that shown in Exhibit 5-5.

(b) Suppose that in addition to the change in part a, the unit time for scheduling a production run decreased from four hours per run to three hours per run. Determine the new total time-driven activity-based costs assigned to each of the four products (flavors) and prepare an income statement similar to that shown in Exhibit 5-5 but also showing the total cost of unused capacity.

LO 3, 5 **5-17** *Assigning activity-based costs in manufacturing, unused capacity, income* Halifax Brass Company manufactures pumps and valves and uses a time-driven activity-based cost (TDABC) system. Last year, Halifax recorded the following data for assigning manufacturing overhead costs to its products:

	UNIT COST ESTIMATES (RATES PER HOUR)	TOTAL UNIT TIME ESTIMATES (HOURS ASSIGNED TO PRODUCTS)		PRACTICAL CAPACITY NOT ASSIGNED TO PRODUCTS (HOURS)
		PUMPS	VALVES	
Machine setups and run time	$20.00 per machine hour	1,500	1,800	300
Labor for setups, receiving, and packing	$30.00 per labor hour	5,000	6,000	200
Engineering (for specializing products)	$80.00 per engineering hour	200	400	50

Halifax also developed the following information on revenues and costs other than manufacturing overhead:

Total revenues	$890,000
Total direct labor cost	$120,000
Total direct materials cost	$90,000
SG&A expenses	$100,000

Required

(a) Using the company's TDABC system, how much manufacturing overhead cost will be assigned to pumps? How much will be assigned to valves?

(b) What is the company's net income? (Assume the company sells the entire amount of the products it produces.)

LO 5 **5-18** *Capacity costs* Ken's Cornerspot, a popular university eatery in a competitive market, has seating and staff capacity to serve about 600 lunch customers every day. For the past two months, demand has fallen from its previous near-capacity level. Concerned about his declining profit, Ken decided to take a closer look at his costs. He concluded that food was the primary cost that varied with meals served; the remaining costs of $3,300 per day were fixed. With demand averaging 550 lunches per day for the past two months, Ken thought it was reasonable to divide the $3,300 fixed costs by the current average demand of 550 lunches to arrive at an estimate of $6 of support costs per meal served. Noting that his support costs per meal had now increased, he contemplated raising his meal prices.

Required

(a) What is likely to happen if Ken continues to recompute his costs using the same approach if demand decreases further?

(b) Advise Ken on choosing a cost driver quantity for computing support costs per meal and explain why you advocate your choice of quantity.

Problems

LO 3, 5 **5-19** *Assigning corporate support costs, activity-based costing* Pick-Up Department Store has developed the following information in order to develop a time-driven ABC model for its accounts receivable department:

ACTIVITY	ESTIMATED WORKER TIME TO PERFORM ACTIVITIES
Manual processing of invoices and cash receipts	1.5 hour
Electronic processing of invoices and electronic funds transfers	0.25 hour
Maintain customer files	1 hour

The time required to process payments of customer invoices depends on whether the customer pays the bill manually or electronically, as shown above. The time to maintain each customer file is the same for all customers. The annual cost of the accounts receivable department is $1,500,000 and the associated practical capacity of accounts receivable labor is 25,000 hours.

Required

(a) What is the capacity cost rate for the accounts receivable department?

(b) Pick-Up's Division 1 has 2,000 small to medium-sized customers who annually generate a total of $20 million in sales, resulting in 8,000 invoices. These customers pay all their invoices manually. What is the annual activity-based cost associated with Division 1's customers?

(c) Pick-Up's Division 2 has 600 large customers who annually generate a total of $20 million in sales, resulting in 1,800 invoices. These customers pay all of their invoices electronically. What is the annual activity-based cost associated with Division 2's customers?

(d) Suppose 60% of Pick-Up's Division 1 customers change their method of payment to electronic next year. How many hours of accounts receivable labor will it require for 2,000 customers, 3,200 manual invoices, and 4,800 electronic invoices? How much will Division 1 be charged for the accounts receivable function? Will Pick-Up's costs decrease because of the shift to 60% electronic invoicing in Division 1?

LO 3, 5 **5-20** *Compute activity-based cost rate, time equations* CAN Company sells multiple products and uses a time-driven activity-based costing system. The company's products must be wrapped individually before shipping. The packaging and shipping department employs 25 people. Each person works 22 days per month on average. Employees in this department work an eight-hour shift that includes a total of 90 minutes for breaks and a meal. The full compensation, including fringe benefits, for each packaging and shipping employee is $3,575 per month.

Required

(a) Using the principles discussed in this chapter and time-driven activity-based costing, what is the rate per hour for each packaging and shipping employee at CAN?

(b) On average, it takes one packaging and shipping employee 16 minutes to prepare a package and label, independent of the number or types of items in the shipment, plus 9 minutes per item to bubble wrap and pack it in the carton. Using CAN's time-driven activity-based costing system, what is the packaging and shipping cost assigned to order A/32, which consisted of 120 items?

LO 3, 4, 5 **5-21** *Forecasting resource capacity using a time-driven ABC system* Refer to the time-driven ABC analysis of forecasting resource capacity for the Madison Dairy ice cream plant example on pages 205–208 of this chapter. Suppose that all the information is the same except for the following:

	VANILLA	CHOCOLATE	STRAWBERRY	MOCHA-ALMOND	TOTAL
Sales volume (gallons)	15,500	13,000	1,600	1,200	31,300
# production runs	18	16	4	3	41

Required

(a) Assuming that only full-time employees can be hired, determine the number of production employees required to meet this production plan. Also, determine the number of machines required for this production plan.

(b) Prepare a pro forma monthly product line income statement similar to that shown in Exhibit 5-7.

(c) What are the company's gross profit and the ratio of gross profit to sales after incorporating the cost of unused capacity?

LO 4   **5-22** *Relationship of the Balanced Scorecard to activity-based costing*   Explain how an activity-based costing model can be linked to a Balanced Scorecard approach.

LO 4   **5-23** *Balanced Scorecard or activity-based costing*   Suppose an organization has not implemented either activity-based costing or a Balanced Scorecard but believes both would be valuable for the organization. However, management is currently willing to undertake only one major change initiative. Advise management on the decision between implementing an activity-based costing model or a Balanced Scorecard.

LO 5   **5-24** *Cost rates for peak- and non–peak-hour capacity usage*   XZ Discount Brokerage is trying to determine the cost of supplying computing resources in order to determine how much to charge for trades. The company's cost analyst is perplexed because XZ has acquired 80 servers to meet peak capacity needs, which occur between 9 A.M. and 5 P.M. local time, but only needs the capacity of 20 servers during the remaining time. The costs associated with each server are $3,696 per month and each server is available for use for 24 hours per day for an average of 22 days per month.

Required

(a) What cost per hour would you advise for peak-hour capacity consumption? Explain why you think this cost rate is appropriate.

(b) What cost per hour would you advise for non–peak-hour capacity consumption? Explain why you think this cost rate is appropriate.

LO 3, 5, 6 (Appendix)   **5-25** *Original activity-based costing and time-driven activity-based costing*   Collins Company uses a traditional activity-based costing system to assign $800,000 of committed resource costs for customer service on the basis of the following information gathered from interviews with customer service personnel:

ACTIVITY	TIME PERCENTAGE	ESTIMATED COST DRIVER QUANTITY
Handle customer orders	60%	6,000 customer orders
Process customer complaints	25%	500 customer complaints
Perform customer credit checks	15%	600 credit checks
	100%	

Required

(a) Compute the activity cost driver rates using this system.

(b) Suppose instead that Collins uses time-driven ABC to assign the $800,000 of committed resource costs to the three activities. Compute the time-driven activity cost driver rates, assuming 20,000 hours of useful work and the following unit time estimates:

ACTIVITY	UNIT TIME (HOURS)
Handle customer orders	1.50
Process customer complaints	8.00
Perform customer credit checks	5.00

(c) Suppose that the quantities of activities this period are 6,000 customer orders, 500 customer complaints, and 600 credit checks. Using the information and activity cost driver rates developed in part b, determine the cost assigned to each of the activities and the estimated hours of unused capacity as well as the associated cost. What actions might managers take when evaluating such information?

(d) Suppose that in the next time period, the quantities of activities change to 8,000 customer orders, 600 customer complaints, and 400 credit checks. Using the information and activity cost driver rates developed in part b, determine the cost assigned to each of the activities and the estimated hours of unused capacity as well as the associated cost.

(e) Explain why the activity cost driver rates computed in part a are different from the rates computed in part b.

LO 3, 6   **5-26** *Activity-based costing in a health care organization*   Riverdale Bone and Joint Surgery specializes in treating injuries related to bones and joints, as well as surgeries such as knee replacements and hip replacements. In addition to performing surgeries, Riverdale offers post-operation treatment. Riverdale would like to develop an activity-based costing system in order to obtain accurate costs regarding the variety of patients that it serves.

Required

(a) What resource units would you advise using to build an activity-based costing system for Riverdale?

(b) After identifying the resource units, what other steps are required to determine the cost of a particular patient?

LO 1, 3   **5-27** *Manufacturing support cost driver rates*   (Adapted from CMA, December 1990) Moss Manufacturing has just completed a major change in its quality control (QC) process. Previously, products had been reviewed by QC inspectors at the end of each major process, and the company's 10 QC inspectors were charged as direct labor to the operation or job. In an effort to improve efficiency and quality, a computer video QC system was purchased for $250,000. The system consists of a minicomputer, 15 video cameras, other peripheral hardware, and software.

    The new system uses cameras stationed by QC engineers at key points in the production process. Each time an operation changes or there is a new operation, the cameras are moved, and a new master picture is loaded into the computer by a QC engineer. The camera takes pictures of the units in process, and the computer compares them to the picture of a good unit. Any differences are sent to a QC engineer who removes the bad units and discusses the flaws with the production supervisors. The new system has replaced the 10 QC inspectors with two QC engineers.

The operating costs of the new QC system, including the salaries of the QC engineers, have been included as manufacturing support in calculating the company's plantwide manufacturing support cost rate, which is based on direct labor dollars.

Josephine Gugliemo, the company's president, is confused. Her vice president of production has told her how efficient the new system is, yet there is a large increase in the manufacturing support cost driver rate. The computation of the rate before and after automation is shown here:

ITEM	BEFORE	AFTER
Budgeted support costs	$1,900,000	$2,100,000
Budgeted direct labor costs	1,000,000	700,000
Budgeted cost driver rate	190%	300%

"Three hundred percent," lamented the president. "How can we compete with such a high manufacturing support cost driver rate?"

Required

(a) Define manufacturing support costs and cite three examples of typical costs that would be included in this category. Explain why companies develop manufacturing support cost driver rates.

(b) Explain why the increase in the cost driver rate should not have a negative financial impact on Moss Manufacturing.

(c) Explain, in great detail, how Moss Manufacturing could change its accounting system to eliminate confusion over product costs.

(d) Discuss how an activity-based costing system may benefit Moss Manufacturing.

LO 1, 3, 4, 6 (Appendix) **5-28** *Original activity-based costing for shared services, outsourcing, implementation issues* Smithers, Inc., manufactures and sells a wide variety of consumer products. The products are viewed as sufficiently profitable, but recently some product-line managers have complained about the charges for the call center that handles phone calls from customers about the products. Product lines are currently charged for call center support costs on the basis of product sales revenues. The manager of product Y is particularly upset because he has just obtained a report that includes the following information for last year:

	PRODUCT X	PRODUCT Y
Number of calls for information	5,000	2,500
Average length of calls for information	10 minutes	6 minutes
Number of calls registering complaints	1,500	300
Average length of complaint calls	12 minutes	6 minutes
Sales volume	$200,000	$750,000

Product Y is simple to use and consumers have little concern about adverse health effects. Product X is more complex to use and has many health hazard warnings on its label. Smithers currently allocates call center support costs using a rate of 10% of net sales dollars. The manager of product Y argues that the current system does not trace call center resource usage to specific products. For example, product Y bears four times the call center costs that product X does, although fewer calls are related to product Y, and the calls consume far less time.

Required

(a) What activity cost driver would you recommend to improve the current system of assigning call center support costs to product lines? Why is your method an improvement?

(b) Suppose Smithers announces that it will now assign call center support costs on the basis of an activity-based cost system that uses minutes of calls (calls for information and calls for complaints) as the activity cost driver. Suppose also that the rate is $1 per minute. Compare the call center cost assignments to product X and product Y under the previous system and the new activity-based cost system.

(c) What actions can the product managers take to reduce the center costs assigned to their product lines under the previous system and the new system? What other functional areas might help reduce the number of minutes of calls for product Y?

(d) Who might resist implementation of the new activity-based cost system? In your response, discuss possible reactions of the call center staff and other staff who might be affected by efforts to reduce minutes of calls.

(e) From the company's point of view, how might the activity-based costing system help in the assessment of whether to outsource the call center activities?

LO 1, 3, 4 (Appendix)   **5-29** *Cost distortions, original activity-based costs*   At its manufacturing plant in Dallas, Texas, Precision Electronics Company manufactures two products, P and Q. For many years, the company has used a simple plantwide manufacturing support cost rate based on direct labor hours. A new plant accountant suggested that the company may be able to assign support costs to products more accurately by using an activity-based costing system that relies on a separate rate for each manufacturing activity that causes support costs.

After studying the plant's manufacturing activities and costs, the plant accountant has collected the following data for last year:

ITEM	P	Q
Units produced and sold	40,000	100,000
Direct labor hours used	120,000	300,000
Direct labor cost	$1,440,000	$6,000,000
Number of times handled	40,000	30,000
Number of parts	12,000	8,000
Number of design changes	1,000	600
Number of product setups	6,000	4,000

The accountant has also determined that actual manufacturing support costs incurred last year were as follows:

COST POOL	ACTIVITY COSTS
Handling	$2,800,000
Number of parts	3,000,000
Design changes	1,600,000
Setups	3,000,000
Total	$10,400,000

The direct materials cost for product P is $160 per unit, whereas for product Q it is $200 per unit.

Required

(a) Determine the unit cost of each product using direct labor hours to allocate all manufacturing support costs.

(b) Determine the unit cost of each product using activity-based costing.

(c) Which of the two methods produces more accurate estimates of job costs? Explain.

(d) Suppose Precision has been determining its product prices by adding a 25% markup to its reported product cost. Compute the product prices on the basis of the costs computed in parts a and b. What do you recommend to Precision regarding its pricing?

(e) What product-level changes do you suggest on the basis of the activity-based cost analysis? Who would be involved in bringing about your suggested changes?

LO 1, 3, 4 (Appendix)   **5-30** *Product cost distortions with traditional costing, original activity-based costing analysis* The Manhattan Company manufactures two models of compact disc players: a deluxe model and a regular model. The company has manufactured the regular model for years; the deluxe model was introduced recently to tap a new segment of the market. Since the introduction of the deluxe model, the company's profits have steadily declined, and management has become increasingly concerned about the accuracy of its costing system. Sales of the deluxe model have been increasing rapidly.

The current cost accounting system allocates manufacturing support costs to the two products on the basis of direct labor hours. The company has estimated that this year it will incur $1.2 million in manufacturing support costs and will produce 5,000 units of the deluxe model and 50,000 units of the regular model. The deluxe model requires four hours of direct labor, and the regular model requires two hours. Material and labor costs per unit and selling price per unit are as follows:

ITEM	DELUXE	REGULAR
Direct materials cost	$50	$40
Direct labor cost	60	30
Selling price	200	100

Required

(a) Compute the manufacturing support cost driver rate for this year.

(b) Determine the cost to manufacture one unit of each model.

(c) The company has decided to trace manufacturing support costs to four activities. The manufacturing support costs traceable to the four activities this year are as follows:

			COST DRIVER UNITS DEMANDED		
ACTIVITY	COST DRIVER	COST	TOTAL	DELUXE	REGULAR
Purchase orders	Number of orders	$200,000	800	200	600
Quality control	Number of inspections	250,000	1,250	650	600
Product setups	Number of setups	400,000	200	100	100
Machine maintenance	Machine hours	350,000	35,000	20,000	15,000
		$1,000,000			

Compute the total cost to manufacture one unit of each model.

(d) Compare the manufacturing activity resources demanded per unit of the regular model and per unit of the deluxe model. Why did the old costing system undercost the deluxe model?

(e) Is the deluxe model as profitable as the company thinks it is under the old costing system? Explain.

(f) What should the Manhattan Company do to improve its profitability? Consider pricing and product-level changes among your suggestions. Who should be involved in implementing your recommendations?

5-31 *Original activity-based costing, activity-based management* (Adapted from CMA, June 1992) Alaire Corporation manufactures several different types of printed-circuit boards; however, two of the boards account for the majority of the company's sales. The first of these boards, a TV circuit board, has been a standard in the industry for several years. The market for this type of board is competitive and, therefore, price sensitive. Alaire plans to sell 65,000 of the TV boards this year at a price of $150 per unit. The second high-volume product, a PC circuit board, is a recent addition to Alaire's product line. Because the PC board incorporates the latest technology, it can be sold at a premium price; this year's plans include the sale of 40,000 PC boards at $300 per unit.

Alaire's management group is meeting to discuss strategies for this year, and the current topic of conversation is how to spend the sales and promotion dollars for next year. The sales manager believes that the market share for the TV board could be expanded by concentrating Alaire's promotional efforts in this area. In response to this suggestion, the production manager said, "Why don't you go after a bigger market for the PC board? The cost sheets that I get show that the contribution from the PC board is more than double the contribution from the TV board. I know we get a premium price for the PC board. Selling it should help overall profitability."

Alaire uses a standard cost system, and the following data apply to the TV and PC boards:

	PER UNIT	
ITEM	TV BOARD	PC BOARD
Direct materials	$80	$140
Direct labor	1.5 hours	4 hours
Machine time	0.5 hour	1.5 hours

Direct labor cost is $14 per hour. Variable manufacturing support costs are applied on the basis of direct labor hours. This year's variable manufacturing support costs are budgeted at $1,120,000, and direct labor hours are estimated at 280,000. Other manufacturing support is applied at $10 per machine hour. Alaire applies a materials handling charge of 10% of materials cost; this materials handling charge is not included in variable manufacturing support costs. Total expenditures for materials this year are budgeted at $10,800,000.

Ed Welch, Alaire's controller, believes that before the management group proceeds with the discussion about allocating sales and promotional dollars to individual products, it may be worthwhile to look at these products on the basis of the activities involved in their production. Welch has prepared the following schedules for the management group:

COSTS	BUDGETED COST	COST DRIVER	ANNUAL ACTIVITY FOR COST DRIVER
Material support costs:			
Procurement	$400,000	Number of parts	4,000,000
Production scheduling	220,000	Number of boards	110,000
Packaging and shipping	440,000	Number of boards	110,000
Total costs	$1,060,000		

(continued)

Costs	Budgeted Cost	Cost Driver	Annual Activity for Cost Driver
Variable support costs:			
Machine setup	$446,000	Number of setups	278,750
Hazardous waste disposal	48,000	Pounds of waste	16,000
Quality control	560,000	Number of inspections	160,000
General supplies	66,000	Number of boards	110,000
Total costs	$1,120,000		
Other manufacturing support costs:			
Machine insertion	$1,200,000	Number of machine insertions	3,000,000
Manual insertion	4,000,000	Number of manual insertions	1,000,000
Wave soldering	132,000	Number of boards	110,000
Total costs	$5,332,000		

Required per Unit	TV Board	PC Board
Parts	25	55
Machine insertions	24	35
Manual insertions	1	20
Machine setups	2	3
Hazardous waste	0.02 pound	0.35 pound
Inspections	1	2

"Using this information," Welch explained, "we can calculate an activity-based cost for each TV board and each PC board and then compare it to the standard cost we have been using. The only cost that remains the same for both cost methods is the cost of direct materials. The cost drivers will replace the direct labor and support costs in the standard cost."

Required

(a) Identify at least four general advantages that are associated with activity-based costing.

(b) On the basis of standard costs, calculate the total contribution expected this year for Alaire Corporation's products: the TV board and the PC board.

(c) On the basis of activity-based costs, calculate the total contribution expected this year for Alaire Corporation's two products.

(d) Explain how the comparison of the results of the two costing methods may impact the decisions made by Alaire Corporation's management group.

Cases

LO 1, 2, 4   **5-32 *Part proliferation: role for activity-based costing***   An article in the *Wall Street Journal* by Neal Templin and Joseph B. White (June 23, 1993) reported on the major changes occurring at General Motors. Its new chief executive officer, John Smith, had been installed after the board of directors requested the resignation of Robert Stempel, the previous chief.

John Smith's North American Strategy Board identified 30 components that could be simplified for 1994 models. GM had 64 different versions of the cruise control/turn signal mechanism. It planned to reduce that to 24 versions the next year and the following year to just 8. The tooling for each one cost GM's A. C. Rochester division about $250,000. Smith said, "We've been talking about too many parts doing the same job for 25 years, but we weren't focused on it." (Note that the tooling cost is only one component of the cost of proliferating components. Other costs include the design and engineering costs for each different component, purchasing costs, setup and scheduling costs, plus the stocking and service costs for every individual component in each GM dealership around the United States.)

GM's proliferation of parts was mind-boggling. GM made or bought 139 different hood hinges, compared with one for Ford. Saginaw's Plant Six juggled parts for 167 different steering columns—down from 250 the previous year but still far from the goal of fewer than 40 by decade's end.

This approach increased GM's costs exponentially. Not only did the company pay far more engineers than competitors did to design steering columns, but it also needed extra tools and extra people to move parts around, and it suffered from quality glitches when workers confused one steering column with another.

Required

(a) How could an inaccurate and distorted product costing system have contributed to the overproliferation of parts and components at General Motors?
(b) What characteristics should a new cost system have that would enable it to signal accurately to product designers and market researchers about the cost of customization and variety?

LO 3, 4 **5-33** *Role for activity-based cost systems in implementing strategy*   Consider the case of the Cott Corporation, a Canadian private-label producer of high-quality cola beverages. Cott is attempting to get grocery retailers to stock its cola beverages as a lower price alternative to the more well-known brands of Coca-Cola and Pepsi-Cola. The international brands deliver directly to the retailer's store and stock their products on the retailer's shelves. Cott, in contrast, delivers to the retailer's warehouse or distribution center, leaving the retailer to move the product to the shelves of its various retail outlets. Cott offers substantially lower prices to the retailers and, in addition, is willing to work with the grocery retailer to customize the cola beverage to the retailer's specification; develop special packaging for the retailer, including labeling the beverage with the retailer's name (a practice known as *retailer branding,* such as Safeway Select Cola); offer a full variety of carbonated beverages (diet, caffeine free, multiple flavors, multiple sizes, and packaging options); and develop a marketing and merchandising strategy for the retailer for the private-label beverage.

Required

Consider how Cott might measure and manage activities and processes and relationships with suppliers and customers. How can Cott build cost systems to help it implement its strategy successfully?

LO 4, 6 **5-34** *Financial versus management accounting: role for activity-based cost systems in privatization of government services*   The mayor of Gotham City is dissatisfied with the rising costs and deteriorating quality of the services provided by the city's municipal workers, particularly in the transportation department: paving roads, repairing potholes, and cleaning the streets. He is contemplating privatizing these services by outsourcing the business to independent, private contractors. The mayor has demanded that his staff develop an activity-based cost system for municipal services before he proceeds with his privatization initiative, declaring, "Introducing competition and privatization to government services requires real cost information. You can't compete if you are using fake money." Currently, the accounting and financial systems of Gotham City report only how much is being spent in each department by type of expenditure: payroll, benefits, materials, vehicles, equipment (including computers and telephones), and supplies.

Required

(a) Before outsourcing to the private sector, why does the mayor want to develop activity-based cost estimates of the current cost of performing these municipal services?
(b) How should the staff estimate capacity cost rates and time demands that are required for an activity-based cost system?
(c) After building activity-based cost models, should this information be shared with the municipal workers? Why or why not? How might the workers use the activity-based cost information?

LO 1, 3, 4, 7 (Appendix)   **5-35** *Comparison of two costing systems, original activity-based costs, implementing change*   The Redwood City plant of Crimson Components Company makes two types of rotators for automobile engines: R361 and R572. The old cost accounting system at the plant traced support costs to four cost pools:

Cost Pool	Support Costs	Cost Driver
S1	$1,176,000	Direct labor cost
S2	1,120,000	Machine hours
P1	480,000	—
P2	780,000	—
	$3,556,000	

Pool S1 included service activity costs related to setups, production scheduling, plant administration, janitorial services, materials handling, and shipping. Pool S2 included activity costs related to machine maintenance and repair, rent, insurance, power, and utilities. Pools P1 and P2 included supervisors' wages, idle time, and indirect materials for the two production departments, casting and machining, respectively.

The old accounting system allocated support costs in pools S1 and S2 to the two production departments using direct labor cost and machine hours, respectively, as the cost drivers. Then the accumulated support costs in pools P1 and P2 were applied to the products on the basis of direct labor hours. A separate rate was determined for each of the two production departments. The direct labor wage rate is $15 per hour in casting and $18 per hour in machining.

DIRECT LABOR HOURS (DLH)

DEPARTMENT	R361	R572	TOTAL	DIRECT LABOR COSTS
Casting (P1)	60,000	20,000	80,000	$1,200,000
Machining (P2)	72,000	48,000	120,000	2,160,000
Total	132,000	68,000	200,000	$3,360,000

MACHINE HOURS (MH)

DEPARTMENT	R361	R572	TOTAL
Casting (P1)	30,000	10,000	40,000
Machining (P2)	72,000	48,000	120,000
Total	102,000	58,000	160,000

ITEM	R361	R572
Sales price per unit	$19	$20
Sales and production units	500,000	400,000
Number of orders	1,000	1,000
Number of setups	2,000	4,000
Materials cost per unit	$8	$10

Now the plant has implemented an activity-based costing system. The following table presents the amounts from the old cost pools that are traced to each of the new activity cost pools:

	OLD COST POOLS				
ACTIVITY COST DRIVERS	S1	S2	P1	P2	TOTAL
P1-DLH	$120,000	$0	$120,000	$0	$240,000
P2-DLH	240,000	0	0	120,000	360,000
Setup hours	816,000	80,000	240,000	540,000	1,676,000
P1-MH	0	260,000	120,000	0	380,000
P2-MH	0	780,000	0	120,000	900,000
Total	$1,176,000	$1,120,000	$480,000	$780,000	$3,556,000

Setups for R572 are 50% more complex than those for R361; that is, each R572 setup takes 1.5 times as long as one R361 setup.

Required

(a) Determine the product costs per unit using the old system. Show all intermediate steps for allocations, including departmental cost driver rates and a breakdown of product costs into each of their components.

(b) Determine the product costs per unit using the new system.

(c) Explain the intuitive reason that the product costs differ under the two accounting systems.

(d) What should Crimson Components do to improve the profitability of its Redwood City plant? Include marketing and product-related changes among your recommendations.

(e) Describe how experienced production and sales managers are likely to react to the new product costs.

LO 1, 2, 3, 4, 5, 7   **5-36 *Time-driven ABC, activity-based management*** Sippican Corporation (A)[10]

The decline in our profits has become intolerable. The severe price cutting in pumps has dropped our pre-tax margin to less than 2%, far below our historical 15% margins. Fortunately, our competitors are overlooking the opportunities for profit in flow controllers. Our recent 10% price increase in that line has been implemented without losing any business.
Robert Parker, President of Sippican Corporation

Robert Parker was discussing operating results in the latest month with Peggy Knight, his controller, and John Scott, his manufacturing manager. The meeting among the three was taking place in an atmosphere tinged with apprehension because competitors had been reducing prices on pumps, Sippican's major product line. Since pumps were a commodity product, Parker had seen no alternative but to match the reduced prices to maintain volume. But the price cuts had led to declining company profits, especially in the pump line (summary operating results for the previous month, March 2006, are shown in Exhibits 5-8 and 5-9).

Exhibit 5-8
Sippican Corporation: Operating Results (March 2006)

Sales		$1,847,500	100%
Direct labor expense		351,000	
Direct materials expense		458,000	
Contribution margin		$1,038,500	56%
Manufacturing overhead			
Machine related expenses	$334,800		
Setup labor	117,000		
Receiving and production control	15,600		
Engineering	78,000		
Packaging and shipping	109,200		
Total manufacturing overhead		654,600	35%
Gross margin		383,900	21%
General, selling and administrative expenses		350,000	19%
Operating income (pretax)		$33,900	1.8%

Source: Robert S. Kaplan.

---

[10] Copyright © 2006 President and Fellows of Harvard College. Harvard Business School Case 9-106-058. This case was prepared by Professor Robert S. Kaplan as the basis for class discussion rather than to illustrate either effective or ineffective handling of an administrative situation. Reprinted by permission of Harvard Business School.

Exhibit 5-9
Product Profitability
Analysis (March
2006)

	Valves	Pumps	Flow Controllers
Direct labor cost[a]	$12.35	$16.25	$13.00
Direct material cost	16.00	20.00	22.00
Manufacturing overhead (at 185%)	22.85	30.06	24.05
Standard unit costs	$51.20	$66.31	$59.05
Target selling price	$78.77	$102.02	$90.85
Planned gross margin (%)	35%	35%	35%
Actual selling price	$79.00	$70.00	$95.00
Actual gross margin	$27.80	$3.69	$35.95
Actual gross margin (%)	35%	5%	38%

[a]Direct labor costs were charged at $32.50 per hour. The average daily compensation for days worked was $195 per day ($3,900 per month divided by 20 working days per month). The hourly rate was calculated by dividing $195 by the 6 hours per day available for productive work.

Source: Robert S. Kaplan.

Sippican supplied products to manufacturers of water purification equipment. The company had started with a unique design for valves that it could produce to tolerances that were better than any in the industry. Parker quickly established a loyal customer base because of the high quality of its manufactured valves. He and Scott realized that Sippican's existing labor skills and machining equipment could also be used to produce pumps and flow controllers, products that were also purchased by its customers. They soon established a major presence in the high-volume pump product line and the more customized flow controller line.

Sippican's production process started with the purchase of semifinished components from several suppliers. It machined these parts to the required tolerances and assembled them in the company's modern manufacturing facility. The same equipment and labor were used for all three product lines, and production runs were scheduled to match customer shipping requirements. Suppliers and customers had agreed to just-in-time deliveries, and products were packed and shipped as completed.

Valves were produced by assembling four different machined components. Scott had designed machines that held components in fixtures so that they could be machined automatically. The valves were standard products and could be produced and shipped in large lots. Although Scott felt several competitors could now match Parker's quality in valves, none had tried to gain market share by cutting price, and gross margins had been maintained at a standard 35%.

The manufacturing process for pumps was practically identical to that for valves. Five components were machined and then assembled into the final product. The pumps were shipped to industrial product distributors after assembly. Recently, it seemed as if each month brought new reports of reduced prices for pumps. Sippican had matched the lower prices so that it would not give up its place as a major pump supplier. Gross margins on pump sales in the latest month had fallen to about 5%, well below the company's planned gross margin of 35%.

Flow controllers were devices that controlled the rate and direction of flow of chemicals. They required more components and more labor, than pumps or valves, for each finished unit. Also, there was much more variety in the types of flow controllers used in industry, so many more production runs and shipments were performed for this product line than for valves. Sippican had recently raised flow controller prices by more than 10% with no apparent effect on demand.

Sippican had always used a simple cost accounting system. Each unit of product was charged for direct material and labor cost. Material cost was based on the prices paid for components under annual purchasing agreements. Labor rates, including fringe benefits, were $32.50 per hour,[11] and were charged

---

[11] The full compensation, including fringe benefits, for direct and indirect employees (other than engineers) was $3,900 per month. Employees worked an average of 20 days per month (holidays and vacations accounted for the remaining 2 to 3 days per month).

Exhibit 5-10
Product Data

PRODUCT LINES	VALVES	PUMPS	FLOW CONTROLLERS
Materials per unit	4 components	5 components	10 components
	2 at $2 = $4	3 at $2 = $6	4 at $1 = $4
	2 at $6 = 12	2 at $7 = 14	5 at $2 = 10
			1 at $8 = $8
Materials cost per unit	$16	$20	$22
Direct labor per unit	0.38 DL hours	0.50 DL hours	0.40 DL hours
Machine hours per unit	0.5	0.5	0.3
Setup hours per run	5	6	12

Source: Robert S. Kaplan.

to products based on the standard run times for each product (see Exhibit 5-10). The company had only one producing department, in which components were both machined and assembled into finished products. The overhead costs in this department were allocated to products as a percentage of production-run direct labor cost. Currently, the rate was 185%. Since direct labor cost had to be recorded anyway to prepare factory payroll, this was an inexpensive way to allocate overhead costs to products.

Knight noted that some companies did not allocate any overhead costs to products, treating them as period, not product, expenses. For these companies, product profitability was measured at the contribution margin level—price less all variable costs. Sippican's variable costs were only its direct material and direct labor costs. On that basis, all products, including pumps, would be generating substantial contribution to overhead and profits. She thought that perhaps some of Sippican's competitors were following this procedure and pricing to cover variable costs.

Knight had recently led a small task force to study Sippican's overhead costs since they had now become much larger than the direct labor expenses. The study had revealed the following information:

1. A setup had to be performed each time a batch of components had to be machined in a production run. Each component in a product required a separate production machine to run the raw material or purchased part to the specifications for the product. Workers often operated several of the machines simultaneously once they had set up the machine. Because of the large number of setups, Sippican had dedicated about 25% of its production workforce to focus exclusively on setups. Some production workers did not operate any machines; they performed only manual assembly work. Their assembly time per product was included in the direct labor hour estimates for each product.

   Sippican operated two 7½-hour shifts each weekday. Each shift employed 45 production and assembly workers, plus 15 setup workers. Workers received two 15-minute breaks each day. They received an average of 30 minutes per day for training and education activities, and all workers—production, assembly, and setup—spent 30 minutes each shift on doing preventive maintenance and minor repairs to the machines.

2. The company had 62 machines for component processing. These machines were generally available for the six hours per shift that production workers were actively engaged in production or setup activities on the machines. Sippican leased the machines. Each machine's operating expenses were about $5,400 per month, including lease payments, supplies, utilities, and maintenance and repairs.

3. The receiving and production control departments employed four people over the two shifts. These personnel ordered, processed, inspected, and moved each batch of components for a production run. It took a total of 75 minutes for all of the activities required to get one batch of components ordered, received, and moved to a machine for processing. This time was independent of whether the components were for a long or a short production run, or whether the components were expensive or inexpensive.

4. The work in the packaging and shipping area had increased during the past couple of years as Sippican increased the number of customers it served. Each shipment took 50 minutes to prepare the packages and labels, independent of the number or types of items in the shipment, plus 8 minutes per item to bubble wrap and pack in the carton, whether the item was a valve, pump, or flow controller. The packaging and shipping area employed 14 people in each of the two shifts (28 in total).

Employees in the receiving, production control, packaging, and shipping departments worked a 7½-hour shift that included two 15-minute breaks per day, and 30 minutes, on average, for training and education.

5. Sippican employed eight engineers for designing and developing new product varieties. Engineers' total compensation was $9,750 per month. Much of their time was spent modifying flow control products to conform to customer requests. Engineers worked 7½-hour shifts. After breaks, training, education, and professional activities, engineers supplied about 6 hours of productive work per shift.

Knight's team had collected the data shown in Exhibit 5-11 based on operations in March 2006. The team felt that this month was typical of ongoing operations.

Required

(a) Calculate the practical capacity and the capacity cost rates for each of Towerton's personnel resources: brokers, account managers, financial planners, principals, and customer service representatives.

(b) Calculate the practical capacity and the capacity cost rates for each of Sippican's resources: production and setup employees, machines, receiving and production control employees, shipping and packaging employees, and engineers.

(c) Using these capacity cost rates and the production data in Exhibits 5-10 and 5-11, calculate revised costs and profits for Sippican's three product lines. What difference does your cost assignment have on reported product costs and profitability? What causes any shifts in cost and profitability?

(d) Could this approach be extended to service companies and to companies much larger and more complex than Sippican? What would be the barriers and difficulties with implementing time-driven ABC in practice?

(e) On the basis of the revised cost and profitability estimates, what actions should Sippican's management team take to improve the company's profitability?

LO 3, 5, 7   **5-37 *Activity-based budgeting, Balanced Scorecard, and strategy*** Sippican Corporation (B)[12]

Exhibit 5-11
Monthly Production and Operating Statistics (March 2006)

	VALVES	PUMPS	FLOW CONTROLLERS	TOTAL
Production (units)	7,500	12,500	4,000	24,000
Machine hours (run time)	3,750	6,250	1,200	11,200
Production runs	20	100	225	345
Setup hours (labor and machines)	100	600	2,700	3,400
Number of shipments	40	100	200	340
Hours of engineering work	60	240	600	900

Source: Robert S. Kaplan.

---

[12]Copyright © 2006 President and Fellows of Harvard College. Harvard Business School Case 9-106-060. This case was prepared by Professor Robert S. Kaplan as the basis for class discussion rather than to illustrate either effective or ineffective handling of an administrative situation. Reprinted by permission of Harvard Business School.

Refer to Case 5-36, the Sippican Corporation (A) case, which required time-driven ABC analysis. Sippican's senior executive committee met to consider the implications from its time-driven ABC model. Frankly all had been shocked to learn that their apparently highest margin product line, flow controllers, could actually be losing money because of its many shipments, short production runs, and heavy use of engineering time. The team contemplated action steps to restore profitability.

After some deliberation, the executive team crafted a new strategy that involved the following principles:

Improve Revenue Quality: Product Focus and Menu-Based Pricing

- Focus on core products: valves and pumps.
- Increase market share in valves by offering discounts for large orders.
- Reduce discounting for pumps, especially in small order sizes.
- Aggressively raise prices for small orders of flow controllers.

Productivity

- Reduce set-up times.

Based on the new strategy, Peggy Knight developed the forecasted monthly sales and production plan shown in Exhibit 5-12. She wondered whether the shift in product mix, new pricing model, and forecasted productivity improvement in setup times would be sufficient to restore Sippican's historic margins. Sippican's machines were leased monthly and had staggered expiration times; Knight believed she could, on short notice, make 10% to 15% adjustments up or down to accommodate changes in demand for machine capacity. Also, Knight felt that she had some flexibility with the size and composition of the labor force as well. The company had recently hired quite a few production employees on short-term contracts to meet the expanded demand for the newly introduced flow controller line.

Required

(a) Estimate the resource demands from Knight's forecasted sales production plan in Exhibit 5-12.
(b) Prepare a pro forma product line income statement based on the new plan.
(c) Comment on the magnitude of the change in profit with the new plan in relation to the change in production and sales under the previous plan.

Exhibit 5-12
Forecasted Monthly Sales and Production Plan

	VALVES	PUMPS	FLOW CONTROLLERS	TOTAL
Forecasted price	$75	$80	$110	
Forecasted sales (units)	10,000	12,000	2,500	24,500
Number of production runs	40	40	50	130
Number of shipments	40	70	100	210
Total direct labor hours	3,800	6,000	1,000	10,800
Setup labor hours per run	4.0	4.8	9.6	
Total setup hours	160	192	480	832
Machine hours: run + setup	5,160	6,192	1,230	12,582
Engineering hours	60	240	400	700

Source: Robert S. Kaplan.

Exhibit 5-13
Towerton
Monthly Income
Statement (000)

Sales	$4,024
Professional staff	
Brokers	1,246
Account managers	136
Financial planners	141
Support personnel	
Principals	325
Customer service representatives	146
Space	300
Computer server expenses	241
Other information technology	169
Total costs	2,704
Margin	1,320
Margin %	32.8%
S, G & A (unallocated corporate expenses)	1,300
Operating income	20
Operating margin	0.5%

Source: Robert S. Kaplan.

LO 3, 4, 5, 6   **5-38 *Activity-based costing, service company*** Towerton Financial Services[13]
Towerton Financial Services, a brokerage firm, started with a focus on stock trading and mutual funds. As the business grew, Towerton diversified into two new product lines, investment account management and financial planning. Although revenue has grown with the new product lines, Towerton's management is disappointed with the firm's profitability. (See Exhibit 5-13 for the most recent monthly income statement, which is typical for the company.)

Towerton's three groups of professional staff deal directly with customers across the four product and service lines. *Brokers* execute stock trades and mutual fund transactions and provide advice and recommendations. However, Towerton's brokerage customers make their own buy and sell decisions. Towerton charges a flat fee per stock trade that depends on the total amount of assets a customer has on deposit with the company. Last month, these fees averaged $8.80 per transaction. For mutual fund transactions, Towerton charges 1.5% of the value of the mutual fund shares purchased. This fee averaged $41.45 per mutual fund transaction last month. There is no charge when customers later sell their shares.

Investment account managers actively manage customers' investments by buying and selling stocks to meet customer objectives. These managers meet initially with customers to learn about their investment goals, interests, and risk tolerance. Thereafter, the parties meet quarterly to review account performance and investment strategy. Towerton charges each customer an annual asset management fee of 1.5% of the customer's assets under management.

Financial planners prepare financial plans for customers. The planners help customers develop a budget and determine how much to save and how much insurance to purchase. Towerton charges $1,200 for the first financial plan and $125 per hour thereafter for ongoing advice. Planners typically meet quarterly with customers to discuss any needed changes in plans.

Among the support personnel, *principals* manage and supervise brokers, investment account managers, and financial planners. *Customer service representatives* handle customer requests over the telephone for sales and account services.

Towerton uses two types of computer equipment: servers and desktop computers. Servers, in centralized clusters, process customer transactions, maintain customer accounts, and perform various administrative functions. Server capacity is measured in millions of computer instructions processed (MIPS). Towerton also leases a desktop computer for every employee.

---

[13] *Source:* Robert S. Kaplan.

Towerton's remaining expenses include office space rental and miscellaneous corporate expenses. Office space consists of individual offices for each of the professional staff and support personnel, as well as conference rooms for face-to-face meetings with customers to open accounts or service existing accounts. Miscellaneous expenses include administrative expenses for finance, human resources, audits, taxes, professional fees, and compliance.

Because of management's concern about the company's profitability, Towerton's accountants have gathered the following information:

1. After taking into account weekends, holidays, and vacations, the professional staff and support personnel work about 20 days per month on average.
2. Brokers, account managers, financial planners, and principals show up for 8 hours of work per day, but spend an average of 1.5 hours per day on breaks, training, education, and professional activities, with the remaining workday spent interacting with customers.
3. Like the other personnel, customer service representatives show up for 8 hours of work per day, but they spend an average of 1 hour per day on breaks, training, and education.
4. Each server costs $3,168 per month and operates 24 hours per day for 22 days each month. The cost per server hour is therefore $6. The server processing capacity is 50 MIPS per hour. Peak server usage occurs for 8 hours each day; during these hours, all 76 servers are operated. During the nonpeak hours, only 19 of the servers are operated. Towerton has computed the cost per MIPS as $0.12 for nonpeak hours and $0.30 for peak hours.
5. The costs per month in Exhibit 5-14 include compensation, fringe benefits, and the costs of space assigned on the basis of square feet of space occupied and individual information technology resources used for other than for customer-related activities.

Towerton's enterprise resource planning (ERP) system provided the activity report, average time utilizations, and peak and nonpeak transactions detailed in Exhibits 5-15, 5-16, and 5-17, respectively.

Required

(a) Calculate the practical capacity and the capacity cost rates for each of Towerton's personnel resources: brokers, account managers, financial planners, principals, and customer service representatives.

(b) Using the data in Exhibits 5-15, and 5-16, calculate the time utilization for each category of personnel for each of the four product lines.

(c) Using the data in Exhibit 5-17, calculate the MIPS during peak usage for each of the product lines and the MIPS during nonpeak usage for each of the product lines.

(d) Assume that the average price per mutual fund trade is $41.45. Prepare an income statement showing costs and profits for each of Towerton's four product lines, as well as the cost of unused capacity. What are reasons for the large differences in profits across the product lines?

(e) What actions might Towerton's management team take to improve the company's profitability?

Exhibit 5-14
Monthly Resources and Costs per Person

	NUMBER OF PEOPLE	COST PER PERSON PER MONTH
Professional staff		
Brokers	230	$6,787
Account managers	18	$8,954
Financial planners	20	$8,828
Support personnel		
Principals	30	$12,932
Customer service representatives	42	$4,192

Source: Robert S. Kaplan.

Exhibit 5-15
Activity Levels
per Month

	STOCK TRADING	MUTUAL FUND TRADING	ACCOUNT MANAGEMENT	FINANCIAL PLANNING
Number of transactions	305,288	26,325	5,400	
Average account balance maintained			$60,000	
Number of new accounts opened	595	255	175	130
Number of total accounts maintained	29,750	12,750	1,200	900
Number of calls to customer service center (other than new product sales)	47,600	11,475	1,320	540
Number of customer meetings servicing existing accounts	3,570	765	480	569

Source: Robert S. Kaplan.

Exhibit 5-16
Time Utilization:
Contact Minutes

	STOCK TRADING	MUTUAL FUND TRADING	ACCOUNT MANAGEMENT	FINANCIAL PLANNING
Brokers				
New accounts (minutes per new account opened)	60	60		
Existing accounts (minutes per transaction)	5	5		
Meetings with existing accounts (minutes per meeting)	20	20		
Account Managers				
New accounts (minutes per new account opened)			240	
Existing accounts (minutes per transaction)			10	
Meetings with existing accounts (minutes per meeting)			60	
Financial Planners				
New accounts (minutes per new account opened)				600
Existing accounts (minutes per transaction)				
Meetings with existing accounts (minutes per meeting)				90
Principals				
New accounts (minutes/new account opened)	10	10	20	60
Existing accounts (minutes/transaction or account)	0.5	0.5	4	
Customer Service				
New accounts (minutes per new account opened)	12	12	18	18
Existing accounts (minutes per call)	5	5	7	10

Source: Robert S. Kaplan.

Exhibit 5-17
Number of Transactions Processed by Servers

Transactions	MIPS per Transaction	Stock Trading		Mutual Fund Trading		Investment Account Management Services		Financial Planning		Total	
		Peak	Non-Peak	Peak	Non-Peak	Peak	Non-Peak	Peak	Non-Peak	Peak	Non-Peak
Order placements, trades and order clearing and settlement activities	1.4	305,288	0	0	26,325	54,750	31,000	0	0	360,038	57,325
Account balance inquiries	0.1	52,695	23,730	52,695	23,730	35,130	15,820	35,130	15,820	175,650	79,100
Quotation requests	0.1	332,400	177,100	249,300	132,825	166,200	88,550	83,100	44,275	831,000	442,750
Balance transfers	0.7	0	75,000	0	60,000	0	15,000	0	0	0	150,000
Account statement preparation	0.9	0	29,750	0	12,750	0	8,750	0	6,500	0	57,750
Total		690,383	305,580	301,995	255,630	256,080	159,120	118,230	66,595	1,366,688	786,925

Source: Robert S. Kaplan.

Chapter

Measuring and Managing Customer Relationships

After completing this chapter, you will be able to:

1. Assign marketing, selling, distribution, and administrative costs to customers.

2. Measure customer profitability.

3. Explain the differences between a low- and a high-cost-to-serve customer.

4. Calculate and interpret the "whale curve" of cumulative customer profitability.

5. Explain why measuring customer profitability is especially important for service companies.

6. Describe the multiple actions that a company can take to transform breakeven and loss customers into profitable ones.

7. Appreciate the value of the pricing waterfall to trace discounts and allowances to individual customers.

8. Align salespersons' incentives to achieving customer profitability and loyalty.

9. Understand why calculating customer lifetime value is valuable to a business.

10. Explain why companies need nonfinancial measures of customer satisfaction and loyalty.

An Unprofitable Customer at Madison Dairy

Jerold Browne, CEO of Madison Dairy, had just received a quarterly report that summarized the profitability of all of the company's customers. He was surprised to see that Verdi, a retail chain of 133 specialty ice cream shops and one of Madison's oldest customers, had become one of Madison's most unprofitable customers. Despite annual sales to Verdi of more than $4 million, Madison had just incurred a quarterly operating loss of $100,000 with this customer. Browne had known that producing ice cream for Verdi was expensive, with its special recipes, multiple flavors, and direct store delivery to its multiple outlets. Until viewing this report, however, Browne had believed that the higher prices per gallon charged to Verdi exceeded the extra costs of these special services. He could now see that the small lot production and labeling, frequent deliveries of less-than-truckload quantities to multiple locations, and the high degree of follow-up calls to respond to the customer's service requests had led to a highly unprofitable customer. He wondered how he should break the news to Mr. Rancantore, the chain's owner, who took such pride in having founded a successful retail chain.

In Chapter 5, we illustrated how to use activity-based costing to assign factory expenses, such as indirect labor and machinery, to individual products. But an organization's expenses are not limited to its factories. Companies, in addition to the costs of producing their products and services, also incur **marketing, selling, distribution, and administrative (MSDA) expenses**. Most of these expenses are independent of the volume and mix of products that the company produces, so that they cannot be traced through causal relationships to products (as we did in Chapter 5). Many of these expenses are incurred to market and sell products to customers through multiple distribution channels. And, like the different demands by products for factory resources, customers and channels differ considerably in their use of MSDA resources.

For example, consider a mutual fund company that markets products, such as retirement investment programs, directly to companies and also markets investment and retirement programs to millions of retail customers. The cost of reaching company clients is much lower than the cost of marketing, selling, and supporting its millions of small retail customers. In addition the size of a typical company relationship is many times larger than an individual customer's retail account. Companies need to understand the cost of selling through various channels to diverse customer segments. In this chapter, we show how to extend activity-based costing to trace MSDA expenses directly to customer orders and to individual customers.

This chapter's focus on customers also links us back to the Balanced Scorecard strategy framework introduced in Chapter 2. The costing concepts introduced in Chapters 3, 4, and 5 enable companies to calculate financial metrics related to product and process costs. Metrics such as gross margins and product-line profitability can appear in the financial perspective of the Balanced Scorecard (BSC), while the process perspective can include metrics related to the costs of production and purchasing processes. But if the only information that managers have about customers is their financial performance, then they may take actions that improve financial performance in the short-term but damage long-term customer relationships. Managers, therefore, need both financial and nonfinancial metrics to manage their performance with customers. In this chapter, we introduce nonfinancial customer metrics that can appear in the BSC's customer perspective. We will describe some common customer metrics, such as customer satisfaction, loyalty, and willingness to recommend, that many companies select for their Balanced Scorecard's customer perspective and that serve as leading indicators of future revenue and profit performance in the financial perspective.

Many companies today are already quantifying their customer relationships by using nonfinancial metrics on satisfaction and loyalty, but they do not trace MSDA costs to customers to facilitate an accurate measurement of customer profitability. Although the nonfinancial customer metrics are certainly valuable, as we will discuss later in the chapter, an excessive focus on improving customer performance with only these metrics can lead to deteriorating financial performance. Companies, in order to achieve high customer satisfaction and loyalty scores, may offer special features, highly customized products and services, and highly responsive customer service. This careful attention creates satisfaction and loyalty. But at what price? Companies run the risk of going beyond being customer focused to being customer obsessed, and when asked by customers to "Jump," they simply reply, "How high?"

To balance the pressure to meet and exceed customer expectations, companies should also be measuring the cost to serve each customer and the profits earned, customer by customer. Measures such as percentage of unprofitable customers and dollars or Euros lost in unprofitable customer relationships provide valuable balancing metrics for a company's strategy and its Balanced Scorecard. The ability to accurately calculate such metrics represents an important role for activity-based costing in a company's BSC.

MEASURING CUSTOMER PROFITABILITY: EXTENDING THE MADISON DAIRY CASE

We illustrate the assignment of marketing, selling, distribution, and administrative expenses to customers by considering another division of Madison Dairy, one that produces and sells many dairy products (including yogurt, sour cream, milk, and ice cream) to large wholesalers, distributors, and retailers. Currently, the division has annual revenues of $3,000,000; its MSDA expenses are about $900,000, or 30% of revenues. The division has two important customers, Carver and Delta, with approximately the same sales revenue. In the past, Gene Dempsey, the division's controller, allocated MSDA expenses to customers as a percentage of sales revenue leading to the following customer profitability statement for the two customers:

	CARVER	DELTA
Sales	$320,000	$315,000
Cost of goods sold	190,000	195,000
Gross margin	$130,000	$120,000
MSDA expenses at 30% of sales	96,000	94,500
Operating profit	$34,000	$25,500
Profit percentage	10.6%	8.1%

Both customers seemed highly profitable for the company. Dempsey, however, did not believe that these two customers were equally profitable. He knew that the account manager for Delta spent a huge amount of time on that account. The customer required a great deal of hand-holding and was continually inquiring whether Madison could modify products to meet its specific needs. Many technical resources, in addition to marketing resources, were required to service the Delta account. Delta also tended to place many small orders for special products, required expedited delivery, and tended to pay slowly, increasing the demands on Madison's ordering, invoicing, and accounts receivable processes. Carver, on the other hand, ordered only a few products and in large quantities, placed its orders predictably and with long lead times, and required little sales and technical support. Dempsey believed that Carver was a much more profitable customer for Madison than the financial statements were currently reporting.

Dempsey launched an activity-based cost study of the company's MSDA costs. He formed a multifunctional project team that included representatives from the marketing, sales, technical, and administrative departments. The team developed capacity cost rates for all of the resources in these support departments (such as the accounts receivable department). It then estimated the time demands on the various resources to obtain and process customer orders, to distribute the orders to customers, and to service each customer. This enabled them to assign the $900,000 in MSDA expenses down to every customer. The picture of relative profitability of Carver and Delta shifted dramatically, as shown here:

ABC CUSTOMER PROFITABILITY ANALYSIS

	CARVER	DELTA
Sales	$320,000	$315,000
Cost of goods sold	190,000	195,000
Gross margin	$130,000	$120,000
Gross margin percentage	40.6%	38.1%
Marketing and technical support	7,000	54,000
Travel to customers	1,200	7,200
Service customers	4,000	42,000
Handle customer orders	1,400	26,900
Ship to customers	12,600	42,000
Total MSDA activity expenses	26,200	172,100
Operating profit	$103,800	$(52,100)
Profit percentage	32.4%	(16.5%)

As Dempsey suspected, Carver Company was far more profitable than calculated in his previous report, which had allocated MSDA costs as a fixed percentage of revenues. Carver's ordering and support activities placed few demands on the company's MSDA resources, so almost all of the gross margin earned on the products sold to it dropped to the operating margin bottom line. Delta Company, in contrast, was now seen to be Madison's most unprofitable customer. While Dempsey and other managers at Madison intuitively sensed that Carver was a more profitable customer than Delta, none had had any idea of the magnitude of the difference.

We summarize some of the differences in high- and low-cost-to-serve customers in Exhibit 6-1.

Exhibit 6-1
Characteristics of High- and Low-Cost-to-Serve Customers

HIGH COST-TO-SERVE CUSTOMERS	LOW COST-TO-SERVE CUSTOMERS
• Order custom products	• Order standard products
• Small order quantities	• High order quantities
• Unpredictable order arrivals	• Predictable order arrivals
• Customized delivery	• Standard delivery
• Change delivery requirements	• No changes in delivery requirements
• Manual processing; high order error rates	• Electronic processing (EDI) with zero defects
• Large amounts of pre-sales support (marketing, technical, and sales resources)	• Little to no pre-sales support (standard pricing and ordering)
• Large amounts of post-sales support (installation, training, warranty, field service)	• No post-sales support
• Pay slowly (have high accounts receivable from customer)	• Pay on time (low accounts receivable)

As we will learn later in the chapter, companies can still make money with high-cost-to-serve customers, and lose money with low-cost-to-serve customers, but the information on the MSDA costs incurred for each customer is vital for effective management of the customer relationship.

Reporting and Displaying Customer Profitability

One of the most important empirical regularities in business and economics is the 80–20 rule, originally formulated about 100 years ago by an Italian economist, Vilfredo Pareto. As originally stated, Pareto found that 80% of a region's land was owned by 20% of the population. It was subsequently extended to show that 80% of a region's income or wealth was earned or held by the top 20%. For our purposes, Pareto's interesting discovery applies to products and customers as well (see the distribution shown in Exhibit 6-2). When companies rank products and customers from the highest volume to the lowest, they generally find that their top-selling 20% of products or customers generate 80% of total sales. Interestingly, the 80–20 curve also produces a 40–1 rule. By studying Exhibit 6-2, you can see that the lowest volume 40% of products and customers generates only 1% of total sales.

Although the 80–20 law applies well to sales revenues, it does not apply to profits. A graph of cumulative profits versus customers, constructed from an ABC customer profitability analysis, generally has a very different shape, which we call a **whale curve**. Exhibit 6-3 shows a typical whale curve of cumulative customer profitability. In this exhibit, customers are ranked on the horizontal axis from most profitable to least profitable (or most unprofitable). The whale curve of cumulative profitability in Exhibit 6-3 shows that the most profitable 20% of customers generated about 180% of total profits; this is the peak, or hump of the whale above sea level. The middle 60% of customers about break even, and the least profitable 20% of customers lose 80% of total

Exhibit 6-2
Product and Customer Diversity: Pareto's 80–20 (or 40–1) Rule

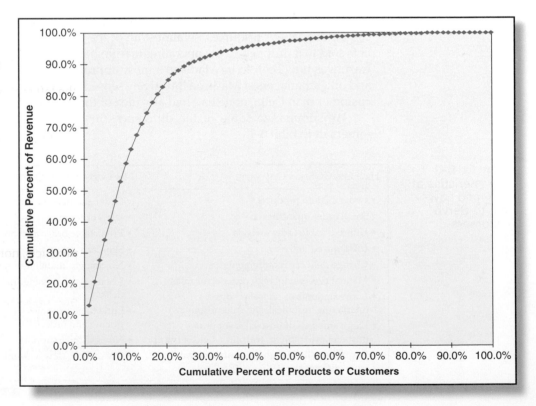

Exhibit 6-3
A Typical "Whale Curve" of Cumulative Customer Profitability

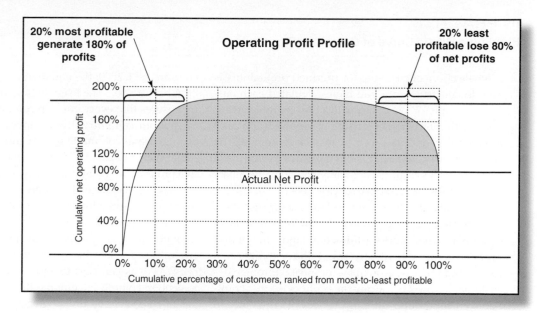

20% most profitable generate 180% of profits

Operating Profit Profile

20% least profitable lose 80% of net profits

Cumulative net operating profit

200%
160%
120%
100%
80%
40%
0%

Actual Net Profit

0%   10%   20%   30%   40%   50%   60%   70%   80%   90% 100%

Cumulative percentage of customers, ranked from most-to-least profitable

profits, leaving the company with its 100% of total profits ("sea level" in the whale curve represents the company's actual reported profits). The hump (or maximum height) of a cumulative profitability curve generally hits 150% to 250% of total profits, and this height is usually achieved by the most profitable 20% to 40% of customers.

Another interesting finding on most company's whale curves is that some of the largest customers, such as Delta for Madison Dairy, fall on the far right-hand side of the curve. They are among the company's most unprofitable. In retrospect, this finding should not be unexpected. A company cannot lose a large amount of money with a small customer because it does not do enough business with it to incur large losses. Only a large customer, demanding high discounts from list price and also making many demands on a company's technical, sales, distribution, and administrative resources, can be highly unprofitable. Large customers are typically a company's most profitable or its most unprofitable. They are rarely in the middle of the whale curve.

High-profit customers, such as Carver, appear in the left section of the profitability whale curve (Exhibit 6-3). Companies can celebrate the high margins that they earn on products and services sold to such customers. These customers should be cherished and protected. Because they could be vulnerable to competitive inroads, the managers of companies serving such customers should be prepared to offer discounts, incentives, and special services to retain the loyalty of these valuable customers, particularly were a competitor to begin selling to this customer.

Customers like Delta appear on the right tail of the whale curve, dragging the company's profitability down to sea level with their low margins and high cost to serve. The high cost of serving such customers can be caused by their unpredictable order patterns, small order quantities for customized products, nonstandard logistics and delivery requirements, and large demands on technical and sales personnel. One telecommunications equipment company, after doing such a customer profitability study, learned that for 20 percent of the orders in the previous year, the up-front cost of getting the order (the marketing, sales, and technical resources used to win the order) exceeded the size of the order. Even if the company could have produced, delivered, and installed the product at zero cost, it would still have lost money on the order. The opportunity for a company to identify its unprofitable customers and then transform them into profitable ones is perhaps the most powerful benefit that a company's managers can receive from an ABC system.

A whale curve of customer (or product) profitability is easy to construct once you have calculated each customer's profit (or loss). Start with a two-column spreadsheet with the customer's name or identification code in column A and its profit or loss in column B. The spreadsheet should have as many rows as you have customers; let's assume a company has 2,000 customers (and, therefore, 2,000 active spreadsheet rows). Use the spreadsheet's *Data Sort* command to rank the customers from most to least profitable, based on the data in column B. After running this command, the highest profit customer should be in row 1, the next highest in row 2, and the least profitable—or most unprofitable—customer in row 2,000. Copy the profit of the most profitable customer into column C of row 1. The entry in column C of all other rows is the cumulative profit from all previous customers (in the cell above) plus the profit of the current customer, which appears in column B of that row. For example, the equation for cell C10 (row 10, column C) would be "= C9 + B10."

After copying this equation into rows 2 through 2,000 (the last row), the entry in C2000 should be the total operating profit of the company (the sum of profits earned from all 2,000 customers). In column D, calculate the ratio of the entry in column C divided by the entry in cell C2000; the equation in cell D10 would be "= C10/C$2000." The $ sign in front of the row 2000 entry ensures that every entry in column D is divided by the bottom cell entry, the company's total operating profit. Format column D so that entries appear as "%" rather than a decimal. Column D contains the cumulative profitability by number of customers.

The number in cell D10 represents the percentage of total profits earned by the most profitable 10 customers in the company. The entries in column D increase through all of the profitable customers, and then decrease back down to 100% (which should be the entry in cell D2000) as you start to add in the unprofitable customers. In column E, compute the cumulative percentage of customers by dividing each customer's rank by 2000. For the most profitable customer, this is 1/2000. For each subsequent customer, add 1/2000 to the cumulative total. Use the spreadsheet's graphing capabilities to produce a curve where the *y* axis represents the entries in column D and the *x* axis represents the entries in column E. The height of the whale's hump represents the profits earned by all of the profitable customers (generally 150% to 250%), and the decline in the curve from the hump back to sea level (which represents 100% of profits) is the amount lost by the unprofitable customers.

An unprofitable banking customer receives extensive customer service but maintains low balances and conducts many manual transactions per month.

Customer Costs in Service Companies

Service companies must focus, even more than manufacturing companies, on customer costs and profitability because the variation in demand for organizational resources is much more customer driven than in manufacturing organizations.

How much technical and personal service a customer requires affects the profitability of the transaction.

Alamy Images
Royalty Free

A manufacturing company producing standard products can calculate the cost of producing the products without regard to how their customers use them; the manufacturing costs are *customer independent*. Only the costs of marketing, selling, order handling, delivery, and service of the products might be customer specific. For service companies, in contrast, customer behavior determines the quantity of demands for organizational resources that produce and deliver the service to customers.

To illustrate, consider a standard product from a service company, such as a checking account in a bank. It is relatively straightforward, using ABC methods, to calculate all of the costs associated with a checking account. These can be easily matched with the product's revenues, such as interest earned on monthly balances and the fees charged to customers for services. The analysis will reveal whether such a product is, on average, profitable or unprofitable. But such an average look at the product will hide the enormous variation in profitability across all customers using this product. One customer may maintain a high cash balance in his checking account; make very few deposits, withdrawals, balance inquiries, or service requests; and use only electronic channels (i.e., automatic teller machines and the Internet). Another customer may manage her checking account balance very closely, keeping only the minimum amount on hand, and use her account heavily by making many small withdrawals and deposits via manual transactions with bank tellers. The second customer's checking account may be highly unprofitable under current pricing arrangements. Customer balances or sales volume are poor proxies for profitability. Small-balance customers can be quite profitable and large-balance customers can be highly unprofitable.

As another example, customers of a telecommunications company can order a basic service unit in several different ways—through a phone call, a letter, or a visit to a local retail outlet. The customer may order two phone lines at once or just one; engineers may have to appear to install the new line, or they may make a change at the local switching center. The customer may make only one request or several and can pay either by direct debit over the Internet, by a telephone banking transfer, by a mailed check, or in person. The cost of each option is quite different. Therefore, measuring revenues and costs at the customer level provides the company with far more relevant and useful information than at the product level.

Manufacturing and service companies alike have many options to transform their breakeven or loss customers into profitable ones:

- Improve the processes used to produce, sell, deliver, and service the customer.
- Deploy menu-based pricing to allow the customer to select the features and services it wishes to receive and pay for.
- Enhance the customer relationship to improve margins and lower the cost to serve that customer.
- Use more discipline in granting discounts and allowances.

Process Improvements

Managers should first examine their internal operations to see where they can improve their own processes to lower the costs of serving customers. If most customers are migrating to smaller order sizes, companies should strive to reduce the costs of processes such as setup and order handling so that customer preferences can be accommodated without raising overall prices. For example, Madison Dairy could strive to become more efficient in handling orders by encouraging customers to access a purchasing web page and place their orders over the Internet. This would substantially lower the cost of processing large quantities of small orders. If customers have a preference for suppliers offering high variety, manufacturing companies can try to customize their products at the latest possible stage, as well as use information technology to enhance the linkages from design to manufacturing so that greater variety and customization can be offered without cost penalties.

Activity-Based Pricing

Pricing is the most powerful tool a company can use to transform unprofitable customers into profitable ones. **Activity-based pricing** establishes a base price for producing and delivering a standard quantity for each standard product. In addition to this base price, the company provides a menu of options, with associated prices, for any special services requested by the customer. The prices for special services on the menu can be set simply to recover the activity-based cost to serve, allowing the customer to choose from the menu the features and services it wishes while also allowing the company to recover its cost of providing those features and services to that customer. Alternatively, the company may choose to earn a margin on special services by pricing such services above the costs of providing the service. Pricing surcharges could be imposed when designing and producing special variants for a customer's particular needs. Discounts would be offered when a customer's ordering pattern lowers the company's cost of supplying it.

Activity-based pricing, therefore, prices orders, not products. When managers base prices on valid cost information, customers shift their ordering, shipping, and distribution patterns in ways that lower total supply chain costs to the benefit of both suppliers and customers.

Managing Relationships

Companies can transform unprofitable customers into profitable ones by **managing customer relationships**, which includes persuading them to use a greater scope of the company's products and services. The margins from increased purchases contribute to covering customer-related costs that do not increase proportionately with volume, such as the cost of the salesperson assigned to the account. Companies can establish minimum order sizes from unprofitable customers, so that the margins from higher volumes more than cover the costs of processing an order and setting up a production run for the customer.

Customers of service companies often have more than one relationship with them. Consider a commercial bank with a basic entry-level product: commercial loans. The interest spread on such loans—the difference between the bank's effective borrowing rate and the rate it charges the customers—may be insufficient to cover the bank's cost of making and sustaining the loan because of intense competition and the customer's low use of the lending relationship. However, the bank may make enough profit on other services that the customer uses—for example, investment banking services and corporate money management—that in aggregate the customer is a highly profitable one. Alternatively, however, a small borrower who uses no other commercial banking or investment banking services may be quite unprofitable. In this case, the bank could ask the customer to expand its use of the loan facility (that is, borrow more) and use other and more profitable services offered by the bank's services.

A customer of a telecommunications company may have, in addition to a basic landline phone account, a high-speed data line, an Internet line, a television cable connection, a maintenance and service contract, and equipment rentals. Therefore, before taking drastic action with a customer who has an unprofitable basic landline phone account, the company's managers should understand all of the relationships it has with the customer and act on the basis of total relationship profitability, not just on the basis of the profitability of a single product.

As one example of how a commercial bank dealt with an unprofitable customer, the loan officer tried to fire an unprofitable corporate customer, who had only a single banking relationship and did not use its banking facility intensively. The officer shared the economics of the unprofitable relationship with the customer and suggested that it seek other financial institutions for its borrowing needs. The customer, however, wanted to retain its relationship with the bank and offered to find ways to increase the bank's profitability on this account. The CFO offered to travel to New York for periodic meetings, rather than have the loan officer visit its Midwestern headquarters. He also offered to use more of the bank's products and services so that the relationship could be transformed into a profitable one for the bank.

Some customers may be unprofitable only because it is the start of the relationship with the company. The company may have incurred high costs to acquire the customer, and the customer's initial purchases of products or services may have been insufficient to cover its acquisition and maintenance costs. No action is required at this point. The company expects and hopes that the customer's purchases of products and services will increase and soon become profitable, including recovering any losses incurred in the start-up years. Companies can afford to be more tolerant of newly acquired unprofitable customers than they can of unprofitable customers they have served for 10 or more years. Later in this chapter, we will discuss customer lifetime profitability, a more formal way of managing newly acquired unprofitable customers.

The Pricing Waterfall

Beyond the factors already discussed, heavy discounting and granting of special allowances can also lead to breakeven or highly unprofitable customers. Before confronting a customer with an explicit price increase, the company should examine the many ways it has already reduced the effective price the customer actually pays. Exhibit 6-4 shows how a producer of kitchen appliances had offered multiple discounts and allowances to one of its largest customers, a major home improvement

Exhibit 6-4
Pricing Waterfall Chart

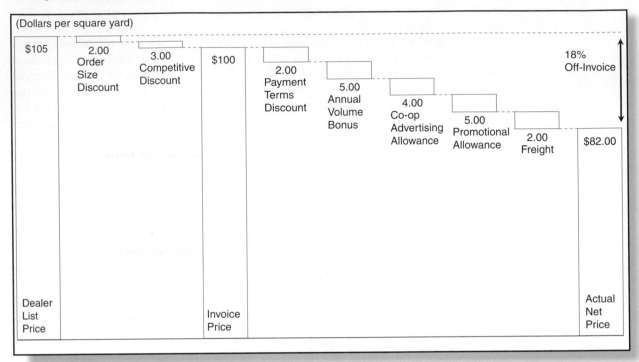

retail chain. This chart is commonly referred to as the **pricing waterfall** because of the multiple revenue leaks from list price caused by special allowances and discounts granted to obtain the order and build customer loyalty. In this exhibit, the list price started out at $105. The salesperson offered a 2% volume discount since the retailer had ordered at least 10 units of the product. He offered another nearly 3% discount from list price to match what the retailer claimed was an attractive offer from a competitor, bringing the invoice price down to $100 per unit. These discounts, however, were only the start of several other deductions from list price.

The company gives all of its retail customers a 2% discount ($2) if they pay the invoice in full within 10 days. Separately, to encourage large purchases throughout the year, the company offered an annual volume bonus of up to 5% based on the retailer's total annual purchases. Retailers also received cooperative advertising allowances of up to 4% for featuring the company's products in its print advertisements. The sale of this batch of products occurred near the end of a calendar quarter when the company was trying to encourage additional sales, so it offered a 5% promotional allowance for purchasing units that could be shipped before the end of the quarter. Finally, the company had agreed to pay the freight for transporting the appliances to the retailer's distribution center. The freight cost amounted to $2 per unit, or an additional 2% deduction from the invoiced price.

Each of these discounts and allowances seemed like a small concession in order to get the order, encourage a high volume of sales, and receive payment promptly. The discounts were granted by different organizational units: The salesperson had the discretion to offer a discount to get the order in the face of competitive pressure, the finance department granted discounts to encourage prompt payment and also receive a signal when customers are in some financial difficulty and do not take advantage of the attractive purchase discount, the company's CEO wanted to generate sales in the last week of the reporting quarter, and the marketing department wanted to motivate a high volume of revenues from the customer for the entire year. Yet Exhibit 6-4 reveals that the total quantity of discounts and allowances on this one order produced a total revenue leak of $23 (nearly 23%) from the original list price.

Companies, like the one illustrated above, fail to see all of the revenue leaks from list price because they record the discounts and allowances in different systems and make the revenue deductions at different times of the year. For example, the prompt payment discount may be recorded by the finance department in an aggregate income statement account (sales deductions); the finance department also lumps all freight costs into a general financial statement account labeled as transportation expenses. It does not link either the purchase discount or the freight expense back to a customer or an individual order. The volume discount may be refunded to the customer only once it has accumulated sufficient volume to qualify, and it is not linked back to the individual transactions that qualified for the volume discount. With discounts and allowances recorded into different accounts and at different times, no manager sees the complete picture shown in Exhibit 6-4 and consequently no one realizes how much revenue loss occurs with individual orders and customers.

One company, attempting to understand better its discounting policies, produced the chart shown in Exhibit 6-5. This exhibit showed that the quantity of discounts provided to customers in the previous year bore no relationship to the volume or the cost-to-serve individual customers. The downward sloping diagonal line suggests a plausible discounting policy in which low-cost-to-serve customers can receive discounts from list price, whereas high-cost-to-serve customers would receive little to no discounting. Yet the many companies above this diagonal line show that large discounts (some as high as 60%) had been granted to customers who had high service costs, while many customers who had low service costs (below the diagonal) received few discounts. In addition, many of the high-cost-to-serve customers receiving large discounts were not the highest volume customers either (as shown by the smaller size

Exhibit 6-5
One Company's Discounting Policy Was Unrelated to Its Cost to Serve Individual Customers

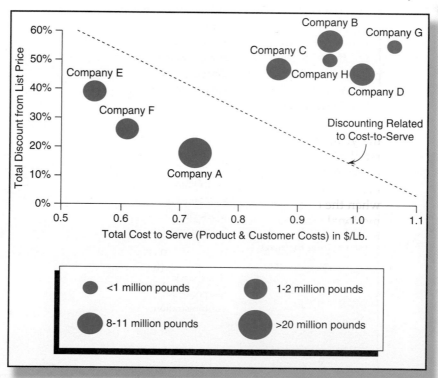

of their circles on this exhibit). This is an example of a company with little apparent discipline or economic rationality in its discounting policies.

To remedy this problem, companies are now extending their activity-based costing systems to trace all revenue deductions, as well as promotional costs and allowances, to individual orders and customers so that they can calculate actual, realized profit or loss, customer by customer. Exhibit 6-6 shows how one company calculates an operating income statement for every customer. It performs this calculation every quarter for every customer so that it can see the actual profit and loss of each customer,

Exhibit 6-6
Comprehensive
Customer
Operating Income
Statement

		CUSTOMER A	% OF SALES
Sales	**Total Revenues**	**1,518**	**104.8%**
	Less: Sales Adjustments		
	Sales Returns & Allowances	1	0.1%
	Sales Discounts	27	1.9%
	Service Discounts	0	0.0%
	Display Discounts	0	0.0%
	Customer Specific Program	21	1.5%
	Rebates	9	0.6%
	Restocking Fees	1	0.1%
	Returns	9	0.6%
	Other Deductions	2	0.1%
	Total Sales Adjustments	70	4.8%
Net Sales		**1,448**	**100.0%**
Production Costs			
	Materials	680	47.0%
	Support	30	2.1%
	Preparation	78	5.4%
	Drawing and Annealing	182	12.6%
	Finishing	205	14.2%
	Volume Related Costs	35	2.4%
	Storage (Raw Materials)	14	1.0%
	Carrying Costs	7	0.5%
	Freight (Inbound)	17	1.2%
Total Production Costs		**1,248**	**86.2%**
Gross Profit		**200**	**13.8%**
Other Expenses			
	Distribution	52	3.6%
	Commissions	69	4.8%
	Marketing	44	3.0%
	Sales Support	27	1.9%
Total Selling Expenses		**192**	**13.3%**
	Sales Service	10	0.7%
	Corporate & IT	15	1.0%
	Administration	107	7.4%
Total Administrative Expenses		**132**	**9.1%**
Operating Income		**(124)**	**(8.6)%**

Exhibit 6-7
Mapping
Customer
Profitability

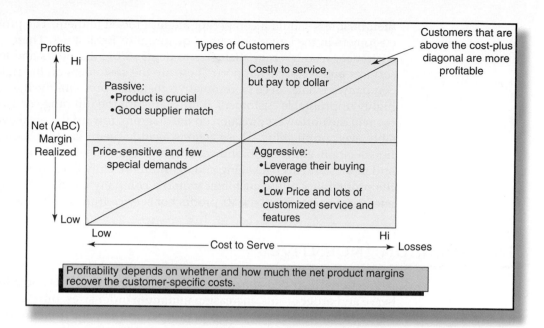

Profitability depends on whether and how much the net product margins recover the customer-specific costs.

including all revenue deductions and allowances. In this company, a salesperson, clutching a well-annotated package of all of his customers' operating income statements, walked up to a senior finance officer to thank him for the quarterly summary: "This is my Bible; it's how I manage and run my business."

Exhibit 6-7 shows one additional way to summarize the net contribution from each customer. A customer's position in this diagram is determined by two parameters, the x and y coordinates. The y or vertical position is determined by the gross margins from all products sold to the customer. The gross margin equals the net revenues received (after deducting all discounts and allowances in the pricing waterfall) less all costs of producing the products purchased by the customer during the period. The costs come from the company's activity-based costing system so they represent the cost of the actual demands on the company's resources to develop and produce the products purchased by the customer. The x or horizontal position represents the sum of all MSDA costs associated with serving the customer and processing and fulfilling its orders. Customers above the diagonal line are profitable. Those below are unprofitable; that is, the gross margins from the products and services sold do not cover all the costs required to market, sell, distribute to, and service the customer.

Exhibit 6-7 shows that companies can make profits with customers in multiple ways. For customers in the upper right-hand corner, a company can afford to spend a great deal on transportation, technical support, and service because of the high gross margins on the products and services sold to this customer. In the lower left-hand quadrant, a company can make money with even a highly discounted customer, such as Wal-Mart or a "big box" retailer, as long as the cost of servicing that customer is low. Looking back at Exhibit 6-1, Wal-Mart has many of the characteristics of a low-cost-to-serve customer: It purchases a limited variety of products in large quantities, with predictable orders, standard deliveries to its distribution centers, and pays within 30 days. So even though Wal-Mart demands the lowest prices from its suppliers, it can still be a supplier's most profitable customer because of its large purchasing volume and low cost to serve.

Companies love having customers in the upper left-hand quadrant of Exhibit 6-7. These customers are price insensitive, demand few discounts, and are low cost to serve. Such customers should be cherished and nurtured, including dedicating customer service teams to them and being prepared to compete aggressively to retain their business should a competitor attempt to sell to them. The problems occur with customers in the lower right-hand quadrant of Exhibit 6-7. These are typically large customers who leverage their size to demand big discounts and lots of customized services and technical support. These are the customers on the right-hand edge of a company's whale curve of cumulative customer profitability. If a company has such highly unprofitable customers, it must attempt the full range of actions to transform them in the northwest direction on the diagram, toward the breakeven point and possibly even profitability. These actions include menu-based pricing, product mix rationalization, elimination of discounts and allowances, and moving to larger orders and more standard packaging and distribution. Only if all such actions fail to restore the profitability of the customer would a company consider "firing" a customer by encouraging it to purchase its product or service from an alternative supplier.

SALESPERSON INCENTIVES

The actions described above—repricing, relating discounts and allowances to cost to serve and order profits, increasing minimum order sizes, purchasing a broader scope of products and services—attempt to repair the damage from unprofitable customers. Even better would be avoiding unprofitable customers in the first place. Many breakeven or unprofitable customer relationships occur because salespeople have incentives to generate sales not profits. A typical salesperson's compensation plan sets minimum quotas and commissions based on sales revenue, and it ties bonuses and rewards (including luxurious vacation trips) to achieving sales revenues above a stretch target. Such **salesperson incentives** and compensation arrangements encourage salespeople to close deals and generate revenues without regard to the cost of fulfilling the special arrangements negotiated in the deal and the impact of discounts and allowances granted to close the deal.

In one office products company, a salesperson signed the largest contract in the company's history with a prominent customer. The contract was won, however, by committing the company to delivering every item to the desk of the person requesting a resupply of any item—whether a single pad of writing paper, a small package of pens, or a ream of paper for a desktop printer. When all of the costs of this contract were eventually collected and attributed to this customer relationship, the company discovered that the salesperson had created the company's most unprofitable customer.

Companies base salespeople's compensation and rewards on revenues because it is a simple measure, generally easy to calculate (though often missing the subsequent discounts and allowances booked against the contract), and consistent with the salesperson's mission to generate sales. Another reason is that, until the recent development of activity-based costing, companies lacked the ability to trace MSDA costs, as well as the actual product margins, to individual customers. So lacking a valid, calculable measure of customer profitability, companies focused on generating revenues but not profits from their customers.

Companies can now use their time-driven activity-based costing system to create customer-specific profit and loss statements even when they have thousands or, for some financial service companies, millions of customers. This ability has also been enabled by greatly expanded computing power and new enterprise resource planning (ERP) and customer relationship management (CRM) software systems that can electronically capture all of the features of sales and production orders. Companies now use the information to base salesperson incentives on order and customer profits, not just sales. Salespeople can still accept breakeven or loss orders in order to penetrate a new account or to keep an overall highly profitable and loyal customer happy. But they accept this transaction for future benefit, understanding that these unprofitable orders may not contribute to their sales quota and definitely will not be eligible for a selling commission. The capability of management accounting today to calculate order and customer profitability provides management with an important new tool to align salespersons' incentives with improvements in the company's financial performance.

LIFE-CYCLE PROFITABILITY

Many service companies invest considerable resources in marketing campaigns to attract new customers. If the company does not know about the characteristics of what makes a profitable customer, such companies may spend a great deal of money to attract many unprofitable customers. By knowing the characteristics of profitable customers, companies can direct their marketing efforts to specific segments that are most likely to yield profitable customers.

Because of the high acquisition costs and the time required to establish a broad and deep relationship (such as across multiple product offerings), even attractive new customers may be initially unprofitable. The high cost of acquisition in the initial year of the relationships could cause the customer to fall into the unprofitable quadrant in Exhibit 6-7. Companies need to distinguish the economics of their newly acquired customers from those who have been customers for many years. Thus, in addition to recognizing cross-sectional variation of demands by customers—across multiple products and services—companies must also forecast the longitudinal variation of customers over time to calculate their total life-cycle profitability.

As a specific example, consider a company that has just spent $5 million on a campaign to acquire new customers. The campaign yielded 5,000 new customers, or an average cost of $1,000 per customer acquired.

- Customer A purchased products and services that generated a net margin of $300 per year (after deducting all production, and MSDA costs attributable to the relationship). Customer A, however, left for a competitor after three years.
- Customer B purchased products and services yielding a net margin of $275 per year, and defected after five years.

The company's accounting system recorded that Customer A was more profitable than B because of the $25 higher annual profits per year that it generated. The system, however, failed to see that the three years of $300 net margin did not repay the initial $1,000 acquisition cost so that A was actually a loss customer over its lifetime with the company. Customer B, in contrast, generated sufficient net margin over its five years of relationship to cover its initial acquisition cost.[1]

If you are familiar with algebra and net present value techniques, you can study the equation below, which is a general formulation for calculating **customer lifetime value (CLV)**.

$$\text{CLV} = \sum_{t=1}^{t=n} \frac{(M_t - c_t) \times (\text{retention rate}_t)^{t-1}}{(1 + i)^t} - \text{Initial acquisition cost}$$

---

[1] To do this calculation correctly, the company should calculate the discounted present value of the cash flows from Customer B to determine whether the five years of $275 net margin not only repaid the initial $1,000 acquisition cost but also the time value of the money invested in this customer at the start of the relationship. Calculating discounted present values is not covered in this textbook—you will learn this technique in your first finance course. If you are already familiar with the technique, you can verify that Customer B is profitable for companies whose cost of capital is less than 11.6%.

where

M_t = Margin (revenue less cost) from customer in year t
c_t = Any additional costs-to-serve (and retain) customer in year t
i = Cost of capital (e.g., 10%)

If M_t, c_t, and r_t are about the same each year, and n is large:

$$\text{CLV} \approx \frac{M - c}{i + (1 - r)} - \text{Acquisition cost}$$

(r = retention rate period to period)

The equation assumes that the company can estimate the probability of retaining a customer from one year to the next, which it calls the retention rate, r. The customer's profit each year is its margin, M, calculated as total net revenues (after deducting discounts, promotions, and allowances) less all the costs to produce, market, distribute, and sell to the customer, less any additional promotions, c, to retain the customer each year. The discounted net cash flows from the customer for all of the years that it remains a customer are compared to the initial acquisition cost to obtain the total value to the company from the lifetime relationship with this customer.

Many service companies (banks, mobile telecommunication companies, Internet service providers) spend a great deal of money to acquire new customers, particularly young customers attending colleges, even though their profits in the year of acquisition and for several years afterwards are negative or, at best, slightly positive. The service companies make such investments because they want to become the lifetime provider to these customers as they obtain good jobs and become successful in their careers. If a company is following such a customer lifetime value strategy, then it should be tracking, for each of its customers, how much it spent to acquire the customer, and then the profits earned each year in the relationship. The critical parameters for calculating customer lifetime value are:

- Initial acquisition cost.
- Profits or losses earned each year.
- Any additional costs incurred to retain the customer each year.
- The duration of the relationship.

Some banks have highly sophisticated analytic systems that allow them to estimate these parameters based on the demographic characteristics of a potential or newly acquired customer. The analytics help guide the bank's promotion strategies and campaigns to attract customers with the highest expected lifetime value. For example, RBC Financial Group in Canada uses an analytic model of a customer's future profitability based on age, tenure with the bank, number of products and services already used at the bank, and the customer's potential to purchase additional products and services, grow account balances, and generate fee-based income.[2] The bank assigns a personal account representative to its estimated high lifetime value customers, ensures that their phone calls get picked up quickly, and provides them with ready access to credit at attractive terms.

Another financial institution that calculates lifetime profitability for all of its customers produced the table shown in Exhibit 6-8 to illustrate the success of its marketing programs. At first glance (the top row in the exhibit), the bank appears to have

---

[2] V. G. Narayanan, "Customer Profitability and Customer Relationship Management at RBC Financial Group," HBS No. 102-043 (Boston: Harvard Business School Publishing, 2002).

Exhibit 6-8
Summary of
Annual Change
in a Retail Bank's
Customer
Acquisition
and Retention

CATEGORY	LOST	GAINED	DIFFERENCE
Number of households (HH)	45,310	40,249	(5,061)
Loans and deposits per HH	$39,051	$77,883	$38,832
Revenue per HH per month	$61	$108	$47
Services per HH	1.8	2.5	0.7
Percent HH with only one service	52%	33%	+19%

had a disappointing year because it had a net loss of more than 5,000 customers. But the subsequent lines show that this was desirable attrition since the newly acquired customers had larger account balances, higher revenues per account, and used more banking services than the departing customers. The bank's marketing director said, "The quality of the new households in all measurable respects is better compared to the lost households." This is a good example of a company that is consciously trying to attract and retain customers with high lifetime profitability.

MEASURING CUSTOMER PERFORMANCE WITH NONFINANCIAL METRICS

The material covered so far in this chapter focuses only on financial measurements (e.g., cost to serve, discounts and allowances, profitability), related to a company's customer relationships. As the section on lifetime customer profitability helps us realize, short-term metrics of customer cost and profitability may cause a company to take actions that work well to improve customer profitability metrics but put at risk the company's long-term relationship with the customer. Harking back to the Balanced Scorecard discussion in Chapter 2, a company cannot measure and manage its customer relationships with financial metrics alone, even valuable and accurate metrics such as profitability. Companies need to supplement their financial measurements with nonfinancial measures of their customer relationship.

Customer Satisfaction

Most companies today attempt to calculate some metrics on **customer satisfaction**. The company, or an independent market research company, sends a survey to a recent purchaser or user of the company's products and services.[3] The survey, from a company such as Madison Dairy, starts by asking a general question such as this:

	5. VERY SATISFIED	4. SOMEWHAT SATISFIED	3. NEITHER SATISFIED OR DISSATISFIED	2. SOMEWHAT DISSATISFIED	1. VERY DISSATISFIED
Based on your recent purchasing [or service] experience, how satisfied are with you with Madison Dairy?					

[3] A template for constructing a customer satisfaction survey can be found at http://www.loyaltyrules.com/loyaltyrules/acid_test_customer.html (accessed August 19, 2010).

The survey would then continue asking for responses, on a similar five-point scale (from Very Satisfied to Very Dissatisfied), to specific aspects of the purchase or service experience, such as the quality of the product or service, the ease of ordering, the friendliness and responsiveness of Madison's sales, technical, and administrative personnel, and the responsiveness of the company to customer complaints and concerns.

Writing a customer survey may seem simple but getting valid responses from a high percentage of customers requires specialized expertise. Companies generally use three approaches: mail surveys, telephone interviews, and personal interviews. These techniques range in cost from low to high, respectively, but response rates and valuable insights also range from low to high across them. Specialized marketing research firms offer companies expertise in psychology, market research, statistics, and interviewing techniques, as well as considerable numbers of personnel and computing power capable of conducting customer satisfaction surveys and summarizing and interpreting the results for the sponsoring company.

Some customer satisfaction surveys become public information. J.D. Power and Associates conducts satisfaction surveys of consumers who recently purchased a new automobile. J.D. Power's annual rankings of automotive customers' satisfaction are eagerly anticipated and publicized, and can have a strong influence on which brands will be purchased in the subsequent year. In 2010, Toyota dropped 15 places in the J.D. Power rankings, from 6th to 21st, largely because of widely publicized recalls due to problems with brakes, sudden acceleration, and poorly fitted floor mats. Because of the success of its automotive ratings and rankings, J.D. Power now offers customer satisfaction ratings of boats, home appliances, credit cards, retail banks, home-builders, insurance companies, telecom providers, airlines, airports, hotels, and rental car agencies. The American Customer Satisfaction Index (ACSI) measures customer satisfaction annually for more than 200 companies in 45 industries. Several studies have found significant correlations between a company's ACSI score and its future stock price, suggesting that a change in a company's customer satisfaction score is a leading indicator of its future financial performance.

Customer Loyalty

Although customer satisfaction scores are important, experts now agree that it is a mistake for a company to use the satisfaction score as its only customer metric. A customer's satisfaction is an attitude or belief stemming from a feeling that the product or service has generally delivered on the customer's expectation of performance. But attitudes and beliefs are not actions; a customer's attitude toward a product or a company does not readily translate into the desired behavior of repeated and increased purchases of the product or service, or customer loyalty. An influential study in the 1990s[4] found that in highly competitive industries, characterized by low differentiation among products, many substitutes, and low cost of switching (automobiles and personal computers are examples), only customers who give the company the highest satisfaction score (a 5 in a 5-point scale, or 9 or 10 on a 10-point scale) are likely to repurchase the company's product or service. Customers that report they are "somewhat" or "generally" satisfied may defect to a competitor that offers a lower price or incrementally better features.

Loyal customers are valuable for several reasons:

1. Loyal customers have a greater likelihood to repurchase, and the costs to retain them are generally much lower than the cost to acquire an entirely new customer.

---

[4] T. O. Jones and E. Sasser, "Why Satisfied Customers Defect," *Harvard Business Review* (November–December 1995): 88–99.

2. Loyal customers can persuade others, through word of mouth, to become new customers; they can become references for potential future customers.
3. Loyal customers are less likely to defect when a competitor offers a similar product at the same or slightly lower price.
4. Loyal customers are often willing to pay a price premium to retain a known and trusted relationship with a key supplier.
5. Loyal customers are willing to collaborate with the supplier to improve performance and develop new products.

Companies can measure *loyalty* directly by actual repeat purchasing behavior. Companies that can readily identify all of their customers—for example, industrial companies, distributors and wholesalers, newspaper and magazine publishers, computer on-line service companies, banks, credit card companies, and long-distance telephone suppliers—can readily measure customer retention from period to period. Beyond just retaining customers, many companies will want to measure customer loyalty by the percentage growth of business with existing customers and account share, which represents a company's percentage of a customer's spending in its product or service category. For example, a clothing retailer might estimate the percentage of a consumer's wardrobe that it supplies, a bank can measure the percentage of a customer's wealth that it manages, and a food company, the percentage of a consumer's stomach that it fills.

When companies cannot easily identify individual customers to measure their retention and repeat purchasing behavior, they often invest in loyalty programs that provide incentives to customers to reveal themselves when they are making a purchase. Companies, as diverse as gambling casinos (Harrah's, for example) and retailers (such as Staples), now give customers discounts or cash and service rebates to reward their frequent purchases and repeat business. Loyalty metrics can include percentage of customers from a previous period who make at least one purchase in the current period and the period-to-period growth in business with a targeted customer.

One scholar has proposed that companies view their customer satisfaction and loyalty along a five-stage hierarchy[5]:

1. Satisfied customers, as measured by how well a customer's expectations have been met or exceeded in an individual transaction or long-term relationship.
2. Loyal customers, as measured by the customer devoting an increasing "share of wallet" for repeat purchases from the same supplier.
3. Committed customers, those who not only purchase frequently from the supplier but also tell others about the supplier's great products and service.
4. Apostle customers, committed customers who have credibility and authority when they recommend the supplier to friends, neighbors, and colleagues. For example, respected and opinion-leading surgeons have great credibility when they attest to their satisfaction with a new medical instrument.
5. Customer "owners," who take responsibility for the continuing success of the supplier's product or service. For example, some of Southwest Airlines' most loyal customers are willing to interview prospective flight attendants to help select the ones they would most want to serve them. Procter & Gamble has established an interactive site so that its loyal customers can provide feedback on existing products and suggestions for improving them or for entirely new products.

A company should strive to have more of its customers in categories 3, 4, and 5 above, since their willingness to recommend the company to others and to collaborate

---

[5] J. Heskett, "Beyond Customer Loyalty," *Managing Service Quality*, Vol. 12, No. 6 (2002): 355–357.

with it to continually improve product features and service makes them far more valuable, with a much higher customer lifetime value, than customers who are merely satisfied with the most recent transaction. To measure whether their customers have moved beyond "loyalty" to commitment, apostle, and ownership behavior, many companies are now using a new metric, the net promoter score.

The Net Promoter Score

With so much attention focused on satisfying customers and measuring how well a company is performing on customer satisfaction metrics, consumers are getting bombarded with more and more requests for surveys, and many of these have become too long and complicated to fill out or respond to during phone surveys. Some researchers, despite the claims by ACSI and other customer surveys organizations, find low correlations between customer satisfaction scores and future revenue growth. Fred Reichheld, a leading strategy consultant, has concluded from his extensive research that retention rate, a traditional customer loyalty metric, is a poor indicator of a customer's loyalty. Customers often remain with their current supplier because of inertia, high switching costs, or the current lack of an alternative supplier. For example, in the 1990s, Internet service provider AOL had a high market share and low attrition rates. But when telecommunication companies began to offer low-cost, reliable, and fast Internet access, many AOL customers defected rapidly to alternative suppliers. AOL had failed to create true loyalty among its customer base. Similarly, US Airways had a high market share at the Philadelphia airport, but when Southwest Airlines chose Philadelphia as its new hub, many of US Airways long-time customers switched their loyalty immediately to the lower price, more reliable airline. US Airways had not built true loyalty among its large customer base and when a credible alternative arose, it was much too late for US Airways to make up for the lost opportunity.

Reichheld claims that the variable most strongly correlated with future growth and profits is a customer's *willingness to recommend*. He referred to the response to the question "How likely is it that you would recommend [Company xyz] to a friend or colleague?" as the single best question a company can ask about its customers' loyalty.[6] Reichheld and colleagues developed the following 10-point scale for customers to respond to this question as follows:

1.	2.	3.	4.	5.	6.	7.	8.	9.	10.

Extremely unlikely   Neutral   Extremely likely

They labeled the customers who gave the company a 9 or 10 score as the "promoters." They called those who gave a 7 or 8 score the "passively satisfied," and those who gave a 1 to 6 score the "detractors." The evidence suggested that customers who were "promoters" were the only truly loyal customers, and that "detractors" could harm the company's reputation and brand value. Based on this work, many companies now calculate a **net promoter score (NPS)** defined as the percentage of customers who are promoters (score of 9 or 10) less the percentage that are detractors (score of 1 through 6). An airline's net promoter score could, by itself, explain variation in a company's growth rate over a three-year period. No airline could grow revenues without increasing its percentage of promoters over detractors. The median NPS, across 400 companies in

---

[6] F. Reichheld, "The One Number You Need to Grow," *Harvard Business Review* (December 2003), 46–54; F. Reichheld, *The Ultimate Question: Driving Good Profits and True Growth* (Boston: Harvard Business Press, 2008).

28 industries based on 130,000 customer survey responses during 1999–2002, was only 16% and quite a few companies had negative NPSs. Since 2002, the average NPS of surveyed companies has dropped below 10%. Intuit (the producer of Quicken software), eBay, Amazon.com, and the specialty insurance company USAA have among the highest NPSs. The power of the net promoter score is that for customers to make a recommendation to a friend and colleague, the company must satisfy them along two dimensions: (1) The product or service must offer superior value for the money and they feel good about the relationship they have with the company and (2) they are confident that the company will treat their friends and colleagues well should problems emerge. After its founding, Quicken grew rapidly to several hundred million dollars of sales with only a handful of actual salespeople. Its thousands of customers served voluntarily and spontaneously as salespeople when they told their friends, neighbors, and colleagues about the functionality and ease of use of their new electronic checking program.

Earlier in the chapter, we discussed how using activity-based costing to calculate the profitability of individual orders and customers enables a company to shift its sales force incentives from revenues to profits. Many companies are also using customer satisfaction metrics and the net promoter score to reward sales and service personnel. If you are ever asked by the salesperson who sold you an automobile or the service manager who oversaw the service performed under the company's warranty if there was anything preventing you from giving them the highest score on a telephone or Internet survey that might be done in the next week, you can be confident that their bonus depends on having provided you with a high degree of satisfaction with the transaction. One hotel placed a card on the nightstand next to the bed asking the visitor to talk with the hotel manager if there was some aspect of their stay that would cause them not to score the hotel stay as anything less than a 9 or 10 on a survey. While such "coaching" of customers is not desirable, the use of customer satisfaction and loyalty metrics in compensating a sales and service worker certainly gets the attention of front-line employees to be highly focused on creating a great customer experience.

EPILOGUE TO MADISON DAIRY

Jerold Browne, CEO of Madison Dairy, set up a lunch meeting with Mr. Rancantore, the owner of the Verdi retail chain of specialty ice cream stores. After a pleasant meal, Rancantore inquired about the purpose of the meeting. Browne explained that Madison had just installed a new customer profitability system and he saw, for the first time, that the company was incurring large losses producing and delivering products to Verdi and servicing the multiple requests from Verdi's store managers. But Browne told the owner not to be overly concerned since he would propose several options to correct this problem.

Browne described option 1, continue business as usual, with some small modifications for delivery and service responsiveness, but add an 11% price increase that would cover the extra costs Madison incurred in meeting Verdi's special requests. Rancantore, unsure about whether he could absorb such a large price change, blinked several times and asked what other options were available.

Browne indicated that the second option would be to keep prices exactly where they were but that instead of producing products using Verdi's special recipes, ingredients, and labels, Madison would supply the chain with product made under its own brand, which it was already producing in large quantities for its many supermarket customers. It would use its standard packaging and weekly deliveries. The savings from using products and labels already produced in large quantities would enable Verdi to become a profitable customer of Madison's without any price increase.

Rancantore blinked several more times, as he visualized his differentiation advantage disappearing if he offered his customers the same products that they could buy cheaper in supermarkets. He asked about any other options.

Browne replied quickly that Verdi always had the option of finding another supplier willing to meet Verdi's special demands at the current price, but that for Madison to remain as a supplier, Mr. Rancantore would have to choose between the first two options. Several days later, Rancantore called back to say he would accept the price increase. He wanted to retain the quality, unique flavors, and services that Madison provided, and felt that his customers were loyal and likely willing to continue to buy even as he passed on some of the price increase to them. Browne was pleased both with the process and the outcome. Rather than continue to suffer losses with an important customer, or be forced to abandon the customer, he had been able to have a constructive conversation, based on the actual facts on the profitability of the relationship, and offer two alternatives that the customer could choose from in order to retain Madison as its supplier. The data gave Browne the insights about where he could achieve the savings to offset the potential loss of $4 million in annual revenues if he lost the customer's account, and this insight gave him the ability to adopt a strong position in the negotiations.

SUMMARY

The long-term sustainable success of a company will be determined by how well a company performs for and with its customers. Historically, however, management accounting information had focused on measures of product and process performance and paid little attention to how well the company was doing with its customers. In effect, these companies operated in a "field of dreams"-type product-focused mentality: If we build it, customers will come and buy it. This may have worked up through the 1970s, when the world was limited by available productive capacity. But as companies in countries around the world recovered from the destruction of World War II, a shift in power occurred from producers to customers. While operating efficiency remains a high priority for almost all companies, companies today need an intense focus on their targeted customers. They need to understand what their customers' expectations are for their products and services and measure whether they are meeting and exceeding these expectations. Customer satisfaction, loyalty, account share, and willingness to recommend a company's products are important metrics that companies should be continually capturing and analyzing.

Companies must strive, however, not only for happy, loyal customers, but also for profitable customers. Measuring accurately the gross margins earned by selling to individual customers and also tracing the discounts, allowances, and MSDA costs associated with each customer enable a company to see which are its most profitable and unprofitable customer relationships. This information then becomes the basis of targeted actions—process improvement, activity-based pricing, disciplined discounts and allowances, enhanced relationships—that transform breakeven and unprofitable customers into profitable ones. The information on the highly profitable customers enables the company to focus special attention and services to retain and grow the business with these excellent accounts. The ability to measure and manage customer relationships is indeed one of the primary benefits derived from excellent management accounting information.

KEY TERMS

activity-based pricing, 250
customer lifetime value (CLV), 257
customer loyalty, 260
customer satisfaction, 259
managing customer
  relationships, 250

marketing, selling, distribution, and administrative (MSDA) expenses, 243
net promoter score (NPS), 262

pricing waterfall, 252
salesperson incentives, 256
share of wallet, 261
whale curve, 246

ASSIGNMENT MATERIALS

Questions

6-1 Why are nonfinancial measures alone insufficient for managing relationships with customers? **(LO 5)**

6-2 What are the characteristics of high-cost-to-serve customers? **(LO 3)**

6-3 "Companies should avoid high cost-to-serve customers because they are unprofitable." Do you agree with this statement? Explain. **(LO 2, 3)**

6-4 What is a whale curve? **(LO 4)**

6-5 In which section of the whale curve do (a) highly profitable and (b) least profitable customers appear? **(LO 4)**

6-6 Why must service companies, even more so than manufacturing companies, focus on customer costs and profitability? **(LO 5)**

6-7 Provide an example of how customers may use a specific company's resources or services very differently. **(LO 3)**

6-8 What are four broad groups of actions that managers might use to transform unprofitable customers into profitable ones? **(LO 6)**

6-9 What is activity-based pricing? **(LO 6)**

6-10 Why did companies traditionally base salespersons' compensation on revenues? How has this practice changed? **(LO 8)**

6-11 What are the critical parameters for calculating customer lifetime value? **(LO 9)**

6-12 "The only nonfinancial measure for customer relationships that our company should focus on is customer satisfaction." Do you agree with this statement? Explain. **(LO 10)**

6-13 Provide three reasons why customer loyalty provides benefits to companies. **(LO 10)**

6-14 Why might customer retention rate be a poor measure of customer loyalty? **(LO 10)**

6-15 List and describe the five stages of a hierarchy for categorizing customer satisfaction and loyalty. Which companies that you know or deal with as a consumer create the highest form of loyalty for you? **(LO 9)**

6-16 What is the net promoter score and why is it recommended for use by companies? **(LO 10)**

Exercises

LO 1 **6-17** *Assigning marketing, distribution, and selling expenses to customers* Titan Company's cost system assigns marketing, distribution, and selling expenses to customers using a rate of 30% of sales revenue. The new controller has discovered that Titan's customers differ greatly in their ordering patterns and interaction with Titan's sales force. Because the controller believes Titan's cost system does not accurately assign marketing, distribution, and selling expenses to customers, she developed an activity-based costing system to assign these expenses to customers. She then identified the following marketing, distribution, and selling costs for two customers, Gordon and Sylvester:

	GORDON	SYLVESTER
Sales representative travel	$45,000	$8,000
Service customers	90,000	12,000
Handle customer orders	10,000	1,000
Ship to customers	75,000	20,000

The following additional information is available:

	GORDON	SYLVESTER
Sales	$450,000	$550,000
Cost of goods sold	$250,000	$355,000

Required

(a) Using the current cost system's approach of assigning marketing, distribution, and selling expenses to customers using a rate of 30% of sales revenue, determine the operating profit associated with Gordon and with Sylvester.

(b) Using the activity-based costing information provided, determine the operating profit associated with Gordon and with Sylvester.

(c) Which of the two methods produces more accurate assignment of marketing, distribution, and selling expenses to customers? Explain.

LO 1.3   **6-18** *Activity-based costing of order entry costs*   Hampstead Company's order entry department has 20 order entry operators. The cost associated with these 20 operators (salaries, fringe benefits, and supervision, as well as occupancy and equipment costs) is $873,600 per year. After taking into account vacations and holidays, Hampstead calculated that each operator worked about 1,920 hours per year. Allowing for breaks, training, and other time off, each operator provided about 1,560 hours of productive work each year. Hampstead uses time-driven activity-based costing for its order entry operations.

Required

(a) What is the rate per hour for each order entry employee for Hampstead's activity-based costing system?

(b) On average, it takes an order entry employee about 0.1 hour to enter the basic customer information for a manual customer order. In addition, manual orders require an operator to spend an additional 0.02 hour to enter each line item on the order. An operator spends an average of 0.06 hour to check the information on an electronic order, but no further entries are needed for specific line items. What is the order entry cost associated with each of the following two orders?

   (1) A manual order with 10 line items

   (2) An electronic order with 10 line items.

LO 4   **6-19** *Whale curve*   Wright Company, a new systems consulting company, is concerned about the profitability of its customers during the past year. The company has prepared the following data:

Customer	Profit	Customer	Profit
1	$221,000	14	83,000
2	−40,000	15	−179,000
3	−143,000	16	14,000
4	217,000	17	50,000
5	22,000	18	−191,000
6	9,000	19	−90,000
7	101,000	20	30,000
8	−200,000	21	−10,000
9	259,000	22	87,000
10	96,000	23	−158,000
11	208,000	24	−100,000
12	233,000	25	75,000
13	264,000		

Required

(a) Prepare a whale curve, as described in this chapter.
(b) What percentage of total profits did the most profitable 20% of the customers generate?
(c) What percentage of total profits did the least profitable 20% of the customers lose for the company?

LO 2, 6, 7   **6-20 *Increasing customer profitability***   For each of the categories below, provide a specific example of how a company might transform its breakeven or loss customers into profitable ones:
  a. Process improvements
  b. Activity-based (menu-based) pricing
  c. Managed customer relationships
  d. Disciplined discounts and allowances.

LO 7   **6-21 *Pricing waterfall***   Refer to the pricing waterfall chart in Exhibit 6-4.

Required

(a) What circumstances result in firms often failing to be aware of all of the discounts and allowances granted on a customer order?
(b) Once a firm becomes aware of pricing waterfalls leading to undesirably large sales discounts, what steps might the firm take to manage discounts with more discipline?

LO 7   **6-22 *Benefits of managing discounts***   The Harveys Company has recently become aware of the large amount of total discounts on its orders and would like to know the impact on profit. The company computed its operating profit as follows:

Sales	$250,000
Variable costs	100,000
Contribution margin	$150,000
Fixed costs	70,000
Operating profit	$80,000

Required

(a) Suppose Harveys could reduce its sales discounts by 8%, resulting in an 8% increase in revenues but no changes in variable or fixed costs. By what percentage would operating profit increase? How does this percentage compare to the percentage reduction in sales discounts?
(b) Refer to the original information in this problem. Suppose Harveys' salespeople discount sales another 6%, with no change in variable or fixed costs. By what percentage would operating profits decrease? How does this percentage compare to the percentage increase in sales discounts?
(c) Consider the ratio of operating profit to sales. How does this ratio relate to the percentage change in operating profit, for a given percentage change in the sales discount?

LO 1, 2, 8   **6-23 *Salespersons' incentives, customer profitability***   In response to how the sales incentives might be contributing to falling profits despite growing sales, Chan Company's controller has produced the following information on last year's sales to two customers that purchased a variety of products from the company:

	CUSTOMERS	
	CARLSON	DONNER
Sales	$450,000	$400,000
Cost of goods sold	180,000	80,000
MSDA expenses, excluding sales commissions	320,000	65,000

Required

(a) Which customer is more profitable for the company?

(b) Compare a sales incentive scheme that pays 2% of sales revenue to an incentive scheme that pays 4% of customer profit. How will each scheme affect salespersons' desire to increase sales to each customer?

LO 9   **6-24** *Customer lifetime value calculation*   Compute the customer lifetime value for Customer 421 based on the data below for the first six years of the customer relationship. Costs (c_t) were incurred to promote customer retention to a rate of 0.8 in years 1 through 6.

	CUSTOMER 421
Initial acquisition cost	$600
n = number of years retained	6
r = retention rate for each of the n years retained	0.8
Cost of capital	0.1
M_t = margin from customer in year t	
M_1	$250
M_2	300
M_3	325
M_4	350
M_5	375
M_6	400
c_1	60
c_2	50
c_3	50
c_4	50
c_5	40
c_6	40

LO 10   **6-25** *Net promoter score calculation*   Don's, a fast-food chain, has conducted a survey to collect data on customer satisfaction and perception of its food quality and service. Data for responses to the question "How likely is it that you would recommend Don's to a friend or colleague?" appear below.

SCORE	NUMBER OF RESPONSES
1	49
2	253
3	276
4	231
5	64
6	764
7	875
8	982
9	914
10	1,392
Total	6,000

Required

What is Don's net promoter score?

Problems

LO 1, 2, 5 **6-26** *Customer profitability* A credit card company has classified its customers into the following types for customer profitability analysis:

1. Applies for credit card in response to a low introductory interest rate; transfers balance to new account, but when the low introductory rate expires, the customer transfers the balance to an account with a different credit card company that has offered a low introductory rate.
2. Charges a large dollar volume of purchases; pays balance in full and on time each month.
3. Carries a high balance; pays only the minimum required payment but pays regularly with occasional late payment.
4. Carries a high balance; pays at least the minimum required payment but does not pay in full and always pays on time.
5. Carries a low balance; pays at least the minimum required payment but does not pay in full and always pays on time.
6. Does not use the account but does not close the account.

The following facts pertain to the credit card company's operations:

- Merchants pay the credit card company a percentage of the dollar sales on each credit card transaction.
- Customers pay no interest on charges for purchases if the balance is paid in full and on time each month.
- The credit card company charges a late fee if the customer's payment is late.
- The credit card company incurs costs to send statements to inactive customers.

Required

Given the preceding information, which customer types would you expect to be the most desirable or profitable, the next most profitable, and so on for the credit card company on a long-term basis? Explain your ranking.

LO 1, 2, 3, 5, 6 **6-27** *Customer profitability analysis, original activity-based costing* Kronecker Company, a growing mail-order clothing and accessory company, is concerned about its growing MSDA expenses. It therefore examined its customer ordering patterns for the past year and identified four different types of customers, as illustrated in the following table. Kronecker sends catalogs and flyers to all its customers several times a year. Orders are taken by mail or over the phone. Kronecker maintains a toll-free number for customers to use when placing orders over the phone. Kronecker prides itself on the personal attention it provides shoppers who order over the phone. All purchases are paid for by check or credit card. Kronecker has a very generous return policy if customers are not satisfied with the merchandise received. Customers must pay return shipping charges, but their purchase price is then fully refunded.

	CUSTOMER TYPE 1	CUSTOMER TYPE 2	CUSTOMER TYPE 3	CUSTOMER TYPE 4
Initial sales	$1,000	$1,000	$2,500	$3,000
Number of items returned	0	4	2	24
Dollar value of items returned	0	$200	$500	$1,500
Number of orders per year	1	6	4	12
Number of phone orders per year	1	0	0	12
Time spent on phone placing orders	0.25 hour	0	0	1 hour
Number of overnight deliveries	1	0	0	12
Number of regular deliveries	0	6	4	0

Prices are set so that cost of goods sold is on average about 75% of the sales price. Customers pay actual shipping charges, but extra processing is required for overnight deliveries. Kronecker has developed the following activity cost driver rates for its support costs:

ACTIVITY	ACTIVITY COST DRIVER RATE
Process mail orders	$5 per order
Process phone orders	$80 per hour
Process returns	$5 per item returned
Process overnight delivery requests	$4 per request
Maintain customer relations (send catalogs and respond to customer comments or complaints)	$50 per year

Required

(a) Using activity-based costing, determine the yearly profit associated with each of the four customers described.

(b) Comment on which customers are most profitable and why.

(c) What advice do you have for Kronecker regarding managing customer relationships with the different types of customers represented?

LO 2, 4 **6-28** *The 80–20 rule and whale curve* Write an essay to explain how the 80–20 graph for sales revenues would be prepared and describe typical findings with respect to proportions of products and customers generating percentages of sales. Also, describe how a whale curve is prepared and typical findings with respect to proportions of customers generating percentages of cumulative customer profitability.

LO 7 **6-29** *Pricing waterfall* Randolph Company's product mix has become more diverse over the past few years. Consequently the company undertook an activity-based costing initiative to develop accurate costs for production, as well as marketing, selling, distribution, and administration. The company set list prices that would provide a profit regardless of whether the customer orders were complex or routine. Nevertheless, profits have been falling. The company's management team decided to examine discounts that had been granted to determine whether these are the reason for poor profit performance.

Management was surprised to learn that customers were taking advantage of a large number of possible discounts or allowances, including the following:

1. Volume discount if 20 or more units are ordered	2%
2. Pay in full in 15 days	3%
3. Cooperative advertising allowance for featuring the company's products in its advertisements	4%
4. Take a large shipment before the end of the quarter in advance of an expected seasonal increase in demand	5%
5. Online ordering discount	2%
6. Rebate on sales during specific promotional periods	2%

The management team believed that some discounting was necessary to acquire and retain large customers. On deeper investigation, they learned that some of their smaller customers, who were often the most cost conscious, took advantage of every discount or allowance offered. To compare discounts or allowances taken, they compared Customer 1 and Customer 2.

Customer 1 is a long-time customer with sales of $200,000 at list prices. This customer takes advantage of each discount or allowance listed in the preceding table. Moreover, this customer has been a loyal customer since Randolph Company's inception. In appreciation, Randolph's sales representative offers free freight, which amounts to 3% of the customer's list-price purchases from Randolph.

Customer 2 is a more recently acquired customer with sales of $1,000,000 at list prices. This customer only takes advantage of items 1, 3, and 5 in the preceding table.

Required

(a) Compute the total sales discount percentage for Customer 1 and for Customer 2.
(b) Why might Randolph Company's management team have been unaware of the potentially large total discounts offered to its customers?
(c) What advice do you have for Randolph Company regarding managing its discounts and allowances?

LO 9   **6-30**   *Customer lifetime value calculations*   KEM Company has begun studying customer lifetime value for its customers and has prepared the information below for selected customers. For simplicity, management has assumed that for a given customer, the retention rate is the same every year until the customer departs. For Customer 4, costs (c_t) were incurred to promote customer retention in years 1 and 2.

	CUSTOMERS			
	1	2	3	4
Initial acquisition cost	$1,000	$1,000	$1,000	$1,000
n = number of years retained	5	3	5	5
r = retention rate for each of the n years retained	1	1	0.9	1
Cost of capital	0.1	0.1	0.1	0.1
M_t = margin from customer in year t				
M_1	$275	$300	$275	$275
M_2	275	300	275	275
M_3	275	300	275	300
M_4	275	—	275	300
M_5	275	—	275	300
c_t = additional costs-to-serve and retain customer in year t				
c_1	$0	$0	$0	$50
c_2	0	0	0	25
c_3	0	0	0	0
c_4	0	—	0	0
c_5	0	—	0	0

Required

(a) Compute the customer lifetime value for each customer for the stated number of years.
(b) Discuss the reasons for differences in customer lifetime value between Customers 1 and 2, Customers 1 and 3, Customers 1 and 4, and Customers 3 and 4.

(c) Compute the customer lifetime value for Customers 1, 2, and 3 assuming that n is very large and the numbers in the table remain about the same each year.

(d) How does information on a customer's estimated lifetime value help a company manage its customer acquisition and loyalty programs?

LO 10 **6-31** *Net promoter score* In which industries would you expect the net promoter score to have the greatest predictive power for repeat purchases and growth? The least predictive power for repeat purchases and growth?

Cases

LO 1, 2, 3, 6, 8 **6-32** *Pricing, customer profitability, managing customer relationships* Read the *Wall Street Journal* article "Survival Strategies: After Cost Cutting, Companies Turn toward Price Increases" by Timothy Aeppel (September 18, 2002, p. A1). The article reports "an all-out search for new ways to charge more money without raising prices."

Required

(a) How did Jergens, Inc., use an activity-based costing approach to justify the price for an order of odd-size metal locating fasteners?

(b) What issues arose in Goodyear Tire & Rubber's pricing to distributors? What was Goodyear's response?

(c) What was the outcome of Emerson Electric's decision to depart from cost-based pricing? How can a product costing system contribute to undercosting a low-volume or customized product?

(d) How did Wildeck influence customers to purchase products and services that are more profitable to Wildeck? How did Wildeck respond to a competitor's lower priced storage-rack protector? What role should a cost system play in such decisions?

(e) Why was Union Pacific not concerned if it lost its less profitable customers? Will dropping unprofitable customers always lead to an immediate increase in profit?

LO 1, 2, 3, 5, 6, 9 **6-33** *Time-driven activity-based costing, activity-based management* Midwest Office Products[7]

John Malone, general manager of Midwest Office Products (MOP), was concerned about the financial results for calendar year 2003. Despite a sales increase from the prior year, the company had just suffered the first loss in its history (see summary income statement in Exhibit 6-9).

Exhibit 6-9
Midwest Office Products: Income Statement, January–December 2003

Sales	$42,700,000	122.0%
Cost of items purchased	35,000,000	100.0%
Gross margin	7,700,000	22.0%
Personnel expense (warehouse, truck drivers)	2,570,000	7.3%
Warehouse expenses (excluding personnel)	2,000,000	5.7%
Freight	450,000	1.3%
Delivery truck expenses	200,000	0.6%
Order entry expenses	840,000	2.4%
General and selling expenses	1,600,000	4.6%
Interest expense	120,000	0.3%
Net income before taxes	($80,000)	(0.2)%

Source: Robert S. Kaplan.

[7] Copyright © 2004 President and Fellows of Harvard College. Harvard Business School Case 9-104-073. This case was prepared by Professor Robert S. Kaplan as the basis for class discussion rather than to illustrate either effective or ineffective handling of an administrative situation. Reprinted by permission of Harvard Business School.

Midwest Office Products was a regional distributor of office supplies to institutions and commercial businesses. It offered a comprehensive product line ranging from simple writing implements (such as pens, pencils, and markers) and fasteners to specialty paper for modern high-speed copiers and printers. MOP had an excellent reputation for customer service and responsiveness.

Warehouse personnel at MOP's distribution center unloaded truckload shipments of products from manufacturers, and moved the cartons into designated storage locations until customers requested the items. Each day, after customer orders had been received, MOP personnel drove forklift trucks around the warehouse to accumulate the cartons of items and prepare them for shipment.

MOP ordered supplies from many different manufacturers. It priced products to its end-use customers by first marking up the purchased product cost by 16% to cover the cost of warehousing, order processing, and freight; then it added another 6% markup to cover the general, selling, and administrative expenses, plus an allowance for profit. The markups were determined at the start of each year, based on actual expenses in prior years and general industry and competitive trends. Midwest adjusted the actual price quoted to a customer based on long-term relationships and competitive situations, but pricing was generally independent of the specific level of service required by that customer, except for desktop deliveries.

Typically, MOP shipped products to its customers using commercial truckers. Recently, MOP had introduced a desktop delivery option in which Midwest personnel personally delivered supplies directly to individual locations at the customer's site. Midwest had leased four trucks and hired four drivers for the desktop delivery service. Midwest charged a price premium (up to an additional 5% markup) for the convenience and savings such direct delivery orders provided to customers. The company believed that the desktop delivery option would improve margins and create more loyal customers in its highly competitive office supplies distribution business.

Midwest had introduced electronic data interchange (EDI) in 1999, and a new Internet site in 2000, which allowed customer orders to arrive automatically so that clerks would not have to enter data manually. Several customers had switched to this electronic service because of the convenience to them. Yet Midwest's costs continued to rise. Malone was concerned that even after introducing innovations such as desktop delivery and electronic order entry, the company could not earn a profit. He wondered about what actions he should take to regain profitability.

Distribution Center: Activity Analysis

Malone turned to his controller, Melissa Dunhill, and director of operations, Tim Cunningham, for help. Tim suggested:

If we can figure out, without going overboard of course, what exactly goes on in our distribution center, maybe we can get a clearer picture about what it costs to process orders and serve our customers.

Distribution center manager, Wilbur Smith, spoke with Melissa and Tim about the operations at the center:

All we do is store the cartons, process the orders, and get them ready to ship to customers, either by commercial freight or using the desktop delivery option.

Wilbur described some details of these activities:

The amount of warehouse space we need and the people to move cartons in and out of storage and get them ready for shipment just depends on the number of cartons. All items have about the same inventory turnover so space and handling costs are proportional to the number of cartons that go through the facility.

We use commercial freight for normal shipments, and the cost is based more on volume than on anything else. Each carton we ship by commercial carrier costs about the same, regardless of the weight or distance. Of course, any carton that we deliver ourselves, through our new desktop delivery service, avoids the commercial shipping charges but does use our trucks and drivers.

The team talked with one of the truck drivers doing desktop deliveries:

An average delivery takes about three hours. But delivery times can be as short as 30 minutes for nearby customers, and up to eight hours for delivery to a distant customer. We also spend different times once we arrive at a customer's site. Some customers have only a single dropoff point, while others require us to deliver individual cartons to different locations at their site.

Melissa and Tim next checked on the expenses of entering and validating customer order data at the distribution center. The order entry expenses included the data processing system, the data entry operators, and supervisors. They spoke with Hazel Nutley, a data entry operator at Midwest for 17 years.

All I do is key in the orders, line by line by line. I start by entering the customer ID and validating our customer information. Beyond that, the only thing that really matters is how many order lines I have to enter. Each line item on the order has to be entered separately. Of course, any order that comes in through the EDI system or Internet page sets up automatically without any intervention from me. I just do a quick check to make sure the customer hasn't made an obvious error, and that everything looks correct. This validity check takes about the same time for all electronic orders; it doesn't depend on the number of items ordered.

Melissa and Tim collected information from company databases and learned the following:

- The distribution centers processed 80,000 cartons in 2003. Of these, 75,000 cartons were shipped by commercial freight. The remaining 5,000 cartons were shipped under the desktop delivery option. Midwest made 2,000 desktop deliveries during the year (the average desktop delivery was for 2.5 cartons).
- People felt that handling, processing, and shipping 80,000 cartons per year was about the capacity that could be handled with existing people and space resources.
- The total compensation for truck drivers was $250,000 per year. Each driver worked about 1,500 hours per year doing the desktop delivery service. This was also the maximum time available from each truck, after subtracting maintenance and repair time.
- Midwest employed 16 order entry operators. The $840,000 of order entry costs in Midwest's income statement included the salaries, fringe benefits, supervision, occupancy, and equipment costs for the operators.
- With vacations and holidays, each operator worked about 1,750 hours per year. But allowing for breaks, training, and other time off, the order entry supervisor believed that operators provided about 1,500 hours per year of productive work.
- Operators required about 9 minutes (0.15 hour) to enter the basic information on a manual customer order. Beyond this basic setup time for a manual order, operators took an additional 4.5 minutes (0.075 hour) to enter each line item on the order. The operators spent an average of 6 minutes (0.10 hour) to verify the information on an electronic order.
- Some customers paid their invoices within 30 days, while others took 90 to 120 days to pay. Midwest had recently taken out a working capital loan to help finance its growing accounts receivables balance. The current interest rate on this loan was 1% per month on the average loan balance.

Understanding Order Costs and Profitability

Melissa looked through recent orders and found five that seemed representative of those received during the past year (see Exhibit 6-10). The orders all involved cartons containing merchandise costing about $500 to acquire from manufacturers to which the normal 22% markup had been realized. Orders requiring direct delivery had an additional 4% to 5% surcharge. Although each of these orders had been priced in the standard way for cost recovery and profit margins, Melissa wondered what profits Midwest Office Products had really earned on each of these orders.

Exhibit 6-10
Midwest Office Products: Five Orders

ORDER	1	2	3	4	5
Price	$610	$634	$6,100	$6,340	$6,100
Acquisition cost	500	500	5,000	5,000	5,000
Number of cartons in order	1	1	10	10	10
Number of cartons shipped commercially	1	0	10	0	10
Desktop delivery time (hours)	—	4	—	4	—
Manual order	No	Yes	No	Yes	Yes
Number of line items in order	1	1	10	10	10
Electronic order	Yes	No	Yes	No	No
Payment period (months)	1	4	1	4	4

Source: Robert S. Kaplan.

Required

(a) Based on the interviews and the data in the case, estimate the following:
   (1) The cost of processing cartons through the facility
   (2) The cost of entering electronic and manual customer orders
   (3) The cost of shipping cartons on commercial carriers
   (4) The cost per hour for desktop deliveries.

(b) Using this capacity cost rate information, calculate the cost and profitability of the five orders in Exhibit 6-10. What explains the variation in profitability across the five orders?

(c) On the basis of your analysis, what actions should John Malone take to improve Midwest's profitability? Include suggestions for managing customer profitability.

(d) Suppose that currently, Midwest processes 40,000 manual orders per year, with a total of 200,000 line items entered, and 30,000 electronic orders.

   (1) How much unused practical capacity does the company have?
   (2) If the company's efforts to encourage customers who order manually to change to electronic ordering results in 20,000 manual orders per year (100,000 line items entered) and 50,000 electronic orders, how many order entry operators will the company require? If order entry resource costs can be reduced in proportion to the number of employees, what will be the cost savings from the changes?
   (3) Returning to the original information in part d, if the company's process improvement efforts result in a 20% reduction in time to perform each of the three order entry activities, how many order entry operators will the company require? If order entry resource costs can be reduced in proportion to the number of employees, what will be the cost savings from the process improvements?

Chapter 7

Measuring and Managing Process Performance

After completing this chapter, you will be able to:

1. Explain the theory of constraints.
2. Compare the different types of facilities layouts: process, product, and group technology.
3. Explain lean manufacturing.
4. Describe the concept of the cost of quality.
5. Demonstrate the value of just-in-time manufacturing systems.
6. Explain kaizen costing.
7. Discuss the various kinds of benchmarking approaches.
8. Calculate the cost savings resulting from reductions in inventories, reductions in production cycle time, improvements in production yields, and reductions in rework and defect rates.

Blast from the Past Robot Company

For the past 10 years, the Blast from the Past Robot (BFTPR) Company of Worthington, Ohio, has been producing high-quality reproduction tin toy robots that had originally been produced in Japan during the 1950s and 1960s. Many of these toys such as Robby the Robot and Gort were tied into famous science fiction films such as *Forbidden Planet* and *The Day the Earth Stood Still*.

In today's market, original toy robots cost thousands of dollars and only the most rabid collectors are willing to pay such prices. BFTPR was able to produce reproduction robots that could be purchased often for a fraction of the price of the originals to satisfy those seeking nostalgia on a limited budget.

The company prided itself on faithfully reproducing robots. Using parts from the original robots, the company cast individual pieces and then assembled them. Their best-selling toy was a mechanical toy robot called Mr. Mechanical that performed several functions such as lighting up, moving forward and backward with its arms moving up and down.

276

Blast from the Past Robot Company's Mr. Mechanical
Photo courtesy of S. Mark Young

The robot, which was also "aged" to look more vintage, was fashioned after the original Robby the Robot from Forbidden Planet. It commanded a 40% market share. In early 2011, however, Mr. Mechanical experienced a large drop in sales and market share. After some investigation, this loss was attributed to a significant decrease in the quality of the product and to general delays in getting it to customers. Customers complained that the toy robots failed to perform many of their functions and simply stopped working after several days. The number of returns was astronomical.

Top management decided that the quality of the toy robot needed to be improved dramatically so that the company could regain its reputation and market share. Apparently, the quality problem was due to deterioration of equipment and an out-of-date production process. Morale among the workers was also poor. Neva Dominguez, senior manager of manufacturing, was asked to conduct a thorough investigation and arrive at recommendations for change and improvement.

After several weeks of study, Neva and a cross-functional team of management and shop floor personnel documented numerous shop floor problems:

1. A disorganized, sloppy production system in which piles of both work-in-process and raw materials inventories were scattered over the shop floor
2. A lengthy and complex flow of production
3. The use of outdated machinery.

In addition, the quality of the computer chip that allowed the robot to perform its functions was found to be highly variable, and thus there were as many defective robots sent back for rework as acceptable ones. Neva, a proponent of lean manufacturing, a philosophy centered on producing the highest quality product with the lowest level of waste and inefficiency, had just completed a benchmarking study of another company that had implemented the just-in-time (JIT) manufacturing philosophy. She believed that the BFTPR Company could benefit greatly from implementing JIT. The JIT system seemed to have many advantages, such as streamlining the production process and improving facilities layout, eliminating waste, reducing raw and work-in-process inventories, and generally creating an environment in which producing quality products was rewarded. Further, costs would be easier to control if the company had a well-designed and well-understood production process. Neva's report to top management raised several questions:

1. Should many of the existing machines, including the major injection-molding machine, be replaced?
2. What should the company do about the local vendor who produced the faulty computer chips?
3. Would it make sense to implement an entirely new production process such as JIT?

After a month of study, top management decided to implement the JIT approach. The cost of implementation and worker training amounted to $300,000. Management personnel wanted to be able to assess the return (benefits) from their investment in JIT. They were adamant that Neva and her team carefully monitor the quality of products and the changes in the amount of rework. The cost of rework was part of a calculation the company made to determine what it called the *cost of quality*.

After the first year, Neva plotted a graph of the rates of major rework, which required scrapping the robot, and minor rework, which included repairs such as realignment of parts and gears. The graph is shown in Exhibit 7-1. Major rework had declined by about 2.5%, whereas the minor rework rate showed a larger decrease of 6.6%.

Exhibit 7-1
BFTPR: Major and Minor Rework Rates

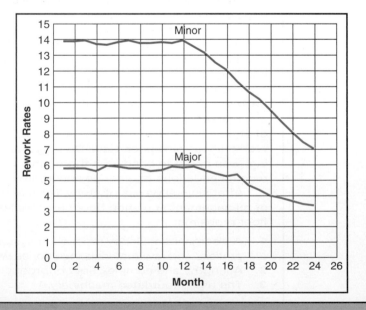

Neva believed that improvement in yield rates should improve cycle time—the time it took to produce the robot from start to finish. On average, she found that cycle time had indeed decreased from 16.4 days to 7.2 days and that the work-in-process inventory had decreased from $1,774,000 to $818,000, for a savings of $956,000.

Neva knew that the transition to a full JIT system would take some time, but she also wondered what the bottom-line effect on company profits would be for the year. Would the benefits of less rework, yield increases, and cycle time and inventory reductions be sufficient to offset the $300,000 implementation costs?

In this chapter, we will discuss many issues related to how management accounting information is used to measure and manage process decisions. This chapter presents three types of facility designs—(1) process layouts, (2) product layouts, and (3) group technology—all of which can be used to help organizations reduce costs. We follow this with a discussion of how organizations can reduce costs by using a lean manufacturing approach aimed at improving the quality of their processes and reducing cycle time. The JIT manufacturing system, originally developed by Toyota, is presented as a system that integrates many of the ideas we discuss in the chapter. Benchmarking will also be introduced as a way in which organizations can find out what their competition is doing and to take the best methods from what they observe.

PROCESS PERSPECTIVE AND THE BALANCED SCORECARD

As we noted in Chapter 2, the process perspective of the Balanced Scorecard identifies the key operations management, customer management, innovation, and regulatory and social processes in which the organization must excel to achieve its customer, revenue growth, and profitability objectives. In this chapter we discuss the operations management processes that allow organizations to produce products and services and deliver them to customers. Objectives for these processes include streamlining operations through lean manufacturing; improving the cost, quality, and cycle times of processes; and using benchmarking as a way to obtain information for competitive purposes. These tools form the basis of decisions about the organization's activities and processes, as we saw in the case of the BFTPR Company.

FACILITY LAYOUT SYSTEMS

Determining the right kind of facility layout for an operation is a critical part of managing operations. Managers must consider the entire operations process within a facility and consider the amount of space required, the demand for the product or service produced, and the number of operations that are needed. In this section we discuss the three general types of facility designs: (1) process layouts, (2) product layouts, and (3) group technology.

Regardless of the type of facility design, a central goal of the design process is to streamline operations and thus increase the operating income of the system. One method that can guide this process for all three designs is the theory of constraints (TOC).

This theory maintains that operating income can be increased by carefully managing the bottlenecks in a process. A bottleneck is any condition that impedes or constrains the efficient flow of a process; it can be identified by determining points at which excessive amounts of work-in-process inventories are accumulating. The buildup of inventories also slows the cycle time of production.

The TOC relies on the use of three measures: (1) the throughput contribution; (2) investments, and (3) operating costs. The **throughput contribution** is the difference between revenues and direct materials for the quantity of product sold; **investments** equal the materials costs contained in raw materials, work-in-process, and finished goods inventories; and **operating costs** are all other costs, except for direct materials costs, that are needed to obtain throughput contribution. Examples of operating costs are depreciation, salaries, and utility costs.

The TOC emphasizes the short-run optimization of throughput contribution. Its planning horizon is typically one month. For this short time period, almost all of an organization's costs will be fixed and unavoidable, which explains why TOC concentrates on maximizing short-run contribution margin. At first, this seems contrary to the view of activity-based costing (ABC), presented in Chapters 5 and 6, but ABC's planning horizon is quarterly, annually, and longer. For these horizons, managers have the ability to decrease resources that are in excess supply and not needed for current or future production, and also add to the supply of resources that would otherwise create bottlenecks. The ability of managers to adjust resource capacity to meet current and future demands is why ABC treats the resource capacity costs as relevant for decisions about products and customers. In fact, therefore, TOC and ABC are entirely compatible with TOC providing insights for short-run profit optimization and ABC providing managers with signals about how to optimize performance over longer periods of time. In this way, TOC and ABC can be used simultaneously and productively by organizations.

Process Layouts

To understand why inventories stockpile in conventional processing systems and thus increase cycle time, we must understand the conventional way in which factory or office facilities are organized. In a **process layout** (sometimes called a job shop or functional layout), all similar equipment or functions are grouped together. Process layouts exist in organizations in which production is done in small batches of unique products. The product follows a serpentine path, usually in batches, through the factories and offices that create it. In addition to these long production paths, process layouts are also characterized by high inventory levels because it is necessary to store work in process in each area while it awaits the next operation. Often a product can travel for several miles within a factory as it is transformed from raw materials to finished goods.

For example, the process associated with a loan application at a bank may occur as follows: The customer goes to the bank (a moving activity). The bank takes the loan application from the customer (a processing activity). Loan applications are accumulated (a storage activity) and passed to a loan officer (a moving activity) for approval (both a processing and an inspection activity). Loans that violate standard loan guidelines are accumulated (a storage activity) and then passed (a moving activity) to a regional supervisor for approval (a processing activity). The customer is contacted when a decision has been made (a processing activity), and if the loan is approved, then the loan proceeds are deposited in the customer's account (a processing activity).

In most banks, work in process is stockpiled at each of the processing points or stations. Loan applications may be piled on the bank teller's desk, the loan officer's desk, and the regional supervisor's desk. Work-in-process inventory, such as bank loan applications, accumulates at processing stations in a conventional organization for three reasons:

1. Handling work in batches is the most obvious cause of work-in-process inventory in a process layout system. Organizations use batches to reduce setting up, moving, and handling costs; however, batch processing increases the inventory levels in the system because at each processing station all items in the batch must wait while the designated employees process the entire batch before moving all parts in the batch to the next station.

2. If the rate at which each processing area handles work is unbalanced—because one area is slower or has stopped working because of problems with equipment, materials, or people—work piles up at the slowest processing station. Such scheduling delays create another reason why inventory levels increase in a process layout system.

3. Since supervisors evaluate many processing area managers on their ability to meet production quotas, processing station managers try to avoid the risk of having their facility idle. Many managers deliberately maintain large stocks of incoming work in process so that they can continue to work even if the processing area that feeds them is shut down. Similarly, to avoid idling the next processing station and suffering the resulting recriminations, managers may store finished work that they can forward to supply stations further down the line when their stations are shut down because of problems.

Some organizations have developed innovative approaches to eliminating many of the costs related to moving and storing, which are significant non–value-added costs associated with process layout systems.

Product Layouts

In a **product layout** (sometimes called a flow-shop layout), equipment is organized to accommodate the production of a specific product; an automobile assembly line or a packaging line for cereal or milk, for example, is a product layout. Product layouts exist primarily in companies with high-volume production. The product moves along an assembly line beside which the parts to be added to it have been stored. Placement of equipment or processing units is made to reduce the distance that products must travel.

Product layout systems planners often can arrange for raw materials and purchased parts to be delivered directly to the production line where and when they are needed. Suppose that an assembly line is scheduled to handle 600 cars on a given day. The purchasing group knows that these 600 automobiles require 2,400 regular tires and 600 spare tires. Under ideal conditions, the purchasing group will arrange delivery of small batches of these tires to the assembly line as frequently as they are needed. However, because each batch of tires from the supplier incurs some related ordering, transportation, and delivery costs, planners may arrange for a few days' worth of tires to be delivered at a time.

Consider the work in process in a cafeteria setting. People pass by containers of food and take what they want. Employees organize the food preparation activities so that the containers are refilled just as they are being emptied—not one unit at a time. For example, the cook does not make and replace one bowl of soup at a time because the setup costs of making soup in this fashion will be prohibitively expensive. Reducing setup costs, however, allows for the reduction of batch sizes (the size of the containers) along the line. This reduces the level of inventory in the system and, therefore, costs. It also improves quality while increasing customer satisfaction. The ultimate goal is to

Peugeot assembly line. In this assembly line, each workstation is designed to perform a specific process. Thus, the car is constructed as it moves down the line and ultimately emerges as a finished product.

Alamy Images

IN PRACTICE

Manufacturing a CD

A CD or compact disc is an optical digital audio disc that contains up to 74 minutes of hi-fi stereo sound. CDs were first introduced into the U.S. market in 1983. CDs are plastic platters that are recorded on one side and can store between 650 and 700 MB of information. Audio tracks are recorded as microscopic pits in a groove that starts at the center of the disc and spirals outward to the edge.

Manufacturing a CD typically usually requires a process layout involving six major steps. The first step is to make a glass master, which is an exact copy of the source material, such as a song. The master is made by taking a glass disc that is coated with a very thin layer of light-reactive material. Digital data 1's and 0's are carved by a laser into the CD as pits (low spots) and lands (high spots).

In the second step a mold is made on metal stampers of the contents of the disc. The disc itself is too fragile to be used in the replication process. The metal stampers are then attached to injection molding machines. In the third step, the metal stamper is put into a mold and polycarbonate plastic is injected into it. The stamper imprints data pits into the plastic. The fourth step involves placing a layer of reflective material directly onto the polycarbonate plastic so that the laser can then read what is on the disc. Aluminum is next applied to the back of the disc

Shutterstock

to create the reflective surface. In the fifth step, this layer is then coated with an acrylic lacquer for protection and is cured under UV light.

The final step involves silk-screening a face label onto the cured lacquer in inks cured with a UV light. This creates the finished product as shown below.

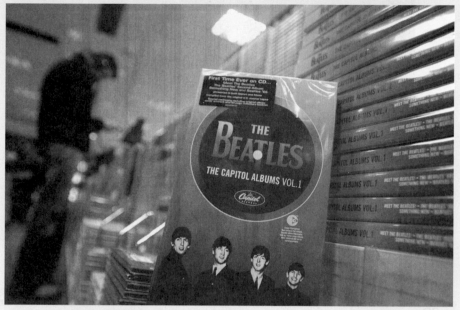

A boxed set of Beatles CDs.
Getty Images Editorial

reduce setup costs to zero and to reduce processing time to as close to zero as possible so that the system can produce and deliver individual products just as they are needed.

Group Technology

The third approach to facilities layout, **group technology** (sometimes called cellular manufacturing), refers to the organization of a plant into a number of cells so that within each cell all machines required to manufacture a group of similar products are arranged in proximity to each other. As Exhibit 7-2 illustrates, the shape of a cell is often U shaped, which allows workers convenient access to required parts. The machines in a group technology layout are usually flexible and can be adjusted easily or even automatically to make different products. Often when group technology is introduced, the number of employees needed to produce a product can be reduced because of the new work design. The U shape also provides better visual control of the workflow because employees can observe more directly what their coworkers are doing.

INVENTORY COSTS AND PROCESSING TIME

Inventory and Processing Time

Not only does batch production create inventory costs, but it also creates the delays associated with storing and moving inventory. These delays increase cycle times, thereby reducing service to customers. Delays can happen at any stage of the production cycle, even before manufacturing begins. For example, because of high setup

Exhibit 7-2
Group Technology
Layout

Group technology or cellular manufacturing is built on the principle of grouping machines together in one place to reduce waiting time and increase visual control.

http://ti2.com.au/ web/ti2images/ LineLayout.jpg

costs, a manufacturer may require that a product be manufactured in some minimum batch size. If a customer order is less than the minimum batch size and if the order cannot be filled from existing finished goods inventory, then the customer must wait until enough orders have accumulated to meet the minimum batch size requirement. It may take a loan officer only 5 minutes to read and approve a loan application at the bank; however, the application may have to wait for several hours or even days before it reaches the loan officer because having a clerk run back and forth with each new loan application when it arrives is too expensive.

Inventory-Related Costs

Demands for inventory lead to huge costs in organizations, including the cost of moving, handling, and storing the work in process, in addition to costs due to obsolescence or damage. Many organizations have found that factory layouts and inefficiencies that create the need to hold work-in-process inventory also hide other problems, leading to excessive costs of rework.

For example, in batch operations, workers near the end of a process—downstream—often find batch-size problems resulting from the way workers earlier in the process—upstream—have done their jobs. When work is performed continuously on one component at a time, however, workers downstream can identify an upstream problem in that component almost immediately and correct it before it leads to production of more defective components.

Costs and Benefits of Changing to a New Layout: An Example Using Group Technology

Pinsky Electric Corporation is a leader in the manufacturing of small electrical appliances for household and industrial use. It produces a variety of electrical valve controls at its plant in Pasadena, California. Until recently, the plant was organized into five production departments: casting, machining, assembly, inspection, and packing.

Now the plant layout has been reorganized to streamline production flows and introduce group technology. In the following sections we will take an extended look at both the old and the new work flows, identify the benefits of the new system, and compare the costs and benefits of the two.

The plant manufactures 128 different products that have been grouped into eight product lines for accounting purposes, based on common product features and production processes. Under the old plant layout, the 128 products followed a similar sequence of steps in the manufacturing process (see Exhibit 7-3). Manufacturing of panels for valve controls occurred in large batches in the casting department. Then the manufactured panels were stored in a large work-in-process storage area located near the machining department, where they remained until the lathes and drilling machines were free.

After machining, the panels were stored until they were requisitioned for assembly, during which switches and other components received from outside suppliers were placed onto each panel. Another storage area located near the assembly department was used for work in process awaiting inspection or packing, which occurred before the panels were packed for shipping. Finally, the packed valve control panels were stored in the finished goods warehouse until they were shipped to distributors and other customers.

This production flow required storage of work-in-process inventory for a long time and at several times before the beginning of the next production stage. As mentioned, manufacturing cycle time is measured as the time from the receipt of the raw materials from the supplier to the delivery of the finished goods to the distributors and customers. At Pinsky, cycle time was 28 days $(5 + 1 + 9 + 1 + 1 + 4 + 1 + 2 + 1 + 3)$ under the old plant layout. The 4 days during which switches and other components were kept as inventory were not added to the processing time, the time expended for the product to be made, because the time spent in inventory represented parallel time with other production activities, such as work-in-process storage and machining. Therefore, the storage requirements for switches and other components did not prolong the time for the total production activity in the plant.

To evaluate how much of the old cycle time was spent in inventory, we need to know how organizations assess the efficiency of their manufacturing processes. One widely used measure, which would be a key operating metric in a company's Balanced Scorecard process perspective, is processing cycle efficiency (PCE). PCE is calculated as follows:

$$\text{PCE} = \text{Processing time}/(\text{Processing time} + \text{Moving time} + \text{Storage time} + \text{Inspection time})$$

Of the 28 days required for the manufacturing cycle under Pinsky's old system, only 4 days were spent on actual processing [(1 casting) + (1 machining) + (1 assembly) + (1 packing)]. The other 24 days were spent in non–value-added activities, such as moving, storage, and inspection. The amount of time that materials spent in inventory could be as long as 24 days. The PCE formula reveals that processing time equaled 14.3% $(4 \div 28)$ of total cycle time. These results are representative of many other plants that manufacture products from mechanical or electronic components. We will see shortly how the PCE changes for Pinsky after its reorganization.

Reorganization

A primary objective of the reorganization of the Pinsky plant layout was to reduce the production cycle time (another key BSC process metric). The plant was reorganized into eight manufacturing cells (corresponding to the eight product lines) in addition to the casting department. Each cell focused on the manufacturing of similar products belonging to the same product line.

Exhibit 7-3
Pinsky Electric
Corporation:
Production Flows
and Average Time
under Old Plant
Layout

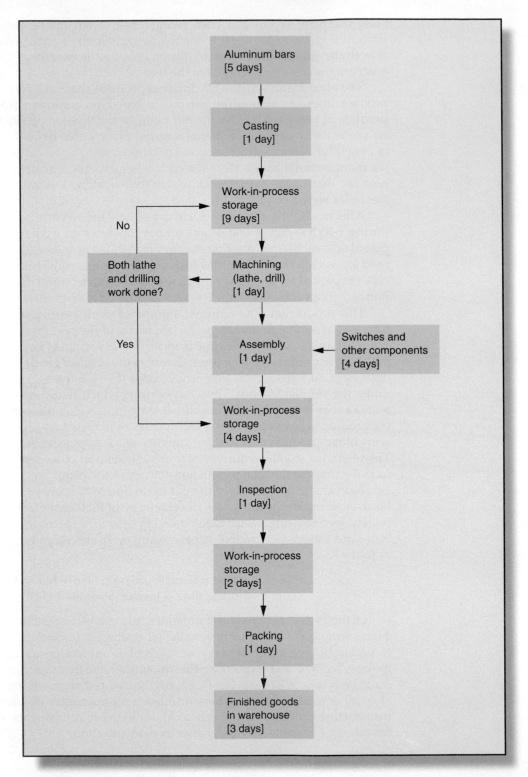

Exhibit 7-4 depicts the production flows under the new plant layout. While the casting department remains a separate department, the other four operations—machining, assembly, inspection, and packing—are now located in proximity to each other within each manufacturing cell. Aluminum panels received from the casting

Exhibit 7-4
Pinsky Electric Corporation: Production Flows and Average Time under New Plant Layout

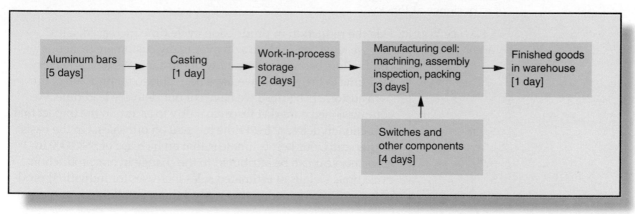

department are lathe machined, drilled, and assembled in the manufacturing cells. Workers in the cells also are responsible for inspection and packing operations. Thus, material handling distances and the time required to move a panel from one process to the next are greatly reduced.

Pinsky Electric also made a transition toward JIT production. The change required that there be no work-in-process inventories among the various stages of operations in the manufacturing cells because panel production flowed immediately from lathe to drilling to assembly to inspection to packing operations. As a result of these steps, the time between operations has been greatly reduced as production is pulled from one stage to the next on the basis of orders for the finished product.

When comparing Exhibits 7-3 and 7-4, notice that Pinsky Electric Corporation did not reduce the amount of time spent on actual manufacturing when it changed the plant layout. The time spent on manufacturing operations after the change (see Exhibit 7-4) is the same as the time spent before the change (see Exhibit 7-3). However, the cycle time is reduced substantially in the new plant layout from 28 to only 12 days. Thus, PCE changes from 14.3% to 33.3% (4 ÷ 12). This significant improvement in efficiency over the previous layout comes from eliminating the need for work-in-process inventory between many of the manufacturing operations.

Analysis of Costs and Benefits

Has this change helped improve the profitability of the Pasadena plant? Kaylee Young, the Pasadena plant controller, identified the following costs associated with the implementation of the changes in the plant layout:

Moving machines and reinstallation	$600,000
Training workers for group technology	+ $400,000
Total costs	$1,000,000

Kaylee also identified three types of benefits resulting from the plant reorganization: (1) an increase in sales because of the decrease in production cycle time, (2) a reduction in inventory-related costs because of the decrease in the amount and handling of work-in-process inventory, and (3) an improvement in quality since defective processes are detected much faster (at the next processing stage), before many defective items have been produced.

Kaylee interviewed several production and sales managers to assess the extent of these benefits. She began with Vicki Mulligan, a senior sales manager with 17 years of experience at Pinsky:

KAYLEE YOUNG: Has the reduction in production cycle time increased sales?

VICKI MULLIGAN: Yes, we have been able to win over many customers from our competitors because we can now quote a much shorter delivery lead time to them. Also, we have been able to retain some of our own customers because we have cut our delivery lead time. We commissioned a market research study to ascertain the impact that reduction in delivery lead time has had on our sales. On the basis of this study, our best estimate is that an increase of $880,000 in sales this year can be attributed to the change in our production cycle time. Details of estimated sales increases for individual products are also provided in this study. I think you'll find it interesting.

Kaylee next turned to her analyst, Bob Phillips, to collect the information necessary to assess the profitability of the sales increase. He returned the next day with several detailed cost accounting reports.

BOB PHILLIPS: I've prepared a detailed analysis of the costs for all our products. Here is a summary that gives the totals for all 128 products (see Exhibit 7-5). I began with the estimate of the increase in sales for each of the 128 products. Here is an example for product TL32 (see Exhibit 7-6). I multiplied the 800-unit sales increase by the direct materials cost of $7.00 per unit and direct labor cost of $4.00 per unit. Using our time-driven ABC system, I also included support costs of $5.50 per unit. The $10,000 profit is obtained by calculating the difference between the $23,200 increase in sales revenue and the $13,200 in costs. The summary in Exhibit 7-5 displays the totals of similar revenue and cost numbers across all of our 128 products.

Exhibit 7-5
Pinsky Electric Corporation: Impact of Increase in Sales on Profit

Increase in sales revenue		$880,000
Increase in costs:		
Direct materials	$245,000	
Direct labor	140,000	
Support resources	194,000	579,000
Net increase in profit		$301,000

Exhibit 7-6
Pinsky Electric Corporation: Impact of Increase in Sales of Product TL32

Increase in sales	(800 units × $29 price per unit)		$23,200
Increase in costs:			
Direct materials	(800 units × $7 cost per unit)	$5,600	
Direct labor	(800 units × $4 cost per unit)	3,200	
Support resources	(800 units × $5.50 cost per unit)	4,400	$13,200
Net increase in profit			$10,000

KAYLEE YOUNG: Thanks, Bob, for all your efforts. I see that our best estimate is that the increase in sales resulting from the lower production cycle time has generated a profit of $301,000 this year.

Kaylee next met with Megan McDermott, production and inventory manager at the Pasadena plant, to find out how the reduction in the level of work-in-process inventory affected the consumption of support resources:

KAYLEE YOUNG: Has the change in the plant layout led to changes in the handling and storage of work-in-process inventory?

MEGAN MCDERMOTT: Yes, we have been able to make many changes. We don't need a materials-handling crew to move work-in-process inventory from lathes to drilling machines to storage areas on the shop floor. Nor do we need to move and store work-in-process inventory between the assembly, inspection, and packing stages. We did not reduce the number of materials handling workers immediately, but as work patterns stabilized a few weeks after the change in the plant layout, we reduced our materials handling crew from 14 to only 8 workers.

KAYLEE YOUNG: Were there any other changes in the workload of people performing these support activities?

MEGAN MCDERMOTT: With an almost 70% reduction in work-in-process inventory, down from $2,270,000 to $690,000, we had a corresponding decrease in inventory-related transactions. We did not require as much record keeping for the movement of materials into and out of storage. We expect to be able to reduce our shop-floor-stores staff by 75%, from four workers to only one. So far we have reassigned only one worker, but two more will be reassigned to other production-related tasks next week.

KAYLEE YOUNG: So far we have talked about personnel. Were any other resources freed up as a result of the reduction in work-in-process inventory?

MEGAN MCDERMOTT: Yes, we need only one-third of the storage space we used earlier for work-in-process inventory. The extra space is idle at present, however, because we haven't yet found an alternative use for it. I don't believe there was any proposal to use that extra space in the three-year facilities plan prepared last month, but eventually as production activity expands, we should be able to place new manufacturing cells in the space formerly used to store work-in-process inventory.

KAYLEE YOUNG: But you don't expect any immediate benefit to arise from the availability of the extra storage space?

MEGAN MCDERMOTT: Yes, that's correct. But there is one more benefit that you shouldn't forget. When some panels are produced in large batches and stored awaiting the next stage of processing, we always find that some of them get damaged in handling, and at times some of them become obsolete because the customer no longer requires them. The change to JIT production in the manufacturing cells and the elimination of much of our work-in-process inventory have resulted in a reduction in materials scrap and obsolescence cost from 0.32% of materials cost to only 0.12%.

KAYLEE YOUNG: Thank you, Megan. The information you've provided will be very useful in evaluating the impact of the change in the plant layout.

Kaylee and Vicki sat in Kaylee's office to analyze the information they had collected so far. Support costs pertaining to plant space included building depreciation, insurance, heating, lighting, janitorial services, building upkeep, and maintenance. Kaylee and Vicki decided that the costs associated with the extra storage space were at present a sunk cost with no cost savings yet realized from freeing up this space.

A check of the materials handling activity costs indicated that the annual wages of workers in this grade averaged $21,000, with 35% more, or $7,350 ($21,000 × 0.35), added for fringe benefits. The total materials handling cost savings, therefore, was $170,100 ($28,350 × 6) because the crew size was reduced by six workers.

In a similar fashion, Megan determined that the annual wages of stores personnel averaged $26,400. With a 35% fringe benefit rate and an expected reduction of three workers, the total annual cost savings was $106,920 ($26,400 × 1.35 × 3).

The financing of inventories can involve significant costs. Kaylee estimated the interest rate on bank loans to finance the investment in inventories to be 12% per year. The work-in-process inventory was reduced by $1,580,000 ($2,270,000 − $690,000). This reduced the cost of inventory financing correspondingly by $189,600 ($1,580,000 × 0.12).

Finally, Kaylee determined that the total annual materials cost was $31,000,000. If the rate of materials, scrap, and obsolescence had remained at the previous 0.32% of materials cost, this loss would have been $99,200 ($31,000,000 × 0.0032). But because of the reduction in the rate to 0.12%, the cost of materials scrap and obsolescence was reduced to only $37,200 ($31,000,000 × 0.0012). This represents a cost savings of $62,000 ($99,200 − $37,200).

Summary of Costs and Benefits

Kaylee then summarized the information on cost savings resulting from the change in the plant layout (see Exhibit 7-7). she estimated that annual benefits were $829,620. In comparison, the one-time costs of implementing the change were only $1,000,000. If benefits from the changed layout continue to accrue at the same rate for at least three more months, the total benefits will exceed the amount that Pinsky invested in the project:

$$\$829,620 \times 15/12 = \$1,037,025$$

More specifically, the process improvements from the investment would repay the front-end cost in $1,000,000/$829,620 = 1.205 years.

Exhibit 7-7
Pinsky Electric Corporation: Annual Benefits Resulting from the Change in Plant Layout

Contribution from increased sales:			
Sales increase	(Exhibit 7-5)	$880,000	
Incremental manufacturing costs	(Exhibit 7-5)	579,000	$301,000
Cost savings from work-in-process inventory reduction:			
Cost of financing investment in work-in-process inventory		$189,600	
Cost of materials handling labor		170,100	
Cost of stores labor		106,920	
Cost of materials scrap and obsolescence		62,000	528,620
Total benefits			$829,620

The Pinsky case study introduces several important concepts. We have identified several different ways in which new manufacturing practices can improve a plant's profitability. In particular, we have seen that financing is a principal inventory-related cost. It is important to consider this cost, although financing costs are often not emphasized in many traditional cost accounting systems. Streamlining manufacturing processes also reduces the demand placed on many support-activity resources. Analyzing the use of support resources in production helps to identify the total potential cost savings that can be realized from more efficient product flows.

Many new manufacturing practices are designed to promote continuous improvement in manufacturing performance by enabling workers to learn and innovate. In this example, changing to a manufacturing cell layout led to improvements in production

IN PRACTICE
History of Lean Manufacturing

The history of lean manufacturing is summarized well in the chart below. Lean manufacturing can trace its roots back as far as Eli Whitney, who invented the cotton gin and the concept of interchangeable parts. Early pioneers' work, such as Frederick Taylor and Frank Gilbreth's time and motion studies, Henry Ford's assembly line, Taiichi Ohno and Shigeo Shingo's just-in-time system based on stockless production, and the quality movement pioneered by Edwards Deming and Joseph Juran, were all critical to the development of lean manufacturing.

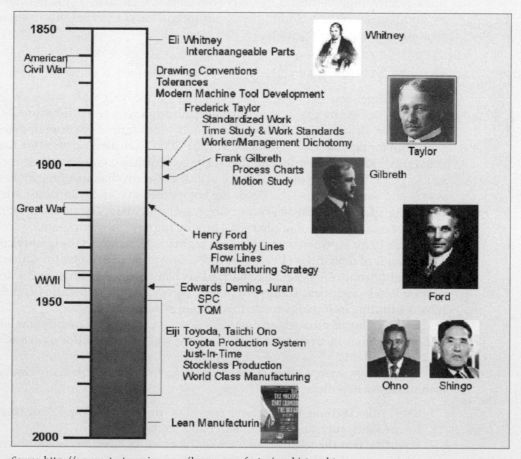

Source: http://www.strategosinc.com/lean_manufacturing_history.htm

yield rates and quality and, consequently, improvements in overall plant productivity. In addition, revenues also can increase from shorter lead times to customers.

Lean manufacturing or lean production, often just called "lean," is another new manufacturing approach. Lean's central philosophy is that any resource spending that does not create value for the end customer is wasteful and must be eliminated. Value is defined as any action or process for which a customer would be willing to pay. Lean manufacturing is a generic process management philosophy derived from the legendary Toyota Production System that is associated with just-in-time manufacturing. We will discuss this topic in depth later in the chapter.

COST OF NONCONFORMANCE AND QUALITY ISSUES

The preceding example shows that cost reduction has become a significant factor in the management of most organizations. Reducing costs, however, involves much more than simply finding ways to cut product design costs by, for example, using less expensive materials. The premise underlying cost reduction efforts today is to decrease costs while maintaining or improving product quality in order to be competitive.

An emphasis on quality has been a focal point for business worldwide since the 1980s when quality circles (typically unpaid groups of workers who voluntarily tried to solve quality issues) and total quality management (TQM), now known as continuous quality improvement (CQI), were developed. CQI takes a systems view of quality and focuses on how to improve both internal and external processes related to customers using objective data.

Quality Standards

Global competition led to the development of the ISO 9000 series of standards beginning in 1987 by the International Organization for Standardization (ISO), headquartered in Geneva. These international quality standards have been updated several times and the new standard is called ISO 9001–2008. Company certification under these standards indicates to customers that management has committed their company to follow procedures and processes that will ensure the production of the highest quality goods and services. These standards are comprehensive and companies interested in becoming ISO 9000 registered must comply with regulatory agencies, meet or exceed customer requirements or implement a quality improvement program.

In the 1990s Motorola introduced Six Sigma, which moved the quality criterion of three standard deviations (1 defect in 100) that was developed by the father of statistical quality control, Walter Shewhart, to six standard deviations, or 3.4 defects per million items produced. Trainers in the Six Sigma system, known as Black Belts, and new computing technology made this system possible.

If the quality of products and services does not conform to quality standards, then the organization incurs a cost known as the **cost of nonconformance (CONC) to quality standards**.

Quality may mean different things to different people. It usually can be viewed as hinging on two major factors:

1. Satisfying customer expectations regarding the attributes and performance of the product, such as in functionality and features.
2. Ensuring that the technical aspects of the product's design and performance, such as whether it performs to the standard expected, conform to the manufacturer's standards.

Costs of Quality Control

This section focuses on how to interpret **quality costs** from a management accounting point of view. Companies have discovered that they can spend as much as 20% to 30% of total manufacturing costs on quality-related processes such as detection and correction of internal and external failure. The best known framework for understanding quality costs classifies them into four categories:

1. Prevention costs.
2. Appraisal costs.
3. Internal failure costs.
4. External failure costs.

Experience shows that it is much less expensive to prevent defects than to detect and repair them after they have occurred.

Prevention Costs

Prevention costs are incurred to ensure that companies produce products according to quality standards. Quality engineering, training employees in methods designed to maintain quality, and statistical process control are examples of prevention costs. Prevention costs also include evaluating and training suppliers to ensure that they can deliver defect-free parts and materials and better, more robust product designs. Such suppliers earn a **certified supplier** designation.

Appraisal Costs

Appraisal costs relate to inspecting products to make sure they meet both internal and external customers' requirements. Inspection costs of purchased parts and materials and costs of quality inspection on an assembly line are considered to be appraisal costs. Examples include inspection of incoming materials, maintenance of test equipment, and process control monitoring.

Internal Failure Costs

Internal failure costs result when the manufacturing process detects a defective component or product before it is shipped to an external customer. Reworking defective components or products is a significant cost of internal failures. The cost of downtime in production is another example of internal failure. Engineers have estimated that the cost of defects rises by an order of magnitude for each stage of the manufacturing process during which the defect goes undetected. For example, inserting a defective $1 electronic component into a subassembly leads to $10 of scrap if detected at the first stage, $100 at the next stage, and perhaps $10,000 if not detected for two more stages of assembly.

External Failure Costs

External failure costs occur when customers discover a defect. All costs associated with correcting the problem—repair of the product, warranty costs, service calls, and product liability recalls—are examples of external failure costs. For many companies, this is the most critical quality cost to avoid. Not only are costs required to fix the problem in the short run, but customer satisfaction, future sales, and the reputation of the manufacturing organization also may be in jeopardy over the long run. Exhibit 7-8 provides examples of the quality costs in each category.

This information is compiled in a **cost-of-quality (COQ) report**, developed for several reasons. First, it illustrates the financial magnitude of quality factors. Often managers are unaware of the enormous impact that rework has on their costs.

Exhibit 7-8
Examples of
Quality-Related
Costs

PREVENTION COSTS	APPRAISAL COSTS
Quality engineering	Inspection/testing of incoming materials
Quality training	Maintenance of test equipment
Statistical process control	Process control monitoring
Supplier certification	Product quality audits
Research of customer needs	
INTERNAL FAILURE COSTS	EXTERNAL FAILURE COSTS
Downtime due to defects	Product liability lawsuits
Waste	Repair costs in the field
Net cost of scrap	Returned products
Rework costs	Product liability recalls
	Service calls
	Warranty claims

Second, COQ information helps managers set priorities for the quality issues and problems they should address. For example, one trend that managers do not want to see is a very high percentage of quality costs coming from external failure of a product. External quality problems are expensive to fix and can greatly harm the reputation of the product or organization producing the product. Third, the COQ report allows managers to see the big picture of quality issues and allows them to try to find the root causes of their quality problems. Fixing the problem at its root will have positive ripple effects throughout the organization, as so many quality issues are interrelated.

JUST-IN-TIME MANUFACTURING

A comprehensive and effective manufacturing system that integrates many of the ideas discussed in this chapter is **just-in-time (JIT) manufacturing**. Recall that the Blast from the Past Robot Company implemented this system in the opening vignette to this chapter.

JIT manufacturing requires making a product or service only when the customer, internal or external, requires it. It uses a product layout with a continuous flow—one with no delays once production starts. This means there must be a substantial reduction in setup costs in order to eliminate the need to produce in batches; therefore, processing systems must be reliable.

Implications of JIT Manufacturing

JIT manufacturing is simple in theory but hard to achieve in practice. Some organizations hesitate to implement JIT because with no work-in-process inventory, a problem anywhere in the system can stop all production. For this reason, organizations that use JIT manufacturing must eliminate all sources of failure in the system. The production process must be redesigned so that it is not prohibitively expensive to process one or a small number of items at a time. This usually means reducing the distance over which work-in-process has to travel and using very adaptable people and equipment that can handle all types of jobs.

At the core of the JIT process is a highly trained workforce whose task is to carry out activities using the highest standards of quality. When an employee discovers a problem with a component he or she has received, it is the responsibility of that employee to call immediate attention to the problem so that it can be corrected. Suppliers must be able to produce and deliver defect-free materials or components just when they are required. In many instances, companies compete with suppliers of the same components to see who can deliver the best quality. At the end of a performance period, the supplier who performs the best will obtain a long-term contract. Preventive maintenance is also employed so that equipment failure is a rare event.

Consider how JIT manufacturing can be used at a fast-food restaurant. Some use a JIT, continuous-flow product layout, while others use batch production in a process layout. In fact, some fast-food restaurants combine both approaches into hybrid systems that use a batch approach to production and keep inventories at predefined levels. For example, the restaurant may use racks or bins to hold food ready to be sold to the customer and have employees start another batch of production when the existing inventory falls below a line drawn on the bin or rack. At off-peak times, the restaurant may produce to order.

The motivation to use the JIT approach is to improve the quality of the food and to reduce waste by eliminating the need to discard food that has been held in the bin too long. The motivation to use batch production is to sustain a certain level of inventory to reduce the time the customer has to wait for an order. As processing time and setup costs drop, the organization can move closer to JIT manufacturing and reduce the waste and quality problems that arise with batch production.

JIT Manufacturing and Management Accounting

JIT manufacturing has two major implications for management accounting. First, management accounting must support the move to JIT manufacturing by monitoring, identifying, and communicating to decision makers the sources of delay, error, and waste in the system. Balanced Scorecard process metrics related to a company's ability to implement a JIT production system include:

1. Defect rates.
2. Cycle times.
3. Percent of time that deliveries are on time.
4. Order accuracy.
5. Actual production as a percent of planned production.
6. Actual machine time available compared with planned machine time available.

Conventional production systems use performance metrics based on labor and machine utilization ratios. These metrics encourage large batch sizes and high levels of production. The result is large inventory quantities that lead to long manufacturing cycle times. Therefore, the use of conventional labor and machine productivity ratios is inconsistent with the JIT production philosophy, in which operators are expected to produce only what is requested, when it is requested, and on time. The second implication is that the clerical process of management accounting is simplified by JIT manufacturing because there are fewer inventories to monitor and report.

JIT manufacturing has been a benefit to many organizations. Those interested in implementing this system need to remember several things. First, any significant management innovation, such as ABC or JIT, requires a major cultural change for an organization. Because the central ideas behind JIT are the streamlining of operations and the reduction of waste, many people inside companies are ill prepared for the change. JIT also can alter the pace of work and the overall work discipline of the organization. It can cause structural changes in such areas as the arrangement of shop floors. Finally, because JIT relies on teamwork, often individuals have to subordinate their own interests to those of the team. Some employees find this difficult, especially if they have come from a work environment where they worked on a single component in relative isolation or if their personalities are not team oriented.

IN PRACTICE

Using Lean Manufacturing in a Hospital Setting

According to Dr. Gary Kaplan, CEO of Virginia Mason Hospital, after studying their hospital's infrastructure, senior management at Virginia Mason hospital determined it was designed for them and not their patients. Patients complained that they had to hurry to be on time for scheduling but once they were there they had long waits to see a doctor.

Management decided to look for better ways to improve quality, safety, and patient satisfaction. Using the lean manufacturing approach originally developed at Toyota, Virginia Mason tailored the Japanese model to fit the health care environment.

Over the years Kaplan and 200 company employees visited manufacturing plants at Toyota and Yamaha. Much of their time was spent learning how to cut out waste. According to the production system

there are seven wastes. Three of the most critical wastes are wasting time, such as patients waiting for a doctor or for test results to come back; inventory waste, having more materials and information than is necessary; and overproduction waste, producing more than is necessary.

One example of reducing waste relates to the number of pamphlets and brochures that the hospital has on hand. Historically, the hospital over-ordered these brochures and filled closets with them. After installing a Kanban system, which signals the need to restock the brochures, thousands of dollars were saved and the clutter was reduced.

The hospital also developed standardized instrument trays for surgeries and procedures. This saved hundreds of dollars because instruments that were not

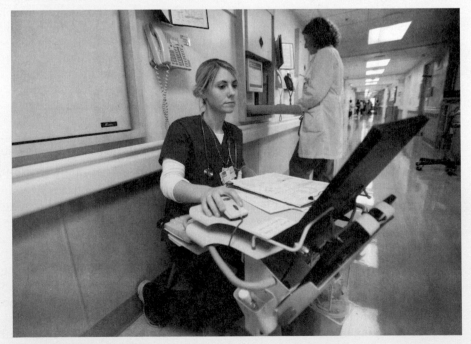

Paul Joseph Brown Photography

needed were not used. In the past, unused but opened instruments had to be thrown away.

Another innovation was a flip chart showing the level of mobility in physical therapy patients. The chart shows the level of what the patient can and cannot do, and each nurse or physician who comes in the room doesn't have to waste time searching charts or asking questions.

Further, instead of waiting until the end of the day to go though a stack of patient records, doctors now write comments and recommendations immediately after seeing the patient before going to see the next one. The time saved increases the time a physician can spend with a patient.

Virginia Mason has also redesigned their facilities to make patient and staff work flow more productive. Overtime and labor expenses were reduced by $500,000 in one year and productivity was increased by 93%. Overall hospital efficiency has been greatly improved.

Source: Cherie Black, "To Build a Better Hospital, Virginia Mason Takes Lessons from Toyota Plants," *Seattle Post-Intelligencer* (March 15, 2008), retrieved November 30, 2010, from http://www.seattlepi.com/local/355128_lean15.html

KAIZEN COSTING

The lean manufacturing approach has been successfully implemented in many companies. What has not kept pace with these operational changes are the finance and cost management systems. Kaizen costing is a system that provides relevant data to support lean production systems. Kaizen costing focuses on reducing costs during the manufacturing stage of a product. *Kaizen* is the Japanese term for making improvements to a process in small, incremental amounts rather than through large innovations. Kaizen's incremental approach is appropriate since products are already in the manufacturing process, making it difficult to make large changes to reduce costs.

Kaizen costing is tied into the profit-planning system. In the Japanese automobile industry, for example, an annual budgeted profit target is allocated to each plant. Each automobile has a predetermined cost base that is equal to the actual cost of that automobile in the previous year. All cost reductions use this cost base as their starting point. Kaizen costing's goal is to ensure that a product meets or exceeds customer requirements for quality, functionality, and prices in order to effectively compete.

The *target reduction rate* is the ratio of the target reduction amount to the cost base. This rate is applied over time to all variable costs and results in specific target reduction amounts for materials, parts, direct and indirect labor, and other variable costs. Then management makes comparisons of actual reduction amounts across all variable costs to the preestablished targeted reduction amounts. If differences exist, variances for the plant are determined. Kaizen costing's goal is to ensure that actual production costs are less than the cost base. However, if the cost of disruptions to production is greater than the savings due to kaizen costing, then it will not be applied. Exhibit 7-9 illustrates one example of determining the total amount of kaizen costs across multiple plants in a Japanese automobile plant.

Comparing Traditional Cost Reduction to Kaizen Costing

The kaizen costing system is quite distinct from a traditional standard costing system in which the typical goal is to meet the cost standard while avoiding unfavorable variances. Under kaizen costing, the goal is to achieve cost reduction targets that are continually adjusted downward. Variance analysis under a standard cost system compares actual to standard costs. Under the kaizen costing system,

Exhibit 7-9
Computing Kaizen Costs for Plants

Cost savings in Japanese automobile plants involve reducing both committed (fixed) and flexible (variable) costs. Since fixed costs are believed necessary for growth, the main emphasis is on reducing variable costs.

In this example, the total amount of kaizen costs in all plants determined in a kaizen planning meeting is designated as C in the formulas that follow:

Amount of actual cost per car in the last period (A)	=	Amount of actual cost in the last period	$\div$	Actual production in the last period
Estimated amount of actual cost for all plants in this period (B)	=	Amount of actual cost per car in the last period (A)	$\times$	Estimated production in this period
Kaizen cost target in this period for all plants (C)	=	Estimated amount of actual cost for all plants in this period (B)	$\times$	Target ratio of cost decrease to the estimated cost

The target ratio of cost decrease to the estimated cost is based on attaining the target profit for the year.

The kaizen cost target for each plant is determined in the following manner:

Assignment ratio (D)	=	Costs controlled directly by each plant	$\div$	Total amount of costs controlled directly by plants
Total kaizen cost for each plant	=	Kaizen cost target in this period for all plants (C)	$\times$	Assignment ratio (D)

The amount of kaizen cost for each plant is subdivided to each division and subdivisions as cost reduction goals.

variance analysis compares the target costs with actual cost reduction amounts. Kaizen costing operates outside the standard costing system, in part because standard costing systems in Japan are used only for financial accounting reports.

Another key difference between standard and kaizen costing has to do with the assumptions about who has the best knowledge to improve processes and reduce costs. Traditional standard costing assumes that engineers and managers know best because they have the technical expertise and can determine procedures that workers are required to perform according to preset standards and procedures. Under kaizen costing, workers are assumed to have superior knowledge about how to improve processes because they actually work with the manufacturing processes used to produce products. To facilitate the process, information on actual costs must be shared with front-line employees, which is a significant change for many companies. Thus, another central goal of kaizen costing is to give workers the responsibility and control to improve processes and reduce costs. Exhibit 7-10 summarizes the differences in philosophy between standard costing and kaizen costing methods.

Concerns about Kaizen Costing

Kaizen costing also has been criticized for the same reasons as target costing in the research, development, and engineering stage (discussed in Chapter 8): The system places enormous pressure on employees to reduce every conceivable cost. To address the problem, some Japanese automobile companies use a grace period in manufacturing just before a new model is introduced. This period, called a *cost-sustainment period*, provides employees with the opportunity to learn any new procedures before the company imposes kaizen and target costing goals on them.

Another concern has been that kaizen costing leads to incremental rather than radical process improvements. This can cause myopia as management tends to focus on the details rather than the overall system.

Exhibit 7-10
Comparison of Standard Costing to Kaizen Costing

Standard Costing Concepts	Kaizen Costing Concepts
Cost control system concept	Cost reduction system concept
Assumes stability in current manufacturing processes	Assumes continuous improvement in manufacturing
Goal is to meet cost performance standards	Goal is to achieve cost reduction standards
Standard Costing Techniques	**Kaizen Costing Techniques**
Standards are set annually or semiannually	Cost reduction targets are set and applied monthly, and continuous improvement (Kaizen) methods are applied all year long to meet targets
Cost variance analysis involves comparing actual to standard costs	Cost variance analysis involves target Kaizen costs versus actual cost reduction amounts
Cost variance investigation occurs when standards are not met	Investigation occurs when target cost reduction (Kaizen) amounts are not attained
Who Has the Best Knowledge to Reduce Costs?	**Who Has the Best Knowledge to Reduce Costs?**
Managers and engineers develop standards as they have the technical expertise	Workers are closest to the process and thus know best

BENCHMARKING

In the opening vignette, Neva Dominguez used benchmarking to find out that her competition was using the JIT manufacturing system to produce its products. Her research and discussions with another local firm provided her with much information, as discussed next.

Organizations interested in new ways to improve their operations usually choose one of three ways to learn about and adopt a method:

1. The first is to bring in outside consultants to implement a particular method. Outside consultants can be effective but costly.
2. A second approach is for organizational members to develop their own systems internally with little or no assistance from outside consultants. Although this approach can be satisfying, it can be highly costly and time consuming, especially if the organization fails in its first few attempts at change.
3. The third approach, known as **benchmarking**, requires that organizational members first understand their current operations and approaches to conducting business and then look to the best practices of other organizations for guidance on improving.

Benchmarking is a way for organizations to gather information regarding the best practices of others. It is often highly cost effective, because organizations can save time and money by avoiding the mistakes that other companies have made or by not reinventing a process or method that other companies have already developed and tested. Since its inception benchmarking has undergone many changes. Most notably, the once cumbersome process that took six to nine months has now been streamlined and has become a fast and flexible tool. Thus, selecting appropriate benchmarking partners (discussed later in this chapter) is a critical aspect of the process. The benchmarking process typically consists of five stages that include several organizational/diagnostic, operational, and informational factors. We present each stage here by listing its key factors. Exhibit 7-11 depicts the benchmarking process.

Exhibit 7-11
Stages of the Benchmarking Process

STAGES OF THE BENCHMARKING PROCESS	FACTORS TO CONSIDER
Stage 1: Internal study and preliminary competitive analyses	Preliminary internal and external competitive analyses Determine key areas for study Determine scope and significance of the study

Stage 2:
Developing long-term commitment to the benchmarking project and coalescing the benchmarking team
	Developing long-term commitment to the benchmarking project:
	    Gain senior management support
	    Develop a clear set of objectives
	    Empower employees to make change
	Coalescing the benchmarking team:
	    Use an experienced coordinator
	    Train employees

Stage 3: Identifying benchmarking partners	Size of partners Number of partners Relative position within and across industries Degree of trust among partners

Stage 4:
Information-gathering and-sharing methods
	Type of benchmarking information:
	    Product
	    Functional (process)
	    Strategic (includes management accounting methods)
	Method of information collection:
	    Unilateral
	    Cooperative
	    Database
	    Indirect/third party
	    Group
	Determine performance measures
	Determine the benchmarking performance gap in relation to performance measures

Stage 5: Taking action to meet or exceed the benchmark	Comparisons of performance measures are made

Stage 1: Internal Study and Preliminary Competitive Analyses

In this stage, the organization decides which key areas to benchmark for study, such as the company's activities, products, or management accounting methods. Then the company determines how it currently performs on these dimensions by initiating both preliminary internal competitive analyses using internal company data and preliminary external competitive analyses using, for example, industry comparisons of quality from publications such as *Consumer Reports* or reports from J. D. Power and Associates. Both types of analyses will determine the scope and significance of the study for each area. Another key factor to remember is that these analyses are not limited only to companies in a single industry. Thus, for example, although Kaylee Young works in the toy industry, she could do competitive analyses in any type of organization.

Stage 2: Developing Long-Term Commitment to the Benchmarking Project and Coalescing the Benchmarking Team

In this stage, the organization must develop its commitment to the benchmarking project and coalesce a benchmarking team. Because significant organizational change can take several years, the level of commitment to benchmarking has to be long term rather than short term. Long-term commitment requires (1) obtaining the support of senior management to give the benchmarking team the authority to spearhead the changes, (2) developing a clear set of objectives to guide the benchmarking effort, and (3) empowering employees to make change.

The benchmarking team should include individuals from all functional areas in the organization. An experienced coordinator is usually necessary to organize the members' team and develop training in benchmarking methods. Lack of training often leads to failure of the implementation.

Stage 3: Identifying Benchmarking Partners

The third stage of benchmarking includes identification of partners—willing participants who know the process. Some critical factors are as follows:

1. Size of the partners.
2. Number of partners.
3. Relative position of the partners within and across industries.
4. Degree of trust among partners.

Size

The size of the benchmarking partner will depend on the specific activity or method being benchmarked. For example, if an organization wants to understand how a huge organization with several divisions coordinates its suppliers, then the organization would probably seek another organization of similar size for benchmarking. However, size is not always an important factor. For example, DaimlerChrysler Corporation, a huge corporation, studied L.L. Bean's warehousing method of flowcharting wasted motion. As a result, Chrysler implemented a method that led to significant changes in the ways that its workers were involved in organizational problem solving.

Number

Initially, it is useful for an organization to consider a wide array of benchmarking partners. However, organizations must be aware that as the number of partners increases, so do issues of coordination, timeliness, and concern over proprietary information disclosure. Researchers argue that today's changing business environment is likely to encourage firms to have a larger number of participants because increased competition and technological progress in information processing increases benchmarking benefits relative to costs.

Relative Position within and across Industries

Another factor is the relative position of the organization within an industry. In many cases, industry newcomers and those whose performance on leading indicators has declined are more likely to seek a wider variety of benchmarking partners than those who are established industry leaders. Those who are industry leaders may benchmark because of their commitment to continuous improvement.

Degree of Trust

From the benchmarking organization's point of view, developing trust among partners is critical to obtaining truthful and timely information. Most organizations, including industry leaders, operate on a quid pro quo basis, with the understanding that both organizations will obtain information they can use.

Stage 4: Information Gathering and Sharing Methods

Two dimensions relating to information gathering and sharing emerge from the literature: (1) the type of information that benchmarking organizations collect and (2) methods of information collection.

Type of Information

Firms interested in benchmarking can focus on three broad classes of information: *Product benchmarking* is the long-standing practice of carefully examining other organizations' products. *Functional* (process) *benchmarking* is the study of other organizations' practices and costs with respect to functions or processes, such as assembly or distribution. *Strategic benchmarking* is the study of other organizations' strategies and strategic decisions, such as why organizations choose one particular strategy over another. Since management accounting methods have become an integral part of many organizations' strategies, benchmarking of these methods would occur as part of the management accounting function.

Methods of Gathering Information

Management accountants play a key role in gathering and summarizing information used for benchmarking. Two major methods are used to collect information for benchmarking. The most common can be described as **unilateral (covert) benchmarking**, in which companies independently gather information about one or several other companies that excel in the area of interest. Unilateral benchmarking relies on data that companies can obtain from industry trade associations or clearinghouses of information.

A second method is **cooperative benchmarking**, which is the voluntary sharing of information through mutual agreements. The major advantage of cooperative benchmarking is that information sharing occurs both within and across industries. Cooperative benchmarking has three subcategories: database, indirect/third-party, and group benchmarking.

Companies that use **database benchmarking** typically pay a fee and in return gain access to information from a database operator. The database operator collects and edits the information prior to making it available to users. In most cases, there is no direct contact with other firms, and the identity of the source of the data often is not revealed. The database method has the advantage of including a large amount of information in one place; however, insights regarding what the data mean for the firm and how to use the information often are not available.

Indirect/third-party benchmarking uses an outside consultant to act as a liaison among firms engaged in benchmarking. The consultant supplies information from one party to the others and handles all communications. Often the consultant participates in the selection of partners. Because the members may be competitors, they pass information through a consultant so that members remain anonymous. This approach requires that the sources of the information remain confidential.

Participants using **group benchmarking** meet openly to discuss their methods. They coordinate their efforts, define common terminology, visit each other's sites, and generally have a long-run association. Typically, firms that engage in cooperative benchmarking abide by a code of conduct that they agree on prior to the study. As in most interactions, direct contact offers the opportunity for better understanding of the other parties involved and usually is the most effective benchmarking method. This method also is the most costly to implement; therefore, firms must evaluate the cost–benefit trade-offs.

After the information gathering process is complete, the participants conducting the benchmarking study determine a **benchmarking (performance) gap** by comparing their organization's own performance with the best performance that emerges from the data. The performance gap is defined by specific performance measures on which the firm would like to improve. Performance measures may include reduced defectives, faster on-time delivery, increased functionality, or reduced life-cycle product costs. Other, more qualitative measures may include better employee decisions concerning ways to work or solve problems, increased motivation and satisfaction, and improved cooperation and coordination among work groups and employees.

Financial gains such as reduced product costs usually occur as a result of addressing the relevant nonfinancial measures involved. Since most financial gains may take a significant amount of time to be felt, organizations should monitor the nonfinancial variables in the short term. Simply judging the effects of a benchmarking effort in the short term on the basis of financial indicators may lead to premature abandonment of what has been learned during the benchmarking project.

Stage 5: Taking Action to Meet or Exceed the Benchmark

In the final stage, the organization takes action and begins to change as a result of the benchmarking initiative. After implementing the change, the organization makes comparisons to the specific performance measures selected. In many cases,

IN PRACTICE
Benchmarking Mobile Web Experiences

Benchmarking can be used in many different contexts. Trey Harvin, CEO of dotMobi, stated in a recent article, "Benchmarking allows businesses to see their sites in relation to the sites of their industry peers, which will also help drive the creation of more good sites for consumers to use."

As an example dotMobi has come up with a five-dimensional approach that benchmarks the mobile web experience of users when accessing websites using mobile technology. The five key metrics that they have derived are:

- Discoverability: how readily a consumer can find the mobile website using different URLs
- Readiness: how well the mobile website renders on popular mobile devices
- Availability: the percentage of successful transactions or the availability of a Web page

- Response time: how long each page takes to download and the duration of an entire transaction
- Consistency: how well the mobile website performs on different mobile carriers, in different geographies and time frames.

"As dotMobi announced in a recent study, there are now more than 1.1 million Web sites designed for mobile users, and that number is continuing to grow at an incredibly fast pace. Helping consumers better understand which of those sites will offer them a good experience—no matter what handset or operator they're using—will help increase the use of the mobile Web," said Harvin. "Benchmarking allows businesses to see their sites in relation to the sites of their industry peers, which will also help drive the creation of more good sites for consumers to use."

Source: dotMobi, "Benchmarks that Measure Five Critical Dimensions of Success for Mobile Websites," *CircleID* (April 21, 2009), retrieved November 30, 2010, from http://www.circleid.com/posts/20090421_gomez_dotmobi_benchmarks_measure_mobile_websites

the decision may be to perform better than the benchmark to be more competitive. The implementation stage, especially the change process, is perhaps the most difficult stage of the benchmarking process, as the buy-in of organizational members is critical for success.

EPILOGUE TO BLAST FROM THE PAST ROBOT COMPANY

We return now to see how the Blast from the Past Robot Company fared after its adoption of the JIT manufacturing system. BFTPR succeeded in decreasing its major rework rate from 5.8% to 3.3% and its minor rework rate from 13.6% to 7.0%. Major rework required scrapping the robot. Minor rework required correcting the alignment of robot body parts or fixing the ways the gears were functioning, and it had to be done in a specially designated rework area. Minor rework did not cycle back to the beginning of the process but instead went to a different processing area where direct labor and indirect labor costs were incurred.

As a result of the improvements in rework rates, average production cycle time was reduced by 9.2 days, from 16.4 days to 7.2 days. Average work-in-process inventory was reduced from $1,774,000 to $818,000. Neva Dominguez, BFTPR Company's senior manufacturing manager, now had to prepare a report for her chief executive officer detailing how these improvements had affected the company's profits.

Production Flows

Neva began by obtaining the new production flowchart shown in Exhibit 7-12. She wanted to assess how the change to the JIT system was progressing. In the first step, the arms and legs of the robot were produced via an injection-molding process in plastic. To accomplish this, metal molds were designed for each component. A measured amount of polypropylene in the form of granules was fed into a horizontal heated cylinder where it was forced into a closed cold mold by a plunger. The liquid plastic entered the mold by means of a channel that led directly into the mold. Runners fed off the channel and moved the liquid plastic to each individual cavity. On cooling, the plastic took the shape of the mold. The process was designed so that each channel produced enough components for 60 robots.

Workers now assembled the various components using the JIT manufacturing system. Other components, such as the computer chip, nylon gears, wheels, and various parts, were added as the production process continued. Although BFTPR was striving to eliminate defective robots through the JIT process, achieving this goal was going to take some time. Thus, at the end of the process, any defective robots were rejected and returned for rework or scrapping, depending on the defect. Several finishing operations and inspections were performed next. Any excess plastic, or flashing, from the molding process was eliminated. The toy robot was then polished to a high gloss. During this process, each robot was inspected. A separate rework area was set aside for correcting the defects and reinserting the robots to ensure that no defects remained. Robots that passed inspection, either before or after rework, were packed and made available for shipment to customers. Neva concluded that the integration of the JIT system into the overall production flow was relatively successful.

Exhibit 7-12
BFTPR Company:
Production
Flowchart

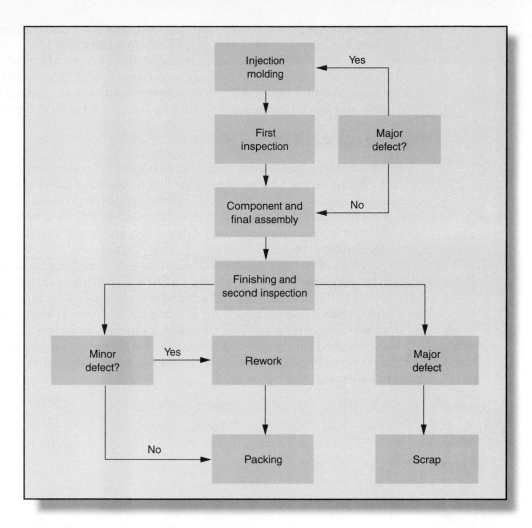

Effects on Work-in-Process Inventory

Neva next turned her attention to records for work-in-process inventory. She had already found that the average work-in-process inventory decreased by $956,000 after the implementation of the JIT system. She determined from meetings with production personnel that some work-in-process inventory was still maintained between each pair of successive process stages because each batch of robots had to await the completion of work on the preceding batch. Neva could find no detailed records to identify the change in work-in-process inventory. The number of major and minor defects, however, directly influenced it. When defect rates were high, inventory of rejected robots would build up, awaiting rework or scrap. More important, production supervisors sought to accumulate a large inventory of work in process in stages occurring after the two inspection points to enable them to keep busy when many robots were rejected. Therefore, production managers attributed the reduction in work-in-process inventory entirely to reductions in defect rates.

Effect on Production Costs

An important part of Neva's analysis was an assessment of the impact that the improvement in defect rates had on production costs. Direct materials costs included the cost of the plastic content and the cost of the gears and the computer chip in the robot. The average cost of this type of chip in a robot was $58.

Neva also collected information about direct labor and time-driven ABC support costs for each stage of the production process. Exhibit 7-13 includes these costs presented on a unit (robot) basis. The support costs include material handling, indirect labor and machine time for setup of molds for each batch, and power.

Cost of Rework

Remembering that rework costs are considered internal failure costs, what is the cost of a major defect detected during the first inspection following the injection-molding stage? Because a robot with a major defect cannot be processed further, all operations must be repeated, incurring the conversion costs again. Neva summarized the costs associated with the correction of a major defect and found that they were $42 per robot (see Exhibit 7-14).

This estimation includes additional support costs because they represent the cost of the entire mold-making, casting, and first-inspection operations that were repeated to rectify the major defect. Neva found it somewhat easier to assess the costs of correcting minor defects, which are detected at the second inspection and do not require the rejection of the entire robot. Instead, such minor defects require additional rework operations. Therefore, the additional costs of correcting minor defects are only the rework costs. Neva did some new analyses and determined that the cost or rework per robot equaled the following:

Direct rework labor	$24
Support	12
Total cost	$36

Exhibit 7-13
BFTPR Company: Conversion Costs per Robot by Production Stages

	INJECTION MODELING	FIRST INSPECTION	COMPONENT AND FINAL ASSEMBLY	FINISHING AND SECOND INSPECTION	PACKING
Direct labor (including fringe benefits)	$14	$10	$20	$8	$6
Support	14	4	14	3	10
Total costs	$28	$14	$34	$11	$16

Exhibit 7-14
BFTPR Company: Cost per Unit (Robot) for the Correction of a Major Defect

TYPE OF COST	AMOUNT
Conversion costs for injection molding:	
Direct labor	$14
Support	14
Costs of first inspection:	
Direct labor	10
Support	4
Total costs	$42

BFTPR manufactures and sells 180,000 robots each year. Before implementation of the JIT system, on average, 10,440 (180,000 × 0.058) major defects and 24,480 (180,000 × 0.136) minor defects occurred each year. Now, only 5,940 (180,000 × 0.033) major defects and 12,600 (180,000 × 0.070) minor defects occur, representing a reduction of 4,500 and 11,880 defects, respectively. Therefore, the cost savings of correcting fewer defects because of the JIT system are $189,000 ($42 × 4,500) for major rework and $427,680 ($36 × 11,880) for minor rework:

	MAJOR DEFECTS	MINOR DEFECTS
Before JIT	10,440	24,480
After JIT	5,940	12,600
Reduction	4,500	11,880
Cost per correction	× $42	× $36
JIT cost reduction	$189,000	$427,680

Cost of Carrying Work-in-Process Inventory

Neva turned next to the problem of evaluating the cost savings resulting from the reduction in the amount of work-in-process inventory. Interest rates on bank loans to finance the investment in inventories averaged 12.5% per year. With a reduction of $956,000 in work-in-process inventory ($1,774,000 − $818,000), the cost of financing also decreased by $119,500 ($956,000 × 0.125).

In addition, Neva estimated that support costs for various production stages included a total cost of $30 per batch (of 60 robots) that pertained to activities such as work-in-process, inventory handling, and storage. With the 53.89% reduction in work-in-process inventory [100 × ($956,000 ÷ $1,774,000)], Neva estimated these related costs would also decrease by about 30% or, equivalently, by about $9 per batch ($30 × 0.30). With an annual production of 180,000 robots in 3000 batches (180,000 ÷ 60), Neva expected a decrease of $27,000 in the costs of work-in-process inventory handling and storage costs ($9 × 3,000). As in the case of Pinsky Electric Corporation, however, Neva's estimate of $27,000 represented the reduction in the demand for these activities because of the reduction in work-in-process inventory. Over time, these costs should decrease by this amount, but for the reduction to actually occur, the plant management must identify the personnel and other resources committed to this activity and eliminate the resources not required because of the reduction in the demand for them.

Benefits from Increased Sales

Neva finally decided to evaluate whether the reduction in the production cycle time had resulted in any gains in sales. For this purpose, she met with the marketing manager, Emma Rothschild. Emma pointed out that annual sales had remained stable at around 180,000 robots for the past three years; however, she did believe that the improvement in the production cycle time had had an impact on sales. Because of increased competition in the robot market, Emma had expected to lose sales of about 2,000 robots. But the reduction of 6.5 days in the production cycle time had permitted her to respond more aggressively to market demand by offering the robots to customers with a much shorter lead time. Emma believed that the shorter production cycle time led to maintaining sales of about 2,000 robots that otherwise would have been lost. As a result, BFTPR had not lost any market share in this market segment.

Neva determined that the average net selling price (the net of sales commission and shipping costs) for these 2,000 robots was $250. Exhibit 7-15 presents her list of the

Exhibit 7-15
BFTPR Company:
Additional Costs
of Production per
Robot

TYPE OF COST	COST PER ROBOT
Direct materials:	
Chip	$58.00
All others	32.00
Incremental conversion costs:	
Injection molding	28.00
First inspection	14.00
Component and final assembly	34.00
Second inspection	11.00
Packing	16.00
Prorated rework costs:	
Major defects[a]	1.43
Minor defects[b]	2.71
Total incremental costs	$197.14
Average net sales price	$250.00
Contribution margin per robot	$52.86

$$^a \frac{33}{1,000 - 33} \times \$42 = \$1.43$$

$$^b \frac{70}{1,000 - 70} \times \$36 = \$2.71$$

additional costs for the production of these robots. Notice in Exhibit 7-15 that rework costs are prorated over the good units of production. For example, additional costs for major rework are $42 for each robot that requires rework. For every 1,000 robots produced, an average of 33 robots (1,000 × 3.3%) now require major rework. Therefore, the company obtains 967 good robots (1,000 − 33). The total additional major rework cost for 33 robots is $1,386 ($42 × 33), which is borne by the 967 good robots at the rate of $1.43 ($1,386 ÷ 967) per good robot.

The profit is estimated to be $52.86 per robot, or $105,720 in total for the 2,000 robots ($52.86 × 2,000). Without the JIT system and the consequent reduction in cycle time, this contribution from sales would have been lost.

Summary of Costs and Benefits

Exhibit 7-16 displays Neva's summary of the benefits from the quality improvement program. Total estimated annual benefits of $868,900 are much greater than the one-time costs of $300,000 spent on the JIT system and worker training discussed in this chapter's opening vignette.

Exhibit 7-16
BFTPR Company:
Summary of
Annual Benefits
Resulting from
the JIT System

Reduction in network costs:		
Major rework	$189,000	
Minor rework	427,680	$616,680
Reduction in work-in-process inventory-related costs:		
Financing costs	119,500	
Inventory handling and storage-activity costs	27,000	146,500
Contribution from sales increases resulting from		
improved production cycle time		105,720
Total annual benefits		$868,900

SUMMARY

Managers need various types of costs and other functional information to assess the impact of process decisions, such as improved plant layouts that streamline production operations. A detailed evaluation of implemented actions may shed light on ways to increase the benefits derived from them. Managers can choose from three general types of facility designs: (1) process layout, in which all similar equipment or functions are grouped together, (2) product layouts, in which equipment is organized to accommodate the production of a specific product, and (3) cellular manufacturing, in which a plant is divided into a number of cells so that within each cell all machines required to manufacture a group of similar products are arranged in close proximity. Managers can also apply the tools of JIT or lean manufacturing, kaizen, and benchmarking to improve their operations.

Finally, the implementation of a JIT or lean manufacturing system has many positive effects on the levels of work-in-process inventory, the cost of support activities of handling and storing work-in-process inventory, and the amounts of major and minor rework. Further, it reduces cycle times so that there are shorter lead times to fulfilling customer orders. All these changes have a very tangible and quantifiable bottom-line effect.

KEY TERMS

appraisal costs, 293
benchmarking, 299
benchmarking (performance)
   gap, 303
certified supplier, 293
cooperative benchmarking, 302
cost of nonconformance (CONC)
   to quality standards, 292
cost-of-quality (COQ) report, 293
cycle time, 279
database benchmarking, 302

external failure costs, 293
group benchmarking, 302
group technology, 283
indirect/third-party
   benchmarking, 302
internal failure costs, 293
investments, 280
just-in-time (JIT) manufacturing, 294
kaizen costing, 297
lean manufacturing, 292
operating costs, 280

prevention costs, 293
process layout, 280
processing cycle
   efficiency (PCE), 285
processing time, 285
product layout, 281
quality costs, 293
theory of constraints (TOC), 279
throughput contribution, 280
unilateral (covert)
   benchmarking, 302

ASSIGNMENT MATERIALS

Questions

7-1 There are three types of facility designs: process layouts, product layouts, and group technology. Define these three designs in the context of facility layout systems. **(LO 2)**

7-2 What is the theory of constraints? Name its measures. **(LO 1)**

7-3 What is a bottleneck? **(LO 1)**

7-4 Describe the lean manufacturing approach. **(LO 3)**

7-5 What is meant by the phrase *cost of nonconformance* in relation to quality? **(LO 4)**

7-6 Waste, rework, and net cost of scrap are examples of what kinds of quality costs? **(LO 4)**

7-7 Quality engineering, quality training, statistical process control, and supplier certification are what kinds of quality costs? **(LO 4)**

7-8 List three examples for each of the following quality costing categories:
   a. Prevention costs
   b. Appraisal costs
   c. Internal failure costs
   d. External failure costs. **(LO 4)**

7-9 How is a just-in-time manufacturing system different from a conventional manufacturing system? **(LO 5)**

7-10 What creates the need to maintain work-in-process inventory? Why is work-in-process inventory likely to decrease on the implementation of group technology, just-in-time production, and quality improvement programs? **(LO 2, 5)**

7-11 Why are production cycle time and the level of work-in-process inventory positively related? **(LO 2, 5)**

7-12 State the advantages of the group technology layout of facility design. (LO 2)

7-13 What are two types of financial benefits resulting from a shift to group technology, just-in-time production, or continuous quality improvements? (LO 2, 5)

7-14 What are the goals of kaizen costing? (LO 6)

7-15 When is a cost variance investigation undertaken under kaizen costing? (LO 6)

7-16 How is traditional standard costing different from kaizen costing? (LO 6)

7-17 What is benchmarking, and why is it used? (LO 7)

7-18 What are the five stages of the benchmarking process? (LO 7)

7-19 What are the three broad classes of information on which firms interested in benchmarking can focus? Describe each. (LO 7)

7-20 What stage of the benchmarking process is the most important for benchmarking

management accounting methods? Why? (LO 7)

7-21 What are the two general methods of information gathering and sharing when undertaking a benchmarking exercise? (LO 7)

7-22 What are the three types of information gathering and sharing used under the cooperative form of benchmarking? (LO 7)

7-23 What is a benchmarking (performance) gap? (LO 7)

7-24 What is the additional cost of replacing one unit of a product rejected at inspection and scrapped? (LO 4, 8)

7-25 What is the additional cost if a unit rejected at inspection can be reworked to meet quality standards by performing some additional operations? (LO 4, 8)

7-26 What costs and revenues are relevant in evaluating the profit impact of an increase in sales? (LO 8)

Exercises

LO 2, 5 **7-27** *Facilities layout* How would you classify the layout of a large grocery store? Why do you think it is laid out this way? Can you think of any way to improve the layout of a conventional grocery store? Explain your reasoning. (*Hint:* Think about JIT, cycle time, and so on.)

LO 4 **7-28** *Quality cost categories* Regarding the quality costing categories, how do prevention costs differ from appraisal costs? How do internal failure costs differ from external failure costs?

LO 4 **7-29** *Quality cost categories* Of the four quality costing categories, which quality cost is the most damaging to the organization? Explain.

LO 5, 8 **7-30** *JIT manufacturing and cost savings* Lloyds Company introduced JIT manufacturing last year and has prepared the following data to assess the benefits from the change:

CATEGORY	BEFORE THE CHANGE	AFTER THE CHANGE
Production cycle time	75 days	30 days
Inventories	$250,000	$60,000
Total sales	$1,600,000	$2,000,000
Costs as percentage of sales:		
Direct materials	20%	10%
Direct labor	20%	15%
Variable support	25%	15%
Fixed support	10%	5%

Inventory financing costs are 20% per year. Support costs are based on a time-driven activity-based costing analysis. Estimate the total financial benefits that resulted from the switch to JIT manufacturing operations.

LO 8 **7-31** *Inventory carrying costs* XYZ Corporation produces 50,000 videophones per year. The company estimates its direct material costs for the videophone to be $600 per unit and its conversion (direct labor plus support) costs to be

$480 per unit. Annual inventory carrying costs, not included in these costs, are estimated to be 10%. XYZ's average inventory levels are estimated as follows:

Direct material	1 month of production
Work in process (100% complete for materials and 50% for conversion)	2 months of production
Finished goods	½ month of production

Compute the annual inventory carrying costs for XYZ Corporation.

Problems

LO 1   **7-32**   *ABC and TOC*   Discuss the similarities and differences between activity-based costing and the theory of constraints, as well as situations in which one approach might be preferable to the other.

LO 2, 5, 8   **7-33**   *Relevant cost and revenues: changes in facility layout*   To facilitate a move toward JIT production, PQ Company is considering a change in its plant layout. The plant controller, Mike Ross, has been asked to evaluate the costs and benefits of the change in plant layout. After meeting with production and marketing managers, Mike has compiled the following estimates:

- Machine moving and reinstallation will cost $85,000.
- Total sales will increase by 25% to $1,500,000 because of a decrease in production cycle time required under the new plant layout. Average contribution margin is 40% of sales.
- Inventory-related costs will decrease by 20%. Currently, the annual average carrying value of inventory is $360,000. The annual inventory financing cost is 10%.

Required

Should PQ implement the proposed change in plant layout? Support your answer.

LO 2, 5   **7-34**   *Cycle time efficiency and JIT*   James Company is considering installing a JIT manufacturing system in the hope that it will improve its overall processing cycle efficiency. Data from the traditional system and estimates for the JIT system are presented here for their output:

TIME CATEGORY	TRADITIONAL SYSTEM	JIT SYSTEM
Storage	5 hours	1.5 hours
Inspection	1 hour	10 minutes
Moving	2 hours	15 minutes
Processing	2 hours	75 minutes

Required

(a) Calculate processing cycle efficiency (PCE) under the traditional and JIT systems for the output.
(b) Strictly based on your PCE calculations above, should James Company implement the JIT system? Explain.

LO 2, 5, 8   **7-35**   *JIT and group technology*   You are a manufacturing manager faced with the decision about how to improve manufacturing operations and efficiency. You have been studying both group technology and JIT manufacturing systems. Your boss expects you to prepare a report covering the costs and benefits of each approach.

Required

Write a detailed memorandum discussing the costs and benefits of group technology versus JIT.

LO 8   **7-36** *Quality improvement programs and cost savings*   Gurland Valves Company manufactures brass valves that meet precise specification standards. All finished valves are inspected before being packed and shipped to customers. Rejected valves are returned to the initial production stage to be melted and recast. Such rework requires no new materials in casting but requires new materials in finishing. The following unit cost data are available:

Costs	Casting	Finishing	Inspection	Packing	Total
Direct materials	$200	$15	$0	$10	$225
Direct labor	115	120	30	15	290
Variable support	124	176	40	20	360
Fixed support	65	89	16	10	180
	504	410	86	55	1,055

As a result of a quality-improvement program, the reject rate has decreased from 7.5% to 5%, and the number of rejects has decreased by $(7.5\% - 5\%) \times (20,000)$ units. Improvements in reject rates have also led to a decrease in work-in-process inventory from $420,000 to $300,000. Inventory carrying costs are estimated to be 12% per year. Estimate the annual cost savings as a result of the quality improvement, assuming that capacity costs as indicated by the time-driven ABC support costs can be reduced if not needed.

LO 2, 4   **7-37** *Group technology and processing cycle efficiency*   Steve Martin's company, Whisper Voice Systems, is trying to increase its processing cycle efficiency (PCE). Because Steve has a very limited budget, he has been searching for a way to increase his PCE by using group technology. One of Steve's manufacturing managers, Cheryl Jones, has been studying group technology and claims that with minimal cost that includes downtime in the operation, she can rearrange existing machinery and workers and improve PCE. Steve is quite skeptical about this and decides to allow Cheryl to rearrange a small part of his operation. For Steve to be satisfied, he has stated that PCE must increase by 15%. PCE data before and after the rearrangement are as follows:

Time Category	Before Rearrangement	After Rearrangement
Inspection	40 minutes	15 minutes
Moving	60 minutes	5 minutes
Processing	60 minutes	15 minutes
Storage	80 minutes	15 minutes

Does the change in PCE meet Steve's requirement? Why or why not?

LO 2   **7-38** *Facilities layout*   One aspect of facilities layout for McDonald's is that when customers come into the building, they can line up in one of several lines and wait to be served. In contrast, customers at Wendy's are asked to stand in one line that snakes around the front of the counter and to wait for a server to become available.

Required

(a) What is the rationale for each approach?

(b) Which approach do you favor from (1) a customer's perspective and (2) management's perspective? Explain.

7-39 *Quality of customer service*   Read "Everyone Likes to Laud Serving the Customer; Doing It Is the Problem," by Carol Hymowitz (*Wall Street Journal*, February 27, 2006, p. B1).

Required

(a) According to the article, what measures are commonly used to evaluate customer service representatives, and what measure(s) should be used?

(b) Explain how the prevention, appraisal, and external failure aspects of the cost-of-quality framework might be applied to customer service processes. In your response, include a discussion of which of the three aspects companies should focus on and illustrate how evaluation measures may affect performance in customer service processes.

LO   **7-40** *Quality costing: balancing category costs*   Managers concerned with improving quality sometimes have a difficult balancing act, given the four types of quality costs they have to manage. As a new manager, you are trying to figure out a strategy for managing $2 million of quality costs; your total quality costs cannot exceed 4% of sales.

Required

You need to decide how much should go into each of the four quality-cost categories. How would you go about allocating these costs? What trade-offs would you have to make as you allocate the costs?

LO 4   **7-41** *Preparing a cost-of-quality report*   The following data have just been gathered on last year's quality-related costs at the Becker Company:

COST CATEGORY	AMOUNT
Supplier certification	$300,000
Product quality audits	500,000
Warranty claims	115,000
Returned products	50,000
Statistical process control	400,000
Product liability lawsuits	80,000
Quality engineering	175,000
Rework costs	415,000
Quality training	225,000
Inspection of and testing of incoming materials	450,000
Process control monitoring	250,000
Repair costs in the field	120,000
Waste	60,000
Product recalls	135,000
Net cost of scrap	225,000
Downtime due to defects	200,000

Total sales last year were $80,000,000.

Required

(a) Prepare a cost-of-quality report that groups costs into prevention, appraisal, internal failure, and external failure. Also show costs as a percentage of sales.

(b) Interpret the data and make recommendations to Becker's management.

7-42 *Preparing a cost-of-quality report* The following information shows last year's quality-related costs for the Watson Company:

ITEM	AMOUNT
Waste	$980,000
Warranty claims	4,300,000
Downtime due to defects	480,000
Research of customer needs	60,000
Quality training	70,000
Maintenance of test equipment	220,000
Product liability lawsuits	1,410,000
Rework costs	1,200,000
Quality engineering	$630,000
Returned products	2,145,000
Process control monitoring	505,000
Inspection of and testing of incoming materials	400,000
Supplier certification	65,000
Repair costs in the field	1,145,000
Statistical process control	325,000
Product recalls	2,750,000
Net cost of scrap	1,190,000
Product quality audits	275,000

Total sales for the year were $110,000,000.

Required

(a) Prepare a cost-of-quality report that groups costs into prevention, appraisal, internal failure, and external failure. Also show costs as a percentage of sales.

(b) Interpret the data and make recommendations to Watson's management.

LO 6   **7-43 *Kaizen versus standard costing*** What factors differentiate kaizen costing from standard costing?

LO 6   **7-44 *Kaizen costing: knowledge*** According to the kaizen costing approach, who has the best knowledge to reduce costs? Why is this so?

LO 6   **7-45 *Kaizen meaning*** What do the terms *kaizen* and *kaizen costing* mean?

LO 6   **7-46 *Kaizen costing*** Under what condition will the cost savings due to kaizen costing not be applied to production?

LO 6   **7-47 *Kaizen costing: managerial issues*** Kaizen costing is a method that many Japanese companies have found effective in reducing costs.

Required

(a) What are the biggest problems in using kaizen costing?

(b) How can managers overcome these problems?

LO 7   **7-48 *Benchmarking partners*** What are the key factors in identifying benchmarking partners? Explain why these factors are important.

LO 7   **7-49 *Benchmarking mobile web experiences*** As a manager asked to benchmark another organization's mobile web experience provided to users, on what factors would you gather information? Why?

LO 6   **7-50 *Standard costing versus kaizen costing*** Many companies are interested in adopting a kaizen costing approach to reducing costs. However, they are not sure how their current standard costing system will fit with the kaizen costing approach.

Required

How do the standard costing system and the kaizen costing system differ? Can the two systems coexist? Explain.

LO 6   **7-51 *Kaizen costing versus standard costing*** Your organization, located in Worthington, Ohio, is contemplating introducing kaizen costing to help with cost reduction. As someone who has an understanding of management accounting, you have been asked for your opinion. Specifically, some of your colleagues are wondering about the differences between standard costing and kaizen costing.

Required

Write a report discussing the following:

(a) The similarities and differences between standard costing and kaizen costing
(b) Under what conditions kaizen costing can be adapted to U.S. organizations.

LO 7   **7-52 *Benchmarking: field exercise with other students*** Assume that you are an average student who has a desire to be one of the best students in class. Your professor suggests that you benchmark the working habits of the best student in the class. You are somewhat skeptical but decide to take on the challenge.

Required

How would you go about this benchmarking exercise? In answering this question, describe the process that you would undertake in benchmarking the best student, the factors that you would try to study, and how you would implement changes to your working habits.

LO 7   **7-53 *Benchmarking: field exercise in a company*** Benchmarking a product, process, or management accounting method takes a great deal of time and effort. Companies have many choices when it comes to conducting a benchmarking study. For example, in following the five stages of the benchmarking process, companies have to decide how to proceed, who to select as benchmarking partners, and what information they are willing to share and to gather.

Required

Locate a company in your local community that has engaged in a benchmarking study. Try to arrange a visit to the company (perhaps through your professor, relative, or friend) in order to talk to employees who have been involved in the benchmarking effort. Using the five-stage process, critique the approach that this company followed. What are the similarities and differences between what this company did and the process described in this chapter? Be specific about the procedures that were used and the variables that were assessed. Finally, what were the results of the benchmarking exercise at this company? Was it a success or a failure? Why?

Cases

LO 2   **7-54 *Facilities layout, value-added activities*** Woodpoint Furniture Manufacturing produces various lines of pine furniture. The plant is organized so that all similar functions are performed in one area, as shown in Exhibit 7-17. Most pieces of furniture are made in batches of 10 units.

Raw materials are ordered and stored in the raw materials storage area. When an order is issued for a batch of production, the wood needed to complete that batch is withdrawn from the raw materials storage area and taken to the saw area. There the wood is sawed into the pieces that are required for the production lot.

Exhibit 7-17
Woodpoint
Furniture
Manufacturing

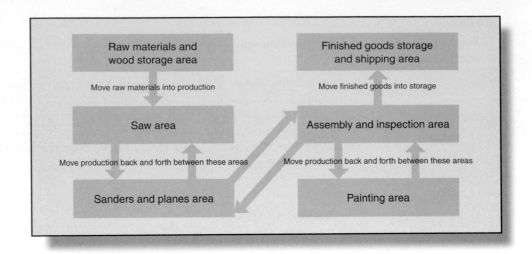

The pieces are then transferred to the sanding and planing area, where they are stored await-ing processing in that area. When the machines are free, any sanding or planing is done on all the pieces in the batch. Any pieces that are damaged by the planing or sanding are reordered from the saw area. The other pieces in the lot are set aside in a storage area when pieces have to be reordered from the saw area.

When all of the pieces have been sanded or planed, the pieces are then transferred to the assembly area, where they are placed in a large bin to await assembly. Pieces are withdrawn from the bin as assembly proceeds. Defective pieces are returned to the saw or sand and plane area, where they are remanufactured.

As assembly proceeds or when assembly is completed, depending on the product, any required painting or staining is done in the painting area. Pieces to be stained or painted are transferred back and forth on a trolley between the assembly and paint areas. The paint department has a storage area for pieces awaiting painting. Whenever assembly is halted to await pieces that have been sent for painting and staining, the rest of the pieces in that batch are put into the storage bin to await the return of the stained or painted pieces.

When assembly is completed, the quality inspector checks the product. Any defective products are returned to the appropriate department for rework. When the product is approved, it is pack-aged and put into final storage to await an order by the customer.

Required

(a) Chart the process (that is, specify, from start to finish, the activities used) for making furniture at Woodpoint Furniture Manufacturing. Which activities do you think add value from the customer's perspective?

(b) What performance indicators do you think are critical in evaluating the performance of this manufacturing operation from the standpoint of customers and the company?

LO 2, 3, 5   **7-55 *Facilities layout, lean manufacturing, brand management, value-added activities***
Some firms in the fashion industry have adopted lean or just-in-time approaches to maintain or in-crease their competitive advantage. Read the following articles or other resources to address the ques-tions below: "Brand-New Bag: Louis Vuitton Tries Modern Methods On Factory Lines" (C. Passariello, *The Wall Street Journal*, October 9, 2006, p. A1) and "Zara Thrives By Breaking All Rules" (K. Capell, *BusinessWeek*, October 20, 2008, p. 66).

Required

(a) Compare Louis Vuitton's previous and current processes for making a bag. For example, how many people and days are required, what are the workers' degrees of specialization, and what improvements have resulted?

(b) How did Louis Vuitton's previous process for making bags support the company's value proposition?

(c) How have practices from competitors such as Zara changed Louis Vuitton's view of what its target customers want? Has Louis Vuitton's value proposition changed? If so, how well will the new process support the company's value proposition?

(d) What performance indicators do you think are critical in evaluating the performance of this manufacturing operation from the standpoint of customers and the company?

LO 4   **7-56 *Cost-of-quality framework, health care*** Johnson & Johnson (www.jnj.com), a major health care and pharmaceutical firm, voluntarily recalled a number of its products in 2010 because of quality problems. These products included hip-repair implants, contact lenses, and over-the-counter medications.

Required

Using information from the company's website, the business press, or other sources, develop responses to the following:

(a) What specific quality problems were reported?

(b) What are some examples of external failure costs related to the recalls? What financial estimates are available?

(c) What new prevention or appraisal costs will the company incur in response to the quality problems?

LO 4   **7-57 *Relevant costs, qualitative factors, cost-of-quality framework, environmental issues*** Kwik Clean handles both commercial laundry and individual customer dry cleaning. Kwik Clean's current dry cleaning process involves emitting a pollutant into the air. In addition, the commercial laundry and dry cleaning processes produce sediments and other elements that must receive special treatment before disposal. Pat Polley, Kwik Clean's owner, is concerned about the cost of dealing with increasingly stringent laws and environmental regulations. Recent legislation requires Kwik Clean to reduce its amount of air pollution emissions.

To reduce pollution emissions, Polley is considering the following two options:

- *Option 1:* Invest in equipment that would reduce emissions through filtration. The equipment would involve a large capital expenditure but would bring Kwik Clean into compliance with current regulations for emissions.

- *Option 2:* Invest in a new dry cleaning process that would eliminate current air pollution emissions, partly by using a different solvent than the one currently used. This option would require an even larger capital expenditure than option 1, but the new equipment would reduce some operating costs. Moreover, Kwik Clean might be able to market its environmentally safer process to increase business.

In evaluating the two options and current operations, Polley has enumerated the following items:

1. The price and quantity of solvent used in current operations (and option 1).
2. The price and quantity of the new solvent that would be used in option 2.
3. The purchase price of new equipment for option 1 and for option 2.
4. The cost of removing old equipment and installing new equipment under option 2.
5. The purchase price of the filtration equipment in option 1 as well as the useful life of the equipment.

6. The purchase price of the current equipment and its remaining useful life.
7. The salvage value of the current equipment, which would be sold under option 2.
8. Polley's salary and fringe benefits.
9. Labor costs for current operations (and option 1) and option 2; labor costs would be lower under option 2 than under option 1.
10. Training costs associated with the new equipment in option 2.
11. Legal fees paid to handle paperwork associated with hazardous waste liabilities connected with the sediments produced when cleaning commercial laundry by the current operations (the same sediments would be produced with the equipment in option 2).
12. Storage and disposal costs associated with the sediments produced when cleaning commercial laundry.
13. Insurance for the equipment and workers; under option 2, insurance fees would be reduced from the current level.

Polley was concerned about recent events that were publicized locally. A newspaper article reported that the Occupational Safety and Health Administration fined one of Polley's competitors several thousand dollars for unsafe employee working conditions related to handling solvents. Another business incurred a very expensive cleanup for accidental hazardous waste leakage that contaminated the soil. The leakage received major attention in the local television and radio news broadcasts and was headlined in the local newspapers.

Required

(a) Which costs are relevant to Polley's decision to choose either option 1 or option 2?
(b) What qualitative factors is Polley likely to consider in choosing either option 1 or option 2?
(c) Explain how the cost-of-quality framework of prevention, appraisal, internal failure, and external failure might be applied to operations with environmental pollution, where *failures* are defined as accidental spillage or leakage of hazardous wastes or as illegal levels of pollutants. On which of the four cost-of-quality categories would you advise Polley to focus her attention?

LO 2, 4   **7-58 *Customer service processes, non–value-added activities***   Daniel Morris purchased a 42-inch plasma television, manufactured by TVCO, from a local electronics store that permits customers to return defective products within 30 days of purchase. Approximately 45 days after Daniel's purchase, the TV began to malfunction periodically. Because Daniel could not return the TV to the local store, he turned to the warranty information and found that the warranty included picking up the approximately 100-pound TV from the owner's home, repairing the TV, and delivering the repaired TV to the owner's home. TVCO's customer service process for handling warranty repairs is as follows:

1. The customer calls Customer Service (CS) to request authorization of the TV repair.
2. CS requests the customer to mail or fax the receipt, TV model number, and serial number.
3. On receipt of the information, CS locates a nearby repair shop to perform the repair.
4. CS forwards the repair request to the Warranty Department (WD) for approval.
5. On approval, WD informs CS so that CS can inform the customer and fax authorization for the repair to the approved repair shop.
6. The customer contacts the designated repair shop to arrange for the TV pickup. The repair shop picks up the TV.
7. The repair shop diagnoses the problem and orders parts.
8. On receipt of the parts, the shop repairs the TV and delivers it to the customer.
9. If the TV cannot be repaired, TVCO replaces the defective TV with a new one.

Accordingly, Daniel called CS to request authorization to repair the TV and faxed the receipt, TV model number, and serial number to CS. CS located a repair shop (RS1) 30 miles from Daniel's city of Anytown. On obtaining WD's approval, CS faxed authorization for the repair to the approved repair shop. Daniel contacted RS1 to arrange for the TV pickup, but RS1 refused to pick up the TV, stating that Daniel's location is too far away. After several more phone calls to CS, with wait times before talking to a CS representative ranging from 25 to 45 minutes, CS authorized another repair shop, RS2. RS2 picked up the TV, and Daniel informed RS2 that he planned to move to Othertown in two weeks and therefore hoped the TV could be repaired by then. RS2 did not look at the TV until Daniel called eight days later to check on progress. RS2 then diagnosed the problem and contacted TVCO for parts for the repair and was told that parts would not be available for several weeks. Because of his impending move to another city, Daniel requested RS2 to return the TV to him, thinking that he would get the TV repaired in Othertown.

After moving to Othertown, Daniel again called CS to request authorization for the TV repair. After several phone calls with sizable wait times before talking to CS, and several miscommunications between CS and WD that led Daniel to talk to a supervisor, CS located RS3 in Othertown. However, RS3 was backlogged and would not pick up the TV for at least a week. RS3 picks up only on weekdays during regular working hours. Moreover, the technician would not look at the TV for at least 10 days after the TV arrived in the shop. Given the length of time that had now passed since Daniel's first contact with CS, Daniel found this situation unacceptable, so he called CS and asked to talk to a supervisor. The supervisor suggested other approved stores for the repair.

Daniel found RS4, which was willing to pick up the TV at a day's notice and diagnose problems as soon as possible so that parts could be ordered. Daniel called CS to arrange for authorization, and CS promised to call back soon. After a week with no response, Daniel called CS and was told that WD refused to authorize RS4 to perform the repair because WD thought Daniel still lived in Anytown and RS4 was too far from Anytown. Daniel called the supervisor again, and after a week the supervisor arranged for authorization for RS4 to do the repair. RS4 picked up the TV; by now, more than two months had passed since Daniel first contacted CS, and RS4 could not provide a definite date for completion of the repair. However, as promised, RS4 diagnosed the problem shortly after the TV arrived in the shop and ordered the apparently appropriate part. Disappointingly, changing the part did not correct the problem. TVCO suggested that RS4 try changing another part but could not provide an estimated date of arrival for the part. After Daniel's further phone calls, TVCO agreed to exchange the defective TV for a new one. By this time, more than three months had passed since Daniel first contacted CS.

Required

(a) Assuming that TVCO has a performance measurement system for CS, what measures do you think the company is using to evaluate CS performance?

(b) What measures reflect what the customer is concerned about?

(c) What changes in the warranty service approval process might improve the process from the customer's perspective?

(d) Compare how RS3 and RS4 have designed their repair process and explain to RS3 how it can reduce the time spent on non–value-added activities.

LO 8   **7-59** *Cost savings: replacement decision*   Rossman Instruments, Inc., is considering leasing new state-of-the-art machinery at an annual cost of $900,000. The new machinery has a four-year expected life. It will replace existing machinery leased one year earlier at an annual lease cost of $490,000 committed for five years. Early termination of this lease contract will incur a $280,000 penalty. There are no other fixed costs.

The new machinery is expected to decrease variable costs from $42 to $32 per unit sold because of improved materials yield, faster machine speed, and lower direct labor, supervision, materials handling, and quality inspection requirements. The sales price will remain at $56. Improvements in quality, production cycle time, and customer responsiveness are expected to increase annual sales from 36,000 units to 48,000 units.

The variable costs stated earlier exclude the inventory carrying costs. Because the new machinery is expected to affect inventory levels, the following estimates are also provided. The enhanced speed and accuracy of the new machinery are expected to decrease production cycle time by half and, consequently, lead to a decrease in work-in-process inventory level from 3 months to just 1.5 months of production. Increased flexibility with these new machines is expected to allow a reduction in finished goods inventory from 2 months of production to just 1 month. Improved yield rates and greater machine reliability will enable a reduction in raw materials inventory from 4 months of production to just 1.5 months. Annual inventory carrying cost is 20% of inventory value.

Category	Old Machine	New Machine
Average per unit cost of raw materials inventory	$12	$11
Average per unit cost of work-in-process inventory	25	20
Average per unit cost of finished goods inventory	46	36
Variable cost per unit sold	42	32

Required

(a) Determine the total value of annual benefits from the new machinery. Include changes in inventory carrying costs.

(b) Should Rossman replace its existing machinery with the new machinery? Present your reasoning with detailed steps identifying relevant costs and revenues.

(c) Discuss whether a manager evaluated on the basis of Rossman's net income will have the incentive to make the right decision as evaluated in part b.

LO 2, 4   **7-60** *Customer service processes, non–value-added activities*   Precision Systems, Inc. (PSI).[1] Precision Systems, Inc. (PSI) has been in business for more than 40 years and has generally reported a positive net income. The company manufactures and sells high-technology instruments (systems). Each product line at PSI has only a handful of standard products, but configuration changes and add-ons can be accommodated as long as they are not radically different from the standard systems.

Faced with rising competition and increasing customer demands for quality, PSI adopted a total quality improvement program in 1989. Many employees received training and several quality initiatives were launched. Like most businesses, PSI concentrated on improvements in the manufacturing function and achieved significant improvements. However, little was done in other departments.

In early 1992, PSI decided to extend its total quality improvement program to its order entry department, which handles the critical functions of preparing quotes for potential customers and processing orders. Order processing is the first process in the chain of operations after the order is received from a customer. High-quality output from the order entry department improves quality later in the process, and allows PSI to deliver higher quality systems both faster and cheaper, thus meeting the goals of timely delivery and lower cost.

As a first step, PSI commissioned a cost of quality (COQ) study in its order entry department. The study had two objectives:

- To develop a system for identifying order entry errors
- To determine how much an order entry error costs.

PSI's Order Entry Department

PSI's domestic order entry department is responsible for preparing quotations for potential customers and taking actual sales orders. PSI's sales representatives forward requests for quotations to the order entry department, though actual orders for systems are received directly from customers. Orders for parts are also received directly from customers. Service-related orders (for parts or repairs), however, are generally placed by service representatives. When PSI undertook the COQ

---

[1] *Source:* Institute of Management Accountants, *Cases from Management Accounting Practice, Volume 12.* Adapted with permission.

study, the order entry department consisted of nine employees and two supervisors who reported to the order entry manager. Three of the nine employees dealt exclusively with taking parts orders, while the other six were responsible for system orders. Before August 1992, the other six were split equally into two groups: One was responsible for preparing quotations, and the other was responsible for taking orders.

The final outputs of the order entry department are the quote and the order acknowledgment or "green sheet." The manufacturing department and the stockroom use the green sheet for further processing of the order.

The order entry department's major suppliers are (1) sales or service representatives; (2) the final customers who provide them with the basic information to process further; and (3) technical information and marketing departments, which provide configuration guides, price masters, and similar documents (some in printed form and others online) as supplementary information. Sometimes the printed configuration guides contain information in the format the order entry requires, but other times it does not.

At times there are discrepancies in the information available to order entry staff and sales representatives with respect to price, part number, or configuration. These discrepancies often cause communication gaps between the order entry staff, sales representatives, and manufacturing.

An order entry staff provided the following example of lack of communication between a sales representative and manufacturing with respect to one order.

If the sales reps. have spoken to the customer and determined that our standard configuration is not what they require, they may leave a part off the order. [In one such instance] I got a call from manufacturing saying when this system is configured like this, it must have this part added. . . . It is basically a no charge part and so I added it (change order #1) and called the sales rep. and said to him, "Manufacturing told me to add it." The sales rep. called back and said, "No [the customer] doesn't need that part, they are going to be using another option . . . so they don't need this." Then I did another change order (#2) to take it off because the sales rep. said they don't need it. Then manufacturing called me back and said, "We really need [to add that part] (change order #3). If the sales rep. does not want it then we will have to do an engineering special and it is going to be another 45 days lead time. . . ." So, the sales rep. and manufacturing not having direct communication required me to do three change orders on that order; two of them were probably unnecessary.

A typical sequence of events might begin with a sales representative meeting with a customer to discuss the type of system desired. PSI's sales representatives have scientific knowledge that enables them to configure a specific system to meet a customer's needs. After deciding on a configuration, the sales representative then fills out a paper form and faxes it or phones it in to an order entry employee, who might make several subsequent phone calls to the sales representative, the potential customer, or the manufacturing department to prepare the quote properly. These phone calls deal with such questions as exchangeability of parts, part numbers, current prices for parts, or allowable sales discounts. Order entry staff then keys in the configuration of the desired system, including part numbers, and informs the sales representative of the quoted price. Each quote is assigned a quotation number. To smooth production, manufacturing often produces systems with standard configurations in anticipation of obtaining orders from recent quotes for systems. The systems usually involve adding on special features to the standard configuration. Production in advance of orders sometimes results in duplication in manufacturing, however, because customers often fail to put their quotation numbers on their orders. When order entry receives an order, the information on the order is reentered into the computer to produce an order acknowledgment. When the order acknowledgment is sent to the invoicing department, the information is reviewed again to generate an invoice to send to the customer.

Many departments in PSI use information directly from the order entry department (these are the internal customers of order entry). The users include manufacturing, service (repair), stockroom, invoicing, and sales administration. The sales administration department prepares commission payments for each system sold and tracks sales performance. The shipping, customer support (technical support), and collections departments (also internal customers) indirectly use order entry information. After a system is shipped, related paperwork is sent to customer support to maintain a service-installed database in anticipation of technical support questions that may arise. Customer support is also responsible for installations of systems. A good order acknowledgment (i.e., one with no errors of any kind) can greatly reduce errors downstream within the process and prevent later non–value-added costs.

Cost of Quality

Quality costs arise because poor quality may—or does—exist. For PSI's order entry department, poor quality or nonconforming "products" refer to poor information for further processing of an order or quotation (see Exhibit 7-18 for examples). Costs of poor quality here pertain to the time spent by the order entry staff and concerned employees in other departments (providers of information, such as sales or technical information) to rectify the errors.

Class I Failures

Class I failure costs are incurred when nonconforming products (incorrect quotes or orders) are identified as nonconforming before they leave the order entry department. The incorrect quotes or orders may be identified by order entry staff or supervisors during inspection of the document. An important cause of Class I failures is lack of communication. Sample data collected from the order entry staff show that they encountered more than 10 different types of problems during order processing (see Exhibit 7-18 for examples). Analysis of the sample data suggests that, on average, it takes 2.3 hours (including waiting time) to rectify errors on quotes and 2.7 working days for corrections on orders. In determining costs, the COQ study accounted only for the time it actually takes to solve the problem (i.e., excluding waiting time). Waiting time was excluded because employees use this time to perform other activities or work on other orders. The total Class I failure costs, which include only salary and fringe benefits for the time it takes to correct errors, amount to more than 4% of order entry's annual budget for salaries and fringe benefits (see Exhibit 7-19).

Class II Failures

Class II failure costs are incurred when nonconforming materials are transferred out of the order entry department. For PSI's order entry department, "nonconforming" refers to an incorrect order acknowledgment as specified by its users within PSI. The impact of order entry errors on final (external) customers is low because order acknowledgments are inspected in several departments, so most errors are corrected before the invoice (which contains some information available on the

Exhibit 7-18
Examples of Failures

1. Incomplete information on purchase order
2. Transposition of prices on purchase order
3. More than one part number on order acknowledgment when only one is required
4. Incorrect business unit code (used for tracking product line profitability) on the order acknowledgment
5. Freight terms missing on the purchase order
6. Incorrect part number on order acknowledgment
7. Incorrect shipping or billing address on the order acknowledgment
8. Credit approval missing (all new customers have a credit approval before an order is processed)
9. Missing part number on order acknowledgment
10. Customer number terminated on the computer's database (an order cannot be processed if customer number is missing)
11. Incorrect sales tax calculation on the order acknowledgment
12. Part number mismatch on purchase order

Exhibit 7-19
Estimated Annual Failure Costs (as a Percentage of Order Entry's Annual Salary and Fringe Benefits Budget)

	ORDER ENTRY	OTHER DEPARTMENTS	TOTAL COSTS
Class I failure costs			
Quotations	1.1%	0.4%	1.5%
Orders	0.9%	1.7%	2.6%
Total Class I failure costs	2.0%	2.1%	4.1%
Class II failure costs			
Order acknowledgments	2.6%	4.4%	7.0%
Change orders	2.6%	—	2.6%
Final customers	0.02%	0.1%	0.12%
Return authorizations	1.9%	—	1.9%
Total Class II failure costs	7.12%	4.5%	11.62%
Total failure costs	9.12%	6.6%	15.72%

order acknowledgment) is sent to the final customer. Corrections of the order entry errors do not guarantee that the customer receives a good quality system, but order entry's initial errors do not then affect the final customer. Mistakes that affect the final customer can be made by individuals in other departments (e.g., manufacturing or shipping).

Sample data collected from PSI's users of order entry department information show that more than 20 types of errors can be found on the order acknowledgment (see Exhibit 7-18 for examples). The cost of correcting these errors (salary and fringe benefits of order entry person and a concerned person from another PSI department) accounts for approximately 7% of order entry's annual budget for salaries and fringe benefits (see Exhibit 7-19).

In addition to the time spent on correcting the errors, the order entry staff must prepare a change order for several of the Class II errors. A change order may be required for several other reasons that cannot necessarily be controlled by order entry. Examples include (1) changes in ship-to or bill-to address by customers or sales representatives, (2) canceled orders, and (3) changes in invoicing instructions. Regardless of the reason for a change order, the order entry department incurs some cost. The sample data suggest that for every 100 new orders, order entry prepares 71 change orders; this activity accounts for 2.6% of order entry's annual budget for salaries and fringe benefits (see Exhibit 7-19).

Although order entry's errors do not significantly affect final customers, customers who find errors on their invoices often use the errors as an excuse to delay payments. Correcting these errors involves the joint efforts of the order entry, collections, and invoicing departments; these costs account for about 0.12% of order entry's annual budget (see Exhibit 7-19).

The order entry staff also spends considerable time handling return authorizations when final customers send their shipments back to PSI. Interestingly, more than 17% of the goods returned are because of defective shipments, and more than 49% fall into the following two categories: (1) ordered in error and (2) 30-day return rights. An in-depth analysis of the latter categories suggests that a majority of these returns can be traced to sales or service errors. The order entry department incurs costs to process these return authorizations, which account for more than 1.9% of the annual budget (see Exhibit 7-19). The total Class I and Class II failure costs account for 15.72% of the order entry department's annual budget for salaries and fringe benefits. Although PSI users of order entry information were aware that problems in their departments were sometimes caused by errors in order entry, they provided little feedback to order entry about the existence or impact of the errors.

Changes in PSI's Order Entry Department

In October 1992, preliminary results of the study were presented to three key persons who had initiated the study: the order entry manager, the vice president of manufacturing, and the vice president of service and quality. In March 1993, the final results were presented to PSI's executive council, the top decision-making body. During this presentation, the CEO expressed alarm not only at the variety of quality problems reported, but also at the cost of correcting them. As a consequence, between October 1992 and March 1993, PSI began working toward obtaining the International Organization for Standardization's ISO 9002 registration for order entry and manufacturing practices, which it received in June 1993.

The effort to obtain the ISO 9002 registration suggests that PSI gave considerable importance to order entry and invested significant effort toward improving the order entry process. Nevertheless, as stated by the order entry manager, the changes would not have been so vigorously pursued if cost information had not been presented. COQ information functioned as a catalyst to accelerate the improvement effort. In actually making changes to the process, however, information pertaining to the different types of errors was more useful than the cost information.

Required

(a) Describe the role that assigning costs to order entry errors played in quality improvement efforts at Precision Systems, Inc.

(b) Prepare a diagram illustrating the flow of activities between the order entry department and its suppliers, internal customers (those within PSI), and external customers (those external to PSI).

(c) Classify the failure items in Exhibit 7-18 as internal failures (identified as defective before delivery to internal or external customers, that is, Class I failures) or external failures (nonconforming "products" delivered to internal or external customers, that is, Class II failures) with respect to the order entry department. For each external failure item, identify which of order entry's internal customers (that is, other departments within PSI who use information from the order acknowledgment) will be affected.

(d) For the order entry process, how would you identify internal failures and external failures, as defined in question (c)? Who would be involved in documenting these failures and their associated costs? Which individuals or departments should be involved in making improvements to the order entry process?

(e) What costs, in addition to salary and fringe benefits, would you include in computing the cost of correcting errors?

(f) Provide examples of incremental (fairly low-cost and easy to implement) and breakthrough (high-cost and relatively difficult or time consuming to implement) improvements that could be made in the order entry process. In particular, identify prevention activities that can be undertaken to reduce the number of errors. Describe how you would prioritize your suggestions for improvement.

(g) Discuss the issues that PSI should consider if it wishes to implement a web-based ordering system that permits customers to select configurations for systems.

(h) What nonfinancial quality indicators might be useful for the order entry department? How frequently should data be collected or information be reported? Can you make statements about the usefulness of cost-of-quality information in comparison to nonfinancial indicators of quality?

Chapter 8

Measuring and Managing Life-Cycle Costs

After completing this chapter, you will be able to:

1. Describe the total-life-cycle costing approach for managing product costs.
2. Explain target costing.
3. Compute target costs.
4. Calculate the breakeven time for a new product development project.
5. Select nonfinancial measures for product development processes.
6. Identify environmental costing issues.

Chemco International

Marais Young has just been appointed controller of a specialty chemical company after serving several years as senior manager of the manufacturing division. Although her performance was excellent in that division, she continually struggled with the narrow scope of the company's management accounting system.

The system focused solely on assigning the costs of the manufacturing process to products and did not provide any insight into premanufacturing and postmanufacturing costs, such as the cost of developing products and disposing of toxic waste from the production process and the used chemicals that had been returned by customers. Competition in the chemicals industry had increased dramatically, and Marais knew she needed to understand the total costs over the entire life cycle of the company's products.

She has heard that some companies in the industry have adopted an approach imported from Japan called target costing, which helps engineers lower the costs of products during the design and development stage. In addition, the variety of products produced by the company have different hazards and toxicities associated with them. With the cost of environmental compliance rising rapidly, Marais wanted to trace safety, take-back, recycling, and disposal costs to individual products in the same way that activity-based costing now allows the tracing of manufacturing costs to individual products, and MSDA costs to individual customers. She believed that better costing systems would help the company's managers and product and process engineers make better decisions about how to design, produce, recycle, and dispose of products over their entire life cycle.

MANAGING PRODUCTS OVER THEIR LIFE CYCLE

In the past several chapters, we have focused on measuring and improving product, customer, and process performance. Companies, however, should not only improve the profitability from existing products but also create new products and services. Successful innovation drives customer acquisition and growth, margin enhancement, and customer loyalty. Without innovation, a company's advantage in the marketplace will eventually be imitated, forcing it to compete solely on price for commodity products and services.

Companies, such as Apple, become the industry's leader and earn exceptional profits by bringing innovative products—well matched to targeted customers needs and expectations—to the market fast and efficiently. Product innovation is a prerequisite to even participate in some dynamic, technologically based industries, such as pharmaceuticals, specialty chemicals, semiconductors, telecommunications, and media.

Companies that continually bring new products to the market quickly must also be concerned about the environmental impact from their innovation, as customers discard their now obsolete products. Societal concerns about pollution have caused companies such as Xerox, HP, and Sony to measure the total life-cycle costs of their products, including the impact of raw material extraction, energy consumption during use, and, finally, salvage, recycling, and disposal. We refer to total-life-cycle costing (TLCC) as the approach companies now use to understand and manage all costs incurred in product design and development, through manufacturing, marketing, distribution, maintenance, service, and, finally, disposal (see Exhibit 8-1). Managing life-cycle costs is also known as managing costs "from the cradle to the grave."

The innovation process itself is expensive. One automotive component supplier discovered that it incurred 10% of its expenses during product design and development, whereas its entire production direct labor costs were 9% of expenses. Yet it monitored and controlled direct labor expense tightly, whereas its design and development group had hardly any management accounting system to monitor its rate of expenditure in R&D or to measure the performance of the new products that it released to the production department.

Beyond managing the costs of product development, engineers and managers must plan ahead for a product's production costs once its design and development have been

Exhibit 8-1
Cycle Comprising the Total-Life-Cycle Costing Approach

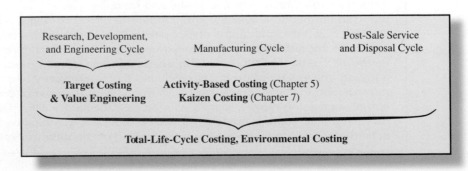

completed. After products reach the manufacturing stage, the opportunities for substantial cost reduction may be limited. Companies have learned that most of a product's costs are designed in during the research and development stages. And many companies are now planning for the postproduction costs of retrieving, recycling, and salvaging their products (referred to as product take-back) after their customers are finished using them.

Consider the situation faced by managers of the Burleson Company who have just learned about a new product concept that may revolutionize their business. Their initial research suggests to them that they can manufacture the product at a reasonably low cost, especially given the new technology that they have just acquired. They begin to consider how they can reorganize their operations to accommodate the production of the new product. Because they have only some preliminary ideas about the feasibility of product design, they approach their research, development, and engineering (RD&E) division for further investigation. The report from the RD&E group tells them that the product can be produced, but the cost of developing prototypes is 20 times more than the average prototype costs. RD&E confirms, however, that the actual cost to manufacture the product after the first year will be low as Burleson gains experience with the new technology. Thus, the initial life-cycle cost of the product may be high, but unit manufacturing costs should be relatively low. With this new information, managers of the division have to determine whether they should forge ahead with developing the new product in light of its high R&D costs, low manufacturing costs, and the opportunity costs of committing their scarce engineers for this project.

Each part of a company's value chain—new product development, production, distribution, marketing, sales, and postsales service and disposal—is typically managed by a different organizational function. Although costs may be collected and traced to each function, companies need a total-life-cycle perspective that integrates the trade-offs and performance over time and across functional units. From the company's perspective, total-life-cycle product costing integrates RD&E, manufacturing, and postsales service and disposal. Let us look at each.

Research, Development, and Engineering Stage

The research, development, and engineering (RD&E) stage consists of three substages:

1. *Market research*, during which emerging customer needs are assessed and ideas are generated for new products.
2. *Product design*, during which scientists and engineers develop the technical specifications of products.
3. *Product development*, during which the company creates features critical to customer satisfaction and designs prototypes, production processes, and any special tooling required.

By some estimates, 80% to 85% of a product's total life-cycle costs are committed by decisions made in the RD&E stage of the product's life (see Exhibit 8-2). Decisions made during this cycle can have a huge impact on the costs incurred in later stages. Spending an additional dollar in better design can often save $8 to $10 in manufacturing and postmanufacturing activities, by reducing the costs of design changes, service costs, and take-back and recycling costs.

Manufacturing Stage

After the RD&E stage, the company enters the manufacturing stage, in which it spends money—on materials, labor, machinery, and indirect costs—to produce and distribute the product. This stage offers little opportunity for engineering decisions to reduce product costs through redesign decisions since most costs have already been

Exhibit 8-2
Total-Life-Cycle
Costing:
Relationship
between
Committed Costs
and Incurred
Costs

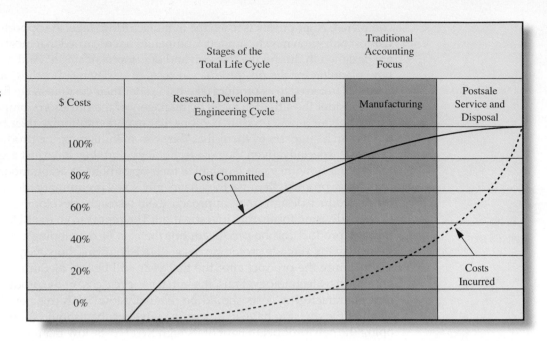

determined during the RD&E stage. In Exhibit 8-2, the lower curve illustrates how costs are incurred over both the RD&E and the manufacturing cycle. For moderate to long life-cycle products, the costs incurred during RD&E will be less than 10% of total-life-cycle costs. But the decisions made during the RD&E stage will determine 80% of the costs that will be incurred in subsequent stages. Traditional cost accounting and process improvement methods focus their attention on the manufacturing stage. This is the role for product and process costing, facilities layout, kaizen, benchmarking, and just-in-time manufacturing (discussed in Chapters 4 through 7). These methods help reduce product costs during the manufacturing stage. But they ignore the potential for effective cost management during the RD&E stage.

Postsale Service and Disposal Stage

In the third stage, companies incur costs for **postsale service and disposal**. Although the costs for service and disposal are committed in the RD&E stage, the actual service stage begins once the first unit of a product is in the hands of the customer. Thus, this stage overlaps somewhat with the manufacturing stage. It typically consists of three substages:

1. Rapid growth from the first time the product is shipped through the growth stage of its sales.
2. Transition from the peak of sales to the peak in the service cycle.
3. Maturity from the peak in the service cycle to the time of the last shipment made to a customer; disposal occurs at the end of a product's life and lasts until the customer retires the final unit of a product.

Disposal costs include those associated with eliminating any harmful effects associated with the end of a product's useful life. Products whose disposal could involve harmful effects to the environment, such as nuclear waste or other toxic chemicals, can incur very high salvage, recycling, and disposal costs.

A breakdown of costs for each of the functional life cycles will differ, depending on the industry and specific product produced. Exhibit 8-3 illustrates four types of products and the variation of costs over their total life cycles. For example, the manufacturing

Exhibit 8-3
Percentage of Life-Cycle Costs Incurred across Four Types of Products

STAGE OF LIFE CYCLE	TYPE OF PRODUCT			
CYCLE	COMBAT JETS	COMMERCIAL AIRCRAFT	NUCLEAR MISSILES	COMPUTER SOFTWARE
RD&E	21%	20%	20%	75%[a]
Manufacturing	45%	40%	60%	[a]
Service and disposal	34%	40%	20%	25%
Average length of life cycle	30 years	25 years	2 to 25 years	5 years

[a]For computer software, both RD&E and manufacturing are often tied directly together.

costs of the commercial aircraft company are approximately 40% of total incurred costs. RD&E and postsale service and disposal incur 20% and 40%, respectively. An understanding of total-life-cycle costs encourages product engineers to select product designs that make them easier to service and easier and less costly to dispose of at the end of their useful life. Computer software development during the RD&E stage creates and debugs the software code. It can cost 100 times more to correct a software defect during its operating stage than to prevent or catch the bug in the design phase.

TARGET COSTING

Japanese engineers in the 1960s developed an approach called **target costing** to help them consider manufacturing costs early in their design decisions. Target costing helps engineers design new products that meet customers' expectations and that can be manufactured at a desired cost. Target costing is an important management

Japanese camera companies use target costing to lower the manufacturing costs of a new generation of products during its research, development, and engineering stage.

Reuters Limited

Exhibit 8-4
A Comparison of the Process of Traditional U.S. and Japanese Cost Reduction Methods

TRADITIONAL U.S. COST REDUCTION	JAPANESE TARGET COSTING
Market research to determine customer requirements	Market research to determine consumer needs and price points
⇩	⇩
Product specification	Production specification and design
⇩	⇩
Design	Target selling price (S_{tc})
⇩	(and target product volume)
Engineering	
⇩	−
Supplier pricing	
⇩	Target profit (P_{tc})
ESTIMATED COST (C_t)	=
(if too high, return to design phase)	
Desired profit margin (P_t)	TARGET COST (C_{tc})
=	⇩
	Value engineering / Supplier cost reduction
	(Both value engineering and collaboration with suppliers are used to achieve the target costs for each component)
Expected selling price (S_t) − Estimated cost (C_t)	
⇩	⇩
Manufacturing	**Manufacturing**
⇩	⇩
Periodic cost reduction	Continuous cost reduction

accounting method for cost reduction during the design stage of a product's life cycle and one that can explicitly help to manage total-life-cycle costs.

The traditional product development method followed in the United States and other Western companies is shown as the left-hand column in Exhibit 8-4. It starts with market research into customer requirements for the new product, and the price they are willing to pay for a product that performs according to those requirements. From this research, engineers determine the product's specifications to deliver the desired performance. They then perform detailed product design and engineering for the product to meet its specifications.

After the product has been completely designed, the development team requests prices from raw materials and component suppliers, and production cost estimates from manufacturing engineers. This leads to the first estimate of the product's cost (C_t), where t indicates a product cost estimate derived from this traditional, sequential design and development process. The team then estimates the product's profit margin (P_t) by subtracting the estimated cost from the expected selling price (S_t), which has also been determined during the initial market research. The new product's profit margin is the difference between the expected selling price and the estimated production cost[1] as expressed in the following equation:

$$P_t = S_t - C_t$$

---

[1] Robin Cooper developed the structure for comparing costs in this manner in "Nissan Motor Company, Ltd.: Target Costing System," HBS No. 9-194-040 (Boston: Harvard Business School Publishing, 1994).

Another widely used approach, the cost-plus method, adds the desired profit margin for the product P_{cp} to the expected product cost (C_{cp}) where cp indicates numbers derived from the cost-plus method. This calculation yields the selling price (S_{cp}). In equation form, this relationship is expressed as follows:

$$S_{cp} = C_{cp} + P_{cp}$$

In both the traditional and cost-plus methods, product designers do not attempt to achieve a particular cost target. The company either accepts the profit margin allowed as the difference between the market-determined selling price and the estimated product cost, or it attempts to set the price sufficiently high to earn the desired margin over the product's cost, without paying much attention to customers' willingness to pay. In both methods, product development engineers do not attempt to actively influence the product's cost. They design the product to meet its specifications and accept the costs as the consequence of their design and development decisions.

Target costing, in contrast, strives to actively reduce a product's cost during its RD&E stage rather than wait until the product has been released into production to start the cost reduction, or kaizen, process. As previously noted, cost reduction during the manufacturing stage is generally more costly and less effective than during the RD&E stage. In target costing (see right-hand column of Exhibit 8-4), both the sequence of steps and the way of thinking about determining product costs differ significantly from traditional costing. Although the initial steps—market research to determine customer requirements and product specification—appear similar to traditional costing, target costing introduces some important differences. First, market research under target costing is not a single event as it often is under the traditional approach. Rather, the approach is *customer driven*, with customer input obtained continually throughout the process. Second, the product engineers attempt to design costs out of the product before design and development ends and manufacturing begins. This approach is particularly effective since, as previously stated, 80% or more of a product's total-life-cycle costs get committed during the RD&E cycle (review Exhibit 8-2). Third, target costing uses the total-life-cycle concept by adopting the perspective of minimizing the cost of ownership of a product over its useful life. Thus, not only are costs such as the initial purchase price considered, but so are the costs of operating, servicing, maintaining, repairing, and disposing of the product.

In a third target costing innovation, the engineers set an allowable cost for the product that enables the targeted product profit margin to be achieved at a price that customers are willing to pay. With this approach, a target selling price and target product volume are chosen on the basis of the company's perceived value of the product to the customer. The target profit margin results from a long-run profit analysis that is often based on return on sales (net income ÷ sales). Return on sales is the most widely used measure because it can be linked most closely to profitability for each product. The **target cost** is defined as the difference between the target selling price and the target profit margin. (Note that tc indicates numbers derived under the target costing approach.) This relationship for the target costing approach is shown in the following equation:

$$C_{tc} = S_{tc} - P_{tc}$$

Once the target cost has been set for the entire product, the engineers next determine the target costs for each component in the product. The **value engineering process** examines the design of each component to determine whether it is possible to reduce costs while maintaining functionality and performance. In some cases, the engineers can change the product's or component's design, substitute new materials, or modify and improve the manufacturing process. For example, a product redesign may enable the same functionality to be achieved but with fewer parts or with more common rather than unique parts.

Recall from activity-based costing that it is less expensive to produce 10% more from an existing production run than to change over to switch to a low-production run for a specialty component. It is less expensive to order 10% more of a component from an existing supplier than to find a new vendor to order a low quantity of a specialty component. All of these decisions and trade-offs are best made during the RD&E stage when the product's design is still fluid rather than during the manufacturing stage when it is far more costly to do a major redesign of a product. Several iterations of value engineering usually are needed before the final target cost gets achieved.

Two other differences characterize the target costing process. First, throughout the entire process, **cross-functional product teams** made up of individuals representing the entire value chain—both inside and outside the organization—guide the process. For example, it is not uncommon for a team to consist of people from inside the organization (such as design engineering, manufacturing operations, management accounting, and marketing) and representatives from outside the organization (including suppliers, customers, distributors, and waste disposers).

A second difference is that suppliers play a critical role in making target costing work. Often the company asks its suppliers to participate in finding ways to reduce the cost of specific components or an entire subassembly or module. Companies offer incentive plans to suppliers who come up with the largest cost reduction ideas. As companies work more closely with their suppliers during the RD&E stage, they use a set of methods collectively known as **supply chain management**. Supply chain management develops cooperative, mutually beneficial, long-term relationships between buyers and suppliers. The benefits are many. For example, as trust develops between buyer and supplier, decisions about how to resolve cost reduction problems can be made with shared information about various aspects of each other's operations. In some organizations, the buyer may even expend resources to train the supplier's employees in some aspect of the business, or a supplier may assign one of its employees to work with the buyer to understand a new product. Such interactions are quite different from the short-term, arms-length relationships that are characteristic of a transactions-based buyer–seller relationship.

A Target Costing Example

How does target costing actually work in practice?[2] We illustrate the target costing process with an example drawn from actual experiences but using a hypothetical company, Kitchenhelp, Inc.

Among other products, Kitchenhelp manufactures coffeemakers. Market research has identified eight features of a coffeemaker that are important to customers:

1. Coffee tastes and smells like espresso.
2. The coffeemaker is easy to take apart and clean.
3. Capacity is at least six cups.
4. The coffeemaker has an attractive design (since it is continually visible as it sits on a kitchen counter).
5. The coffeemaker has a clock timer to start automatically at a designated time.
6. The grinder performs well with different kinds of coffee beans.
7. The coffeemaker keeps the coffee warm after making it.
8. The coffeemaker automatically shuts off after a designated time period.

---

[2] We thank Shahid Ansari, Jan Bell, Tom Klammer, and Carol Lawrence for allowing us to use this example from their book *Target Costing* (Boston: Houghton Mifflin Company, 2004).

These customer requirements become the basis for the engineering design of the coffeemaker. Engineers must ensure that the product encompasses all of the features that are important to customers. Assume that Kitchenhelp's current coffeemaker unit costs $50 to manufacture. Management has decided that the cost of the new unit has to be reduced to broaden its appeal to a much larger customer audience.[3] Product engineers perform cost analysis and value engineering to reduce the cost of each of the coffeemaker's components.

Cost Analysis

For Kitchenhelp, cost analysis involves determining what components of the coffeemaker (heating element, control panel, or grinder) to target for cost reduction and then assigning a cost target to each of these components. Cost analysis also focuses on the interaction between components and parts. Often a reduction in the cost of one component may be more than offset by a cost increase elsewhere. For example, decreasing the cost of the outer shell of the coffeemaker by making it smaller may increase the costs of shrinking the size of the control panel, electronic circuitry, and heating element. Cost analysis requires five subactivities:

1. **Develop a list of product components and functions.** Cost reduction efforts start by listing the various product components and identifying the functions that they perform and their current estimated cost. The initial product design and cost estimates provide this information. The list tells us what components and functions are needed to satisfy customer requirements and what it might cost to provide these functions. Exhibit 8-5 shows a diagram of the various components of the proposed coffeemaker.

2. **Perform a functional cost breakdown.** Each of the various parts and components of the coffeemaker performs a specific function. The next step is to identify that function and to estimate the cost. The functional cost breakdown is shown in

Exhibit 8-5
Major Components of Kitchenhelp's Proposed Coffeemaker

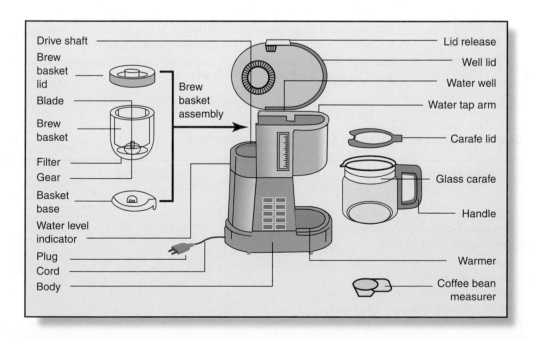

---

[3] To simplify the example, we assume that selling, general, and administrative costs stay the same, although in practice these costs can change as well.

Exhibit 8-6
Functional Cost
Breakdown for
Kitchenhelp's
Coffeemaker

		COST	
COMPONENT	FUNCTION	AMOUNT	PERCENT
Brew basket	Grinds and filters coffee	$9	18%
Carafe	Holds and keeps coffee warm	2	4
Coffee warmer	Keeps coffee warm	3	6
Body shape and water well	Holds water and encasement	9	18
Heating element	Warms water and pushes it	4	8
Electronic display panel	Controls grinder/clock settings	23	46
Total		$50	100%

Exhibit 8-6. For example, the function of the brew basket is to grind and filter coffee. The current estimated cost is $9 for the basket, which represents 18% of the total manufacturing cost for this product. To keep the example simple, we have combined several functions and components for the coffeemaker. At a detail level, the brew basket or the electronic control panel will be broken into several subcomponents. The total for all components is $50.

3. **Determine the relative importance of customers' requirements.** Engineers often have a different view of a product's functionality than customers. Recall that Kitchenhelp had identified eight features important to its customers. The engineer's view of a product as a collection of functions must be reconciled with a customer's view of a product as a set of performance features. To connect a product's functions to the features that customers want, engineers first assess the relative importance that customers place on the various features. They conduct a formal survey of prospective customers asking them to rank the relative importance of the product's eight features. The results from this survey are shown in Exhibit 8-7. The importance ranking is based on a scale from 1 to 5, where a 5 means that the feature is very important and a score of 1 indicates that it is unimportant. From this exhibit, we learn that the taste and smell of coffee is the most important feature, and multiple grinder settings is the least important.

Exhibit 8-7
Customer Feature Ranking for Kitchenhelp's Coffeemaker

CUSTOMER REQUIREMENTS	CUSTOMER RANKING			RELATIVE RANKING
	1 NOT IMPORTANT		5 VERY IMPORTANT	IN PERCENT
Coffee tastes and smells like espresso			5	20%
Coffeemaker is easy to clean			4	16
Looks nice		2		8
Has 6+ cup capacity			3	12
Starts automatically at designated time			4	16
Works well with different coffee beans	1			4
Keeps the coffee warm			3	12
Automatically shuts off			3	12
Total				100%

The last column of Exhibit 8-7 converts the raw scores for the importance of features into a relative ranking of features. The total feature score is 25 (calculated as $5 + 4 + 2 + 3 + 4 + 1 + 3 + 3 = 25$) and each feature's score gets expressed as a percentage of this total score of 25. For example, coffee taste has a ranking of 20% (a score of 5 out of 25) indicating that 20% of the total value a customer derives from this coffeemaker comes from the taste of the coffee.

4. **Relating features to functions.** Engineers can now convert the relative rankings of features into an importance ranking for each product function. Since components carry out the functions of a product and are the key design parameters, this step relates customer rankings to the components that best meet that particular requirement. The engineers use a tool called a quality function deployment (QFD) matrix for displaying the information about these three variables—features, functions (components), and competitive evaluation—in a matrix format.

The QFD matrix (see Exhibit 8-8 for Kitchenhelp's coffeemaker) highlights the relationships among competitive offerings, customer requirements, and design parameters. The QFD matrix summarizes the information about product functions from Exhibit 8-6 with customer rankings from Exhibit 8-7. It adds two other pieces of information that have been collected during market research: the correlation between a component or design parameter and customer requirements and information about how customers evaluate competitor offerings on these same features.

The matrix shows that the requirement that the coffee taste like espresso has a high correlation with the design of the brew basket and the heating element. Similarly, how many cups the coffeemaker can hold is correlated to the water well and carafe size. It also shows that taste, the most important feature to a customer, is currently rated at 3 for Kitchenhelp and 2 for its competitor. This tells Kitchenhelp that while it is ahead of the competition, it still is far from the customer's ideal taste experience. On appearance, the competition obviously has a better looking product, with a rating of 5. However, the customer ranking for this feature is 2, which suggests that Kitchenhelp should not spend much of its resources to improve the coffeemaker's appearance.

Exhibit 8-8
A QFD Matrix for Kitchenhelp's Coffeemaker

COMPONENTS OR FUNCTIONS →	BREW BASKET	CARAFE	COFFEE WARMER	BODY/ WATER WELL	HEATING ELEMENT	DISPLAY PANEL	COMPARISON COMPETITOR VS. OUR PRODUCT 1 2 3 4 5	CUSTOMER FEATURE RANKING
CUSTOMER REQUIREMENTS ↓								
Tastes/smells like espresso	▲				▲		■ ❑	5
Easy to clean	●	●		▲			❑ ■	4
Looks nice				▲		▲	❑ ■	2
Has 6+ cup capacity		▲		▲			■ ❑	3
Starts automatically on time						▲	❑ ■	4
Works with different beans	○					▲	■ ❑	1
Keeps the coffee warm		●	▲				■ ❑	3
Automatic shutoff						▲	❑ ■	3

Correlation of design parameters and customer requirements:
▲ = Strong correlation
● = Moderate correlation
○ = Weak correlation

Comparative competitor rankings:
■ = Competitor ranking
❑ = Our ranking

Exhibit 8-9
Kitchenhelp Coffeemaker: Percentage Contribution of Each Component to Customer Requirements

Components → Customer Requirements ↓	Brew Basket	Carafe	Coffee Warmer	Body/ Water Well	Heating Element	Display Panel	Relative Feature Ranking
Tastes/smells like espresso	50% × 20 = 10					50% × 20 = 10	20%
Easy to clean	30% × 16 = 4.8	10% × 16 = 1.6		60% × 16 = 9.6			16
Looks nice				60% × 8 = 4.8		40% × 8 = 3.2	8
Has 6+ cup capacity		50% × 12 = 6		50% × 12 = 6			12
Starts automatically on time						100% × 16 = 16	16
Has multiple grinder settings	5% × 4 = 0.2					95% × 4 = 3.8	4
Keeps the coffee warm		20% × 12 = 2.4	80% × 12 = 9.6				12
Automatic shutoff						100% × 12 = 12	12
Converted component ranking	15.0	10.0	9.6	20.4	10.0	35.0	100%

5. **Develop relative functional rankings.** The QFD matrix enabled the engineers to convert feature rankings into functional or component rankings, shown as a general association in Exhibit 8-8. This is valuable but the engineers still need one additional piece of information: the percentage that each component contributes to a customer feature, as shown in Exhibit 8-9. You can see in this exhibit that the feature "Tastes/ smells like espresso" depends on the design of the brew basket and heating element (an association also shown in Exhibit 8-8). Engineers feel that the brew basket and heating element component contribute equally to the "taste" feature, and they assign each a 50% contribution to taste. The relative value ranking of the "taste" feature is 20%. Therefore, since both components contribute equally, they assign each of the two components a value ranking of 10%. The last row of Exhibit 8-9 shows *each component's approximate value to a customer* by adding up all the value contributions from a component to all customer-desired features. You can see that the brew basket component has an overall value of 15% to a customer, and that the carafe has a value of 10%. Note that the last row and last column add up to 100%. They are simply different views of customer values. The last column represents the value of each feature, and the last row represents the value of each component that delivers the desired features.

Conduct Value Engineering
Once the five-step cost analysis has been completed, engineers start the value engineering (VE) activity. During VE, engineers analyze the functions of the various components and attempt to improve the components' and product's design to lower overall cost without reductions in required performance, reliability, maintainability, quality, safety, recyclability, and usability. For example, the purpose or function of a heating element is to heat water to a desired temperature. Value engineering asks how the function of raising room temperature water to 110 degrees within three minutes can be accomplished at a lower cost. It analyzes both product and manufacturing process design and reduces costs by generating ideas for simplifying both.

Exhibit 8-10
Value Index for Kitchenhelp's Coffeemaker

COMPONENT OR FUNCTION	COMPONENT COST (% OF TOTAL) (EX. 8-6)	RELATIVE IMPORTANCE (EX. 8-9) (IN %)	VALUE INDEX (COL 3 ÷ 2)	ACTION IMPLIED
Brew basket	18	15.0	0.83	Reduce cost
Carafe	4	10.0	2.50	Enhance
Coffee warmer	6	9.6	1.60	Enhance
Body shape and water well	18	20.4	1.13	O.K.
Heating element	8	10.0	1.25	Enhance
Electronic display panel	46	35.0	0.76	Reduce cost
	100%	100%		

Value engineering is a key activity within target costing and consists of the following two subactivities:

1. **Identify components for cost reduction.** Choosing which components to select requires computing a **value index**. This is the ratio of the value (degree of importance) to the customer and the percentage of total cost devoted to each component. For the coffeemaker, the value information appears in the last row of Exhibit 8-9, and the relative cost information is in the last column of Exhibit 8-6. Both of these quantities are expressed as percentages. Exhibit 8-10 shows the value index calculation and its implications for cost reduction. Components with a value index of less than 1 are candidates for value engineering. Components with a high value index are candidates for enhancement since we are spending too little for a feature that is important to the customer. These components present an opportunity to enhance the product. Cost and relative importance are plotted in Exhibit 8-11.

The optimal value zone in Exhibit 8-11 indicates the value band in which no action is necessary. The optimal value zone is based on the experience and opinions of target costing team members. The zone is usually wider at the bottom of the value index chart, where low importance and low cost occur, and narrower at the top, where features are important and cost variations are larger. The area of the graph above the optimal value zone indicates components that are candidates for cost reduction. Items below the zone are candidates for enhancement.

Exhibit 8-11
Value Index Chart
for Kitchenhelp's
Coffeemaker

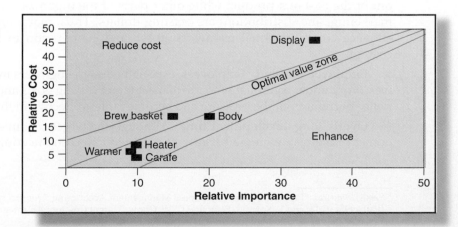

Exhibit 8-12
Kitchenhelp
Coffeemaker:
Electronic Display
Panel Value
Engineering Ideas
to Reduce Cost

PANEL SUBCOMPONENT	COST REDUCTION IDEA
Power supply	**Reduce** wattage—more than needed in current design.
Flexible circuit	**Eliminate** flexible circuit. Use wiring harness.
Printed wire board	**Standardize** board specifications. Use mass-produced unit.
Clock timer	**Combine** with printed wire board.
Central processor chip	**Substitute** standard 8088 chip instead of custom design.
Heater connector	**Rearrange** layout of board to heater connection.

2. **Generate cost reduction and function enhancement ideas.** Engineers engage in creative thinking and brainstorming to identify what can be reduced, eliminated, combined, substituted, rearranged, or enhanced to provide the same or higher level of functionality from a component at less cost. Exhibit 8-12 lists several of the cost reduction ideas that Kitchenhelp's engineers have proposed to reduce the cost of the electronic display panel, the prime target for cost reduction identified by the value index. Perhaps reducing the number of parts, simplifying the assembly, and not overengineering the product beyond what a customer needs will lower cost. Finally, testing and implementing ideas is the last subactivity within value engineering. Promising ideas are evaluated to ensure that they are technically feasible and acceptable to customers.

Concerns about Target Costing

Although target costing has some obvious advantages, some studies of target costing indicate potential problems in implementation, especially if a focus on meeting the target cost diverts attention away from the other elements of overall company goals.[4] Consider the following examples:

1. **Lack of understanding of the target costing concept.** For many in the West, target costing is not a mainstream concept. Without a clear understanding of the benefits, many senior executives reject the idea.

2. **Poor implementation of the teamwork concept.** Teamwork and trust issues can lead to significant problems in implementing target costing. In some cases, companies put excessive pressure on subcontractors and suppliers to conform to schedules and reduce costs. This can lead to alienation or failure of the subcontractor. Sometimes design engineers become upset when other parts of the organization are not cost conscious; they argue that they exert much effort to squeeze pennies out of the cost of a product while other parts of the organization (administration, marketing, and distribution) are wasting dollars. Thus, many organizations must enhance cross-functional teamwork, trust, and cooperation to succeed at target costing.

3. **Employee burnout.** Employees, especially design engineers in Japanese companies, work under continual pressure to meet target costing goals and eventually experience burnout from the pressure and become far less effective in their jobs.

4. **Overly long development time.** Although the target cost might be met, development time may increase because of repeated value engineering cycles to reduce

---

[4] See M. Sakurai, "Past and Future of Japanese Management Accounting," *Journal of Cost Management* (Fall 1995): 1–14; and Y. Kato, G. Boer, and C. W. Chow, "Target Costing: An Integrated Management Process," *Journal of Cost Management* (Spring 1995): 39–51.

Target Costing and the Mercedes-Benz M-Class

In the early 1990s, Mercedes-Benz wanted to develop a new line of SUVs, the Mercedes-Benz M-Class. Production began in 1997 at the Tuscaloosa plant in Alabama. Mercedes decided to use target costing to help them define costs before they were committed. Mercedes relied on a number of customer, design, product, and marketing clinics before manufacturing the product and determined that safety, comfort, economy, and styling were the four key characteristics that customers were concerned about. Engineers determined that the key components for the automobile were the chassis, transmission, air conditioner, electrical system, and other systems.

Using an approach very similar to the one used for design and development of the Kitchenhelp coffeemaker, Mercedes determined the relationships among customer requirements and engineering components. What follows is an illustration of how the final value index for the Mercedes-Benz M-Class might look. The value index shows that both the chassis and the air conditioner could be enhanced, while the transmission, electrical system, and other systems' costs could be reduced.

COMPONENT OR FUNCTION	COMPONENT COST (% OF TOTAL)	RELATIVE IMPORTANCE (%)	VALUE INDEX	ACTION IMPLIED
Chassis	20	33	1.65	Enhance
Transmission	25	20	0.80	Reduce cost
Air conditioner	5	7	1.40	Enhance
Electrical systems	7	6	0.86	Reduce cost
Other systems	43	35	0.81	Reduce cost

Source: Professor Thomas L. Albright, "Use of Target Costing in Developing the Mercedes-Benz M Class," class presentation, University of Alabama.

costs, ultimately leading to the product coming late to market. For some types of products, being six months late may be far more costly than having small cost overruns.

Companies may find it possible to manage many of these factors, but organizations interested in using the target costing process should be aware of them before immediately attempting to adopt this cost reduction method. The behavioral issues associated with motivating employees to meet ambitious targets are particularly important to consider. We will discuss these issues more fully in Chapter 9. Despite these concerns, target costing does provide engineers and managers with a great tool at the time of greatest leverage, the RD&E stage, to reduce total-life-cycle product costs.

A survey conducted by Kobe University of Japanese companies showed that of those responding, 100% of transportation equipment manufacturers, 75% of precision equipment manufacturers, 88% of electrical manufacturers, and 83% of machinery manufacturers stated that they used target costing.[5] These companies had been experiencing diminishing returns from their kaizen costing and just-in-time production systems and were looking for new opportunities to reduce manufacturing and service costs by focusing on cost reduction activities that could be accomplished during the RD&E stage.[6]

In the United States, target costing has gained momentum as a management method; however, it is not only a method of cost control but also a comprehensive

---

[5] See Kato et al., "Target Costing."
[6] See R. Cooper and R. Slagmulder, *Target Costing and Value Engineering* (Portland, OR: Productivity Press, 1997).

approach to profit planning and cost management. Companies such as Boeing, Texas Instruments, Eastman Kodak, and DaimlerChrysler have successfully adopted target costing in their businesses.[7]

BREAKEVEN TIME: A COMPREHENSIVE METRIC FOR NEW PRODUCT DEVELOPMENT

New product development requires work to be performed by many of an organization's departments: marketing, engineering, finance, operations, sales, and service. In many companies, the work in these various departments is not coordinated well; each department does its own job by receiving inputs from one or more departments, performing its work, and, when finished, handing its work output to another department. Such fragmented, compartmentalized activities lead to poor hand-offs between departments, delays, high costs, and frequent errors.

Product development delays are particularly problematic since delaying the launch of a product into the market by six months can cost a company up to 35% of the product's lifetime profits, a far more consequential loss than exceeding the project's R&D budget by 10%. Target costing, as we described, does an excellent job of reducing total-life-cycle costs. But like all cost-based measures, it does not reflect all of the economic factors associated with creating value for customers and shareholders. Companies that are attempting to manage an intangible asset such as their new product pipeline are particularly in need of nonfinancial measures, the motivation for the Balanced Scorecard that we discussed in Chapter 2.

Several decades ago, Hewlett-Packard engineers developed a comprehensive metric for the product development process, called the **breakeven time (BET)**, to motivate and measure the benefits from cross-functional integration during the product development cycle.[8] BET measures the length of time from the project's beginning until the product has been introduced and generated enough profit to pay back the investment originally made in its development (see Exhibit 8-13). BET brings together in a single measure three critical elements in an effective and efficient product development process. First, for the company to break even on its RD&E process, its investment in the product development process must be recovered. So BET requires tracking the entire cost of the design and development process.[9] It provides incentives to make the product development process faster and less costly. Second, BET stresses profitability. It encourages marketing managers, manufacturing personnel, and design engineers to work together to develop a product that meets real customer needs, including offering the product through an effective sales channel at an attractive price, and at a manufacturing cost that enables the company to earn profits that can repay the product development investment cost. Third, BET is denominated in time: it encourages the launch of new products faster than the competition so that higher sales can be earned sooner to repay the product development investment.

Beyond the technical aspects of the BET measure, which we will illustrate shortly, success in improving the comprehensive measure encourages collaboration and

---

[7] See J. Dutton and M. Ferguson, "Target Costing at Texas Instruments," *Journal of Cost Management* (Fall 1996): 33–38.

[8] Charles H. House and Raymond L. Price, "The Return Map: Tracking Product Teams," *Harvard Business Review* (January–February 1991): 92–100; also Marvin L. Patterson, "Designing Metrics," Chapter 3 in *Accelerating Innovation: Improving the Process of Product Development* (New York: Van Nostrand Reinhold, 1993).

[9] For financial reporting purposes, research and development expenses are expensed each reporting period (fiscal year quarter) so many companies never accumulate in one account the total spending on a project over the multiple periods required for the RD&E stage.

Exhibit 8-13
Illustration of
Breakeven Time

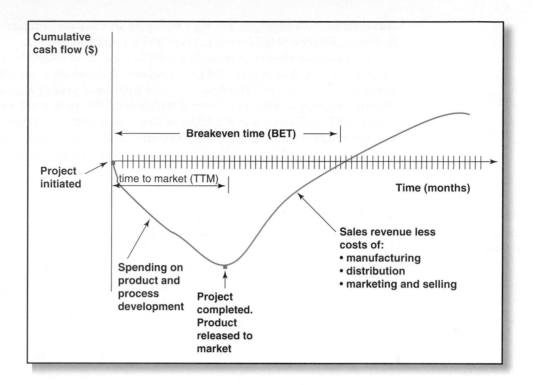

integration across organizational functions. It allows people from different disciplines to come together at the start of every product development project to estimate the time and money they require to perform their tasks, and the impact of their efforts on the success of the entire project. The metric facilitates discussion and decision making during the project among people from the multiple functions as more information about the project, customers, and competitors becomes available.

The breakeven time graph (see Exhibit 8-13) plots cumulative profits on the y or vertical axis, and elapsed time on the x or horizontal axis. Initially, the company spends on market research and on developing the technical specifications for the new product, such as its features, target cost and price, feasibility of the proposed manufacturing technology and processes, and preliminary project plan. These initial costs, at the start of the project, cause the project's profit curve to head in the negative direction since the project is unprofitable at this point. If the project is approved for further development, additional costs get incurred for product development, value engineering, building prototypes, testing, and doing the engineering changes to develop a feasible product along with its associated manufacturing processes. The RD&E stage ends when the company makes a commitment to produce, sell, and deliver the product.

As production gears up during the manufacturing stage, sales get realized and, as assumed in Exhibit 8-13, if the sales revenues exceed the production, marketing, sales, and distribution costs of the product, the cumulative profitability curve finally heads upward. Eventually, the company hopes that the profits earned over the initial years of the product's launch will repay its front-end marketing research and all RD&E costs. BET measures how long it takes for these initial costs to be recovered. Of course, the goal is not just to break even but to earn a substantial profit from the new product launch. To keep the analysis simple, the HP engineers found that a focus on the time required just to break even on the project stimulated a productive and collaborative dialogue among employees in the marketing, engineering, manufacturing, finance, sales, logistics, and service departments.[10]

We illustrate these points with a simple numerical example. Consider the data shown in panel A of Exhibit 8-14 for Greyson Technology's launch of a new digital communications device. The project's cross-functional project team prepared the data shown in panel A after extensive discussion of the new product's specification's, estimated RD&E time, and the likely selling price, manufacturing cost, rate of sales, and incremental marketing, distribution, sales, and service costs. The team anticipated that market research and subsequent product development would take seven quarters

Exhibit 8-14
Greyson Technology New Product Introduction

Panel A

	Y1, Q1	Y1, Q2	Y1, Q3	Y1, Q4	Y2, Q1	Y2, Q2	Y2, Q3	Y2, Q4	Y3, Q1	Y3, Q2	Y3, Q3	Y3, Q4
Market research*	(100)	(50)										
Product development*		(80)	(200)	(200)	(200)	(200)	(60)					
Selling price							20	20	20	19	19	18
Cost per unit							12	11	10	10	10	10
Margin/unit							8	9	10	9	9	8
Sales quantity*							25	40	50	50	50	50
Contribution*							200	360	500	450	450	400
MSDA expenses*							80	100	120	120	120	120
Product profit*							120	260	380	330	330	280
Quarterly profit/loss*	(100)	(130)	(200)	(200)	(200)	(200)	60	260	380	330	330	280
Cumulative profit/loss*	(100)	(230)	(430)	(630)	(830)	(1,030)	(970)	(710)	(330)	–	330	610

Panel B

	Y1, Q1	Y1, Q2	Y1, Q3	Y1, Q4	Y2, Q1	Y2, Q2	Y2, Q3	Y2, Q4	Y3, Q1	Y3, Q2	Y3, Q3	Y3, Q4
Market research*	(100)	(50)										
Product development*		(100)	(250)	(250)	(250)	(250)						
Selling price						22	22	22	22	20	20	20
Cost per unit						12	11	10	10	10	10	10
Margin/unit						10	11	12	12	10	10	10
Sales quantity*						30	40	50	50	50	50	50
Contribution*						300	440	600	600	500	500	500
MSDA expenses*						80	100	120	120	120	120	120
Product profit*						220	340	480	480	380	380	380
Quarterly profit/loss*	(100)	(150)	(250)	(250)	(250)	(30)	340	480	480	380	380	380
Cumulative profit/loss*	(100)	(250)	(500)	(750)	(1,000)	(1,030)	(690)	(210)	270	650	1,030	1,410

*In thousands

---

[10] As introduced at HP and illustrated here, the BET metric does not account for the time-value of money. This is a significant omission for most development projects where the BET is measured in several years. It is a simple extension to use net present value techniques (not discussed in this textbook) to calculate a discounted breakeven time metric, which will always be longer than the undiscounted version described in this chapter.

(20 months) to launch the new product, and a total of $1,090,000 of spending over this time period. Once launched, the team expected that the product would have a selling price of $20 per unit, cost per unit of $12, and first quarter sales of 25,000 units. It also estimated the MSDA expenses associated with this new product ($80,000 in the initial quarter, increasing up to $120,000 in future quarters). The team anticipated some modest production cost reductions due to learning effects and application of kaizen costing during the first few months of production. It also forecasted that as the market for the device matured and lower cost competitors entered, the selling price and margins would begin to erode.

Combining all of these data—product development time and cost, selling prices, production costs, sales quantities over time, and MSDA expenses—the example shows a BET of 30 months; the product recovers its $1,090,000 development costs at the end of the second quarter in year 3. Although the actual calculation of BET is simple, its calculation requires the active participation of key employees from multiple departments to provide information on new product features and functionality, development time and cost, expected selling price and volumes, and expected manufacturing and MSDA costs over the product's useful lifetime.

The BET metric allows the product development team to conduct sensitivity analyses on key parameters in the product's development process. Many companies, when financial difficulties arise, respond by slowing down the spending on new product development. But this action will delay the time when the product comes to the market; at this later date, the product will likely be be a follower, not a product leader; as such, it will command a lower selling price and generate lower sales volumes. Quarterly financial reporting shows the benefits from reduced spending on RD&E but not the loss in future revenues and profits from bringing the product to market a year or two later. By having a metric such as BET readily available, perhaps Greyson's managers will see that reducing the spending on RD&E now causes a much larger loss in future cash flows.

Consider the alternative scenario shown in panel B of Exhibit 8-14 in which the development team contemplates accelerating product development by spending more during the RD&E stage. For example, they plan to raise spending by $50,000 per quarter to $250,000 between year 1, quarter 3, and year 2, quarter 2. Because of the higher and more intensive spending, Greyson launches the product three months earlier. This brings the product to market faster, opening up a longer lead time before competitors can offer rival products with similar functionality. As a consequence, the initial selling price is 10% higher and opening period sales are also somewhat higher. Even with the higher total spending on RD&E in the panel B scenario, Greyson breaks even on the project in the middle of year 3, quarter 1, five months earlier than in the original scenario. Of course, the sustainable profits, beyond the breakeven time, are also substantially higher in the panel B scenario because of the advantages from being the first-to-market with the new technology.

Among the other scenarios to consider might be a product with less innovative functionality, which would require a shorter and less expensive development time, but also lower market share, and lower selling price and a longer BET. Conversely, the development team can also debate, at the start of the project, the consequences from a longer and more expensive product development process caused by attempting to meet highly demanding specifications from the marketing study.

The BET metric is not a decision-making tool. It does, however, offer a means by which a multifunctional product development team can conduct productive discussions and make trade-offs between the time, cost, and functionality of new product proposals along with the product's anticipated sales volume and prices, and production and other organizational costs.

The BET metric is a good example of the use of a nonfinancial measure to supplement financial measures, such as target cost, for managing a company's total-life-cycle costs. Before turning to additional **nonfinancial measures of innovation**, we first mention other financial measures that companies use to motivate and evaluate the success of their innovation and product development processes. Companies, such as 3M, that have a strategy to continually introduce new products measure their success by the percentage of sales from products launched within, say, the past 24 months. Another financial metric of new product success would be the gross margin of newly introduced products. Companies that rely only on an innovation metric such as percentage of revenues from new products might find that their engineers begin to introduce new products that are merely line extensions of existing products. For example, the laser-jet printer when first introduced was a major new product platform. But versions 2.0, 3.0, and 4.0 of this product, while representing incremental new design features, were basically built off of the original product platform innovation. The new versions replace, some would say cannibalize, existing versions so sales from the new products will increase. But over time, the company's products will become stale, copied by competitive offerings, and prices and margins will decline.

A truly innovative new product, such as Amazon.com's Kindle e-book reader and Apple's iPad, generates far higher margins than existing products. So an attractive financial metric for evaluating the success of new product introductions would be *gross margins from new products*. Version 1.0 of a revolutionary product will enjoy high margins, whereas the release, 10 years later, of version 9.0 of this product will earn the same or lower margins than the version it replaced.

Financial measures alone, however, cannot drive a company's success in new product development. Companies, especially those following a strategy of innovation and product leadership, need nonfinancial measures to motivate and evaluate their innovation activities. Let's look at several objectives and measures that can appear in the process perspective of a company's Balanced Scorecard to evaluate the effectiveness and efficiency of its innovation process.

Market Research and Generation of New Product Ideas

Some typical objectives and measures for the market research and idea generation stage include the following:

Objectives for Generating New Ideas	Measures
Anticipate future customer needs.	• Time spent with targeted customers learning about their future opportunities and needs • Number of new projects launched based on customer input
Discover and develop new, more effective, or safer products/services.	• Number of new projects or concepts presented for development • Number of new value-added services identified

Design, Development, and Launch of New Products

Once ideas for new products and services have been accepted, we can think of various objectives and measures to guide the RD&E stage:

Objectives for Managing the RD&E Process	Measures
Develop innovative new products offering superior performance.	• Potential value of products in project pipeline • Customer feedback and revenue projections based on prototypes of products in pipeline • Number of patents; number of patent citations[11]
Reduce product development cycle time.	• Number of projects delivered on time • Average time spent by projects at the development, test, and launch stages of the development process • Total RD&E time: from idea to market
Manage development cycle cost.	• Actual vs. budgeted spending on projects at each development stage
Launch the new product into production	• Manufacturing cost of new products: actual vs. target cost • Number of failures or returns of new products from customers • Warranty and field service costs • Consumer satisfaction or complaints about new products launched

The new product development process is one of the most important that organizations perform if they are to avoid extreme price competition on nondifferentiated products and services. Yet many companies' management accounting systems focus only on operations and production costs and do not apply the same rigor and discipline to their innovation processes. As a consequence, their innovation processes take longer, incur higher costs, and deliver products that are more expensive to produce than they need to be. In this chapter, we have introduced new management accounting tools, such as target costing and nonfinancial metrics, to improve both the effectiveness and the efficiency of innovation processes.

IN PRACTICE
Life-Cycle Revenues: The Case of Motion Pictures

In this chapter, we have discussed life-cycle costing. The other side of this issue is life-cycle revenues. The motion picture industry provides a good example where we can examine life-cycle revenues.

In 2008, consumers worldwide spent more than $50 billion watching U.S. movies in a variety of formats. Until the early 1970s, consumers in the United States had only a few ways in which they could enjoy a movie: They could see it during its theatrical release, attend a film festival or revival, or view it long after theatrical release on one of the three major television networks (ABC, NBC, or CBS). During this era, the main sources of revenues for the studios came from theatrical release, international sales, and network television.

Today the viewing options for consumers and, hence, the revenue streams for the studios have increased significantly as content delivery systems continue to evolve. Because studios rely on a variety of revenue streams, new technologies allow the industry to remain viable in turbulent times. Nevertheless, the theatrical release of a movie is still the single most important indicator of success and offers a critical means by which to evaluate industry trends.

(continued)

---

[11] Number of patents and patent citations has been identified in B. Lev, *Intangibles: Management, Measurement, and Reporting* (Washington, DC: Brookings Institution Press, 2001): 57–61, as a key indicator of research output.

To maximize their television license revenue, studios divide the licensing of their movies into discrete time periods, known as "windows of exhibition," as listed in the following table:

WINDOWS OF EXHIBITION FOR MOVIES

SOURCES	WINDOW
Domestic box office (theaters)	Initial theatrical release 2 weeks to 6 months
Home video (VHS/DVD)	Exclusive window of only 6 weeks before release to pay-per-view
Pay-per-view	Exclusive window from 2 to 6 weeks before release to premium channels
Premium pay channels (pay TV)	Exclusive window for up to 18 months before release to network and cable TV
Network (free) and cable TV	Up to 12 to 18 months before release to syndication
Syndication	60 months on either network television or cable network

Note: Omitted from the distribution channels and windows are foreign sales, hotel and airline viewings, college campus showings, the video game sector, consumer products merchandising, and theme parks. Foreign sales usually begin after the initial theatrical release in the United States. Each territory has different windows for different channels. Video games based on blockbuster movies sometimes earn equivalent revenues as theatrical releases.

Domestic Box Office. In 2008, overall box office performance reached an all-time high of $9.8 billion and, although this number may be seen as good news, the percentage of the population that actually goes to a movie theater to watch a movie has been in decline. Second, box office revenues have reached this record level due primarily to the large increases in ticket prices. Third, in 2008, movie piracy, especially illegal downloads from the Internet, has reduced studios' revenues by more than $6.1 billion.

Faced with a decline in patrons at the box office, increased competition from other entertainment options, and piracy of its content, the major studios are constantly assessing new revenue streams. Currently, the major sources of revenue (outside of theater releases) come from home video; network, satellite, and cable television; international distribution; the Internet; and mobile devices.

Home Video. The development of home video tapes in VHS format in the mid-1970s as a highly profitable post-theatrical release option fundamentally altered the economic structure of the film industry and its market practices. In 1997, the first digital versatile disc (DVD) players were sold in the United States. DVDs quickly became the industry standard and today VHS tapes are no longer produced for new films. In 2008, DVD sales accounted for $16.2 billion, and DVD rentals generated revenues of $7.5 billion; however, DVD sales are on the decline. Based on a 9% drop in 2008, projections are that DVD sales will decline 8% in 2009. The decline is attributed to the high price of DVDs, the downturn in the economy, and the popularity of DVD rental sites.

Industry analysts suggest that DVDs will be replaced by Blu-ray discs (although market penetration of Blu-ray has been much slower than anticipated) once the price of Blu-ray players and Blue-ray discs drops significantly. Some suggest that all physical discs will be phased out and that consumers will then obtain their films by direct streaming from Internet sources like Netflix and iTunes or via satellite.

As the table above shows, after the initial theatrical run (which lasts from 2 weeks to 6 months), the next window is for home video, which lasts up to 6 weeks with guaranteed exclusivity. According to Larry Gerbrandt, senior analyst at Paul Kagan & Associates, a little known secret in the home video rental market is that the video rental companies make their largest profits from late fees.

Pay-per-View (PPV). The next window is pay-per-view (PPV), which allows subscribers to cable and satellite television to order movies directly through a joint venture that licenses the films from all of the major studios. Initially this window was timed to open about seven months after the theatrical release to avoid delaying or competing with the video release. But when studios began releasing DVDs in the late 1990s and their popularity soared, the window had to be moved up when cable and satellite suppliers complained that they received their movies too late to compete with DVDs. Despite claims that PPV would provide another strong cash stream, the six studios' revenues from it have remained relatively modest.

Premium Pay Channels. The next window, which opens one year after the movie is released in theaters, is premium pay channels. The three major pay TV channels are HBO, Showtime, and Starz. This window remains open for up to 18 months. The licensing fee to show a major studio movie over a one-year period is based on domestic box office performance and can be as high as $20 to $25 million for a blockbuster, although the average is more like $7 million per film.

Network or Cable TV. The fifth window is network or free television. This interval lasts between 12 and 18 months. The networks and cable stations compete to determine who will obtain the rights to broadcast each film. Typically, fees range from $3 to $15 million for a movie depending on the box office success of the title and number of runs.

When television was born in the 1940s, the Hollywood studios initially viewed it more as a threat than an opportunity. In time, however, the studios discovered that it was quite profitable to license movies to television. The six major studios earned revenues of about $17.7 billion in 2005 by licensing their movies and TV series to television networks and stations

Syndicated TV. The final window is syndicated television stations. Syndicated television means that local stations can bid for the right to show the movie and can air it for up to five years. In the largest TV markets, studios may charge up to $5 million for syndicated television rights to a strong film.

International Distribution. The international box office has accounted for slightly under half of the major studios' total income from theatrical markets since the 1960s. Internationally, the market for U.S. films continues to grow. It has been estimated that in 2008, foreign consumers spent nearly $18 billion watching U.S. movies (the worldwide box office is $28 billion, including nearly $10 billion of domestic box office revenue). The largest foreign consumers of films are those in the United Kingdom, Japan, Germany, France, Spain, and Australia/New Zealand. Of course, not all of the $18 billion in revenues went to U.S. studios—the exhibitors kept approximately 50% of box office receipts.

Television licensing is equally profitable overseas. Studios typically sell their movies to foreign television networks in blocks of 6 to 10 films. The license fee for the package is then allocated across the movies at the studio's discretion. In 2003, overseas TV licensing was valued at approximately $1.76 billion, half from conventional broadcast stations and networks and the other half from pay TV.

The overseas non-theatrical market grew in the late 1980s as a result of the growth of cable and video. The home video market became a larger source of overseas revenue for Hollywood studios than the overseas theatrical market in the 1990s. It has been predicted that the overseas revenue from U.S. movies is expected to increase to $41.6 billion by 2011.

Internet and Mobile Technology. As has been the case historically, new technology will pave the way for perhaps the most significant revenue streams yet to come. The rate at which the new technology (e.g., smart phones) penetrates the market is the limiting factor for new product (e.g., downloadable movies) proliferation. Hollywood has taken note of how file sharing almost destroyed the music industry and it is now preparing to deal with a similar threat. Like their experience with television and home video, the film industry is trying to determine a new revenue-generating model to exploit the Internet as a new revenue source.

The greatest concern is protecting copyright. Studios fear that once a film is released online in digital format, that they will lose all control over its subsequent use and distribution. In one effort to maintain control over online content, the studios are working with the computer industry to build copy-protection technology into its hard drives. For instance, Microsoft has developed a digital rights management system that tries to stop DVD-restricted content from playing while unsigned software is running in order to prevent the unsigned software from accessing the content. DVD rental companies and studios have come up with a new business model although it will take some time for digital downloading and video-on-demand (VOD) to become significant revenue streams. Netflix and Blockbuster, through an alliance with TiVo, the digital video recording service, are creating a digital entertainment service that reportedly will allow customers to order a movie online, which will then be loaded onto their TiVo sets, providing DVD-quality movies on demand. Walt Disney recently joined News

(continued)

Group and Universal Studios to finance and supply content to Hulu.com. Walt Disney will not only supply archived TV programs but also titles from Disney's movie library. Hulu operates on a revenue-sharing basis with its content partners.

Already, consumers can download films directly to their iPods, iPhones, and other mobile devices. It was estimated that the number of those so-called smart phones would reach 2.6 billion worldwide by 2011. It is no stretch to see, then, that movie downloads potentially offer a significant revenue source for the movie studios, assuming they can put in place the right business models. Predictions are hard to make, but it has been estimated that revenues from Internet movie downloads in the United States and Western Europe may potentially reach $1.3 billion in the next couple of years.

Getty Images Inc.—Stone Allstock

Source: Adapted from S. Mark Young, James J. Gong, and Wim A. Van der Stede, "The Business of Making Money with Movies," *Strategic Finance* (February 2010): 35–40.

ENVIRONMENTAL COSTING

We have now, for total-life-cycle costing (TLCC), developed management accounting tools to help manage the front-end product development cycle, and the long middle production and operations stage. But all good things eventually have to end and companies must also deal with cost issues at the end of a product's life. In today's business environment, environmental remediation, compliance, and management have become critical aspects of enlightened business practice. **Environmental costing** involves selecting suppliers whose philosophy and practice in dealing with the environment match those of buyers, disposing of waste products during the production process, and incorporating postsale service and disposal issues into management accounting systems.

Controlling Environmental Costs

Activity-based costing, as introduced in Chapter 5, can be easily applied to the measurement, management, and reduction of environmental costs. First, identify the processes that cause environmental costs to be incurred. Second, assign the organizational costs associated with these processes. Third, assign those costs to the individual products, distribution channels, and customers that cause the environmental issues or

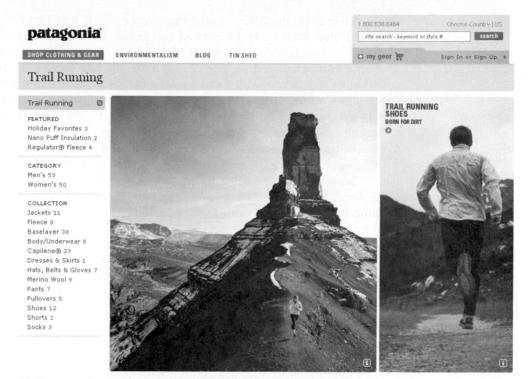

On Patagonia's website, you can track the impact of specific products on the environment, an issue of concern to many of its customers.

that benefit from processes associated with the prevention or **remediation** of environmental impact. You can't manage when you don't measure so by measuring and making managers and employees aware of the environmental costs associated with their design, production, distribution, and consumption activities, they have more ability to control and reduce them.

BMW uses parts made of recycled plastics and parts that can be recycled. So-called green manufacturing and potential legislation for companies to take back used components illustrate decision making based on the total-life-cycle costing concept.

Companies can reuse, refurbish, or dispose of a product's components safely and reduce total-life-cycle product costs.

BMW of North America, LLC

When applying ABC for environmental costing, first remove all environmentally related costs from general overhead cost pools. Then trace these costs, using the ABC methodology, directly to products and services. For example, costs such as pollution control equipment and the use of raw materials and energy can be directly traced to products. Also, some hidden and less tangible costs and benefits, such as the capital costs for emissions monitoring equipment, expenses for monitoring and testing, and product liability costs, can also be traced to the products that benefit from such spending. Removing environmental costs from overhead costs and accurately allocating them to specific products results in far fewer distortions in product costing and more attention directed to reducing the environmentally related costs of individual products.

Activity-based costing also applies at the end of a product's life cycle. This is particularly important in Europe where environmental legislation is increasingly forcing companies to be responsible for the "take-back" and disposal of products at their end of life, and to remediate land used for production facilities. Companies wishing to minimize product take-back, recycling, and site cleanup costs need to recognize and consider environmental costs during product and process design stages where they have the greatest influence. A comprehensive ABC model will help identify all of the activities and the total resource costs related to preventing and remediating expected environmental damage. Current environmental costs must be correctly attributed to both existing products and past products. A failure to recognize in today's production costs the costs of future disposal, recycling, and remediation will underestimate the total costs of producing today's products.

Environmental costs fall into two categories: explicit and implicit. *Explicit costs* include the direct costs of modifying technology and processes, costs of cleanup and disposal, costs of permits to operate a facility, fines levied by government agencies, and litigation fees. *Implicit costs* are often more closely tied to the infrastructure required to monitor environmental issues. These costs are usually administration and legal counsel, employee education and awareness, and the loss of goodwill if environmental disasters occur.

Toshiba introduced environmental accounting to provide information about the company's environmental management initiatives. Exhibit 8-15 illustrates Toshiba's model for weighing both environmental costs and benefits using a framework that assesses internal and external benefits, environmental risks, and competitive advantages. Toshiba reduced its total environmental costs by 10.5% in FY2009 compared with FY2008.[12] Exhibit 8-16 shows the estimated environmental impact from

Exhibit 8-15
Environmental Accounting as an Environmental Management Tool

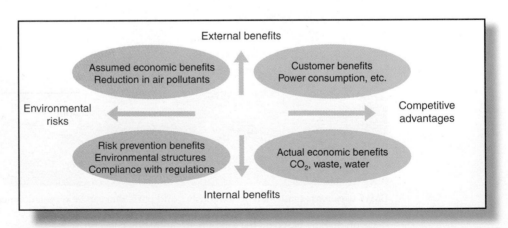

---

[12] This information was adapted from Toshiba's website, http://www.toshiba.co.jp/env/en/management/account.htm

Exhibit 8-16
Toshiba Semiconductor's Environmental Summary

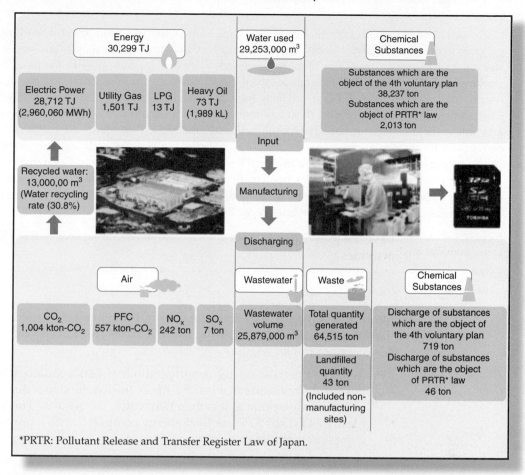

*PRTR: Pollutant Release and Transfer Register Law of Japan.

Toshiba's semiconductor division. Exhibit 8-17 shows a similar summary of energy and resource consumption produced by the Sony Group.

Xerox in its 2009 report "Nurturing a Greener World through Sustainable Innovations and Development," provides extensive documentation and measurement on

Exhibit 8-17
Sony Group's Total Environmental Impact

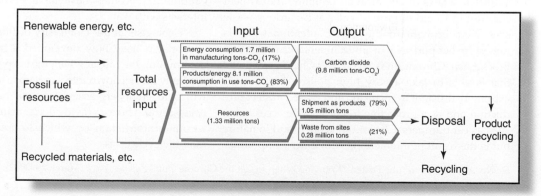

The Cisco Take-Back and Recycle Program

Cisco has introduced a take-back and recycling program to decrease the costs associated with tracking, storing, and managing excess or obsolete Cisco networking and IT assets. This program enables customers and partners to ship Cisco products back to Cisco, where they will be recycled in an environmentally safe manner using processes that comply with all current and future regulations.

A manager at Dimension Data, a leading IT services provider and value reseller of Cisco products, commented "Many companies, when they issue tenders are asking for environmental policies regarding recycling old products. By working diligently with Cisco, to re-use or recycle end-of-useful-life products, we can . . . comply with the [takeback] directive. We have an environmental and social responsibility to maximize the use of such programs."

Cisco, in turn, works with a recycler to ensure that the highest standards are met and conducts audits of its facilities as well as downstream smelters and processors. In this way, Cisco ensures that only 0.5% of what is sent to the recycler ends up in landfill sites, a percentage that is far below any legislative target.

Source: Cisco website, retrieved August 21, 2010, from http://www.cisco.com/web/about/ac227/ac228/ac231/docs/DimensionDataCS.pdf

its efforts to reduce total-life-cycle consumption of energy, solid waste disposal, and harmful emissions. Much of the success arises from decisions made in the RD&E stage. For example:

> Xerox engineers used light emitting diode (LED) technology in newly designed printheads that last the life of the machine to reduce sleep mode power consumption to less than two watts. The results? The Xerox Work Centre 7435 uses 30% less total energy compared with a previous comparable model.

These are good examples of the emerging importance of how management accounting systems help make companies and their stakeholders more aware of a company's total environmental impact and the actions that engineers and managers can take, early in a product's life cycle to reduce a company's environmental footprint.

Scientific Progress and the Reduction of Environmental Costs: The Case of Chromium in Groundwater

The toxic effects of chemical chromium-6 (hexavalent chromium) found in groundwater at hazardous waste sites were brought to the public attention by Julia Roberts in her portrayal of environmental crusader Erin Brockovich. Chromium is an odorless, hard gray metal that is able to take a very high polish. The metal is extremely resistant to corrosion and is used in steel production and as a protective in automotive accessories, such as car bumpers. Chromium is not found in nature but is the result of interactions with other compounds. Chromium becomes hexavalent chromium when it interacts with water.

Geologists at the University of Illinois at Urbana–Champaign have now developed a new method for determining the rate at which the suspected carcinogen naturally breaks down into a less toxic form. The results will help engineers assess when a major cleanup is necessary and hence provide decision makers with more accurate information by which to assess chromium's total-life-cycle costs.

Source: Adapted from Julie Foster, "Knowing When to Get the Chrome Out," *BusinessWeek* (March 25, 2002): 43.

SUMMARY

We present the total-life-cycle costing concept as a method that accumulates product costs over a product's entire life cycle, from design and development, through production, and culminating with salvage and disposal. We have introduced new management accounting tools that help managers measure and manage a product's total-life-cycle cost, including target costing, RD&E performance metrics, such as breakeven time, and environmental costing. Target costing and environmental costing must begin in the RD&E stage so that engineers and managers can control and reduce costs throughout the life cycle while still delivering desired customer performance and features.

KEY TERMS

breakeven time (BET), 340
cross-functional product teams, 332
environmental costing, 348
manufacturing stage, 327
nonfinancial measures
  of innovation, 344
postsale service and disposal
  stage, 328

quality function deployment (QFD)
  matrix, 335
remediation, 349
research, development,
  and engineering (RD&E) stage, 327
supply chain management, 332

target cost, 331
target costing, 329
total-life-cycle costing (TLCC), 326
value engineering process, 331
value index, 337

ASSIGNMENT MATERIALS

Questions

8-1 Explain why total-life-cycle costing is a "from the cradle to the grave" approach. **(LO 1)**

8-2 What are the three major stages of the total-life-cycle costing approach in a manufacturing situation? **(LO 1)**

8-3 What is the difference between a postsale service cost and a disposal cost? **(LO 1)**

8-4 What are the three substages of the RD&E stage of total-life-cycle costing? **(LO 1)**

8-5 What three substages typically occur in the postsale service and disposal stage of total-life-cycle costing? **(LO 1)**

8-6 What is a target cost? **(LO 2)**

8-7 List the steps that are adopted under target costing for determining the cost of a product. **(LO 2)**

8-8 What is a quality function deployment matrix, and how does it relate to value index computations for target costing? **(LO 2, 3)**

8-9 What is cost analysis? **(LO 2, 3)**

8-10 What is a value index? **(LO 2)**

8-11 Which variables does the QFD matrix display information about? **(LO 2, 3)**

8-12 What does the breakeven time (BET) metric for the product development process measure? **(LO 4)**

8-13 What three critical elements does the BET metric bring together? **(LO 4)**

8-14 What desirable behavioral consequences are likely as people focus on improving the BET metric? **(LO 4)**

8-15 Explain why using *percentage of revenues from new products* as a performance metric may fail to stimulate the creation of highly innovative products. **(LO 5)**

8-16 What are some nonfinancial measures that a company might use in order to motivate achieving the objective of anticipating future customer needs? **(LO 5)**

8-17 What are some nonfinancial measures that a company might use in order to motivate achieving the objective of reducing product development cycle time across an array of products? **(LO 5)**

8-18 What activities are included in environmental costing? **(LO 6)**

8-19 What are some examples of explicit and implicit environmental costs? **(LO 6)**

Exercises

LO 1   **8-20**   *Total-life-cycle costing*   Explain how the total-life-cycle costing approach differs from traditional product costing.

LO 1   **8-21**   *Benefits of total-life-cycle costing*   Explain the benefits of using a total-life-cycle costing approach to product costing.

LO 1   **8-22**   *Problems with traditional accounting focus*   What is the traditional accounting focus in managing costs over the total life cycle of a product? What is the problem with this focus?

LO 1   **8-23**   *Costs committed versus costs incurred*   Review Exhibit 8-2, showing the relationship between committed costs and incurred costs over the total life cycle of a product. Explain what the diagram means and what the implications are for managing costs.

LO 1   **8-24**   *Postsale service and disposal stage*   When does the disposal phase of the postsale service and disposal stage of a product begin and end?

LO 2   **8-25**   *Target costing*   List the salient features of target costing.

LO 2, 3   **8-26**   *Value engineering*   What is value engineering? What are the subactivities performed under it?

LO 2, 3   **8-27**   *Cost analysis*   What are the different subactivities that must be performed during cost analysis?

LO 2   **8-28**   *Implementing target costing*   From a behavioral point of view, what potential problems can occur when implementing a target costing system?

LO 2   **8-29**   *Benchmarking a target costing system*   As a manager asked to benchmark another organization's target costing system, on what factors would you gather information? Why?

LO 3   **8-30**   *Target costing equation*   Express the target costing relationship in equation form. How does this equation differ from the two other types of traditional equations relating to cost reduction? Why is this significant?

LO 3   **8-31**   *Target costing calculations*   Refer to the Kitchenhelp Coffeemaker example in the chapter. Suppose that Exhibits 8-6 and 8-7 remain the same but that engineers developed different numerical correlations, shown below, for the QFD matrix in Exhibit 8-8.

| | COMPONENTS OR FUNCTIONS | | | | | |
CUSTOMER REQUIREMENTS	BREW BASKET	CARAFE	COFFEE WARMER	BODY/WATER WELL	HEATING ELEMENT	DISPLAY PANEL
Tastes/smells like expresso	0.7				0.3	
Easy to clean	0.5	0.1		0.4		
Looks nice		0.1		0.5		0.4
Has 6+ cup capacity		0.5		0.5		
Starts automatically on time						1
Has multiple grinder settings	0.1					0.9
Keeps the coffee warm		0.2	0.8			
Automatic shutoff						1

Required

(a) Prepare an exhibit similar to Exhibit 8-9 showing percentage contributions of each component to customer requirements.

(b) Prepare a value index exhibit similar to Exhibit 8-10. Which components are candidates for cost reduction?

LO 4   **8-32** *Breakeven time for new product development*   Refer to Exhibit 8-14 regarding Greyson Technology's launch of a new digital communications device. Suppose that Greyson reduced the quarterly spending on product development in panel A, which delayed launching the new product for two quarters, at which time the selling price and sales volume would be lower. Specifically, assume the following:

	Y_1, Q_1	Y_1, Q_2	Y_1, Q_3	Y_1, Q_4	Y_2, Q_1	Y_2, Q_2	Y_2, Q_3	Y_2, Q_4	Y_3, Q_1
Market research (000)	$ (100)	$ (50)							
Product development (000)			$ (80)	$ (150)	$ (150)	$ (150)	$ (150)	$ (150)	$ (150)	$ (60)

	Y_3, Q_1	Y_3, Q_2	Y_3, Q_3	Y_3, Q_4	Y_4, Q_1	Y_4, Q_2	Y_4, Q_3	Y_4, Q_4
Selling price	$ 19	$ 18	$ 18	$ 17	$ 17	$ 16	$ 15	$ 15
Sales quantity (000)	25	35	45	50	50	50	40	30

Required

Assuming that the cost per unit remains $10 and the MSDA expenses remain $120,000 per quarter, determine the difference between the breakeven time metrics under the initial assumptions in panel A and the new assumptions.

LO 4   **8-33** *Breakeven time for new product development*   Refer to Exhibit 8-14 regarding Greyson Technology's launch of a new digital communications device. Suppose that Greyson reduced the quarterly spending on product development in panel A, which delayed launching the new product for two quarters, at which time the selling price and sales volume would be lower. Specifically, assume the following:

	Y_1, Q_1	Y_1, Q_2	Y_1, Q_3	Y_1, Q_4	Y_2, Q_1	Y_2, Q_2	Y_2, Q_3	Y_2, Q_4	Y_3, Q_1
Market research (000)	$ (100)	$ (50)							
Product development (000)			$ (80)	$ (150)	$ (150)	$ (150)	$ (150)	$ (150)	$ (150)	$ (60)

	Y_3, Q_1	Y_3, Q_2	Y_3, Q_3	Y_3, Q_4	Y_4, Q_1	Y_4, Q_2	Y_4, Q_3	Y_4, Q_4
Selling price	$ 18	$ 17	$ 17	$ 16	$ 15	$ 15	$ 15	$ 15
Sales quantity (000)	20	30	40	45	45	35	30	20

After Y4, Q4, the competitive price is expected to remain at $15 and the maximum sales will be 20,000 units.

Required

Assuming that the cost per unit remains $10 and the MSDA expenses remain $120,000 per quarter, determine the breakeven time metric under the new assumptions.

LO 6   **8-34** *Activity-based costing for environmental costs*   How can a firm use activity-based costing to help control and reduce environmental costs?

Problems

LO 3 **8-35** *Target costing calculations* A major car manufacturer developed the following information as part of its target costing efforts:

Customer Importance Rating by Category

CATEGORY	IMPORTANCE
Safety	140
Comfort and convenience	120
Economy	40
Styling	60
Performance	140
Total	500

Target Cost by Function Group

FUNCTION GROUP	TARGET COST
Chassis	$1,400
Transmission	280
Air conditioner	100
Electrical system	700
Other function groups	4,520
Total	$7,000

Quality Function Deployment (Correlation) Matrix

CATEGORIES	Function Group				
	CHASSIS	TRANSMISSION	AIR CONDITIONER	ELECTRICAL SYSTEM	OTHER FUNCTION GROUPS
Safety	0.3	0.1		0.1	0.5
Comfort and convenience	0.3		0.1	0.1	0.5
Economy	0.2	0.2	0.1	0.1	0.4
Styling	0.1				0.9
Performance	0.3	0.2		0.1	0.4

Required

(a) Prepare an exhibit similar to Exhibit 8-9 showing percentage contributions of each function group to categories of customer requirements.
(b) Prepare a value index exhibit similar to Exhibit 8-10.
(c) Which function groups are candidates for cost reduction?

LO 1 **8-36** *Total-life-cycle costing* Consider the following situation: Your manager comes to you and says, "I don't understand why everyone is talking about the total-life-cycle costing approach to product costing. As far as I am concerned, this new approach is a waste of time and energy. I think we should just stick to what we know, and that is the traditional approach to product costing."

Required

Write a memorandum critiquing your manager's view. In the memo, discuss the benefits of adopting the total-life-cycle costing approach.

LO 1   **8-37**   *Total-life-cycle costing versus traditional methods*   Gregoire Grant is a traditional manufacturing manager who is concerned only with managing costs over the manufacturing cycle of the product. He argues that since traditional accounting methods are focused on this cycle, he should not bother with the RD&E cycle because it is separate from his area of manufacturing.

Required

Write an essay discussing Gregoire's views. What types of structural and functional changes in organizations may be necessary to help Gregoire overcome his traditional view?

LO 3   **8-38**   *Target costing: unit cost*   Graham Company is contemplating introducing a new type of mobile phone to complement its existing line of mobile phones. The target price of the mobile phone is $100; annual sales volume of the new phone is expected to be 800,000 units. Graham Company has a 20% return-on-sales target.

Required

Compute the unit target cost per mobile phone.

LO 3   **8-39**   *Target costing: return on sales*   Mark Bell, president of Caremore, Inc., an electronics manufacturer in Seattle, Washington, has been trying to decide whether one of his product-line managers, Roger Twickenham, has been achieving the companywide return-on-sales target of 35%. Mark has just received data from the new target costing system regarding Roger's operation. Roger's sales volume was 640,000 with an average selling price of $750 and expenses totaling $264 million.

Required

Determine whether Roger's return-on-sales ratio has met the companywide target. Has Roger done a good or a poor job? Explain.

LO 2   **8-40**   *Target costing: implementation issues*   Pierre LeBlanc, manager of Centaur Corporation, is thinking about implementing a target costing system in his organization. Several managers have taken him aside and have expressed concerns about implementing target costing in their organization.

Required

As an expert in target costing, you have been called in to discuss these concerns and offer advice on overcoming them. Write a memorandum discussing common concerns that managers have about target costing. In the memo, state how you would remedy these concerns.

LO 2, 3   **8-41**   *Traditional cost reduction versus target costing*   Traditional cost reduction in the United States differs significantly from the Japanese method of target costing.

Required

Discuss the similarities and differences in the process by which cost reduction under both systems occurs. Be specific in your answer.

LO 2   **8-42**   *Benchmarking for target costing*   As a manager interested in implementing target costing, you are contemplating three approaches. The first is to bring in an outside consultant; the second is to develop your own system inside your organization with little to no outside assistance; and the third is to engage in a benchmarking project with several other firms.

Required

Critique each of these approaches, discussing their pros and cons. On what basis will you select your approach to implementing target costing? Explain.

LO 2, 3   **8-43 *Target costing versus traditional cost reduction methods***   According to this chapter, the target costing and traditional cost reduction methods approach the relationships among cost, selling price, and profit margin quite differently.

Required

Write an essay that illustrates how the target costing and traditional cost reduction methods differ, using the appropriate symbols and equations. In addition to the equations, describe how the processes differ in deriving costs.

LO 2   **8-44 *Target costing and service organization***   Imagine that you are the manager of a large bank. Having heard about a management accounting method called *target costing*, you are wondering whether it can be applied to the banking industry. In particular, you are trying to determine how to benchmark other organizations to gain more information.

Required

Can target costing be applied to the banking industry? To what products or services can target costing be applied?

Cases

LO 6   **8-45 *Environmental costs, activity-based costing***   Bevans Co. makes two products, Product X and Product Y. Bevans has produced Product X for many years without generating any hazardous wastes. Recently, Bevans developed Product Y, which is superior to Product X in many respects. However, production of Product Y generates hazardous wastes. Because of the hazardous wastes, Bevans now must deal with hazardous waste disposal, governmental environmental reports and inspections, and safe handling procedures.

Bevans Co. uses an indirect cost rate based on machine hours to assign manufacturing support costs to its two products. Because of concerns about the accuracy of the product costing system, Joel Dempsey, the controller, undertook an activity-based costing analysis of the manufacturing support costs, including an analysis of the support costs related to Product Y's generation of hazardous wastes. The resulting cost information, as well as machine hours and number of units, is summarized in the following table:

	PRODUCT X	PRODUCT Y
Direct costs (material plus labor)	$9,000,000	$4,000,000
Environmental support costs	—	$14,000,000
Nonenvironmental support costs	$22,000,000	$29,000,000
Total machine hours	10,000,000	6,000,000
Number of units	100,000,000	40,000,000

Required

(a) Compute product costs per unit for Products X and Y using the current indirect cost rate based on machine hours for manufacturing support costs.
(b) Compute product costs per unit for Products X and Y using the activity-based costing figures provided in the table.

(c) Explain the reasons for the differences in cost for each product using the two cost systems.

(d) Bevans has been selling Products X and Y at a price equal to 1.5 times the product cost computed using the machine-hour–based cost driver rate for manufacturing support costs. Compute these prices and provide recommendations to Bevans' management concerning profit improvement through pricing changes and cost reduction through manufacturing improvements.

LO 6   **8-46 *Explicit and implicit environmental costs***   Refer to Case 7-57, which describes Kwik Clean's environmental costs.

Required

(a) Of the costs listed by Pat Polley, identify which are explicit and which are implicit environmental costs.

(b) Should Polley identify any other environmental costs?

(c) Prepare a memo to Polley explaining how an activity-based costing approach can help her control and reduce Kwik Clean's environmental costs.

LO 2 **8-47**   *Target costing*   Mercedes-Benz All Activity Vehicle (AAV)[13]

Introduction

During the recession beginning in the early 1990s, Mercedes-Benz (MB) struggled with product development, cost efficiency, material purchasing, and problems in adapting to changing markets. In 1993, these problems caused the worst sales slump in decades, and the luxury car maker lost money for the first time in its history. Since then, MB has streamlined the core business, reduced parts and system complexity, and established simultaneous engineering programs with suppliers.

In their search for additional market share, new segments, and new niches, MB started developing a range of new products. New product introductions included the C-Class in 1993, the E-Class in 1995, the new sportster SLK in 1996, and the A-Class and M-Class All Activity Vehicle (AAV) in 1997. Perhaps the largest and most radical of MB's new projects was the AAV. In April 1993, MB announced it would build its first passenger vehicle–manufacturing facility in the United States. The decision emphasized the company's globalization strategy and desire to move closer to its customers and markets.

Mercedes-Benz United States International used function groups with representatives from every area of the company (marketing, development, engineering, purchasing, production, and controlling) to design the vehicle and production systems. A modular construction process was used to produce the AAV. First-tier suppliers provided systems rather than individual parts or components for production of approximately 65,000 vehicles annually.

The AAV Project Phases

The AAV moved from concept to production in a relatively short period of time. The first phase, the concept phase, was initiated in 1992. The concept phase resulted in a feasibility study that was approved by the board. Following board approval, the project realization phase began in 1993, with production commencing in 1997. Key elements of the various phases are described next.

---

[13] Institute of Management Accountants, *Cases from Management Accounting Practice, Volume 15*. Adapted with permission. The case author, Tom Albright, wishes to express his gratitude to Ola Kallenins, Johnathan DeHart, Jason Hoff, Henrik Jonsson, Iosef Pfau, and Günther Thuss of Mercedes-Benz for their generous contributions to the development of this case.

Concept Phase, 1992–1993

Team members compared the existing production line with various market segments to discover opportunities for new vehicle introductions. The analysis revealed opportunities in the rapidly expanding sports utility vehicle market that was dominated by Jeep, Ford, and GM. Market research was conducted to estimate potential worldwide sales opportunities for a high-end AAV with the characteristics of a Mercedes-Benz. A rough cost estimate was developed that included materials, labor, overhead, and one-time development and project costs. Projected cash flows were analyzed over a 10-year period using net present value (NPV) analysis to acquire project approval from the board of directors. The sensitivity of the NPV was analyzed by calculating "what-if" scenarios involving risks and opportunities. For example, risk factors included monetary exchange rate fluctuations, different sales levels due to consumer substitution of the AAV for another MB product, and product and manufacturing costs that differed from projections.

On the basis of the economic feasibility study of the concept phase, the board approved the project and initiated a search for potential manufacturing locations. Sites located in Germany, other European countries, and the United States were evaluated. Consistent with the company's globalization strategy, the decisive factor that brought the plant to the United States was the desire to be close to the major market for sports utility vehicles.

Project Realization Phase, 1993–1996

Regular customer clinics were held to view the prototype and to explain the new vehicle concept. These clinics produced important information about how the proposed vehicle would be received by potential customers and the press. Customers were asked to rank the importance of various characteristics, including safety, comfort, economy, and styling. Engineers organized in function groups designed systems to deliver these essential characteristics. However, MB would not lower its internal standards for components, even if initial customer expectations might be lower than the MB standard. For example, many automotive experts believed that the superior handling of MB products resulted from manufacturing the best automobile chassis in the world. Thus, each class within the MB line met strict standards for handling, even though these standards might exceed customer expectations for some classes. MB did not use target costing to produce the lowest price vehicle in an automotive class. The company's strategic objective was to deliver products that were slightly more expensive than competitive models. However, the additional cost would have to translate into greater perceived value on the part of the customer.

Throughout the project realization phase, the vehicle (and vehicle target cost) remained alive because of changing dynamics. For example, the market moved toward the luxury end of the spectrum while the AAV was under development. In addition, crash test results were incorporated into the evolving AAV design. For these reasons, MB found it beneficial to place the design and testing team members in close physical proximity to other functions within the project to promote fast communication and decision making. Sometimes new technical features, such as side air bags, were developed by MB. The decision to include the new feature on all MB lines was made at the corporate level because experience had shown that customers' reactions to a vehicle class can affect the entire brand.

Production Phase, 1997

The project was monitored by annual updates of the NPV analysis. In addition, a three-year plan (including income statements) was prepared annually and reported to the headquarters in Germany. Monthly departmental meetings were held to discuss actual cost performance compared with standards developed during the cost estimation process. Thus, the accounting system served as a control mechanism to ensure that actual production costs would conform to target (or standard) costs.

Target Costing and the AAV

The process of achieving target cost for the AAV began with an estimate of the existing cost for each function group. Next, components of each function group were identified with their associated costs.

Cost reduction targets were set by comparing the estimated existing cost with the target cost for each function group. These function groups included the following: doors, sidewall and roof, electrical system, bumpers, power train, seats, heating system, cockpit, and front end. Next, cost reduction targets were established for each component. As part of the competitive benchmark process, MB bought and tore down competitors' vehicles to help understand their costs and manufacturing processes.

The AAV manufacturing process relied on high-value-added systems suppliers. For example, the entire cockpit was purchased as a unit from a systems supplier. Thus, systems suppliers were part of the development process from the beginning of the project. MB expected suppliers to meet established cost targets. To enhance function group effectiveness, suppliers were brought into the discussion at an early stage in the process. Decisions had to be made quickly in the early stages of development.

The target costing process was led by cost planners who were engineers, not accountants. Because the cost planners were engineers with manufacturing and design experience, they could make reasonable estimates of costs that suppliers would incur in providing various systems. Also, MB owned much of the tooling, such as dies to form sheet metal, used by suppliers to produce components. Tooling costs are a substantial part of the one-time costs in the project phase.

Index Development to Support Target Costing Activities

During the concept development phase, MB team members used various indexes to help them determine critical performance, design, and cost relationships for the AAV.[14] To construct the indexes, various forms of information were gathered from customers, suppliers, and their own design team. Although the actual number of categories used by MB was much greater, Table 1 illustrates the calculations used to quantify customer responses to the AAV concept. For example, values shown in the "Importance" column resulted from asking a sample of potential customers whether they consider each category extremely important when considering the purchase of a new MB product. Respondents could respond affirmatively to all categories that applied.

To gain a better understanding of the various sources of costs, *function groups* were identified together with target cost estimates. (MB also organizes teams called function groups whose role is to develop specifications and cost projections.) As shown in Table 2, the relative target cost percentage of each function group was computed.

TABLE 1 Relative Importance Ranking by Category

CATEGORY	IMPORTANCE	RELATIVE PERCENTAGE
Safety	32	41%
Comfort	25	32
Economy	15	18
Styling	7	9
Total	79	100%

TABLE 2 Target Cost and Percentage by Function Group

FUNCTION GROUP	TARGET COST	PERCENTAGE OF TOTAL
Chassis	$x,xxx	20%
Transmission	x,xxx	25
Air conditioner	xxx	5
Electrical system	xxx	7
Other function groups	x,xxx	43
Total	$x,xxx	100%

---

[14] All numbers have been altered for proprietary reasons; however, the tables illustrate the actual process used in the development of the AAV.

TABLE 3 Function Group Contribution to Customer Requirements

FUNCTION GROUP	CATEGORY			
	SAFETY	COMFORT	ECONOMY	STYLING
Chassis	50%	30%	10%	10%
Transmission	20	20	30	
Air conditioner		20		5
Electrical system	5		20	
Other function groups	25	30	40	85
Total	100%	100%	100%	100%

Table 3 summarizes how each function group contributes to the consumer requirements identified in Table 1. For example, safety was identified by potential customers as an important characteristic of the AAV; some function groups contributed more to the safety category than others. MB engineers determined that chassis quality was an important element of safety (50% of the total function group contribution).

Table 4 combines the category weighting percentages from Table 1 with the function group contribution from Table 3. The result is an importance index that measures the relative importance of each function group across all categories. For example, potential customers weighted the categories of safety, comfort, economy, and styling as 0.41, 0.32, 0.18, and 0.09, respectively. The rows in Table 4 represent the contribution of each function group to the various categories. The importance index for the chassis is calculated by multiplying each row value by its corresponding category value and summing the results: $(0.50 \times 0.41) + (0.30 \times 0.32) + (0.10 \times 0.18) + (0.10 \times 0.09) = 0.33$.

As shown in Table 5, the target cost index is calculated by dividing the importance index by the target cost percentage by function group. Managers at MB used indexes such as these during the concept design phase to understand the relationship of the importance of a function group to the target cost of a function group. Indexes less than 1 may indicate a cost in excess of the perceived value of the function group. Thus, opportunities for cost reduction consistent with customer demands, may be identified and managed during the early stages of product development. Choices

TABLE 4 Importance Index of Various Function Groups

FUNCTION GROUP	CATEGORY				
	SAFETY 0.41	COMFORT 0.32	ECONOMY 0.18	STYLING 0.09	IMPORTANCE INDEX
Chassis	0.50	0.30	0.10	0.10	0.33
Transmission	0.20	0.20	0.30		0.20
Air conditioner		0.20		0.05	0.07
Electrical system	0.05		0.20		0.06
Other function groups	0.25	0.30	0.40	0.85	0.35
Total	1.00	1.00	1.00	1.00	

TABLE 5 Target Cost Index

FUNCTION GROUP	(A) IMPORTANCE INDEX	(B) % OF TARGET COST	(C) TARGET COST INDEX = A/B
Chassis	0.33	0.20	1.65
Transmission	0.20	0.25	0.80
Air conditioner	0.07	0.05	1.40
Electrical system	0.06	0.07	0.86
Other function groups	0.35	0.43	0.81
Total		1.00	

made during the project realization phase were largely irreversible during the production phase because approximately 80% of the production cost of the AAV was for materials and systems provided by external suppliers.

The AAV project used a streamlined management structure to facilitate efficient and rapid development. The streamlined MB organization produced an entirely new vehicle from concept to production in four years. Using the target costing process as a key management element, MB manufactured the first production AAV in 1997.

Required

(a) What is the competitive environment faced by MB as it considers launching the AAV?

(b) How has MB reacted to the changing world for luxury automobiles?

(c) Using Cooper's cost, quality, and functionality chart,[15] discuss the factors on which MB would have to compete with other automobile producers, such as Jeep, Ford, and GM.

(d) How does the AAV project link with MB's strategy in terms of market coverage?

(e) Explain the process of developing an importance index for a function group or component. How can such an index guide managers in making cost reduction decisions?

(f) How does MB approach cost reduction to achieve target costs?

(g) How do suppliers factor into the target costing process? Why are they so critically important to the success of the MB AAV?

(h) What role does the accounting department play in the target costing process?

---

[15] Robin Cooper, *When Lean Enterprises Collide* (Boston: Harvard Business School Press, 1995).

Chapter 9

Behavioral and Organizational Issues in Management Accounting and Control Systems

After completing this chapter, you will be able to:

1. Understand the meaning of control.
2. Identify the characteristics of well-designed management accounting and control systems.
3. Discuss key behavioral considerations in the design of a management accounting and control system.
4. Explain the human resources management model of motivation.
5. Apply the ethical control framework to decisions.
6. Discuss task and results control methods.
7. Understand how the Balanced Scorecard can be used to align employees to corporate and business unit objectives.
8. Discuss motivation and dysfunctional behavior in management control systems.
9. Discuss the importance of employee empowerment in the design of management accounting and control systems.
10. Recognize the behavioral issues in budgeting.
11. Discuss the links between different incentive systems and performance.

Advanced Cellular International

Wayne Jagielski has just been appointed controller of a large cellular phone manufacturer. He is on the fast track, having graduated with a dual concentration in strategy and management accounting from a large Midwestern business school only four years earlier. Before going back to school, Wayne worked as a management consultant. His most recent job as a senior manager in one of the manufacturing divisions has been challenging; however, he has performed relatively well despite the low morale of company employees.

On the basis of his experience as a consultant, Wayne has decided to design a management accounting and control system (MACS) that will generate relevant information and motivate the right kinds of behavior from company employees. At a management briefing, Eddie Yueh, a senior vice president, mentioned to him that several managers and their employees were expressing concerns about the proposed changes to the MACS. They wanted to know how the system was designed, whether their performance would be assessed differently, and whether their compensation plans would be altered. They also were uncertain about how the new MACS would affect employee behavior and help achieve organizational strategies.

As he listened to the discussion, Wayne realized that he had committed a major error in his approach—he had not involved enough key people in system design. He wanted to achieve several goals with the new MACS. First, he wanted to design a system whose operation on a day-to-day basis was consistent with the company's ethical and cultural norms of behavior. Second, because the previous system had relied myopically on narrow, short-term financial goals, he wanted to encourage broader thinking for all employees through the use of multiple performance measures. In particular, he wanted to encourage a work environment that fostered creativity. Third—and this is where he had really faltered—he wanted to make sure that people were motivated to work at the company. To this end, he had thought about various types of compensation systems to reward superior performance, but he had not considered asking more employees to participate in overall system design. Would they resist the changes that he was proposing? Could a Balanced Scorecard approach provide some important guidance overall?

Shutterstock

WHAT ARE MANAGEMENT ACCOUNTING AND CONTROL SYSTEMS?

The preceding chapters explored different types of cost management systems and the ways the information they generate is used in a variety of decision contexts. A cost management system is the central performance measurement system at the core of a larger entity known as a **management accounting and control system (MACS)**. In this chapter, we discuss the role that MACS play in helping decision makers determine whether organization-, business-, and operational-level strategies and objectives are being met. We begin by presenting the concept of control and then delineate the technical and behavioral characteristics of a well-designed MACS. Further, we discuss how MACS can be used to motivate behavior, how ethical issues are addressed, the possible dysfunctional consequences that can occur when MACS are poorly designed, and how incentives are used.

The Meaning of "Control"

Broadly speaking, a MACS generates and uses information that helps decision makers assess whether an organization is achieving its objectives. The term *control* in management accounting and control refers to the set of procedures, tools, performance measures, systems, and incentives that organizations use to guide and motivate all employees to achieve organizational objectives. A system is in control if it is on the path to achieving its strategic objectives, and deemed out of control otherwise.

For the process of control to have meaning and credibility, the organization must have the knowledge and ability to correct situations that it identifies as being out of control; otherwise, control serves no purpose. As described in Chapter 1, the process of keeping an organization in control consists of the following four stages:

1. *Plan*—Develop an organization's objectives, choose activities to accomplish the objectives, and select measures to determine how well the objectives were met.
2. *Do*—Implement the plan.
3. *Check*—Monitor by measuring and evaluating the system's current level of performance; compare feedback about the system's current level of performance to the planned level in order to identify discrepancies and prescribe corrective action.
4. *Act*—Take appropriate actions to return the system to an in-control state.

Regardless of whether an organization makes video games, helps clean up the environment, or flies people around the world, the same basic control process applies. Where control processes may differ across different types of organizations lies in determining which are the most appropriate types of performance measures to be used. In the following section, we discuss the technical and behavioral characteristics that designers consider when developing a MACS.

CHARACTERISTICS OF A WELL-DESIGNED MACS

Technical Considerations

Technical factors fall into two categories: (1) the relevance of the information generated and (2) the scope of the system. The relevance of information is measured by four characteristics:

1. **Accurate:** As discussed throughout this text, inaccurate information is not relevant or useful for decision making because it is misleading. Designers have to

develop a system that leads to the most accurate information possible, subject to a cost–benefit trade-off. For example, more accurate product costs can be obtained by using systems that trace costs more directly from support activities to products.

2. **Timely:** Accurate information that is late is also of little use for decision making. The MACS must be designed so that the results of performance measurement are fed back to the appropriate units in the most expedient way possible. The proliferation of high-speed computers, local-area networks, and many other forms of technology make the process of providing feedback a real-time possibility in many, if not all, systems.

3. **Consistent:** Designers must structure the MACS to provide a consistent framework that can be applied globally across the units or divisions of an entity. Consistency means that the language used and the technical methods of producing management accounting information do not conflict within various parts of an organization. For example, if two divisions use different costing systems, it is more difficult to understand and compare results across divisions. If one division of an organization uses activity-based costing principles and another division, especially one that is very similar in goals and function to the first, uses volume-based overhead allocation methods, then the information system does not meet the consistency criterion. Consider the difficulties that would arise if divisions classified the same expense differently, that is, if fringe benefits of workers were classified as direct labor expenses in one division but as indirect labor expenses in another.

4. **Flexible:** MACS designers must allow employees to use the system's available information in a flexible manner so that they can customize its application for local decisions. If flexibility is not possible, an employee's motivation to make the best decision may be lessened for the decision at hand, especially if different units engage in different types of activities. For example, if one division of a company located in Pasadena undertakes new product development and another division in Monterey performs final assembly, each division probably will have different data needs and may use different cost drivers in making its decisions. The performance measures for managing new product development in Pasadena will be quite different from the factors that the Monterey assembly division must use to manage effectively. A well-designed MACS should be able to accommodate the local needs of each division. If not, inaccurate ad hoc local systems may develop, leading to poor decisions and confusion between the company's division and upper management.

The scope of the MACS must be comprehensive and include all activities across the entire value chain of the organization. For example, historically, many MACS measure and assess performance in only one part of the value chain—the actual production or throughput process. In this case, the performance of suppliers, the design activities, and the postproduction activities associated with products and services are ignored. Without a comprehensive set of information, managers can make only limited decisions.

Behavioral Considerations

Because human interests and motivation can vary significantly, a major role for control systems is to motivate behavior congruent with the desires of the organization.

The rest of the chapter turns to the second set of characteristics related to MACS design. Four major behavioral characteristics should be considered when designing a MACS:

1. Embedding the organization's ethical code of conduct into MACS design.
2. Using a mix of short- and long-term qualitative and quantitative performance measures (or the Balanced Scorecard Approach).

3. Empowering employees to be involved in decision making and MACS design.
4. Developing an appropriate incentive system to reward performance.

Wayne Jagielski's dilemma at the beginning of this chapter highlights a key issue that plagues major companies. Although many managers want to do what is best for their companies, they often try to implement new systems without considering the behavioral implications and consequences of using a MACS. Unless they pay careful attention to these factors, goal congruence may not occur, motivation could be low, and, worst of all, employees may be encouraged to engage in dysfunctional behavior.

Note, however, that these four characteristics do not simply arise by accident in every MACS. Rather, companies that have a MACS often subscribe to a particular worldview of the role of management that we label the human resource management model of motivation. The development of this view is discussed next, followed by a detailed discussion of the four characteristics.

THE HUMAN RESOURCE MANAGEMENT MODEL OF MOTIVATION

One of the earliest attempts at understanding the role of management, developed at the turn of the 20th century, was the scientific management school. The underlying philosophy was that most people found work objectionable, that individuals cared little for making decisions or exercising creativity on the job, and that money was the driving force behind performance. Management believed that employees should follow highly detailed, prescribed procedures and that behavior should be monitored and controlled very carefully through time-and-motion studies.

The human relations movement was the next significant step in the development of managerial views on motivation. This movement recognized that people had needs that went well beyond performing a simple repetitive task at work and that financial compensation was only one aspect of what workers desired. Employees wanted respect, discretion over their jobs, and a feeling that they contributed something valuable to their organization. The human relations movement was the impetus for developing ways to improve morale and job satisfaction and the overall quality of working life.

Perhaps the most contemporary management view of motivation is the human resources model of motivation (HRMM). Based on initiatives to improve the quality of working life and the strong influence of Japanese management practices, HRMM introduces a high level of employee responsibility for and participation in decisions in the work environment. The central assumptions of HRMM are that organizations operate under a system of beliefs about the values, purpose, and direction of their organization; that people find work enjoyable; and that people desire to participate in developing objectives, making decisions, and attaining goals in their work environment. Individuals are motivated by both financial and nonfinancial means of compensation. This model also assumes that employees have a great deal of knowledge and information about their jobs, the application of which will improve the way they perform tasks and benefit the organization as a whole. Individuals are assumed to be highly creative, ethical, and responsible, and they desire opportunities to effect change in their organizations.

The human resource model is the basis of the presentation of the four behavioral considerations in MACS design that follows. Next, the organization's ethical code of conduct is discussed.

THE ORGANIZATION'S ETHICAL CODE
OF CONDUCT AND MACS DESIGN

A boundary system is a set of standards relating to acceptable behavior in an organization. At the center of many boundary systems is a set of ethical principles, and thus a well-designed MACS should incorporate the principles of an organization's code of ethical conduct to guide and influence behavior and decision making. Ethics is a discipline that focuses on the investigation of standards of conduct and moral judgment. A MACS design that incorporates ethical principles can provide decision makers with guidance as they face ethical dilemmas. Recent scandals in corporate America have greatly heightened the need for a renewed emphasis on ethical judgment and decision making.

Managers often play a significant role in MACS design. Their behavior and decision making are guided by the organization's code of ethical conduct and the ethical standards under which they abide. The ethical framework embedded in system design is extremely important because it will influence the behavior of all users. The key user group—managers—interacts a great deal with the MACS. Often managers are subject to intense pressures from their job circumstances and from other influential organizational members to suspend their ethical judgment in certain situations. These pressures include the following:

1. Requests to tailor information to favor particular individuals or groups.
2. Pleas to falsify reports or test results.
3. Solicitations for confidential information.
4. Pressures to ignore a questionable or unethical practice.

To incorporate ethical principles into the design of a MACS and help managers deal effectively with the types of situations listed above, system designers might attempt to ensure the following:

1. That the organization has formulated, implemented, and communicated to all employees a comprehensive code of ethics. This is often accomplished through the organization's beliefs system.
2. That all employees understand the organization's code of ethics and the boundary systems that constrain behavior.
3. That a system in which employees have confidence exists to detect and report violations of the organization's code of ethics.

Avoiding Ethical Dilemmas

Most organizations attempt to address ethical considerations and avoid ethical dilemmas by developing a code of ethics. Although no universal hierarchy of ethical principles exists, five categories capture the broad array of ethical considerations: legal rules, societal norms, professional memberships, organizational or group norms, and personal norms.

This hierarchy is listed in descending order of authority. For example, an action that is prohibited by law should be unacceptable by society, by one's profession, by the organization, and then by each individual. However, an action that is legally and socially acceptable, such as strategically underestimating product costs, may be professionally unacceptable and, in turn, unacceptable to the organization and its employees. Unfortunately, any hierarchy of this sort has a number of gray areas, but it nevertheless provides general guidelines for understanding and dealing with ethical problems that arise.

This ethical hierarchy provides a set of constraints on a decision. In this scheme, ethical conflicts occur when one system of values diverges from a more fundamental system. For example, suppose that the organization's code of ethics commits it to meeting only the letter of the law regarding disclosure of a product defect in one of its manufactured goods that could prove hazardous to consumers. However, a broader societal expectation is that organizations should be aggressive in identifying and disclosing potential product defects. An individual decision maker dealing with this situation may face an ethical conflict when the organizational code of ethics implies doing nothing about the defect since there is no definitive evidence of a product problem. In such cases, broader societal expectations would imply that disclosure is necessary because there is persistent evidence of a problem.

Dealing with Ethical Conflicts

Organizations that formulate and support specific and unambiguous ethical codes can create an environment that will reduce ethical conflicts. One step in avoiding ambiguity or misunderstanding is to maintain a hierarchical ordering of authority, which means that the organization's stated code of ethics should not allow any behavior that is either legally or socially unacceptable. Because most professional codes of ethics reflect broad moral imperatives, such as loyalty, discretion, and competence, an organization would create public relations problems for itself if its stated code of ethics conflicted with a professional code of ethics.

Another critical variable that can reduce ethical conflicts is the way in which the chief executive and other senior managers behave and conduct business. If these individuals demonstrate exemplary behavior, other organizational members will have role models to emulate. Organizations whose leaders exhibit unethical behavior cannot expect their employees to behave according to high ethical standards.

In some cases, when organizations develop a formal code of ethics, they can create the potential for explicit ethical conflicts with the code itself to arise. The conflicts that appear most in practice are those between the law and the organization's code of ethics, between the organization's practiced code of ethics and common societal expectations, and between the individual's set of personal and professional ethics and the organization's practiced code of ethics. Any conflicts that remain relate primarily to personal values and norms of behavior that were acceptable prior to the adoption of the organization's new code of ethics but that are now in question.

Conflicts between Individual and Organizational Values

People bring personal codes of ethics with them into an organization. If the organization's code of ethics is more stringent than an individual's code, conflicts may arise. However, if adherence to the organization's ethical code is required and enforced, it is possible to diminish ethical conflicts if, as part of the employment contract, the individual is asked and expected to pursue a more stringent code of ethics. Another possible (and probably more desirable) outcome is that individuals may raise their own ethical standards without conflict.

Difficult issues may arise when an individual's personal code of ethics prohibits certain types of behavior that are legal, socially acceptable, professionally acceptable, and acceptable to the organization. Potential for conflicts in such situations will arise when the action that is unacceptable to the individual is desirable to the organization. As an example, an employee may have deep religious objections to conducting business in any form on a holy day. Working for an organization may require that the

IN PRACTICE
Does Cheating at Golf Lead to Cheating in Business?

Almost a decade ago, Starwood Hotels and Resorts commissioned a study of high-ranking corporate executives to see if they were less than honest on the golf course. The results of the study showed that 82% of these executives admitted to various kinds of cheating behavior. Another informal study of a dozen CEOs polled by *USA Today* revealed that these CEOs also bent the rules when they play, in part, because they saw their competitors doing the same.

Are there consequences for this behavior? Jeff Harp, former president of Summit National Bank in Fort Worth, Texas, states that he has denied loans after seeing CEOs cheat at golf. Since he is in the business of trying to assess honesty, he feels that if one can cheat at golf, one can cheat on a loan application. However, there may be a bigger societal issue.

Ken Siegel, an organizational psychologist who has been interviewing executives for 25 years, says that executives who cheat and lie and then deny it may be deluding themselves and others. "They lose the ability to distinguish what is honest and what is not," Siegel says. "Lies are getting bigger and bigger. We're seeing this played out everywhere now, from Tyco to Enron."

In 2009 another study was conducted by Duke University. A survey of 17,000 golfers found that there were four kinds of cheating behavior: stating that you got a lower than actual score on a hole, moving a ball slightly to improve your lie, claiming you lost your first ball and dropping a second ball, and kicking your ball to a better position.

David Rynecki, an author who has written extensively about golf, says that golf is "an 18-hole character test," from which one can learn a great deal about your competitor. This not only includes whether they cheat or not but how passionate they are and whether they fit with you and your company. Said Dan Ariely, one of the authors of the Duke study, "First of all, I think cheating in golf is kind of a good example for

how we think about day-to-day tasks. The fact that people can take a mulligan or how they can cheat on golf, I think tells us that's there a lot of corner bending that we see in the business world. And what I worry about is that once we start in this path of immorality, even with small bending of rules and cutting corners here and there, that this tendency could become bigger and bigger and really a part of the collective understanding of how business is actually done."

Food for thought.

Getty Images—Photodisc—Royalty Free

Source: Adapted from Del Jones, "Cheating at Golf Is Par for the Course for CEOs," *Salt Lake City Tribune* (June 30, 2002); David Rynecki, "An 18-Hole Character Test," *Business Week* (May 28, 2007): 92–95; and behavioral economist, Dan Ariely, quoted from http://marketplace.publicradio.org/display/web/2009/10/06/pm-ariely-golf-q

person, under these circumstances, do things that he or she finds unacceptable. In this case, the individual is confronted with a personal choice. Unfortunately, the employee may have little institutional support in this situation but can lobby within or outside the organization to prohibit working on a holy day. This tactic may be effective, or the affected employee may choose not to work for that organization, depending on what he or she values most. As a practical matter, employees faced with ethical conflicts must make sure to document the events and discussions and list the parties involved so that a case can be made.

Conflicts between the Organization's Stated and Practiced Values

In some cases, employees will observe management or even senior management engaged in unethical behavior, such as management fraud. This type of conflict is the most difficult because the organization is misrepresenting its ethical system, forcing the employee to make a choice between going public with the information or keeping it quiet. In this setting, the employee is in a position of drawing attention to the problem by being a whistle-blower, which many have found to be a lonely and unenviable position. In many instances, though, whistle-blowers have chosen personal integrity over their loyalty to an organization.

Experts who have studied this problem advise that the individual should first ensure that the facts are correct and that a conflict does exist between the organization's stated ethical policy and the actions of its employees in practice. Second, by speaking with superiors, the individual should determine whether this conflict is institutional or whether it reflects the decisions and actions of only a small minority of employees. Faced with a true conflict, the individual has several choices, including the following:

1. Point out the discrepancy to a superior and refuse to act unethically. This may lead to dismissal, the need to resign from the organization, or the experience of suffering hidden organization sanctions.
2. Point out the discrepancy to a superior and act unethically. The rationale for this choice, which is incorrect, is that the employee believes that this affords protection from legal sanctions.
3. Take the discrepancy to a mediator in the organization if one exists.
4. Work with respected leaders in the organization to change the discrepancy between practiced and stated ethics.
5. Go outside the organization to publicly resolve the issue.
6. Go outside the organization anonymously to resolve the issue.
7. Resign and go public to resolve the issue.
8. Resign and remain silent.
9. Do nothing and hope that the problem will dissolve.

Although most experts recommend following alternative 4 on this list, it is beyond the scope of this chapter to discuss the efficacy of any of these alternatives other than to mention that there are circumstances that can make any of them appropriate. If the organization is serious about its stated code of ethics, it should have an effective ethical control system to ensure and provide evidence that the organization's stated and practiced ethics are the same. Part of this control system should include a means for employees to point out inconsistencies between stated practices and ethics without fear of retribution. For example, some organizations rely on an ombudsman, while others rely on the internal audit function or an external auditor. Any organization that does not provide a system to protect employees in these situations either is not taking its code of ethics seriously or has an inadequate ethical control system.

The Elements of an Effective Ethical Control System

To promote ethical decision making, management should implement an **ethical control system**. The elements of an ethical control system should include the following:

1. A statement of the organization's values and code of ethics written in practical terms, along with examples so that the organization's employees can relate the statement to their individual jobs.
2. A clear statement of the employee's ethical responsibilities for every job description and a specific review of the employee's ethical performance as part of every performance review.
3. Adequate training to help employees identify ethical dilemmas in practice and learn how to deal with those they can reasonably expect to face.
4. Evidence that senior management expects organization members to adhere to its code of ethics. This means that management must do the following:
   - Provide a statement of the consequences of violating the organization's code of ethics.
   - Establish a means of dealing with violations of the organization's code of ethics promptly, ruthlessly, and consistently with the statement of consequences.
   - Provide visible support of ethical decision making at every opportunity.
   - Provide a private line of communication (without retribution) from employees directly to the chief executive officer, chief operating officer, head of human resource management, or someone else on the board of directors.
5. Evidence that employees can make ethical decisions or report violations of the organization's stated ethics (i.e., be the whistle-blower) without fear of reprisals from superiors, subordinates, or peers in the organization. This proof usually takes the form of an organization mediator who has the authority to investigate complaints, wherever they lead, and to preserve the confidentiality of people who report violations.
6. An ongoing internal audit of the efficacy of the organization's ethical control system.

Steps in Making an Ethical Decision

Formal training is part of the process of promoting ethical decision making. After gathering the facts relating to a particular decision and evaluating the alternative courses of action, the decision maker can eliminate possible courses of action that are ethically unacceptable. The decision model in Exhibit 9-1 is one approach to eliminating unacceptable alternatives.

In summary, the organization's code of ethics is integral to MACS design. Both designers and users of the system should remember this fact and rectify any deviations from the code of ethics that the system explicitly or implicitly promotes.

Motivation and Congruence

In addition to fostering ethical behavior and decision-making, a central issue in MACS design is how to motivate appropriate behavior at work. When designing jobs and specific tasks, system designers should consider the following three dimensions of motivation:

1. Direction, or the tasks on which an employee focuses attention.
2. Intensity, or the level of effort the employee expends.
3. Persistence, or the duration of time that an employee will stay with a task or job.

Exhibit 9-1
Decision Model for Resolving Ethical Issues

---

1. **Determine the Facts–What, Who, Where, When, How**

   What do we know or need to know, if possible, that will help us define the problem?

2. **Define the Ethical Issue**
   - List the significant stakeholders
   - Define the ethical issues

   Identify precisely what the ethical issue is, for example, conflict involving rights, questions over limits of disclosure obligation, and so on.

3. **Identify Major Principles, Rules, Values**

   Determine key principles such as integrity, quality, respect for persons, societal benefits, and costs.

4. **Specify the Alternatives**

   List the major alternative courses of action, including those that represent some form of compromise or point between simply doing or not doing something.

5. **Compare Values and Alternatives**

   Determine if there is one principle or value (or a combination) that is so compelling that the proper alternative is clear, for example, correcting a defect that is almost certain to cause loss of life.

6. **Assess the Consequences**

   Identify short- and long-term positive and negative consequences for the major alternatives. The common short run focus on gains or losses needs to be measured against long-run considerations.

7. **Make Your Decision**

   Balance the consequences against your primary principles or values and select the alternative that best fits.

Consistent with theories of individual motivation, careful attention to motivation is a key step for the organization and its employees to align their respective goals; this alignment is known as achieving **goal congruence**. The alignment of goals occurs as employees perform their jobs well and are helping to achieve organizational objectives; they are also attaining their own individual goals, such as obtaining promotions, earning financial bonuses, or advancing their careers in other ways.

In a frictionless world, as employers and employees align their goals, employers could simply rely on the concept of **employee self-control**, in which employees monitor and regulate their own behavior and perform to their highest levels. Even if goals are aligned, however, different types of tasks require different levels of skill, precision, responsibility, initiative, and uncertainty. In most situations, managers try to establish systems that they do not have to personally monitor on a regular basis. The hope is that if these systems are well designed, the manager has much more time to attend to other concerns. These are called **diagnostic control systems**. These are feedback systems that monitor organizational outcomes and correct any deviations from predetermined performance standards. Typically, there is little debate about the nature of the system, and the systems tend to run in a routine fashion.

However, if a large degree of strategic uncertainty offers threats and opportunities that could alter the operating assumptions of a business, managers have to spend much more time monitoring the decisions and actions of their subordinates. Such a system is called an **interactive control system**.[1] Unlike diagnostic systems, interactive systems force a dialogue among all organizational participants about the data coming out of the system and what action to take.

---

[1] See R. Simons, *Levers of Control* (Boston: Harvard Business School Press, 1995).

Task and Results Control Methods

At the core of diagnostic and interactive systems are two common methods of control: task control and results control.

Task Control

Task control is the process of finding ways to control human behavior so that a job is completed in a prespecified manner. Task control can be separated into two categories: preventive control and monitoring. In **preventive control**, much, if not all, of the discretion is taken out of performing a task because of the precision required or the nature of the materials involved. For example, tasks that require very careful handling, such as making silicon wafers, or those that use precious metals, such as gold, often are controlled carefully or are performed by machines or computers. This is not to say that machines are infallible but rather that the degree of error is probably less than that experienced with humans. Naturally, as the accomplishment of a task requires increasingly greater judgment, the building of preventive control systems becomes more difficult.

Monitoring refers to inspecting the work or behavior of employees while they are performing a task. Monitoring can be accomplished using listening devices or through surveillance. For example, all of us have experienced the situation in which a (sometimes annoying) phone message tells us that the conversation we are about to have with a company representative may be "monitored to ensure quality control." Since monitoring, or listening in to a conversation in this case, is often done randomly, the employee does not know when it will occur and thus will be disciplined to act in a consistent, professional manner at all times. Monitoring also can be accomplished using surveillance. For example, cameras or "eyes in the sky" are used to observe the actions and behaviors of croupiers at gambling casinos.

Monitoring, however, can have its negative consequences. Some employees feel that being monitored causes them unnecessary stress. These same employees believe that monitoring also undermines the level of trust between employers and employees.

IN PRACTICE
Monitoring in the Workplace

For the past decade, the number of organizations that have been installing electronic performance monitoring systems to observe employee behavior at work has been steadily increasing. Estimates are that over a quarter of the entire U.S. workforce works under these systems. In addition, 66% of employers monitor Internet connections and the monitoring of e-mail and phone lines is also on the rise. This Orwellian "Big Brother" concept is supported by companies but denounced by employees.

Companies state that the advantages of such systems are that they improve productivity and the quality of work, they reduce human supervision costs, they overcome issues of subjectivity in performance evaluations, and they help in the security of company information and property.

As you might guess, employees are not very happy about such systems stating that they feel that their privacy is violated, that the organization does not trust them, that it reduces their dignity at work, and creates unnecessary tension and stress in the workplace.

Since it appears that these monitoring systems are here to stay, what can organizations do to help mitigate the negative effects that these systems have on employees? First, the reason for the system should be explained to all employees. Second, employees should be able to participate in system design and implementation. Third, monitoring should be restricted only to performance-related activities and not to other activities (such as lunch or coffee breaks). Fourth, an

(continued)

organization should not rely solely on monitoring data to assess an employee's performance and, finally, management should be open to system design changes.

Getty Images, Inc.—Stone Allstock

Source: American Management Association, *2007 Electronic Monitoring and Surveillance Survey*, retrieved from http://www.amanet.org/research/2008

Task control is most appropriate in the following situations:

1. When there are legal requirements to follow specific rules or procedures to protect public safety, such as in the manufacture of prescription drugs and critical aircraft components and in the operation of nuclear power generation facilities
2. When employees handle liquid assets (or other precious assets) to reduce the opportunity for temptation and fraud
3. When the organization can control its environment and eliminate uncertainty and the need for judgment. In such instances, the organization can develop specific rules and procedures that employees must follow.

Results Control

Rather than directly monitoring and directly controlling tasks, results control systems focus on measuring employee performance against stated objectives. For **results control** to be effective, the organization must have clearly defined its objectives, communicated them to appropriate organization members, and designed performance measures consistent with the objectives. For example, salespeople are often evaluated on the basis of the volume of sales they made during a specific time interval. The organization sets standards of performance against which the actual results of an employee's performance are compared. For another example, consider a business unit head who must improve her organization's financial performance relative to a prespecified target.

In some instances, task and results controls are used in tandem. As mentioned, phone calls by company salespeople often are monitored to control behavior; however, in addition, these same salespeople often have a weekly sales quota to reach. This is particularly true of salespeople from major long-distance carriers.

Results control is most effective in the following situations:

1. When organization members understand the organization's objectives and their contribution to those objectives.
2. When organization members have the knowledge and skill to respond to changing situations by taking corrective actions and making sound decisions.
3. When the performance measurement system is designed to assess individual contributions so that an individual can be motivated to take action and make decisions that reflect his or her own and the organization's best interests.

Central to the design of results control systems is the development of a performance measurement system that fully reflects the multiple objectives and goals of an organization. This issue is discussed in the following section.

USING A MIX OF PERFORMANCE MEASURES: A BALANCED SCORECARD APPROACH

The Need for Multiple Measures of Performance: Non–Goal-Congruent Behavior

The old saying "What gets measured gets done" indicates that the ways in which organizations and individuals measure performance send signals to all employees and stakeholders about what the organization considers as its priorities. If organizations choose performance measures without careful consideration, non–goal-congruent behavior can occur. For example, suppose a firm sets up a performance evaluation system that rewards a vendor only on the basis of on-time delivery of a product. In all likelihood, on-time delivery will be the variable on which the vendor's employees will focus. Since this evaluation would not consider the quality of the goods sent, vendors who supply the merchandise may sacrifice quality for the sake of meeting promised delivery dates, or they may quote excessively long lead times to ensure that deliveries are not late. Either action could work to the long-term detriment of the organization and the vendor.

Department store managers have discovered that when salespeople are compensated using sales quotas, their attention is focused on selling as much expensive merchandise as possible. Employees faced with such a situation initially may find that their sales volume is increasing, but as the competition for customers develops, the work environment may become hostile as salespeople dispute about customers or sales. Another consequence of relying solely on commissions as a motivating tool is that other aspects of the sales function, such as straightening merchandise or restocking shelves, may become lower priorities. Also, customers may return merchandise that has been oversold to them.

Dysfunctional Behavior

Occasionally, employees are so motivated to achieve a single goal that they engage in dysfunctional behavior. With respect to performance measurement, **dysfunctional behavior** refers to employees knowingly manipulating or falsifying performance measures. To illustrate, consider again a company whose single performance measure is whether employees attain their sales quotas. If an employee is worried about being fired and if there are no other ways to demonstrate good performance, the employee might alter his or her actions specifically in an attempt to manipulate a performance indicator through job-related acts. This is known as **gaming the performance indicator**.

As an example, a salesperson might ask his coworker to give him credit for the colleague's sales bookings, or the salesperson may have his friends come into the store, buy merchandise, and return it 30 days later. The salesperson might engage in data falsification by knowingly altering sales booking records in his or her favor. Data falsification is considered illegal, and the accounting profession has recently witnessed the dire consequences of employees engaged in such activities.

Another form of dysfunctional behavior is smoothing, a form of earnings management that occurs when individuals accelerate or delay the preplanned flow of data without altering the organization's activities. For example, a manager who is close to meeting a performance target, such as a net income or ROI number, may decide to defer expenses incurred in the current period to a future period. Similarly, the manager may attempt to book future revenues into the current period to increase net income. Over the long term, such behavior will lead to the same bottom-line financial outcomes, but the cost to the organization is that it does not have a clear picture of performance for a defined time period. Excessive amounts of smoothing are probably the result of inappropriate standards or a poorly conceived reward system.

In addition to setting up boundary systems so that employees have a clear understanding of what is considered appropriate and inappropriate behavior, organizations also can design performance measurement systems that encourage the desired behavior. One possibility is to use multiple performance measures that reflect the complexities of the work environment and the variety of contributions that employees make. In many of today's manufacturing and service environments, employees or associates are being cross-trained to perform a variety of tasks. For example, at all of the major automobile manufacturers including Toyota, DaimlerChrysler, Nissan, General Motors, Ford, Honda, and BMW, employees are organized into self-managed work teams that follow a product's manufacture from beginning to end. Thus, organizations have an opportunity to design multiple measures to assess the work that is actually being done. Using multiple performance measures also will cause employees to recognize the various dimensions of their work and to be less intent on trying to maximize their performance on a single target at the expense of other aspects of their jobs.

Using the Balanced Scorecard to Align Employees to Corporate Goals and Business Unit Objectives

In addition to using multiple performance measures, MACS designers have to expand their views of the kinds of performance measures to use. For example, only fairly recently have managers become aware of the need for measures of quality, speed to market, cycle time, flexibility, complexity, innovation, and productivity. Historically, some of these measures, such as quality, were in the hands of industrial engineers, while others, such as speed to market or flexibility, were not measured at all.

Managers should keep in mind other new organizational realities. Faced with increasing competitive pressures, many organizations have begun to move away from traditional hierarchical organizations with many layers of management, referred to as *tall organizations*, to those with fewer and fewer layers, or *flat organizations*. General Electric, for example, has reduced its hierarchical structure significantly. As the barriers between functional areas such as engineering design, manufacturing, accounting, finance, and marketing are eliminated, employees are working increasingly in cross-functional teams.

Another significant corresponding change is the use of business process reengineering, in which designers begin with a vision of what organizational participants would like their process or product to look like or how they would like it to function and then radically redesign it. Such an approach is significantly different from starting with an existing product or process and then making slight incremental changes. Further, reengineering design changes have led to the need for new informational requirements and measures related to the costs and benefits of innovation. Thus, new measures of performance must take into account group-level performance measures and cross-functional business process measures, not just departmental efficiency and spending measures.

The traditional focus of performance measures in management accounting has been on quantitative financial measures such as cost and profit rather than quantitative nonfinancial and qualitative measures. Examples of quantitative nonfinancial measures include yield, cycle time, schedule adherence, number of defects, market share, and customer retention. Variables such as the image of a product or service, the level of caring of the staff in a hospital, or the reputation of a company are examples of qualitative variables. Although they may be more subjective than quantitative variables, many qualitative variables can now be assessed using psychometric methods developed in the behavioral sciences. Customer satisfaction, for example, is a qualitative measure, which can now be quantified by using psychological scales. Clearly, measures such as customer satisfaction and employee morale are crucial for both the short- and the long-term success of any organization.

Change Management

As discussed in Chapter 2, MACS sometimes have to be redesigned to be congruent with an organization's new strategy. In particular, a firm may develop a new Balanced Scorecard strategy map to communicate and support implementation of the new strategy. Research has shown that the single most important factor in making major changes to an organization is having top management support, often at the level of the CEO and other senior managers. The change process often relies on a champion who is charged with spearheading the process. The most effective champions are those with strong entrepreneurial and communications skills, who have great respect in the organization and have the resources to carry out the change. The champion usually coalesces an implementation team composed of a wide variety of employees with different skills who represent key parts of the organization such as systems, accounting, finance, marketing, human resources, and strategy.

One organizational phenomenon that is often encountered by designers is resistance to change on the part of employees. Employees at all levels may feel threatened as new changes are suggested. One of the biggest threats is the potential loss of jobs or being reassigned to a new job, increases in the amount of work or responsibility in an existing job, changes in the workplace environment, changes in compensation, or just the threat of uncertainty and anxiety.

EMPOWERING EMPLOYEES TO BE INVOLVED IN MACS DESIGN

Empowering employees in MACS design requires two essential elements: allowing employees to participate in decision making and ensuring that employees understand the information they are using and generating.

Participation in Decision Making

Organizations often do not realize that their greatest asset is the people they employ. Encouraging participation has a twofold benefit for organizations. First, research has suggested that employees who participate in decision making evince better morale and greater feelings of job satisfaction. In many instances, these heightened feelings translate into increased productivity as employees begin to feel that they have some ownership and control over what they do at work.

Second, except in highly automated industries, people (not machines) still perform the major portion of work and have superior information and understanding with regard to how work is best accomplished and, consequently, how to improve products and processes. For example, employees in the Sydney branch of ANZAC Company will know more about the way their branch functions than will the people at central headquarters located in Melbourne. Therefore, MACS designers should strongly consider enlisting the participation of the Sydney employees. The same concept applies within a division. Assembly-line operators usually know more about the process on which they work than their managers do. Research has shown that participation and communication between local and central offices and between superiors and subordinates result in the transmission of critical information to which central management would otherwise not have access.

Education to Understand Information

The second critical element of empowering employees is to ensure that they understand the information they use and on which they are evaluated. Many executives believe that only managers need to understand the information generated by the MACS. Recently, it has become evident to many managers that employees at all levels must understand the organization's performance measures and the way they are computed in order to be able to take actions that lead to superior performance. For example, if employees do not understand how their actions affect a variable such as cycle time (the time it takes for a product or service to be produced or performed from start to finish), they will not know how to alter their actions to improve cycle time performance. If employees in a manufacturing plant are performing unnecessary actions on an assembly line or are idle, for example, the cycle time performance of their group will be affected. Similarly, at the point of service, or the point where organizational employees interact with customers, delays in the processing of claims also will increase cycle time.

Consider an airline whose intent is to improve its public image. From time to time, some airlines ask customers to fill out a customer satisfaction survey. If flight attendants have not been educated regarding how each of their actions (such as being rude or slow to produce service) directly affects customer satisfaction, the airline has failed to do its part to ensure satisfactory performance of one of its key indicators for flight attendants. This is also true in many other types of service organizations. In restaurants or department stores, customers often become frustrated with the level of service. For example, assigning waitpersons in a restaurant to too many tables can cause them to forget customer requests, or if they have annoying personal habits or are extremely clumsy, customers remember the negative experience and may not return. Consider a department store in which sales personnel may be too pushy, too difficult to find for service, or arrogant. A customer may become irritated with such an experience and vow never to shop at that store again.

Unless restaurant owners and department store managers educate their employees about how their actions affect customer perceptions of service quality and repeat business, the energy devoted to improving customer satisfaction is wasted. Studies have shown that, on average, five times as many customers who are dissatisfied with a product or service tell other people about their experience than do customers who are satisfied with a product or service. Thus, the reputation of organizations that offer a poorly produced product or a poorly delivered service can be ruined rather quickly. In general, poor or nonresponsive service by employees who have direct contact with customers is usually evidence of poor management, poor training, and poor education rather than an indicator that the employee is not a good worker.

For MACS to function well, employees have to be constantly reeducated as the system and its performance measures change. Without continuous updating of everyone's education, companies cannot be leaders or even players in international markets. In the United States, lack of training is a severe problem. For example, some studies have shown that U.S. employees receive only one-tenth the training of Japanese employees. Thus, U.S. management cannot expect its employees to be globally competitive if management does not supply them with the necessary training. Ultimately, the concept of continuous education should become so ingrained in employees that continually mastering new skills becomes a job requirement. Organizations that foster such an environment have been labeled learning organizations.

BEHAVIORAL ASPECTS OF MACS DESIGN: AN EXAMPLE FROM BUDGETING

One area of MACS design that has been well studied from a behavioral point of view is the budgeting process. While we discuss the technical aspects of budgeting in Chapter 10, we highlight the behavioral issues in this chapter.

Most organizations use budgets as a financial representation of their strategy. The process of developing budgets is often a long one and can sometimes be contentious. Because of the human factor involved in the entire process, budgets often do not develop in a smooth, frictionless manner. How do people try to affect the budget and, in turn, how do budgets affect people's behavior? These questions have led social scientists to undertake extensive studies about the human factors involved in budgeting.

Whether developing a family budget, a budget for a small company, or a budget for a major multinational company, it is important to be aware that the ways in which people interact with budgets are essentially the same. This section presents two related behavioral issues in budgeting:

1. *Designing the budget process*—How should budgets be determined, who should be involved in the budgeting process, and at what level of difficulty should the budget be set to have the greatest positive influence on people's motivation and performance?
2. *Influencing the budget process*—How do people try to influence or manipulate the budget to their own ends?

Designing the Budget Process

Where do the data that planners use to prepare the master budget and supporting plans come from? How should budgets be determined, and who should be involved in the budgeting process? Three common methods of setting budgets are authoritative, participative, and consultative.

Authoritative Budgeting

Authoritative budgeting occurs when a superior informs subordinates what their budget will be without requesting input. The benefit to the organization is that the process is straightforward and efficient—it allows superiors to assign budgets and promotes overall coordination among subunits in the organization because it is done from a single perspective. Managers who want to impose a budget in a top-down manner often want control and have authoritarian aspects to their personalities.

One disadvantage of imposing budgets is that superiors usually have less information about the process being budgeted than the subordinate. In authoritative budgeting situations, the superior indicates the goals to the subordinates, and subordinates who have high aspirations for the coming year regarding new goals may become frustrated and debilitated. A second problem is the lack of motivation and commitment to the budgeted goals because of the lack of employee participation in establishing the budget. Worse yet, if the superior sets high goals and provides only a small budget for resource spending, motivation can decrease significantly, and individuals and the organization can fail to attain their goals.

Research shows that the most motivating types of budgets are those that are tight, that is, those with targets that are perceived as ambitious but attainable. Companies such as Boeing and General Electric have implemented what are known as *stretch targets*. In the past, both companies used an incremental approach in which targets from the previous year were increased slightly. Stretch targets exceed previous targets by a significant amount and usually require an enormous increase in a goal over the next budgeting period. Stretch budgeting means that the organization will try to reach much higher goals with the current budget. The rationale is that stretch targets push an organization to its limits. The thinking is that only in this manner will companies completely reevaluate the ways in which they develop and produce products and services. While some employees thrive in this type of environment, the pace of work and the difficulty of achieving stretch targets can frustrate many and cause others to quit their jobs. Further, whereas employees may be able to push themselves very hard to meet the stretch target in the short run, they may not be able to sustain a high level of effort in every subsequent period. Organizations need to make sure that they provide resources and a plan so that employees believe that stretch targets are achievable.

Participative Budgeting

Participative budgeting is an approach to budget setting that uses a joint decision-making process in which all parties agree about setting the budget targets. Allowing employees to participate in decision making provides an opportunity for them to use information that they develop through their training or experience on the job to jointly set their goals and negotiate the level of their budgets. Participation has many benefits for employees, such as greater feelings of commitment to the budget and, therefore, a higher level of motivation to attain goals and keep within the budget.

Research on participative budgeting has shown that employees who participate in the budgeting process generally feel greater job satisfaction and higher morale because they feel greater control over their jobs. In some instances, higher levels of performance can result. Allowing participation offers an additional benefit for management because it often induces subordinates to reveal their private information, reveals data about how well they can perform their jobs, or allows the introduction of new ideas that may help improve existing processes. As a result of discussing the budget jointly, subordinates indirectly reveal this information and their level of aspiration to management. It then can be incorporated into the planning process.

Consultative Budgeting

Consultative budgeting occurs when managers ask subordinates to discuss their ideas about the budget but no joint decision making occurs. Instead, the superior solicits the subordinates' ideas and determines the final budget alone. For many large organizations in which complete participation is impractical, consultation is the norm. A variant of the consultative form of budgeting may occur when subordinates believe their input will be used directly in setting the budget—even though their superior really has no intention of considering their input. This process is called pseudoparticipation and can have a debilitating effect on subordinates if they find out that the superior was insincere.

Influencing the Budget Process

Clearly, the budgeting process is neither simple nor mechanical. It highlights the need for interactions about resource allocation, organizational goals, and human motivation and performance. In large organizations, as in families, budgets represent the outcomes of negotiations among individuals. Some individuals will do all they can to increase the size of their budgets because they believe a large budget is a symbol of power and control.

Although the budget is used as a tool for planning, coordinating, and resource allocation, it also serves to measure performance and serves ultimately to control and influence behavior. In addition, many managers have their incentive compensation tied directly to budget and goal attainment. When incentives and compensation are tied to the budget, some managers engage in behavior that is dysfunctional to their organizations. Managers have been known to play budgeting games in which they attempt to manipulate information and targets to achieve as high a bonus as possible. One well-known way that managers engage in budgeting games is through the participation process.

Participation has provided employees the opportunity to affect their budgets in ways that may not always be in the best interests of the organization. For example, subordinates might ask for more resources than they need to accomplish their budget objectives. This results in a misallocation of resources for the organization as a whole. Another risk is that subordinates will distort information by claiming that they are not as efficient or effective at what they do as they really are, thereby attempting to lower management's expectations of their performance. Subordinates may want some additional cushion in performance requirements in case there is an unforeseen change in the work environment that detrimentally affects resources or impairs their ability to meet the budget. If subordinates succeed in this type of negotiation, they will find it easy to meet or exceed their budgeted objectives. Again the organization suffers because it is not obtaining the most accurate information available to assess and thereby improve its operations. Both these acts—requiring excess resources and distorting performance information—fall under the heading of creating budget slack.

Consider a manager who is worried that a supplier will be unwilling to sell raw materials at a historically budgeted price. The manager may decide to increase the allowance requested for purchasing raw materials, which would build slack into this budget line item. The request leads to the assignment of excess resources for this purpose and, hence, fewer resources for other purposes. Other distortions can arise from arbitrary increases in resource requests because the resulting established standard costs for products will be incorrect. Further, subordinates are also concerned about standards or budgets that are too difficult to attain: If their bonuses are based on attaining a budget, they will opt for an easier budget. To counter the problem of low target setting, management may design an incentive system that provides higher levels of bonuses based on attaining higher targets.

Budgeting games can never be eliminated, although some organizations have devised methods to decrease the amount of budget slack. They can use an iterative process to formulate the budget, for example, developing a very lengthy budgeting cycle that may last as long as a year. Then subordinate managers submit a preliminary budget, which is modified by senior management and sent back to subordinate managers for modification. The modifications usually require justification in painful detail for each line item. This process continues for several iterations until senior managers are convinced that they have eliminated as much slack as possible from the subordinate manager's budget. The other benefit of this approach is that by the time both parties agree to the budget, everyone has developed a strong commitment to it. This commitment gives everybody involved the confidence that they can achieve their goals for the coming year.

DEVELOPING APPROPRIATE INCENTIVE SYSTEMS TO REWARD PERFORMANCE

The final behavioral consideration in MACS design is to consider the most appropriate reward systems to further motivate employees. The following presentation begins with a focus on both intrinsic and extrinsic rewards and continues with a discussion of the many types of financial reward systems that organizations use. A number of different theories of human motivation exist, including expectancy theory, agency theory, and goal-setting theory. Each theory stresses different aspects of motivation. Because the debate regarding these theories is so extensive, readers must decide to which theory they subscribe.[2]

Organizations use both intrinsic and extrinsic rewards to motivate employees. Intrinsic rewards are those that come from within an individual and reflect satisfaction from doing the job and from the opportunities for growth that the job provides. In some cases, intrinsic rewards reflect the nature of the organization and type of work one is performing. For example, volunteering at a day care center offers no financial compensation but instead provides the volunteer with the feeling or reward that he or she is helping children learn. Even in jobs where people are financially compensated, one of management's most challenging tasks is to design jobs and develop

Rewards in organizations don't have to be monetary. In many cases getting recognition through trophies, certificates, and plaques can be highly motivating.
Alamy Images Royalty Free

---

[2] Readers are referred to S. E. Bonner, and G. B. Sprinkle, "The Effects of Monetary Incentives on Effort and Task Performance: Theories, Evidence, and a Framework for Research," *Accounting, Organizations, and Society* (May/July 2002): 303–345.

an organizational environment and culture that lead employees to derive intrinsic rewards just by working. Organizations also hope that through the hiring process they can find a good match between a specific type of job and a specific individual. Because of how intrinsic rewards are derived, manufacturing accounting information has no effect on them.

Based on assessed performance, **extrinsic rewards** are any rewards that one person provides to another to recognize a job well done. Examples of commonly used extrinsic rewards are meals, tips, cash bonuses, stock bonuses, and recognition in newsletters and on plaques. Extrinsic rewards reinforce the notion that employees have distinguished themselves from the organization. Many people believe that extrinsic rewards also reinforce the common perception that the wage compensates the employee for a minimally acceptable effort and that the organization must use additional rewards or compensation to motivate the employee to provide additional effort.

Choosing between Intrinsic and Extrinsic Rewards

Many compensation experts believe that organizations have not made enough use of intrinsic rewards. They claim that, given proper management leadership, intrinsic rewards may have motivational effects as strong as or even stronger than extrinsic rewards. The issue of the effectiveness of intrinsic and extrinsic rewards is a topic of heated debate in the management literature. Some argue that people who expect to receive a reward for completing a task or for doing that task successfully do not perform as well as those who expect no reward at all. Others argue that, although this result holds true over a wide range of tasks, people, and rewards, the result is strongest when the job requires creative skills. For some, pay may not be a motivator. This argument is built around the idea that the preoccupation with extrinsic rewards undermines the effectiveness of reward systems and that the design of organizations and jobs should allow employees to experience intrinsic rewards.

The issue remains unresolved. However, one thing is clear: Most organizations have ignored and continue to ignore the role of intrinsic rewards in motivation and blindly accept the view that only financial extrinsic rewards motivate employees. Many people believe that financial extrinsic rewards are both necessary and sufficient to motivate superior performance. Both systematic and anecdotal evidence suggests, however, that financial extrinsic rewards are not necessary to create effective organizations and that performance rewards do not necessarily create them. Whether nonfinancial extrinsic and intrinsic rewards are more or less effective than financial extrinsic rewards in motivating behavior is an unresolved matter. However, both nonfinancial extrinsic and intrinsic rewards have a role to play in most organizations.

Beyond the debate about the relative effectiveness of intrinsic and extrinsic rewards, some people argue that incentive compensation programs in any form are unacceptable. They suggest that organizations must strive to be excellent to survive in a complex and competitive world. Thus, superior and committed performance is necessary for all employees in organizations and is part of the contract of employment, not something that merits additional pay.

Conversely, a large number of organizations rely on extrinsic monetary rewards to motivate performance. Since employees often engage in social comparisons of how they are performing at work, extrinsic monetary rewards are a tangible indicator of how well one is doing relative to others. These organizations base their reward systems to a large extent on information and measures provided by management accounting systems. The remainder of this section focuses on the kinds of extrinsic rewards that are most commonly used in organizations.

Extrinsic Rewards Based on Performance

Incentive compensation plans, or pay-for-performance systems, are reward systems that provide monetary (extrinsic) rewards based on measured results. Pay-for-performance systems base rewards on achieving or exceeding some measured performance. The underlying philosophy of this system is based on the adage "You get what you measure and reward." Thus, organizations need performance measurement systems that gather relevant and reliable performance information. The reward can be based on absolute performance, performance relative to some plan, or performance relative to that of some comparable group. Measures of absolute performance include the following:

1. The number of acceptable quality units produced (such as a piece-rate system).
2. The organization's results (such as profit levels or an organization's Balanced Scorecard measures of customer or employee satisfaction, quality, and rate of successful new product introductions).
3. The organization's share price performance (such as stock option plan).

Examples of rewards based on relative performance are those tied to the following:

1. The ability to exceed a performance target level (such as paying a manager for accomplishing his or her goals under budget or paying a production group a bonus for beating a benchmark performance level).
2. The amount of a bonus pool (such as sharing in a pool defined as the organization's reported profits less a stipulated return to shareholders).
3. The degree to which performance exceeds the average performance level of a comparable group.

Occasionally, compensation policy can be affected by government regulations. For example, since 1994, for the purpose of computing taxable income, most organizations in the United States cannot claim as an expense the portion of any employee's salary that exceeds $1 million. This will certainly (1) reduce the use of salary and perquisites (such as company cars and club memberships) and (2) increase the use of variable pay based on performance.

Effective Performance Measurement and Reward Systems

The following six attributes of a measurement system must be in place in order to motivate desired performance:

1. **The employees must understand their jobs and the reward system and believe that it measures what they control and contribute to the organization.** This attribute ensures that the employee perceives the reward system as fair and predictable. If employees do not understand their jobs or how to improve their measured performance, a reward system based on performance measures is ineffective. In this case, employees perceive no relationship between effort and performance and, ultimately, outcomes. Similarly, if the reward system is complex, employees are unable to relate perceived performance improvements to changes in outcomes, and the motivational effect of the reward system will be lost. Additionally, if the reward system does not measure employees' controllable performance, they conclude that measured performance is independent of their efforts, and again the incentive effect of the reward system is lost. Specifying and developing a clear relationship among effort, performance, and results and ensuring that all employees understand this relationship is a critical management role. Therefore, the centerpiece of incentive compensation systems is the performance measurement system, which becomes the focus of the employees' attention. The

decisions that employees make in pursuing the performance measures that ultimately provide valued personal outcomes move the organization toward achieving its goals if the performance measures are aligned with the organization's goals.

2. **Related to the first attribute, designers of the performance measurement system must make a careful choice about whether it measures employees' inputs or outputs.** In general, the greatest alignment between employees' and the organization's interests is provided when the performance measurement system monitors and rewards employee outputs that contribute to the organization's success. However, outputs often reflect circumstances and conditions that are beyond the employee's control, and when they do, the perceived link between individuals' efforts and measured results is reduced, thereby decreasing the motivation provided by the reward system. Under circumstances when outcome measurement is problematic, organizations often choose to monitor and reward inputs (such as employee learning, demonstrated skill, and time worked). For example, in some manufacturing organizations, employees can take on-site night classes to increase their skills. Once these classes are completed and the new skills mastered, the employees are moved to a higher wage level. The choice of the mix of performance measures and the decision about whether those measures are input based, output based, or a combination of measures make up one of the most difficult tasks in the design of performance measurement and compensation systems.

3. **The elements of performance that the performance measurement system monitors and rewards should reflect the organization's critical success factors.** This attribute ensures that the performance system is relevant and motivates intended performance that matters to the organization's success. Moreover, the performance measurement system must consider all facets of performance so that employees do not sacrifice performance on an unmeasured element for performance on an element that the reward system measures. This is the role and purpose of measuring and rewarding employees across a set of balanced and comprehensive measures, as proposed in the Balanced Scorecard. For example, if a supervisor tells a telephone operator that productivity (such as the number of help requests handled per shift) is important, the operator may sacrifice the quality and courtesy offered to customers in order to handle as many questions as possible.

4. **The reward system must set clear standards for performance that employees accept.** Standards help employees assess whether their skills and efforts create results that the performance measurement system captures and reports as outcomes. This attribute determines employees' beliefs about whether the performance system is fair. If performance standards are either unspecified or unclear to employees, the relationship between performance and outcome is ambiguous and thereby reduces the motivational effect of the performance reward system.

5. **The measurement system must be calibrated so that it can accurately assess performance.** This attribute ensures that the performance measurement system establishes a clear relationship between performance and outcome.

6. **When it is critical that employees coordinate decision making and other activities with other employees, the reward system should reward group rather than individual performance.** Many organizations now believe that, to be effective, employees must work well in teams. These organizations are replacing evaluations and rewards based on individual performance with rewards and evaluations based on group performance.

In most organizations, pay is more than simply what is required to keep an employee from leaving the organization. Pay is part of the complex bundle of factors that motivate people to work in the organization's best interests. Therefore, organizations must consider pay issues within the larger context of motivation.

Conditions Favoring Incentive Compensation

Not all organizations are suited to incentive compensation systems. Centralized organizations require most of the important operating decisions to be made in the head office. Such organizations are unsuited to incentive compensation systems for their front-line employees because employees in these organizations are expected to follow rules and have no authority to make decisions. In fact, it is more appropriate to call compensation systems in these organizations enforcement systems because employment continues only if people follow the rules and standard operating procedures. Here the task of the management accountant is to design internal control systems and conduct internal audits to verify that people are following rules and procedures.

Incentive compensation systems work best in organizations in which employees have the skill and authority to react to conditions and make decisions. We previously discussed organizations that face continually changing environments—ones in which it is either impractical or impossible to develop standard operating procedures to deal with these changing conditions. Such organizations can develop incentive compensation systems that motivate employees to identify changes in the environment, to apply their skills and knowledge accordingly, and to make decisions that best reflect the organization's goals.

When the organization has empowered its employees to make decisions, it can use incentive compensation systems to motivate appropriate decision-making behavior. In these organizations, the focus of control changes from telling people what to do to asking employees to use their skills and delegated authority to do their best to help the organization achieve its stated objectives.

Incentive Compensation and Employee Responsibility

The incentive compensation system must focus primarily on outcomes that the employee controls or influences. Consider an incentive compensation plan that rewards the performance of a production worker only when the sales department meets its sales target. Assuming that the worker is responsible only for the amount of resources used in the production of a product and its quality, it would be demotivating to base the employee's compensation on a sales target because the sales department, and not the production department, controls the level of sales.

Employees' incentive compensation should reflect the nature of their responsibilities in the organization. Employees whose roles are to plan, coordinate, and control day-to-day activities should receive rewards based on their ability to manage these daily operations effectively and to make the best short-term use of available resources. Their rewards should be tied to short-term controllable performance measures, such as efficiency and the ability to meet customer quality and service requirements. Employees whose roles are to plan long-term projects, such as building new facilities or acquiring significant capital equipment, should be rewarded on the basis of the long-term growth or improvement in the organization's operations that results from their strategic choices. These rewards should be based on the organization's performance compared with its stated objectives. In some cases, rewards also can be based on how an organization's performance compares with that of other, similar organizations. This mix of rewarding both short- and long-term outcomes is consistent with the goals of the Balanced Scorecard approach discussed in Chapter 2.

Rewarding Outcomes

Another consideration in the design of effective incentive compensation systems is the manner in which performance is measured. Incentive compensation schemes tie rewards to the outputs of employee performance rather than to such inputs as their level of effort. Moreover, incentive compensation based on outcomes requires that organization members understand and contribute to the organization's objectives.

However, rewards can be based on inputs in three instances:

- When it is impossible to measure outcomes consistently.
- When outcomes are affected by factors beyond the employee's control.
- When outcomes are expensive to measure.

Input-based compensation measures the time, knowledge, and skill level that the employee brings to the job, with the expectation that the unmeasured outcome is correlated with these inputs. Many organizations use some form of knowledge-based remuneration. This type of remuneration bases the rate of pay on an employee's training and job qualifications, which can be upgraded by on-the-job training. The employee's compensation is the product of the number of hours worked (time input) and the hourly rate (a reflection of the deemed level of skill input). Organizations use knowledge-based pay to motivate employees to continuously upgrade their job skills, thereby allowing them to receive a higher base pay.

Managing Incentive Compensation Plans

Considerable evidence indicates that organizations have mismanaged incentive compensation plans, particularly those for senior executives. Many articles have appeared in influential business periodicals arguing that executives, particularly executives of U.S. corporations, have been paid excessively for mediocre performance.

Experts debate whether compensation systems motivate goal-seeking behavior and whether they are efficient, that is, whether they pay what is needed and no more. Some studies show a positive correlation between executive compensation and shareholder wealth. Other studies report finding no correlation (or even a negative one) between organization performance and executive compensation. Until recently, shareholder value was decreasing, while executive compensation was climbing. Some believe it is particularly inappropriate for companies to continue operating compensation systems in which executive rewards bear no relation to corporate performance.

This executive is smiling since sales are going up and he expects a bonus. It could be argued that the executive is simply doing his job and that as long as he is compensated fairly, no bonus is necessary. What do you think?

Alamy Images Royalty Free

Despite economic data showing an association between executive compensation and company performance, many professionals still argue that the amounts are excessive and reflect high status rather than good performance. The issue of fairness has also surfaced. Surveys indicate that, on average, chief executive officers in the United States earn 300 times the amount of the lowest paid employee. In Japan, however, the relationship is only 30 times the lowest paid worker. That these questions are raised reflects perceptions of unfairness and a degree of cynicism that average people feel about the role of incentive compensation in organizations.

Types of Incentive Compensation Plans

The most common incentive compensation plans are cash bonuses, profit sharing, gain sharing, stock options, performance shares stock, stock appreciation rights, participation units, and employee stock ownership plans. These different plans pose varying challenges for the management accounting system.

We can group compensation plans into two broad categories: (1) those that rely on internal measures, invariably provided by the organization's management accounting system, and (2) those that rely on performance of the organization's share price in the stock market.

Management accountants get involved in the first group of plans—those that revolve around rewards based on performance that the organization's management accounting system monitors and reports. Most employees who participate in financial incentive plans take the plans very seriously. These people are both interested in and concerned about the performance measurement system that monitors and reports the performance measures used to compute and distribute financial rewards. Many practicing management accountants have found that the most contentious debates arise from issues relating to performance measurement used for financial rewards. Therefore, management accountants take the matter of developing performance measures for financial reward systems very seriously.

Organizations use many other forms of stock-related incentive compensation plans, including performance shares stock, stock appreciation rights, participation units, and employee stock ownership plans that are beyond the scope of issues in management accounting. These plans provide incentive compensation to the participants when the stock price increases. The idea behind such plans is to motivate employees to act in the long-term interests of the organization by engaging in activities that increase the organization's market value. Therefore, all of these plans assume that stock markets will recognize exceptional behavior in the form of increased stock prices.

Cash Bonus

A cash bonus plan—also called a lump-sum reward, pay for performance, or merit pay—pays cash on the basis of some measured performance. Such a bonus is a one-time award that does not become part of the employee's base pay in subsequent years.

Cash bonuses can be fixed in amount and triggered when measured performance exceeds the target, or they can be proportional to the level of performance relative to the target. They can be based on individual or group performance, and they can be paid to individuals or groups.

For example, in the late 1980s, General Motors eliminated automatic salary increases based on increases in the cost of living and replaced them with a pay-for-performance system that rewarded managers based on their results. Managers were required to group their employees into four groups: high performers (the top 10%), good performers (the next 25%), average performers (the next 55%), and low performers (the last 10%). Supervisors used these groupings to award merit pay and to enforce salary differences based on assessed performance.

Profit Sharing

Profit sharing is a cash bonus calculated as a percentage of an organization's reported profit. Profit sharing is a group incentive compensation plan focused on short-term performance.

All profit-sharing plans define what portion of the organization's reported profits is available for sharing, the sharing formula, the employees who are eligible to participate in the plan, and the formula for each employee's share.

Many profit-sharing plans are based on residual income, now called economic value added. In such plans, the reported profit will be reduced by some percentage (say, 15%) of the shareholders' investment in the organization. This allotment provides the shareholders with the required return on their investment. The resulting pool is shared between employees and shareholders on some fractional basis, such as 40% for employees and 60% for shareholders. The plan also may specify a limit on the total amount of profits that can be distributed to employees. In addition, the profit-sharing plan specifies how it will distribute the money in the pool to each employee: Some plans provide equal distribution; others distribute the bonus pool on the basis of the employee's performance relative to individual performance targets.

IN PRACTICE

UNIBANCO—Tying the Balanced Scorecard to Compensation

Unibanco, with more than US $23 billion in total assets, is the fifth largest bank in Brazil, and the third largest in the private sector. Unibanco started its Balanced Scorecard project in 2000 by building a company scorecard and scorecards for its four major business units: insurance and pension, retail, wholesale, and asset (wealth) management. During 2001, senior executives launched a communication campaign to inform all 27,000 employees about the new strategy and the method for managing the strategy. It used the Schürmann family of Brazil, famous for traveling the world in a sailboat, to give talks to 2,000 managers at various bank locations on how "we're all in the same boat," and that each crew member has to know the destination for them to contribute to the objective of the boat reaching its destination successfully. Advertisements and articles about the Painel de Gestão (management panel) and the relevant indicators appeared on the corporate intranet portal and the internal TV network, in the internal monthly magazine, and in personal e-mails sent to every manager. The successful sailing campaign branded the scorecard concept for employees and made everyone aware that their everyday actions affected the success of the company strategy. Several years later, in 2004, Unibanco launched a 2-10-20 campaign: the goals were to achieve by the 80th anniversary year in 2006, R2 billion in income, R10 billion

in equity, and a 20% return-on-equity. The communications program promoted the 2-10-20 slogan everywhere, including in elevator displays.

People were encouraged to tell the story of how their actions led to successful outcomes. Each monthly issue of the internal magazine selected the best stories to celebrate the individuals and teams that had achieved significant results on key performance indicators. Annually, Unibanco provided a presidential reward for initiatives that achieved breakthrough results for a strategic theme.

In 2002, Unibanco adapted an existing personnel management tool, the management agreement between each employee and his or her manager. The first page of the revised management agreement described the unit's and the bank's strategic themes. Employees then created their personal management agreement, with their supervisors, aligned to the unit and bank's strategic themes. The management agreement had employee objectives in the four BSC perspectives that were clearly linked to one or more unit and corporate strategic themes. For example, an employee in the marketing department, helping to create a campaign to stimulate new accounts, would have a financial objective related to the estimated lifetime value of new accounts acquired. An employee producing an output used by another bank unit would treat the

(continued)

value delivered to the other unit as a customer objective. Unibanco used the management agreement in every employee's recognition and bonus plan. For the learning and growth objective in the management agreement, the human resources group helped employees determine the competencies—knowledge, skills, and behavior— they required to reach the objectives in their three other management agreement perspectives.

Unibanco's previous compensation program assigned a total compensation pool to each unit based on the unit's financial performance. The bank modified this program by adding two additional elements of variable pay. First, it added (or subtracted) a percentage

to the compensation pool based on the lead (nonfinancial) indicators on the unit's Balanced Scorecard; another percentage was added or subtracted based on the company's performance. The company included a corporate bonus component so that employees would think about the total bank's performance, not just the performance of their decentralized unit.

From 1999 to 2004, Unibanco's employee "comprehension of the company's mission and vision" rose from 72% to 83%. Earnings per share increased from 5.57 in 1999 to 9.45 in 2004, with expectations of continued substantial increases in future years (to reach the 2-10-20 targets).

Source: R. Kaplan and D. Norton, *The Execution Premium: Linking Strategy to Operations for Competitive Advantage* (Boston: Harvard Business School Press, 2008).

In the performance compensation approach, employees receive a performance score that reflects how well they achieved specific performance goals for that year. The employee's score divided by the total scores of all employees in the profit-sharing agreement is the individual's share of the pool total. Some profit-sharing plans distribute rewards to each employee in an amount proportional to the base wage or salary because the plans' designers believe this reflects the employee's contribution to the overall result.

Profit-sharing plans require a number of contributions from the organization's accounting systems in general and from the management accounting system in particular. First, the organization must prepare a means to calculate profits. This process usually is monitored and attested to by an external auditor. Second, when a deduction is to be made from the pool that is based on the owners' investment, the management accounting system must provide a measure of invested capital. Third, when the profit sharing is based on some measured level of performance (for example, a composite score that reflects the employee's ability to meet a set of performance targets), the management accounting system must provide the underlying measures of performance and the overall performance score.

Gain Sharing

Gain sharing is a system for distributing cash bonuses from a pool when the total amount available is a function of performance relative to some target. For example, employees in a designated unit receive bonuses when their performance exceeds a performance target. Gain sharing is a group incentive, unlike the pay-for-performance cash bonus, which is an individual reward. In its usual form, gain sharing provides for the sharing of financial gains in organizational performance. The gain-sharing plan usually applies to a group of employees within an organization unit, such as a department or a store. It uses a formula to specify the amount and distribution of the rewards and a base period of performance as the benchmark for comparing subsequent performance. This benchmark is not changed unless a major change occurs in process or technology. When performance exceeds the base period performance, the gain-sharing plan pays a bonus pool.

Gain sharing promotes teamwork and participation in decision making. It requires employees to have the skills to participate and the organization to encourage participation. Consider these companies that have used gain sharing effectively:

- The Herman Miller Company, a furniture manufacturer that is frequently rated as one of the 10 best managed U.S. corporations, has used a gain-sharing plan for many years. The company also uses a strategy of employee involvement that supports and enhances the motivational effect of the gain-sharing plan.

- Grumman Corporation developed a performance bonus plan for the crew in its Long Life Vehicle project that it used in conjunction with its Grumman quality program. Employees focused on processes that involved rework, scrap, and excessive maintenance costs. Half the savings from improved performance were divided equally among the crew members working on the project.

The three most widely used gain-sharing programs are improshare, the Scanlon plan, and the Rucker plan:

1. **Improshare** (improved productivity sharing) determines its bonus pool by computing the difference between the target level of labor cost given the level of production and the actual labor cost (the direct labor efficiency variance; see Chapter 10 for details). The plan specifies how the difference will be shared between the shareholders and the employees and how to calculate the amount distributed to each employee.

2. The **Scanlon plan** is based on the following formula, computed using the data in some base period:

Base ratio = Payroll costs/Value of goods or services produced

For example, if in the base period payroll costs are $25 million and the deemed value of production or service is $86 million, the base ratio would be 0.29 ($25 million ÷ $86 million). In any period in which the ratio of labor costs to the value of production or service is less than the base ratio, the deemed labor savings are added to a bonus pool. Therefore, continuing the previous example, if actual payroll costs were $28 million in a period when the deemed value of production was $105 million, the amount added to the bonus pool would be as follows:

Amount added to bonus pool = (Value of production this period × Base ratio)
− Actual payroll costs
= ($105,000,000 × 0.29) − $28,000,000
= $2,450,000

When labor costs are more than the base ratio, some organizations deduct the difference from the bonus pool. Periodically, usually once a year, the pool is apportioned between the company and the employees in the pool using the plant ratio, which is often 50%/50%.

3. The **Rucker plan** is based on the following formula, which reflects the data from a representative period:

Rucker standard = Payroll costs/Production value

where production value is measured as Net sales – Inventory change – Materials and supplies used. As in the Scanlon plan, the idea of the Rucker plan is to define a baseline relationship between payroll costs and the value of production and then to reward workers who improve efficiency. Efficiency is measured as lowering the ratio of payroll costs to the value of production. When actual costs are less than the Rucker standard, the employees receive a bonus.

For gain-sharing plans to work, they must reflect performance levels that are reasonable. As might be expected, management and the employees who are subject to these plans often have very different ideas about what is fair. Management usually seeks tighter standards or targets, and employees want the opposite. These plans require that management, the management accountant, and employees participate in seeking the performance level that will serve as the standards or benchmarks for the plans. Many management accountants relish their role as the honest brokers between management and the employees who are subject to these plans.

The people who designed gain-sharing plans believed, from the beginning, that monthly or even weekly performance awards are best because they provide rapid feedback and, therefore, additional motivation, because rewards reinforce the desired type of behavior. However, although rapid feedback may improve the motivational effect of rewards (expectancy), short-cycle feedback can put strains on the organization's management accounting system when the need for recording and accruing labor costs increases both the cost and potential for error in the management accounting system.

Since gain-sharing plans are team-based rewards, they have the associated problem that some team members may not be doing their fair share and could earn rewards based on the work of others. For example, students often complain about group projects, particularly when they cannot choose their own groups, because someone in the group often refuses to do or is incapable of doing the work. Students, like employees, are often uncomfortable about disciplining, or reporting, their peers. The early proponents of gain sharing recognized this phenomenon and observed that for gain sharing to work, the organizational culture must promote cohesive relationships within the group and between the group and management.

In addition, corporate culture has a significant effect on the potential of gain-sharing plans. These programs rely on employee commitment and involvement. Therefore, a corporate culture that respects employees, encourages their involvement, and actively supports employee learning and innovation reinforces the motivational potential of a gain-sharing program.

Like all incentive programs, gain-sharing programs work best when they are simple to understand and monitor. A test of this attribute is whether employees can do the math to compute their own bonuses. In addition, such programs should be perceived as fair, as being directly affected by employee performance, and as being conducive to promoting teamwork.

Gain-sharing plans usually rely on performance measures reported by an organization's management accounting system, which plays a primary supporting role in the gain-sharing process. Most gain-sharing plans focus on management accounting measures relating to labor costs and the relationship of actual labor cost to some standard, or budgeted, level of labor cost. Therefore, the key issues in performance measurement relate to measuring labor costs accurately and consistently and to having the ability to establish a cost standard that is perceived as fair.

Stock Options and Other Stock-Related Compensation Plans

Judging by the published remarks of compensation experts, stock options are the most widely known, misused, and maligned approach to incentive compensation. A stock option is the right to purchase a unit of an organization's stock at a specified price, called the option price.

A common approach to option pricing is to set the option price at about 105% of the stock's market price at the time the organization issues the stock option. This method is intended to motivate the employee who has been granted the stock option to act in the long-term interests of the organization, thereby increasing the value of the firm so that the market price of the stock will exceed the option price. For this reason, compensation system designers usually restrict stock options to senior executives because they believe that these people have the greatest effect on increasing the market value of the organization. Others have argued, however, that operations staff, as they carry out short-term operating plans, can make significant and sustainable process improvements. This would provide the organization with a competitive advantage, thereby increasing the organization's market value.

The critics of stock option plans have argued that organizations have been too generous in rewarding senior executives with stock options. For example, the organization may issue a senior executive many thousands of stock options with an option price that is very near (or even below) the market price at the time the stock option is issued. This is an implementation issue, not a fundamental defect of stock options. Some critics have argued, however, that stock price increases often reflect general market trends that have nothing to do with the performance of the individual organization. For this reason, many incentive compensation experts have argued that the stock option price should be keyed to the performance of the organization's shares relative to the performance of the prices of comparable shares. In this case, the stock option would be valuable only if the organization's share price increases more rapidly than the share prices of comparable organizations. Since management accountants are often involved in studies or systems that rely on external benchmarks, organizations sometimes delegate the role of developing the appropriate performance standards for relative stock option plans to a team that includes a management accountant.

In general, the use of employee stock ownership plans assumes that employees will work harder when they have an ownership stake. Avis, the automobile rental company, used an employee stock ownership plan to improve employee motivation, resulting in both higher sales and a higher margin on sales. Salomon Brothers, a Wall Street investment house, provided huge bonuses for high-performing employees during the 1980s and early 1990s. For example, one bond trader was paid a $23 million bonus in 1990. Reacting to this, Salomon Brothers' largest shareholder, Warren Buffett, whom *Forbes* magazine identified as the wealthiest person in the United States in 1993 and who was interim chairman at the time, indicated that he wanted Salomon Brothers employees to earn rewards through owning shares, not by free riding on the owners' investment. To align the interests of the firm's employees and its shareholders and provide for more reasonable performance rewards, Buffett, through the Salomon Brothers Compensation Committee, developed an incentive plan that paid employees up to half their pay in company stock, issued at below-market prices, but that could not be sold for at least five years after issue. However, Buffett failed to weigh a consideration that is vital in designing any compensation plan, namely, how other investment banking firms were compensating their employees. While some people applauded the rationality of Buffett's plan, many employees left the firm to join other investment banking firms that were using compensation practices similar to the ones abandoned at Salomon Brothers. These departures precipitated a crisis that eventually led to the scrapping of the new plan.

EPILOGUE TO ADVANCED CELLULAR INTERNATIONAL AND CHAPTER SUMMARY

In the opening vignette to this chapter, Wayne Jagielski thought he had not been careful enough to involve employees in designing his new MACS. He wondered whether there were other behavioral considerations that he needed to take into account and manage. This chapter outlined four key behavioral characteristics that make up a well-designed MACS. The choice of the four characteristics is based largely on an acceptance of the human resources model of human motivation. Understanding these characteristics should provide Wayne guidance for designing his new MACS.

The first is embedding the organization's ethical code of conduct into MACS design. At the core of a well-designed MACS is the organization's ethical code of conduct. Ethical codes of conduct help organizations deal with ethical dilemmas or conflicts between individuals and organizational values and those that exist between the organization's stated and practiced values. The elements of an effective ethical control system were presented together with a specific decision model that can be applied when attempting to resolve ethical issues.

Organizations spend a lot of time determining how to motivate employees. One way is to align the goals of employees with those of the organization. However, even if goals are aligned, organizations cannot always rely on employee self-control to achieve targeted performance. In many instances, organizations must set up task or results control systems. Task control uses either preventive control devices or relies on monitoring, whereas results control focuses on comparing actual results to desired performance. Development and use of the right kinds of performance measures are tied directly into the second behavioral characteristic, which involves using a mix of short- and long-term qualitative and quantitative performance measures. This is the Balanced Scorecard approach. Even in the best control systems, employees often attempt to engage in non–goal-congruent behavior and we illustrated this within a budgeting context. One of the most challenging aspects of control system design is to find ways to mitigate these problems.

The third characteristic is empowering employees to be involved in decision making and MACS design. This characteristic acknowledges that people are the organization's greatest asset. Providing a voice through participation has a twofold benefit. First, participation in decision making has been shown to increase employee morale, commitment to a decision, and job satisfaction. Second, by allowing employees to participate, the organization is able to gather information about jobs and processes from the individuals who are closest to those jobs and processes. Such information provides managers with insights that they would not normally be able to obtain simply by performing cursory inspections of how people are working. Continuing to educate employees in the information they are using and being evaluated on is another critical aspect of employee involvement. For example, without a clear understanding of how their actions translate into a score on a performance measure, employees are left without direction and may take actions detrimental to the organization.

Both intrinsic and extrinsic rewards are used by organizations to motivate employees. However, intrinsic rewards come from inside an individual and may simply be the result of an employee liking a specific job. Organizations try to hire individuals who will match a particular job and thus be intrinsically motivated. However, even if intrinsic motivation exists, many organizations still rely on extrinsic rewards, such as financial incentives, for motivational purposes.

Developing an appropriate incentive system to reward performance is the fourth characteristic. This chapter discussed the characteristics of an effective performance measurement system and the most common ways of rewarding results, including cash bonus, gain sharing, and stock options.

Finally, this chapter provided examples of behavioral and organizational issues that arise in relation to budgets, an important part of management and control systems. Because budgets are developed and implemented through people, we must consider the effects that budgets and budgeting have on people and how people affect budgets and budgeting. Research suggests that involving those subject to budgets in the budgeting process increases their commitment to the budget if people believe that they are contributing to the setting of targets and standards. In this regard, research also suggests that stretch targets, which are targets deemed difficult but achievable by the people subject to the target, are the most effective in motivating performance levels.

KEY TERMS

Questions

9-1 What does *control* refer to in the context of a management accounting and control system? (LO 1)

9-2 What are the four stages involved in keeping an organization in control? (LO 1)

9-3 What two broad technical considerations must designers of management and control systems address? (LO 2)

9-4 What four components should MACS designers consider when addressing the relevance of the system's information? (LO 2)

9-5 What are the four major behavioral considerations in MACS design? (LO 3)

9-6 What is the primary difference between the scientific management view of motivation and the human resources model view? (LO 3)

9-7 What is the human relations movement view of motivation? (LO 4)

9-8 What different types of unethical pressures are managers subjected to? (LO 5)

9-9 What are some choices that individuals can make when ethical conflicts arise? (LO 5)

9-10 What is an ethical control system, and what are its key elements? (LO 5)

9-11 What are the three key dimensions of motivation? (LO 6)

9-12 What is employee self-control? (LO 6)

9-13 How do diagnostic control systems differ from interactive control systems? (LO 6)

9-14 What is task control? List the two categories of task control. (LO 6, 7)

9-15 What is monitoring? (LO 6, 7)

9-16 What are the two ways in which monitoring is accomplished? (LO 6, 7)

9-17 List three quantitative financial measures of performance each in a manufacturing organization and a service of your choice. (LO 8)

9-18 List three quantitative nonfinancial measures of performance each in a manufacturing organization and a service organization. (LO 8)

9-19 How does results control differ from task control? (LO 6, 7)

9-20 List three qualitative measures of performance. (LO 8)

9-21 What is meant by the term *smoothing*? (LO 6, 8)

9-22 What is data falsification? (LO 6, 8)

9-23 What is the single most important factor in making major changes to an organization? (LO 6, 8)

9-24 What is an example of gaming the performance indicator? (LO 6, 8)

9-25 What are two essential elements in employee empowerment in MACS design? (LO 9)

9-26 What are the two interrelated behavioral issues in budgeting? (LO 10)

9-27 What are the three most common methods of setting a budget? (LO 10)

9-28 How does consultative budgeting differ from participative budgeting? (LO 10)

9-29 What is stretch budgeting? (LO 10)

9-30 What are *budgeting games*? (LO 10)

9-31 What does *pseudoparticipation* mean? (LO 10)

9-32 What is an intrinsic reward? (LO 11)

9-33 What is incentive compensation? (LO 11)

9-34 What are the six attributes of effective performance measurement systems? (LO 11)

9-35 What are the two broad categories of group compensation plans? (LO 11)

9-36 What are the features of a cash bonus plan? (LO 11)

9-37 How do profit and gain sharing differ? (LO 11)

9-38 What are the three most widely used gain sharing programs? (LO 11)

9-39 What is a stock option plan? (LO 11)

Exercises

LO 1   **9-40** *Achieving objectives*   Eni Corporation's mission statement includes the following: "Our mission is to continuously improve the company's value to shareholders, customers, employees, and society." Interpret how each of Eni Corporation's stakeholder groups may interpret "the company's value" in the mission statement and, given each group's interpretation, how it may be measured for each group.

LO 2   **9-41** *Achieving relevance in MACS design*   Identify the four components that MACS designers should consider when addressing the relevance of the system's information and explain why each component is important.

LO 4   **9-42**   *Managerial approaches to motivation*   How do the scientific management, human relations, and human resource schools differ in their views on human motivation?

LO 5   **9-43**   *Characteristics of a MACS: ethical framework*   List and describe the hierarchy of ethical considerations.

LO 5   **9-44**   *Ethical conflicts*   What should a person do if faced with a conflict between his or her values and those of the organization?

LO 5   **9-45**   *Ethical conflicts*   What should a person do if the organization's stated values conflict with practiced values? What are the individual's choices? Why do you think such conflicts exist?

LO 6, 7   **9-46**   *Choosing an approach to control*   Think of any setting in need of control. Explain why you think that task control or results control would be more appropriate in the setting that you have chosen. Do not use an example from the text.

LO 6, 8   **9-47**   *Suitability of control methods*   What are the situations under which task control is most appropriate?

LO 6, 11   **9-48**   *Effectiveness of control methods*   What are the situations under which results control is most effective?

LO 6   **9-49**   *Controllable performance*   Why should performance measurement systems and rewards focus on performance that employees can control?

LO 6, 7   **9-50**   *Tailoring performance measurement to the job*   In a company that takes telephone orders from customers for general merchandise, explain how you would evaluate the performance of the company president, a middle manager who designs the system to coordinate order taking and order shipping, and an employee who fills orders. How are the performance measurement systems similar? How are the performance measurement systems different?

LO 6, 11   **9-51**   *Characteristics of a MACS: rewards*   Can goal congruence be increased if rewards are tied to performance? Explain.

LO 6   **9-52**   *Non–goal-congruent behavior*   What distinguishes data falsification from gaming activities?

LO 6   **9-53**   *Non–goal-congruent behavior*   List some methods of gaming performance indicators.

LO 6   **9-54**   *Non–goal-congruent behavior*   Can you think of instances when gaming behavior is appropriate in an organization?

LO 4, 9   **9-55**   *Characteristics of a MACS: participation*   What are the advantages for the individual in being able to participate in decision making in the organization, and what are the advantages for the organization in allowing the individual to participate in decision making?

LO 10   **9-56**   *Method of designing the budget*   How does participation in the budgeting process differ from consultation?

LO 10   **9-57**   *Budget slack*   What are the pros and cons of building slack into the budget from (1) the point of view of the employee building in slack and (2) from a senior manager's point of view?

LO 10   **9-58**   *Budgeting games*   What are budgeting games, and why do employees engage in them?

LO 11   **9-59**   *The nature of intrinsic and extrinsic rewards*   Do you believe that people value intrinsic rewards? Give an example of an intrinsic reward that you would value and explain why. Why are extrinsic rewards important to people? If you value only extrinsic rewards, explain why.

LO 11   **9-60**   *Choosing what to reward*   Explain when one would reward outcomes or outputs, reward inputs, or use knowledge-based pay.

LO 11 **9-61** *Choosing the reward level*   You work for a consulting firm and have been given the assignment of deciding whether a particular company president is overpaid both in absolute terms and relative to presidents of comparable companies. How would you undertake this task?

LO 11 **9-62** *Using cash bonuses*   When should an organization use a cash bonus?

LO 11 **9-63** *Using profit sharing*   When should an organization use profit sharing?

LO 11 **9-64** *Using gain sharing*   When should an organization use gain sharing?

LO 11 **9-65** *Using stock options*   When should an organization use stock options?

LO 11 **9-66** *Rewarding group performance*   How would you reward a group of people that includes product designers, engineers, production personnel, purchasing agents, marketing staff, and accountants whose job is to identify and develop a new car? How would you reward a person whose job is to discover a better way of designing crash protection devices in cars? How are these two situations similar? How are they different?

Problems

LO 3, 4 **9-67** *MACS design motivation*   Explain why an understanding of human motivation is essential to MACS design.

LO 3 **9-68** *Behavioral considerations in MACS design*   List the four key behavioral considerations in MACS design and explain the importance or benefits of each.

LO 5 **9-69** *Relationship between ethics in golf and business*   Refer to "Does Cheating at Golf Lead to Cheating in Business?" in the In Practice box on page 347. Discuss reasons why individuals might feel justified in cheating at golf and whether individuals who cheat at golf are likely also to cheat in business.

LO 5 **9-70** *Ethical issues*   Suppose you are the chief executive officer of a manufacturing firm that is bidding on a government contract. In this situation, the firm with the lowest bid will win the contract. Your firm has completed developing its bid and is ready to submit it to the government when you receive an anonymously sent packet containing a competitor's bid that is lower than yours. If your firm loses the bid, you may need to lay off some employees, and your profits will suffer. What are some possible options in this situation, what are the possible consequences, and what would you do?

LO 5 **9-71** *Ethical issues*   During data collection for the transition from an old management accounting system to a new activity-based cost management system, you see a manager's reported time allotments. You know that the data supplied by the manager are completely false. You confront the manager, and she states that she is worried that if she reports how she actually spends her time, her job will be altered, and it will also be found out that she is really not performing very well. She implores you not to tell anyone because she has needed to take time off to care for her chronically ill parents and needs the pay to help cover her parents' medical expenses. What actions should you take? Explain.

LO 5 **9-72** *Ethical issues*   You are a management accountant working in the controller's office. Rick Koch, a very powerful executive, approaches you in the parking lot and asks you to do him a favor. The favor involves falsifying some of his division's records on the main computer. The executive states that if you do not do as he asks, he will have you fired. What do you do? Explain.

LO 6, 7 **9-73** *Approaches to control*   Cite two settings or jobs where each of the following approaches to control would be appropriately applied. Identify what you feel is the definitive characteristic of the setting that indicates the appropriateness of the approach to control that you have identified:

a. Preventive control

b. Monitoring

c. Results control

LO 2, 3, 6, 8   **9-74** *Characteristics of MACS: types of information*   Under what circumstances should both quantitative and qualitative performance measures be used to evaluate employee, work group, and divisional performance? Provide examples to support your answer.

LO 3, 6   **9-75** *Evaluating system performance*   Suppose that you are the manager of a production facility in a business that makes plastic items that organizations use for advertising. The customer chooses the color and quantity of the item and specifies what is to be imprinted on the item. Your job is to ensure that the job is completed according to the customer's specifications. This is a cutthroat business that competes on the basis of low price, high quality, and good service to the customer. Recently you installed a just-in-time manufacturing system. How would you evaluate the performance of this system given the characteristics of your organization?

LO 9   **9-76** *Characteristics of MACS design: participation and education*   Explain how participating in decision making and being educated to understand information received in an organization contribute toward employee empowerment in MACS design.

LO 10   **9-77** *Methods of setting budgets*   Megan Espanoza, manager of the Wells Division of Mars, Inc., a large credit card company, recently received a memorandum describing the company's new budgeting process for the coming year. The new process requires Megan and the other division managers to submit a budget proposal outlining their operating plans and financial requirements. Management would then study the proposals and determine the budget for each division.

Required

(a) What is this form of budgeting called?

(b) What are the pros and cons of this approach? Explain.

LO 9   **9-78** *Methods of designing budgets*   Budgets are usually set through one of three methods: participation, authority, or consultation.

Required

Write an essay stating the circumstances under which each method is most appropriate. If you disagree with a particular method, justify your answer.

LO 9   **9-79** *Budgeting: motivational issues*   Manoil Electronics manufactures and sells electronic components to electronics stores. The controller is preparing her annual budget and has asked the sales group to prepare sales estimates. All members of the sales force have been asked to estimate sales in their territory for each of the organization's 10 major products.

The marketing group is paid a salary and a commission based on sales in excess of some target level. You have discovered that the sales manager uses the sales estimates to develop the target levels at which commissions begin. Specifically, the sales manager takes the sales estimate, adds 10%, and the result becomes the sales hurdle level. If sales are less than the hurdle level, no commissions are paid. If sales are above the hurdle level, commissions are paid at varying rates.

Required

(a) What is the motivation of the sales force if they know the relationship between their estimate and the target level of sales?

(b) What is the likely consequence of basing the organization's budgets on these estimates?

(c) If you were the controller in this situation and were responsible for both the reward system and the budgeting system, what would you do?

LO 10　**9-80** *Budget slack*　Mike Shields was having dinner with one of his friends at a restaurant in Memphis. His friend, Woody Brooks, a local manager of an express mail service, told Mike that he consistently overstated the amount of resources needed in his budget requests for his division. He also told Mike that year after year he was able to obtain the budget requested. When Mike asked him why he did this, Woody replied, "It's a dog-eat-dog world out there. If I'm going to succeed and move up the ladder, I've got to perform well. Having those extra resources really helps!"

Required

Write an essay discussing Woody's point of view related to budgeting. Is he justified in his approach? Explain.

LO 11　**9-81** *Characteristics of MACS design: rewards*　What are some pros and cons of tying an individual's pay to performance?

LO 11　**9-82** *Designing reward structures*　Answer the following two questions about the organization units listed below:

- What behavior should be rewarded?
- What is an appropriate incentive compensation system?
  - **a.** A symphony orchestra
  - **b.** A government welfare office
  - **c.** An airline complaint desk
  - **d.** A control room in a nuclear power–generating facility
  - **e.** A basketball team

LO 6, 11　**9-83** *Designing a compensation plan*　Suppose that you are the owner/manager of a house-cleaning business. You have 30 employees who work in teams of three. Teams are dispatched to the homes of customers where they are directed by the customer to undertake specific cleaning tasks that vary widely from customer to customer.

Your employees are unskilled workers who are paid an hourly wage of $9. This wage is typical for unskilled work. Turnover in your organization is quite high. Generally, your best employees leave as soon as they find better jobs. The employees that stay are usually ones who cannot find work elsewhere and have a poor attitude.

The hourly rate charged customers per team hour is $40. That is, if a team spends 1.5 hours in a customer's home, the charge is $60.

You want to develop an incentive system to use in your organization. You would like to use this incentive system to motivate good employees to stay and motivate poor workers either to improve or to leave. What type of system would you develop? If the system relies on any measurements, indicate how you would obtain these measurements.

LO 6, 11　**9-84** *Motivating desired performance*　DMT Biotech is a biotechnology research and development company that designs products for the needs of life science researchers. The company consists of an administrative unit, a research laboratory, and a facility used to develop prototypes of and produce new products. The major costs in this company are the salaries of the research staff, which are substantial.

In the past, the research scientists working at DMT Biotech have been rewarded on the basis of their proven scientific expertise. Salaries of these research scientists are based on the level of education achieved and the number of research papers published in scientific journals. At a recent board of directors meeting, an outside director criticized the research and development activities with the following comments:

> There is no question that we have the most highly trained scientists in our industry. Evidence of their training and creativity is provided by the number of research publications they generate. However, the knowledge and creativity are not translating into patentable inventions and increased sales for this company. Our organization has the lowest rate of new product introduction in our industry, and we have one of the largest research and development teams. These people are too far into basic research, where the rewards lie in getting articles published. We need these people to have more interest in generating ideas that have commercial potential. This is a profit-seeking organization, not a university research laboratory.

Required

(a) Assuming that the director's facts are correct, do you agree that this is a problem?

(b) The board of directors has ordered the president of DMT Biotech to increase the rate of new product introduction and the time devoted to new product development. How should the president go about this task?

LO 11   **9-85** *Profit-sharing plan at Hoechst Celanese*   Hoechst Celanese, a pharmaceutical manufacturer, has used a profit-sharing plan, the Hoechst Celanese Performance Sharing Plan, to motivate employees. To operationalize the plan, the Hoechst Celanese executive committee set a target for earnings from operations (EFO). This target was based on the company's business plans and the economy's expected performance. The performance sharing plan also used two other critical values: the earnings from operations threshold amount and the earnings from operations stretch target. The targets for 2010 are shown here:

Threshold EFO	Target EFO	Stretch EFO
$300 M	$400 M	$500 M

Earnings from Operations

The plan operates as follows. If earnings from operations fall below the threshold value, there is no profit sharing. If earnings from operations lie between the threshold amount and the target, the profit-sharing percentage is prorated between the threshold award of 1% and the target payment of 5%. For example, if earnings from operations were $385 million, the profit-sharing percentage would be 4.4%:

$$\text{Profit-sharing percentage} = 1\% + \{4\% \times [(385 - 300)/(400 - 300)]\} = 4.4\%$$
$$\text{Profit-sharing pool} = 4.4\% \times \$385,000,000 = \$16,940,000$$

If earnings from operations are between the target and the stretch target, the profit-sharing percentage is prorated between the target payment of 5% and the stretch-sharing payment of 10%. For example, if earnings from operations were $450 million, the profit-sharing percentage would be 7.5%, and the profit-sharing pool would be $33.75 million:

$$\text{Profit-sharing percentage} = 5\% + \{5\% \times [(450 - 400)/(500 - 400)]\}$$
$$= 7.5\%$$
$$\text{Profit-sharing pool} = 7.5\% \times \$450,000,000 = \$33,750,000$$

If earnings from operations equal or exceed the stretch target level, the profit-sharing pool would be $50 million:

$$\text{Profit-sharing pool} = 10\% \times \$500,000,000 = \$50,000,000$$

Required

(a) List, with explanations, what you think are desirable features of the Hoechst Celanese Performance Sharing Plan.
(b) List, with explanations, what you think are the undesirable features of the Hoechst Celanese Performance Sharing Plan.
(c) The EFO for 2010 was $480 million. Compute the size of the profit-sharing pool.
(d) In 2011, the Performance Sharing Plan parameters were as follows: threshold EFO—$420 million; target EFO—$490 million; and stretch EFO—$560 million. What do you think of the practice of raising the parameters from one year to the next?

LO 11 **9-86 *Profit sharing*** Peterborough Medical Devices makes devices and equipment that it sells to hospitals. The organization has a profit-sharing plan that is worded as follows:

The company will make available a profit-sharing pool that will be the lower of the following two items:

1. 45% of income before taxes in excess of the target profit level, which is 20% of net assets, or
2. $8 million.

The individual employee is paid a share of the profit-sharing pool equal to the ratio of that employee's salary to the total salary paid to all employees.

Required

(a) If the company earned $60 million before taxes and had net assets of $100 million, what amount would be available for distribution from the profit-sharing pool?
(b) Suppose that Marge Watson's salary was $55,000 and that total salaries paid in the company were $22 million. What would Marge's profit share be?
(c) What do you like about this profit-sharing plan?
(d) What do you dislike about this profit-sharing plan?

LO 11 **9-87 *Gain sharing*** Sakura Snack Company manufactures a line of snack foods, such as cheese crackers, granola bars, and cookies. The production workers are part of a gain-sharing program that works as follows: A target level of labor costs is set that is based on the achieved level of production. If the actual level of labor costs is less than the target level of labor costs, the difference is added to a cumulative pool that is carried from year to year. If the actual level of labor costs exceeds the target level, the amount of the excess is deducted from the cumulative pool.

If the balance of the pool is positive at the end of any year, the employees receive half the balance of the pool as part of a gain-sharing plan, and the balance of the pool is reset to zero. If the balance of the pool is negative at the end of any year, the employees receive nothing, and the negative balance is carried to the following year.

In any year when the target level of costs exceeds the actual level of costs, the target level for the following year is based on the actual level of cost performance in the previous year.

Required

(a) Suppose that the target level of performance is set using the following labor use standards: (1) 0.25 labor hour per case of snack food A, (2) 0.30 labor hour per case of snack food B, (3) 0.40 labor hour per case of snack food C, and (4) 0.15 labor hour per case of snack food D. During the last year, production levels of snacks A, B, C, and D were 300,000 cases, 220,000 cases, 430,000 cases, and 280,000 cases, respectively. The company used 320,000 labor hours during the year, and the average cost of labor was $20 per hour. What is the amount available for distribution to employees under this gain-sharing program, assuming no prior balance in the pool?

(b) What do you like about this program?

(c) What do you dislike about it?

LO 11 **9-88** *Scanlon plan* Knox Company manufactures consumer products such as cleansers, air fresheners, and detergents. During a recent quarter, the value of the products made was $50 million, and the labor costs were $6 million. The company has decided to use a Scanlon plan with this quarter being used to establish the base ratio for the plan.

The formula is to be applied quarterly with differences, positive or negative, added to the bonus pool. The pool is to be distributed on a 40%/60% basis between the employees and the company at the end of the fourth quarter.

The following production and cost levels were recorded during the first year of the plan's operation:

Quarter	Production Value	Payroll Costs
1	$45,000,000	$2,475,000
2	60,000,000	3,480,000
3	55,000,000	3,575,000
4	48,000,000	2,832,000

Required

(a) How much would be distributed to the employees at the end of the year?

(b) What assumptions does the Scanlon plan make about the behavior of payroll costs?

(c) What formula should be used to determine each employee's share?

(d) Management proposes to adjust the base ratio using the lowest ratio experienced in any year. Do you think this is a good idea?

LO 11 **9-89** *Choosing what to reward* During the late 1970s, Harley-Davidson, the motorcycle manufacturer, was losing money and was very close to bankruptcy. Management believed that one of the problems was low productivity and, as a result, asked middle managers to speed up production. The employees who made the motorcycles were told that the priority was to get the motorcycles made and shipped on schedule, which was usually very tight. Middle managers were judged by their ability to meet shipment schedules.

Required

(a) What is the rationale that would lead to a desire to speed production in the face of increasing costs and declining productivity?

(b) What type of behavior do you think this performance measurement system would create in the sense of the priorities that middle management would establish for the production process?

(c) What type of problems would this performance measurement system create?

(d) How, if at all, would you modify this system?

LO 11 **9-90** *Characteristics of MACS design: participation versus imposition* Denver Jack's is a large toy manufacturer. The company has 100 highly trained and skilled employees who are involved with six major product lines, including the production of toy soldiers, dolls, and so on. Each product line is manufactured in a different city and state. Denver Jack has decided to make all of the production decisions for the toy lines himself, including which products to eliminate. The managers of each toy line believe he is making a mistake.

Required

What are the pros and cons of Denver Jack's approach?

LO 11 **9-91** *Evaluating a compensation plan* Beau Monde, Inc., a manufacturer and distributor of health and beauty products, made the following disclosure about its compensation program:

> Our compensation philosophy is based on two simple principles: (1) We pay for performance and (2) management cannot benefit unless our shareholders benefit first.
>
> Executive compensation at Beau Monde consists of three elements: base salary, bonus, and stock awards. Frankly, we see base salaries and the underlying value of restricted stock as what you have to pay to get people in the door—fixed costs, if you will. Incentives, in the form of annual cash bonuses and gains tied to increases in the price of our stock, are the performance drivers of our pay equation—the variable costs.
>
> The first element is base salary. Our philosophy is to peg salary levels at median competitive levels. In other words, we pay salaries that are sufficient to attract and retain the level of talent we require.
>
> The second element of our executive compensation is our bonus plan. This plan is based on management by objectives. Each year, the compensation committee approves objectives and performance measures for the corporation, our divisions, and our key individual managers. At year end, bonuses are paid on the basis of measurable performance against these objectives.
>
> The third element of our executive compensation program is stock incentives, namely, restricted stock and stock options.
>
> Our restricted stock program is very straightforward. Stock option grants are made each year at market value. Our options vest over time periods of two to six years to encourage long-term equity holding by management.
>
> In 1998, we instituted an innovative stock incentive plan called the Stock Option Exchange Program. Under this program, management can purchase stock options by exchanging other forms of compensation, such as the annual bonus or restricted stock, for the options. The price

charged for the options is determined by an independent investment banker using pricing mechanics.

Our compensation committee is made up entirely of independent outside directors. We have no interlocking directorates, in which I serve on the compensation committee of one of my director's companies and he or she serves on mine. The compensation committee uses outside advisers chosen independently to ensure that recommendations are fair to all shareholders.

Required

Evaluate this incentive compensation plan.

LO 11   **9-92** *The mix of salary and commission*   Belleville Fashions sells high-quality women's, men's, and children's clothing. The store employs a sales staff of 11 full-time employees and 12 part-time employees. Until recently, all sales staff were paid a flat salary and participated in a profit-sharing plan that provided benefits equal to about 5% of wages. Recently, the manager and owner of Belleville Fashions announced that in the future all compensation would be commission based. The initial commission rate was set equal to the rate that would have caused the actual wage bill based on the old system to be equal to what the wage bill would have been under the commission system. Profit sharing was discontinued.

Required

(a) What do you think of this change?
(b) Describe some of the reactions that the owner might hear from the sales staff when announcing this change.
(c) Do you think that the method of determining the commission rate was appropriate?
(d) Describe what you think will happen under the new system.

LO 11   **9-93** *Salary and job responsibilities*   Marie Johnston, the manager of a government unemployment insurance office, is paid a salary that reflects the number of people she supervises and the number of hours that her subordinates work.

Required

(a) What do you think of this compensation scheme? What incentives does this compensation scheme provide to Marie?
(b) What would you recommend as an appropriate performance measurement and reward system?

LO 11   **9-94** *Distributing a bonus pool*   Four broad approaches to distributing the proceeds of a bonus pool in a profit-sharing plan are listed here:

1. Each person's share is based on salary.
2. Each person receives an equal share.
3. Each person's share is based on position in the organization (larger payments to people at higher levels).
4. Each person's share is based on individual performance relative to some target.

Required

(a) Give two reasons to support each alternative.
(b) Give two reasons to oppose each alternative.
(c) Pick the alternative that you think is best and support your choice with an argument of no more than 100 words.

Cases

LO 3, 6 **9-95** *Characteristics of MACS design: types of information* Chow Company is an insurance company in Hong Kong. Chow hires 55 people to process insurance claims. The volume of claims is extremely high, and all claims examiners are kept extremely busy. The number of claims in which errors are made runs about 10%. If a claim has an error, it must be corrected by the claims examiners. After looking at the data, Judy Choy, senior manager of the division, was not satisfied with the volume of claims processed. She instructed Anne Wu, the manager, to motivate the claims examiners to work faster. Judy believes that the claims examiners are working as fast as they possibly can. She is also concerned that, by working faster, the examiners will make more errors.

Required

(a) How should Anne Wu handle this situation?
(b) On what performance measures is the organization relying?
(c) What performance measures should the organization use?

LO 5 **9-96** *Ethical control frameworks* In December 2002, *Time* magazine named Cynthia Cooper, Coleen Rowley, and Sherron Watkins as its Persons of the Year. Cynthia Cooper was vice president of internal audit for WorldCom and informed the firm's audit committee that the firm had improperly treated billions of dollars as capital expenditures rather than properly treating them as period expenses. Coleen Rowley was an FBI attorney who wrote a 13-page memo describing deficiencies in the FBI. Sherron Watkins was vice president at Enron and informed chairman Kenneth Lay of her serious concerns about Enron's financial reporting. Select one of the two accounting-related situations (WorldCom or Enron) to answer the following questions on the basis of the *Time* magazine Person of the Year articles or other articles.

Required

(a) How did Cooper and Watkins become aware of financial reporting problems within their companies?
(b) Which of the nine alternatives listed on page 372 (or other variation) did Cooper or Watkins take? How did the public become aware of their concerns?
(c) What pressures did Cooper or Watkins face to suspend their ethical judgments or drop their concerns? Who would have benefited if Cooper or Watkins had dropped their concerns?
(d) What information is reported in the article about WorldCom's or Enron's code of ethics, communication of the code, and system of reporting violations of the code?
(e) What role did personal norms play in Cooper's and Watkins's decisions to report the problems they had discovered?
(f) What consequences did Cooper and Watkins face for reporting the problems?
(g) If you had been in Watkins's or Cooper's place, what would you have done?

LO 8, 11 **9-97** *Compensation tied to Balanced Scorecard, degree of difficulty of target achievement* Discuss Case 2-48.

LO 6, 8, 11 **9-98** *Multiple performance measures to evaluate and reward performance; subjective evaluation* Citibank: Performance Evaluation[3]

Frits Seegers, President of Citibank California, was meeting with his management team to review the performance evaluation and bonus decisions for the California branch managers. James

---

[3] Copyright © 1997 President and Fellows of Harvard College. Harvard Business School Case 9-198-048. This case was prepared by Doctoral Candidate Antonio Dávila and Professor Robert Simons as the basis for class discussion rather than to illustrate either effective or ineffective handling of an administrative situation. Reprinted by permission of Harvard Business School.

McGaran's performance evaluation was next. Frits felt uneasy about this one. McGaran was manager of the most important branch in the Los Angeles area, and his financials were impressive. A year ago he would have received "above par" rating with full bonus. But last year, the California Division of Citibank had introduced a new performance scorecard to highlight the importance of a diverse set of measures in achieving the strategic goals of the division. Among the new measures introduced was a customer satisfaction indicator. Unfortunately, James McGaran had scored "below par" on customer satisfaction.

Frits looked at Lisa Johnson, the area manager supervising James McGaran. Frits had read Lisa's comments (Exhibit 9-2). The comments were very positive, but Lisa had not wanted to give a final recommendation until she had discussed it with Frits. She knew that James' case would be watched closely by many managers within the division.

The Financial District Branch

James McGaran was manager of the most important of the 31 branches in the Los Angeles area. Located in Los Angeles's financial district, James's branch had a staff of 15 people, revenues of $6 million, and $4.3 million in profit margin. The customer base was very diverse. Individual customers ranged from people who worked in the financial district with sophisticated retail banking needs to less informed individuals banking for convenience. Business customers were sophisticated buyers who demanded high service quality and knowledgeable employees who could satisfy their financial needs. "Mom and pop" businesses, the dominant segment in other regions, were also present but to a much lesser extent. Competition was intense. Two competitors—Bank of America and Wells Fargo—had offices less than a block away from James's branch.

James joined Citibank in 1985 as assistant branch manager. He had worked in the banking industry since 1977. Within a year, in 1986, he was promoted to manager of a small branch. He progressed quickly through the ranks until 1992 when he was given the responsibility of managing the Financial District office. His performance in this office had exceeded expectations every single year. He had delivered impressive financial results for four years in a row. In 1996, when the division expanded its performance indicators to include non-financial measures, it became apparent that his branch's customer satisfaction ratings did not follow the same pattern as its financial performance.

James reported to Lisa Johnson, Los Angeles area manager. Lisa was a long time employee of Citibank. She joined the company in 1978 in Chicago and moved to California in early 1988. Her area was the biggest in the division and included two regions that had previously been managed separately. Lisa was a hands-on manager who spent a lot of time in the branches supporting the managers and becoming familiar with the events in each branch.

New Performance Scorecard

Citibank was a niche player in the California market. It had eighty branches compared with four hundred offices of its biggest competitor. Citibank's strategy in California was to build a profitable franchise by providing relationship banking combined with a high level of service to its customers. Service was delivered face to face (in the branch) or remotely, depending on the wishes of the customers. Customers' service expectations rose in line with their net worth, as did their profitability for the bank. These customers demanded high levels of service with careful personal attention and a broad selection of financial products. Citibank provided a broad array of services including a dense network of ATM machines, 24 hour banking, and home banking.

Financial measures had dominated Citibank's performance evaluation in the past. But top managers in the division felt that these measures were poor vehicles to communicate the high service strategy of the bank. Frits Seegers wanted people in the division to have a broader view of the business and focus their attention on those dimensions that were critical to the long term success of the franchise.

To reflect the importance of non-financial measures as leading indicators of strategy implementation, the California Division developed a Performance Scorecard. It complemented existing

Exhibit 9-2
James McGaran's Year-End Performance for 1996

	Below Par	Par	Above Par	YEAR-END PERFORMANCE ASSESSMENT
FINANCIAL			☐	James had an exceptional year. The branch grew $56 million or 39% in footings, ranking #1 in the marketplace. Contribution margin was $4.3 million for the year, ranking the branch #1 in the marketplace. Expenses were $88.5 thousand better than plan for the year. Contribution margin improved by 48% from 4Q95 to 4Q96.
Revenue $6 million / $1.7 million / $4.3 million — Total / Above plan				
STRATEGY IMPLEMENTATION			☐	The branch enjoyed strong growth in business, professional, and retail. Citigold began to pick up in the third and fourth quarter. The branch's new household acquisition of 21% was impressive. Annualized attrition was 12% in 1996. James grew balances in all business segments: retail balances improved $2.4 million, Citigold increased $18 million, and business and professional increased $34.8 million.
CUSTOMER SATISFACTION	☐			Full-year service scores showed mixed results, 66 1Q, 63 2Q, 54 3Q, 72 4Q. James identified areas of opportunity and put corrective measures in place that allowed him to improve service scores substantially by year-end.
CONTROL			☐	The branch received two "5" audit ratings in 1996. James is a very conscientious manager and works closely with his SCM to ensure operational compliance all times. Due to the sheer volume of transactions, the branch sustained substantial operating and fraud losses, over $137 thousand full-year. Some of these losses were from prior years, others were beyond branch control. Still, there is room for improvement in this area.
Operating losses $81,960 / Fraud losses $55,920				
PEOPLE			☐	James is an excellent people manager. His Viewpoint results were amongst the best in the Area. He is a team-builder in his branch and motivates his people to go above and beyond. James had minimal turnover in 1996. James is one of the most consistent managers in the Area. His daily meetings are well-planned and productive. He instills focus and discipline in his branch. James is viewed as a team-player in the Area. He is quick to volunteer to help his peers or participate on special projects. James has been working on his MBA and has nearly completed the comprehensive Credit training program.
Performance Management / Teamwork / Training / Development / Employee Statisfaction				
STANDARDS			☐	James has very high standards for himself and those in his employ. He is well respected for his strong leadership skills. He showed sincere concern for his customer service scores and did whatever was necessary to improve customer satisfaction. James and his team are very involved in the local community. James has taken an active role in developing a business network within the community. He also served as a board member on the American Heart Walk campaign. James's people are also involved in various community groups.
Leadership / Business Ethics / Integrity / Customer Interaction / Focus / Community Involvement / Contribution to Overall Business				
OVERALL EVALUATION			☐	This has been an exceptional year for James. From a financial perspective, his branch was rated #1 in the marketplace. His willingness and ability to look outside the box to close a deal are admired and respected. He has done an excellent job refining his management style, becoming one of the most effective leaders and coaches in the marketplace. James is dedicated to the success of the business, as evidenced by his willingness to work weekends, holidays, and during his vacation to ensure customer satisfaction, operational control, and financial growth. James is an outstanding manager. Congratulations on a job well done!!

Signed by Area Manager: _____

Approved by Regional President: _____

financial measures with new measures reflecting important competitive dimensions in the bank's strategy. The initial version was pre-tested in 1995 and, starting in the first quarter of 1996, Performance Scorecard goals and performance data became a central management tool to implement strategy and evaluate performance.

The Performance Scorecard was built around six different types of measures: financial, strategy implementation, customer satisfaction, control, people, and standards (see Exhibits 9-3 to 9-6).

Financial measures were obtained from the regular accounting system and focused primarily on total revenue and profit margin against targets.

Strategy implementation measures tracked revenue for different types of target customer segments relevant to the strategy of the branch. James's Performance Scorecard focused primarily on revenues from retail customers—households, businesses, and professionals.

Customer satisfaction was measured through telephone interviews with approximately twenty-five branch customers who had visited the branch during the past month. Customer satisfaction scores were derived from questions that focused on branch service as well as other Citibank services like 24 hours phone banking and ATM services. An independent research firm was responsible for administering the survey under the guidance of the division's Relationship Satisfaction department. Given the current strategy of the bank, which focused on customer service as a key differentiator, Frits Seegers considered the customer satisfaction measure as critical to the long term success of his division. He saw it as a leading indicator of future financial performance. If customer satisfaction deteriorated, it was only a matter of time before it showed in the financials.

Control measures reported the evaluation by internal auditors on the branch's internal control processes. Branches had to score at least par (defined as 4 on a scale of 1 to 5) to be eligible for any bonus. If the rating was below 4, the branch's business was considered at risk and did not meet the minimum requirements for effective control.

People and Standards were non-quantifiable ratings determined subjectively by the branch manager's boss. The "people" measure focused on the proactive efforts of the manager to develop and communicate with subordinates, to encourage area training programs, and to be a role model to more junior people. Standards included an assessment of a manager's involvement in community groups, trade associations, and business ethics.

Each component of the Scorecard was scored independently into one of three rating categories: "below par," "par," or "above par." For those measures that could be measured quantitatively— financial, strategy implementation, customer satisfaction, and control—pre-defined performance thresholds determined where performance fell in this three-level scale. However, ratings related to people and standards lacked an appropriate objective indicator: in these cases performance was determined subjectively by the branch manager's superior.

In addition, the manager's boss gave a global rating for each of the six components of the Scorecard and an overall rating for the branch manager.

Performance and Incentives

The performance planning process started in October with a negotiation process between Frits Seegers and his area managers. At the end of this initial stage, Performance Scorecard targets for the upcoming year were established for the division and for each area. These targets were cascaded down the organization. Area managers negotiated with branch managers to determine their financial targets and strategy implementation goals for the year. At the end of this process, the targets for branch managers were added up to ensure that they equaled or exceeded the area's targets.

Customer satisfaction and control goals were common to all branches in the division. For customer satisfaction, the 1996 goal was to achieve a rating of at least 80.

Financial, strategy implementation, customer satisfaction, and control targets formed the quantitative basis for *ex post* performance evaluation. Each quarter, area managers received branch information with the actual numbers for each of these measures and a comparison with the

Exhibit 9-3
James McGaran's Performance Scorecard for the First Quarter of 1996

	Below Par	Par	Above Par	1996 RESULTS 1st quarter	2nd quarter	3rd quarter	4th quarter	1996 GOALS 1st quarter	2nd quarter	3rd quarter	4th quarter
FINANCIAL											
Revenue			✓	1,250,094				1,134,276	1,206,442	1,325,692	1,416,242
Expense		✓		421,430				403,586	417,972	414,900	414,900
Margin			✓	828,664				730,690	788,470	910,792	1,001,342
STRATEGY IMPLEMENTATION											
Total Households	✓			3,228							
New to bank households		✓		257							
Lost to bank households		✓		(93)							
Cross-sell, splits, mergers households			✓	4							
Retail asset balances			✓	$ 5,578							
Market share			✓	1.8%							
CUSTOMER SATISFACTION	✓			Score 66 Goal 80 — The branch has shown significant and sustained improvement in customer satisfaction.							
CONTROL											
Audit			✓	Score 4 Goal 4 — The branch demonstrates strong operational control.							
Legal / Regulatory			✓								
PEOPLE											
Performance Management			✓	James is a strong manager. He has inculcated a disciplined sales process and reinforces it with a daily focus on how the business, branch, and individuals are doing vs. goal.							
Teamwork			✓								
Training / Development			✓	James is currently working on his MBA degree.							
Self			✓								
Other			✓	James works closely with his staff, coordinating the necessary training programs either in branch or in the classroom. His daily meeting and coaching sessions have allowed him to increase the knowledge and professionalism of his people.							
Employee Satisfaction			✓								
STANDARDS											
Leadership			✓	James provides clear and concise direction in his branch. He acts professionally, earning the respect of his staff, colleagues, and customers. James has built a cohesive team and leads by example.							
Business Ethics / Integrity			✓	James consistently upholds all bank standards and ensures appropriateness of action for himself and his staff.							
Customer Interaction / Focus			✓	Excellent progress in customer interaction.							
Community Involvement			✓	James proactively develops and implements effective programs to enhance Citibank's image as socially responsible. He and his staff are involved in a number of community groups in Los Angeles.							
Contribution to Overall Business			✓	James makes significant contribution to the business. The branch is currently the highest revenue and margin producer in the market place. James and his team grew revenue by $142.2 million or 16%.							
OVERALL EVALUATION			✓	James takes complete ownership of his branch and leverages internal and external relationships to grow the business and solve problems. He has demonstrated his ability to consistently outperform the branch's aggressive financial goals.							

Signed by Area Manager: _____

Exhibit 9-4
James McGaran's Performance Scorecard for the Second Quarter of 1996

	Below Par	Par	Above Par	1996 RESULTS 1st quarter	2nd quarter	3rd quarter	4th quarter	1996 GOALS 1st quarter	2nd quarter	3rd quarter	4th quarter
FINANCIAL			✓								
Revenue				1,254,876	1,486,172			1,141,612	1,213,744	1,332,865	1,423,454
Expense				421,430	378,959			403,586	436,276	436,806	437,282
Margin				833,446	1,107,213			738,026	777,468	896,059	986,172
STRATEGY IMPLEMENTATION			✓								
Total Households				3,403	3,438						
New to bank households				257	162						
Lost to bank households				(93)	(119)						
Cross-sell, splits, mergers households				4	(7)						
Retail asset balances				$5,578	$5,402						
Market share				1.8%	1.8%						

	Below Par	Par	Above Par	
CUSTOMER SATISFACTION	✓			Score 63 Goal 80 — The score is down 3 points. James and his team need to work on customer satisfaction.
CONTROL			✓	
Audit				Score 5 Goal 5 — An exceptional score given the size and complexity of the branch.
Legal / Regulatory				
PEOPLE			✓	James fosters a strong sense of teamwork, as evidenced by his Viewpoint results and employee satisfaction scores. James maintains very high development standards for himself and his staff.
Performance Management				
Teamwork				He is currently working on his MBA degree and should graduate in 1997. James also actively promotes cross-training and self-development.
Training / Development				
Self				
Other				
Employee Satisfaction				
STANDARDS			✓	James is recognized throughout the business as one of California's finest managers. He has demonstrated strong leadership skills and a keen understanding of the business.
Leadership				
Business Ethics / Integrity				The branch, under James's leadership, has made a major contribution to the marketplace. The branch's margin contribution of $1,108M, exceeds the next closest branch by 53%.
Customer Interaction / Focus				
Community Involvement				
Contribution to Overall Business				
OVERALL EVALUATION			✓	James had another exceptional quarter. The branch exceeded its margin goal by 22%. Total margin contribution improved 33%, total footings increased by 9.4%, and revenue increased 18.4%. Congratulations on another outstanding quarter.

Signed by Area Manager: _[signature]_

Exhibit 9-5
James McGaran's Performance Scorecard for the Third Quarter of 1996

	Below Par	Par	Above Par	1996 RESULTS 1st quarter	2nd quarter	3rd quarter	4th quarter	1996 GOALS 1st quarter	2nd quarter	3rd quarter	4th quarter
FINANCIAL											
Revenue			✓	1,254,876	1,486,172	1,593,690		1,141,612	1,213,744	1,429,974	1,423,454
Expense			✓	421,430	395,216	378,458		403,586	436,276	445,688	437,282
Margin			✓	833,446	1,090,956	1,215,232		738,026	777,468	984,286	986,172
STRATEGY IMPLEMENTATION											
Total Households			✓	3,409	3,445	3,511					
New to bank households		✓		257	162	152					
Lost to bank households		✓		(93)	(119)	(100)					
Cross-sell, splits, mergers households		✓		4	(7)	13					
Retail asset balances			✓	$ 5,578	$ 5,402	$ 5,437					
Market share			✓	1.8%	1.8%	1.8%					

	Below Par	Par	Above Par	
CUSTOMER SATISFACTION	✓			Score 54 Goal 80 — Service scores continued to deteriorate in the 3rd. quarter. The branch ran short of one teller and desperately needs another two CBCs to offload the day time traffic in the branch.
CONTROL				
Audit		✓		Not reviewed this quarter.
Legal / Regulatory		✓		
PEOPLE				
Performance Management			✓	James has a very focused and disciplined sales process in his branch. His daily sales meetings have become the "model" for the Area.
Teamwork			✓	James is currently working on his MBA degree and participating in the Commercial program.
Training / Development			✓	Employee satisfaction is high in the branch, as evidenced by James's positive Viewpoint results.
Self			✓	
Other			✓	
Employee Satisfaction			✓	
STANDARDS				
Leadership			✓	James is highly respected in the Area as a seasoned manager and leader.
Business Ethics / Integrity			✓	James and his team are very involved in the local community.
Customer Interaction / Focus		✓		James makes a tremendous contribution to the Area and the business. He has a "can do" attitude and often finds ways to make deals happen despite systems and back-office constraints.
Community Involvement			✓	
Contribution to Overall Business			✓	
OVERALL EVALUATION		✓		James had another exceptional quarter. Financials improved in all aspects. Expenses were below plan and his contribution margin is the highest in the marketplace.

Signed by Area Manager: _Lawrence_

Exhibit 9-6
James McGaran's Performance Scorecard for the Fourth Quarter of 1996

	Below Par	Par	Above Par	1996 RESULTS 1st quarter	2nd quarter	3rd quarter	4th quarter	1996 GOALS 1st quarter	2nd quarter	3rd quarter	4th quarter
FINANCIAL											
Revenue			✓	1,254,876	1,486,172	1,593,690	1,636,056	1,141,612	1,213,744	1,429,974	1,580,534
Expense			✓	421,430	395,216	378,458	456,061	403,586	436,276	445,688	454,076
Margin			✓	833,446	1,090,956	1,215,232	1,179,995	738,026	777,468	984,286	1,126,458
STRATEGY IMPLEMENTATION			✓								
Total Households			✓	3,409	3,445	3,511	3,503				
New to bank households		✓		257	162	152	102				
Lost to bank households		✓		(93)	(119)	(107)	(128)				
Cross-sell, splits, mergers households			✓	4	(7)	20	18				
Retail asset balances			✓	$ 5,578	$ 5,402	$ 5,437	$ 5,510				
Market share			✓	1.8%	1.8%	1.8%	1.8%				

CUSTOMER SATISFACTION ✓ Score 72 Goal 80

Congratulations to James and his team for their improvement in service results.

CONTROL
- Audit ✓ Score 5 Goal 5 — James maintains strong operational control in his branch.
- Legal / Regulatory ✓

PEOPLE ✓

James is an exceptional performance manager. He communicates clear and concise expectations and manages his people to their best potential.

- Performance Management ✓ — James is a consummate team player and fosters the same behavior in his branch.
- Teamwork ✓
- Training / Development ✓ — Self and employee development are a priority to James. He is currently working on his MBA degree and is attending comprehensive Credit training program.
- Self ✓ — James encourages his staff to develop themselves. He also looks for opportunities for them to attend Area or CitiSource training programs.
- Other ✓
- Employee Satisfaction ✓ — James enjoys a high level of employee satisfaction, as evidenced by his Viewpoint results and low employee turnover.

STANDARDS ✓

James is highly regarded as an effective leader and coach. His daily sales meetings have become the model for the other branches in the Area.

- Leadership ✓ — It's been a difficult year meeting customer expectations in the branch but James and his team have done an outstanding job managing the challenge.
- Business Ethics / Integrity ✓
- Customer Interaction / Focus ✓ — James is very involved in the local community and proactively looks for opportunities for himself and his staff to create an awareness with local groups and establish Citibank as a model corporate citizen.
- Community Involvement ✓
- Contribution to Overall Business ✓

OVERALL EVALUATION ✓

James has done an exceptional job. The branch was rated #1 in the marketplace. It generates the highest revenue and makes the greatest margin to the business. They have done all that while maintaining a 5 rated audits. Exceptional quarter and outstanding year!!

Signed by Area Manager: _Eric Jackson_

quarterly objectives. This information, together with the subjective scores that the area manager gave for the People and Standards ratings, formed the basis for the quarterly and yearly evaluation of branch managers.

Year-end performance evaluation was determined jointly by a team led by Frits Seegers. The team comprised the area managers, including Lisa Johnson, and managers from human resources, quality, and finance. Frits believed that having a team jointly evaluate performance of every branch manager gave consistency to the process throughout the division. It was this team that was now meeting to decide James's performance evaluation for the year.

In addition to other motivational elements associated with the yearly evaluation, a branch manager's bonus was linked to his or her final Performance Scorecard rating. A "below par" rating did not carry any bonus. A "par" rating generated a bonus of up to 15% of the basic salary (for branch managers with a salary in the lower part of the salary bracket, the bonus could reach 20%). An "above par" rating could mean as much as 30% bonus.

Without "par" ratings in *all* the components of the Scorecard, a manager could not get an "above par" rating.

Performance of the Financial District Branch

Frits reviewed the 1996 performance evaluation forms for James McGaran. His financials were outstanding—20% above target. According to Lisa Johnson, James's branch "had generated the highest revenue and made the greatest margin contribution to the business of any branch in the system." His strategy implementation scores were in the "par" to "above par" range, although Lisa Johnson had given him an "above par" rating in three quarters. James had maintained an "above par" rating in the control scorecard and Lisa Johnson had rated him exceptionally where she had the discretion to do so.

However, customer satisfaction was "below par". A branch obtained a "par" rating if it scored 74 to 79. If customer satisfaction was above 80 or it had improved 6 points with no regression during 2 quarters and it was above the market average (77), then the branch got an "above par" rating.

Lisa and Frits were aware that a strict application of the new policies for performance evaluation meant that James could get at most a "par" evaluation for the year. But James's branch was the largest and toughest branch in the division. He had a demanding clientele and challenging competition. It was difficult to manage such a diverse set of indicators, and the customer satisfaction measure was sometimes hard to reconcile with demonstrated financial performance. James had discussed with Lisa his concerns regarding the adequacy of the survey. Customers rated not only their branch, but also other Citibank services such as ATM's that were out of the control of branch managers. Thus, it was possible that these centralized services were not providing adequate support to the sophisticated customers of James's branch.

Notwithstanding these concerns, James had worked hard to improve the customer satisfaction rating during the last quarter. He had made some changes in his staff to improve the score. One person in the branch was now dedicated to greeting the customer when arriving at the office and helping with any problems that may arise. He also held branch meetings and coached branch employees to focus their attention on improving customer satisfaction.

James gave a lot of importance to his ratings. It was a matter of pride to be "above par" and show that he was able to successfully run the hardest branch in the division. He had felt very disappointed when, in two quarters of the year, his rating had been only par. His branch was difficult and he was delivering the best financial performance in the division. He thought that his efforts deserved an above par rating, even if customer satisfaction was somewhat lagging.

Frits reviewed James's scorecards for each quarter of 1996 (Exhibits 9-3 to 9-6). His financials were exceptional, but only in the last quarter was he able to pull customer satisfaction to an acceptable level. If the performance evaluation team gave James an "above par" people could think that the division was not serious about its non-financial measures. James had been "below par" in customer satisfaction for all quarters of 1996 and, if this measure was truly important, he should not get an "above par" rating. On the other hand, he deserved the above par given his excellent performance in other dimensions. James was a reference point for a lot of other branch managers.

Frits held the summary scorecard in his hand (Exhibit 9-2) and turned to Lisa Johnson:

"Lisa, I've read over your comments and reviewed James's quarterly scorecards. All that now remains is ticking off the six boxes on this summary form and deciding on an overall performance rating for James . . . What do you recommend?"

Required

(a) Why has Citibank introduced its Performance Scorecard? What benefits does Citibank expect the Performance Scorecard to provide?

(b) What cause-and-effect linkages are implied in the Performance Scorecard?

(c) What characteristics are desirable for measures used to evaluate and reward performance? Discuss the Performance Scorecard's measures in relation to the characteristics you identified.

(d) Assume that you are Lisa Johnson. Complete Exhibit 1 to evaluate James's performance and explain your rationale for your rating on each of the six dimensions and the overall evaluation.

Chapter 10

Using Budgets for Planning and Coordination

After completing this chapter, you will be able to:

1. Explain the role of budgets and budgeting in organizations.
2. Demonstrate the importance of each element of the budgeting process.
3. Explain the different types of operating budgets and financial budgets and the relationships among them.
4. Describe the way organizations use and interpret budgets.
5. Develop and use what-if and sensitivity analyses—budgeting tools used by budget planners.
6. Compute and interpret common variances used by managers.
7. Identify the role of budgets in service organizations and not-for-profit organizations.
8. Understand the criticisms leveled against traditional budgeting and the "beyond budgeting" approach.

California Governor Prepares "Terrible Cuts" to Close Budget Deficit

Determining California's state budget seems to be harder every year. In August, 2010 the headlines reported that California Governor Arnold Schwarzenegger will seek "terrible cuts" to eliminate an $18.6 billion budget deficit facing the U.S. state through June 2011.

Schwarzenegger, who introduced his revised budget plans on May 14, said that he will not seek tax increases to bolster California's finances. The main problem was the shortfall in income tax revenue, which was $3.6 billion, or 26 percent less than expected.

Schwarzenegger's newest plan will revise proposals introduced earlier in the year to account for the tax-collection shortages. In January, the governor stated that California may have to eliminate entire welfare programs, including the main one that provides cash and job assistance to families

---

below the poverty line. Legislation adopted during the emergency session ordered by Schwarzenegger did reduce the $1.4 billion from the deficit.

In September 2010, Democrats introduced a series of bills to raise as much as $2.9 billion annually by imposing a 10% severance tax on oil production in the state. This would repeal the corporate-tax breaks approved last year to encourage job growth. During 2009–2010, the governor and lawmakers have had difficulty redrawing the budget fast enough to make up for revenue lost amid rising unemployment.

The financial strains have left California with the lowest credit rating among U.S. states.

The State Capitol building in Sacramento has been the site of one of the most contentious budgeting processes in California in recent years.
Shutterstock

DETERMINING THE LEVELS OF CAPACITY-RELATED AND FLEXIBLE RESOURCES

Thus far in this book, we have focused on how costs are created by short- and long-term decisions. We called costs that varied with the activity level in the firm *variable costs*; costs that did not change with changes in activity levels we called *fixed*, or *capacity-related*, costs. For decisions affecting the short term, the firm's fixed costs are considered to be given and fixed. So the costs that are relevant to the firm in the short run, since they are the only ones that are controllable, are variable costs.

In this chapter, we discuss the budgeting process, which determines the planned level of most variable costs. Chapter 5 illustrates forecasting and planning for intermediate-term capacity resources in conjunction with activity-based costing (ABC). Specifically, in the Madison Dairy ice cream plant example, the firm's controller used a time-driven ABC model to understand how different products used the factory's resources in different quantities. This led to insights about possibilities for process improvements and repricing in order to generate higher sales and profit. The ABC model enabled the controller to accurately forecast the personnel and equipment resources needed to handle the planned increase in sales and production. Budgeting also includes discretionary spending, such as for machine maintenance, research and development, advertising, and employee training. These discretionary costs do not supply the firm with capacity to produce, but they do provide support for the organization's strategy by enhancing its performance potential. For example, systematic maintenance increases machine reliability and lowers the lifetime costs of equipment, successful research and development increases the organization's future profit potential by developing new products, advertising increases profit potential by making products more attractive to customers, and employee training enhances employees' ability to undertake their assigned roles as expected. Once authorized, discretionary spending **budgets** are committed or fixed—that is, they do not vary with levels of production or service.

THE BUDGETING PROCESS

The Role of Budgets and Budgeting

Most families have developed a financial plan to guide them in allocating their resources over a planning period. Usually the plan reflects spending priorities and demands, including specific spending categories such as the mortgage, utilities, property taxes, and essential items such as food and clothing. Family budgets often are the result of negotiations among parents, children, and others such as relatives and creditors reflecting their different priorities and objectives. For example, money left over after required spending on food, clothing, medicine, insurance, and shelter may go into savings or be used for other purposes; one parent may want to use most of the disposable income for a vacation, while another may want to use the money to paint the house. Within the same household, teenagers may ask their parents for help in

The budgeting process involves a great deal of input and negotiation with many people in an organization.
Shutterstock

financing the purchase of a used car. The family budget is a planning tool, but it also serves as a control on the behavior of family members by setting limits on what can be spent in each budget category. Without a budget, the family would not have a way to monitor and control its spending by categories of spending. Without such monitoring and control, a family can easily succumb to unexpected debt and severe financial difficulties.

Budgets serve the same purpose for managers within the business units of an organization and are a central part of the design and operation of management accounting systems. Exhibit 10-1 shows the central role budgets play and the relationship between planning and control. Note the distinct but linked steps for each function—three for planning and two for control.

As in households, budgets in organizations reflect in quantitative terms how to allocate financial resources to each part of an organization—each department or division or other distinct part—based on planned activities and short-run objectives of that part of the organization. For example, a bank manager may want to increase the bank's local market share, which may require a larger spending budget than the previous year's for local advertising, implementing a staff training program to improve customer service, and renovating the building to make it more appealing to customers.

Keep in mind always: A budget is a quantitative expression of the planned money inflows and outflows that reveals whether the current operating or business plan will meet the organization's financial objectives. Budgeting is the process of preparing budgets.

Budgets also provide a way to communicate the organization's short-term goals to its employees. Asking organization unit managers to undertake budgeting activities can accomplish two things: (1) reflect how well unit managers understand the organization's goals, so that they can align their activities and spending priorities with those goals, and (2) provide an opportunity for the organization's senior planners to correct misperceptions about the organization's goals. Suppose an organization recognized quality as a critical factor for its success and wanted to promote

Exhibit 10-1
Planning and Control and the Role of Budgets

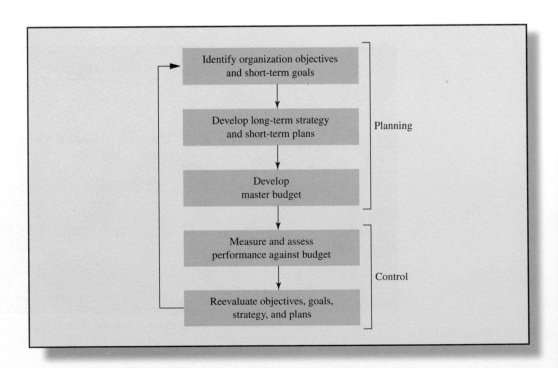

quality awareness among its employees. If a department prepared a budget that reflected no expenditures for employee quality training, a senior planner would recognize that the organization's goal with respect to quality had not been communicated properly to the person who should have recognized the need for quality training.

Budgeting also serves to coordinate the many activities of an organization. For example, budgets show the effect of sales levels on purchasing, production, and administrative activities and on the number of employees that must be hired to serve customers. In this sense, budgeting is a tool that promotes coordination of the organization's activities and helps identify coordination problems. Suppose the sales force plans to significantly expand sales. By comparing selling plans with manufacturing capacity, planners might discover that the manufacturing operations are unable to meet the planned increased level of sales. The kind of coordination needed can be accomplished through powerful desktop computers and software; with the computer and software, planners can simulate the effect of different decisions on the organization's financial, human, and physical resources. Simulation analysis—which is, simply, what-if analysis—helps managers choose a course of action among many alternatives by identifying a decision's consequences in a complex system with many interdependencies.

By considering the interrelationships among operating activities, a budget helps to anticipate potential problems and can serve as a tool to help provide solutions to these problems. For example, canneries engage in seasonal production, consuming large amounts of cash when they build inventory during the canning season. Throughout the year, the cannery sells its inventory and recovers cash. Budgeting reflects this cash cycle, shown in Exhibit 10-2, and provides information to help the organization plan the borrowing needed to finance the inventory buildup early in the cash cycle. If budget planning suggests that the organization's sales potential exceeds its manufacturing potential, the organization can develop a plan to put more capacity in place or to reduce planned sales. It is important for managers to anticipate problems because putting new capacity in place can take several months to several years.

The Elements of Budgeting

Budgeting involves forecasting the demand for four types of resources over different time periods:

1. *Flexible resources that create variable costs*—Flexible resources are those that can be acquired or disposed of in the short term, such as the lumber, glue, and varnish used in a furniture factory or, based on estimates of the number of automobiles to be assembled, the number of tires an automobile assembly plant needs to acquire.

Exhibit 10-2
The Cash Cycle

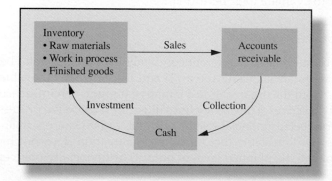

2. *Intermediate-term capacity resources that create fixed costs*—An example is forecasting the need for rental storage space that might be contracted on a quarterly, semiannual, or annual basis.
3. *Resources that, in the intermediate run and long run, enhance the potential of the organization's strategy*—These are discretionary expenditures, which include research and development, employee training, the maintenance of capacity resources, advertising, and promotion. These discretionary expenditures do not provide capacity, nor do they vary with the level of organizational activity.
4. *Long-term capacity resources that create fixed costs*—An example is a new fabrication facility for a computer chip manufacturer, which might take several years to plan and build and might be used for 10 years.

The framework for budgeting in organizations is discussed in the following sections. The discussion begins with the budgeting process and leads to formulation of the master budget. Two major types of budgets make up the master budget:

1. **Operating budgets** summarize the level of activities such as sales, purchasing, and production.
2. **Financial budgets**, such as balance sheets, income statements, and cash flow statements, identify the expected financial consequences of the activities summarized in the operating budgets.

Behavioral Considerations in Budgeting

As we discussed in Chapter 9, it is important to understand the behavioral issues that arise from the participants in the budget-setting process and the kinds of games that people engaged in the budgeting process sometimes play with budgets.

Game playing with budgets is inherent in the budgeting process. Budget planners solicit information from managers or employees who are in the best position to know performance potential—such as sales, production potential, and costs. This information is then incorporated into the budget that is later used to evaluate actual performance. This creates the incentive for managers to misrepresent their information—a process known as gaming the budgeting process.

For example, a production machine operator might understate the machine's production potential in order to secure a lower budget or standard for output, thus making after-the-fact evaluations of actual performance to budget look favorable. A sales manager might understate the sales potential in a region in order to have a lower target set for sales.

To avoid this potential for managers to misrepresent their information, many students of budgeting have proposed that the information that managers provide not be used later to evaluate their performance.

Budget Components

Exhibit 10-3 summarizes different components of the budget. The dashed lines from the expected financial results (boxes 11 and 12) show how the estimated financial consequences from the organization's tentative budgets can influence the organization's plans and objectives. The dashed lines illustrate a recursive process in which planners compare projected financial results with the organization's financial goals. If initial budgets prove infeasible (because the organization does not have the capacity to produce or sell the planned level of output) or financially unacceptable (because the

Exhibit 10-3
The Master Budget

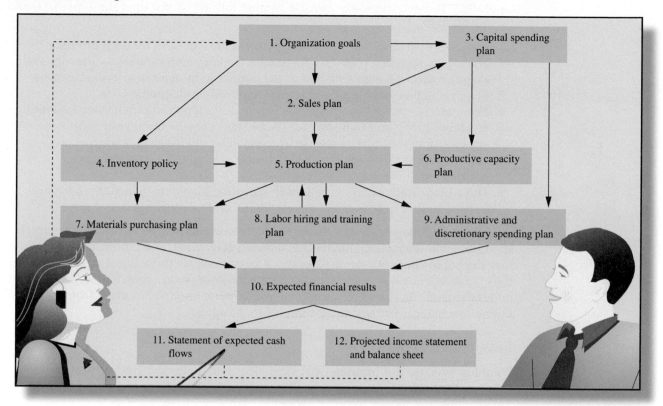

proposal plan does not yield the desired target level of profits), planners repeat the budgeting cycle with a new set of decisions until the results are both feasible and financially acceptable.

The budgeting process describes the acquisition, production, selling, and logistical activities performed during the budget period. Planners can select any budget period, but they usually choose one year to conform to the organization's external reporting cycle. A one-year budget period is assumed in the following discussion.

The master budget process in Exhibit 10-3 includes two broad sets of outputs: (1) the plans or operating budgets that operating personnel use to guide operations (sales plan [box 2], capital spending plan [box 3], production plan [box 5], productive capacity plan [box 6], materials purchasing plan [box 7], labor hiring and training plan [box 8], and the administrative and discretionary spending plan [box 9]), and (2) the expected or projected financial results [boxes 11 and 12]. Planners usually present the expected, or projected, financial results, in three forms:

1. A statement of expected cash flows.
2. The projected balance sheet.
3. The projected income statement.

Managers call the projected statement of cash flows, balance sheet, and projected income statement **pro forma financial statements** (*pro forma* means provided in advance).

Operating Budgets

Operating budgets typically consist of the following six operating plans (see Exhibit 10-3):

1. The sales plan (box 2) identifies the planned level of sales for each product.
2. The capital spending plan (box 3) specifies the long-term capital investments, such as buildings and equipment, that must be made to meet activity level objectives.
3. The production plan (box 5) schedules required production.
4. The materials purchasing plan (box 7) schedules required purchasing activities.
5. The labor hiring and training plan (box 8) specifies the number of people the organization must hire or release to achieve its activity level objectives and, based on those numbers, the needed hiring, training, and counseling out policies requirements.
6. The administrative and discretionary spending plan (box 9) includes administration, staffing, research and development, and advertising.

Operating budgets specify the expected resource requirements of selling, capital spending, manufacturing, purchasing, labor management, and administrative activities during the budget period. Operations personnel use those plans represented in the operating budget to guide and coordinate the level of various activities during the budget period. At the same time, operations personnel record data from current operations that can be used to develop future budgets.

Financial Budgets

Planners prepare the projected balance sheet and projected income statement to estimate the financial consequences of investment, production, and sales plans.
Planners use the statement of projected cash flows in two ways:

1. To plan when excess cash will be generated so that it can be used to make short-term investments rather than simply holding cash during the short term.
2. To plan how to meet any cash shortages.

THE BUDGETING PROCESS ILLUSTRATED

The budgeting process can be frustrating and time consuming. Some organizations invest thousands of hours over many months to prepare the budget documents just described. We will illustrate an entire budgeting process with a simplified yet comprehensive exercise that covers many of the budgeting elements that we have just described.

Oxford Tole Art, Buoy Division

Oxford Tole Art sells high-quality wood and metal objects, new and antique, painted by the owner, Gael Foster. Until recently, each object was unique and Gael did all of the work herself. Two years ago, Gael developed a new product line that she intended to sell in larger volumes because she wanted to expand her business. The new products are two models of painted fishing buoys: Santa, a buoy painted to look like Father Christmas, and Danny Buoy, a buoy painted to look like an Irish fisherman. Gael set up a new operation for this new product: Oxford Tole Art, Buoy Division (hereafter called Oxford Tole Art). Gael did the planning for this operation and hired a manager, April Cheung, to handle the daily operations of the new business.

The production process begins when Gael purchases used fishing buoys from local fishers for $2.25 each. An artist sands the used buoys to remove old paint and

Buoys serve many functions, but the ones shown above serve as markers in maritime channels to indicate where hazardous or administrative areas exist. They allow boats and ships to navigate safely.

Shutterstock

debris and applies a base coat of primer paint. When the base coat is dry, the artist hand paints the image of the Santa or the fisherman onto the buoy. Once the image dries, the artist applies a finishing coat of varnish. When the varnish dries, the artist wraps the finished buoy in packing material and inserts it into a specifically designed mailing container that Oxford Tole Art ships directly to the customer.

Oxford Tole Art has two types of customers: retail and dealer. Retail orders arrive by mail and are prepaid. The retail price per unit, including packing and shipping charges, is $80. If capacity exceeds retail demand, Gael sells to dealers at the lower per unit price of $55. Because dealers will buy other products from other suppliers, Gael loses dealer orders that she is not able to fill immediately.

Sales to dealers are on account; stated terms call for the dealers to pay the full amount of the invoice within 30 days of billing. Receipts from dealers, however, are often delinquent. Typically only 30% of dealers pay in the month following the sale, 45% pay in the second month following the sale, 20% pay in the third month following the sale, and 5% of sales to dealers are never collected.

Oxford Tole Art hires local artists to paint the buoys. Because of local employment conditions, Oxford Tole Art must hire artists for periods of three months. The artists receive a fixed monthly salary of $2,000 and work a maximum of 160 hours per month. April, the Oxford Tole Art manager, makes staffing decisions at the start of each quarter, beginning January 1. The total time to sand, apply the base coat, paint, and pack each buoy is 0.8 labor hour.

Paint costs $3.15 for each buoy. Other manufacturing costs, including sandpaper, brushes, varnish, and other supplies, amounts to $2.75 per buoy. Packing materials cost $1.95 per buoy, and shipping by courier costs $7.50 per buoy. Oxford Tole Art purchases for cash all flexible resources in the month they are needed.

Oxford Tole Art rents space in a local industrial park where the artists work on the buoys. The one-year lease stipulates that rent is to be paid quarterly and in advance. Oxford Tole Art can rent production space of several sizes that would provide enough space to produce the following monthly capacities in buoys: 600, 800, 1,000, and 1,200. The quarterly rents for each of these units are $3,600, $4,800, $6,000,

Shop Space Type	Shop Capacity (Number of Buoys)	Quarterly Rent
A	600	$3,600
B	800	4,800
C	1,000	6,000
D	1,200	7,200

and $7,200, respectively. All production takes place to order, and Oxford Tole Art acquires supplies only as needed.

Insurance, heating, lighting, and business taxes are $20,000 per year, and advertising expenses amount to $40,000 per year. April Cheung receives $30,000 per year to supervise the operation, manage the raw materials acquisitions, handle all of the order taking and billing, and do the accounting.

All operating expenses are incurred and paid in equal monthly installments.

Realized sales for October, November, and December 2010 and forecasted demand for 2011 appear in Exhibit 10-4. Based on this forecasted demand, Gael and April have decided to rent an 800-capacity unit for 2011 and hire two painters in the first quarter, two painters in the second quarter, one painter in the third quarter, and three painters in the fourth quarter.

Gael plans to withdraw $20,000 from the company at the start of each six-month period for a total of $40,000 per year as her compensation for acting as owner and planner. She also wants to maintain the entire firm's cash in a separate bank account for her business with a minimum cash balance of $5,000 (see Exhibit 10-5). She has arranged a $50,000 line of credit with her bank to provide her with short-term funds for the company. At the start of each month, the bank charges interest at the rate of 1% on the outstanding balance of the line of credit as of the end of the previous month. The bank pays interest at the rate of 0.6% on any cash in excess of $5,000 held in the account. The bank pays interest on the first day of each month based on the balance in the account at the end of the previous month.

Exhibit 10-4
Oxford Tole Art:
Forecasted Unit
Demand,
2010–2011

	DEMAND		
MONTH	RETAIL	DEALER	TOTAL
October 2010*	275	510	785
November 2010*	420	425	845
December 2010*	675	175	850
January 2011	100	375	475
February 2011	105	400	505
March 2011	95	425	520
April 2011	115	350	465
May 2011	75	300	350
June 2011	60	250	310
July 2011	50	300	350
August 2011	55	325	380
September 2011	75	300	375
October 2011	150	300	450
November 2011	290	350	640
December 2011	350	400	750

*Actual

Exhibit 10-5
Oxford Tole Art:
Proposed Balance
Sheet, January
2011

Cash	$5,000	Owner's equity	$34,948
Accounts receivable	29,948		
Total assests	$34,948	Total liabilities and owner's equity	$34,948

Demand Forecast

An organization's goals provide the starting point and the framework for evaluating the budgeting process (see Exhibit 10-3, box 1). At Oxford Tole Art, the goals are to produce high-quality products and to be profitable. To assess the plan's acceptability, Gael compares the tentative operating plan's projected financial results with the organization's financial goals.

The budgeting process in Exhibit 10-3 is influenced strongly by the demand forecast, which is simply an estimate of sales demand at a specified selling price. Organizations develop demand forecasts in many ways. Some use market surveys conducted either by outside experts or by their own sales staff. Other organizations use statistical models to generate demand forecasts from trends and forecasts of economic activity in the economy and the relation of past sales patterns to this economic activity. Other companies simply assume that demand will either grow or decline by some estimated rate over previous demand levels.

Regardless of the approach used to develop the demand forecast, the organization must prepare a sales plan for each major line of goods or services (see Exhibit 10-3, box 2). The sales plan provides the basis for acquiring the necessary factors of production, such as labor, materials, production capacity, and cash. Production plans are sensitive to the sales plan; therefore, most organizations develop budgets on computers so that planners can readily explore the effects of changes in the sales plan on production plans.

Choosing the amount of detail to present in the budget involves making trade-offs. A greater level of detail in the forecast improves the chances that the budgeting process will identify potential bottlenecks and problems by specifying the exact timing of production flows in the organization. However, forecasting and planning in great detail for each item among thousands of items in production can be extremely expensive and overwhelming to compute. Most organizations rely on the judgment of their production planners to strike a balance between the need for detail and the cost and practicality of detailed scheduling. Planners do this by grouping products into pools so that each product in a given pool places roughly equivalent demands on the organization's resources so that planning is simplified. Because Oxford Tole Art has one product, a painted buoy with only two variations, its budget can be detailed and comprehensive. Organizations with many products and services may choose, however, to budget at a more aggregated level, such as by product line. For example, production in a plant making headache capsules might budget by the product line rather than by individual stock-keeping units.

The Production Plan

Planners match the completed sales plan with the organization's inventory policy and capacity level to determine a production plan (Exhibit 10-3, box 5). The plan identifies the required production in each of the interim periods making up the annual budget period. Budget periods, such as a year, may have interim periods comprised of days, weeks, or months, depending on the information needs of the people managing the acquisition, manufacturing, selling, and distribution activities.

Planners use the inventory policy (Exhibit 10-3, box 4) and the sales plan (Exhibit 10-3, box 2) to develop the production plan (Exhibit 10-3, box 5). Therefore, the inventory policy is critical and has a unique role in shaping the production plan. Some organizations have a policy of producing goods for inventory and, therefore, attempt to keep a predetermined, or target, number of units in inventory at all times. This inventory policy often reflects a level production strategy that is characteristic of an organization with highly skilled employees or equipment dedicated to producing a single product. A level production strategy reflects a lack of flexibility. Highly skilled production workers cannot be used to do various jobs in the organization; therefore, they must be kept busy in the job they know. Similarly, dedicated equipment that can be used for only one job must be kept busy to justify its expense. In such organizations, monthly sales draw down the inventory levels, and the production plan for each month attempts to restore inventory levels to their target levels.

Other organizations have an inventory policy of producing for planned sales in the next interim period within the budget period. Organizations moving toward a just-in-time inventory policy produce goods to meet the next interim period's demand as an intermediate step along the path to moving to a full just-in-time inventory system in which only an order can trigger production, as does Toyota. Each interim period becomes shorter and shorter until the organization achieves just-in-time production. In this setting, the inventory target is the level of next week's or next month's planned sales, and the scheduled production is the amount required to meet the inventory target. Implementing a just-in-time inventory policy requires flexibility among employees, equipment, and suppliers and a production process that has little potential for failure. In organizations using a just-in-time inventory strategy, demand drives the production plan directly—that is, the production in each interim period equals the next interim period's planned sales. This is the inventory policy that Oxford Tole Art uses (Exhibit 10-3, box 4).

The just-in-time manufacturing process requires just-in-time delivery which means that direct materials are delivered to a facility just when they are needed. Trucks such as these can make up to 12 deliveries a day to the same plant.
Shutterstock

Developing the Spending Plans

Once planners have identified a feasible production plan, they can make tentative resource commitments. The purchasing group prepares a materials purchasing plan to acquire the raw materials and supplies that the production plan requires (Exhibit 10-3, box 7). Materials purchasing plans are driven by the cycle of the organization's production plans (which may be hourly, daily, weekly, monthly, or even longer) and the suppliers' production plans. The organization's production plans notify suppliers of the quantity of materials they should supply and when those materials must be delivered. Because sales plans and production plans change during the year, the organization and its suppliers must be able to quickly adjust their plans based on information received during the operating period. For example, a manufacturer of a fashion item might find that demand is far outpacing expectations and supply. The manufacturer would have to signal to its suppliers that it will require more raw materials. At some point, however, the production and materials supply plans have to be locked in place and no additional changes made. For example, commitment to a production schedule in a large automotive assembly plant happens about eight weeks before production takes place. This gives suppliers and the assembly plant managers the time to put raw materials supply in place and schedule the production.

The personnel and production groups prepare the labor hiring and training plan (Exhibit 10-3, box 8). This plan works backward from the date when the personnel are needed to develop hiring and training schedules that will ensure the availability of these personnel. This plan can include both expansion and contraction activities. For example, when an organization is contracting, it will use retraining plans to redeploy employees to other parts of the organization or will develop plans to discharge employees from the organization. The discharge plans for laid-off employees may include retraining and other activities to help them find new jobs. Because discharging employees reflects moral, ethical, and legal issues and may involve high severance costs, many organizations attempt to avoid layoffs unless no other alternative can be found.

Other decision makers in the organization will prepare an administrative and discretionary spending plan that summarizes the proposed expenditures on such activities as research and development, advertising, and training (Exhibit 10-3, box 9). Discretionary expenditures provide the infrastructure required by the proposed production and sales plan. Discretionary, as used here, means the actual sales and production levels do not drive the amount spent; rather, the senior managers in the organization determine the amount of discretionary expenditures. Once determined, however, the amount to be spent on discretionary activities becomes fixed for the budget period because it is unaffected by product volume and mix.

If a fast-food restaurant plans to make 3,000 hamburgers during some budget period, it knows the quantity of materials it will use because there is a physical, or engineered, relationship among ingredients such as meat, buns, condiments, packages, and the number of hamburgers made. However, no direct physical, or engineered, relationship exists among the number of hamburgers sold and the discretionary amounts spent on items like advertising and employee training.

Finally, the appropriate authority in the organization approves the capital spending plan for putting new productive capacity in place (Exhibit 10-3, box 3). Because capital spending projects usually involve time horizons longer than the period of the operating budget, a long-term planning process rather than the one-year cycle of the operating budget drives the capital spending plan. The spending plans for material, labor, and support resources are based on a forecast of the activities the organization must complete to achieve the production targets identified in its production plan. As the planning period unfolds and time reveals the actual production requirements, production planners make commitments to detailed production schedules and the required related purchasing requirements.

Choosing the Capacity Levels

At Oxford Tole Art, the following three types of resources determine the monthly production capacity:

1. *Flexible resources that the organization can acquire in the short term, such as paint and packing supplies*—If suppliers either do not deliver these resources or deliver unacceptable resources, production may be disrupted. This problem was not identified as an issue for Oxford Tole Art, but it is a practical concern for many organizations. Organizations such as Wal-Mart spend a great deal of time and money developing supplier relationships so that they can purchase inventory if and only when needed and so that they will receive zero-defect materials.

2. *Capacity resources, such as painters, that the organization must acquire for the intermediate term*—Between July 1 and September 30, Oxford Tole Art plans to employ one painter. Because each painter works 160 hours per month and because each buoy requires 0.8 hour to complete, the monthly capacity provided by intermediate-term activity decisions between July 1 and September 30 is 200 (= 160/0.8) units.

3. *Capacity resources, such as building a factory, that the organization must acquire for the long term*—Gael plans to rent a shop that provides a monthly capacity of 800 units. Gael needs just a simple setting with a relatively short commitment period. Other organizations may take several years to acquire long-term capacity that may last for 10 years or longer, and the cost is justified only if it is used that long. Consider the amount of time an oil company takes to build an oil refinery or the time that a municipality needs to build a hospital. Capacity resources are expensive and are called *committed* because they are the same regardless of how much of the facility is used and because the level of capacities and fixed costs are very difficult to change in the short term. Therefore, capacity resources impose financial risk on the organization.

As indicated in Exhibit 10-6, the nature of the resources determines whether they are short term, intermediate term, or long term. Many organizations develop sophisticated approaches to choose a production plan that balances the use of short-term, intermediate-term, and long-term capacity to minimize committed resource idle time.

Exhibit 10-6
Summary of
Capacity Types and
Commitment Time

TERM	TYPE OF CAPACITY ACQUIRED	EXAMPLES
Flexible resources required in short term (less than several weeks)	Provides the ability to use existing capacity	Raw materials, supplies, casual labor
Committed resources acquired for the intermediate term (several weeks to six months)	General purpose capacity that is transferrable among organizations given time	Employees, general-purpose equipment, specialty raw materials
Committed resources acquired for the long-term (more than six months)	Special purpose capacity that is customized for the organization's use	Buildings, special-purpose equipment

For example, the size and number of service areas in a bank represent the capacity available for use during any period provided by long-term building decisions. The level of long-term capacity chosen reflects the organization's assessment of its long-term growth trend. For Oxford Tole Art, which is renting capacity, long-term capacity is defined by the lease stipulations and equals one year. If Oxford Tole Art were building this capacity, its long-term capacity would be defined by the time needed to plan and build the facility.

The number of full-time staff employed by a bank determines the long-term capacity available for the intermediate term. For example, if the plan were to acquire capacity that the organization could use increasingly as sales grew, the intermediate-term capacity decisions would put in place other elements that require intermediate-term commitments. These would include defining the number of people and banking equipment necessary to allow the bank to use its long-term capacity. The intermediate-term capacity decision reflects the longer of either the duration needed to put intermediate-term capacity in place or the duration of the contracting period for intermediate-term capacity. For Oxford Tole Art, this is the contracting period for artists, which is three months.

The number of part-time or temporary staff employed by a bank determines its capacity on a day-to-day basis. Such short-term capacity decisions reflect the cyclical demands that the bank may face daily, weekly, monthly, or annually. The short-term capacity decision reflects the time needed to put short-term capacity in place. For Oxford Tole Art, this is the time that suppliers require for delivery, which is assumed to be nearly instantaneous. However, if Oxford Tole Art had to order and wait for supplies, it would become very important to plan acquisitions so that in the very short term, such as hourly, Oxford Tole Art would not have to stop production while it waited for supplies to arrive. In this sense, supplies provide the short-run capacity to use longer term capacity.

Organizations use many different approaches to plan capacity, and it is important to understand how production planners choose capacity levels. The process that Oxford Tole Art used was to choose a level of shop capacity (either 600, 800, 1,000, or 1,200 units) and then to hire the number of painters in each quarter that, given the forecasted demand and chosen shop capacity, provided the highest level of expected profits.

The resource-consuming activities for Oxford Tole Art can be classified into three groups that are common to most organizations:

1. *Activities that create the need for resources and, therefore, resource expenditures in the short term*—For Oxford Tole Art, these short-term activities include the purchasing, preparation, painting, packing, and shipping of buoys. Acquiring the resources for these short-term activities requires expenditures that vary directly with the production levels because the inventory policy is to produce only to order.
2. *Activities undertaken to acquire capacity for the intermediate term*—For Oxford Tole Art, this is the quarterly acquisition of painting capacity, that is, hiring the painters to paint the buoys.
3. *Activities undertaken to acquire or support capacity needed for the long term*—For Oxford Tole Art, this includes annually choosing the level of shop capacity, the level of advertising, the manager and manager's salary, and expenditures for such items as insurance and heat.

Planners classify activities by type because they plan, budget, and control short-, intermediate-, and long-term expenditures differently. Analysts evaluate short-term activities by considering efficiency: Did we accomplish this task with the fewest possible resources and effectiveness? Did we achieve what we set out to accomplish? They also ask questions such as the following:

1. Is this expenditure necessary to add to the product value perceived by customers?
2. Can the organization improve how it performs this activity?
3. Would changing the way this activity is done provide more satisfaction to customers?

Analysts evaluate intermediate- and long-term activities by using efficiency and effectiveness considerations and asking questions such as these:

1. Are alternative forms of capacity available that are less expensive?
2. Is this the best approach to achieve our goals?
3. How can we improve the capacity selection decision to make capacity less expensive or more flexible?

Choosing the capacity plan—making the commitments to acquire intermediate- and long-term capacity—commits the firm to its intermediate- and long-term expenditures. Choosing the production plan—that is, choosing the level of the short-term activities—fixes the short-term expenditures that the budget summarizes.

Handling Infeasible Production Plans

Although the relationship between planning and production at Oxford Tole Art is a simple one, the company's planning process reflects how planners use forecasted demand to plan activity levels and provide required capacity. If planners find the tentative production plan infeasible because projected demand exceeds available capacity, they must make provisions to acquire more capacity or reduce the planned level of production. For example, if the labor market is tight and Oxford Tole Art can hire only two artists between January and June, Gael would have to revise her capacity and production plans to reflect this constraint.

Interpreting the Production Plan

Exhibit 10-7 summarizes the production plan that Oxford Tole Art has developed for 2011. Three factors drive planning:

1. Demand, which is the quantity customers are willing to buy at the stated price.
2. The capacity levels chosen.
3. Production output quantity.

Oxford Tole Art starts no production until it receives an order. Therefore, production is the minimum of total demand and production capacity. In equation form, we write this in general form as follows:

Production = Minimum (total demand, production capacity)

The general form can be applied to Oxford Tole Art:

Production capacity = Minimum (shop capacity, painting capacity, supplies capacity)

Remember that for Oxford Tole Art,

Total demand = Retail demand + Dealer demand

In Oxford Tole Art's case, the production capacity is the minimum of the long-term capacity (the productive capacity of the shop), the intermediate-term capacity

Exhibit 10-7
Oxford Tole Art: Demand, Capacity, and Sales Data, 2011

	Jan.	Feb.	March	April	May	June	July	Aug.	Sept.	Oct.	Nov.	Dec.
Retail demand	100	105	95	115	75	60	50	55	75	150	290	350
Dealer demand	375	400	425	350	300	250	300	325	300	300	350	400
Total demand	475	505	520	465	375	310	350	380	375	450	640	750
Shop capacity	800	800	800	800	800	800	800	800	800	800	800	800
Painting capacity	400	400	400	400	400	400	200	200	200	600	600	600
Production capacity	400	400	400	400	400	400	200	200	200	600	600	600
Total units made and sold	400	400	400	400	375	310	200	200	200	450	600	600
Retail units made and sold	100	105	95	115	75	60	50	55	75	150	290	350
Dealer units made and sold	300	295	305	285	300	250	150	145	125	300	310	250

(the painting capacity provided by hiring artists), and the short-term capacity (the capacity provided by the short-term acquisition of materials). For example, in August the retail demand is 55 units and the dealer demand is 325 units, totaling 380 units. The shop capacity is 800 units, and the painting capacity is 200 units. Therefore, production capacity, which is the minimum of the shop capacity and painting capacity, is 200 units. Planned production and sales of 200 units represents the minimum of total demand (380 units) and production capacity (200 units).

The Financial Plans

Once the planners have developed the production, staffing, and capacity plans, they can prepare a financial summary of the tentative operating plans. The financial results for Oxford Tole Art implied by the production plan developed in Exhibit 10-7 appear in the following exhibits:

- Exhibit 10-8 presents the cash flows expected from the production and sales plan.
- Exhibits 10-9 and 10-10 summarize the projected balance sheet and income statement, respectively, expected as a result of the production and sales plans.

(These exhibits are examples of the elements in boxes 11 and 12 in Exhibit 10-3.)

Planners use the projected balance sheet as an overall evaluation of the net effect of operating and financing decisions during the budget period and the income statement as an overall test of the profitability of the planners' proposed activities. To keep it simple, this example ignores taxes. Taxes are part of the budgeting and cash flow estimation process of all organizations.

Understanding the Cash Flow Statement

The cash flow statement in Exhibit 10-8 is organized into three sections:

1. *Cash inflows* from retail cash sales and collections of dealer receivables.
2. *Cash outflows* for flexible resources that are acquired and consumed in the short term (buoys, paint, other supplies, packing, and shipping) and cash outflows for capacity resources that are acquired and consumed in the intermediate term and long term (painters, shop rent, manager's salary, other shop costs, interest

Exhibit 10-8
Oxford Tole Art Cash Flow Forecast, 2011

CASH INFLOWS	JAN.	FEB.	MARCH	APRIL	MAY	JUNE	JULY	AUG.	SEPT.	OCT.	NOV.	DEC.
Retail sales	$8,000	$8,400	$7,600	$9,200	$6,000	$4,800	$4,000	$4,400	$6,000	$12,000	$23,200	$28,000
Dealer collections												
1 month	$2,887	$4,950	$4,868	$5,033	$4,703	$4,950	$4,125	$2,475	$2,392	$2,062	$4,950	$5,115
2 months	10,519	4,331	7,425	7,301	7,549	7,054	7,425	6,188	3,713	3,589	3,094	7,425
3 months	5,610	4,675	1,925	3,300	3,245	3,355	3,135	3,300	2,750	1,650	1,595	1,375
Total cash inflows	$27,016	$22,356	$21,818	$24,834	$21,497	$20,159	$18,685	$16,363	$14,855	$19,301	$32,839	$41,915
Cash outflows												
Flexible resources:												
Buoys	$900	$900	$900	$900	$844	$698	$450	$450	$450	$1,013	$1,350	$1,350
Paint costs	1,260	1,260	1,260	1,260	1,181	977	630	630	630	1,418	1,890	1,890
Other manufacturing costs	1,100	1,100	1,100	1,100	1,031	853	550	550	550	1,238	1,650	1,650
Packing costs	780	780	780	780	731	605	390	390	390	878	1,170	1,170
Shipping costs	3,000	3,000	3,000	3,000	2,813	2,325	1,500	1,500	1,500	3,375	4,500	4,500
Committed resources:												
Painters' salaries	$4,000	$4,000	$4,000	$4,000	$4,000	$4,000	$2,000	$2,000	$2,000	$6,000	$6,000	$6,000
Shop rent	4,800	0	0	4,800	0	0	4,800	0	0	4,800	0	0
Manager's salary	2,500	2,500	2,500	2,500	2,500	2,500	2,500	2,500	2,500	2,500	2,500	2,500
Other shop costs	1,667	1,667	1,667	1,667	1,667	1,667	1,667	1,667	1,667	1,667	1,667	1,667
Advertising costs	3,333	3,333	3,333	3,333	3,333	3,333	3,333	3,333	3,333	3,333	3,333	3,333
Interest paid	0	163	127	95	81	48	17	208	177	160	231	145
Total cash outflows	$23,340	$18,703	$18,667	$23,435	$18,181	$17,006	$17,837	$13,228	$13,197	$26,382	$24,291	$24,205
Net operating cash flow this month	**$3,676**	**$3,653**	**$3,151**	**$1,399**	**$3,316**	**$3,153**	**$848**	**$3,135**	**$1,658**	**$(7,081)**	**$8,548**	**$17,710**
Financing operations:												
Opening cash	$5,000	$5,000	$5,000	$5,000	$5,000	$5,000	$5,000	$5,000	$5,000	$5,000	$5,000	$5,000
Cash withdrawn	(20,000)	0	0	0	0	0	(20,000)	0	0	0	0	0
Cash available	(11,324)	8,653	8,151	6,399	8,315	8,155	(14,152)	8,134	6,658	(2,079)	13,548	22,710
Opening loan	0	16,324	12,671	9,520	8,121	4,806	1,652	20,803	17,669	16,010	23,089	14,541
Borrowing made	16,324	0	0	0	0	0	19,152	0	0	7,079	0	0
Borrowing repaid	0	3,653	3,151	1,399	3,315	3,155	0	3,134	1,658	0	8,548	14,541
Ending loan	16,324	12,671	9,520	8,121	4,806	1,652	20,803	17,669	16,010	23,089	14,541	0
Ending cash	$5,000	$5,000	$5,000	$5,000	$5,000	$5,000	$5,000	$5,000	$5,000	$5,000	$5,000	$8,168

Exhibit 10-9
Oxford Tole
Art Projected
Balance Sheet,
December 31, 2011

Cash	$8,168		
Accounts receivable	27,445	Owner's equity	$35,613
Total assets	$35,613	Total liabilities and owner's equity	$35,613

Revenue		$279,134
Flexible resources expenses:		
Buoys	$10,204	
Paint	14,285	
Other suppliers	12,471	
Packing	8,843	
Shipping	34,013	$79,816
Contribution margin		$199,318
Committed resource expenses:		
Painters' salaries	$48,000	
Shop rent	19,200	
Other shop costs	20,000	
Manager's salary	30,000	117,200
Other expenses:		
Advertising	$40,000	
Interest paid	1,452	41,452
Net income		$40,666

paid, and advertising costs). The difference between cash inflows from revenues and cash outflows from expenditures is called the net cash flows from operations.

3. *Results of financing operations.* For each month, the format of the cash flow statement is as follows:

$$\text{Cash inflows} - \text{Cash outflows} = \text{Net cash flow}$$

In January, for example, ending cash was as follows:

$$\text{Ending cash} = \text{Operating cash flow} + \text{Opening cash}$$
$$+ \text{Effects of financing operations}$$
$$= \$3,676 + \$5,000 + (-\$20,000 + \$16,324)$$
$$= \$5,000$$

To understand the derivation of the numbers in Oxford Tole Art's cash flow statement, study the numbers for July to ensure that you can follow the calculations.

Cash Inflows Section

Recall that the pattern of collections at Oxford Tole Art is as follows:

1. Retail orders are paid for with the order at a retail price per unit of $80.
2. Sales to dealers for $55 per unit are on account with a typical collection pattern being 30% in the month following the sale, 45% in the second month following the sale, 20% in the third month following the sale, and 5% never collected.

Exhibit 10-11
Oxford Tole Art:
Summary of Cash
Collections, July
2011

ITEM	CALCULATION	
Retail sales from July (see Exhibit 10-7)	50 × $80 =	$4,000
30% of June dealer sales*	30% × 250 × $55 =	4,125
45% of May dealer sales	45% × 300 × $55 =	7,425
20% of April dealer sales	20% × 285 × $55 =	3,135
Total		$18,685

*Sales equals units sold multiplied by the selling price of $55 per unit.

Therefore, in July, Oxford Tole Art will collect (1) all of the retail sales for July, (2) 30% of the dealer sales from June, (3) 45% of the dealer sales from May, and (4) 20% of the dealer sales from April. Exhibit 10-11 summarizes these July collections.

Cash Outflows Section

Exhibit 10-12 summarizes the cash outflow numbers for July. Because Oxford Tole Art pays cash for flexible resources, this equation applies for each flexible resource purchased:

$$\text{Cash outflow} = \text{Units of flexible resource purchased} \times \text{Price per unit of flexible resource}$$

For expenditures on capacity resources—that is, resources acquired in the intermediate or long term—the following equation applies for each resource:

$$\text{Cash outflow} = \text{This month's expenditure for that capacity resource}$$

Financing Section

The financing section of the cash flow statement summarizes the effects on cash of transactions that are not a part of the normal operating activities. This section includes the effects of issuing or retiring stock or debt and buying or selling capital

Exhibit 10-12
Oxford Tole Art: Cash Outflow Calculations, July 2011

ITEM	AMOUNT	FORMULA	CALCULATION
Flexible resources:			
Buoy cost	$450	July production × Price per buoy	200 × $2.25
Paint cost	630	July production × Paint cost per buoy	200 × $3.15
Other supplies cost	550	July production × Other supplies cost per buoy	200 × $2.75
Packing costs	390	July sales × Packing cost per buoy	200 × $1.95
Shipping costs	1,500	July sales × Shipping cost per buoy	200 × $7.50
Committed resources:			
Painters' salaries	$2,000	Number of painters in July × Monthly salary	1 × $2,000
Shop rent	4,800	Units of capacity × Capacity cost per unit	800 × $6
Manager's salary	2,500	Annual salary ÷ 12	$30,000 ÷ 12
Other shop costs	1,667	Annual other costs ÷ 12	$20,000 ÷ 12
Interest paid	17	June ending loan balance × 1%	$1,652 × 1%
Advertising costs	3,333	Annual advertising ÷ 12	$40,000 ÷ 12

Exhibit 10-13
Format of
Financing Section
of Cash Flow
Statement

	Net cash flow from operations	$848
+	Opening cash	15,000
±	Cash invested or withdrawn*	(20,000)
±	Cash provided or used in issuing or retiring stock or debt	0
=	Cash available before short-term financing	(14,152)
±	Cash used or provided by short-term financing	19,152
=	Ending cash	$5,000

*In the case of a private business such as Oxford Tole Art, this refers to the capital transactions by the owner.

assets. Exhibit 10-13 shows a common format used in the financing section of the cash flow statement with the corresponding numbers for July. Note that the format of the financing section of the cash flow statement is as follows:

Net operating cash flow + Opening cash ± Cash from financing activities
= Ending cash

The major sources and uses of cash in most organizations are (1) operations, (2) investments or withdrawals by the owner in an unincorporated organization, (3) long-term financing activities related to issuing or retiring stock or debt, and (4) short-term financing activities.

Short-term financing often involves obtaining a line of credit, secured or unsecured, with a financial institution. The line of credit allows an organization to borrow up to a specified amount at any time. The line of credit is secured if the organization has pledged an asset that the financial institution can seize if the borrower defaults on any of the bank's requirements. The financial institution sets a limit on the line of credit, and the borrower, in the example of Oxford Tole Art, pays the specified interest at specified periods, such as monthly, on the outstanding balance borrowed. See the "Ending loan" row in Exhibit 10-8 and note that Oxford Tole Art's line of credit balance varies between $0 and $23,089 during the year, well within the limit of $50,000 that Gael negotiated with the bank.

The format of the financing section of the cash flow statement in Exhibit 10-8 for Oxford Tole Art does not follow the format used in Exhibit 10-13. The financing section of Oxford Tole Art's cash flow statement provides information about the line-of-credit balance. Many organizations include the line-of-credit information in the cash flow statement because financial statement readers should be aware of the limits that can potentially constrain operations.

Using the Financial Plans

Oxford Tole Art's cash flow statement, shown in Exhibit 10-8, contains a short-term financing plan that suggests that, if events unfold as expected, Oxford Tole Art's cash balance increases only modestly during the year because of the $40,000 withdrawal that Gael will make from the business. Therefore, the company will use its line-of-credit agreement heavily. It will be borrowing from the bank for 11 of the 12 months in the year.

Organizations can raise money from outsiders by borrowing from banks, issuing debt, or selling shares of equity. A cash flow forecast helps an organization identify if and when it will require external financing. The cash flow forecast also shows whether any projected cash shortage will be temporary or cyclical, which can be met by a line-of-credit arrangement, or whether it will be permanent, which would require either or all of a long-term loan from a bank, further investment by the current owners, or investment by new owners. Based on the information provided by the cash flow forecast, organizations can plan the appropriate mix of external financing to minimize the long-run cost of capital.

The projected income statement and balance sheet provide a general assessment of the operating efficiencies at Oxford Tole Art. If Gael feels that these projected results are unacceptable, she must take steps to change the organizational processes that create the unacceptable results. For example, if the employees consistently use more quantities of any factor of production than competitors use, such as paint, labor, or capacity, Gael should attempt to modify procedures and, therefore, resource use to be able to compete profitably with competitors.

Suppose April has studied the projected financial results in the initial budget plans and has decided that the 14.6% profit margin on sales ($40,666 ÷ $279,134 from Exhibit 10-10) is too low. April has reached this conclusion because Oxford Tole Art is in the craft industry, in which competitors often duplicate attractive products quickly, resulting in short periods of product profitability. After determining that this profit margin on sales is too low, the manager may develop a marketing program or a cost reduction program to improve the cost/revenue performance at Oxford Tole Art.

Using the Projected Results

The operating budgets, like the production plan, hiring plan, capital spending plan, and purchasing plan for materials and supplies, provide a framework for developing expectations about activity levels in the upcoming period. Planners also use the operating budgets to test the feasibility of production plans. As the budget period unfolds, production and operations schedulers will make more accurate forecasts and base their production commitments on them. Thus, planners use the budget information to accomplish the following:

1. *Identify broad resource requirements*—This helps develop plans to put needed resources in place. For example, April can use the activity forecast to plan when the organization will have to hire and train temporary help.
2. *Identify potential problems*—This helps to avoid problems or to deal with them systematically. For example, April can use the statement of operating cash flows to identify when the business will need short-term financing from its bank. This will help April negotiate with a bank lending officer for a line of credit that is both competitive and responsive to Oxford Tole Art's needs. The forecasted cash flows also will identify when the buoy business will generate cash that Gael can invest in other business opportunities.
3. *Compare projected operating and financial results*—These comparisons within an organization serve as a measure for comparison with the operating and financial results of competitors. Such a comparison to plan can be used as a test of the efficiency of the organization's operating processes. The differences between planned and actual costs at Oxford Tole Art will focus April's attention on understanding whether the plans were unrealistic or whether the execution of a sound business plan was flawed. This signals the need for improved planning, better execution, or both.

WHAT-IF ANALYSIS

The cost–volume–profit analysis discussed in Chapter 3 provided insights into how revenues, costs, and profits respond to changes in the quantity of product made and sold. However, that analysis assumed a constant product mix. Now, powerful desktop computers and electronic spreadsheet software make it possible to consider product mixes (and much more) so that managers can evaluate alternative strategies.

Using a computer for the budgeting process, managers can explore the effects of alternative marketing, production, and selling strategies. For example, at Oxford Tole Art, April may consider raising prices, opening a retail outlet, or using different employment strategies. Such alternative proposals can be evaluated in a what-if analysis.

April may ask, "What if I decrease prices on my retail products by 5% and then sales increase by 10%? What will happen to my profits?" The answer: Oxford Tole Art profits will fall from $40,666 to $39,103. (This revised profit number was found by inserting the revised price and demand schedule in the spreadsheet that was used to prepare the original budget figures.) Therefore, this proposed price adjustment is undesirable.

April may also wonder, "What if retail sales would increase by 50% if Oxford Tole Art opened a retail outlet that would cost $40,000 per year to operate (including all costs). The retail outlet orders would be shipped by courier to the customer's address. What would happen to my profits?" In this case, Gael would use the same shop capacity; the painters hired in the year's four quarters would be three, two, two, and four, respectively; and projected profit would increase to $56,553.

The structure and information required to prepare the master budget can be used easily to provide the basis for what-if analysis. (It took only several seconds to answer April's questions using the spreadsheet developed to prepare the Oxford Tole Art cash flow forecast. This spreadsheet is available from this text's website for you to try what-if analysis on your own.)

Evaluating Decision-Making Alternatives

Suppose April is considering renting a machine to automatically sand the buoys and apply the primer coat. The capacity of the machine is 1,300 buoys per month. This machine will reduce the painting time per buoy from 0.8 to 0.5 hour but will increase other shop costs from $20,000 to $35,000. The reduction in painting time per buoy allows Oxford Tole Art to reduce the number of painters needed for any level of scheduled production.

Exhibit 10-14 shows the revised estimated income statement reflecting the rental of the sanding and priming machine. Renting this machine will increase projected net income from the original level of $40,666 to $57,490, a 41% increase of $16,824.

Sensitivity Analysis

What-if analysis is only as good as the model used to represent what is being evaluated. The model must be complete, it must reflect relationships accurately, and it must use accurate estimates. A model that is incomplete, fails to reflect relationships accurately, or uses unreasonable estimates will not provide good estimates of a plan's results. If the model is complete and reflects capacity, cost, and revenue relationships accurately, the remaining issue is the accuracy of the data used. Planners test planning models by varying the model estimates. Suppose one machine represents a bottleneck for manufacturing operations. Then the productivity (output per hour) of that machine is a key estimate for the production plan. The production planner could test the effect of errors in the estimate of the machine's productivity on the production plan

Exhibit 10-14
Oxford Tole Art:
Projected Income
Statement,
December 31, 2011

Revenue		$326,943
Flexible resources expenses:		
Buoys	$12,263	
Paint	17,168	
Other suppliers	14,988	
Packing	10,628	
Shipping	40,875	$95,920
Contribution margin		$231,023
Committed resource expenses:		
Painters' salaries	$48,000	
Shop rent	19,200	
Other shop costs	35,000	
Manager's salary	30,000	132,200
Other Expenses:		
Advertising	$40,000	
Interest paid	1,332	41,332
Net income		$57,490

by varying the productivity number by 10% or 20% above and below the estimate used in the planning budget.

If small forecasting errors of an estimate used in the production plan change the plan, we say that the model is sensitive to that estimate. If the performance consequences (for example, profits) from a bad estimate are severe, planners may want to invest time and resources to improve the accuracy of their estimates. For example, suppose an organization has the production capacity to accept only one of two possible orders. Order 1 promises revenues of $1,000,000 and expected costs of $750,000. Order 2 promises revenues of $800,000 and has costs of $600,000. Based on this information, order 1—with an expected profit of $250,000—looks like a better prospect than order 2, which has a profit of $200,000. Note, however, that the profit associated with order 1 is uncertain, whereas the profit associated with order 2 is certain. Suppose that, with further investigation, planners decide that the costs associated with order 1 could be anywhere between $720,000 and $780,000. This would not affect the decision because even if the worst costs are realized for order 1, profits will still be $220,000, which is more than the $200,000 associated with order 2. However, if the costs associated with order 1 could be anywhere between $680,000 and $820,000, certain circumstances (when costs are more than $800,000) after the fact will have planners wishing they had accepted order 2. This is an example of sensitivity analysis.

Sensitivity analysis is the process of selectively varying a plan's or a budget's key estimates for the purpose of identifying over what range a decision option is preferred. In the preceding example, order 1 is preferred if its costs are $800,000 or less. Sensitivity analysis enables planners to identify the estimates that are critical for the decision under consideration. For example, the labor that Oxford Tole Art needs to make each product is an important factor in its planning budget. Small changes in the estimate of this factor, which is the key productive resource, produce large changes in the projected or planned profit. If Oxford Tole Art can develop a process or can redesign the product so that labor time needed to make a buoy would be reduced by 10%, from 0.8 to 0.72 hour per buoy, projected profit would increase 31% from $40,666 to $53,229. This is a signal to April that designing and running the manufacturing process so that the artists can work as efficiently as possible are critical to the success of her business.

COMPARING ACTUAL AND PLANNED RESULTS

To understand results, such as production and financial outcomes, organizations use variance analysis to compare planned or budgeted results in the master budget with actual results.

Variance Analysis

Budgets are prepared for specific periods so that managers can compare actual results for the period with the planned results for that period. **Variance analysis** has many forms and can result in complex measures, but, as shown in Exhibit 10-15, its basis is very simple—an actual cost or actual revenue amount is compared with a target cost or target revenue amount to identify the difference, which is called a **variance**. For example, a manager might compute the cost of labor that went into making an aircraft and compare that cost with the planned cost of labor for making that aircraft. A variance represents a departure from what was budgeted or planned. What caused the variance and the size of that variance will trigger an investigation to determine its cause and what should be done to correct that variance.

Budgeted, or planned, costs can come from three sources:

1. *Standards established by industrial engineers,* such as cost of steel that should go into an automobile door based on the door's specifications.
2. *Previous period's performance,* such as the average cost of steel per door that was made in the last budget period.
3. *A performance level achieved by a competitor*—usually called a *benchmark* and based on best-in-class results—such as the cost of steel per comparable door achieved by a competitor who is viewed as the most efficient.

The financial numbers used in variance analysis for flexible resources are the product of a price and a quantity component:

$$\text{Planned, or budgeted, amount} = \text{Standard price per unit} \times \text{Budgeted quantity}$$

while

$$\text{Actual amount} = \text{Actual price per unit} \times \text{Actual quantity}$$

Variance analysis explains the difference between planned costs and actual costs by evaluating differences between standard prices and actual prices and budgeted

Exhibit 10-15
Comparison of Actual Cost to Budgeted Cost to Identify the Variance

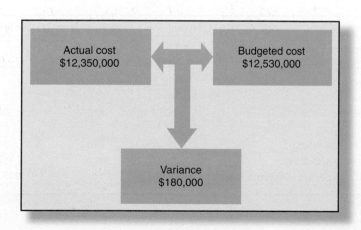

quantities and actual quantities. Managers focus separately on prices and quantities because in most organizations one department or division is responsible for the acquisition (thereby determining the actual price) of a resource and a different department uses (thereby determining the quantity of) the resource.

A variance is a signal that is part of a control system for monitoring results, and thus variances provide a signal that operations did not go as planned. Supervisory personnel use variances as overall checks on how well the people who are managing day-to-day operations are doing what they should be doing. When compared to the performance of other organizations engaged in comparable tasks, variances show the effectiveness of the control systems that operations people are using.

Basic Variance Analysis

Variance analysis helps managers understand the source of the differences—the variances—between actual costs and budgeted costs. If managers learn that specific actions they took on some jobs helped lower the actual costs of these jobs, they can pursue further cost savings by repeating those actions on similar jobs in the future. If they can identify the factors causing actual costs to be higher than expected, managers may be able to take the necessary actions to prevent those factors from recurring in the future. If they learn that cost changes are likely to be permanent, they can update their cost information when bidding for future jobs.

We will now study a specific example that illustrates the nature and role of variances.

Canning Cellular Services

Canning Cellular Services (CCS) is a national provider of cellular phone services. Cellular services are highly competitive and, as in any competitive industry, CCS depends on cost control to be profitable. For this reason CCS has undertaken a major study to understand the behavior of its costs and to provide a continuing basis for cost reduction. The two major costs in the cellular business are equipment costs and personnel costs.

As part of its effort to control personnel costs, CCS has documented in euros (€) the costs associated with connecting a new customer and estimated it to be €95.50. Exhibit 10-16 reports the results of the study, which identified three relevant costs: direct materials costs, direct labor costs, and support costs.

The *direct materials costs* relate to the welcoming package provided to each new customer. This package defines the range and nature of the various cellular services offered by CCS.

Exhibit 10-16
Canning Cellular Services: Total Cost per Activated Customer

	UNIT	COST/UNIT	TOTAL COST
Direct material:			
Welcoming package	1.00	€25.00	€25.00
Direct labor:			
Sales staff	0.50	25.00	12.50
Technical staff	0.25	40.00	10.00
Support cost:			
Data processing	0.20	15.00	3.00
System activation	0.15	300.00	45.00
Total cost per activated customer			€95.50

The *direct labor costs* include two components: One is the cost of the salesperson, who describes the various services available and writes up the sales contract. On average, the salesperson spends 0.5 hour with each new customer and is paid €25 per hour. The other component is the cost of the sales staff employees who activate new cellular telephones by calling the control center and providing electronic serial numbers and such customer-related information as names, addresses, and payment details. This requires 0.25 hour of time per phone, and sales staff are paid €40 per hour.

The support costs are comprised of two components. One is the salaries of the data processing staff who enter customer-related information into the CCS customer database. This information is used for billing and advertising purposes. On average, it takes 0.20 hour to enter the information for each customer, and the data processing clerks are paid €15 per hour. The other component is the system activation cost. This includes the cost of the computing and data processing systems that support the process of entering each new customer into the system and activating the customer on the system. On average, the activation process takes 0.15 hour on the computer, and the cost of computer time is estimated at €300 per hour.

Based on these cost estimates and the projected addition of 1 million new customers during fiscal 2011, CCS developed the estimate of costs for the upcoming year (see Exhibit 10-17.)

The document summarizing these costs—variously referred to as budgeted costs, estimated costs, projected costs, target costs, or forecasted costs, but all identify the same costs—is called the **master budget**. Note that the budgeted costs of €95,500,000 depend on the following:

1. The projected volume of activity, which in this example is 1 million customers.
2. The standards for the quantity of each of the budgeted items.
3. The standards for the cost per unit of each of the budgeted items.

If any of these items differs from the forecasted amount, the actual total costs will differ from the master budget total.

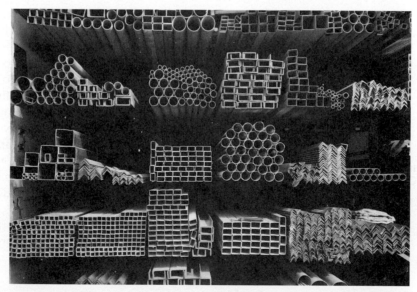

The costs of direct materials such as these metal rods, brackets, and extrusions are significant costs of a manufactured product. Purchasing has to carefully consider what quantities to buy in order to get the best price without stockpiling too much inventory.
Shutterstock

Exhibit 10-17
Canning Cellular
Services: Master
Budget

	UNITS/CUSTOMER USE	COST/UNIT	TOTAL COST
Direct material:			
Welcoming package	1.00	€25.00	€25,000,000
Direct labor:			
Sales staff	0.50	25.00	12,500,000
Technical staff	0.25	40.00	10,000,000
Support cost:			
Data processing	0.20	15.00	3,000,000
System activation	0.15	300.00	45,000,000
Total customer-related costs			€95,500,000

	MASTER BUDGET	ACTUAL COSTS	DIFFERENCE
Direct material:			
Welcoming package	€25,000,000	€29,700,000	€4,700,000
Direct labor:			
Sales staff	12,500,000	14,850,000	2,350,000
Technical staff	10,000,000	10,890,000	890,000
Support cost:			
Data processing	3,000,000	3,960,000	960,000
System activation	45,000,000	42,900,000	(2,100,000)
Total customer-related costs	€95,500,000	€102,300,000	€6,800,000

First-Level Variances

Several weeks after year-end 2011, the company comptroller forwarded to the manager of new customer accounts the summary shown in Exhibit 10-18, which displays the **first-level variances** for different cost items. The first-level variance for a cost item is the difference between the actual costs and the budget or planned costs for that cost item. By convention, variances are computed by subtracting budget costs from actual costs. Therefore, variances are "favorable" if the actual costs are less than the estimated master budget costs—that is, if the variance is negative. "Unfavorable" variances arise when actual costs exceed estimated budget costs—that is, when the variance is positive. In this example, the first-level cost variance for sales staff, for example, is €2,350,000 unfavorable.

Sharon Mackenzie, the manager of new customer accounts, was surprised by the report because she had directed her staff to undertake specific initiatives related to employee training and equipment improvement, both intended to reduce costs. Not only had costs not decreased, but they had increased by €6,800,000, which was significant. There was no explanation in this exhibit to help Sharon understand what went wrong. Therefore, Sharon demanded an explanation for why costs had not decreased following the cost-cutting initiatives.

Decomposing the Variances

Following up on Sharon's demand, the financial group prepared Exhibit 10-19 and forwarded it to her. Fred Liang, the CCS comptroller, explained to Sharon that Exhibit 10-19 uses a **flexible budget**, in which the forecast in the master budget is adjusted for the

Exhibit 10-19
Canning Cellular Services: Master Budget, Flexible Budget, and Actual Results Summary

	MASTER BUDGET 1,000,000			FLEXIBLE BUDGET 1,100,000			ACTUAL RESULTS 1,100,00		
	U/C	COST	TOTAL	U/C	COST	TOTAL	U/C	COST	TOTAL
Direct material:									
Welcoming package	1.00	€25.00	€25,000,000	1.00	€25.00	€27,500,000	1.00	€27.00	€29,700,000
Direct labor:									
Sales staff	0.50	25.00	12,500,000	0.50	25.00	13,750,000	0.45	30.00	14,850,000
Technical staff	0.25	40.00	10,000,000	0.25	40.00	11,000,000	0.22	45.00	10,890,000
Support cost:									
Data processing	0.20	15.00	3,000,000	0.20	15.00	3,300,000	0.24	15.00	3,960,000
System activation	0.15	300.00	45,000,000	0.15	300.00	49,500,000	0.12	325.00	42,900,000
Total customer-related costs			€95,500,000			€105,050,000			€102,300,000

difference between planned volume and actual volume. Therefore, the flexible budget reflects a cost budget or forecast based on the level of volume that is actually achieved rather than the planned volume—and it is the planned volume that underlies the master budget. Fred referred Sharon to Exhibit 10-19, which provides the details of the flexible budget calculations. A cost difference between a master budget and flexible budget is a **planning variance** because it reflects the difference between planned activity and actual activity. Planning variances arise entirely because the planned volume of activity was not realized. Therefore, based on the result that 1.1 million new customers were added instead of the planned 1 million, the projected, or budgeted, level of costs is now €105,050,000.

Sharon immediately noted three facts when she reviewed Exhibit 10-19:

1. The number of actual customers exceeded the number of customers used to forecast costs.
2. The actual unit cost of four of the five items in the budget exceeded the standard unit cost used to develop the forecast.
3. The per-unit use of both labor items and one of the two support costs was lower, reflecting the results of the process improvements that Sharon had commissioned. The per unit use of the other support item was higher, but only because midway through the year Sharon had developed a more comprehensive form that required more input for new customers.

Sharon asked the finance group to isolate the effects of these various price and use variances.

Planning and Flexible Budget Variances

In response, the finance group provided Sharon with the additional information shown in Exhibit 10-20. Fred explained that the differences between the flexible budget and the actual results—the **flexible budget variances**—reflect variances from the budget level of costs adjusted for the actual level of activity. He further explained that since the flexible budget identifies the budgeted level of costs for the activity levels achieved, Sharon's focus should be on these variances to determine whether the cost-cutting activities had been successful. Because the total flexible budget variance was –€2,750,000—a favorable variance—overall costs were lower than the

Exhibit 10-20
Canning Cellular Services: Second-Level Variance Summary

	MASTER BUDGET	PLANNING VARIANCE	FLEXIBLE BUDGET	FLEXIBLE BUDGET VARIANCE	ACTUAL RESULTS
Direct material:					
Welcoming package	€25,000,000	€2,500,000	€27,500,000	€2,200,000	€29,700,000
Direct labor:					
Sales staff	12,500,000	1,250,000	13,750,000	1,100,000	14,850,000
Technical staff	10,000,000	1,000,000	11,000,000	(110,000)	10,890,000
Support cost:					
Data processing	3,000,000	300,000	3,300,000	660,000	3,960,000
System activation	45,000,000	4,500,000	49,500,000	(6,600,000)	42,900,000
Total customer-related costs	€95,500,000	€9,550,000	€105,050,000	€(2,750,000)	€102,300,000

budgeted costs for the achieved level of activity. Fred pointed out to Sharon that the planning variance and flexible budget variance are called **second-level variances**, which together add up to the first-level variance.

Sharon was pleased with this information but still concerned. She pointed out to Fred that these flexible budget variances reflect both quantity variances—the difference between the planned and the actual use rates per unit of output—and price variances—the difference between the planned and the actual price per unit of the various cost items. Sharon asked Fred to prepare an exhibit that would highlight the incremental effects of quantity differences and the incremental effects of price variances.

Quantity and Price Variances for Material and Labor

Direct material flexible budget variances and direct labor flexible budget variances can be decomposed further into **efficiency variances**—also called **quantity variances**—and **rate variances**—also called **price variances**. We can refer to these as **third-level variances** because together they explain the flexible budget component of the second-level variance. In Exhibit 10-20, the amount of direct materials used equals the volume of production achieved (1.1 million units produced, that is, customers served) multiplied by the actual use rate, which was 1, giving an actual quantity of direct materials use of 1.1 million. The flexible budget allowance is the volume of production achieved (1.1 million customers) multiplied by the planned or target quantity use rate, which was 1, giving a planned, or budgeted, quantity of direct materials of 1.1 million.

Material Quantity and Price Variances
The material quantity variance can be calculated from the following relationship:

$$\text{Quantity variance} = (AQ - SQ) \times SP$$
$$= (1,100,000 - 1,100,000) \text{ units} \times €25 \text{ per unit}$$
$$= 0$$

where

AQ = Actual quantity of materials used
SQ = Standard quantity of materials allowed for the production level achieved
SP = Estimated or standard price of materials

The material price variance for direct materials is calculated using the following relationship:

$$\text{Price variance} = (AP - SP) \times AQ$$
$$= (€27 - €25) \text{ per unit} \times 1{,}100{,}000 \text{ units}$$
$$= €2{,}200{,}000 \text{ (unfavorable)}$$

where

$$AP = \text{Actual price of materials}$$
$$SP = \text{Estimated or standard price of materials}$$
$$AQ = \text{Actual quantity of materials used}$$

We have now decomposed the total variance for the cost of the welcoming package, which is the direct material in this example, into a material quantity variance and a material price variance. When we add these two third-level variances together (€0 + €2,200,000 unfavorable), we obtain the total flexible budget variance for direct materials (€2,200,000 unfavorable).

The logic of decomposing the variances is easily verified by adding the algebraic formulas for material quantity and price variances. The sum of the decomposed variances is as follows:

$$\text{Sum of decomposed variances} = \text{Quantity variance} + \text{Price variance}$$
$$= [(AQ - SQ) \times SP] + [(AP - SP) \times AQ]$$
$$= (AQ \times SP) - (SQ \times SP)$$
$$\quad + (AP \times AQ) - (SP \times AQ)$$
$$= (AP \times AQ) - (SQ \times SP)$$
$$= \text{Actual cost} - \text{Budgeted cost}$$
$$= \text{Flexible budget variance}$$

What does this variance and its decomposition tell Sharon, who is the manager ultimately responsible for these costs? They tell her that the quantity used was consistent with the number of customers, no more and no less. They also tell her that the cost of €27 per unit exceeded the standard, or budgeted, cost of €25 per unit. Perhaps this cost increment reflected changes in the welcoming package or perhaps additional costs billed by the supplier. Given the magnitude of the variance—€2, or 8% of the target cost—Sharon would follow up to determine its cause. However, it is important to point out that as a good manager, Sharon might already be well aware of the variance and its cause and that the value of the variance analysis is to confirm its amount.

Material Quantity and Price Variances: A General Approach

Many people find that a diagram makes calculating variances easier. To prepare such a diagram, we define one more variable, PQ, the actual quantity of raw materials purchased. This additional variable allows one to handle situations where the amount of raw materials purchased differs from the amount of raw materials used. Here are the terms that you will see in Exhibit 10-21:

Total Cost: The actual cost of the acquired raw materials = purchased quantity (PQ) × actual price (AP).

Price Adjusted Cost: The cost of acquired materials using the standard price = purchased quantity (PQ) × standard price (SP).

Price Adjusted Quantity: The cost of materials used using the standard price = quantity used (AQ) × standard price (SP).

Flexible Budget Cost: The cost of the standard quantity of materials = standard quantity (SQ) × standard price (SP).

Exhibit 10-21
Direct Materials
Flexible Budget
Variance Analysis

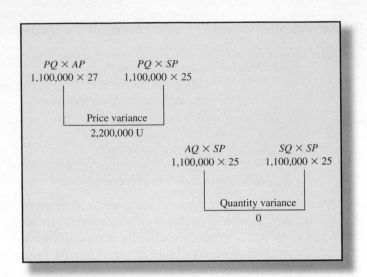

$PQ \times AP$
$1{,}100{,}000 \times 27$

$PQ \times SP$
$1{,}100{,}000 \times 25$

Price variance
2,200,000 U

$AQ \times SP$
$1{,}100{,}000 \times 25$

$SQ \times SP$
$1{,}100{,}000 \times 25$

Quantity variance
0

Exhibit 10-22
A Graphical
Approach to Direct
Materials Flexible
Budget Variance
Analysis

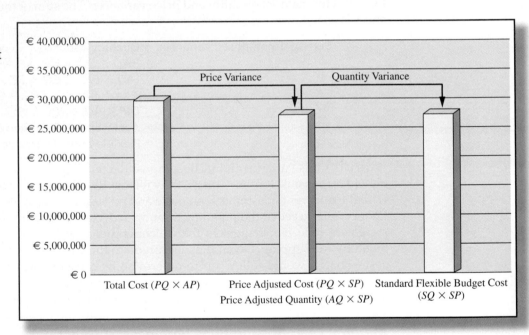

Where the quantity acquired is the quantity used, as is the case in the CSS example, the price-adjusted cost and the price-adjusted quantity are equal.

Exhibit 10-21 diagrams the flexible budget variances for direct materials costs, and Exhibit 10-22 illustrates a graphical approach representing these variances when the price-adjusted cost and the price-adjusted quantity are equal.

Efficiency and Wage Rate Variances for Direct Labor Costs
The labor cost variances are determined in a way similar to that described for material quantity and price variances. The formulas are as follows:

$$\text{Labor efficiency variance} = (AH - SH) \times SR$$
$$\text{Labor rate variance} = (AR - SR) \times AH$$

where

> AH = Actual number of direct labor hours
> AR = Actual wage rate
> SH = Number of direct labor hours allowed given the level of output achieved
> SR = Standard wage rate

Note that while it is common to use the terms *price* and *quantity* for the material variances, it is common to use the terms *rate* and *efficiency* for the comparable labor variances. The total cost variance for labor is computed as follows:

$$
\begin{aligned}
\text{Efficiency variance} + \text{Rate variance} &= (AH - SH) \times SR + (AR - SR) \times AH \\
&= (AH \times SR) - (SH \times SR) \\
&\quad + (AR \times AH) - (SR \times AH) \\
&= (AR \times AH) - (SR \times SH) \\
&= \text{Actual cost} - \text{Budgeted cost} \\
&= \text{Flexible budget variance}
\end{aligned}
$$

To compute the efficiency and rate variance for the sales staff, the total hours of sales staff used is 495,000 (0.45 × 1,100,000 hours), and the total budgeted level of hours, given the achieved level of production, is 550,000 (0.5 × 1,100,000 hours).

Therefore, the efficiency variance for sales staff labor cost is as follows:

$$
\begin{aligned}
\text{Efficiency variance} &= (AH - SH) \times SR \\
&= (495{,}000 - 550{,}000) \times €25 \\
&= -€1{,}375{,}000 \text{ (favorable)}
\end{aligned}
$$

The efficiency efforts commissioned by Sharon evidently paid off in terms of fewer hours used of sales staff time than planned for the achieved level of income, resulting in cost savings of €1,375,000.

The price or rate variance for sales staff labor is as follows:

$$
\begin{aligned}
\text{Rate variance} &= (AR - SR) \times AH \\
&= (€30 - €25) \text{ per hour} \times 495{,}000 \text{ hours} \\
&= €2{,}475{,}000 \text{ (unfavorable)}
\end{aligned}
$$

In other words, for the number of hours worked, the sales staff was paid €2,475,000 more than was planned when the master budget was developed. This increase might reflect a corporate-wide wage adjustment that is beyond Sharon's control, or perhaps it reflects the hiring of more skilled and qualified sales staff who were responsible for the favorable efficiency variance. These facts would be established by an investigation, which would be triggered by a variance this size.

Exhibit 10-23 shows another way to visualize direct labor variances. As required, the sum of the rate variance and the efficiency variance equals the total flexible budget variance for sales staff costs. Total flexible budget variance for sales staff cost = −€1,375,000 + €2,475,000 = €1,100,000 (unfavorable).

Efficiency and Wage Rate Variances for Direct Labor Costs: A General Approach

Following are the terms we need to diagram the flexible budget variances for direct labor costs:

Total Cost: The actual cost of direct labor = actual labor hours (AH) × actual labor rate (AR).

Price Adjusted Quantity: The cost of direct labor quantity using the standard price = actual labor hours (AH) × standard labor rate (SR).

Exhibit 10-23
Visualizing the
Direct Labor Cost
Variances

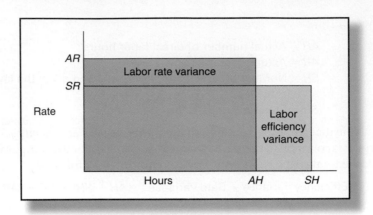

Exhibit 10-24
Direct Labor
Flexible Budget
Variance Analysis

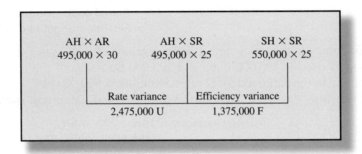

Exhibit 10-25
A Graphical
Approach to Direct
Labor Flexible
Budget Variance
Analysis

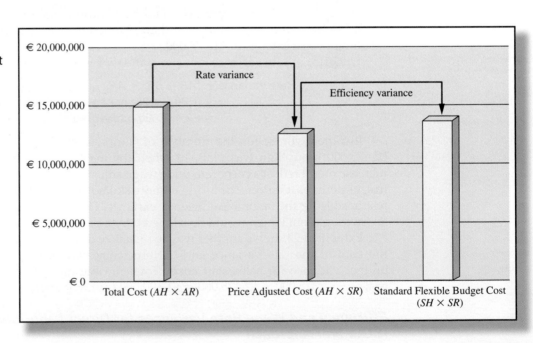

Flexible Budget Cost: The cost of the standard quantity of labor = standard labor hours (*SH*) × standard labor rate (*SR*).

Exhibit 10-24 diagrams the flexible budget variances for direct labor costs, and Exhibit 10-25 shows a graphical approach to representing these variances.

Detailed Analysis of Support Activity Cost Variances

What about support costs? Support costs can reflect variable, or fixed, costs. The quantity of fixed costs may not change from period to period, but the spending on them may fluctuate. Engineers can travel, take courses, vacation, quit, and be replaced with someone else. Thus, it is possible and desirable to monitor spending variances on capacity-related resources, even when one cannot monitor efficiency variances that will show up as changes in used and unused capacity.

What about variable support costs? Such support costs reflect behind-the-scenes operations that are proportional to the volume of activity but are not directly a part of the product or service provided to the customer. For example, an indirect support cost in a factory would be the wages paid to employees who move work in process around the factory floor as the product is being made.

At CCS, these support costs reflect (1) the time and cost of the equipment and personnel who input customer data each time a new customer is added to the CCS customer file, and (2) the time and cost of equipment and personnel each time a new customer is activated on the computers that control access to the cellular system.

An investigation by Sharon revealed that the cost of the data processing staff had two components: a wage rate and a system access charge incurred when the data processor was accessing the system. These cost components are summarized in Exhibit 10-26.

The actual hourly clerical wage is €10, and for each hour the clerk works, the database is, on average, accessed for 0.1 hour. The system access fee is €50. This yields a total cost of €15 per data processing clerk hour. When an aggregate rate per hour is constructed in this way, the rate variance will reflect both the amount and the cost of the components used to compute the rate. With this understanding of how the rate was computed for a flexible support item, cost analysis can be used to investigate the variance associated with a support cost item.

In view of the size of the variance associated with system activation costs, Sharon directed Fred to analyze its source. Exhibit 10-27 summarizes the calculation used to develop the €300 hourly charge for the hourly activation rate, which has two components. One component reflects the wage paid to the sales staff, which is €40 per hour. The other component is the system access fee, which is charged at the rate of €520 per hour of access. On average, the sales staff accesses the activation system for half an hour for each hour worked, yielding the blended rate of €300 per hour, which was used in developing the budget.

Exhibit 10-26
Canning Cellular Services: Clerical Budgeted Cost per Hour

	UNITS	RATE	TOTAL
Clerical wage	1	€10.00	€10.00
Computer access time	0.1	50.00	5.00
Total cost per hour			€15.00

Exhibit 10-27
Canning Cellular Services: Technical Staff Budgeted Hourly Cost Calculation

	UNITS	RATE	TOTAL
Technical staff	1	€40.00	€40.00
Computer access time	0.5	520.00	€260.00
Total cost per hour			€300.00

Exhibit 10-28
Canning Cellular
Services: Actual
Calculation of
Technical Staff
Cost per Hour

	Units	Rate	Total
Technical staff	1	€55.00	€55.00
Computer access time	0.45	600.00	€270.00
Total cost per hour			€325.00

Exhibit 10-29
Canning Cellular Services: Analysis of System Activation Flexible Budget Variance

Due to labor use	$[(1,100,000 \times 0.12 \times 1) - (1,100,000 \times 0.15 \times 1)] \times €40 = €1,320,000$ F
Due to labor rate	$1,100,000 \times 0.12 \times 1 \times (€55 - €40) = €1,980,000$ U
Due to additional computer use	$[(1,100,000 \times 0.12 \times 0.45) - (1,100,000 \times 0.15 \times 0.5)] \times €520 = €12,012,000$ F
Due to additional access rate	$1,100,000 \times 0.12 \times 0.45 \times (€600 - €520) = €4,752,000$ U

Investigation yielded the information in Exhibit 10-28 to explain the actual access fee. Note that the actual rate differs from the budget rate for three reasons: (1) The wage paid to the sales staff was €15 higher than the budgeted rate, (2) the computer access time per hour worked by sales staff was lower than budgeted, and (3) the rate for computer access time was higher than budgeted.

These three elements, combined with the data in Exhibit 10-19, allow Fred to develop the information in Exhibit 10-29, which explains the total flexible budget variance for system activation support costs.

Sales Variances

We have studied how managers factor cost variances into different components in order to signal to management where costs deviated from the plan or target amounts. What about revenues? To illustrate a common approach to variance analysis for sales, consider Danny's Bagel Barn.

Danny sells three types of bagels: regular, superior, and deluxe, which are priced at $0.40, $0.55, and $0.70, respectively. Exhibit 10-30 displays the sales budget that Danny prepared for July.

During July, Danny experienced intense sales competition from Maggie's Bagel Factory on his regular and superior bagel lines. Danny cut his prices for those two lines.

Exhibit 10-30
Danny's Bagel Barn: Planned Sales for July

	Products						
	Regular		Superior		Deluxe		
	Data	% Total	Data	% Total	Data	% Total	Total
Unit Price	$0.40		$0.55		$0.70		
Unit Sales	10,000	50.00%	6,000	30.00%	4,000	20.00%	$20,000
Total	$4,000		$3,300		$2,800		$10,100

Exhibit 10-31
Danny's Bagel Barn: Actual Sales for July

	PRODUCTS						
	REGULAR		SUPERIOR		DELUXE		
	DATA	% TOTAL	DATA	% TOTAL	DATA	% TOTAL	TOTAL
Unit price	$0.35		$0.50		$0.80		
Unit sales	9,000	42.86%	7,000	33.33%	5,000	23.81%	21,000
Total	$3,150		$3,500		$4,000		$10,650

Even with the price cut, Danny sold fewer regular bagels than planned. However, the price cut on the superior bagels resulted in higher than planned sales. Exhibit 10-31 summarizes the July results.

Danny notes that revenues were $550 higher than planned ($10,650 − $10,100) and would like to know how the price changes and volume changes each contributed to this difference between planned and actual results.

Managers undertake the reconciliation between actual and planned sales revenue in two steps. The first step isolates the effect of sales volume differences, and the second step isolates the effect of sales price differences.

Sales Volume Effects

In a firm with multiple products, volume-related revenue differences can arise in two ways:

1. *Because the mix (the percentage of the total of each product's sales) was different than planned.* This is called the **sales mix variance**, and *for each product*, the sales mix variance is computed as follows:

   > Actual total sales units of all products × (Actual sales mix percentage of this product − Planned sales mix percentage of this product) × Planned revenue per unit of this product

   Here is the sales mix variance for each of the products:

   Regular: 21,000 × (0.4286 − 0.5000) × $0.40 = −$600 (unfavorable). (Note that now we are dealing with revenues, so a negative variance is unfavorable.) This means that because sales of the regular bagel made up less than the planned percentage of total sales, revenues of $600 were lost on this product.
   Superior: 21,000 × (0.3333 − 0.3000) × $0.55 = $385 (favorable). This means that because sales of the superior bagel made up more than the planned percentage of total sales, revenues of $385 were gained on this product.
   Deluxe: 21,000 × (0.2381 − 0.2000) × $0.70 = $560 (favorable). This means that because sales of the deluxe bagel made up more than the planned percentage of total sales, revenues of $560 were gained on this product.

2. *Because the volume of sales was different than planned.* This is called the **sales quantity variance** and *for each product*, the sales quantity variance is computed as follows:

   > (Actual total sales units of all products − Planned total sales units of all products) × Planned sales mix percentage of this product × Planned revenue per unit of this product

Here is the sales quantity variance for each of the products:

Regular: $(21{,}000 - 20{,}000) \times 0.5000 \times \$0.40 = \$200$ (favorable). This means that because of the overall increase in sales, if the regular bagel's sales mix percentage had remained as planned, then an increase in sales revenues of $200 would have been realized on this product.

Superior: $(21{,}000 - 20{,}000) \times 0.3000 \times \$0.55 = \$165$ (favorable). This means that because of the overall increase in sales, if the regular bagel's sales mix percentage had remained as planned, then an increase in sales revenues of $200 would have been realized on this product.

Deluxe: $(21{,}000 - 20{,}000) \times 0.2000 \times \$0.70 = \$140$ (favorable). This means that because of the overall increase in sales, if the regular bagel's sales mix percentage had remained as planned, then an increase in sales revenues of $140 would have been realized on this product.

Sales Price Effects

The sales volume and sales mix variances explain the difference between planned and actual revenues because of volume-related effects. What remains to consider is the effect on revenues of differences between actual and planned selling prices. This is the **sales price variance**.

For each product, the sales price variance is computed as follows:

Actual number of units sold $\times$ (Actual price per unit $-$ Planned price per unit)

Here are the sales price variance calculations:

Regular: $9{,}000 \times (0.35 - 0.40) = -\$450$ (unfavorable). This means that because Danny was unable to sell the regular bagels at the planned price of $0.40 per unit, $450 of revenues were lost on the 9,000 units of sales.

Superior: $7{,}000 \times (0.50 - 0.55) = -\$350$ (unfavorable). This means that because Danny was unable to sell the superior bagels at the planned price of $0.55 per unit, $350 of revenues were lost on the 7,000 units of sales.

Deluxe: $5{,}000 \times (0.80 - 0.70) = \$500$ (favorable). This means that because Danny was able to sell the deluxe bagels at a price that exceeded the planned price of $0.70 per unit, $500 of revenues were gained on the 5,000 units of sales.

Exhibit 10-32 summarizes the sales variances for Danny's July operations. Note that, as required, the total of the variances equals the difference between the actual and planned revenues ($10,650 − $10,100).

Exhibit 10-32
Danny's Bagel Barn: Sales Variance Summary

| | PRODUCTS | | | |
	REGULAR	SUPERIOR	DELUXE	TOTAL
Price variance	$(450)	$(350)	$500	$(300)
Sales mix variance	(600)	385	560	345
Sales quantity variance	200	165	140	505
Total	$(850)	$200	$1,200	$550

THE ROLE OF BUDGETING IN SERVICE AND NOT-FOR-PROFIT ORGANIZATIONS

We have focused on the role of budgeting in manufacturing organizations up to this point. Budgeting serves a slightly different but equally relevant role in natural resource companies, service organizations, and not-for-profit (NFP) organizations such as charitable organizations and government agencies. As in manufacturing organizations, budgeting helps nonmanufacturing organizations perform their planning function by coordinating and formalizing responsibilities and relationships and communicating the expected plans. Exhibit 10-33 summarizes the focus of the budgeting process in manufacturing, natural resource, service, and NFP organizations.

In the natural resources sector, the focus is on balancing demand with the availability of natural resources, such as minerals, fish, or wood. Because the natural resource supply often constrains sales, success requires managing the resource base effectively to match resource supply with potential demand.

In the service sector, the focus is on balancing demand and the organization's ability to provide services, which is determined by the level and mix of skills in the organization. Although the service sector often uses machines to deliver products to customers, most operations remain labor paced—that is, they operate at a pace dictated by their human operators. Therefore, people rather than machines usually represent the capacity constraint in the service sector. Planning in the service sector must consider the time needed to put skilled new people in place as sales increase. Planning is critical in high-skill organizations, such as in a consulting business, because people capacity is expensive and services cannot be inventoried when demand falls below capacity.

In NFP organizations, the focus of budgeting has been to balance revenues raised by taxes or donations with spending demands. In government agencies, planned cash outflows, or spending plans, are called **appropriations**. Appropriations set limits on a government agency's spending. Governments worldwide are facing increased pressures to eliminate deficits without raising tax revenues. Therefore, many governments are looking for ways to eliminate unnecessary expenditures and to make necessary expenditures more efficient rather than just ensuring that government agencies do not spend more than they have been authorized to spend. As part of the planning process, these agencies must establish priorities for their expenditures and improve the productivity with which they deliver services to constituents.

PERIODIC AND CONTINUOUS BUDGETING

The basic budgeting process described in this chapter involves many organizational design decisions, such as the length of the budget process, the basic budget spending assumptions, and the degree of top management control.

Exhibit 10-33
Focus of Budgeting in Different Organizations

Organization Type	Main Focus of Budgeting Process
Manufacturing	Sales and manufacturing activities
Natural resource	Sales, resource availability, and acquisition
Service	Sales activities and staffing requirements
NFP	Raising revenues and controlling expenditures

The budget process described for Oxford Tole Art is performed on an annual budget cycle or, generally, a **periodic budget** cycle. Gael, the owner, prepares budgets periodically for each planning period. Although planners may update or revise the budgets at anytime during the budget period, periodic budgeting is typically performed once per budget period.

In a **continuous budget** cycle, as one budget period—usually a month or a quarter—passes, planners drop the current budget period from the master budget and add a future budget period in its place. Therefore, if Oxford Tole Art used continuous budgeting with a one-year cycle, April would drop one month from the beginning of the budget period and add a month to the end of the budget period as each month passes, at the same time making any changes in the estimates of the original months 2 through 12 that appear appropriate given new information that arrived during period 1. For example, at the end of February 2011, April would drop February 2011 from the budget and add February 2012.

The length of the budget period used in continuous budgeting reflects the competitive forces, skill requirements, and technology changes that the organization faces. The budget period must be long enough for the organization to anticipate important environmental changes and adapt to them and yet short enough to ensure that estimates for the end of the period will be reasonable and realistic. Advocates of periodic budgeting argue that continuous budgeting takes too much time and effort and that periodic budgeting provides virtually the same benefits at a lower cost. Advocates of continuous budgeting argue that it keeps the organization planning and assessing and thinking strategically year-round rather than just once a year at budget time.

CONTROLLING DISCRETIONARY EXPENDITURES

Organizations use three general approaches to budget discretionary expenditures for items such as spending on research and development:

1. Incremental budgeting.
2. Zero-based budgeting.
3. Project funding.

Each has benefits relative to the others.

Incremental Budgeting

Incremental budgeting bases a period's expenditure level for a discretionary item on the amount spent for that item during the previous period. If the total budget for discretionary items increases by 10%, each discretionary item is allowed to increase 10%. This basic model has variations. For example, if the total spending on all discretionary items is allowed to increase by 10%, all discretionary spending may experience an across-the-board increase of 5%, and the remaining 5% increase in total spending may be allocated to discretionary items based on merit, such as a high level of performance on an existing project that can be expanded, or based on need, such as a promising new project.

Some people have criticized incremental budgeting because it does not require justification of the organization's goals for discretionary expenditures. Incremental budgeting includes no provision to reduce or eliminate expenditures as the organization changes, nor does it have a mechanism to provide disproportionate support to discretionary items that will yield substantial benefits.

Zero-Based Budgeting

Zero-based budgeting (ZBB) requires that proponents of discretionary expenditures continuously justify every expenditure. (*Note:* ZZB is inappropriate for budgeting costs that vary in proportion to production, such as the amount of wood used in a furniture factory, since by their nature they are inevitable once the manufacturing decision is made.) For each planning period, in ZBB, the starting point for each budget line item is zero.

ZBB arose, in part, to combat indiscriminate incremental budgets, which are based on a percentage adjustment of the previous period's budget. Because incremental budgeting requires very little thought, it often results in misallocation of resources. Proponents also proposed ZBB to control projects that, once activated, take on a life of their own and resist going out of existence, such as a government department that is created for one purpose and is not disbanded when that purpose has been achieved or is no longer required.

Under ZBB, planners allocate the organization's scarce resources to the spending proposals they think will best achieve the organization's goals. While this seems logical, the zero-based approach to planning discretionary expenditures is controversial. This approach to project budgeting has been used primarily to assess government expenditures. In profit-seeking organizations, ZBB has been applied only to discretionary expenditures, such as research and development, advertising, and employee training.

Traditionally, ZBB ideas do not apply to engineered costs—that is, short-term costs that have an identifiable relationship with some activity level. Engineered costs are controlled by measuring and using reports of the amounts of resources consumed by operating activities and by the cost variances described earlier. However, even for engineered costs, ZBB could be effective when combined with the reengineering approach. For example, reengineering a product or process involves developing a vision of how a product should perform or how a process should work independently of current conditions. It is possible to use ZBB as a tool to provide baseline costs to new products or processes.

Project funding requires detailed scrutiny of data in order to determine how much discretionary spending should occur in a very specific time period.
Alamy Images Royalty Free

Project Funding

Critics of ZBB complain that it is expensive because it requires so much employee time to prepare. These critics have proposed an intermediate solution between the two extremes of ZBB and incremental budgeting to mitigate the disadvantages of each. The intermediate solution is called project funding and is a proposal for discretionary expenditures with a specific time horizon or sunset provision. Projects with indefinite lives, which are sometimes called *programs*, should be continuously reviewed to ensure that they are living up to their intended purposes.

Advocates of discretionary expenditures state their requests as project proposals that include project duration and cost for each period during a project's life. Planners approve no discretionary spending for projects that have indeterminate lengths or indeterminate spending amounts. If the planners approve the project, they agree to provide the level of support requested in the plan. Requests to extend or modify the project must be approved separately. The advantage of providing sunset provisions is that they strike a balance between the high cost resulting from the need for close scrutiny and continuous justification provided by ZBB and the much lower cost of incremental budgeting.

MANAGING THE BUDGETING PROCESS

Who should manage and oversee the budgeting process? Many organizations use a budget team, headed by the organization's budget director, sometimes the controller or the chief financial officer, to coordinate the budgeting process. The budget team usually reports to a budget committee, which generally includes the chief executive officer, the chief operating officer, and the senior executive vice president. The composition of the budget committee reflects the role of the budget as the planning document that reflects and relates to the organization's strategy and objectives. The danger of using a budget committee is that it may signal to other employees that budgeting is relevant only to senior management. Senior management must take steps to ensure that the organization members affected by the budget do not perceive the budget and the budgeting process to be beyond their control or responsibility.

Criticisms of the Traditional Budgeting Model and the "Beyond Budgeting" Approach

In this chapter we have discussed the traditional model of budgeting. The traditional approach was developed in the 1920s for cost control purposes. As organizations grew and became more complex, senior management relied increasingly on the budgeting process to control the complexity of multiple divisions, diverse product lines, and new technologies and to motivate managers to achieve specific goals. Today's budgeting process in large organizations is often a yearlong process involving thousands of people and enormous quantities of time and resources.

According to critics the traditional budgeting process has gone unchecked for too long. The traditional model was useful when market conditions were stable, competition and the need for continual innovation were not as intense as they are today, and customers were not as demanding. Critics claim that the traditional budgeting process is an outmoded ritual that hamstrings organizations and managers and prevents them from being able to respond to a constantly changing environment. It reflects a top-down approach to organizing that is inconsistent with the need to be flexible and adapt to changing organizational circumstances. Further, it focuses on controls (such as meeting the target budget) rather than on helping the organization achieve its strategic objectives. Resource allocations are also driven by politics rather than strategy—that is, political power in the organization drives resource allocations rather than the strategic needs that drive traditional budgeting.

As an alternative, leading critics such as Jeremy Hope and Robin Fraser[1] have proposed a "beyond budgeting" approach. The beyond budgeting approach differs in two fundamental ways from traditional budgeting. First, traditional budgets are based on fixed annual plans that tie managers to predetermined actions. In the beyond budgeting approach, targets are developed based on stretch goals tied to peers, competitors, and key global benchmarks. These targets are reviewed and modified if necessary and managers are more motivated to achieve these goals since the goals represent measures that link directly to the competition rather than an internal artificial goal. Second, the beyond budgeting model provides a more decentralized way of managing. Rather than relying on traditional hierarchical and centralized management, managers are much more accountable to their teams and work groups since the targets directly pertain to what they are doing. This provides everyone with a more direct sense of responsibility and is more motivating. While the arguments for the beyond budgeting approach are sound, it has been difficult for many organizations to switch to this approach because it requires a fundamental shift not only in thinking but also in the way entire organizations operate.

EPILOGUE TO THE CALIFORNIA BUDGET CRISIS

On September 24, 2010, Governor Arnold Schwarzenegger and state lawmakers agreed to a compromise to close the $19.1 billion deficit and give California a budget. The agreement ended the state's record three-month impasse that began on July 1, 2010. The deal was reached after a grueling five-hour negotiating session among the Governor and Democratic and Republican heads of the Senate and the State Assembly. A relieved

Budgeting is often not a game for the feint of heart. The process can be extremely contentious as evidenced by these lawmakers.

Getty Images, Inc.—Getty News

---

[1] J. Hope and R. Fraser, *Beyond Budgeting: How Managers Can Break Free from the Annual Performance Trap* (Boston: Harvard Business School Press, 2003).

Darrell Steinberg, the Senate president pro tem, emerged from the meeting simply saying, "We have a comprehensive agreement. The new budget deal neither raises taxes as desired by Democrats nor does it gut the state's welfare system as desired by Republicans. Pundits have already predicted even more fireworks for the next budget cycle. As we can all see from this example, the technical side of the budgeting process is quite easily managed compared to the effects of politics and human behavior.

SUMMARY

This chapter discussed how organizations use budgets to plan what they are going to do during a budget period—which is usually one year—to allocate resources to various projects, and to monitor progress toward achieving financial objectives.

We saw that there are two types of budgets: Operating budgets describe the various activities (for example, hiring people, acquiring machinery and raw materials, producing, and distributing) that the organization plans to undertake during the budget period, whereas financial budgets describe the expected financial consequences (in particular, cash flows and expected profits) of those planned activities.

Budgeting, the process of preparing budgets, allows the organization to evaluate whether prospective plans are feasible and have the potential to achieve the organization's objectives. When done properly, budgeting coordinates activities toward achieving the organization's objectives and provides a means of involving organization members in the budgeting process and through this involvement increasing employee commitment to achieving the budget objectives.

The Oxford Tole Art example provided an extended illustration of the budgeting process and showed how organizations commit to and budget for variable costs (such as raw materials and paint) and short- and long-term fixed costs (such as painters and production facilities).

The chapter discussed what-if analysis, a modeling tool that explores the effects on scheduled activities and financial results as key assumptions (such as employee productivity, materials costs, or product prices) are changed. We saw that what-if analysis allows decision makers to determine how sensitive plans are to the underlying assumptions, which, in turn, may suggest either contingency planning or additional investment to make estimates more accurate.

The chapter described variance analysis, which involves comparing actual results to planned results and, when the variance (the difference between the planned and actual results) is deemed significant, undertaking an investigation to determine its cause. In this sense, a variance is like a warning signal—it signals that someone was not as expected but not what or why—that requires investigation.

The chapter discussed some different approaches to the traditional budgeting model illustrated by Oxford Tole Art. Whereas periodic budgeting involves developing a budget for each budget period, continuous budgeting involves rolling the budget forward each month. So, for example, as January of this year is completed, a budget for January of next year is added to the budget. In this way the budget period is continuously maintained.

A common approach to budgeting, often found in governments, is incremental budgeting. In this approach, this year's budget is based on an incremental adjustment of last year's budget. For example, each budget unit is told to increase sales by 10% or to cut costs by 5%. Most students of budgeting consider this approach to be practical but ineffectual since it does not recognize the specific and differential opportunities facing different units in the organization. For example, one division may face a mature and declining market for its products and find it difficult to maintain let alone increase its sales, whereas another product division may be competing in an expanding market where sales increases come relatively easily. Asking both divisions to increase sales by 10% does not reflect the differential opportunities facing the two divisions.

Managers monitor and evaluate discretionary expenditures (such as advertising, research and development, and employee training) differently than expenditures that are tied to and driven by acquisition, production, and distribution activities where activity measures and outcomes are readily measured. Because it is very difficult to measure the outcome of discretionary expenditures (for example, how do we measure the effect on profits of advertising), managers usually control these expenditures through spending budgets that are often tied to sales (for example, research and development will be 5% of sales). As we saw, this type of control does not evaluate whether the money is being well spent, and managers continue to search for ways to measure the benefits of discretionary expenditures.

Finally, the chapter considered some alternatives to, and complaints about, traditional budgeting. The concern is that organizations often prepare budgets slavishly and then tie performance to achieving budgeted performance. Some people believe that this approach inhibits both organization flexibility and innovation (better to achieve the budget than be innovative by redirecting funds to another project). In summary, most organizations continue to use some form of budgeting to plan, allocate resources, and coordinate organization activities. The well-known limitations associated with the traditional budgeting model continue to be addressed by modifications, such as those described in this chapter.

KEY TERMS

appropriations, 455	master budget, 443	sales price variance, 454
budget, 419	operating budgets, 422	sales quantity variance, 453
budgeting process, 418	periodic budget, 456	second-level variances, 446
continuous budget, 456	planning variance, 445	sensitivity analysis, 440
efficiency (quantity) variance, 446	price (rate) variances, 446	third-level variances, 446
financial budgets, 422	pro forma financial statements, 423	variance, 441
first-level variance, 444	project funding, 458	variance analysis, 441
flexible budget, 444	quantity (efficiency) variances, 446	what-if analysis, 439
flexible budget variances, 445	rate (price) variance, 446	zero-based budgeting (ZBB), 457
incremental budgeting, 456	sales mix variance, 453	

ASSIGNMENT MATERIALS

Questions

10-1 What is budgeting? (LO 1)

10-2 What is the difference between variable and capacity-related costs? (LO 1)

10-3 A student develops a spending plan for a school semester. Is this budgeting? Why? (LO 1)

10-4 Does a family need a budget? If so, explain its role in such a setting. (LO 1)

10-5 What is a production plan? Give an example of one in a courier company. (LO 2, 3)

10-6 What are the different elements of an operating budget? (LO 3)

10-7 Would a labor hiring and training plan be more important in a university that is hiring faculty members, or a municipal government office that hires casual workers to do unskilled work? Why? (LO 2, 3)

10-8 What is the relationship between a demand forecast and a sales plan? (LO 4)

10-9 What is a demand forecast? Why is it relevant in budgeting? (LO 4)

10-10 Is employee training an example of a discretionary expenditure? Why? (LO 4)

10-11 What does a labor hiring and training plan do? (LO 4)

10-12 What is an example of a capacity-related expenditure? (LO 4)

10-13 "Budgeting involves forecasting the demand for different types of resources over different time periods." Do you agree with this statement? Explain. (LO 3, 4)

10-14 What does the phrase *gaming the budgeting process* mean? (LO 3)

10-15 What is a line of credit? How is it useful to a small organization? (LO 4)

10-16 What are three broad uses for budget information? (LO 4)

10-17 What are the similarities and differences between what-if and sensitivity analyses? (LO 5)

10-18 What is a variance? How is a dashboard warning light that indicates low oil pressure like a variance? (LO 6)

10-19 How does analysis of reasons for variances between actual and estimated costs help managers? (LO 6)

10-20 What is a flexible budget? (LO 6)

10-21 What are the sources from which budgeted or planned costs are generated? (LO 6)

10-22 Why is it useful to decompose a flexible budget variance into a rate (price) variance and an efficiency (quantity) variance? (LO 6)

10-23 "If more experienced workers work on the job than were planned when developing the labor standards, the labor efficiency variance is likely to be favorable, but the labor rate variance is likely to be unfavorable." Do you agree with this statement? Explain. (LO 6)

10-24 What effect will the purchase and use of cheaper, lower quality materials likely have on price and quantity (efficiency) components of both materials and labor variances? (LO 6)

10-25 What two steps are taken to reconcile the difference between actual and planned sales revenue? (LO 6)

10-26 What is an appropriation? Give an example of one in a university. (LO 7)

10-27 What is zero-based budgeting? (LO 7)

10-28 You are planning your expenditures for the upcoming school semester. You assume that this year's expenditures will equal last year's plus 2%. What approach to budgeting are you using? (LO 4)

10-29 You are willing to donate to worthy organizations. However, you believe strongly that each request for a donation should be evaluated on the basis of its own merits. You would not feel bad in any year if you donated nothing. What approach to budgeting are you using? (LO 4)

10-30 What are some criticisms of the traditional budgeting model? (LO 1, 4, 8)

10-31 What are two fundamental ways in which the beyond budgeting approach differs from traditional budgeting? (LO 1, 4, 8)

Exercises

LO 2, 3 **10-32** *Budgeting information* Consider a company that sells prescription drugs. It has salespeople who visit doctors and hospitals to encourage physicians to prescribe its drugs. The company sells to drugstores. Salespeople are evaluated based on the sales in their territories. For each, income is a salary plus a bonus if actual sales exceed planned sales. To plan operations, this company needs to develop estimates of total sales. Where should it get this information?

LO 1, 4, 8 **10-33** *Budgeting and planning* Some people say that budgets are great for planning but not for control. What do you think they mean? Do you agree with this sentiment? Explain.

LO 1, 4, 7 **10-34** *Budgeting: types of resources in a university* For a university, identify a cost that you think is controllable in the short term and explain why. Identify a cost that you think is controllable in the intermediate term and explain why. Identify a cost that you think is controllable in the long term and explain why. What does this cost structure imply about the university's flexibility in responding to changing student demands and enrollment?

LO 1, 2, 3, 4 **10-35** *Financial budgets* Many managers consider the pro forma financial statements to be the most important product of the master budgeting process. Why do you think they believe this?

LO 1, 2, 4, 7 **10-36** *Consulting company: types of resources* Budgeting allows an organization to identify broad resource requirements so that it can develop plans to put needed resources in place. Use an example to illustrate why this might be valuable in a consulting company that provides advice to clients.

LO 1, 2, 3, 4 **10-37** *Canning company: budgeting process* Budgeting allows an organization to identify potential problems so that plans can be developed to avoid these problems or to deal with them systematically. Give an example of how budgeting might serve this role in a company that buys vegetables and cans them.

LO 3, 4 **10-38** *Financial budgets: cash flows* Monthly cash budgets of inflows and outflows are an important part of the budgeting process in most organizations. In the course of preparing a cash budget, the organization must estimate its cash inflows from credit sales. Suppose that in response to projected cash shortfalls, the organization decides to speed its collections of credit sales. What effect can this have on the organization?

LO 1, 3, 4 **10-39** *Machine shop: comparing financial and operational results* Budgeting allows an organization to compare its projected operating and financial results with those of competitors as a general test of the efficiency of the organization's operating processes. Explain how this might be valuable for a machine shop that does custom machining work for its customers.

LO 2, 3 **10-40** *Merchandising firm purchases budget* Boynton Company sells a variety of recycling bins. The company estimates that it will sell 40,000 units of bin BLX in April. The company expects to have 6,000 units of BLX in inventory on April 1 and would like 5,000 units of BLX in inventory on April 30. How many units of BLX will Boynton budget to purchase in April?

LO 2, 3 **10-41** *Manufacturing firm production and purchases budget* Glynn Company is preparing a budget to determine the amount of part G12 to produce for the first quarter of the year, and the amount of resin to purchase for part G12. The company desires to have 25% of the next month's estimated sales of G12 in inventory at the end of each month. Glynn has a very reliable supplier of resin and therefore desires an ending inventory of only 10% of resin needs for the next month's production. Each unit of G12 requires half a pound of resin. Projected sales of G12 for January, February, and March are 50,000 units, 60,000 units, and 54,000 units, respectively.

Required

(a) How many units of part G12 will Glynn budget to produce in January and February?
(b) How many pounds of resin will Glynn budget to purchase in January and February?

LO 5 **10-42** *What-if analysis* Cathey Company is considering replacing its existing cutting machine with a new machine that will help reduce its defect rate. Relevant information for the two machines includes the following:

COST ITEM	EXISTING MACHINE	NEW MACHINE
Monthly fixed costs	$64,000	$40,000
Variable cost per unit	$35	$40
Sales price per unit	$80	$80

Required

(a) Determine the sales level, in number of units, at which the costs are the same for both machines.
(b) Determine the sales level in dollars at which the use of the new machine results in a 20% profit on sales (profit/sales) ratio.

LO 2, 3, 5 **10-43** *Sensitivity analysis* Sensitivity analysis is an important component of any budgeting exercise. Which estimates do you think will be most crucial in developing a master budget? Why?

LO 5, 7 **10-44** *Sensitivity analysis: cost cutting* A university faced with a deficit reacts by cutting resource allocations to all faculties and departments by 8%. Do you think this is a good approach to budgeting? Why or why not?

LO 6 **10-45** *Variance analysis, material and labor* The following information is available for Mandalay Company:

ACTUAL	
Materials:	15,000 pounds purchased at $6 per pound; used 12,500 pounds
Direct labor:	2,000 hours at $10 per hour
Units produced:	500
STANDARD	
Materials:	30 pounds per unit at a price of $7 per pound
Direct labor:	4 hours per unit at a wage rate of $11 per hour

Required

(a) Determine the material price variance based on the quantity of materials purchased.
(b) Determine the material quantity variance.
(c) Determine the direct labor rate variance.
(d) Determine the direct labor efficiency variance.

LO 6 **10-46** *Variance analysis, material and labor* Pharout Company uses a standard cost system. Job 007 was for the manufacture of 1,000 units of the product X. The company's standards for one unit of product X are as follows:

QUANTITY		PRICE
Direct material	10 ounces	$5 per ounce
Direct labor	5 hours	$10 per hour

The job required 9,800 ounces of raw material costing $58,800. A favorable labor rate variance of $2,250 and an unfavorable labor efficiency variance of $1,000 also were determined for this job.

Required

(a) Determine the direct material price variance for job 007 based on the actual quantity of materials used.
(b) Determine the direct material quantity variance for job 007 based on the actual quantity of materials used.
(c) Determine the actual quantity of direct labor hours used on job 007 based on the actual quantity of materials used.
(d) Determine the actual labor costs incurred for job 007.

LO 6 **10-47** *Variance analysis, material and labor* Each unit of product B has standard requirements of 8 pounds of raw material at a price of $25 per pound and 1 hour of direct labor at $12 per hour. To produce 20,000 units of this product, product B actually required 180,000 pounds of the raw material costing $27 per pound. The job used a total of 18,000 direct labor hours costing a total of $198,000.

Required

(a) Determine the material price variances for product B.
(b) Determine the material quantity variance for product B.

(c) Assume that the materials used on this job were purchased from a new supplier. Would you recommend continuing with this new supplier? Why or why not?

(d) Determine the direct labor rate variance for product B.

(e) Determine the direct labor efficiency variance for product B.

LO 6 **10-48** *Standard costs versus actual costs for materials* Assembly of product P13 requires two units of component X, one unit of component Y, and two units of component Z. Job J372 produced 200 units of P13. The following information pertains to material variances for this job, analyzed by component:

	COMPONENT		
	X	Y	Z
Price variance	1000 U	750 F	450 U
Quantity variance	2500 U	1000 U	800 F

The actual material prices were $2 more, $3 less, and $1.50 more per unit for components X, Y, and Z, respectively, than their standard material prices per unit.

Required

(a) Determine the number of materials units consumed of each type of component.

(b) Determine the standard materials price per unit of each type of component.

LO 4 **10-49** *Master and flexible budgets* An organization plans to make a product in batches of 36,000 units. Planned production is 1,800,000 units, and actual production is 1,944,000 units. What are the planned (master budget) number of batches and the flexible budget number of batches?

Problems

LO 2, 3 **10-50** *Operating budgets: production plan* Borders Manufacturing is developing a sales and production plan as part of its master budgeting process. Following are the projected monthly sales, which occur uniformly during each month, for the upcoming year:

BORDERS MANUFACTURING
PROJECTED MONTHLY SALES

MONTH	UNIT SALES
January	8,742
February	9,415
March	7,120
April	8,181
May	7,942
June	9,681
July	2,511
August	2,768
September	2,768
October	2,283
November	1,542
December	1,980
January	8,725

Production for each month equals one-half of the current month's sales plus one-half of the next month's projected sales. Develop the production plan for Borders Manufacturing for the upcoming year.

LO 2, 3, 4 **10-51** *Operating budgets: labor hiring and production plan* Mira Vista Planters provides reforestation services to large paper products companies. It must hire one planter for every 10,000 trees that it has contracted to plant each month. New employees are hired in the month needed, on the first day of the month. An employee must receive one week of evaluation and training before being profitably employed and therefore works three out of four weeks in the month hired. New employees are paid full wages for all four weeks. For every five prospective employees who enter training, three are deemed suitable for employment. When cutbacks occur, employees are laid off on the first day of the month. Every employee laid off receives severance pay equal to one week's salary, which is on average $400, regardless of how long the layoff will last. Laid-off employees inevitably drift away, and new hires must be trained. The organization will have two trained employees on January 1 and wants to have at least one trained employee at the end of each month.

The company has been offered the following contracts for the upcoming year. Each monthly contract is offered on an accept or reject basis; that is, if a monthly contract is accepted, it must be completed in full. Partial completion is not acceptable. The revenue per tree planted is $0.20.

MIRA VISTA PLANTERS
MONTHLY TREE PLANTING CONTRACTS

MONTH	TREES
January	8,692
February	5,765
March	8,134
April	34,400
May	558,729
June	832,251
July	1,286,700
August	895,449
September	733,094
October	203,525
November	29,410
December	9,827

Required

Prepare a labor plan for the upcoming year, indicating the following for each month:

(a) Whether you feel the company should accept or reject the proposed planting contract.
(b) How many people will be hired for training. (Recall that an employee is not available for planting during the week of training and that only three of the five employees accepted for training can be hired.)
(c) How many people will be laid off.

LO 2, 3, 7 **10-52** *Operating budgets: labor hiring plan* Hotel Holiday Home is planning its operations for the upcoming year. The hotel has 100 units. The following table presents the average number of daily rentals expected for each of the 12 months of the next year.

The hotel hires housekeeping staff on a weekly basis. Each person can clean 20 rooms per day. Employees must be hired for the entire week at a wage of $4,000 per employee per month. Because of the hotel's location in a midsize city, trained people are always available to work on short notice.

The hotel does not own its linen and towels but rents them from a rental agency in a nearby city. The rental contract must be signed for a quarter and for a fixed amount of linen and towels. Therefore, the hotel must sign four contracts for the 12-week tourist season. The contract provides the linen required for each room for $10 per night.

HOTEL HOLIDAY HOME AVERAGE NUMBER OF DAILY RENTALS

MONTH	AVERAGE UNITS RENTED	MONTH	AVERAGE UNITS RENTED
1	70	7	90
2	35	8	75
3	50	9	65
4	60	10	90
5	80	11	100
6	100	12	100

Required

Prepare a weekly budget for the hotel showing the following:

(a) The number of housekeeping staff to employ
(b) The number of linen and towel units to contract.

LO 2, 3, 7 **10-53** *Financial budgets: expense budget* During the school year, the Happy Valley School band arranges concert dates in many communities. Because only part of the school's travel expenses are covered by the concert admission fees, the band raises money to help defray its operating expenses through events in the local community such as car washes.

To estimate its expenses for the upcoming year, the band's manager has estimated the number of concert dates for each of the school months, January through September. For each concert, the manager estimates hotel costs of $1,000, food costs of $500, bus rental costs of $600, and other costs of $300.

The following table presents the number of planned concerts during the upcoming year:

HAPPY VALLEY SCHOOL BAND SCHEDULED CONCERTS

MONTH	SCHEDULED CONCERTS	MONTH	SCHEDULED CONCERTS
January	4	June	8
February	6	July	6
March	5	August	4
April	2	September	5
May	3		

Required

Prepare a monthly schedule estimating the band's travel expenses.

LO 2, 3, 7 **10-54** *Financial budgets: cash inflows* Worthington Company makes cash (20% of total sales), credit card (50% of total sales), and account (30% of total sales) sales. Credit card sales are collected in the month following the sale, net a 3% credit card fee. This means that if the sale is $100, the credit card company's fee is $3, and Worthington receives $97. Account sales are collected as follows: 40% in the first month following the sale, 50% in the second month following the sale, 8% in the third month following the sale, and 2% never collected.

The following table identifies the projected sales for the next year:

WORTHINGTON COMPANY PROJECTED SALES

MONTH	SALES	MONTH	SALES
January	$12,369,348	July	$21,747,839
February	15,936,293	August	14,908,534
March	13,294,309	September	11,984,398
April	19,373,689	October	18,894,535
May	20,957,566	November	21,983,545
June	18,874,717	December	20,408,367

Prepare a statement showing the cash expected each month from the collections from these sales.

LO 2, 3   **10-55** *Operating budgets: materials purchasing plan*   Masefield Dairy is preparing a third-quarter budget (July, August, and September) for its ice cream products. It produces five brands of ice cream, and each uses a different mix of ingredients. Its suppliers deliver ingredients just in time, provided that they are given two months' notice. The following table indicates the units of weight or volume of each type of ingredient required per unit of each product:

MASEFIELD DAIRY REQUIRED INGREDIENTS

	PRODUCT				
INGREDIENTS	A	B	C	D	E
Ingredient 1	1	2	1	1	1
Ingredient 2	2	0	3	1	4
Ingredient 3	0	1	2	4	0
Ingredient 4	1	3	0	2	2
Ingredient 5	0	2	1	0	2
Ingredient 6	3	1	3	0	1

The following table summarizes the estimated unit sales for each product in each of the months in the third quarter:

MASEFIELD DAIRY ESTIMATED UNIT SALES

PRODUCT	JULY	AUGUST	SEPTEMBER
A	194,675	162,033	129,857
B	104,856	98,375	76,495
C	209,855	194,575	170,654
D	97,576	75,766	55,966
E	47,867	39,575	20,958

Prepare a monthly purchases budget for the ice cream ingredients.

LO 2, 3, 7   **10-56** *Financial budgets: wages and expense budgets*   Nathaniel's Motor Shop does major repair work on automobile engines. The major cost in the shop is the wages of the mechanics. The shop employs nine mechanics who are paid $750 each for working a 40-hour week. The workweek consists of five days of eight hours each. Employees actually work seven hours each day because they are given one hour of breaks each day. They are highly skilled and valued by their employer, so these mechanics are paid whether or not there is work available for them to do. They are also paid $30 for every overtime hour or partial overtime hour they work.

The machine shop industry estimates that for every mechanic hour actually worked in a shop like this, the employee consumes about $25 of variable support items, such as lubricants, tool parts, and electricity.

The motor shop estimates that the following work will be available each week during the next 10 weeks:

NATHANIEL'S MOTOR SHOP ESTIMATED WORK

WEEK	HOURS OF WORK	WEEK	HOURS OF WORK
1	255	6	280
2	330	7	260
3	300	8	300
4	285	9	340
5	325	10	355

Develop a weekly budget of mechanic wages and variable support costs.

LO 2, 3 **10-57** *Financial budgets: cash outflows* Country Club Road Nurseries grows and sells garden plants. The nursery is active between January and October each year. During January, the potting tables and equipment are prepared. The potting and seeding are done in February. In March and April, the plants are cultivated, watered, and fertilized. May and June are the peak selling months. July, August, and September are the peak months for visiting customers in their homes to provide them with advice and help solve their problems. During October, the equipment and buildings are secured for the winter months, and in November and December, full-time employees take their paid holidays, and the business is closed.

The nursery employs 15 full-time staff and, depending on the season, up to 20 part-time staff. The full-time staff members are paid an average salary of $2,700 per month and work 160 hours per month.

The part-time staff members are paid $10 per hour. Because the nursery relies on local students for part-time work, there is no shortage of trained people willing to work the hours that are available. The ratio of full-time employee hours worked to part-time employee hours worked is as follows: January, 5:1; February, 5:1; March, 3:1; April, 3:1, May, 1:1; June, 1:1; July, 1:1; August, 1:1; September, 2:1; and October, 4:1. Because part-time students are used mainly for moving and selling activities, their work creates very little incremental support costs.

Fixed costs, other than wages, associated with this operation are about $55,000 per month. The cost drivers in this operation are the activities that the full-time employees undertake. These cost drivers are proportional to the hours worked by the full-time employees. The variable costs depend on the season and reflect the common employee activities during that season. Average variable costs per employee hour worked are as follows: January, $15; February, $15; March, $15; April, $15; May, $5; June, $5; July, $20; August, $20; September, $20; and October, $10. These variable costs include both support items such as power and water and direct items such as soil and pots. Assume that all expenses are paid in the month they are incurred.

On the basis of the information provided, determine the cash outflows for the upcoming year.

LO 2, 3   **10-58 *Budgeted cash flows and income statement***   In September, TEE Company, a merchandising firm that sells one product, assembled the following information and estimates to prepare a budget for October. Expected sales are 40,000 units at a price of $32 per unit. The cost of merchandise purchases is expected to be $20 per unit. Selling and administrative expenses are estimated at $350,000, of which $20,000 is depreciation. The October 1 cash balance is expected to be $40,000.

TEE estimates that 70% of each month's sales are collected in the month of sale and the remaining 30% is collected in the month after sale. Expected sales for September are $1,000,000. The company pays for 20% of its merchandise purchases during the month of purchase, and pays the remaining 80% during the month following purchase. Merchandise purchases for September are estimated to be $880,000 and the purchase cost per unit is $20. All other out-of-pocket expenses are paid for in cash.

Required

(a) TEE plans to purchase 38,000 units of merchandise in October. Prepare a cash budget or statement of estimated cash flows for October for the company.

(b) Prepare a budgeted income statement (for external reporting purposes) for the month ended October 31 for TEE Company.

LO 2, 3   **10-59 *Master budget***   Adams Company, a merchandising firm that sells one product, estimates it will sell 12,000 units of its product at $60 per unit in December. In November, the company prepared other information to prepare a budget for December, as shown here:

Merchandise inventory, December 1	2,000 units
Desired merchandise inventory for December 31	3,000 units
Cost per unit of merchandise purchases	$40
Selling and administrative expenses	$200,000
Cash balance, December 1	$30,000
November sales	$600,000

- The company estimates that 60% of each month's sales are collected in the month of sale and that the remaining 40% is collected in the month after sale.
- The $200,000 of selling and administrative expenses includes $40,000 of depreciation.
- The company pays for half of merchandise purchases during the month of purchase and pays the remainder during the month following purchase. Estimated merchandise purchases for November are $340,000.
- All other out-of-pocket expenses are paid for in cash.

Required

(a) How many units of merchandise will Adams budget to purchase in December? What is the dollar amount of Adams' budgeted merchandise purchases for December?

(b) Prepare a budgeted income statement for the month ended December for Adams Company.

(c) Prepare a statement of estimated cash flows for the month ended December for Adams Company.

LO 2, 3, 7 **10-60** *Operating budgets: labor hiring plan* Merryweather Insurance Company manages a medical insurance program for its clients. Employees of client firms submit claims for reimbursement of medical expenses. Merryweather processes these claims, checks them to ensure that they are covered by the claimant's policy, notes whether the claimant has reached any limit on coverage, computes any deductible, and issues a check for the claimant's refund.

Three types of employees work in the claims processing department: managers, officers, and clerks. The managers are paid $60,000 per year, the officers are paid $50,000 per year, and the clerks are paid $30,000 per year. For every 200,000 claims processed per year, Merryweather plans to use one manager, four clerks, and three officers.

Last year, the company processed 4.5 million medical claims and employed 24 managers, 70 officers, and 90 clerks.

Required

(a) Compute the excess costs or cost savings relating to the claims processing staff.
(b) How would you interpret these results? What additional information would you ask for if you were making a determination of the clerical group's processing efficiencies?

LO 3, 4, 5 **10-61** *Budgeted profit, what-if analysis* The Monteiro Manufacturing Corporation manufactures and sells folding umbrellas. The corporation's condensed income statement for the year ended December 31, 2011, follows:

Sales (200,000 units)		$1,000,000
Cost of goods sold		600,000
Gross margin		400,000
Selling expenses	$150,000	
Administrative expenses	100,000	250,000
Net profit (before income taxes)		$150,000

Monteiro's budget committee has estimated the following changes for 2012:

30% increase in number of units sold
20% increase in material cost per unit
15% increase in direct labor cost per unit
10% increase in variable indirect cost per unit
5% increase in indirect fixed costs
8% increase in selling expenses, arising solely from increased volume
6% increase in administrative expenses, reflecting anticipated higher wage and supply price levels

Any changes in administrative expenses caused solely by increased sales volume are considered immaterial.

Because inventory quantities remain fairly constant, the budget committee considered that for budget purposes any change in inventory valuation can be ignored. The composition of the cost of a unit of finished product during 2011 for materials, direct labor, and manufacturing support, respectively, was in the ratio of 3:2:1. In 2011, $40,000 of manufacturing support was for fixed costs. No changes in production methods or credit policies were contemplated for 2012.

Required

(a) Compute the unit sales price at which the Monteiro Manufacturing Corporation must sell its umbrellas in 2012 in order to earn a budgeted profit of $200,000.

(b) Unhappy about the prospect of an increase in selling price, Monteiro's sales manager wants to know how many units must be sold at the old price to earn the $200,000 budgeted profit. Compute the number of units that must be sold at the old price to earn $200,000.

(c) Believing that the estimated increase in sales is overly optimistic, one of the company's directors wants to know what annual profit is likely if the selling price determined in part a is adopted but the increase in sales volume is only 10%. Compute the budgeted profit in this case.

LO 5   **10-62** *Breakeven analysis, what-if analysis*   The Himal Ice Cream Company produces a single product: a chocolate cup that sells for $2.50 per cup. The variable costs for each cup (sugar, chocolate, milk, wrapper, and labor) total $1.50. The total monthly fixed costs are $720,000. Last month, cup sales reached 1 million. However, the president of Himal Ice Cream Company was not satisfied with its performance and is considering the following options to increase the company's profitability:

1. Increase advertising.
2. Increase the quality of the cup's ingredients and simultaneously increase the selling price.
3. Increase the selling price with no change in ingredients.

Required

(a) The sales manager is confident that an intensive advertising campaign will double sales volume. If the company president's goal is to increase this month's profits by 80% over last month's, what is the maximum amount that can be spent on advertising that doubles sales volume?

(b) Assume that the company increases the quality of its ingredients, thus increasing variable costs to $2 per cup. By how much must the selling price per unit be increased to maintain the same breakeven point in units?

(c) Assume next that the company has decided to increase its selling price to $4 per cup with no change in advertising or ingredients. Compute the sales volume in units that would be needed at the new price for the company to earn the same profit as it earned last month.

LO 5   **10-63** *Breakeven point, what-if analysis*   Premier Products, Inc., is considering replacing its existing machine with a new and faster machine that will produce a more reliable product and will turn around customer orders in a shorter period. This change is expected to increase the sales price and fixed costs but not the variable costs:

Cost Item	Old Machine	New Machine
Monthly fixed costs	$120,000	$250,000
Variable cost per unit	14	14
Sales price per unit	18	20

Required

(a) Determine the breakeven point in units for the two machines.

(b) Determine the sales level in units at which the use of the new machine will achieve a 10% target profit-to-sales ratio.

(c) Determine the sales level in units at which profits will be the same for either the old or the new machine.

(d) Which machine represents a lower risk of incurring a loss? Explain why.

(e) Determine the sales level in units at which the profit-to-sales ratio will be equal with either machine.

LO 5   **10-64 *What-if-analysis***   Tenneco, Inc., produces three models of tennis rackets: standard, deluxe, and pro. Following are the sales and cost information for 2011:

ITEM	STANDARD	DELUXE	PRO
Sales (in units)	100,000	50,000	50,000
Sales price per unit	$30	$40	$50
Variable manufacturing cost per unit	$17	$20	$25

Fixed manufacturing support costs are $800,000, and fixed selling and administrative costs are $400,000. In addition, the company pays its sales representatives a commission equal to 10% of the price of each racket sold.

Required

(a) If the sales price of deluxe rackets decreases 10%, its sales are expected to increase 30%, but sales of standard rackets are expected to decrease 5%, as some potential buyers of standard rackets will upgrade to deluxe rackets. What will be the impact of this decision on Tenneco's profits?

(b) Suppose that Tenneco decides to increase its advertising by $50,000 instead of cutting the price of deluxe rackets. This is expected to increase sales of all three models by 2% each. Is this decision advisable?

(c) The incentive created by sales commissions has led Tenneco's sales force to push the higher priced rackets more than the lower priced ones. Is this in the best interests of the company?

LO 5   **10-65 *Breakeven point, what-if analysis***   The following information pertains to Texas Company's budgeted income statement for the month of June 2011:

Sales (1,500 units at $400)	$600,000
Variable cost	240,000
Contribution margin	$360,000
Fixed cost	432,000
Net loss	($72,000)

Required

(a) Determine the company's breakeven point in both units and dollars.

(b) The sales manager believes that a $48,000 increase in the monthly advertising expenses will result in a considerable increase in sales. How much of an increase in sales must result from increased advertising in order to break even on the monthly expenditure?

(c) The sales manager believes that an advertising expenditure increase of $48,000 coupled with a 10% reduction in the selling price will double the sales quantity. Determine the net income (or loss) if these proposed changes are adopted.

LO 5   **10-66 *Breakeven point, what-if analysis***   Air Peanut Company manufactures and sells roasted peanut packets to commercial airlines. Following are the price and cost data per 100 packets of peanuts:

Estimated annual sales volume = 11,535,700 packets	
Selling price	$35.00
Variable costs:	
Raw materials	$16.00
Direct labor	7.00
Manufacturing support	4.00
Selling expenses	1.60
Total variable costs per 100 packets	$28.60
Annual fixed costs:	
Manufacturing support	$192,000
Selling and administrative	276,000
Total fixed costs	$468,000

Required

(a) Determine Air Peanut's breakeven point in units.

(b) How many packets does Air Peanut have to sell to earn $156,000?

(c) Air Peanut expects its direct labor costs to increase by 5% next year. How many units will it have to sell next year to break even if the selling price remains unchanged?

(d) If Air Peanut's direct labor costs increase by 5%, what selling price per 100 packets must it charge to maintain the same contribution margin-to-sales ratio?

LO 6   **10-67** *Planning and flexible budget variances*   Tang Company's production performance report for April includes the information shown below. Prepare a flexible budget for the items shown and compute the flexible budget cost variances and planning cost variances for each item. Indicate whether the variances are favorable or unfavorable for each item.

	ACTUAL	MASTER BUDGET
Volume	80,000	90,000
Manufacturing costs:		
Direct materials	$550,000	$630,000
Direct labor	225,000	247,500
Fixed manufacturing support	400,000	420,000
Total	$1,175,000	$1,297,500

LO 6   **10-68** *Variance analysis*   The Sudbury, South Carolina, plant of Saldanha Sports Company has the following standards for its soccer ball production:

Standards:	
Material (leather) per soccer ball	0.25 yard
Material price per yard	$16
Direct labor hours per soccer ball	0.20 hour
Wage rate per direct labor hour	$10 per hour
Variable support cost rate	$15 per direct labor hour
Actual results for October:	
Used 13,000 yards of raw material, purchased for $205,150	
Paid for 8,240 direct labor hours at $9.50 per hour	
Incurred $131,840 of variable support costs	
Manufactured 40,000 soccer balls	

Required

Determine the following variances for October:

(a) Total direct material cost variance
(b) Total direct labor cost variance
(c) Total variable support cost variance
(d) Direct material price variance
(e) Direct material quantity variance
(f) Direct labor rate variance
(g) Direct labor efficiency variance
(h) Variable support rate variance
(i) Variable support efficiency variance.

LO 6 **10-69** *Variance analysis*   The North Point plant of Englehart Electronics Company has the following standards for component C93:

Standards:	
Material	2 units of material B
Material price	$10 per unit of B
Direct labor	1 hour
Wage rate	$10 per direct labor hour
Variable support cost rate	$25 per direct labor hour

Actual results for May:

   Used 4,200 units of B, purchased at $9.75 per unit of B
   Paid for 2,000 direct labor hours at $11 per hour
   Incurred $48,000 of variable support costs
   Manufactured 2,000 units of component C93

Required

Determine the following variances for May:

(a) Total direct material cost variance
(b) Total direct labor cost variance
(c) Total variable support cost variance
(d) Direct material price variance
(e) Direct material quantity variance
(f) Direct labor rate variance
(g) Direct labor efficiency variance
(h) Variable support rate variance
(i) Variable support efficiency variance.

LO 6 **10-70** *Standard versus actual costs*   For each of the following two jobs manufacturing two different products, determine the missing amounts for items (a) through (h):

ITEM	JOB 321	JOB 322
Units produced	200	(e)
Standards per unit:		
Material quantity	5 pounds	(f)
Material price	$2 per pound	$3 per pound
Labor hours	2 hours	3 hours
Labor rate	$15 per hour	$12 per hour

(continued)

ITEM	JOB 321	JOB 322
Actual consumption:		
Material quantity	(a)	1,000 pounds
Material cost	$2,000	(g)
Labor hours	(b)	(h)
Labor cost	(c)	$5,800
Variance:		
Material quantity	(d)	$100 F
Material price	$50 U	$500 F
Labor efficiency	$100 F	$60 U
Labor rate	$60 U	$200 F

LO 4, 6   **10-71** *Variance analysis, material and labor*   Trieste Toy Company manufactures only one product, Robot Ranger. The company uses a standard cost system and has established the following standards per unit of Robot Ranger:

	STANDARD QUANTITY	STANDARD PRICE	STANDARD COST
Direct materials	3.0 pounds	$12 per pound	$36.00 per unit
Direct labor	1.2 hours	15 per hour	18.00 per unit

During November, the company recorded the following activity:

- The company produced 6,000 units.
- A total of 21,000 pounds of material were used, purchased at a cost of $241,500.
- The company employs 40 persons to work on the production of Robot Ranger. These employees worked an average of 160 hours at an average rate of $16 per hour.

   The company's management wishes to determine the efficiency of the activities related to the production of Robot Ranger.

Required

(a) For direct materials used in the production of Robot Ranger, compute the direct material price variance and the direct material quantity variance.
(b) The direct materials were purchased from a new supplier who is eager to enter into a long-term purchase contract. Would you recommend that Trieste sign the contract? Explain.
(c) For direct labor employed in the production of Robot Ranger, compute the direct labor rate variance and the direct labor efficiency variance.
(d) In the past, the 40 persons employed in the production of Robot Ranger consisted of 16 experienced workers and 24 inexperienced assistants. During November, the company experimented with 20 experienced workers and 20 inexperienced assistants. Would you recommend that Trieste continue the new labor mix? Explain.

LO 6, 7   **10-72** *Variance analysis, hospital (adapted from CMA, June 1989)*   Mountain View Hospital has adopted a standard cost accounting system for evaluation and control of nursing labor. Diagnosis-related groups (DRGs), instituted by the U.S. government for health insurance reimbursement, are used as the output measure in the standard cost system. A DRG is a patient classification scheme that perceives hospitals to be multiproduct firms where inpatient treatment procedures are related to the numbers and types of patient ailments treated. Mountain View Hospital has developed standard nursing times for the treatment of each DRG classification, and nursing labor hours are assumed to vary with the number of DRGs treated within a time period.

The nursing unit on the fourth floor treats patients with four DRG classifications. The unit is staffed with registered nurses (RNs), licensed practical nurses (LPNs), and aides. Following are the standard nursing hours and salary rates:

FOURTH-FLOOR NURSING UNIT STANDARD HOURS

DRG CLASSIFICATION	RN	LPN	AIDE
1	6	4	5
2	26	16	10
3	10	5	4
4	12	7	10

STANDARD HOURLY RATES

RN	$12
LPN	8
Aide	6

Following are the results of operations for the fourth-floor nursing unit for the month of May:

ACTUAL NUMBER OF PATIENTS

DRG 1	250
DRG 2	90
DRG 3	240
DRG 4	140
	720

	RN	LPN	AIDE
Actual hours	8,150	4,300	4,400
Actual salary	$100,245	$35,260	$25,300
Actual hourly rate	$12.30	$8.20	$5.75

The accountant for Mountain View Hospital calculated the following standard times for the fourth floor nursing unit for May:

		STANDARD HOURS/DRG			TOTAL STANDARD HOURS		
DRG CLASSIFICATION	NO. OF PATIENTS	RN	LPN	AIDE	RN	LPN	AIDE
1	250	6	4	5	1,500	1,000	1,250
2	90	26	16	10	2,340	1,440	900
3	240	10	5	4	2,400	1,200	960
4	140	12	7	10	1,680	980	1,400
					7,920	4,620	4,510

The hospital calculates labor variances for each reporting period by labor classification (RN, LPN, aide). The variances are used by nursing supervisors and hospital administration to evaluate the performance of nursing labor.

Required

Calculate the total nursing labor variance for the fourth-floor nursing unit of Mountain View Hospital for May, indicating how much of this variance is attributed to the following for each class of hospital worker:

(a) Labor efficiency

(b) Rate differences.

LO 6 10-73 *Variance analysis* Asahi USA, Inc., based in Denver, Colorado, is a subsidiary of a Japanese company manufacturing specialty tools. Asahi USA employs a standard cost system. Following are the standards per unit of one of its products, tool KJ79. This tool requires a special chrome steel as a direct material.

	STANDARD QUANTITY	STANDARD PRICE	STANDARD COST
Direct materials	8 pounds	$18 per pound	$144
Direct labor	2.5 hours	$8 per hour	20
			$164

During November, Asahi USA started and completed job KJX86 to manufacture 1,900 units of tool KJ79. It purchased and used 14,250 pounds of the special chrome steel for tool KJ79 at a total cost of $270,750. The total direct labor charged to job KJX86 was $37,800. Job KJX86 required 5,000 direct labor hours.

Required

(a) For job KJX86, compute the following and indicate whether the variances are favorable or unfavorable:

(1) Direct material price variance

(2) Direct material quantity variance

(3) Direct labor rate variance

(4) Direct labor efficiency variance.

(b) Provide a plausible explanation for the variances.

LO 6 10-74 *Sales variance analysis* Bakery Extraordinaire sells several types of muffins and scones and also sells carrot bread loaves. Planned prices and sales quantities for February are shown here:

		PLANNED SALES FOR FEBRUARY		
	MUFFINS	SCONES	CARROT BREAD	TOTALS
Unit price	$1.35	$1.75	$2.75	
Unit sales	1,600	3,400	1,000	6,000
Total	$2,160	$5,950	$2,750	$10,860

The actual results for February are shown here:

		ACTUAL SALES FOR FEBRUARY		
	MUFFINS	SCONES	CARROT BREAD	TOTALS
Unit price	$1.55	$1.60	$3.25	
Unit sales	1,400	4,500	1,300	7,200
Total	$2,170	$7,200	$4,225	$13,595

The owner would like to know how the price changes and volume changes each contributed to the $2,735 difference between planned and actual sales revenues.

Required

(a) Compute the sales mix variance for each product line and explain the meaning of each variance you computed.

(b) Compute the sales quantity variance for each product line and explain the meaning of each variance you computed.

(c) Compute the sales price variance for each product line and explain the meaning of each variance you computed.

LO 4, 6   **10-75** *Variances and motivation*   Discuss the possible effect on human behavior of a preoccupation with variances in financial control.

Cases

LO 3, 4, 5   **10-76** *Budget preparation, breakeven point, what-if analysis with multiple products (adapted from CPA, May 1993)*   The following budget information for the year ending December 31, 2011, pertains to Rust Manufacturing Company's operations:

| | PRODUCT | | |
BUDGET ITEM	ACE	BELL	TOTAL COSTS
Budgeted sales in units	200,000	100,000	
Selling price per unit	$40	$20	
Direct materials cost per unit	$8	$3	
Direct labor hours per unit	2	1	
Depreciation			$200,000
Rent			$130,000
Other manufacturing support costs			$500,000
Selling costs			$180,000
General and administrative costs			$40,000

The following information is also provided:

1. Rust has no beginning inventory. Production is planned so that it will equal the number of units sold.
2. The cost of direct labor is $5 per hour.
3. Depreciation and rent are fixed costs within the relevant range of production. Additional costs would be incurred for extra machinery and factory space if production is increased beyond current available capacity.
4. Rust allocates depreciation proportional to machinery use and rent proportional to factory space. Budgeted usage is as follows:

	ACE	BELL
Machinery	70%	30%
Factory space	60%	40%

5. Other manufacturing support costs include variable costs equal to 10% of direct labor cost and also include various fixed costs. None of the miscellaneous fixed manufacturing support costs depend on the level of activity, although support costs attributable to a specific product are avoidable if that product's production ceases. The fixed-cost portion of other manufacturing support costs is allocated between Ace and Bell on the basis of a percentage of budgeted direct labor cost.

6. Rust's selling and general and administrative costs are committed in the intermediate term.
7. Rust allocates selling costs on the basis of number of units sold at Ace and Bell.
8. Rust allocates general and administrative costs on the basis of sales revenue.

Required

(a) Prepare a schedule, using separate columns for Ace and Bell, showing budgeted sales, variable costs, contribution margin, fixed costs, and pretax operating profit for the year ending December 31, 2011.
(b) Calculate the contribution margin per unit and the pretax operating profit per unit for Ace and for Bell.
(c) Calculate the effect on pretax operating profit resulting from a 10% decrease in sales and production of each product.
(d) What may be a problem with the above analysis?

LO 2, 3, 4 **10-77 *Commitment and consumption of labor hours*** Steelmax, Inc., sells office furniture in the Chicago metropolitan area. To better serve its business customers, Steelmax recently introduced a new same-day service. Any order placed before 2:00 P.M. is delivered the same day.

Steelmax hires five workers on an eight-hour daily shift to deliver the office furniture. Each delivery takes 30 minutes on average. If the number of customer orders exceeds the available capacity on some days, workers are asked to work overtime to ensure that all customer orders are delivered the same day. Regular wages are $12 per hour. Overtime wages include a 50% premium in addition to the regular wages.

Steelmax's management has noticed considerable fluctuation in the number of customer orders from day to day during the past three months, as shown here:

DAY OF THE WEEK	AVERAGE NUMBER OF ORDERS
Monday	65
Tuesday	70
Wednesday	80
Thursday	85
Friday	95

Steelmax has decided to pursue a more variable hiring policy. It will reduce the number of delivery workers to four on Mondays and Tuesdays and increase the number to six on Fridays.

Required

(a) Determine the total and unit delivery cost per day under the old hiring policy when the number of daily customer orders is 70, 80, or 90.
(b) For each day of the week, determine the expected total delivery cost per day and the expected delivery cost per customer order based on both the old and the new hiring policy. What is the expected savings per week with the new variable hiring policy?

LO 2, 3, 4, 5 **10-78 *Budgeting: comprehensive problem*** Judd's Reproductions makes reproductions of antique tables and chairs and sells them through three sales outlets. The product line consists of two styles of chairs, two styles of tables, and three styles of cabinets. Although customers often ask Judd Molinari, the owner/manager of Judd's Reproductions, to make other products, he does not intend to expand the product line.

The planning group at Judd's Reproductions prepares a master budget for each fiscal year, which corresponds to the calendar year. It is December 2011, and the planners are completing the master budget for 2012.

Unit prices are $200, $900, and $1,800 for the chairs, tables, and cabinets, respectively. Customers pay (1) by cash and receive a 5% discount, (2) by credit card (the credit card company takes 3% of the revenue as its fee and remits the balance in the month following the month of sale), or (3) on account (only exporters buy on account). The distribution of cash, credit card, and exporter sales is 25%, 35%, and 40%, respectively. Of the credit sales to exporters, Judd's Reproductions collects 30% in the month following the sale, 50% in the second month following the sale, and 17% in the third month following the sale, with 3% going uncollected. Judd's Reproductions recognizes the expense of cash discounts, credit card fees, and bad debts in the month of the sale.

Judd's employs 40 people who work in the following areas: 15 in administration, sales, and shipping; 2 in manufacturing supervision (director and a scheduler); 9 in manufacturing fabrication and assembly (carpenters); and 14 in manufacturing, finishing, and other areas (helpers, cleaners, and maintenance crew).

The carpenter hours required to make the parts for and assemble a chair, table, or cabinet are 0.4, 2.5, and 6, respectively. Production personnel have organized the work so that each carpenter hour worked requires 1.5 helper hours. Therefore, production planners maintain a ratio on average of 1.5 helpers for every carpenter. The company pays carpenters and helpers $24 and $14 per hour, respectively (including all benefits).

Judd's Reproductions guarantees all employees pay for at least 172 hours per month regardless of the hours of work available. When the employees are not doing their regular jobs, they undertake maintenance, training, community service, and customer relations activities. Judd's pays each employee weekly for that week's work. If an employee works 172 hours or less during the month, Judd's still pays the employee for 172 hours at his or her normal hourly rate. The company pays 150% of the normal hourly rate for every hour over 172 that the employee works during the month. Planners add new carpenters if the projected total monthly overtime is more than 5% of the total regular carpenter hours available. Judd's has a policy of no employee layoffs. Any required hiring is done on the first day of each month.

For a factory, Judd's Reproductions rents a converted warehouse that costs $600,000 per year. The company pays rent quarterly beginning January 1 of each year. Judd's pays other fixed manufacturing costs, which include manufacturing supervision salaries and amount to $480,000 annually, paid in equal monthly amounts.

The capital investment policy is to purchase, each January and July, $5,000 of machinery and equipment per carpenter employed during that month. Judd's recognizes depreciation at the rate of 10% of the year-end balance of the machinery and equipment account. Statistical studies of cost behavior have determined that supplies, variable support, and maintenance costs vary with the number of carpenter hours worked and are $5, $20, and $15 per hour, respectively.

The units of wood required for chairs, tables, and cabinets are 1, 8, and 15, respectively. Each unit of wood costs $30. The inventory policy is to make products in the month they will be sold. Two suppliers deliver raw materials and supplies as required. The company pays for all materials, supplies, variable support, and maintenance items on receipt.

Annual administration salaries, fixed selling costs, and planned advertising expenditures are $300,000, $360,000, and $600,000, respectively. Judd's Reproductions makes these expenditures in equal monthly amounts. Packaging and shipping costs for chairs, tables, and cabinets are $15, $65, and $135, respectively. Variable selling costs are 6% of each product's list price. Judd's Reproductions pays packaging, shipping, and variable selling costs as incurred.

Using its line of credit, Judd's Reproductions maintains a minimum cash balance of $50,000. All line-of-credit transactions occur on the first day of each month. The bank charges interest on the line-of-credit account balance at the rate of 10% per year. Judd's pays interest on the first day of each month on the line-of-credit balance outstanding at the end of the previous month. On the first of each month, the bank pays interest at the rate of 3% per year on funds exceeding $50,000 in the company's cash account at the end of the previous month.

Realized sales for October and November and expected sales for December 2011 appear in the following table:

JUDD'S REPRODUCTIONS UNIT SALES 2011

ITEM	OCTOBER	NOVEMBER	DECEMBER
Chairs	900	975	950
Tables	175	188	201
Cabinets	90	102	95

Sales staff estimates the unit demand for 2012 as follows: chairs, 1,000, plus a random number uniformly distributed between 0 and 50, plus 15% of the previous month's sales of chairs; tables, 200, plus a random number uniformly distributed between 0 and 20, plus 15% of the previous month's sales of tables; and cabinets, 100, plus a random number uniformly distributed between 0 and 10, plus 15% of the previous month's sales of cabinets. This estimation process resulted in the demand forecasts and the sales plan found in the following table:

JUDD'S REPRODUCTIONS
PROJECTED UNIT SALES 2012

MONTH	CHAIRS	TABLES	CABINETS
January	1,020	200	109
February	1,191	237	120
March	1,179	243	119
April	1,195	250	126
May	1,200	252	122
June	1,204	255	125
July	1,194	242	123
August	1,199	253	121
September	1,222	243	127
October	1,219	248	126
November	1,207	244	126
December	1,192	255	119

Planners project the Judd's Reproductions balance sheet at January 1, 2012, to be as follows:

JUDD'S REPRODUCTIONS BALANCE SHEET JANUARY 1, 2012

Cash	$50,000	Bank loan	$0
Accounts receivable	575,008		
Machinery (net book value)	360,000	Shareholder's equity	985,008
Total	$985,008	Total	$985,008

Required

(Round quantities up in the problem.)

(a) Prepare a sales forecast, staffing plan, production plan, estimated cash flow statement, pro forma income statement for the year ended December 31, 2012, and pro forma balance sheet at December 31, 2012.

(b) The level of bad debts concerns the Judd's Reproductions controller. If Judd's insists on cash payments from exporters who would be given the cash discount, the sales staff expects that total sales to exporters in 2012 will fall by 5% (sales in 2011 will not be affected). Based on the effect of this change on profitability, is it desirable? (Round sales forecasts to the nearest unit.)

(c) Ignore the changes described in part b and return to the data in the original example. The sales staff is considering increasing the advertising budget from $600,000 to $900,000 and cutting prices by 5% beginning on January 1, 2012. This should increase sales by 30% in 2012. Based on the effect of this change on profitability, is it desirable? (Round sales forecasts to the nearest unit.)

(d) Is there a criterion other than profitability that may be used to evaluate the desirability of the changes proposed in parts b and c? If yes, what is that criterion, and why is it important? If no, why is profitability the sole relevant criterion?

LO 6 **10-79** *Variance and cost analysis, original activity-based costing hierarchy* Peterborough Food produces a wide range of breakfast cereal foods. Its granola products are two of its most important product lines.

Because of the complexity of the granola production process, the manufacturing area in the plant that makes these two product lines is separated from the rest of the plant and is treated as a separate cost center. Exhibit 10-34 presents the activity and cost data for this cost center for the most recent quarter. The plan data in Exhibit 10-34 reflect the master budget targets for the quarter.

The factory accountant estimates that, with the increased production in line 1, the labor-related product-sustaining costs and the other product-sustaining costs for line 1 should increase by $20,000 and $100,000, respectively. The factory accountant also indicates that the decreased production in line 2 would require several quarters to be reflected in lower product-sustaining costs.

The factory accountant indicated that the labor-related business-sustaining costs and the other business-sustaining costs should increase by $0 and $140,000, respectively, given the net increase in production.

Required

Prepare a second-level and third-level variance analysis of costs for the granola line cost center. In your analysis, group costs into unit-related, batch-related, product-sustaining, and business-sustaining costs.

LO 4, 7 **10-80** *Budgeting: motivational issues* Nate Young is the dean of a business school. The university is under strong financial pressures, and the university president has asked all the deans to cut costs. Nate is wondering how he should respond to this request.

The university receives its operating funds from three sources: (1) tuition (60%), (2) government grants (25%), and (3) gifts and endowment income (15%). The money flows into the university's general operating fund. A management committee consisting of the university president, the three vice presidents, and the nine deans allocates funds to the individual schools. The university's charter requires that it operate with a balanced budget.

The initial allocation of funds reflects (1) fixed costs that cannot be avoided, primarily the employment costs of tenured faculty, and (2) fixed costs relating to support items, such as staff, building maintenance, and other operations costs. The balance of funds is allocated to discretionary activities, such as scholarships, program changes or additions, and sports.

The various deans compare their respective funding levels. The basis of comparison is to divide total university expenditures by the number of full-time students to get an average cost per student. Then the average cost per student is multiplied by the number of full-time students to get the target funding for each school. On average, the actual funding for the business school has been about 70% of the target funding, which is the second lowest in the university. (The lowest is the arts school.)

Because of the rapid growth of fixed faculty and administrative costs, the amount of funds allocated to discretionary activities has been declining from a historic level of about 10%. This year, the projected revenues will not even cover the projected fixed costs. In response to this development, the president has called on all deans to "do your best to reduce the level of expenditures."

The president's request has been met with skepticism by many deans, who are notorious for digging in their heels, ignoring requests for spending cuts, and then being bailed out by funds

Exhibit 10-34
Peterborough Food: Granola Line Products

	Line 1 Plan	Line 1 Actual	Line 2 Plan	Line 2 Actual	Total Line 1 Plan	Total Line 1 Actual	Total Line 2 Plan	Total Line 2 Actual	Total Plan	Total Actual
Number of boxes	945,000	1,200,000	1,175,000	945,000						
Number of batches	189	200	235	210						
Units per batch	5,000	6,000	5,000	4,500						
Unit-related costs:										
Materials										
Grams per box	500	515	350	375						
Cost per gram	$0.0030	$0.0027	$0.0050	$0.0055	$1,417,500	$1,668,600	$2,056,250	$1,949,062	$3,473,750	$3,617,662
Packaging										
Units per box	1.0000	1.0600	1.0000	1.0405						
Cost per unit	$0.0450	$0.0420	$0.0380	$0.0410	$42,525	$53,424	$44,650	$40,314	$87,175	$93,738
Labor										
Hours per box	0.013	0.011	0.009	0.010						
Cost per hour	$18.00	$18.25	$18.00	$18.25	$221,130	$240,900	$190,350	$172,463	$411,480	$413,363
Batch-related costs:										
Materials										
Per batch	$1,200	$1,325	$1,525	$1,495	$226,800	$265,000	$358,375	$313,950	$585,175	$578,950
Labor										
Hours per batch	12	11	16	18						
Cost per hour	$18.00	$18.25	$18.00	$18.25	$40,824	$40,150	$67,680	$68,985	$108,504	$109,135
Product-sustaining costs										
Labor					$256,000	$287,000	$305,000	$323,000	$561,000	$610,000
Other					$2,054,000	$2,123,000	$1,927,000	$2,005,000	$3,981,000	$4,128,000
Business-sustaining costs										
Labor									$145,000	$152,000
Other									$4,560,000	$4,740,000
Total all costs					$4,258,779	$4,678,074	$4,949,305	$4,872,774	$13,913,084	$14,442,849

released from other activities or raised to meet the budget shortfall. Many deans believe that the departments that sacrificed and reduced their budgets would only create funds that would be used by the university to support other schools that had made little or no effort to reduce their budgets. Then these schools would be asked to make even more cuts to make up for the lack of cuts in schools that made little progress in cost reduction. On the other hand, the deans also believe that if there were no reaction to the president's initial request for cost reductions, arbitrary cutbacks would be imposed on the individual schools.

In response to this situation, Nate is wondering what to do. He knows that by increasing class sizes slightly, using some part-time instructors, and eliminating some optional courses that seldom attract many students, he can trim about $800,000 from his operating budget of $11,000,000. However, making these changes would create hardships for both the students and faculty in the business school, and given the historic relationship of the school's average funding to its target funding, Nate is wondering whether the business school should be asked to make additional sacrifices.

Nate knows that he has several alternatives:

- Do nothing, arguing that the business school is already cost effective relative to others and that it is time for others to reduce their cost structures.
- Make the cuts that he has identified but stretch them out over a number of years and stop making them if other schools are not doing their share in cutting costs.
- Make the cuts unilaterally and advise the administration that the business school budget can be reduced by about $800,000.

Required

Explain what you would do if you were Nate and why. Your explanations should include your analysis of the motivation of all schools to cut costs in an environment that traditionally has taken advantage of those who cooperate.

Chapter 11

Financial Control

After completing this chapter, you will be able to:

1. Understand and be able to explain the nature and scope of financial control and its important roles both inside and outside organizations.

2. Understand why organizations decentralize decision-making responsibility, the control and motivation issues that arise from this choice, and how organizations approach these control and motivation issues.

3. Understand why organizations use responsibility centers, the type of responsibility center that is appropriate in a given setting, the limitations of the responsibility center approach to evaluating performance, and what performance measures senior management uses to evaluate responsibility center performance.

4. Be able to design and interpret appropriate performance measures to evaluate the performance of each type of responsibility center.

5. Understand why organizations use transfer prices and the types of transfer prices that organizations use.

6. Be able to determine and compute the appropriate transfer price in a particular setting.

7. Understand the nature and scope of return on investment and economic value added approaches to evaluating economic performance and be able to compute return on investment and residual income measures.

Adrian's Home Services

Adrian's Home Services (AHS) provides heating, air conditioning, plumbing, and electrical services to residential customers. AHS is very successful because of its outstanding reputation for quality work. In fact, AHS often has to turn work away because demand exceeds the available capacity. Exhibit 11-1 provides a pretax segment report for the most recent year.

Exhibit 11-1
Adrian's Home Services: Pretax Segment Report

	HEATING	AIR CONDITIONING	PLUMBING	ELECTRICAL	UNALLOCATED	CORPORATE TOTAL
Sales	$1,546,000	$2,344,670	$5,340,000	$3,423,000		$12,653,670
Cost of goods sold	870,000	1,384,000	3,245,000	2,198,000		7,697,000
Gross margin	$676,000	$960,670	$2,095,000	$1,225,000		$4,956,670
Selling, general, and administrative	134,500	456,000	1,324,500	654,000	2,980,000	5,549,000
Income	$541,500	$504,670	$770,500	$571,000		($592,330)
Assets	876,000	958,000	2,176,000	1,127,000	547,000	5,684,000
Shareholders' equity						2,875,000

In view of AHS's outstanding reputation and the heavy demand for its services, Adrian Rose, the primary shareowner and general manager, is unhappy about the business profitability and wonders how it might be improved.

THE ENVIRONMENT OF FINANCIAL CONTROL

What is meant by *financial control*? **Financial control** involves the use of measures based on financial information to assess organization and management performance. The focus of attention could be a product, a product line, an organization department, a division, or the entire organization. Financial control, which focuses on financial results, provides a counterpoint to the Balanced Scorecard view, which links financial results to their presumed drivers. In for-profit organizations, financial control looks at the drivers of profit such as the organization's ability to use its assets effectively and control costs for a given level of sales. In not-for-profit organizations, financial control looks at the organization's ability to use its resources in the most effective way to accomplish its service objectives.

Financial control thus plays an important role in the plan–do–check–act cycle we first discussed in Chapter 1. Financial control summarizes the financial results of operations and compares them to planned results. The purpose is to identify why plans were not achieved and to make the appropriate adjustment.

In Chapter 2 we explored the important role of the Balanced Scorecard as a means to quantify strategy and drive strategy down through the organization's hierarchy. The Balanced Scorecard's cause-and-effect structure reflects management's assessment of what drives success in achieving organizational objectives. In for-profit organizations, success is ultimately measured by generating good financial returns to capital suppliers, using metrics such as return on investment, earnings per share, market share growth, and profit growth.

Because external stakeholders such as investors, stock analysts, and creditors have traditionally relied on financial performance measures to assess an organization's potential, organizations have developed and exploited financial measures to assess performance and target areas for improvement. Recall from the Balanced Scorecard discussion that shortfalls in financial measures signal poor performance but do not identify what has gone wrong. They identify that expectations were not met and that attention, explanation, and possibly even action are needed. For example, falling profits may reflect falling sales, which in turn may reflect customer dissatisfaction with poor quality, poor service, or high prices. Financial measures will highlight the falling profit and sales but not why—that is the role of the nonfinancial measures discussed in Chapter 2.

Financial control is part of the broader topic of organization control we considered in Chapter 9. Financial control is treated separately in this text because of its widespread use in our market-based economy.

FINANCIAL CONTROL

In Chapter 10 we studied variance analysis, which is one of the oldest and most widely used forms of financial control. This chapter focuses on broader issues in financial control, including the evaluation of organization units and of the entire organization.

When managers apply financial control tools to evaluate organization units—for example, to evaluate the profitability of a product or product line—the resulting information is usually used internally and is not distributed to outsiders. Managers, particularly at General Motors during the 1920s, developed this form of **internal financial control** to support decentralizing of decision-making information in large organizations.

Outside analysts developed financial control tools to assess various aspects of organization performance, such as solvency, efficiency, and profitability. Because financial measures reflect how outsiders view the organization, these external financial control tools are relevant for management use and evaluation.

THE MOTIVATION FOR DECENTRALIZATION

Decentralization, the process of delegating decision-making authority to frontline decision makers, evolved for two reasons. First, as organizations became larger, it became increasingly difficult for a central decision maker, or core of decision makers, to make all organizational decisions. Second, as organizations became larger and more geographically dispersed, it became increasingly difficult to gather and transmit information about the organization's environment for evaluation and processing at the organization's center. Therefore, decentralization was a natural development reflecting the need for large organizations to respond more quickly and effectively to important changes in their environment. In turn, decentralization was the phenomenon that prompted the development and use of internal financial control in organizations in the early 1900s.

Because of the difficulty involved in gathering and transmitting information quickly to a central decision maker, most highly centralized organizations are unable to respond effectively or quickly to their environments; therefore, centralization is best suited to organizations that are well adapted to stable environments. Observers of industry practice used to cite power, gas, and telephone utilities and companies such as couriers, fast-food operations, financial institutions, and natural resource industries as examples of organizations facing stable environments. A stable environment meant there were no major information differences between the corporate headquarters and the employees who were responsible for dealing with customers or running the operations that made the organization's goods and services and no changes in the organization's environment that required the organization to adapt. Therefore, there was no need for a rapid response to a changing environment or for

Organizations often delegate important customer service functions to frontline employees. These employees should be well trained so that they can make appropriate choices when dealing with customer complaints.

Shutterstock

delegation of decision making to local managers, and organizations could develop standard operating procedures for its well-understood environment that it expected employees to implement.

In such organizations, technology and customer requirements were well understood, and the product line consisted mostly of commodity products for which the most important attributes were price and quality. When price is critical, so is cost control. To accomplish this, organizations often develop standard operating procedures to ensure that (1) they are using the most efficient technologies and practices to promote both low cost and consistent quality, and (2) there are no deviations from the preferred way of doing things.

For example, McDonald's Corporation has honed its use of standard operating procedures almost to a science. Its kitchen layout, product design, form of raw materials, and prescribed operating procedures are all designed to keep cost low and consistency and quality high. McDonald's is not looking for a chef who wants to be creative either in preparing food or in introducing new menu items. Rather, it wants

IN PRACTICE

Standard Operating Procedures at Mercedes-Benz USA

When Mercedes-Benz built its SUV plant in Tuscaloosa, Alabama, it implemented a manufacturing system that included standard methods and procedures (SMPs). These SMPs specified the exact method in minute detail that workers had to use to complete every task. No variations were permitted—effectively preventing workers from exercising any individual initiative.

someone who can follow standardized procedures to promote consistent quality and low costs. In response to today's increasing competitive pressures and the opening of former monopoly markets to competition, many organizations—even utilities, couriers, and financial institutions that were once thought to face stable environments—are changing the way they are organized and the way they do business. This is necessary because they must be able to adapt quickly in a world where technology, customer tastes, and competitors' strategies are constantly changing. McDonald's is a good example—in the face of increasing health consciousness, during 2003–2005, it experienced franchisee losses and store closures for the first time in its history and had to undertake important changes in its menu, including introducing restaurants that stayed open 24 hours a day.

In the past, banks developed rigid and authoritarian management systems to protect assets and meet regulatory requirements. Although these systems have helped to meet such goals, in many cases they have not served customers well. Providing high-quality customer service means remaining open in the evenings, installing automated teller machines to provide 24-hour banking services, offering online or web-based banking that customers can access via telephone or personal computer, offering new products and services such as credit and debit cards, and responding more quickly, even immediately, to customer requests for car loans, lines of credit, and mortgages.

Being adaptive usually requires that the organization's senior management delegate or decentralize decision-making responsibility to more people in the organization. Decentralization allows motivated and well-trained organization members to identify changing customer requirements quickly and gives frontline employees the authority and responsibility to develop plans to react to these changes.

We can identify many degrees of decentralization. Some organizations restrict most decisions to senior and middle management. Others delegate important decisions about how to make products and serve customers to the employees who perform these activities. The amount of decentralization reflects the organization's trust in its employees, the employees' level of skill and training, the increased risk from delegating decision making, and the employees' ability to make the right choices. It also reflects the organization's need to have people on the front lines who can make good decisions quickly.

To summarize, in decentralization, control moves from task control—where people are told what to do—to results control—where people are told to use their skills, knowledge, and creativity to achieve organization objectives. In financial control, those results are measured in financial terms. For example, a production supervisor would be asked to reduce costs by improving the manufacturing processes.

IN PRACTICE
Evaluating Performance at McDonald's Corporation Restaurants

To promote consistency, McDonald's Corporation develops a SQC (service, quality, and cleanliness) score for each store. Franchises can be terminated if a store fails to maintain an agreed-on SQC performance level. The SQC criteria used to evaluate the store consider performance levels and compliance with standard operating procedures. These criteria include how the customer is greeted, how much time the customer spends in line and at the counter, property cleanliness, and whether products are prepared in the prescribed manner.

RESPONSIBILITY CENTERS AND EVALUATING UNIT PERFORMANCE

A **responsibility center** is an organization unit for which a manager is held accountable. Examples of responsibility centers include a hotel in a chain of hotels, a work station in a production line that makes computer control units, a department in a university or college, the data processing group in a government office that handles claims for payment from suppliers, a claims processing unit in an insurance company, and a shipping department in a mail-order business.

A responsibility center is like a small business, and its manager is asked to run that small business to achieve the objectives of the larger organization. The manager and supervisor establish goals for the responsibility center. Goals provide employees with focus and should therefore be specific and measurable. They also should promote both the long-term interests of the larger organization and the coordination of each responsibility center's activities with the efforts of all the others. The following section explores how this coordination is accomplished for goals that are financial.

Coordinating Responsibility Centers

For an organization to be successful, the activities of its responsibility units must be coordinated. Suppose we divided the operations in a fast-food restaurant into three groups: order taking, order preparation, and order delivery. Imagine the chaos and customer ill will that would be created if the communication links between any two of these organization groups were severed. Unfortunately, in large organizations, sales, manufacturing, and customer service activities are often disjointed, resulting in

Corporate management will delegate many important operating decisions to the manager of this property and, in turn, will hold the manager accountable for achieving specified profit and customer service objectives.

Alamy Images

diminished performance. This need for coordination explains the interest that organizations have in enterprise resource planning systems that focus not only on integrating the organization's activities but also on linking the organization with its suppliers and customers.

Mail and package couriers, such as Federal Express, establish local stations or collection points (called terminals) from which they dispatch trucks to pick up and deliver shipments. Shipments that are bound for other terminals are sent to the Federal Express hub in Memphis, Tennessee, where they are sorted and redirected. The formula for success in the courier business is simple and has two key elements: (1) meeting the service commitment to the customer (i.e., the shipper), politely, on time, and without damage, and (2) controlling costs. The only way to achieve success is to ensure that all pieces of the system work together effectively and to achieve these two critical elements of performance.

Suppose the management of a courier company decided that each terminal is to be treated as a responsibility center. How should the company measure the performance of each terminal, its managers, and its employees?

First, the company can measure efficiency in each terminal. To focus on efficiency, it may measure the number of parcels picked up, sorted, or delivered per route, per employee, per vehicle, per hour, or per shift. To focus on efficiency and customer satisfaction, it may count—for productivity purposes—only those shipments that meet customer requirements, for example, on-time pickup and on-time delivery of an undamaged parcel to the right address.

Second, the organization's ability to meet its service commitment to customers in such a highly integrated operation as a courier business reflects how well the pieces fit together. The company should measure how much each group contributes to the organization's ability to meet its commitments to customers. The following are the two important elements of terminal–hub interaction for a courier:

1. The proportion of the time that the terminal meets its deadlines, that is, whether the trucks and containers are packed and ready to leave for the hub when they are required to leave (this is often called a *percent correct measure*).
2. When terminals are required to sort shipments, the number of shipments sorted to the wrong destination or that travel by the wrong mode (often called a *percent defect measure*).

Third, the company must assess its service to the customer at a more detailed level. For example, it might measure the following:

1. The number of complaints (or percentage of shipments with complaints) the terminal operations group receives.
2. The average time taken by the operations group to respond to complaints.

IN PRACTICE
The High Cost of Coordination

Many organizations invest huge amounts of money in enterprise resource planning (ERP) systems, which are complex and sophisticated computer systems that coordinate the activities of organization units. The goal of ERP systems is to smooth the flow of an order through the credit approval, scheduling, production, and shipping processes so that the customer is provided with a high level of service. Some analysts have put the average cost of an ERP system at about $15 million with one system reputedly costing $400 million. And not all ERP implementations are successful. In 2001, Sobey's, a Canadian grocery chain, reported a $60 million write-off of a failed ERP system.

3. The number of complaints of poor or impolite service received by the company's customer service line.
4. Customer satisfaction.

In general, controlling the activities of responsibility centers requires measuring the nonfinancial elements of performance, such as quality and service, that create financial results in the long run. The key message is that properly chosen nonfinancial measures anticipate and explain financial results. For example, increased employee training that improves operating performance in this period should improve customer satisfaction and therefore revenues and profits in subsequent periods. Focusing on nonfinancial measures of performance such as innovation and employee morale motivates managers to avoid sacrificing long-run performance for short-run performance gains. For example, if we focus only on short-run financial performance, a manager might be motivated to reduce spending on research and development, investment in equipment to improve product quality and customer service, and employee training—thereby impairing long-run performance potential. Therefore, we must always be careful to use financial results as aggregate measures of performance and rely on nonfinancial results to identify the causes or drivers of the financial results.

Responsibility Centers and Financial Control

Organizations use financial control to provide a summary measure of how well their systems of operations control are working. When organizations use a single index to provide a broad assessment of operations, they frequently use a financial number, such as revenue, cost, profit, or return on investment, because these are the measures that their shareholders use to evaluate the company's overall performance.

IN PRACTICE

Nonfinancial Performance Measures at Federal Express: The Service Quality Indicator

Federal Express has developed a measure called its service quality indicator (SQI). The SQI is based on what Federal Express believes are nine key customer requirements. Each of these nine requirements is given a weight indicating the perceived importance of a failure of this requirement to the customer. The nine requirements and their respective weights are:

SERVICE FAILURE	PENALTY AMOUNT
Lost package	50
Damaged package	30
Complaint unresolved	10
Wrong day, late	10
Invoice adjustment required	3
Traces	3
Late pickup stop	3
Missing proof of delivery	1
Right day, late delivery	1

Federal Express tabulates these scores weekly and distributes them throughout the organization. Rewards to senior managers are based on these scores.

Responsibility Center Types

The accounting report prepared for a responsibility center should reflect the degree to which the responsibility center manager controls revenue, cost, profit, or return on investment. When preparing accounting summaries, accountants usually classify responsibility centers into one of four types:

1. Cost centers.
2. Revenue centers.
3. Profit centers.
4. Investment centers.

Cost Centers

Cost centers are responsibility centers in which employees control costs but do not control revenues or investment levels. Virtually every processing group in service operations (such as the cleaning plant in a dry-cleaning business, front-desk operations in a hotel, or the check-clearing department in a bank) or in manufacturing operations (such as the lumber-sawing department in a sawmill or the steelmaking department in a steel mill) is a candidate to be treated as a cost center.

Organizations evaluate the performance of cost center employees by comparing the center's actual costs with budgeted cost levels for the amount and type of work done. Therefore, cost standards and variances figure prominently in cost center reports. Moreover, because organizations often use standards and variances to assess performance, the process of setting standards and interpreting variances has profound behavioral effects on employees, particularly relating to misrepresenting performance potential and performance results.

This machine operator will likely have been given cost, scheduling, and quality targets to achieve. Achieving these targets are the important contributions that this employee makes to the organization's success.

Shutterstock

Other Cost Control Approaches

When an organization unit's mix of products and production levels is constant, it is possible to compare current cost levels with those in previous periods to promote an environment of continuous cost improvement. Interperiod cost comparisons can be misleading when the production mix or the production level is changing. Under such conditions, cost levels between periods are not comparable; however, when circumstances warrant, organizations are often able to plot cost levels on a graph and look for downward cost trends, which imply improved efficiencies in the processes that are creating costs.

Addressing Other Issues in Cost Center Control

Many organizations make the mistake of evaluating a cost center solely on its ability to control and reduce costs. Quality, response time, the ability to meet production schedules, employee motivation, employee safety, and respect for the organization's ethical and environmental commitments are other critical measures organizations often use to assess cost center performance. If management evaluates cost center performance only on the center's ability to control costs, its members may ignore unmeasured attributes of performance such as quality and customer service. Therefore, organizations should never evaluate cost centers using only the center's cost performance.

Revenue Centers

Revenue centers are responsibility centers whose members control revenues but do not control either the manufacturing or the acquisition cost of the product or service they sell or the level of investment made in the responsibility center. Examples are the appliance department in a department store, a regional sales office of a national or multinational corporation, and a restaurant in a large chain of restaurants.

Some revenue centers control price, the mix of stock on hand, and promotional activities. In such centers, revenue will measure most of their value-added activities and will suggest in a broad way how well they carried out their various activities.

Consider the activities of a gasoline and automobile service station owned by a large oil refiner. The service center manager has no control over the cost of items such as fuel, depreciation on the building, power and heating, supplies, and salary rates, but the manager has a minor influence, through scheduling and staffing decisions, on total labor costs. Levels of gasoline sales and repair activities determine all other costs. The service manager also has no control over the wages paid to employees: The head office staff controls them, and the central marketing staff controls all product pricing and promotional activities. The major controllable item in this service station is customer service, which distinguishes its gasoline sales and repair services from those offered in similar outlets and helps to determine the service station's sales levels.

The revenue center approach evaluates the responsibility center based only on the revenues it generates. Most revenue centers incur sales and marketing costs, however, and have varying degrees of control over those costs. Therefore, it is common in such situations to deduct the responsibility center's traceable costs, such as salaries, advertising costs, and selling costs, from its sales revenue to compute the center's net revenue.

Critics of the revenue center approach argue that basing performance evaluation on revenues can create undesirable consequences. For example, sales staff rewarded solely on sales (1) may promote or agitate for a wide product line that in turn may create excessive inventory management costs, or (2) may offer excessive customized services. In general, focusing only on revenues causes organization members to increase their use of activities that create costs to promote higher revenue levels.

Profit Centers

Profit centers are responsibility centers in which managers and other employees control both the revenues and the costs of the products or services they deliver. A profit center is like an independent business, except that senior management, not the responsibility center manager, controls the level of investment in the responsibility center. For example, if the manager of one outlet in a chain of discount stores has responsibility for pricing, product selection, purchasing, and promotion but not for the level of investment in the store, the outlet meets the conditions to be evaluated as a profit center.

Most individual units of chain operations, whether they are stores, motels, or restaurants, are treated as profit centers. It is doubtful, however, that a unit of a corporate-owned fast-food restaurant, such as Burger King, or a corporate-owned hotel, such as Holiday Inn, meets the conditions to be treated as a profit center because the head office makes most purchasing, operating, pricing, and promotional decisions. These units are sufficiently large, however, such that costs can vary because of differences in controlling labor costs, food waste, and the schedule for the facility's hours. Revenues also can shift significantly, depending on how well staff manages the property. Therefore, although these organizations do not seem to be candidates to be treated as profit centers, local discretion often affects revenues and costs enough so that they can be.

Numerous organizations evaluate units as profit centers even though the corporate office controls many facets of their operations. The profit reported by these units is a broad index of performance that reflects both corporate and local decisions. If unit performance is poor, it may reflect (1) an unfavorable condition that no one in the organization can control, (2) poor corporate decisions, or (3) poor local decisions. For these reasons, organizations should not rely only on profit center financial results for performance evaluations. Instead, detailed performance evaluations should include quality, material use (yield), labor use (yield), and service measures that the local units can control.

Investment Centers

Investment centers are responsibility centers in which the managers and other employees control revenues, costs, and the level of investment. The investment center is like an independent business. Perhaps the best example of an organization that uses investment centers is General Electric.

Because these GE units are so diverse, senior management uses return on investment to evaluate each of these business units and their subunits. For example GE Infrastructure includes the subbusinesses of Energy, Technology Infrastructure, GE Capital, Home & Business Solutions, and NBC Universal, while NBC Universal includes the subunit businesses of Network, Film, Television Stations, Entertainment Cable, Television Production, Sports/Olympic Games, and Theme Parks. These are truly diverse portfolios of businesses that must be evaluated in terms of the return on investment each provides.

Exhibit 11-2 summarizes the characteristics of the various types of responsibility centers.

IN PRACTICE
Investment Centers at General Electric in 2010

GE is made up of five businesses, each of which includes a number of units aligned for growth. Here is an organization chart showing those businesses and their subbusinesses.

J. Immelt
Chairman & CEO

Operating entities

J. Rice	J. Krenicki	M. Neal	C. Begley	J. Dineen	D. Joyce	L. Simonelli	J. Zucker
International	*Energy*	*Capital*	*H&BS/CIO*	*Healthcare*	*Aviation*	*Transportation*	*NBCU*

* Included in organizational structure until close of Comcast JV

Staff

B. Comstock	P. Daley	B. Denniston	M. Little	J. Lynch	K. Sherin
Commercial, PR	*BD*	*Legal*	*Global Research*	*HR*	*Finance*

Exhibit 11-2
Responsibility Center Summary

FACTORS	TYPE OF RESPONSIBILITY CENTER			
	COST CENTER	REVENUE CENTER	PROFIT CENTER	INVESTMENT CENTER
Controlled by center management	Costs	Revenues	Costs, revenues	Cost, revenues, and significant control over investment
Not controlled by center management	Revenues, investment in inventory, and fixed assets	Costs, investment in inventory, and fixed assets	Investment in inventory and fixed assets	
Measured by the accounting system	Costs relative to a budget	Revenue relative to a budget	Profit relative to a budget	Return on investment relative to a budget
Not measured by the accounting system	Performance on critical success factors other than cost	Performance on critical success factors other than revenue	Performance on critical success factors other than profit	Performance on critical success factors other than return on investment

Evaluating Responsibility Centers

Using the Controllability Principle to Evaluate Responsibility Centers

Underlying the accounting classifications of responsibility centers is the concept of controllability. The **controllability principle** states that the manager of a responsibility center should be assigned responsibility only for the revenues, costs, or investments responsibility center personnel control. Revenues, costs, and investments that people outside the responsibility center control should be excluded from the assessment of that center's performance. For example, the manager of a production line in a factory should be evaluated based on labor and machine hours used and not based on labor cost and machine cost because labor wage rates and machine costs were determined elsewhere in the organization. Although the controllability principle sounds appealing and fair, it can be difficult, often misleading, and undesirable to apply in practice.

A significant problem in applying the controllability principle is that in most organizations many revenues and costs are jointly earned or incurred. Consider the operations of an integrated fishing products company that is divided into three responsibility centers: harvesting, processing, and marketing and distribution. The harvesting group operates ships that go out to sea to catch various species of fish. The ships return to one of the company's processing plants to unload their catches. The plants process the fish into salable products. The marketing and distribution group sells products to customers.

As in most organizations, the activities that create the final product in this company are sequential and highly interdependent. The product must be of the right species, quality, and cost to be acceptable to the customer. The performance of the harvesting, processing, and marketing and distribution groups jointly determine the organization's success.

Evaluating the individual performance of harvesting, processing, and marketing and distribution requires the firm to consider many facets of performance. For example, it is possible to evaluate harvesting's operations by measuring its ability to do the following:

1. Catch the entire quota allowed.
2. Minimize the waste and damage done to the fish caught.
3. Minimize equipment failures.
4. Control the costs associated with operating the ships.

Appropriate measures can also be developed for processing, and the evaluation of marketing and distribution may be based on their ability to meet delivery schedules and improve market share.

As part of the performance evaluation process, the organization may want to prepare accounting summaries of the performance of harvesting, processing, and marketing and distribution to support some system of financial control. The management accountant undertaking this task immediately confronts the dilemma of how to account for highly interrelated organization centers as if they were individual businesses. For example, costs of harvesting are easy to determine, but what are the harvesting revenues? Harvesting does not control sales or prices—its role is to catch the fish, maintain raw material and product quality, and meet the schedules determined jointly with processing and marketing and distribution.

If the company evaluates harvesting as a cost center, what about indirect organization costs, such as corporate administration, that reflect overhead resources used by the cost center? What about other important performance facets, such as maintaining quality, catching the full quota of fish, and delivering the required species of fish, at the required time, to the processing group? Should harvesting be asked to bear some of the costs of head office groups, such as personnel, planning, and administration, whose services it uses? If so, how should its share of the costs of those services be determined?

We could probably conclude that processing should be evaluated as a cost center, but what about the marketing and distribution group, which, through its general marketing efforts, likely has the greatest impact on sales? What costs does this group control? It does not control harvesting and processing costs. The only costs controlled by marketing and distribution are marketing and distribution costs, which in most integrated fishing products companies are less than 10% of total costs. The harvesting group, through its ability to catch fish and maintain their quality, and the processing group, through its ability to produce quality products, are also influential in determining the organization's sales level. However, some people do not agree that the controllability principle is the best way to view performance evaluation.

Using Performance Measures to Influence versus Evaluate Decisions

Some people argue that controllability is not a valid criterion to use in selecting a performance measure. Rather, they suggest that the choice of the performance measure should influence decision-making behavior.

Consider a dairy that faced the problem of developing performance standards in an environment of continuously rising costs. Because the costs of raw materials, which were between 60% and 90% of the final costs of the various products, were market determined and, therefore, thought to be beyond the control of the various product managers, managers argued that their evaluation should depend on their ability to control the quantity of raw materials used rather than the cost.

The dairy's senior management announced, however, that it planned to evaluate managers on their ability to control total costs. The managers quickly discovered that one way to control raw materials costs was to make judicious use of long-term fixed price acquisition contracts for raw materials. These contracts soon led to declining raw materials costs. Moreover, the company could project product costs several quarters into the future, thereby achieving lower costs and stability in planning and product pricing.

This example shows that managers, even when they cannot control costs entirely, can take steps to influence final product costs. When more costs or even revenues are included in performance measures, managers are more motivated to find actions that can influence incurred costs or generated revenues.

Using Segment Margin Reports

Many problems can occur when organizations treat responsibility centers as profit centers. These problems concern identifying responsibility for the control of sales and costs. In particular, this means deciding how to assign the responsibility for jointly earned revenues and jointly incurred costs. Therefore, as we now consider the form of the accounting reports that accountants prepare for responsibility centers, remember the assumptions and limitations that underlie these reports.

Despite the problems of responsibility center accounting, the profit measure is so comprehensive and pervasive that organizations prefer to treat many of their organization units as profit centers. Because most organizations are integrated operations, the first problem that designers of profit center accounting systems must confront is handling the interactions among the various profit center units.

To address this issue, consider the activities at Earl's Motors, a full-service automobile dealership organized into five responsibility centers: new car sales, used car sales, body shop, service department, and leasing. Each responsibility center has a manager responsible for the profit reported for that unit. The responsibility center managers report to Earl, using the quarterly reports format shown in Exhibit 11-3.

Exhibit 11-3
Earl's Motors: Quarterly Segment Margin Report for the Period of July 1 to September, 2011

Item	New Car Sales	Used Car Sales	Body Shop	Service Department	Lease Sales	Total
Revenue	$976,350	$1,235,570	$445,280	$685,210	$635,240	$3,977,650
Variable costs	764,790	954,850	235,450	427,400	517,360	2,899,850
Contribution margin	$211,560	$280,720	$209,830	$257,810	$117,880	$1,077,800
Other costs	75,190	58,970	126,480	185,280	46,830	492,750
Segment margin	**$136,370**	**$221,750**	**$83,350**	**$72,530**	**$71,050**	**$585,050**
Allocated avoidable costs	69,870	74,650	64,540	65,290	22,490	296,840
Income	$66,500	$147,100	$18,810	$7,240	$48,560	$288,210
Unallocated costs						325,000
Dealership profit						($36,790)

Exhibit 11-3 illustrates a common form of the **segment margin report** for an organization that is divided into responsibility centers. One column is devoted to each profit center. The revenue attributed to each profit center is the first entry in each column. Variable costs are deducted from revenue to determine the contribution margin, which is the contribution made by operations to cover revenue center costs that are not proportional to volume (see "Other costs" in Exhibit 11-3). Examples of these costs are equipment and buildings that the segment uses exclusively.

Next, the segment's fixed costs are deducted from its contribution margin to determine that unit's segment margin, which is the performance measure for each responsibility center. The unit's segment margin measures its controllable contribution to the organization's profit and other indirect costs. Allocated avoidable costs are the organization's administrative costs, such as personnel-related costs and committed costs for facilities. The underlying assumption is that these corporate-level costs can be avoided if the unit is eliminated and the organization has time to adjust its capacity levels by selling excess facilities or by reducing the number of administrative staff. Allocated avoidable costs are deducted from the unit's segment margin to compute its income. Finally, the organization's unallocated costs (sometimes called *shutdown costs*), which represent the administrative and overhead costs incurred regardless of the scale of operations, are deducted from the total of the five profit center incomes to arrive at the dealership's profit.

Evaluating the Segment Margin Report

What can we learn from the segment margin report for Earl's Motors? First, we know that conventional accrual accounting reports a loss of $36,790 for this quarter. This loss may signal a long-term problem, or it may have been expected. Perhaps this quarter is a traditionally slow quarter, and operations in the year's other three quarters make up the deficiency. Perhaps there is a disproportionate amount of committed costs incurred in this quarter, and they will be lower in subsequent quarters.

Many countries have external reporting standards that require organizations to report the financial results for important business segments. Here is part of Honda Motor Co. Ltd.'s segment report that appeared in its financial statements for the year ended March 31, 2010. The business segment information has been prepared in accordance with the Ministerial Ordinance under the Securities and Exchange Law of Japan.

	MOTORCYCLE BUSINESS	AUTOMOBILE BUSINESS	FINANCIAL SERVICES BUSINESS	POWER PRODUCT AND OTHER BUSINESSES	SEGMENT TOTAL	RECONCILING ITEMS	CONSOLIDATED
			YEN (MILLIONS)				
Net sales and other operating revenue:							
External customers	¥1,558,696	¥9,489,391	¥533,553	¥421,194	¥12,002,834	¥ —	¥12,002,834
Intersegment	—	—	15,499	21,571	37,070	(37,070)	—
Total	1,558,696	9,489,391	549,052	442,765	12,039,904	(37,070)	12,002,834
Cost of sales, SG&A and R&D expenses	1,407,409	8,827,726	431,254	420,406	11,086,795	(37,070)	11,049,725
Segment income	151,287	661,665	117,798	22,359	953,109	—	953,109

What Do Segment Margin Statements Tell the Reader?

As we look at the statements for the individual responsibility centers at Earl's Motors, we can see that each showed a positive income. The contribution margin for each responsibility center is the value added by the manufacturing or service-creating process before the costs that are not proportional to volume.

A unit's contribution margin represents the immediate negative effect on corporate income if the unit is shut down. The unit's segment margin is an estimate of the long-term effect of the responsibility center's shutdown on the organization after the fixed capacity used by the unit is either redeployed or sold off. The unit's income is the long-term effect on corporate income after corporate-level fixed capacity is allowed to adjust. For example, if the lease sales operation is discontinued, the immediate effect is to reduce the profit at Earl's Motors by $117,880. After some period of time, however, perhaps a year or even several years, when segment-level capacity has been sold off and corporate-level capacity has been allowed to adjust for this loss of activity, the estimated net effect of closing the lease operation would be to reduce corporate profits by $48,560. The difference between the unit's segment margin and income reflects the effect of adjusting for business-sustaining costs, which are committed in the short run but can be reduced in the long run as the facilities that they reflect are scaled back.

Good or Bad Numbers?

Organizations use different approaches to evaluate whether the segment margin numbers are good or bad. Following are the most popular sources of comparative information:

1. *Past performance*—Is performance this period reasonable, given past experience?
2. *Comparable organizations*—How does performance compare with similar organizations?

Evaluations include comparisons of absolute amounts, such as cost levels and revenue levels, and relative amounts, such as each item's percentage of revenue. For example, in evaluating the performance of Earl's Motors, the manager of the service department may note that variable costs are about 62% of revenue. This may compare favorably with past relationships of variable costs to revenue. By joining an industry group that provides comparative information for dealerships in similar-size communities, however, Earl's Motors may find that, on average, variable costs in automobile dealerships are only 58% of revenue. This suggests that Earl's Motors should investigate why its variable costs are higher than the industry average. Management could make similar evaluations for all cost items in this report.

Interpreting Segment Margin Reports with Caution

The segment margin statement may seem to be a straightforward and interesting approach to financial control. Segment margin statements should be interpreted carefully however, because they reflect many assumptions that disguise underlying issues.

First, like all approaches to financial control, segment margins present an aggregated summary of each organization unit's past performance. It is important to consider other facets relating to critical success factors, such as quality and service, that will affect future profits. For example, companies may use customer surveys to establish a customer satisfaction index for each department, or they might compute quality statistics that report errors or recall rates for each department.

Second, the segment margin report contains arbitrary numbers because they rely on subjective revenue and cost allocation assumptions over which there can be legitimate disagreement. (Accountants often call these arbitrary numbers *soft numbers*). Each subsequent amount shown down each column becomes less controllable by the responsibility center's manager and is affected more by the assumptions used in allocating costs. Although a unit's segment margin is assumed to be controllable, the manager may have less than complete control over the costs used to compute it, and the manager may have almost no control over the costs allocated to compute the unit's income. In a typical refinery, for example, joint use of facilities creates problems when managers attempt to allocate the costs of expensive processes, such as those of the crude distillation unit, to the outputs that it produces (naphtha, distillate, gas, oil, and residuals) (see Exhibit 11-4).

Third, and perhaps most important, the revenue figures reflect important assumptions and allocations that sometimes can be misleading. These assumptions relate to the transfer pricing issue, which focuses on how the revenues the organization earns are divided among the responsibility centers that contribute to earning those revenues.

Cost Allocations to Support Financial Control

Despite the difficulties of measuring responsibility center performance, many organizations want to develop responsibility center income statements. In effect, although revenue and cost allocation rules are arbitrary, people seem satisfied as long as the ones chosen and put in place appear to be fair and consistently applied. Organizations need to design and present responsibility center income statements so that they isolate the discretionary components included in the calculation of each center's reported income. (Exhibit 11-3 presents one possible format.)

The format shown in Exhibit 11-3 helps to identify what the center controls directly. It shows the revenue and variable costs separately from the other costs in the profit calculation, which are the indirect or joint costs that are allocated. Like the allocation of jointly earned revenues, the allocation of indirect or joint costs can cause considerable distortions and can misdirect decision making.

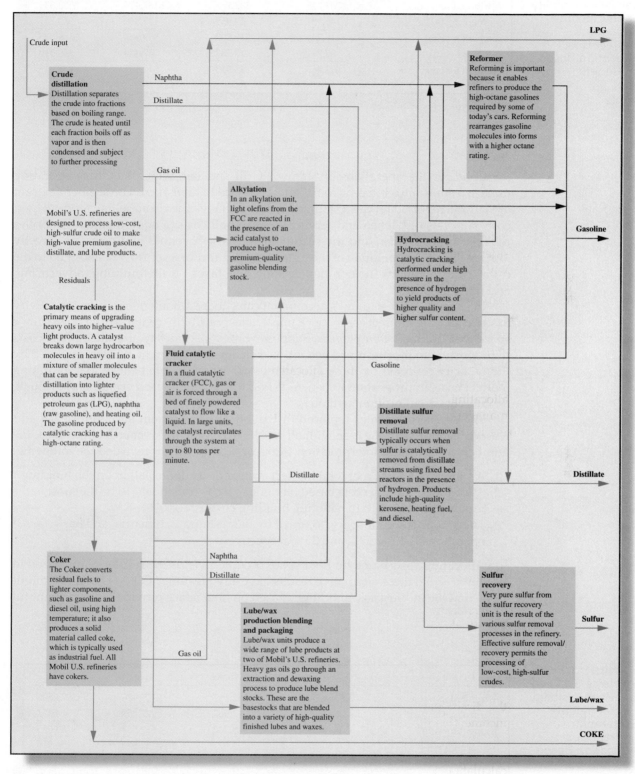

Exhibit 11-5
Shirley's Grill and
Bar Responsibility
Center Income
Statement:
Indirect Cost
Allocation Based
on Benefit

	RESTAURANT	BILLIARDS	BAR	TOTAL
Attributed revenue	$354,243	$32,167	$187,426	$573,836
Segment costs	243,987	12,965	127,859	384,811
Segment margin	$110,256	$19,202	$59,567	$189,025
Allocated costs	87,791	15,289	47,430	150,510
Segment income	$22,465	$3,913	$12,137	$38,515

Consider the operations of Shirley's Grill and Bar, which has three operating units: a restaurant, a billiards room, and a bar (see Exhibit 11-5). The segment margin of $110,256 reported for the restaurant includes all revenues from selling food, all food costs, all costs of kitchen and serving staff, and all costs of equipment and supplies relating to the kitchen and the seating area. These revenues and costs are directly attributable to the operation of the restaurant. Indirect costs of $87,791 allocated to the restaurant operations include depreciation and taxes on the building, advertising, and franchise fees.

In general, the restaurant's accountant can choose among many different activity bases to allocate indirect costs, for example, a responsibility center's direct costs, floor space, and number of employees. Suppose Shirley's decides to allocate indirect costs in proportion to the presumed benefit, as measured by segment margin, provided by the capacity reflected by these allocated costs. Many people believe that allocating indirect costs in proportion to benefit is fair. It is a widely used criterion to evaluate an indirect cost allocation method.

The segment incomes reported in Exhibit 11-5 may seem straightforward and reasonable, but as in the case with all results involving indirect cost allocations, the numbers need careful interpretation. Suppose a cost analysis revealed the following:

1. A significant portion of total indirect costs reflects depreciation on the building.
2. Allocating building costs based on floor space is considered to be the most reasonable approach to handling building costs.
3. The amount of floor space occupied by the restaurant, billiards, and bar operations is 40%, 25%, and 35%, respectively.

Allocating costs based on floor space occupied yields the results summarized in Exhibit 11-6. Do these alternative results have any meaning? On one hand, we might argue that the indirect cost allocations based on floor space provide more meaningful

Exhibit 11-6
Shirley's Grill and
Bar Responsibility
Center Income
Statement:
Indirect Cost
Allocation Based
on Floor Space
Occupied

	RESTAURANT	BILLIARDS	BAR	TOTAL
Attributed revenue	$354,243	$32,167	$187,426	$573,836
Segment costs	243,987	12,965	127,859	384,811
Segment margin	$110,256	$19,202	$59,567	$189,025
Allocated costs	60,204	37,627	52,679	150,510
Segment income	$50,052	($18,425)	$6,888	$38,515

economic results because the floor space allocation reflects depreciation—the major component of indirect costs, and its driver, floor space. On the other hand, even if floor space is the cost driver for indirect costs in the short term, the revised results may suggest nothing significant because the allocated depreciation cost is likely to be a committed cost that cannot be avoided in the short term.

The allocations based on floor space may imply that the contribution to profit per square foot of floor space is lowest in the billiard operation and that Shirley's should reduce the scope of the billiard operations in favor of adding more floor space to the bar or restaurant. This conclusion, however, does not necessarily follow. Suppose that without the billiard operation to attract customers, the bar sales would be cut in half. How could the responsibility center income statements reflect this? They probably cannot. With this supplementary information, it would be possible to determine the economic effect of closing the billiards operation. Conventional segment margin statements cannot capture the interactive effects of such actions.

The message here is that responsibility center income statements have to be interpreted with considerable caution and healthy skepticism. They may include arbitrary and questionable revenue and cost allocations and often disguise interrelationships among the responsibility centers.

TRANSFER PRICING

Transfer pricing is the set of rules an organization uses to allocate jointly earned revenue among responsibility centers. For ease in exposition in the rest of this chapter, we will refer to domestic transfer pricing as simply transfer pricing. Transfer pricing rules can be arbitrary when a high degree of interaction exists among the individual responsibility centers. Exhibit 11-7 shows the possible interactions among the responsibility centers at Earl's Motors.

To understand the issues and problems associated with allocating revenues in a simple organization such as Earl's Motors, consider the activities that occur when a customer purchases a new car. The new car department sells the new car and takes in a used car as a trade. Then Earl's must transfer the used car to the used car department, where it may undergo repairs and service to make it ready for sale, or it may be sold externally, as in the wholesale market.

The value placed on the used car transferred between the new and used car departments is critical in determining the profits of both departments. The new car department would like the value assigned to the used car to be as high as possible because that makes its reported revenues higher; the used car department would like the value to be as low as possible because that makes its reported costs lower.

The same considerations apply for any product or service transfer between any two departments in the same organization. The rule that determines the values of the internal transfers will allocate the organization's jointly earned revenues to the individual profit centers and, therefore, will affect each center's reported profit.

Approaches to Transfer Pricing

There are four main approaches to transfer pricing:

1. Market-based transfer prices.
2. Cost-based transfer prices.

Exhibit 11-7
Earl's Motors:
Transfer Pricing
Interrelationships

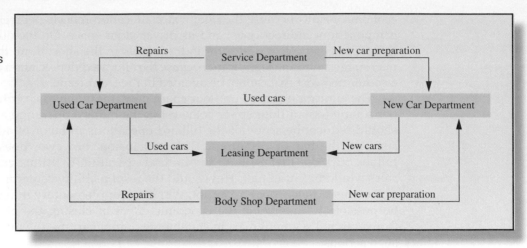

3. Negotiated transfer prices.
4. Administered transfer prices.

It is worthwhile to recall here that the relevance and purpose of transfer prices depend on whether the transfer price has the intended effect on organization decision makers. Transfer prices can have different forms; however, *the goal of using transfer prices is always to motivate the decision maker to act in the organization's best interests.* Accountants must always remember that the primary purpose of producing management accounting numbers is to motivate desirable behavior regarding managers' planning, decision making, and resource allocation activities, not to create accounting reports that meet some aesthetic accounting criteria.

Market-Based Transfer Prices

If external markets exist for the intermediate (transferred) product or service, **market-based transfer prices** are the most appropriate basis for pricing the transferred good or service between responsibility centers. The market price provides an independent valuation of the transferred product or service and how much each profit center has contributed to the total profit earned by the organization on the transaction. For example, the selling division, instead of transferring the good internally, could sell it externally. Similarly, the buying division could purchase externally rather than receiving the internal transfer.

IN PRACTICE

International Transfer Pricing

Under the EU's current tax regimes, the foreign subsidiary of a multinational corporation must pretend to be a stand-alone company. It must account for everything its parent gives it—parts, money, expertise—as if it were bought and sold at arm's length on the market. But the implicit "transfer prices" between different bits of a company are arbitrary and manipulable. A 2002 study by Trade Research Institute, a Miami consultancy, found American firms buying plastic buckets for $973 each and tweezers for $4,896. By overpaying or overcharging its foreign affiliates, a company can spirit losses and profits from one part of the world to another.

Source: The Economist, November 10, 2005.

Unfortunately, such competitive markets with well-defined prices seldom exist. Consider Earl's Motors. Dealers trade used cars in well-organized markets that publish prices. A given used car could be valued using this information. The wholesale value of a used car depends, however, on its mechanical condition, which is only imperfectly observable and at a cost. In addition, the used car's value depends on its visible condition, which is a matter of subjective evaluation. Therefore, it is not clear that it is possible to easily determine an objective wholesale price for a given used car.

Some automobile dealerships avoid this problem by asking the used car manager to value any used car being taken in on trade. This value becomes the transfer price. Because people often react to risk and uncertainty by requiring a margin of safety, the used car manager may discount the perceived value of the used car to provide a margin of safety that covers the repair of any hidden problems that become evident when the car is prepared for resale. If the value is excessively low, however, the new car manager may complain that this impedes the ability of the new car department to sell new cars. Therefore, the new car manager may be given the option to shop a potential trade-in to other used car dealers or sell it at an auction to find a better price. This allows the transfer price to better reflect market forces.

Cost-Based Transfer Prices

When the transferred good or service does not have a well-defined market price, one alternative to consider is a transfer price based on cost. Some common transfer prices are variable cost, variable cost plus some percent markup on variable cost, full cost, and full cost plus some percent markup on full cost. In this context, markups, when used, are intended to provide a return for unallocated corporate-level costs and investment deemed to be supporting product production.

For example, consider a product that has a variable manufacturing cost of $5.00 and allocated fixed manufacturing cost of $3.00. Suppose that the target markup, when used, is 10%. The different possible cost based transfer prices are as follows:

Variable cost	$5.00
Variable cost plus markup	$5.50
Full cost	$8.00
Full cost plus markup	$8.80

The appropriate choice of cost-based transfer price is guided by the same criterion underlying the choice of any transfer price, namely does it provide the incentive for profit center managers to make decisions that are in the organization's best interests?

Proponents of each type of transfer price have arguments to support their respective choices. Economists argue, however, that any cost-based transfer price other than marginal cost (assuming that it can be computed) leads organization members to choose a lower-than-optimal level of transactions, causing an economic loss to the overall organization. For example, if the transfer price is higher than the marginal cost, the supplying unit wants to sell more than the optimal quantity, and the purchasing unit wants to buy less than the optimal quantity. Because supply and demand must be equal and because no organization unit can be forced to buy or sell more than it wants, the amount that is ordered and supplied is always equal to the lesser of what is offered and what is wanted. The dilemma here, however, is that if the supplying division charges marginal cost as the transfer price and marginal costs decline with volume, the marginal cost will be less than average cost, and the supplying division will always show a loss.

Other problems arise when using cost-based transfer prices. Cost-based approaches to transfer pricing do not promote the goal of having the transfer pricing mechanism support the calculation of unit incomes. Moreover, organization units like to be treated as profit centers, not cost centers, because profit centers are considered more prestigious.

Transfer prices based on actual costs provide no incentive to the supplying division to control costs, since the supplier can always recover its costs. This is a well-known problem in government contracting and utility regulation, where prices or rates are often based on actual costs. One solution is to use a standard cost as the transfer price. Under this approach, the difference between the actual costs that a center incurs and the standard costs that are charged out become a measure of the unit's operating efficiency.

Using a cost-based transfer price assumes that the organization can compute a product's cost in a reasonably accurate way. Chapters 4, 5, and 6 showed that developing and operating accurate costing systems present quite a challenge. People are likely to complain and become frustrated if they believe the organization is using an inaccurate costing system for transfer-pricing purposes.

A final problem with cost-based approaches is that they do not provide the proper economic guidance when operations are capacity constrained. When an organization is operating at capacity, production decisions should reflect the most profitable use of the capacity rather than cost considerations only. In this case, the transfer price should be the sum of the marginal cost and the opportunity cost of capacity, where opportunity cost reflects the profit of the best alternative use of the capacity.

One interesting approach to transfer pricing is the so-called dual rate approach, in which the receiving division is charged only for the total variable costs to the point of transfer of producing the unit supplied and the supplying division is credited with the net realizable value (which equals the product's eventual final selling price less all the variable costs needed to complete the product) of the unit supplied. To illustrate, suppose that Fyfe Company produces a product that is started in Division 1 and completed in Division 2. Division 1 incurs a variable cost of $5 to start the product, and Division 2 incurs a variable cost of $3 to complete the product, which is then sold for $20. The transfer price charged to Division 2 when the partially completed product is transferred from Division 1 is $5. The price received by Division 1 is $17. This approach to transfer pricing has the desirable effect of letting marginal cost influence the decisions of the buying division while, at the same time, giving the selling division credit for an imputed profit on the transferred good or service.

Another interesting cost-based approach charges the buying division with the target variable cost in addition to an assignment of the supplying division's committed costs. The assignment should reflect the buying division's share of the supplying division's capacity. For example, if the service department acquired capacity, expecting that 10% of its capacity would be supplied to the new car department, the new car department would receive a lump-sum assignment of 10% of the service department's capacity costs, regardless of the amount of work actually done for the new car department during the period. In this situation, the service department's income is the difference between the actual and target cost of the work it completes.

Cost-based transfer prices raise complex performance measurement, equity, and behavioral issues. Such issues are addressed more thoroughly in advanced texts.

Negotiated Transfer Price

In the absence of market prices, some organizations allow supplying and receiving responsibility centers to negotiate transfer prices among themselves. **Negotiated transfer prices** reflect the controllability perspective inherent in responsibility centers since each division is ultimately responsible for the transfer price it negotiates. Negotiated transfer prices—and therefore production decisions—may, however, reflect the relative negotiating skills of the two parties rather than economic considerations.

Problems arise when negotiating transfer prices because this type of bilateral bargaining situation causes the supplying division to want a price higher than the optimal price and the receiving division to want a price lower than the optimal price. When the actual transfer price is different from the optimal transfer price, the organization as a whole suffers because it transfers a smaller than best number of units between the two divisions.

Administered Transfer Price

An arbitrator or a manager who applies some transfer pricing policy sets **administered transfer prices**, for example, market price less 10% or full cost plus 5%. Organizations often use administered transfer prices when a particular transaction occurs frequently. However, such prices reflect neither pure economic considerations, as market-based or cost-based transfer prices do, nor accountability considerations, as negotiated transfer prices do. Exhibit 11-8 summarizes the four major approaches to transfer pricing.

Transfer Prices Based on Equity Considerations

Administered transfer prices are usually based on cost; that is, the transfer price is cost plus some markup on cost or market. Thus, the transfer price is some function, such as 80%, of the market price. However, sometimes administered transfer prices

Exhibit 11-8
Summary of Transfer Pricing Approaches

APPROACH	MARKET-BASED	COST-BASED	NEGOTIATED	ADMINISTERED
MEASURE USED	MARKET PRICE	PRODUCT COST	DIRECT NEGOTIATIONS	APPLICATION OF A RULE
Advantage	If a market price exists, it is objective and provides the proper economic incentives.	This is usually easy to put in place because cost measures are often already available in the accounting system.	This reflects the accountability and controllability principles underlying responsibility centers.	This is simple to use and avoids confrontations between the two parties to the transfer-pricing relationships.
Problems	There may be no market or it may be difficult to identify the proper market price because the product is difficult to classify.	There are many cost possibilities but any cost other than the marginal cost will not provide the proper economic signal.	This can lead to decisions that do not provide the greatest economic benefits.	This tends to violate the spirit of the responsibility approach.

are based on equity considerations that are designed around some definition of what constitutes a reasonable division of a jointly earned revenue or a jointly incurred cost.

For example, consider the situation in which three responsibility center managers need warehouse space. Each manager has undertaken a study to determine the cost for an individual warehouse that meets the responsibility center's needs. The costs are as follows: manager A—$3 million; manager B—$6 million; and manager C—$5 million. A developer has proposed that the managers combine their needs into a single large warehouse, which would cost $11 million. This represents a $3 million savings from the total cost of $14 million if each manager were to build a separate warehouse. The issue is how the managers should split the cost of this warehouse.

One alternative, sometimes called the *relative cost method*, is for each manager to bear a share of the warehouse cost that is proportional to that manager's alternative opportunity. This would result in the following cost allocations:

Manager A's share = $11,000,000 × $3,000,000/$14,000,000 = $2,357,143
Manager B's share = $11,000,000 × $6,000,000/$14,000,000 = $4,714,286
Manager C's share = $11,000,000 × $5,000,000/$14,000,000 = $3,928,571

This process is fair in the sense of being symmetrical. All parties are treated equally, and each allocation reflects what each individual faces. Another approach, which reflects the equity criterion of ability to pay, is to base the allocation of cost on the profits that each manager derives from using the warehouse. Still another approach, which reflects the equity criterion of equal division, is to assign each manager a one-third share of the warehouse cost. Thus, each of the many different approaches to cost allocation reflects a particular view of equity.

Returning to the example of Earl's Motors, Earl may require that the transfer price for body shop work done for the new and used car departments will be charged out at 80% of the normal market rate. This may seem reasonable and may reflect a practical approach to dealing with the issues associated with market-based and cost-based transfer prices, but this rule is arbitrary and, therefore, provides an arbitrary distribution of revenues and costs among the body shop and the units with which it deals. Administered transfer prices inevitably create cross subsidies among responsibility centers. Subsidies obscure the economic interpretation of responsibility center income and may provide a negative motivational effect if members of some responsibility centers believe that the application of such rules is unfair.

ASSIGNING AND VALUING ASSETS IN INVESTMENT CENTERS

When companies use investment centers to evaluate responsibility center performance, accountants confront all the problems associated with profit centers and some new problems unique to investment centers. The additional problems concern how to identify and value the assets used by each investment center. This task presents troubling questions that have no clear answers.

In determining the level of assets that a responsibility center uses, management must assign the responsibility for (1) jointly used assets, such as cash, buildings, and equipment, and (2) jointly created assets, such as accounts receivable. Once management has assigned the organization's assets to investment centers, they must determine the value of those assets. What cost should be used: historical cost, net book value, replacement cost, or net realizable value? These are all costing alternatives for which supporting arguments can be made (for a more in-depth explanation, see advanced cost accounting texts).

The culmination of the allocation of revenues, costs, and assets to operating divisions is the calculation of the division's return on investment. To consider this, we will consider the DuPont Company, one of the earliest and most prolific users of the return on investment criterion, which is the ratio organizations most often use to evaluate investment center performance.

THE EFFICIENCY AND PRODUCTIVITY ELEMENTS OF RETURN ON INVESTMENT

One of DuPont Company's major challenges as the organization was growing quickly in the late 19th century was to develop a way to manage the complex structure caused by its diverse activities and operations. At this time, most organizations were single-product operations. These organizations approached the evaluation of the investment level of the organization by considering the ratio of profits to sales and the percentage of capacity used. DuPont, however, being a multiproduct firm, pioneered the systematic use of return on investment to evaluate the profitability of its different lines of business. Exhibit 11-9 summarizes DuPont's approach to financial control. At DuPont, the actual exhibit used to summarize operations was extremely detailed and contained as many as 350 large charts that were updated monthly and permanently displayed in a large chart room in the headquarters building.

Exhibit 11-9
The DuPont Company: Return on Investment Control System

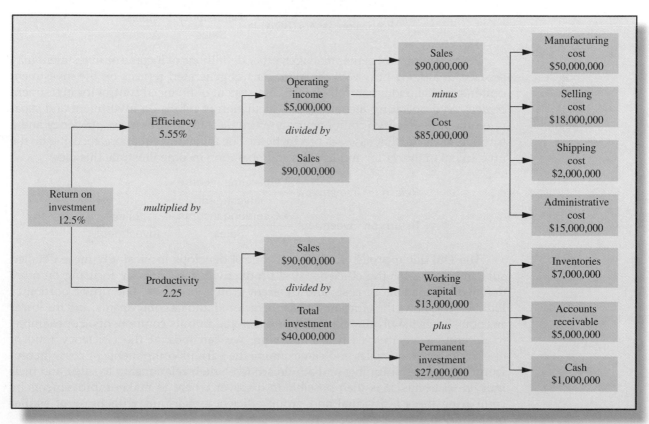

Return on investment, one of the most widely quoted and used financial ratios, is the ratio of income to investment, with varying definitions of income and investment.

$$\text{Return on investment} = \frac{\text{Income}}{\text{Investment}}$$

$$\text{Return on investment (ROI)} = \frac{\text{Income}}{\text{Investment}}$$

$$\text{Return on investment} = \frac{\text{Income}}{\text{Sales}} \times \frac{\text{Sales}}{\text{Investment}}$$

The ratio of operating income to sales (also called *return on sales*, or *sales margin*) is a measure of efficiency; it reflects the ability of the organization or organization unit to control costs at a given level of sales activity. The ratio of sales to investment (often called *turnover*) is a measure of productivity; it reflects the ability to generate sales for a given level of investment.

Shareholders will likely compute the firm's return on investment as return on equity, and may separate this ratio into components as follows:

$$\text{Return on equity (ROE)} = \frac{\text{Net income}}{\text{Sales}} \times \frac{\text{Sales}}{\text{Assets}} \times \frac{\text{Assets}}{\text{Equity}}$$

The ratio of sales to assets (often called *asset turnover*) is a measure of **productivity**: it reflects the ability to generate sales for a given level of assets. The ratio of assets to equity is a measure of financial leverage.

The ratio of assets to equity is usually dropped when evaluating the performance of operating managers and the return on equity measure becomes a return on assets measure.

$$\text{Return on assets (ROA)} = \frac{\text{Net income}}{\text{Sales}} \times \frac{\text{Sales}}{\text{Assets}}$$

For an investment center manager, other definitions of income or investment may be used in judging how well the manager has generated returns on the investment center's capital under control. The DuPont system of financial control for investment centers used operating income in the calculation of return on investment and separated the ratio into two components: a return measure that assesses efficiency and a turnover measure that assesses productivity. The following equations focusing on the investment in the center and its sales and operating income illustrate this idea:

$$\text{Return on investment} = \frac{\text{Operating income}}{\text{Investment}}$$

$$\text{Return on investment} = \frac{\text{Operating income}}{\text{Sales}} \times \frac{\text{Sales}}{\text{Investment}}$$

The DuPont approach to financial control develops increasingly more detailed subcomponents for the efficiency and productivity measures by focusing on more detailed calculations of costs and different groups of assets. The upper portion of Exhibit 11-9 shows the efficiency measure factored into its components; and the lower portion shows the productivity measure factored into its components. For example, to determine whether each is improving, we can look at the efficiency ratio of operating income to sales and can examine the various components of costs (manufacturing, selling, shipping, and administrative), their relationship to sales, and their individual trends. It is then possible to discover where to make improvements by comparing these individual and group efficiency measures with those of similar organization units or competitors.

The productivity ratio of sales to investment allows development of separate turnover measures for the key items of investment: the elements of working capital (inventories, accounts receivable, and cash) and the elements of permanent investment (equipment and buildings). Comparisons of these turnover ratios with those of similar units or those of competitors can suggest where improvements are required.

Assessing Productivity Using Financial Control

The most widely accepted definition of productivity is the ratio of output over input. For example, if a worker produces 50 items in a 7-hour shift, the worker's productivity (often called *labor productivity*) is 7.1 (= 50 ÷ 7) units per hour. Labor-intensive industries such as consultancies, public accounting firms, hospitals, and trades organizations, monitor their labor productivity obsessively because labor costs are a big fraction of total costs.

Organizations develop productivity measures for all factors of production, including people, raw materials, and equipment. For example, in the fishing industry, the ratio of weight of salable final products to the weight of the raw fish is typically around 30%. This ratio of raw material in the finished product to the total quantity of raw material acquired is called *raw material productivity* or *yield*. Most organizations in the natural resource industry keep a close watch on raw material productivity because the cost of raw materials is a large proportion of total costs. For example, Weirton Steel, a U.S. steel products manufacturer, once estimated that each percentage point increase in its raw material yield was equivalent to a $4.7 million decrease in operating costs. This gives a practical example of how organizations can use a financial control number, such as raw material yield, to make inferences about how well the underlying manufacturing operations are working and their effect on income.

Finally, many organizations in continuous process industries, such as paper manufacturing, monitor their machine productivity ratios (output per hour or per shift of machine time). Investment in the machine represents a huge fixed cost invested in capacity, and profitability depends on how well that capacity is used. Again, a measure like machine productivity provides organizations with an effective method to relate process results and financial results.

Questioning the Return on Investment Approach

Despite its popularity, some analysts have criticized return on investment as a means of financial control. Some critics argue that the sole use of any financial measure is too narrow for effective control. They argue that the most effective approach to control is to monitor and assess the organization's critical success factors, such as quality, service, and designing and making products that customers want.

IN PRACTICE
Labor Productivity in a Consultancy

Consultancies track and manage labor costs carefully since they are not only their major costs but these costs are often controllable. A measure consultancies often use is the ratio of labor hours billed to labor hours paid, which is effectively a productivity measure because it divides an output measure (hours billed) by an input measure (hours paid). There are many variations on this theme, but all are focused on the same objective: using resources effectively to achieve the organization's financial objectives.

Fleet costs, such as lease payments and depreciation on aircraft, are major costs in the airline industry. For this reason, airlines focus on what the airline industry calls load factor, which is a productivity measure. Load factor equals the ratio of seats occupied on flights (see the Traffic item in the following table) divided by seats available on flights (see the Capacity item in the following table). The problem with this measure is that it can be increased dramatically by heavy discounting. For this reason, the airline industry focuses on the average revenue earned per passenger mile flown. Here is an excerpt from a financial update issued by the Air France/KLM Group on May 9, 2010. The "Unit Revenue per RPK" is the average revenue (in euros) per passenger kilometer flown and the "Unit Revenue per ASK" is the average revenue (in euros) per available seat kilometer flown. Note carefully the last two numbers in the table. The unit cost per seat kilometer exceeds the unit revenue per seat kilometer which is clearly an undesirable situation for any airline.

	FULL YEAR TO 31ST MARCH		
	2010	2009	CHANGE
Traffic (RPK millions)	202,455	209,060	(3.20)%
Capacity (ASK millions)	251,012	262,356	(4.30)%
Load factor	80.70%	79.70%	1.0 pt
Total passenger revenues (€ m)	16,267	18,832	(13.60)%
Revenues from scheduled passenger business (€ m)	15,489	17,937	(13.60)%
Unit revenue per RPK (€ cts)	7.65	8.58	(10.80)%
Unit revenue per ASK (€ cts)	6.17	6.84	(9.70)%
Unit cost per ASK (€ cts)	6.46	6.78	(4.60)%

Others who accept the need for financial measures still find weaknesses with the return on investment measure. They observe that profit-seeking organizations should make investments in order of declining profitability until the marginal cost of capital of the last dollar invested equals the marginal return generated by that dollar. Unfortunately, financial control based on return on investment may not yield this result.

For example, consider a manager who is evaluated based on return on investment. Suppose that the current average return on investment is 15% and that the manager is contemplating an investment that is expected to return 12%. The manager would be motivated to reject this investment opportunity because accepting it would lower the division's total return on investment and, thus, conflict with what is in the organization's best interests. For example, if the organization's cost of capital were only 10%, the manager should accept the investment because its expected return exceeds the investment's cost of capital.

Using Residual Income

People have responded to this criticism of return on investment by creating a different investment criterion. **Residual income** equals reported accounting income less the economic cost of the investment used to generate that income. For example, if a division's income is $13.5 million and the division uses $100 million of capital, which has an average cost of 10%, residual income can be computed as follows:

$$\text{Residual income} = \text{Income} - \text{Cost of capital}$$
$$= \$13,500,000 - (\$100,000,000 \times 10\%)$$
$$= \$3,500,000$$

In 2007, Siemens reported that it tied performance bonuses for some of its senior executives to the EVA® measure for the operating unit they managed.
Alamy Images

Like return on investment, residual income evaluates income relative to the level of investment required to earn that income. Unlike return on investment, however, residual income does not motivate managers to turn down investments that are expected to earn more than their cost of capital. Under the residual income criterion, managers are asked to do whatever they think is necessary to make residual income as large as possible. For example, recall the previous situation in which the manager faced an investment opportunity with an expected return of 12% when the cost of capital was 10%. If the project requires an investment of $100 million, the residual income if the investment is made and the expected return is realized is $2 million [$100,000,000 × (12% − 10%)]. Therefore, if rewarded based on residual income, the manager will accept this investment opportunity.

Stern Stewart, a consultancy, developed a proprietary tool they call **economic value added (EVA®)**, which is a refinement of the residual income idea. The economic value-added tool adjusts reported accounting income and asset levels for what many consider the biasing effects on current results of the financial accounting doctrine of conservatism. For example, GAAP requires the immediate expensing of research and development costs; yet, when shareholder value analysis income is computed, research and development costs are capitalized and expensed over a certain time period, such as five years. The intent of the adjustments prescribed to compute share-holder value-added income from GAAP income is to develop an income number that better reflects the organization's long-run earnings potential. Many organizations have adopted the economic value-added criterion to evaluate their investments in product lines, divisions, even entire companies.

Organizations can use economic value added to identify products or product lines that are not contributing their share to organization return, given the level of investment they require. These organizations use activity-based costing analysis to assign assets and costs to individual products, services, or customers. This allows them to calculate the EVA by product, product line, or customer.

Organizations can also use economic value added to evaluate operating strategies. Quaker Foods & Beverages, a food manufacturer, used EVA to support its decision in June 1992 to cease *trade loading*, which is the food industry's practice of using promotions to obtain orders for a two- or three-month supply of food from customers.

Organizations Adopt Economic Value Added for Different Reasons

SPX Corporation supplies specialty service tools and original equipment components to the automotive industry. In its 1995 annual report, SPX identified the following reasons for adopting shareholder value analysis:

- It treats the interests of shareholders and management the same, encouraging SPX people to think and act like owners.
- It is easily understood and applied.
- It fits into operational improvement efforts because success requires continuous improvement of EVA®.
- It correlates closer with market value than any other operating performance measure.
- It links directly to investor expectations through EVA® improvement targets.

- It focuses on long-term performance by using a bonus bank and predetermined improvement targets.
- It provides a common language for performance measurement, decision support, compensation, and communication.

The notion of a bonus bank, mentioned in the sixth point, is particularly interesting. In years when performance exceeds the economic value-added target, two-thirds of all bonuses are set aside in a bonus bank that is carried forward and is payable only if the manager achieves economic value-added targets in subsequent years. When performance falls below target, the bonus is negative and is deducted from the bonus bank. The bonus bank turns what is nominally a short-run performance measure and reward into a longer run measure.

Trade loading causes quarterly peaks in production and sales that, in turn, require huge investments in assets, including the inventory itself, warehouses, and distribution centers. Through higher prices, customers pay the costs of the higher inventory levels created by this cyclical pattern of inventory. An article in *Fortune* magazine[1] estimated that trade loading was primarily responsible for the $75 to $100 billion in groceries that were always in transit between manufacturers and consumers and that supporting this inventory "adds some $20 billion to the $400 billion that U.S. consumers annually spend on groceries."

This economic value-added analysis suggests that even though sales levels may be reduced by eliminating price reductions associated with trade loading, it is more profitable for the company and its trading partners to forgo the large inventories and the required warehouse space. Also, to produce food at even levels rather than in peaks reduces the level of production capacity needed. Quaker Foods & Beverages motivated managers to end trade loading by basing bonuses on efficiency and cycle times rather than on annual sales.

A measure of the increasing importance of economic value added in organizations is the seniority of people who are usually appointed to manage EVA implementation projects in organizations. For example, in 1995, Olin Corporation's new president and chief executive officer was heading the company's EVA steering team at the time of his appointment. The results of economic value added suggest interesting insights into financial control applied at all levels of the organization. However, they should be treated with caution. To be an effective motivational and evaluation tool, EVA analysis, like return on investment calculations, requires complex and potentially problematic allocations of assets, revenues, and costs to divisions, product lines, products, or customers, depending on the focus of the analysis. However, many organizations believe that these problems can be solved and that the insights provided by EVA analyses are well worth the effort.

---

[1] Patricia Seller, "The Dumbest Marketing Ploy," *Fortune* (October 5, 1992): 88–94.

THE EFFICACY OF FINANCIAL CONTROL

Although financial control is widely practiced, many people have questioned its true insights and effectiveness. Critics have argued that financial information is delayed—and highly aggregated—information about how well the organization is doing in meeting its commitments to its shareholders and that this information measures neither the drivers of the financial results nor how well the organization is doing in meeting its stakeholders' requirements, a leading indicator of future financial performance.

Financial control may be an ineffective control scorecard for three reasons:

1. Financial control focuses on financial measures that do not measure the organization's other important attributes, such as product quality, the speed at which the organization develops and makes products, customer service, the ability to provide a work environment that motivates employees, and the degree to which the organization meets its legal and social obligations to society. Because these elements and others promote the organization's long-term success, they also need to be measured and monitored. The argument is that financial control measures only the financial results and not how those results were achieved. This limitation of financial control led to the development of the Balanced Scorecard (discussed in Chapter 2). Recall that the Balanced Scorecard uses a range of nonfinancial measures of performance in the area of customer requirements, process characteristics, and learning and growth to both explain and predict financial results. Therefore, the Balanced Scorecard provides a means of managing financial results, which is something not possible when the organization focuses exclusively on financial results since these are an aggregate measure of *what* happened, not *why* it happened.

2. Financial control measures the financial effect of the overall level of performance achieved on the critical success factors, and it ignores the performance achieved on the individual critical success factors. For this reason, many people believe that financial control does not suggest how to improve performance on the critical success factors or on financial performance. Critics argue that, at best, financial results act only as a broad signal of how well the organization manages the tasks that create success on the critical success factors that, in turn, create financial returns. The argument is that effective control begins with measuring and managing the elements or processes that create financial returns rather than measuring the financial returns themselves. The Balanced Scorecard addresses this problem (as discussed in Chapter 2) by focusing on both financial results (such as return on investment) and measures of process performance (such as employee skills, knowledge, and satisfaction; customer satisfaction; cycle times; the rate of process improvement and innovation; and quality) that create the financial results.

3. Financial control is usually oriented to short-term profit performance. It seldom focuses on long-term improvement or trend analysis but instead considers how well the organization or one of its responsibility centers has performed this quarter or this year. This is a result of the misuse of financial control rather than an inherent fault of financial control itself. However, the preoccupation with short-term financial results is debilitating. It motivates an atmosphere of managing short-term financial results that provides disincentives for the types of management and employee initiatives that promote long-term success, particularly in the area of investing in training, equipment, and process changes. One major reason given for taking public organizations private is to provide senior management with the opportunity to manage for long-term results rather than being forced into inappropriate concerns with short-term performance caused by financial analysts who have that preoccupation.

The fundamental issue is that the financial accounting model assumes that all consequences from spending made during the period are reflected in the end-of-period financial metrics. This is fine for spending on operating resources, but breaks down when companies spend to improve their "intangible assets," such as customer relationships, process quality and reliability, new products, employee capabilities and motivation, and databases and information. The expenses get recorded but most of the benefits show up in future periods. So the financial summary is inadequate for measuring the value created during the period (because some or much of the benefits show up in future periods). The converse is also true. Companies can cut back on spending for their intangible assets. The financial results for the period improve – because of reduced spending – but the loss in value will show up in future periods with customer attrition, process breakdowns, lack of new products, and surly, alienated employees. This, of course, is the significant contribution of the Balanced Scorecard, which, by tracking the drivers of future financial performance, provides the opportunity to reflect investments in intangible assets in the current year.

In summary, how should we interpret these facets of financial control? Financial control is an important tool for effective organization control. If used properly, financial results provide crucial help in assessing the organization's long-term viability and in identifying processes that need improvement. It is a tool to be supported by other tools since it is only a summary of performance.

Financial control does not try to measure other facets of performance that may be critical to the organization's stakeholders and vital to the organization's long-term success. It can, however, provide an overall assessment of whether the organization's strategies and decisions are providing acceptable financial returns. Organizations can also use financial control to compare one unit's results with another. This financial benchmarking signal indicates whether the organization's operations control systems, which seek to monitor, assess, and improve performance on the critical success factors, are operating well enough to deliver the desired financial results.

EPILOGUE TO ADRIAN'S HOME SERVICES

Adrian asked Pat Rubinoff, the senior analyst at AHS, to study Exhibit 11-1 and identify how profitability might be improved. After some work Pat returned with the following observations related to getting a better picture of the underlying profitability of the AHS business activities:

1. One of the assets included in Exhibit 11-1 was a residence that Adrian leased for $1 per year from AHS. Pat argued that this property which was carried at book value of $250,000, should be eliminated from the Heat Department's asset base. The cost of maintaining this home was approximately $65,000, which was part of the AHS's unallocated costs. All matters relating to the home and its associated costs were documented and considered part of Adrian's remuneration. Pat recommended eliminating the property from the business statement and the costs from the unallocated costs.

2. AHS donated $400,000 annually to various community charities. These donations were allocated equally to each of the four business areas and were included in the selling, general, and administrative costs for each of the businesses. Pat suggested that $100,000 of costs should be eliminated from each of the operating units.

3. Included in the unallocated selling general and administrative expenses was an amount of $500,000 representing an out-of-court settlement with someone who

had been injured during a fall at AHS's truck compound. Pat argued that this should be eliminated from Exhibit 11-1 to reflect ongoing profit potential since insurance had now been acquired to cover such incidents and the compound was now secured by a locked gate.

4. Finally Pat observed that included in the Heating Division asset base was $250,000 of idle assets relating to oil heating services that the Heating Division no longer provided. Pat believed that these assets could be sold for their book value.

Exhibit 11-10 reflects the results of the changes Pat recommended and the resulting financial ratios.

After studying Exhibit 11-10, Pat reached some important conclusions about the gross margin figures. In all four businesses the ratio of income to sales was about 5% less than the industry standard. Pat attributed this to the higher costs of labor and materials that underlay AHS's quality reputation. Combined with the observation that demand often exceeded capacity, Pat recommended that Adrian implement an across-the-board price increase of 7% to bring the income to sales ratio closer to the industry standards. Exhibit 11-11 summarizes the expected results of the 7% price increase.

Finally when studying the sales to assets ratio for the four businesses, all seemed to be in line with industry standards except for the Electrical Division, which was considerably below the industry average of 4.00. After some investigation Pat discovered that part of the Electrical Division's work was a low-margin business that required considerable investment in assets. Pat recommended exiting this part of the Electrical Division business. This would result in lost sales of approximately $500,000 with an associated gross margin of 25%. Exiting this business would allow the Electrical Division to sell off $200,000 of assets at their book value. Therefore, the reduction of sales, cost of goods sold, and assets would be $500,000, $375,000 [$500,000 × (1 − 0.25], and $200,000, respectively, resulting in the numbers shown in Exhibit 11-12.

Adrian was impressed by this analysis, planned to implement Pat's suggestions, and looked forward to the expected financial results.

Exhibit 11-10
Adrian's Home Services: Reanalysis and DuPont Analysis

	HEATING	AIR CONDITIONING	PLUMBING	ELECTRICAL	UNALLOCATED	CORPORATE TOTAL
Sales	$1,546,000	$2,344,670	$5,340,000	$3,423,000		$12,653,670
Cost of goods sold	870,000	1,384,000	3,245,000	2,198,000		7,697,000
Gross margin	$676,000	$960,670	$2,095,000	$1,225,000		$4,956,670
Selling, general, and administrative	34,500	356,000	1,224,500	554,000	2,480,000	4,649,000
Income	$641,500	$604,670	$870,500	$671,000		$307,670
Assets	626,000	958,000	2,176,000	1,127,000	297,000	5,184,000
Shareholders' equity						2,875,000
Income to sales	41.49%	25.79%	16.30%	19.60%		2.43%
Sales to assets	2.47	2.45	2.45	3.04		2.44
ROA	102.48%	63.12%	40.00%	59.54%		5.93%
Assets to equity						1.80
ROE						10.70%

Exhibit 11-11
Adrian's Home Services: Price Increases and DuPont Analysis

	HEATING	AIR CONDITIONING	PLUMBING	ELECTRICAL	UNALLOCATED	CORPORATE TOTAL
Sales	$1,654,220	$2,508,797	$5,713,800	$3,662,610		$13,539,427
Cost of goods sold	870,000	1,384,000	3,245,000	2,198,000		7,697,000
Gross margin	$784,220	$1,124,797	$2,468,800	$1,464,610		$5,842,427
Selling, general, and administrative	34,500	356,000	1,224,500	554,000	2,480,000	4,649,000
Income	$749,720	$768,797	$1,244,300	$910,610		$1,193,427
Assets	626,000	958,000	2,176,000	1,127,000	297,000	5,184,000
Shareholders' equity						2,875,000
Income to sales	45.32%	30.64%	21.78%	24.86%		8.81%
Sales to assets	2.64	2.62	2.63	3.25		2.61
ROA	119.76%	80.25%	57.18%	80.80%		23.02%
Assets to equity						1.80
ROE						41.51%

Exhibit 11-12
Adrian's Home Services: Results of Dropping Part of Electrical Division

	HEATING	AIR CONDITIONING	PLUMBING	ELECTRICAL	UNALLOCATED	CORPORATE TOTAL
Sales	$1,654,220	$2,508,797	$5,713,800	$3,162,610		$13,039,427
Cost of goods sold	870,000	1,384,000	3,245,000	1,823,000		7,322,000
Gross margin	$784,220	$1,124,797	$2,468,800	$1,339,610		$5,717,427
Selling, general, and administrative	34,500	356,000	1,224,500	554,000	2,480,000	4,649,000
Income	$749,720	$768,797	$1,244,300	$785,610		$1,068,427
Assets	626,000	958,000	2,176,000	927,000	297,000	4,984,000
Shareholders' equity						2,875,000
Income to sales	45.32%	30.64%	21.78%	24.84%		8.19%
Sales to assets	2.64	2.62	2.63	3.41		2.62
ROA	119.76%	80.25%	57.18%	84.75%		21.44%
Assets to equity						1.73
ROE						37.16%

SUMMARY

This chapter explored the scope and nature of financial control—an approach to evaluating operations and management that relies on financial information from internal and external perspectives.

Organizations use financial control information to evaluate how well processes and organization units are fulfilling their objectives. Chapter 10 presented how organizations use budgets and variances to evaluate operating unit and process performance. This chapter considered the different types of responsibility centers and the role of financial information in evaluating organization unit performance. When evaluating an organization unit's profit contribution, organizations use transfer prices to allocate jointly earned revenues to each of the contributing units.

KEY TERMS

administered transfer price 509
controllability principle, 498
cost-based transfer prices, 507
cost centers, 494
decentralization, 488
economic value added (EVA®), 515
financial control, 487

internal financial controls, 488
investment centers, 496
market-based transfer prices, 506
negotiated transfer price, 509
productivity, 512
profit centers, 496
residual income, 514

responsibility center, 491
return on investment, 512
revenue centers, 495
segment margin report, 500
transfer pricing, 505

ASSIGNMENT MATERIALS

Questions

11-1 What does financial control mean? **(LO 1)**

11-2 What is the difference between internal financial control and external financial control? **(LO 1)**

11-3 What are the primary reasons for decentralization of an organization? **(LO 2)**

11-4 What does control mean in a decentralized organization? **(LO 2)**

11-5 What is a responsibility center? **(LO 2)**

11-6 When preparing accounting summaries, how do accountants classify responsibility centers? **(LO 2)**

11-7 What is the assigned responsibility in a profit center? **(LO 3)**

11-8 What is the characteristic of a revenue center? **(LO 3)**

11-9 What is the difference between a cost center and an investment center? **(LO 3)**

11-10 What does the controllability principle state? **(LO 4)**

11-11 How do responsibility centers interact? **(LO 3, 4)**

11-12 How is segment income determined? **(LO 4)**

11-13 What is a soft number in accounting? **(LO 4)**

11-14 What are the two forms of transfer pricing? **(LO 5)**

11-15 What are the four bases for setting a transfer price? **(LO 5)**

11-16 Why do organizations allocate revenues to responsibility centers? **(LO 3, 6)**

11-17 Why do organizations allocate costs to responsibility centers? **(LO 3, 6)**

11-18 What is return on investment? **(LO 7)**

11-19 Name a ratio that measures efficiency and a ratio that measures productivity. **(LO 7)**

11-20 How does productivity (the ratio of sales to investment) affect return on investment? **(LO 7)**

11-21 How is residual income computed? **(LO 7)**

11-22 How does *economic value added* differ from residual income? **(LO 7)**

11-23 Describe specific examples of how firms are using economic value added to evaluate their investments in product lines or divisions, or to evaluate operating strategies. **(LO 7)**

11-24 What are three reasons financial control alone may provide an ineffective control scorecard? **(LO 1, 2)**

Exercises

LO 2   **11-25**   *Issues in decentralization*   What control problem does decentralization create in organizations?

LO 2   **11-26**   *University responsibility centers*   Give an example of a responsibility center in a university.

LO 3   **11-27**   *Cost centers*   Give an example of a responsibility center that is properly treated as a cost center.

LO 3   **11-28**   *Revenue centers*   Give an example of a responsibility center that is properly treated as a revenue center.

LO 3   **11-29**   *Investment centers*   Based on your understanding of how chains are managed, would you agree or disagree that an outlet of a large department store chain should be treated as an investment center? What about the maintenance department within that outlet? What about a single department within the store?

LO 3   **11-30** *Multinational companies and investment centers*   Many multinational companies create wholly owned subsidiaries to do business in the countries or regions where they operate. Are these wholly owned subsidiaries examples of investment centers? Explain.

LO 3   **11-31** *Responsibility centers*   Identify three responsibility centers in a fast-food restaurant and explain how they may interact.

LO 4   **11-32** *Controllability*   Based on your understanding, which of the following does the manager of a cinema control: costs, revenues, profits, and investment?

LO 4   **11-33** *Computing division income*   A home services company offers renovations, as well as heating, air conditioning, and plumbing services, to its customers. Imagine that you are in the process of computing the income for the renovations division. What problems might you encounter in computing this income?

LO 4   **11-34** *Controllability and evaluation*   Suppose you are the manager of a fitness center that is one of many in a chain. Give one example of a cost that you control and one example of a cost you do not control. Why is it important in this setting to distinguish between costs that are controllable and costs that are not controllable?

LO 4   **11-35** *Controllability and motivation*   Give an example of a situation for which invoking the controllability principle would have a desirable motivational effect. Also give an example of a situation for which suspending the controllability principle would have a desirable motivational effect.

LO 6   **11-36** *Effects of transfer price choices*   McCann Company has two divisions, Division C and Division D. Division C manufactures Part C82 and sells it to Division D, and also sells the same part to the outside market for $50 per unit. Division C has capacity to make 400,000 units of C82 per year. The division's fixed costs are $5,000,000 per year and its variable costs per unit are as follows:

Direct materials	$20
Direct labor	12
Variable overhead	8

Part C82 is an essential component for Division D's only product; the division sells 200,000 units per year at a price of $120 per unit. Division D's fixed costs are $4,000,000 per year and its variable costs per unit, excluding the cost of Part C82, are as follows:

Direct materials	$10
Direct labor	25
Variable overhead	10

Required

Suppose Division C's demand for C82 from the outside market is currently 150,000 units per year. By how much will McCann's income decrease if Division D purchases its desired 200,000 units of C82 at $50 per unit from the market rather than from Division C? What transfer price(s) would you suggest to induce both divisions to want Division D to purchase from Division C instead of from the market?

LO 5, 6   **11-37** *Domestic and international transfer pricing*   Organizations might desire to use one transfer pricing system designed to support international transfer pricing and another domestic transfer pricing system designed to achieve motivational objectives. Give a reason why you think organizations would not use two transfer pricing systems—one for international tax purposes and one for motivational purposes.

LO 6   **11-38**   *Choosing transfer prices*   How might a transfer price for logs be chosen in an organization that cuts down trees and processes the logs either in a sawmill to make lumber or in a pulp mill to make paper?

LO 6   **11-39**   *Choosing transfer prices*   In a fishing products company, the harvesting division catches and delivers the fish to the processing division that, in turn, delivers the processed fish to the selling division to sell to customers. How can you determine the appropriate transfer price between harvesting and processing and between processing and selling?

LO 6   **11-40**   *Using market-based transfer prices*   What is the main advantage and the main obstacle in using market-based transfer prices?

LO 4, 6   **11-41**   *Soft numbers*   Why did accountants develop the expression "soft number"?

LO 4, 6   **11-42**   *Allocating costs*   A store is divided into four departments: automotive products, home products, paint, and lumber. How would you assign the building costs, such as depreciation, to each of these departments?

LO 7   **11-43**   *Return-on-investment measurement issues*   Green Company has prepared the following information for three of its divisions:

DIVISION	HISTORICAL COST OF INVESTMENTS	DIVISION OPERATING INCOME
X	$645,000	$70,600
Y	415,000	51,400
Z	588,000	71,250

Required

(a) Compute each division's return on investment and residual income, assuming a 10% cost of capital.

(b) Suppose the net book value of each division's investments is 40% of the historical cost. Using net book value as the measure of investment, compute each division's return on investment and residual income, assuming a 10% cost of capital.

(c) Comment on the division rankings in parts a and b.

(d) If the division managers are rewarded on the basis of return on investment or residual income, will they find it attractive to invest in new, more costly equipment?

LO 7   **11-44**   *Return-on-investment components*   Eta Company would like to examine the sales margin and asset turnover components of return on investment for three of its divisions and has accordingly prepared the following information:

DIVISION	INVESTMENT	DIVISION OPERATING INCOME	SALES
P	$375,000	$75,000	$328,000
Q	1,200,000	144,000	937,000
R	840,000	101,000	675,000

Required

(a) Compute each division's return on investment, sales margin, and asset turnover.

(b) Comment on the divisions' relative rankings on the ratios computed in part a.

(c) Compute each division's residual income, assuming a required return on investment of 10%.

LO 7   **11-45**   *Changes in return-on-investment components*   Division Q's current investment turnover is 2.5 and its return on sales ratio is 0.6. The division is considering a sales promotion that would increase its current return-on-sales ratio by 20% but decrease its investment turnover by 10%.

Required

(a) If the division undertakes this promotion, by what percentage would the return on investment increase or decrease?

(b) If the division undertakes this promotion, by what percentage will the return-on-sales ratio need to increase in order for the return on investment to increase by 20%?

LO 7 **11-46** *Return on investment and residual income*   The following information pertains to VI Division, which has $2,000,000 in investments.

Division sales revenue	$1,350,000
Less division expenses	450,000
Division income	$900,000

The company's cost of capital is 10%.

Required

(a) What is the division's return on investment?

(b) What is the division's residual income?

LO 7 **11-47** *Characteristic return on investment ratios*   For-profit organizations face a requirement to earn at least a minimum-level return on investment. Some businesses rely on high ratios of income to sales; other businesses rely on high ratios of sales to investment. Give an example of each of these types of businesses and explain what this characteristic implies about the business.

LO 7 **11-48** *Productivity ratio*   Give an example of why using units, rather than the value of the products produced, in the numerator of a productivity ratio may give a misleading picture of the process that produced that output.

LO 7 **11-49** *Computing residual income*   A business whose investors require a return on investment of 7% reports an income of $2.5 million on an investment of $30 million. What is the residual income for this business?

LO 7 **11-50** *Residual income in a multiproduct company*   Based on an analysis of operations, a company producing ready-made garments has determined that the incomes provided by its shirt, t-shirt, trouser, and tie product lines are $3.6 million, $8.4 million, $4 million, and $1.2 million, respectively. The accountant believes that the investment levels in these product lines are $40 million, $60 million, $45 million, and $12 million, respectively. Use a residual income analysis to evaluate the performance of each of these product lines, assuming that the organization requires a 10% return on investment.

Problems

LO 2, 3, 4 **11-51** *Choosing responsibility center type*   For each of the following units, identify whether the most appropriate responsibility center form is a cost center, a revenue center, a profit center, or an investment center and explain why you have made that choice.
  a. Appliance section of a department store
  b. A regional sales office
  c. The computer services group in an insurance company
  d. The security department in a department store
  e. A customer service department in a mail-order company
  f. A warehouse used to store goods for distribution in a large city
  g. The souvenir shop of a five-star luxury hotel

11-52 *Allocating common costs to cost centers* You have decided to divide a factory into cost centers. How would you allocate depreciation expense on the factory building to its individual cost centers?

LO 4　**11-53** *Implementing the controllability principle* One of the most widely accepted and longest held beliefs is the controllability principle, which says that organization units and people should be held accountable only for things that they can control.

Required

(a) For any job you choose, give one example of something you should be expected to control and one example of something you should not be expected to control.

(b) Can you think of an example in which making yourself responsible for something that you cannot control would promote a desirable activity?

LO 4　**11-54** *Segment margins* The following is information about Paramount Company's three product lines:

	PRODUCT LINE		
	1	2	3
Revenue	$7,500,000	$2,000,000	$3,750,000
Variable cost percentage of sales	60%	50%	40%
Other costs	$753,000	$317,000	$702,000
Allocated avoidable corporate costs	$312,000	$156,000	$698,000
Allocated unavoidable corporate costs	$575,500	$213,000	$66,500

Required

(a) Construct a segment margin statement for Paramount Company.

(b) Explain why the segment margins reported for an organization unit must be interpreted carefully.

LO 4　**11-55** *Drop unprofitable segments* Perform an Internet search on "close underperforming stores" or similar phrase to locate an example of a company that has closed unprofitable stores or other segments. Explain what issues the company considered in dropping the unprofitable segments and improving profitability of the remaining segments.

LO 5, 6　**11-56** *Transfer prices and division autonomy* You are a government controller. A division manager being audited objects to the transfer price he is being charged by the audit group for the audit services. The manager observes, "If I have to pay for these services, I should be allowed to buy them from an outside supplier who is prepared to offer them to me at a lower price." You have been asked to mediate this dispute. What would you do?

LO 5, 6　**11-57** *Transfer pricing and outside opportunities* Deseronto Electronics manufactures motherboards for computers. The company is divided into two divisions: manufacturing and programming. The manufacturing division makes the board, and the programming division makes the adjustments required to meet the customer's specifications.

　　The average total cost per unit of the boards in the manufacturing division is about $450, and the average total cost per board incurred in the programming division is about $100. The average selling price of the boards is $700. The company is now operating at capacity, and increasing the volume of production is not a feasible alternative.

In the past, the managers of the two divisions have negotiated a transfer price. The average transfer price has been about $500, resulting in the manufacturing division recognizing a profit of about $50 per board and the programming division recognizing a profit of about $100 per board. Each of the managers receives a bonus that is proportional to the profit reported by his or her division.

Karen Barton, the manager of the manufacturing division, has announced that she is no longer willing to supply boards to the programming division. Sam Draper, the senior purchasing executive for Koala Electronics, a computer manufacturer, has indicated that he is willing to purchase, at $650 per unit, all the boards that Karen's division can supply and is willing to sign a long-term contract to that effect. Karen indicated that she offered the boards to the programming division at $625 per board on the grounds that selling and distribution costs would be reduced by selling inside. Neil Wilson, the manager of the programming division, refused the offer on the grounds that the programming division would show a loss at this transfer price.

Neil has appealed to Shannon McDonald, the general manager, arguing that Karen should be prohibited from selling outside. Neil has indicated that a preliminary investigation suggests that he cannot buy these boards for less than about $640 outside. Therefore, allowing Karen to sell outside would effectively doom Neil's division.

Required

(a) What transfer price would you recommend? Why?
(b) What recommendations do you have for the programming division?

LO 7 **11-58** *Return on investment* Michelle Gutierrez, manager of the Components Division of FX Corporation, is considering a new investment for her division. The division has an investment base of $5,000,000 and operating income of $600,000. The new investment of $600,000 supports corporate strategy and is expected to increase operating income by $150,000 next year, an acceptable level of return from corporate headquarters' point of view.

Required

(a) What is the current return on investment (ROI) for the Components Division?
(b) What will the ROI be if Michelle undertakes the new investment?
(c) Suppose Michelle's compensation consists of a salary plus a bonus proportional to her division's ROI. Is Michelle's compensation higher with or without the new investment?

LO 7 **11-59** *Return on investment and residual income* The Newland Flyers operate a major sports franchise from a building in downtown Newland. The building was built in 1940 at a cost of $10,000,000 and is fully depreciated so that it is shown on the company's balance sheet at a nominal value of $1. The land on which the building was built in 1940 was purchased in 1935 for $10,000 and is valued at this amount for balance sheet purposes. The franchise, which is the company's only other major investment, cost $500,000 in 1940.

The current assessed value of the building is $600,000. The assessed value of the land, which is located in a prime urban area, is $40,000,000 and reflects the net value of the property if the current building is demolished and replaced with an office and shopping complex. The current value of the franchise, assuming that the league owners would approve a franchise sale, is $80,000,000.

Required

(a) Ignoring taxes in this calculation, if the team earns an income of approximately $5,000,000 per year, what is the return on investment using net book value, historical cost, and net realizable value as the measures of investment?

(b) Ignoring taxes in this calculation and assuming that the organization's cost of capital is 15%, if the team earns approximately $5,000,000 per year, what is the residual income using net book value and historical cost as the measures of investment?

LO 7 **11-60** *Problems in computing economic value added* A bank is thinking of using economic value added to identify services that require improvement or elimination. What problems may the bank have in computing the economic value added of any of the services that it offers to its customers?

LO 7 **11-61** *Evaluating the potential of economic value added* The owner of a chain of fast-food restaurants has decided to use economic value added to evaluate the performance of the managers of each of the restaurants. What do you think of this idea?

LO 7 **11-62** *Using residual income* As a result of a residual income analysis, the owner of a company that makes and installs swimming pools has decided to shut down the manufacturing operations that show a negative residual income for the current year. Is this necessarily the proper response to this information? Why or why not?

LO 7 **11-63** *Conflicting organization and individual objectives* Strathcona Paper rewards its managers on the basis of the after-tax return on investment of the assets that they manage—the higher the reported return on investment, the higher the reward. The company uses net book value to value the assets employed in the return on investment calculation. The company's cost of capital is assessed as 12% after taxes. The organization's tax rate is 35%.

The manager of the logistics division is faced with an opportunity to replace an aging truck fleet. The current net income after taxes of the logistics division is $7 million, and the current investment base is valued at $50 million. The current net income after taxes and the current investment base, absent any investment in new trucks, are expected to remain at their existing levels.

The investment opportunity would replace the existing fleet of trucks, which have a net book value of about $100,000, with new trucks costing about $50 million net of the trade-in allowance for the old trucks. If kept, the old trucks would last another 5 years and would have no salvage value. The new trucks would last 5 years, have zero salvage value, and increase cash flow relative to keeping the old trucks (through increased revenues and decreased operating costs) by about $16 million per year. If purchased, the new trucks would be depreciated for both accounting and tax purposes on a straight-line basis.

Required

(a) From the point of view of the company, should this investment be made? Support your conclusion with net present value calculations.

(b) From the point of view of the manager, should this investment be made?

(c) If the manager were rewarded on the basis of after-tax residual income, would the manager want to make the investment? Show why or why not.

LO 1, 2, 3, 4   **11-64**   *Strategy and control*   Many people believe that the focus of control in a successful organization reflects the strategic initiatives in the organization. For each of the following organizations, identify what you think are the three most important items assessed by the organization's financial control system and why each is important. For each organization, what critical information is not assessed by the financial control system?
  a. A company selling cable television services to its subscribers
  b. A symphony orchestra
  c. An organization selling canned soup
  d. A government agency responsible for finding jobs for its clients
  e. An auditing firm
  f. A company selling high-fashion clothing.

LO 2   **11-65**   *Organic and mechanistic organizations*   Researchers have defined two extreme forms of organizations. Organic organizations are highly decentralized with few rules. Most people agree that software development companies are very organic. Mechanistic organizations are highly centralized and use many rules to prescribe behavior. Most people agree that government agencies are very mechanistic.

Do you agree with these examples? Give your own examples of each of these types of organizations, along with your reason for giving each organization the chosen classification.

LO 2, 3, 4   **11-66**   *Group and individual conflict*   Think of an example of an organization in which it is important that the various functional areas be closely coordinated to promote the organization's overall success. Show how performance measures that focus solely on the performance of an individual unit could create problems in this organization.

LO 2, 3, 4   **11-67**   *Coordinating divisional activities*   For many years, automobile companies were highly decentralized in terms of functions. The most obvious effect of this heavy decentralization of function was apparent when all the groups needed to work together to accomplish a goal. The highest order of integration occurs in the design of a new automobile.

Reflecting the functional decentralization of automobile manufacturers, the traditional approach to automobile design was for the marketing group to identify a concept. The design group then created an automobile that reflected the marketing group's idea but incorporated engineering requirements and aesthetics identified by the design group. The purchasing group then identified the parts required by the design and made further modifications to it to incorporate parts that could be made or purchased. Finally, the manufacturing group modified the design to reflect the nature and capabilities of the production process. This process took up to four years and usually resulted in a vehicle that was far removed from the initial design.

What was wrong here? How could the process be improved?

LO 1, 2, 3, 4   **11-68**   *Choices in financial control*   Bennington Home Products sells home products. It buys products for resale from suppliers all over the world. The products are organized into groups. A few examples of these groups are floor care products, kitchen products, tool products, and paper products. The company sells its products all over the world from regional offices and warehouses in every country where it operates. Because of differences in culture and taste, the product lines and products within those lines vary widely among countries.

The regional offices have administrative staff that manage the operations, place orders to the corporate office, and undertake the usual office administrative functions, and they have sales staff that do the selling directly to stores within each region. The regional offices are evaluated as investment centers because they have responsibility for revenues, costs, and investment levels. The regional offices make suggestions for new products.

The corporate office manages the regional offices and places the orders received from the regional offices with suppliers. The corporate office does the ordering for three reasons. First, the company believes that one ordering office eliminates duplication in ordering activities. Second, it believes that one office ordering for all of the regional offices gives the organization more power when dealing with suppliers. Third, it is believed that one office can develop the expertise to find and negotiate with suppliers of unique and innovative products.

Required

(a) Describe an appropriate system of financial control at the regional level.
(b) Describe an appropriate system of financial control at the corporate office level.
(c) Explain why the systems of financial control should or need not mesh.

LO 4 **11-69** *Assigning responsibility for uncontrollable events* Some people and organizations believe that the discussion of controllable and uncontrollable events is distracting in the sense that it encourages finger-pointing and an excessive preoccupation with assigning blame. These observers argue that it is more important to find solutions than to identify responsibility for unacceptable or acceptable events.

Required

(a) What do you think of this argument?
(b) As an organization moves away from assessing and rewarding controllable performance, what changes would you expect to see in its organization structure?

LO 6 **11-70** *New product opportunities and transfer pricing* Plevna Manufacturing makes and distributes small prefabricated homes in kits. The kits contain all pieces needed to assemble the home. All that is required is that the builder erect the home on a foundation.

Plevna Manufacturing is organized into two divisions: the manufacturing division and the sales division. Each division is evaluated on the basis of its reported profits. The transfer price between the manufacturing division, where the kits are made, and the selling division, which sells the kits, is variable cost plus 10%, a total of about $33,000. The selling price per kit is about $40,000, and selling and distribution costs are about $5,000 per home kit.

The total costs that do not vary in proportion with volume at Plevna Manufacturing amount to about $2,000,000 per year: about $1,500,000 in manufacturing and about $500,000 in the selling division. The company is currently operating at capacity, which is dictated by the machinery in the manufacturing division. Each kit requires about 10 hours of machine time, and the total available machine time is 5,000 hours per year. Plevna Manufacturing is making and selling about 500 kits per year. Increasing the plant capacity is not a viable option in the foreseeable future.

Willie Scott is the firm's salesperson. Willie has been approached a number of times recently by people wanting to buy cottages to erect on recreational properties. The cottages would be made by modifying the existing home product. The modification process would begin with a completed home kit. The manufacturing division would then incur additional materials and labor costs of $3,000 and three hours of machine time to convert a home kit into a cottage kit.

Willie is proposing that the company split the sales division into two divisions: home sales and cottage sales. The new divisional structure would have no effect on existing administrative, personnel, or selling costs.

Required

Suppose the new division is created. Discuss the issues in choosing a transfer price in this situation. What transfer price for each of the two products, home and cottage kits, would you recommend and why? (If you feel that the appropriate transfer price for each product can be within a range, specify the range.)

LO 1, 7 **11-71** *Decision making with return on investment* You are the manager of a chain of fast-food outlets. You are computing the return on investment for each outlet.

Outlet A, located in a city core, reported a net profit of $250,000. The land on which Outlet A is located was essentially rural when it was purchased for $250,000. Since then, the city has expanded, and the land is now located in the population center. Comparable undeveloped land in the immediate area of the outlet is worth $3,200,000. The net book value of the outlet building and equipment is $400,000. The replacement cost of the building and equipment is $1,500,000. If the outlet building, equipment, and land were sold as a going concern, the sale price would be $2,000,000. It would cost $200,000 to demolish the building and clear the property for commercial development.

Required

(a) What is the return on this investment?
(b) How would you decide whether this outlet should continue to be operated, sold as a going concern, or demolished and the land sold?

Cases

LO 4 **11-72** *Segment analysis, commitment, and consumption of activity resources* Shellie's Lawn and Gardening performs various lawn and garden maintenance activities, including lawn mowing, tree and shrub pruning, fertilizing, and treating for pests. Unlike other lawn and garden businesses in the city, Shellie also specializes in landscape design and planting. Shellie is pleased that her design specialty is so much in demand. However, she is concerned because profits have been falling, even though sales have been growing during the past few years. In an effort to better understand why profits are falling, Shellie prepared the following product-line income statement:

SHELLIE'S LAWN AND GARDEN PRODUCT-LINE INCOME STATEMENT

	LAWN MOWING	LAYOUT DESIGN	OTHER MAINTENANCE	TOTAL
Revenues	$287,500	$218,750	$312,500	$818,750
Direct costs	$156,250	$70,000	$181,250	$407,500
Allocated costs	$131,679	$100,191	$143,130	$375,000
Profit	($429)	$48,559	($11,880)	$36,250

The lawn mowing business involves mowing lawns and trimming edges for customers who generally sign up for the season and pay a flat fee based on the surface area mowed and trimmed. The layout design business involves both designing a garden and lawn layout and installing the design. Other maintenance includes tree and shrub pruning and application of chemicals. The direct costs for each line of business are the costs of the materials and wages of the people who work in that line of business. The remaining costs consist mainly of equipment costs but also include office costs. After some deliberation, Shellie decided to allocate the remaining costs of $375,000 on the basis of revenue, reasoning that revenue is a measure of equipment use.

Required

(a) Based on this product-line income statement, which business is Shellie likely to focus her efforts on? What is the likely result?

A further analysis of the allocated costs produced the information in the following table. General business costs are $50,000, and the remaining $325,000 represents equipment costs. The trucks are shared equally by all segments, but the other equipment is used by only the indicated segment.

SHELLIE'S LAWN AND GARDEN RESOURCE USE INFORMATION

	COST	PRACTICAL CAPACITY HOURS	COST DRIVER RATE PER HOUR	HOURS USED
Trucks and related costs	$50,000	800	$62.50	600
Lawn mowing equipment	37,500	1,500	25.00	1,200
Layout design equipment	150,000	400	375.00	400
Other maintenance equipment	87,500	700	125.00	500
	$325,000			

(b) For each equipment category in the table above, calculate the cost allocated to Shellie's service orders based on the number of hours used, and calculate the cost associated with unused capacity.

(c) Prepare a new product-line income statement with a column for each product line and a column for the total company. For each product line, include the cost of used equipment capacity and the cost of unused capacity that is attributable only to that product line.

(d) Based on your new product-line income statement, what advice do you have for Shellie? How does this advice compare to your response in part a?

LO 2, 3, 4, 7   **11-73 *Choosing an organization structure*** You are a senior manager responsible for overall company operations in a large courier company. Your company has 106 regional offices (terminals) scattered around the country and a main office (hub) located in the geographical center of the country. Your operations are strictly domestic. You do not accept international shipments.

The day at each terminal begins with the arrival of packages from the hub. The packages are loaded onto trucks for delivery to customers during the morning hours. In the afternoon, the same trucks pick up packages that are returned to the terminal in late afternoon and then shipped to the hub, where shipments arrive from the terminals into the late evening and are sorted for delivery early the next day for the terminals.

Each terminal in your company is treated as an investment center and prepares individual income statements each month. Each terminal receives 30% of the revenue from packages that it picks up and 30% of the revenue from the packages it delivers. The remaining 40% of the revenue from each transaction goes to the hub. Each terminal accumulates its own costs. All costs related to travel to and from the hub are charged to the hub. The revenue per package is based on size and service type and not the distance that the package travels. (There are two types of service, overnight and ground delivery, which take between one and seven days, depending on the distance traveled.)

All customer service is done through a central service group located in the hub. Customers access this service center through a toll-free telephone number. The most common calls to customer service include requests for package pickup, requests to trace an overdue package, and requests for billing information. The company has invested in complex and expensive package tracking equipment that monitors the package's trip through the system by scanning the bar code placed on every package. The bar code is scanned when the package is picked up, enters the originating terminal, leaves the originating terminal, arrives at the hub, leaves the hub, arrives at the destination terminal, leaves the destination terminal, and is delivered to the customer. All scanning is done by handheld wands that transmit the information to the regional and then central computer.

The major staff functions in each terminal are administrative (accounting, clerical, and executive), marketing (the sales staff), courier (the people who pick up and deliver the shipments and the equipment they use), and operations (the people and equipment who sort packages inside the terminal).

This organization takes customer service very seriously. The revenue for any package that fails to meet the organization's service commitment to the customer is not assigned to the originating and destination terminals.

All company employees receive a wage and a bonus based on the terminal's residual income. This system has promoted many debates about the sharing rules for revenues, the inherent inequity of the existing system, and the appropriateness of the revenue share for the hub. Service problems have arisen primarily relating to overdue packages. The terminals believe that most of the service problems relate to mis-sorting in the hub, resulting in packages being sent to the wrong terminals.

Required

(a) Explain why you believe an investment center is or is not an appropriate organization design for this company.

(b) Assuming that this organization is committed to the current design, how would you improve it?

(c) Assuming that this organization has decided that the investment center approach is unacceptable, what approach to performance evaluation would you recommend?

LO 1, 2, 3, 4   **11-74 *Computing objectives and organization responsibility***   Baden is a city with a population of 450,000. It has a distinct organization group, called the Public Utilities Commission of the city of Baden, or Baden PUC, whose responsibility is to provide the water and electrical services to the businesses and homes in the city. Baden PUC's manager is evaluated and rewarded on the basis of the profit that Baden PUC reports.

Baden PUC buys electricity from a privately owned hydroelectric facility several hundred miles away for resale to its citizens. Baden PUC is responsible for acquiring, selling, billing, and servicing customers. The maintenance and moving of electric wires within the city are, however, the responsibility of the city of Baden maintenance department, or Baden Maintenance. Baden PUC pays Baden Maintenance for work done on its electrical wires.

Over the years, many squabbles have occurred between Baden Maintenance and Baden PUC. These squabbles have usually involved two items: complaints by customers about delays in restoring disrupted service and complaints by Baden PUC that the rates charged by Baden Maintenance are too high. However, the most recent quarrel concerns a much more serious issue.

On July 12, at about 10:30 A.M., a Baden City employee working in the parks and recreation department noticed an electrical wire that seemed to be damaged. The employee reported the problem to Baden Maintenance at about 12:15 P.M., during his lunch break. At 1:15 P.M., the report was placed on the maintenance supervisor's desk, where it was found at 2:05 P.M., when the supervisor returned from lunch. The maintenance supervisor then called the Baden PUC dispatch office to report the problem and request permission to investigate the report and make any required repairs. The request for repair was placed on the Baden PUC service manager's desk for approval at 2:25 P.M. The service manager received the message at 4:00 P.M., when he returned from a meeting. He approved the work and left a memo for a subordinate to call in the request. The request was then mistakenly called in by a clerk at 4:50 P.M. as a request for routine service and logged by the dispatcher in Baden Maintenance. A truck was dispatched at 3:50 P.M. the following day. When the repair crew arrived at the scene, it discovered that the wire was indeed damaged and that if any of the children playing in the park had touched it, it would have caused instant death.

The incident went unreported for several days until a reporter for the *Baden Chronicle* received an anonymous tip about the episode, verified that it had happened, and reported the incident on the front page of the newspaper as an example of bureaucratic bungling. The public was outraged and demanded an explanation from the mayor, who asked the city manager to respond. The initial response from Baden's city manager—that "everyone had followed procedure"—only fanned the furor.

Required

(a) Was what happened inevitable, given the city of Baden's organization structure? Explain.
(b) Given the existing organization structure, how might this incident have been avoided?
(c) How would you deal with this situation now that it has happened?
(d) Would a change in the organization structure help prevent a similar situation from occurring in the future? Explain.

A

Activity-based pricing Establishes a base price for a proposed customer order based on the estimated cost of producing and delivering the order.

Administered transfer price A transfer price set by some authority in the organization to price the exchange of a good or service between two organization units. For example, the general manager of a car dealership may set the price that the Service Department will bill other organization departments at 75% of the rate charged to external customers.

Applied indirect costs Indirect costs, such as the costs of capacity related resources, that are applied to a cost object.

Appraisal costs The costs related to inspecting materials or products to ensure that they meet both internal and external customer requirements.

Appropriations Planned and approved cash outflows, or spending plans, in government agencies.

Authoritative budgeting A budgeting process that occurs when a superior informs subordinates what their budget will be without requesting input.

Avoidable costs The costs that can be eliminated when a part, product, product line, or business segment is discontinued.

B

Balanced Scorecard A strategic management system that translates an organization's strategy into clear objectives, measures, targets, and initiatives organized by four perspectives.

Benchmarking The process of studying and adapting the best practices of other organizations to improve the firm's own performance and establish a point of reference by which internal performance can be measured.

Benchmarking (performance) gap The gap between actual performance and the performance level of the organization that established the benchmark level of performance.

Breakeven point The level of sales units or sales dollars at which the contribution from sales revenue less variable costs covers fixed costs. At the breakeven point, net income equals zero.

Breakeven time (BET) The length of time required for a new project to pay back its initial investment in research, development and engineering activities.

Budget A quantitative expression of the money inflows and outflows that reveal whether the current operating plan will meet the organization's financial objectives.

Budgeting process The approach used to determine how to allocate financial resources to each part of an organization based on the planned activities and short-run objectives of that part of the organization.

C

Capacity cost rate The cost of supplying capacity for each group of similar resources, such as people and equipment; calculated by dividing the total cost of supplying the resources by their practical capacity, typically measured by the time available to perform productive work.

Capacity-related costs The costs associated with capactiy-related resources.

Capacity-related resources Resources that are acquired and paid for in advance of when the work is done. Capacity-related resources provide the organization with the capacity to make or deliver goods and services.

Cash bonus A payment method that pays cash based on some measured performance. Also called lump-sum reward, pay for performance, or merit pay.

Certified suppliers A set of suppliers that are certified by a company because they are dependable and consistent in supplying high-quality items as needed.

Consultative budgeting A method of budget setting that occurs when managers ask subordinates to discuss their ideas about the budget but no joint decision making occurs.

Consumable resource A resource that is consumed as a result of some activity. Examples of consumable resources are wood used to make furniture and the time of an hourly paid worker who makes the furniture.

Continuous budget A budget that is continuously updated as the current period is dropped from the budget and a new period is added.

Contribution margin Sales less variable costs.

Contribution margin per unit The contribution margin per unit of consumption of a constraining factor of production. For example, the contribution per machine hour.

Contribution margin ratio The ratio of a product's contribution margin to its selling price. It is the fraction of each sales dollar that contributes to covering fixed cost and providing a profit.

Controllability principle States that the manager of a responsibility center should be assigned responsibility only for the revenues, costs, or investments controlled by responsibility center personnel.

Conversion costs   Costs of labor and support activities to convert the materials or product at each process stage.

Cooperative benchmarking   The voluntary sharing of information through mutual agreements.

Cost-based transfer prices   A cost-based transfer price occurs when the price of a good or service exchanged between two organization units is based on the costs incurred by the supplying (selling) organization unit. Cost based transfer prices reflect decisions about which elements of the product or services' cost should be included, such as fixed plus variable or just variable costs, standard or actual costs, and any mark-up over the transferred costs. For example, one cost-based transfer price might be standard variable cost plus a mark up of 34%.

Cost centers   Responsibility centers in which employees control costs but do not control revenues or investment levels.

Cost driver   A cost driver is an activity or variable that causes a cost. For example, increased production volume causes increased investment in production equipment and, in turn, higher levels of machine depreciation. The number of miles driven in a car is the cost driver for the cost of gasoline. The term *cost driver* is also used for the activity whose quantity is the denominator for a cost driver rate or predetermined overhead rate.

Cost driver rate   The amount determined by dividing the activity expense by the total quantity of the activity cost driver.

Cost object   Something for which a cost is computed. Examples of cost objects are a product, a product line, a department, a division, and a geographical area.

Cost of nonconformance (CONC) to quality standards   The cost incurred when the quality of products and services does not conform to quality standards.

Cost of unused capacity   The cost of unused capacity-related resources.

Cost-of-quality (COQ) report   A report that details the cost of maintaining quality production processes and products. The report details prevention, appraisal, internal failure, and external failure costs.

Cost pool   Each subset of total support costs that can be associated with a distinct cost driver.

Cost–volume–profit (CVP) analysis   A study of how costs and profits vary with changes in volume.

Cross-functional product teams   Made up of individuals representing the entire value chain, both inside and outside the organization, to guide the target-costing process.

Customer lifetime value (CLV)   The total profits earned over all time periods of a customer's relationship with the company; measured by subtracting the initial cost of acquiring the customer from the discounted sum of annual net profits during the years that the customer maintains a relationship with the company; often, CLV is estimated prospectively for newly-acquired customers.

Customer loyalty   A measure of the ability of the company to retain existing customers; loyalty can be measured in multiple ways, such as percentage of repeat customers, year-to-year growth in sales with existing customers, and a customers' willingness to recommend the company to other potential customers.

Customer management processes   Processes that select, acquire, retain, and deepen relationships with targeted customers.

Customer perspective   The Balanced Scorecard perspective that identifies objectives and measures for the targeted customer segments, and for the value proposition for customers in these segments.

Customer satisfaction   A measure of how a customer views its current relationship with the company, usually evaluated on a scale where one end represents "extremely satisfied with the relationship," and the other end is "extremely dissatisfied."

Cycle time   The chronological time taken to complete an activity. For example, manufacturing cycle time is the time from start to finish taken to produce a product.

D

Data falsification   The process of knowingly altering company data in one's favor.

Database benchmarking   A policy in which companies usually pay a fee and in return gain access to information from a database operator.

Death spiral   The process by which a company goes out of business through calculating unit cost by allocating overhead to a diminished volume of business, raising prices to cover the high unit costs, losing more business because of higher prices, calculating higher unit costs, setting higher prices to cover them, and, eventually, having no business and very high unit costs.

Decentralization   The process of delegating decision-making authority to front line decision makers.

Diagnostic control systems   Formal information systems that managers use to monitor organizational outcomes and correct deviations from standard measures of performance.

Direct cost   A cost of a resource or activity that is acquired for or used by a single cost object. An example is the cost of leather used to make a leather coat.

Direct labor cost   Direct labor cost refers to the wages paid to workers whose time can be traced reasonably and accurately to a single cost object, usually a product.

Direct materials cost   The cost of materials that can be traced reasonably and accurately to a single cost object, usually a product.

Direct method (for service department allocations)   A method of allocating service department costs that only considers service units provided to production departments (thereby ignoring service units provided to other service departments).

Dysfunctional behavior   Occurs when employees knowingly manipulate or falsify performance measures.

E

Earnings management   Methods by which managers knowingly manipulate the reporting of income.

Economic value added (EVA®)   An estimate of the wealth increment to owners from the current years' operations; measured as adjusted accounting income minus estimated cost of capital for the investment level.

Efficiency (quantity) variance   The difference between the amount of a resource used and the amount allowed, given the level of production, costed at the standard cost of the resource.

Employee self-control   A managerial method in which employees monitor and regulate their own behavior and perform to their highest levels.

Environmental costing   A costing system that calculates the costs that an organization imposes on the environment.

Equivalent unit of production   In process costing, calculated by multiplying the number of partially completed units by the percentage of competition.

Ethical control system   A management control system to ensure and provide evidence that the organization's stated and practiced ethics are the same.

External failure costs   The costs incurred when customers discover a defect.

Extrinsic rewards   Rewards that are given by one person to another to recognize a job well done. Examples include: money, recognition in a corporate newsletter, stock options, or congratulations.

F

Financial accounting   The process of producing financial statements for external constituencies—such as shareholders, creditors, and governmental authorities.

Financial budgets   Budgets that identify the expected financial consequences of the activities summarized in the operating budgets.

Financial control   A process used to assess an organization's success by measuring and evaluating its financial outcomes.

Financial perspective   The Balanced Scorecard perspective that focuses on financial measures of an organization's success, such as return on investment and operating income.

Finished goods inventory   The costs of the resources for completed units that are not yet sold.

First-level variance   Difference between the actual costs and the master budget costs for individual cost items.

Fixed cost   The cost that is associated with capacity-related resources. The amount of fixed costs is related to the planned rather than the actual level of activities.

Fixed manufacturing overhead   Fixed manufacturing overhead refers to the cost of providing production capacity in a factory. Depreciation on factory equipment is an example of fixed manufacturing overhead.

Flexible budget   Reflects a cost budget or forecast based on the level of volume that is actually achieved.

Flexible budget variances   Differences between actual costs and the budget level of costs adjusted for the actual level of activity.

Flexible resources   Resources whose use is proportional to the amount of the resource used. An example of a flexible resource is steel in a steel mill.

Floor price   The floor price is the minimum price that a party to a negotiation will accept.

G

Gain sharing   A system for distributing cash bonuses from a pool when the total amount available is a function of performance relative to some target.

Gaming the performance indicator   An activity in which an employee may to ensure and provide evidence that the organization's stated and practiced ethics are the same.

Goal congruence   The outcome when managers' and employees' goals are aligned with organizational goals.

Group benchmarking   A business alternative in which participants meet openly to discuss their methods.

Group technology   A type of facility layout in which a manufacturing plant is divided into cells. Within each cell all machines required to manufacture a group of similar products are arranged in proximity to each other. This approach is sometimes called cellular manufacturing.

H

Human relations movement   A managerial movement that recognizes that people have needs well beyond performing a simple repetitive task at work and that financial compensation is only one aspect of what workers desire.

Human resources model of motivation (HRMM) A contemporary managerial view that introduces a high level of employee responsibility for and participation in decisions in the work environment.

I

Improshare A gain sharing program that determines its bonus pool by computing the difference between the target level of labor cost given the level of production and the actual labor cost.

Incentive compensation A reward system that provides monetary rewards based on measured results. Also called a pay-for-performance systems.

Incremental budgeting A budgeting process that bases a period's expenditure level for a discretionary item on the amount spent for that item during the previous period.

Incremental cost The amount by which the total costs of production and sales increase when one additional unit of a product is produced and sold.

Indirect cost The cost of a resource that organizations acquire to be used by more than one cost object. An example is the wage paid to a supervisor in a factory that makes different products when the cost object is a product.

Indirect materials Indirect materials are consumable resources that are too costly to trace to individual cost objects. Examples of indirect materials are lubricants used in a factory and office supplies used in a consultancy.

Indirect/third-party benchmarking A technique that uses an outside consultant to act as a liaison among firms engaged in benchmarking.

Innovation processes Processes that develop new products, processes, and services.

Interactive control systems Formal information systems managers use to involve themselves regularly and personally in the decision activities of subordinates.

Internal failure costs The costs incurred when the manufacturing process detects a defective component or product before it is shipped to an external customer.

Internal financial control Application of financial control tools to evaluate organization units, with the resulting information used internally and not distributed to outsiders.

Intrinsic rewards Those rewards that come from within an individual and reflect satisfaction from doing the job and the opportunities for growth that the job provides.

Investment The monetary value of the assets that the organization gives up to acquire a long-term asset.

Investment centers Responsibility centers in which the managers and other employees control revenues, costs, and the level of investment in the responsibility centers.

J

Job order costing A process that estimates the costs of manufacturing products for different jobs required for specific customer orders.

Just-in-time (JIT) manufacturing A production process method in which products are manufactured only as needed.

K

Kaizen costing A costing system that focuses on reducing costs during the manufacturing stage of the total life cycle of a product.

L

Lean manufacturing An approach to manufacturing in which any resource spending that does not create value for the end customer is considered wasteful and should therefore be modified or eliminated.

Learning and growth perspective The Balanced Scorecard perspective that identifies the objectives for employee capabilities, information systems, and organizational climate that will create long-term growth and improvement.

M

Make-or-buy decision A decision in which managers must decide whether their companies should manufacture some parts and components for their products in-house or subcontract with another company to supply these parts and components.

Management accounting The process of supplying managers and employees with financial and nonfinancial information for making decisions and allocating resources, consistent with the strategy, and monitoring, evaluating, and rewarding performance.

Management accounting and control system (MACS) A system that generates and uses information that helps decision makers assess whether an organization is achieving its objectives. The system includes the set of procedures, tools, performance measures, systems, and incentives that organizations use to guide and motivate all employees to achieve organizational objectives. The system also incorporates the plan-do-check-act cycle.

Managing customer relationships The process by which companies choose to improve a customer's profitability by changing policies with it on pricing, discounting, promotions, minimum order size, degree of customization, packaging, and delivery.

Manufacturing overhead cost Manufacturing overhead costs refers to all factory costs that are not considered direct materials or direct labor. Examples of manufacturing overhead costs include depreciation on factory equipment, supervision, utilities, and the cost of supplies such as lubricants.

Manufacturing stage The time periods when a product is produced and distributed to customers; in contrast to the research, development, and engineering stage or the post-sales service and salvage stages.

Market-based transfer prices Transfer prices that are set based on the market price of the good or service transferred between two organization units.

Marketing, selling, distribution, and administrative (MSDA) expenses Generally one or more line items in a standard income statement, below the gross margin line, that include the cost of resources devoted to marketing and selling to customers, distributing products and services to them, and for order handling, credit, invoicing and collections.

Master budget A budget, typically prepared on a yearly basis, that includes operating budgets (for example, sales, purchasing, and production) and financial budgets (for example, balance sheets, income statements, and cash flow statements) that identify the expected financial consequences of the activities reflected in the operating budgets.

Measures Descriptions of how success in achieving Balanced Scorecard objectives will be determined.

Mixed cost A cost that includes fixed and variable components. A mobile telephone bill that includes a basic fixed amount each month and a variable amount that reflects the amount of use is an example of a mixed cost to the consumer.

Monitoring Inspecting the work or behavior of employees while they are performing a task.

Motivation An individual's interest or drive to act in a certain manner.

N

Negotiated transfer price A negotiated price for a good or service transferred between two organization units. For example, after some discussion, the manager of the used car department in an automobile dealership might agree to pay the manager of the new car department $10,000 for a car that was traded in during a new car purchase.

Net promoter score (NPS) A popular customer loyalty metric, measured by the percentage of customers highly willing to recommend the company's product or service less the percentage of customers unwilling to make such a recommendation.

Nonfinancial information Information about a process (such as percent good units produced), a product (such as time taken to fill order), or a customer (such as customer satisfaction) that is not based on information developed in the financial accounting system and is relevant in monitoring the organization's performance on objectives.

Nonfinancial measures of innovation Measures such as number of new products introduced, number of new products co-created with customers, time-to-market, breakeven time, and % of product development milestones achieved, that evaluate the performance of a company's innovation process.

O

Objectives Concise statements in each of the four Balanced Scorecard perspectives that articulate what the organization hopes to accomplish.

Operating budget The document that forecasts revenues and expenses during the next operating period, including monthly forecasts of sales, production, and operating expenses.

Operating costs Costs, other than direct materials costs, that are needed to produce a product or service.

Operations management processes The basic, day-to-day processes by which companies produce their products and services and deliver them to customers.

Opportunity cost The maximum value sacrificed when a course of action is chosen.

Outsourcing The process of buying resources from an outside supplier instead of manufacturing them in-house.

P

Participative budgeting A method of budget setting that uses a joint decision-making process in which all relevant parties agree about setting the budget targets.

Pay-for-performance system Reward system that provides monetary rewards based on measured results. Also called incentive compensation.

Periodic budget A budget that is prepared for a given period, such as a quarter or a year.

Plan-do-check-act cycle A method of budget setting that uses a joint decision-making process in which all relevant parties agree about setting the budget targets.

Planning variance The difference between the planned and flexible budget amount.

Postsale service and disposal stage The portion of the life cycle that begins after the customer has received the product.

Practical capacity The maximum amount of work that can be performed by resources supplied for production or service.

Predetermined overhead rate A predetermined overhead rate, sometimes called a normal overhead rate, is computed by dividing an expected amount of overhead by the quantity of the cost driver that will be used to apply overhead to cost objects. For example, if expected overhead is $1,000,000, the cost driver is machine hours, and the quantity of machine hours is 10,000, then the predetermined overhead rate is $100 per machine hour.

Prevention costs The costs incurred to help ensure that companies produce products according to quality standards (that is, prevent poor quality).

Preventive control An approach to control that focuses on preventing an undesired event.

Price (rate) variances The difference between the amount paid for a resource and the amount that would have been paid if the resource had been purchased at its standard price.

Pricing waterfall A visual representation of all the subtractions, due to discounts, promotions, and allowances, from the list price of a product or service. The pricing waterfall equals the difference between the list price and the cash the company actually receives from the customer for the product or service.

Pro forma financial statements The projected statement of cash flows, balance sheet, and income statement.

Process costing A costing system that computes the cost of each manufacturing process used to make a product.

Process layout A production design in which all similar equipment or functions are grouped together.

Process perspective The Balanced Scorecard perspective that describes how a strategy will be executed. It identifies the operating, customer management, innovation, and regulatory and social processes that are most important to meet the expectations of shareholders and customers.

Processing cycle efficiency (PCE) A measure used to assess the efficiency of a process, the ratio of actual processing time to total elapsed time for the process.

Processing time The time expended to complete a processing activity.

Product layout A production design in which equipment is organized to accommodate the production of a specific product.

Productivity The ratio of outputs produced to inputs consumed.

Profit centers Responsibility centers in which managers and other employees control both the revenues and the costs of the product or service they deliver.

Profit sharing A cash bonus calculated as a percentage of an organization unit's reported profit; a group incentive compensation plan focused on short-term performances.

Project funding A proposal to spend discretionary expenditures with a specific time horizon or sunset provision.

Q

Quality costs The costs incurred on quality-related processes, including *prevention, appraisal, internal failure, and external failure.*

Quality function deployment (QFD) matrix A tool that is typically used for systematically arraying information about the variables of features, functions, and competitive evaluation in a matrix format.

Quantity (efficiency) variances The difference between the amount of a resource used and the amount allowed, given the level of production, costed at the standard cost of the resource.

R

Rate (price) variance The difference between the amount paid for a resource and the amount that would have been paid if the resource had been purchased at its standard price.

Reciprocal method (for service department allocations) A method of allocating service department costs that considers the services provided both to other service departments and to production departments.

Regulatory and social processes Processes that promote meeting or exceeding standards established by regulations and facilitate achievement of desired social objectives.

Relevant cost A cost that changes as a result of making a decision, or a cost that differs between two decision alternatives. For example, the cost of a new piece of production equipment and its operating costs are relevant costs when considering whether to replace an existing piece of equipment with the new one. When considering which of two pieces of production equipment to purchase, the difference between their purchase prices and their operating costs are relevant costs.

Remediation The end-of-life cycle cost to restore a resource, such as water or land, to its original condition after using it for a production process.

Research, development, and engineering (RD&E) stage The first stage of a product's life-cycle in which market research, product design, and product development are performed.

Residual income An accounting-based measure of the increase in shareholder wealth resulting from current operations. Measured as accounting income minus the economic cost of the investment used to generate that income.

Responsibility center An organization unit for which a manager is made responsible.

Results control The process of hiring qualified people who understand the organization's objectives, telling them to do whatever they think best to help the organization achieve its objectives, and using the control system to evaluate the resulting performance, thereby assessing how well they have done.

Return on investment The ratio of net income to invested capital.

Revenue centers Responsibility centers whose members control revenues but do not control either the manufacturing or the acquisition cost of the product or service they sell or the level of investment made in the responsibility center.

Rucker plan   A form of gainsharing program.

S

Sales mix variance   A difference between planned and actual revenue caused by a difference between planned and actual product mix.

Sales price variance   A difference between planned and actual revenue caused by a difference between planned and actual prices for one or several products.

Sales quantity variance   A difference between planned and actual revenue caused by a difference between planned and actual quantity levels.

Salesperson incentives   The contingent payments awarded to salespeople based on actual sales performance, such as quantity or dollars of sales they generated, or the profits earned from their selling activities to customers.

Scanlon plan   A form of gain-sharing program.

Scientific management school   A management movement with the underlying philosophy that most people find work objectionable, that people care little for making decisions or showing creativity on the job, and that money is the driving force behind performance.

Second-level variances   Variances that include both a planning variance and a flexible budget variance that sum to the first-level variance.

Segment margin report   An accounting-based measure of the profit contribution of an organization unit to the overall organization.

Sensitivity analysis   The process of selectively varying a plan's or a budget's key estimates for the purpose of identifying over what range a decision option is preferred.

Sequential method (for service department allocations)   A method of allocating service department costs that proceeds by choosing the order in which the service departments will allocate their costs and then proceeding sequentially through the chosen order.

Share of wallet   Percentage of a customer's spending in a given product or service category that a company captures; for example, a retail clothing store could measure that percentage of a customer's wardrobe that it sells to her, a bank could measure the percentage of a customer's assets it holds or credit sales that it processes.

Smoothing   The act of affecting the preplanned flow of information without altering the organization's activities.

Step variable cost   A step variable cost is a cost that changes in steps as some underlying volume of activity changes. For example the cost of a train of freight cars will increase in steps as the capacity of each car is exceeded and another car gets added to the train.

Stock option   The right to purchase a unit of the organization's stock at a specified price, called the option price.

Strategy   Describes how a company will gain competitive advantage by being different or better than its competitors. Examples of strategies include low cost, complete customer solutions, and product leadership.

Strategy map   A comprehensive visual representation of the linkages among objectives and measures in the four perspectives of the Balanced Scorecard.

Sunk cost phenomenon   The sunk cost phenomenon refers to decision making that is influenced or driven by a previous expenditure or decision. For example, an investor who refuses to sell a share which was purchased for $10 and is now selling for $5 solely because the current price is less than the purchase price is exhibiting the sunk cost phenomenon. From an economic perspective, decision making behavior driven by the sunk cost phenomenon is irrational.

Sunk costs   The costs of resources that already have been committed and cannot be changed by any current action or decision; contrast with *incremental costs.*

Supply chain management   A management system that develops cooperative, mutually beneficial, long-term relationships between buyers and sellers.

T

Target   The level of performance or rate of improvement required for a Balanced Scorecard measure.

Target cost   The difference between the target selling price and the target profit margin.

Target costing   A method of cost planning used during the research, development, and engineering stage to reduce manufacturing costs to targeted levels.

Task control   The process of developing standard procedures that employees are told to follow.

Theory of constraints (TOC)   A management approach that maximizes the volume of production through a bottleneck process.

Third-level variances   Variances that include quantity and price variances that sum to, and therefore explain, the flexible budget variances.

Throughput contribution   The difference between revenues and direct materials for the quantity of product sold.

Time-driven activity-based costing (TDABC)   A new ABC variant that is simple and more powerful since it requires estimating only two parameters: the cost of supplying resource capacity and the quantity of capacity consumed by each transaction, product, and customer. It enables a much simpler ABC model to capture even highly complex operations through the use of time equations.

Time equation   An algebraic representation that predicts the quantity of processing time based on specific order and activity characteristics.

Total-life-cycle costing (TLCC)   Describes the process of managing all costs during a product's lifetime.

Transfer pricing   The set of rules an organization uses to assign prices to products transferred between internal responsibility centers in order to allocate jointly earned revenue among responsibility centers.

U

Unilateral (covert) benchmarking   A process in which companies independently gather information about one or several other companies that excel in the area of interest.

V

Value engineering process   The process of examining each component of a product to determine whether its cost can be reduced while maintaining functionality and performance.

Value index   The ratio of the value of a component to a customer and the percentage of total cost devoted to the component.

Value proposition   Clear and short statement of competitive value that the organization will deliver to its target customers—how it will compete for, or satisfy, customers.

Variable costs   The costs of flexible resources.

Variable overhead   In a manufacturing context, the cost of items that are actually direct costs but are too immaterial (in relation to total product cost) to

trace to individual cost objects. Examples include the cost of glue used to make each piece of furniture, thread for a garment, machine electricity usage, and machine supplies.

Variance   The difference between an actual amount and a target or planned amount.

Variance analysis   A set of procedures managers use to help them understand the source of variances.

W

Whale curve   A plot of cumulative profitability versus the percentage of customers, where customers are ranked from the most profitable to the least profitable. In a typical whale curve, the most profitable 20 percent of customers generate between 150 and 300 percent of the company's profits. The unprofitable customers incur losses that cumulatively bring the company's profits down to 100 percent.

What-if analysis   A process of exploring the effects of changes in estimates on predictions in a financial model.

Work-in-process inventory   The costs of the resources for production not yet completed.

Z

Zero-based budgeting (ZBB)   A budgeting process that requires proponents of discretionary expenditures to continuously justify every expenditure.

SUBJECT INDEX

Q

Quality costs, 293
Quality function deployment (QFD)
    matrix, 335
Quality standards, 292
Quantity (efficiency) variances, 446

R

Rate (price) variances, 446, 447–448
Ratio of assets to equity, 512
Ratio of operating income to sales, 512
Ratio of sales to assets, 512
Ratio of sales to investment, 512
Raw material productivity, 513
Reciprocal method of allocating service
    department costs, 173–174
Regulatory/social processes, 57–58
Reimbursement costs, 88
Relative cost method, 510
Relevant cost, 100, 111–117
Relevant cost analysis, 31, 112
Remediation, 349
Reorganization, of plant layout, 285–287
Report, cost of quality, 293–294
Research, development, and
    engineering (RD&E) stage,
    in total-life-cycle costing,
    326–327, 345
Research in Motion (RIM), 25–26
Residual income, 514–516
Responsibility centers
    coordinating, 490–491
    cost centers, 494–495, 497
    defined, 491
    evaluating, 498–499
    income statements, 502–504
    investment centers, 496, 497
    investment centers, assigning
      and valuing assets in, 510–511
    profit centers, 496, 497
    revenue centers, 495, 497
    types of, 494–497
Results control, 376–377
Retail organizations, cost flows in, 148
Return on capital employed (ROCE),
    60–61
Return on investments, 511–514
Return on sales, 512
Revenue centers, 495, 497
Revenue growth, 50, 51
Reward and incentive programs,
    69, 386
    based on outcomes, 388–389
    cash bonus plans, 390–391
    company example, 391–392
    conditions favoring, 388
    employee responsibility and, 388
    extrinsic rewards, 385–386
    gain sharing, 392–394
    Improshare, 393
    intrinsic rewards, 384–385
    managing, 389–390
    pay-for-performance systems, 386
    performance measurement
      and, 386–387
    profit sharing, 391–392

Rucker plan, 393
Scanlon plan, 393
stock-related, 394–395
types of plans, 390
RIM (Research in Motion), 25–26
Rucker plan, 393

S

Sales margin, 512
Sales mix variance, 453
Salesperson incentives, 256–257
Sales price variance, 454
Sales quantity variance, 453–454
Sales variances, 452–453
Sales volume effects, 453–454
Scanlon plan, 393
Scientific management school, 368
Scope, of strategy, 47–48, 51
Scorecards. *See* Balanced Scorecard
    (BSC); Key performance
    indicator (KPI) scorecards
Second-level variances, 446
Segment margin report, 500–502
Sensitivity analysis, 439–440
Sequential method of allocating service
    department costs, 171–173
Service departments, allocating costs
    of, 170–174
    direct method, 171
    reciprocal method, 173–174
    step-down method, 171–173
Service organizations
    activity-based cost costing in,
      211–213
    cost flows in, 148–149
    customer costs in, 248–249
    role of budgeting in, 455
Service quality indicator (SQI), 493
Share of wallet, 261
Six Sigma system (Motorola), 292
Smoothing, 378
Solver, 115
SQI (service quality indicator), 493
Step-down method of allocating
    service department
    costs, 171–173
Step variable costs, 97
Stock-related compensation plans,
    394–395
Strategy
    advantage and scope of, 47–48
    management accounting and, 28–29
    plan-do-check-act cycle, 29–33
    two principal functions of, 47
Strategy map, Balanced Scorecard, 31,
    49–50
    company example, 60–66
    customer perspective, 51–55
    financial perspective, 50–51
    learning and growth perspective,
      59–60
    process perspective, 55–58
Sunk cost phenomenon, 99
Sunk costs, 98–99
Supply chain management, 332
Support activity cost variances,
    451–452

Survey(s)
    customer satisfaction, 259–260
    determining importance of customer's
      requirements with, 334–335

T

Take-back and recycle program
    (Cisco), 352
Tall organizations, 378
Target cost, 331
Target costing, 87
    company examples, 332–338, 339,
      359–363
    concerns about, 338–340
    cost analysis, 333–336
    cross-functional teams, 332
    supply chain management, 332
    traditional costing methods *vs.*,
      329–332
    value engineering process, 331–332,
      336–338
Target reduction rate, 297
Targets, Balanced Scorecard, 49
Task control, 375–376
Taxes, in budgets, 433
Teach for America (TFA), 68–69
Technical considerations, with
    management accounting
    and control systems (MACS),
    366–367
Theory of constraints (TOC), 279–280
Third-level variances, 446
Throughput contribution, 280
Time-driven activity-based costing
    (TDABC), 196, 208–211
Time equations, 210–211, 213
Total-life-cycle costing (TLCC)
    manufacturing stage, 327–328
    postsale service and disposal stage,
      328–329
    research, development, and
      engineering stage, 326–327
Trade loading, 515–516
Trade Research Institute, 506
Transfer pricing, 505–510
    administered approach to, 509
    based on equity decisions, 509–510
    cost-based approach, 507–509
    domestic, 505
    four main approaches to, 506
    international, 505, 506
    market-based approach, 507
    negotiated approach to, 509
Turnover, 512

U

Unilateral (covert) benchmarking, 302
Unprofitable customers, 242–243

V

Value engineering process, 331–332,
    336–338
Value index, 337

Value propositions, 50, 53–55
Variable costs, 88–89, 149, 211, 507
Variable overhead costs, 152–153
Variance, 441
Variance analysis, 441–442
Variances
    direct labor cost, 449–450
    efficiency (quantity), 446
    first-level, 444
    flexible budget, 445–446
    planning, 445
    price (rate), 446, 447–448
    sales price, 454

sales quantity, 453–454
second-level, 446
support activity cost, 451–452
third-level, 446

W

Whale curve, 246–248
What-if-analysis, 93–94, 439–440
Whistle-blowing, 372
Work-in-process inventory,
    147, 160

Y

Yield (raw material productivity), 513

Z

Zero-based budgeting, 457

Name and Company Index